Diversification and Professionalization in Psychology

Diversification and Professionalization in Psychology offers readers a multicentric perspective on the history of social science and compares the developments in psychology in relation to the developments made in the other social and natural sciences.

This is the second volume about the formation of modern psychology and provides a comprehensive look into the origins and developments of modern psychology. With a large geographical coverage, European developments are put into their own context in their own time. In doing this, the book explores different early schools, from social reductionists like Durkheim, Charles Blondel, and Maurice Halbwachs, to the social debates about relativism in Lévy-Bruhl, early Piaget, the beginnings of ethology, and the semiotic approach of Karl Bühler. These thinkers are placed in relation to the recent upsurge of different social and biological theories of the mind. Throughout, the author develops a detailed presentation of the thematic development of psychology and links the history of psychology to an outline of contemporary psychology.

This is an invaluable introductory text for undergraduate students of the history of psychology and will also appeal to postgraduates, academics, and anyone interested in psychology or the history of science. It will also be of interest to graduate students of psychology, biology, sociology, and anthropology with a theoretical interest in the history of the field.

Csaba Pléh is a Hungarian psychologist and linguist, a member of the Hungarian Academy of Sciences and of the Academia Europeae, and a visiting researcher at the Central European University, Department of Cognitive Science, Hungary. His empirical research is mainly concentrated on the cross-linguistic study of language processing and language development and issues of developmental language disorders.

Diversification and Professionalization in Psychology
The Formation of Modern Psychology
Volume 2

Csaba Pléh

LONDON AND NEW YORK

Cover image: © Getty Images

First published 2024
by Routledge
4 Park Square, Milton Park, Abingdon, Oxon OX14 4RN

and by Routledge
605 Third Avenue, New York, NY 10158

Routledge is an imprint of the Taylor & Francis Group, an informa business

© 2024 Csaba Pléh

The right of Csaba Pléh to be identified as author of this work has been asserted in accordance with sections 77 and 78 of the Copyright, Designs and Patents Act 1988.

All rights reserved. No part of this book may be reprinted or reproduced or utilised in any form or by any electronic, mechanical, or other means, now known or hereafter invented, including photocopying and recording, or in any information storage or retrieval system, without permission in writing from the publishers.

Trademark notice: Product or corporate names may be trademarks or registered trademarks, and are used only for identification and explanation without intent to infringe.

British Library Cataloguing-in-Publication Data
A catalogue record for this book is available from the British Library

Library of Congress Cataloging-in-Publication Data
Names: Pléh, Csaba, author.
Title: Diversification and professionalization in psychology / Csaba Pléh.
Description: Abingdon, Oxon ; New York, NY : Routledge, 2024. | Series: The formation of modern psychology ; volume 2 | Includes bibliographical references and index. | Summary: "Diversification and Professionalization in Psychology offers readers a multicentric perspective on the history of social science and compares the developments in psychology in relation to the developments made in the other social and natural sciences"—Provided by publisher.
Identifiers: LCCN 2023035807 (print) | LCCN 2023035808 (ebook) | ISBN 9781032625799 (hardback ; vol. 2) | ISBN 9781032625775 (paperback ; vol. 2) | ISBN 9781032625805 (ebook)
Subjects: LCSH: Psychology—History. | Psychology—Practice.
Classification: LCC BF81 .P53 2024 (print) | LCC BF81 (ebook) | DDC 150.9—dc23/eng/20230928
LC record available at https://lccn.loc.gov/2023035807
LC ebook record available at https://lccn.loc.gov/2023035808

ISBN: 978-1-032-62579-9 (hbk)
ISBN: 978-1-032-62577-5 (pbk)
ISBN: 978-1-032-62580-5 (ebk)

DOI: 10.4324/9781032625805

Typeset in Times New Roman
by Apex CoVantage, LLC

Please visit the Instructor Resources: www.routledge.com/9781032625775

Contents

List of figures	*vii*
List of tables	*x*
Preface	*xii*
Acknowledgments	*xv*

PART I
Disciplinary developments and eclectics   1

1 Schools of depth psychology: the divisions of psychoanalysis and neo-Freudism   3

2 Individuals and types: the victorious march of personality psychology and measurement   30

3 Motivation and dynamic psychologies   59

4 The victorious march of developmental theories   75

5 Social theories of the mind   100

6 The formation of modern social psychology   164

7 Soviet/Russian psychology   215

PART II
On the road toward contemporary psychology   279

8 Psychology as learning theory: neobehaviorism   281

9	The transformations of experimental psychology: birth and destiny of cognitive psychology	334
10	Roads toward a new psychology at the millennium	397
11	The future of psychology	447

General references	*486*
Author Index	*543*
Subject Index	*554*

Figures

1.1	The appearance in any text of Carl Gustave Jung and Alfred Adler in the PsycINFO database.	5
1.2	Carl Gustave Jung as a young man.	6
1.3	Alfred Adler.	10
1.4	Sándor Ferenczi.	16
2.1	**Character** and **personality** as paper titles in the PsycINFO database.	31
2.2	William Stern.	32
2.3	The different research strategies of differential psychology according to William Stern.	36
2.4	The three basic bodily types proposed by Kretschmer.	44
2.5	The four temperaments and extraversion and neuroticism as basic personality dimensions.	49
2.6	An inkblot similar to the inkblots used by the Rorschach test.	52
2.7	The three-layer theory of intellectual abilities proposed by J. B. Carroll.	57
3.1	The concept of *instinct* and *drive* as titles of papers in the PsycINFO database.	61
3.2	The determination of the Umwelt in Jakob von Uexküll.	65
3.3	The Maslow pyramid of human motives.	73
4.1	The occurrences of the terms "developmental psychology" and "child psychology" in the PsycINFO database over a century.	76
4.2	Jean Piaget.	79
4.3	A classical arrangement to study of object permanence.	87
4.4	Typical Piaget situations for the study of quantity and number constancy.	88
4.5	Number of papers mentioning Piaget according the PsycINFO database.	90
5.1	The presence of social psychology in the general literature was dominant in the 1970–1980s according to Google Ngram.	101
5.2	Papers by subject area in the PsycINFO database showing the importance of social psychology in the 1960s.	101

viii *Figures*

5.3	Maurice Halbwachs.	111
5.4	Sir Frederick Bartlett.	138
5.5	Transformation of a figure during repeated serial reproduction.	142
5.6	Karl Bühler.	151
5.7	Adapted from the three functions of linguistic signs according to Bühler.	155
5.8	The interdisciplinary relations proposed by the different psycho-social theories of the mind.	161
5.9	Assumed causal relations between individual thought and the "external" social determinants.	162
6.1	The first speculative approaches to the social mind.	170
6.2	The popularity of Le Bon and Tarde in the English-language general literature.	181
6.3	Main topics of social psychology.	190
6.4	Kurt Lewin.	199
6.5	The sociometric structure of a family living together.	202
6.6	The mention of *sociometry* and *psychodrama* in the general literature.	203
7.1	Pavlov in his laboratory factory.	234
7.2	Lev Vygotsky.	249
7.3	A. N. Leontiev.	254
7.4	A. R. Luria examining a patient.	258
7.5	S. L. Rubinstein.	261
7.6	A 1930s Soviet cartoon mocking the assumed stigmatizing practice of pedologists.	266
8.1	The essence of the determination of behavior with intervening.	288
8.2	The lens model of perception and action proposed by Egon Brunswik.	290
8.3	The Skinner box arrangement.	293
8.4	Edward Chace Tolman.	295
8.5	References to leading neobehaviorists over half a century in the PsycINFO database.	297
8.6	Clark Leonard Hull.	299
8.7	Burrhus Frederic Skinner.	302
8.8	The three levels of behavioral organization in the vision of Osgood.	324
9.1	Jerome Bruner.	342
9.2	The presence of *behaviorism* and *cognitive psychology* in the PsycINFO database over two generations.	356
9.3	Conceptual trends in all psychology journals in the PsycINFO database.	357

9.4	Human cognition as information processing in the model of Daniel Broadbent.	359
9.5	The Wason task.	362
9.6	An example from the WUG test.	377
9.7	The term "cognitive science" overtakes "cognitive psychology" in the mid-1990s.	381
9.8	The different component disciplines of cognitive science in the Sloan Foundation initiative.	381
9.9	The different version of present-day cognitive research regarding interpretation.	384
9.10	Different trends in representational relations.	386
10.1	Saccadic eye movements while watching a photo.	399
10.2	Eye movements "heat image" while watching a web page.	400
10.3	The multiple determination in present-day psychology.	404
10.4	The fate of the terms *ethology*, *cultural psychology*, and *evolutionary psychology* in the psychological literature.	406
10.5	The abundance-selection model of neural development proposed by Changeux.	423
10.6	Changes in the popularity of **genetics** and **behavior genetics** in the psychological literature.	428
11.1	Membership in the APA sections in the second half of the 20th century.	449
11.2	Psychology profession in Hungary around the millennium.	450
11.3	The fate of the notions "behavior therapy" and "cognitive behavior therapy" in the PsycINFO database.	453
11.4	**Health psychology** and **clinical psychology** as titles of papers in the PsycINFO database during the last decades.	461

Tables

1.1	The instinct pairs of Szondi, with the corresponding disorders, instincts, desires, and pathological tendencies	21
1.2	Comparison of some trends in depth psychology	28
2.1	The European and American traditions of personality psychology according to Allport	31
2.2	Typical social science typologies in the beginning of the 20th century	38
2.3	The typologies of antiquity with the body fluids	43
3.1	Some classical psychological theories from the point of view of belief–desire folk psychology	60
3.2	Correspondence of social instincts and emotions in the hormic system of McDougall	63
3.3	Comparison of some early motivation psychologies	73
4.1	Comparisons of the comprehensive theories of development regarding some key issues	77
4.2	Some of the issues of logical organization in the vision of Piaget, and corresponding developmental research	86
4.3	The stages of intellectual development according to the mature system of Piaget	86
5.1	Basic varieties of Francophone culturalism/sociologism	103
5.2	Differences between collective memory and history writing according to Wertsch and Roediger	122
5.3	A comparison of primitive and rational thought in the conception of Lévy-Bruhl	125
5.4	Some contrasts of the Ebbinghaus and Bartlett paradigms of memory research	145
5.5	Three levels and pools of selection according to Bühler	158
5.6	Students and followers of Karl Bühler and some of their ideas	159
6.1	Presence of classical social psychologists of the experimental trends according to Google Scholar citations	192
7.1	The stages in the work of Pavlov	236
7.2	Stages in the Stalinist questioning of Soviet psychology	262
7.3	Some contrasts of the two views of learning	274

8.1	The scaling theory of psychological measurement	284
9.1	Important factors in forming the modeling approach of cognitive psychology	335
9.2	Some new experimental discoveries and related theories of modern cognitive psychology in the 1960s–1980s	349
9.3	The juxtaposition of connectionist and classical cognitive architecture according to Fodor and Pylyshyn	388
9.4	The fate of rules over half a century of cognitive research	390
9.5	The changes of cognitive psychology over half a century	395
10.1	Some examples from the list of Buss (1995) for psychological mechanisms with an evolutionary base	408
10.2	Two approaches on the application of evolutionary ideas to psychology	412
10.3	Some proposed mental dual systems and their prosed brain equivalents	425
10.4	New biological ideas about the determination of development in the 1960s	429
10.5	Some value choices of the claims about the genetic determination of intelligence promoted by Arthur Jensen	432
11.1	Some alternative visions of applied psychology during the last decades	454
11.2	The main stages of development according to Erikson	458
11.3	The scales used by Kimble to differentiate scientific and softer psychological attitudes	475

Preface

The message of the book

The purpose of this book – in fact, a twin book, with Volume 1 as *laying the foundations of independent psychology* – is to present a more **multicentered vision** of psychology than is usually presented. I parallel developments in psychology with those of other social sciences (anthropology, sociology, education, linguistics) and philosophical disciplines (logic, philosophy of science), as well as relate them to developments in natural science, mainly biology.

Furthermore, this book showcases that **European psychology was and still is continuously present and active** in the modern study of psychology. From the American perspective, the field of psychology became increasingly insular as the framework adopted a more Americo-centric viewpoint from the 1920s on. This is factually true; however, this is not a wholistic treatise on the development of greater psychological studies. In this book, I redress the balance and assay the integral nature of European psychology.

This book, while presenting the leading schools of modern psychology as schools proper, also gives more weight to the typically overlooked, more open, and eclectic schools. In this regard, I firmly believe that there are two attitudes in making science and its history. One may capture these attitudes in the metaphors of Isaiah Berlin (1953), who cites a metaphor that can be traced back to the Ancient Greek poet Archilochus: "A *fox* knows many things, but a *hedgehog* one important thing." Using this metaphor, one can argue that psychology, taken in its entire complexity, represents the fox types more than the hedgehog types. In contrast, the great schools, such as those of Freud and Watson, continuously purported that they were hedgehogs who found THE single unifying principle of the mental world. In this work, I highlight some of these more open, fox-like approaches.

While the books analyze the different schools of psychology, a characteristic feature of Part 1 of Volume 2 is the presentation of the thematic development of psychology in mid-20th century. This is shown by chapters on motivation, personality, and development. As part of this, regarding the new social and biological theories of the mind, Volume 2 specifically endeavors to exhume as many of the most substantial innovations as possible, providing chapters on the early social theories of the mind and the beginnings of social psychology (Chapters 5 and 6). I present reductionist followers of Durkheim (such as Charles Blondel and Maurice Halbwachs); the social debates about relativism in Lévy-Bruhl, the sociological work of early Piaget, the beginnings of ethology; and the schematization and language-based approaches of Frederic Bartlett and Karl Bühler. These theories are early attempts to treat the social mind, while the beginnings and articulation of professional social psychology summarized in Chapter 6 concentrate on the issue of human interaction and its mental representation.

While I attempt to maintain a strict sense of neutrality in presenting the different approaches to psychology, as an experimental psychologist, I do have some preconceptions – despite my adherence to a greater psychological worldview. I believe that the mental world has a biological function. Among those elements involved in representing the world, forming models of the physical world and of our partners is central. I am committed to scientific objectivism, yet at the same time, I believe in the multiplicity of approaches, as well as the value of individual differences. This explains the concentration on the issue of how cognitive psychology has become more and more an approach to study interpreted human cognition and not merely cognition in the abstract sense (Chapters 9 and 10).

A further reason for writing a new book on the history of psychology is the issue of **explanatory models in human and social sciences.** The standard overall treatments still take an almost entirely internalist attitude, that is, talking merely about the seemingly inherent changes of theories. The other extremist approaches are total social reductionist histories that treat the unfolding and changes in psychology as merely resulting from general effects of society. It is in this regard that I attempt to redress the balance, emphasizing an equilibrium of the three layers determining the development of psychology: the intellectual, the personal, and the social should be treated together, as aspects of the real life of the scientist. This aspect comes up in the last two chapters (Chapters 10 and 11). In a non-usual manner, I connect the history of psychology to an outline of contemporary psychology. In this characterization of the last three decades, the issue of social embedding and relations among disciplines dealing with the human mind comes up most clearly. I hope this shall help the identity formation of new generations of psychologists.

Some notes on how to use this book

The book has an accompanying homepage.

Sample PowerPoint presentations, additional texts, and examples for tests could be found there.

The text of the book itself uses two types of boxed texts. Under the title of BIOGRAPHY, I present the professional life of some leading figures of our profession. Under CONTROVERSIES, central dividing issues of the great schools and ages are presented with their impacts on psychology. Educators may find these to be good topics for discussion and/or classwork.

Types of tasks

Each chapter is accompanied at the end by two types of tasks.

Conceptual analysis (CA) homework. The educator may expect a submission of a maximum of two pages, plus references. This task is designed to ask for things such as: comparing and contrasting the two types of conditioning in school settings, relations of unconscious processes, and paraphenomena.

Digital search and analysis (DSA). This task is designed to be a short summary of Internet searches and short statistical comparisons, for example, changes of emotion expressions in professional texts or popular references to empathy in child psychology of the 1970s.

Acknowledgments

This work has a long history as a consequence of a lifetime of teaching the history of psychology in Budapest, Szeged, Vienna, and at Rutgers, New Jersey. I started to write the first Hungarian version in 1982, which was later published in 1992. A further revised Hungarian version was published in 2010.

The English version was prepared in three stages. The first part was conceived in sunny California, at the Stanford University Center for Advanced Studies in the Behavioral Sciences, in 1997. This was followed up by writing the mid- and late 20th-century chapters in Lyon, at Collegium de Lyon, where I was a guest in 2012–2013 and 2016–2017. The book was finalized while I had been a visiting, honorary professor at the Department of Cognitive Science at Central European University, Budapest.

The intellectual outlook of my vision was widely broadened at conferences of CHEIRON and ESHHS, two learned societies of the history of psychology and its neighboring disciplines. At the Stanford CASB, in the jolly company of Steven Shapin and John Toews, I started to be more conscious about what is meant by the complexities of "modernity" in psychology. I started to realize the importance of a way of thought that recognizes separations and mergers in intellectual history in a parallel manner. One has to reconsider relations between nature and culture or between science and society, as highlighted by Bruno Latour. These relations must then be reinterpreted for issues like body and mind, or individuality and community in psychology.

My years in Lyon have naturally caused me to reinterpret the importance of French traditions in psychology. I now embrace an attitude where the constant reinterpretation of the Cartesian tradition, and of the relations between individuals, groups, and society, comes as natural in the form of different knowledge patterns (*epistémé*).

A generation of teaching experience results in substantial changes in the domain as well. What was considered to be modern in the 1970s has itself become history in the new millennium. In the 1970s, the vision of B. F. Skinner, later, neobehavioristic theories of cognition, and humanistic psychology, was part of the present. This long teaching career with this ever-changing subject has reminded me again of the tension between presentist and antiquarian approaches to the history of psychology. It has also reminded me of the relevance of history to understand our recent tensions. With this re-evaluation of the importance of history, I have developed a sort of compromise between an impartial attitude and an attitude that is following the commitments of the active researcher.

Several of my colleagues have been central in the formation of my attitude to writing disciplinary histories. Zsigmond Telegdi, my professor in linguistics, and Ferenc Altrichter, my mentor in philosophy (both in Budapest), taught me the importance of combining conceptual and historical analyses. The influence of Mitchell Asch continued this inspiration, combined with in-depth sociohistorical contextualization. Péter Bodor constantly reminded me of the importance of different versions of the phenomenological attitude, and the centrality of non-positivistic alternatives in late 20th-century psychology. Miklós Győri enlightened me about positivism, and later about the domain-specific interpretation of cognitive development. Talks with Judit Gervain, Zsuzsa Káldy, Kristóf Kovács, and Bence Nánay in the graduate training school at the Invisible College of Budapest have clarified the importance of modern cognitive research in interpreting our history. Eörs Szathmáry, Vilmos Csányi, Anna Fedor, Daniel Dennett, and Dereck Bickerton at the Collegium Budapest have deepened my interpretation of the evolutionary attitude in the history of psychology. Ilona Kovács and Ricardo Luccio deepened my knowledge of the relations between Gestalt theory in history and contemporary research on vision. Gergely Csibra, György Gergely, Ildikó Király, Judit Gervain, Ilona Kovács, and Bálint Forgács taught me to understand how the dramatic changes in contemporary developmental psychology are forcing one to reconsider the historical relations between cognitive and social development. I expanded upon these lessons, integrating a more sociological approach that I learned from Dan Sperber and Olivier Morin at Central European University in Budapest.

Talks with Martin Prinzhorn at the Department of Linguistics at Vienna University, and Steven Harnad in Budapest and Southampton, as well as Tim Crane, Katalin Farkas, Gábor Bródy, and Bálint Forgács at CEU, helped me to correctly see the historical place of my favorite cognitive psychology. The new approaches of the philosopher Kristóf Nyíri on the importance of communicative media in shaping human thought and our self-image have led to a revised vision of representation and skill in the history of psychology as well. György Hunyady provided me with interesting feedback on my chapters on early social psychology.

Talks at Stanford with Alan Code, Judith Aissen, Ellen Spitz, Elemér Hankiss, Siegwart Lindenberg, Judy DeLoache, Gardner Lindzey, and Jerry Clore, as well as Alain Peyraube, Elisabetta Basso, and Hervé Jolly in Lyon, have deepened my understanding of the philosophical underpinning of the history of psychology and its relations to social sciences at large.

At different stages of the evolution of this manuscript, several professional historians of psychology were kind enough to read parts of the manuscript. I am especially thankful for suggestions I received from Judit Mészáros, William Woodward, and Roger Smith. Talks at different CHEIRON and ESHHS meetings with many fellow historians of psychology encouraged me in this never-ending process and gave me interesting insights to ramify some of my proposals.

The last part of the book was discussed with a semester-long seminar organized by Tamás Demeter at the Institute of Philosophy in Budapest, with Kristóf Kovács, Gábor Zemplén, Bálint Forgács, and myself.

Nathaniel Torres corrected my English, and Julia Sávos of the CEU Baby Lab summarized all the corrections. Márton Mundig and Krisztián Gábris helped me with the figures. It was truly a stroke of good fortune to meet Adam Woods, an enthusiastic commissioning editor at Routledge. He convinced me to make a book out of my manuscript. Zoe Thomson contributed to this work with ever-thoughtful suggestions. Together with Maddie Gray, they taught me to appreciate professional editing combined with a friendly atmosphere.

Alongside all my colleagues, I would like to thank the patience of my wife, Ottilia Boross, and my children, Kamilla, Dániel, Aurél, and Krisztián, for being tolerant and sometimes covert influencers of this project.

Budakeszi, Hungary, March 2023

Part I
Disciplinary developments and eclectics

The period between the two world wars was characterized by the growth of the great schools in psychology on both sides of the Atlantic. While these trends were certainly omnivorous, they were not able to integrate psychology as they wished. Depth psychology itself, as shown in Chapter 1, multiplied into diverging sub-schools. There were two developments that broke the image of the overwhelming, all-encompassing dominance of the schools. First, there were developments in specific domains, such as personality, developmental, or social psychology. These "chapter developments" became more and more important since they had clearer connections to the societal issues of applied psychology, such as ability testing, psychotherapy or attitude, and group psychology. As a second factor, there were many important figures in modern psychology who developed their own work in an openly or less openly eclectic manner. The works of Piaget, Bartlett, or Bühler cannot be easily fit into any dominant theory. These people followed the advice of Isaiah Berlin (1953) and became foxes who collect many things, in contrast to the theory-unifier hedgehogs.

Part 1 of this volume presents these disciplinary (or, rather, subdisciplinary) developments and some of the boundary-crossing eclectics. In a way, they have proven to be central in the further development of psychology.

1 Schools of depth psychology
The divisions of psychoanalysis and neo-Freudism

Psychoanalysis permeates culture

A great merit of psychoanalysis recognized by all is to highlight the influence of desires on the world of cognition and behavior. This was recognized rather early on (Holt, 1915). The influence of psychoanalysis due to this, and due to the cultural speculations of Freud, went far beyond the analytic movement proper in the 1920s–1930s. It extended into the 1960s and can even be seen in literary theory today. In psychology, the general attraction of psychoanalysis was connected to the developmental model and the importance of early childhood. Radically different people, even Piaget and Watson, paid tribute early on to the developmental ideas of Freud. Several noted psychologists even tried psychoanalysis, sometimes for intellectual curiosity, like Piaget and, later, Tolman, and sometimes for treating their tensions in life, like Edwin Boring (1940), who even reported about his experiences. Several research programs from other schools who did not share the analytic conception of the exclusiveness and verifying role of clinical data still developed hypotheses for their psychological work using traditional research methods on the basis of the clinically based proposals of Freud. Studies on the relationships between child-rearing practices and personality development were initiated by Sears (1943) in the 1930s at the Iowa Center for Child Development and resulted in a complex theory of socialization based on longitudinal data (Sears et al., 1957). These studies were conducted within a social learning theory promoted by behaviorists, while also relying on psychoanalytic theoretical proposals. Most importantly, while depth psychologies, including the theories of Freud, simultaneously became part of the curriculum, psychoanalysts and representatives of other depth psychology schools were not integrated into faculties of psychology in most countries until the late 1960s.

In order to understand the impact of psychoanalysis, one has to keep in mind that partly due to the cultural message of Freud, psychoanalysis, in the interwar period, went well beyond psychology and psychiatry. Psychoanalysis provided hypotheses and discussion topics to other social sciences and humanities. In **folklore and anthropology**, Freudian ideas about the relations of culture and repression have been widely discussed. The Hungarian ethnographer Géza Róheim (1891–1953) studied the symbolic value of folk rituals and myths (Róheim, 1930) and tried to prove the universality of the Oedipal complex using "mini-psychoanalyses" during

DOI: 10.4324/9781032625805-2

his trips to Australia, where he studied Aboriginals. In his later writings, Róheim softened the psychoanalytic vision pertaining to childhood, claiming that the long childhood of humans was a period for learning culture and practicing curiosity. In the most important anthropological debates, he was still cited as an orthodox Freudian. Bronislaw Malinowski (1884–1942), the Polish British anthropologist, on the other hand, on the basis of his fieldwork on Trobriand Islands and Melanesia, questioned the universality of Oedipal tensions (Malinowski, 1927). The American Margaret Mead (1901–1978) started to claim a relativity in female–male relations and sexual socialization (Mead, 1928, 1975). The debates about the generality–relativity issue are still on. What is important for the history of psychology, however, is that all these discussions were initiated by the universalist biological claims about socialization promoted by Freud himself.

The same is true for the study of literature and art. The idea of sublimation in art following the pioneering studies of Freud (1910/1916) on Leonardo, and the general theory of symbolism in art, appeared as a royal way to analyze the genesis of art. An important step was the work of Ernest Jones (1910) on *Hamlet* as an example for the Oedipal conflict. Some critical voices showed up soon, however. In Soviet Russia, the innovative Bakhtin Circle in the works of Volosinov (1927) and Bakhtin (new edition 1986) had some criticism of the nonsocial nature of the unconscious determination in Freud. Arnold Hauser (1892–1978), the Hungarian/German philosopher of culture, raised the issue that if we are merely looking for libidinal forces and sexual sublimation in art, the specificity of art is lost (Hauser, 1959). In much later developments, the French philosopher and literary scholar Paul Ricoeur (1965), as shown in Chapter 13 of Volume 1, claimed a general similarity between psychoanalysis and literary interpretation. Rather than psychoanalysis providing a hard core for literary interpretation, both are constructive hermeneutic processes. In his view, the novel and the dream are interpreted in a similar way: interpretation is the result of a meaning construction by the analyst and the client, and by the writer and the reader.

All these specific issues do mirror a broader issue. Psychoanalysis became an inspiration of many social science and artistic work. This was shown in direct program impact in the case of the **surrealists** André Breton and Salvador Dali, or the Hungarian poet Attila József. In the 1950s and 1960s, Freudian topics of childhood trauma and the like permeated Hollywood movie making as well.

Parallel to this, a simplified psychoanalytic way of thought and speech became part of everyday discourse as well. Many social critics as well as psychologists noted that the real impact of Freud may be in changing the self-image of humans. Non-conscious determination, the omnipresence of desires and sexuality, and infantile pleasures did change our self-image and thereby became factors of our life (Moscovici, 1961/2008). George Miller, the American cognitive psychologist, summarized the Freudian impact over two generations of psychologists. Freud was less important in the therapies or the tools invented and introduced by him, and more important due to the changes of our self-image.

> Today we are much more aware of the irrational components of human nature and much better able to accept the reality of our unconscious impulses. The

importance of Freudian psychology derives far less from its scientific validity than from the effects it has had on our shared image of man himself.

(Miller, 1969, p. 1067)

These everyday mundane effects notwithstanding, psychoanalysis as a school has been constantly changing. Due to its movement-like character, these changes have taken the form of fraction formations and heresies.

The first schism: the analytic psychology of Jung

Freud repeatedly underlined that the single principle his followers should never give up was the theory of sexuality. However, due to the movement-like organization of psychoanalysis and the strong father/son-like connections between mentors and pupils, some of the direct students of Freud gave up this exact principle. James Putnam (1917) very early on realized that there were two aspects of these schisms. One was the proposition of other unconscious motivational factors besides sexuality, such as competition for dominance (Adler) and the move toward a symbolic integration in adult life (Jung). The other factor is related to general organizational issues: the constant need for revisions within a hierarchically organized movement. The first revolts that showed up in the 1910s, resulting in alternative movements of depth psychology, are still with us. Instead of the vital instincts, they take as a basic explanatory principle something more venerable or more social. We refer to them as **schools of depth psychology**, since they still do accept the idea of unconscious determination.

Figure 1.1 shows that the two first schisms, that of Carl Gustav Jung and Alfred Adler, became part of general psychological literature. Their popularity has even increased recently.

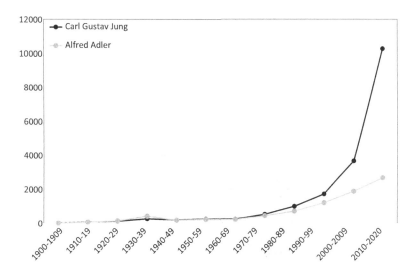

Figure 1.1 The appearance in any text of Carl Gustave Jung and Alfred Adler in the PsycINFO database.

Biography

A prophetic life and a prophetic cult: Carl Gustave Jung

The Swiss psychiatrist Carl Gustav Jung (July 26, 1875, Kesswil, Switzerland–June 6, 1961, Küssnacht, Switzerland) belonged to the inner core of Freud followers in the heroic first years of the movement. His desertion seriously hurt not only Freud but also the entire psychoanalytic movement just taking shape. The young doctor Jung was an associate of Eugen Bleuler at Burghölzli, an innovative psychiatry hospital near Zürich. During his early hospital career, Jung introduced his well-known **association test**. From slowdown of reaction times, from failures to react and bizarre reactions, one can infer the complexes related to the given word (Jung, 1910). Reading Freud and establishing personal contacts with the master provided a key for Jung to interpret these complexes. For a few years, Jung became the president of the favorite organization of Freud, the *International Psychoanalytic Association*. He was the appointed dauphin. The theory of childhood sexuality, however, did not please him, and they separated basically due to this in 1913–1914.

The organizational and intellectual divorce had several motives. There were underlying difference that might also be related to their personal life. Freud saw the sexual element as a key factor in human life, while for Jung the symbolic, more "suprapersonal elements" were crucial. In their personal life, however, as Roudinesco (2016) has shown, the reverse was true. Freud hardly had an active sexual life during his later years, while Jung had a complex and varied sexual life, not merely on the level of fantasy.

Figure 1.2 Carl Gustave Jung as a young man.
Source: Wikimedia commons.

From the separation on, Jung and his followers refer to his system as **analytic or complex psychology**. The Jungians assumed that mental life has a crucial component besides individual unconscious, a **collective unconscious**. Its basic structural elements are the **archetypes** expressing the shared mental frames of humanity, and the alternative roots of personality development. Archetypes most clearly would appear in mythology, religions, and dreams. They are frames of thought about important events in human life. The mother archetype relates to birth, transformation, and nurturance. Archetypes in their origin would be traces of the experience of past generations. In their functionality, they are similar to memes in contemporary culture. Jung traveled widely to support these claims and acquainted himself with primitive cultures and Eastern religions. Richard Noll (1994), the American medical historian and an expert on mystical events and other cultic phenomena, published a controversial book showing Jung as a weakly controlled charlatan. The biological visions of the mind promoted by Ernst Haeckel, and the turn-of-the-century monistic "natural religion" trends, had a great impact on Jung. Three aspects were derived from this influence on the attitude and work of Jung: the inheritance of acquired characteristics, with the idea of recapitulation; a need to maintain a cultic relation with the trans-spiritualized nature; and the interpretation of alternative pathways of personality development. According to Noll, in these mythological matters, Jung remained a superficial amateur, prone to errors and even to distortions. This idea is much challenged by Jung's followers.

Jung organized a huge camp of followers, and the relation between the Freudians and the Jungians are far from friendly. Jung is also a center of discussions about his alleged Nazi sympathies. In the late 1930s, he was president of the German psychotherapy association, but while he tried to promote Jungian psychology in Germany under Hitler, he was never anti-Semitic and clearly not associated with the Nazi cause. Jung wanted to make the society international and with no commitment or preference for worldviews.

There were and are many followers of Jung. In 1948, Jung established a Jung Institute in Zurich, Switzerland, that is still active. There are Jung societies all around the world, and from 1955, an English journal is published under the title *Journal of Analytical Psychology*.

Collective unconscious

Jung has a rather strong standpoint regarding the role of pieces of a more ancient, non-personal kind arising in the unconscious workings of our mind.

> A more or less superficial layer of the unconscious is undoubtedly personal. I call it the *personal unconscious*. But this personal unconscious rests upon a deeper layer, which does not derive from personal experience and is not a personal acquisition but is inborn. This deeper layer I call the *collective*

unconscious. . . . It is identical in all men and thus constitutes a common psychic substrate of a suprapersonal nature which is present in every one of us. . . .

"Archetype" is an explanatory paraphrase of the Platonic *eidos*. . . . we are dealing with archaic or – I would say – primordial types, that is, with universal images that have existed since the remotest times.

(C. G. Jung, 1917, pp. 104, 124–126)

Out of the two basic terms of the supraindividual mental life introduced by Jung, **archetypes**, as a more descriptive term, has become more widespread. *Archetypes* figure over 3,000 times in the PsycINFO database, while **collective unconscious** only about 1,400 times. The Platonist vision of a collective unconscious had followers mainly from the direct affiliates of Jung. The reservations of others have to do with the general individualistic attitude of modern psychology. Modern psychology emerged as a field dealing with the gradually articulated individual and individuality in the process of modernization, which has doubts about collectivistic notions. As an additional factor, in the 1920s–1940s, psychologists became especially suspicious of all group-related essentialist concepts, such as the group mind of McDougall (1920a) (who was, by the way, analyzed by Jung), or the French collective representations, to which Jung actually refers (for details, see Chapters 5 and 6).

There were some exceptions regarding the idea of archetypes and collective unconscious. Besides McDougall, the German writer Thomas Mann (think of *Joseph and his brothers*) and the Hungarian Swiss classical philologist Charles Kerényi (1897–1973) were notable cultural exceptions. Jung and Kerényi collaborated during the Swiss emigration of the Hungarian philologist and published a study of European myths with an eye on archetypes (Jung & Kerényi, 1941).

Personality according to Jung

The relatively reserved appreciation was by far not true for the ideas of Jung about the structure of personality and his methods of psychotherapy. According to the Jungian vision of personality, humans are characterized by a fight of rivaling tendencies. Their essence in Freud was the tension between instincts and culture. In Jung, the tension would be between a more superficial layer responsible for social adaptation and a deeper one representing the more symbolic deeper values of life. Development is a process of individuation where one would learn to pay attention to the symbolic meanings pointing in the far future and referring to the archetypes. Along these lines, while dreams for Freud carry secrets about the past, dreams according to Jungians refer to the future, like the dreams of the Pharaoh in the biblical story of Joseph.

In the process of individuation, different attitudes do develop; among them the most well-known are the **extraverted outer-oriented** and the **introverted inner-oriented types**. As Chapter 2 shows, this has become the foundation of a typology still present in academic psychology, turning it into the most lasting impact of Jung.

In the personality model proposed by Jung, the types work in a complex compensatory economy. Besides the types of directedness, there are types according to the dominance of the different mental processes; there are, for example, thinking and sensing people. Furthermore, the dominant surface organization (**animus**) is complemented by its opposite as a hidden organization, the **anima**. This is related to the continuous presence of female and male role repertories in both genders.

Jung also introduced a new attitude in his **therapeutic interventions**. He is more future- than past-oriented. The past, the childhood, is replaced by forward-looking value choices and individuation as the key issues in psychotherapy. In this regard, the attitude of Jung is echoed by humanistic psychology from the 1960s on. There are similarities between the aims of Jung to reveal the worldviews underlying different religions and the vision of Maslow (1954), who placed the issue of world outlooks on the top of his motivational hierarchy.

The inventions of Jung, in line with his wide public appeal toward the communities looking for salvation in the troubled world of the mid-20th century, were accompanied with emotional enthusiasms and rejections as well. Many of his advocates and his orthodox psychoanalytic adversaries tend to juxtapose him as the representative of a depth psychology of a Christian spirit which is contrasted to psychoanalysis supposedly dominated by a Jewish spirit, or religious skepticism. Jung certainly had religious inspirations and messages as well (Noll, 1994), and his movement continues to be appealing to pastoral psychologists. But to acknowledge their real differences, we do not have to immerse into the world of mutual labeling. The integrity of the Jungian approach with its emphasis on values of a higher order is certainly much more spiritualistic than the quasi-biological vision of Freud. Freud, with his "earthly" libido conception, is a Darwinist evolutionary thinker, in contrast to Jung, who claims aspiration upward, for whom culture is a movement away from the "givens" of situations. They can be contrasted as the biologist versus the idealist, not as the Jew versus the Christian. In their inspirations, both were greatly influenced by the ideas of Haeckel on the recapitulation of phylogenesis in ontogenesis, and both had some Lamarckian ideas about the inheritance of once-upon-a-time experiences and solutions to developmental tensions.

The individual psychology of Adler

While Jung transcended the original libido theory of Freud by moving toward spiritual value orientation, Alfred Adler (1870–1937) moved toward the importance of social relations in individual psychodynamics in his alternative theory. As a young medical practitioner in Vienna, Adler attended the informal Wednesday seminars of Freud and was even the president of the *Viennese Psychoanalytic Association*. Due to their increasing disagreements, however, he left the Freudians in 1911 and established his *Society for Individual Psychology* in 1912.

In the explanation of neurosis, Adler relied on the social situation of the child, rather than on infantile sexuality. The **individual psychology** promoted by Adler looks for the explanation of disorders in social relations and in competition. Sexuality in this way of thought is mainly important as a case for the dominance over the

Figure 1.3 Alfred Adler.

other person. Adler became (among other followers analyzing the impact of family structure) a reference for later feminist psychologies. One of his basic notions is the idea of **compensation**. On the analogy of the organization of some bodily functions, he imagined overcompensation as an organizing principle of the mind. The little child lives in the context of a social (and physical) world of adults characterized by overwhelming power. Feelings of an **inferiority complex** in the child are compensated by feelings of superiority or even omnipotence and a limitless ambition. Neurosis is the result of a contradiction between ambitions and possibilities.

> The inferiority complex leads to a desire for escape and this desire for escape is expressed in a superiority complex, which is nothing more than a goal on the useless and vain side of life offering the satisfaction of false success.
>
> This is the dynamic mechanism of psychological life. More concretely, we know that the mistakes in the functioning of the psyche are more harmful at certain times than at others. We know that the style of life is crystallized in tendencies formed in childhood in the prototype that develops at the age of four or five.
>
> (Adler, 1928, pp. 262–263)

The social world of Central Europe was mapped in detail by Adler to the sibling relations in the family. Adler mainly analyzed multiple boy rivalries. Junior siblings must experience their weakness in relation to their brothers as well, which leads to many revolts and innovations to overcome the context of continuous negative comparisons. Instead of rivalry for sex and love, the main forces of humans are ambition and rivalry for power. Adlerian individual psychology also had close affinity to the cause of education. Adler concentrated on later stages, however. The key for successful education according to this vision was the proper partition of competition, reward, and punishment, depending on the position of children in relative ranks. In Adler's vision of education, vital elements (love) are replaced by many symbolic moments, like ambition and goals (Adler, 1928).

Adler played a central role in depth psychology in Central Europe in the 1920s. With his social engagement, he attracted many young people, and Adlerian societies were formed in large cities of the region. Even for Karl Popper, the experience with psychoanalytic circular explanation, which was so central in his critic of psychoanalysis (Popper, 1959, 1963), was rooted in his association with Adler. With the emphasis on social context, Adler began teaching and lecturing in America and became an important inspiration of later social neo-Freudian theories there. He was also an important source of those theories of motivation and personality that rely on ambition as a special human motivation system, like in the theories of achievement motivation (McClelland, 1953). This association is related to the fact that with his concentration of ambition, the system of Adler proposed a much less deterministic image of humans compared to that of Freud.

There were many questionable studies of birth order effects in his own time. More recently, Adler re-emerged as the inspiration of developmental theories of an evolutionary kind. Sulloway (1996) tried to prove on the basis of biographical data that birth order and life paths, including ideological stances, are related. First-born boys tend to be more conservative, value-preserving, and traditional in their politics, science, and art, trying to emulate their fathers. Younger siblings, on the other hand, tend to be oriented toward revolt and change. As a radical example, in the Russian communist movement, the second-born Lenin was overturning social order, while the firstborn Stalin re-established order. The source of this contingency would be that children born later face a situation where all the good positions were already taken, and their only solution would be to change the situation radically. Mass studies of personality tried to show this proposal with correlations, but sometimes the opposite came out: those born later were more social in their behavioral self-reports. This debate is still ongoing.

The indigenous development of Freudian psychoanalysis

Psychoanalysis in the 1920s–1930s did not change only in its divisions and break-ups. The original Freudian model has also been developing both in the sense of functional, institutional, and geographic expansion and in the sense of intellectually widening toward cultural phenomena, toward a wider array of pathologies and infant development, without giving up the corner stone, libido theory. Some of the extensions are remarkable and interesting, especially regarding the cultural history and the local theories of psychiatry and psychopathology in different cultural settings. After the First World War, psychoanalysis extended from its original German-speaking Central European niche toward Germany, Russia (for about ten years, until the end of the 1920s), England, and the United States.

Institutionally, trainings started to be organized first in Berlin and later in Chicago, and training models with different emphases – the issue of lay analysis, the involvement of traditional medical psychiatry, and especially the nature and topic of training analysis and mentors, later supervision – started to be discussed. Psychoanalysis, besides developing its own training protocols and centers, started to have different role models in relation both to psychology and to medical psychiatry in different cultural contexts. In some contexts, like in France, psychology and psychoanalysis remained separated even in their terminology (see the account in the textbook of French history of psychology by Carroy et al., 2006 and Nicolas, 2002). In other cultures, the main issue became the relation of psychoanalysis and psychiatry as practiced in medical institutions, and in general, there were many points of contention and discussions regarding the training protocols and licensing developed by the psychoanalysts. These were differentiated both from medical- and from philosophy-related psychology training. That is true in most cultural contexts until today, with parallel institutions of psychoanalytic training, either entirely independent or in interaction with clinical psychology training and licensing. In the 1930s, the advent of authoritarian nationalist regimes resulted in racial discrimination and persecution of psychoanalysis, first in Germany and Central Europe, later in many parts of Western Europe as well. The forced exodus mainly to the United States had its own tensions, analyzed by Judit Mészáros (2014), a Hungarian psychoanalyst and historian of psychoanalysis.

The practical clinical extensions of psychoanalysis started in Europe but later flourished on the American scene by the meeting of the exiles and the American medical movements. The Hungarian-born Ferenc-Franz Alexander (1891–1964) became a leading figure in some of these extensions. Alexander, who arrived before the huge exodus, established himself at the Chicago Institute of Psychoanalysis. He became central by trying to propose shorter therapies. That created many tensions in the 1930s, similar to the tensions a generation later created by the proposals of Jacques Lacan to shorten the sessions themselves. To put it more precisely, Lacan (1977) campaigned for variable-length sessions, with the possibility to interrupt the session unexpectedly to initiate symbolic works between the sessions by the patient (Roudineso, 1990).

Alexander was also important in a symbolic manner on the American scene. His involvement of psychoanalysis in Hollywood contributed to the mundane integration of psychoanalysis into American life in the 1950s. Franz Alexander was also a central figure in extending psychoanalysis to criminal justice and to the treatment of physical illnesses toward what has become referred to as psychosomatic medicine (Alexander, 1950). In the thirties, the very influential European-trained psychiatrist at Johns Hopkins University Adolf Meyer (1866–1950), who was spending time both with Jackson and Charcot, allowed and encouraged the integration of psychoanalysis into medical thinking (Meyer, 1928), though he himself stood for a broader psychobiological conception. Alexander also tried to put psychoanalysis to become an integral part of the internist training of would-be psychiatrists. These efforts also proposed making psychoanalysis more scientific. The medical trail was mainly interested in **psychosomatics**, specifically in its relations to neurology, psychiatry, and the work of the general practitioner.

Psychoanalysis in the Freudian variety rooted itself in a slower manner in France, and in a way that involved both the rival indigenous medical psychologies and the alternative art movements, especially surrealism in the footsteps of Breton (Roudinesco, 1994). Ellenberger (1970) analyzed in detail the intellectual-level rivalry for primacy between the Freud tradition and the French dynamic psychology tradition represented by Pierre Janet, both at the medical and Collège de France establishment. With all these impeding factors, the Paris Psychoanalytic Society (*Société psychanalytique de Paris*) was established in 1926. That did not mean, however, a full intellectual integration into French intellectual high society.

There were some early echoes of Freud in the 1920s in France, from non-psychoanalytic circles that were on the periphery in the eye of the clinicians. Charles Blondel (see Chapter 5), starting from the Salpêtrière and later at the reintegrated University of Strasbourg, pursued the clinical dissociation tradition in his first book of seven case studies and an analysis following mainly Janet (Blondel, 1914). He wrote an early French review and a monograph on Freud (Blondel, 1924). Besides presenting the theory of the Austrian intellectual in ironical analogies with Gall, Blondel mainly argued that the overambitious theorizing around the notion of libido may oversimplify the determinations of human mind. Blondel, later as a clinician, unlike Janet, or Freud, claimed qualitative differences between the normal and the pathological. In the French clinical tradition, he was particularly interested in the pathological dissolutions of the traditional, stable Ego. The presence or absence of the Cartesian theater was the main clinical issue for him.

A special role was played in French Freud interpretation by an early left-wing French interpretation of Freud, the **concrete psychology** of George Politzer (1903–1942). He made a name for himself by criticizing Bergson as an irrationalist thinker (Politzer, 1941/2000). Politzer's early French book (1928) on Freud had a double function. It is a critical conceptual analysis and presentation of psychoanalysis and a theoretical introduction of his program for concrete psychology. Politzer's starting point is a sympathy with the dynamicity of psychoanalytic explanations and, at the same time, a critique of Freudian metapsychology, a critique of the introduction of essentialist thing-like structures as the static unconscious. What is to replace the interplay of representations in the vision of Politzer? The proper domain of psychology would be the study of the **human drama** itself.

> The events that arrive to us are of a dramatic nature. We are playing such and such a "role" etc. We have a *dramatic vision of ourselves*: we know that we have been the agent or the witness of such and such an action.... Our *intentions* are also dramatic: we want to get married, go to the movies etc. *We are thinking of ourselves in dramatic terms*.
> (Politzer, 1947, p. 37)

By concentrating on the drama, one could preserve the human character of the phenomena. This program was never worked out as a system of possible social roles and human actions. We have an interaction-based folk psychology program here. Politzer gives everyday examples, like marriage, witnessing, etc., but does not attempt a classification of interactions that would be the case of much later attribution theories. This Hungarian born French philosopher and theoretical psychologist was a Communist resistant who was killed by the German occupying forces in France. With his tragically short life and the missing elaboration of his program of concrete psychology, Politzer still remained a source of hope for an alternative psychology and, for many, an alternative reading of Freud (Roudinesco, 1994).

Innovations of the Budapest school

The efforts of this school were deeply embedded into the network of Budapest – mainly Jewish – intellectual life of the early 20th century that involved embeddedness into a cultural, artistic, and scientific network life (Mészáros, 2014, 2017). This way of life is described in a vivid manner by one of the participants, the latter psychoanalyst Franz Alexander (1960), as a bygone world. His book provides a rich and detailed account of life in the *New York Palace*, a new *art nouveau* turn-of-the-century building in Budapest full of rich bourgeois homes, which was the home of the Alexander family, and at the same time a center for coffeehouse life and journalism. The rich interaction between mathematicians, scientists, medical people, artists, and writers was a peculiar feature of early 20th-century Hungarian intellectual life and, as part of it, of the birth of psychoanalysis as well. As Hungarian intellectual Ferenc Alexander (1960) recalled it, he was influenced by the intensive academic and non-academic networks around his father, Bernát Alexander (1850–1927), himself a noted philosopher, and the intellectual "hub" around turn-of-the-century Budapest at large.

An interesting general feature of early Hungarian psychology in the first decades of the 20th century was the cross talk between cultural networks. Psychoanalysis, experimental psychology, and child study (pedagogy) were characteristically interacting at that time in Budapest. The intellectual consequence of the multiple embedding of Hungarian psychoanalysis was the biological interpretation combined with an interest toward children and intellectual development.

Judit Mészáros (2009), in her analysis of the substantial message of the Budapest school, concentrates on four issues:

- the theory of countertransference;
- the object relations theory in early Ego development;
- the new interpretation of trauma; and
- the synthesis of psychoanalysis with personality testing.

We can add two further aspects to this:

- close ties with natural science; and
- social engagement.

Relations with natural science were central to Hungarian psychoanalysts. In the post-Freud fate of psychoanalysis, there was a constant tension between a biological and a "purely psychological interpretation." Mainstream psychoanalytic thought stays in the solid bases of psychological interpretation, at the same time entertaining a causal mode, an assumed biological determinism of individual behavioral, and mental events. One dominant paradoxical feature of the Hungarian approach, or the Budapest school, was (and still is) a peculiar combination of a more direct biological interpretation of the Freudian message, combined with a softer attitude regarding intervention and therapy. The typical Hungarian way would not lead psychoanalysis into the realms of hermeneutics but rather would try to ground it in natural science. This was paradoxical on two levels. The hard-line biologists preach a softer therapy. And due to the overlapping networks, the biological attitude was combined with an activist social engagement and with a deep interest in arts.

Sándor Ferenczi (1873–1933) was the founder of the Budapest school. While he was a socially engaged practicing medical doctor, he simultaneously elaborated in his theoretical works, especially his *Thalassa: Catastrophes in the development of Genitality*, a rather speculative synthesis of evolutionary biology and libido theory (Ferenczi, 1924/1989). Ferenczi relied on the biogenetic theory also present in Freud (the dramas of ontogenesis repeat events and dramas in phylogenesis) and started to claim that human genitality, including the organization of sexual acts, was a repetition of the great traumas of phylogenesis (the beginning of earthly life after sea-based life) and ontogenesis (birth as suffocation). This connection was rather poetic. The biological attitude implied in it remained, however, a basic feature of the Budapest school. Relations with natural sciences continued to be important for Hungarian psychoanalysts of the next generation. Imre Hermann (1889–1984), in his instinct theory originally published in 1943, tried to combine instincts in the psychoanalytic sense with early observations of then-new ethology. The clinging instinct in humans was related to a biologically relevant clinging to the body of the mother. This new interpretation connected the natural science attitude of the Budapest school to a new interpretation of the sources of pathology. Their basic issue was not the Oedipal complex but the separation from the mother, and most of the pathology could be interpreted as a new effort to reunite with the mother. This makes the connection of the Budapest school biology with the interpretation of early life. Hermann preceded the work of a new generation of British psychoanalysts, like Bowlby (1969), who much later on attempted this kind of synthesis of ethology and psychoanalytic attachment theory.

The natural science inspiration was true on the methodological level too. Hermann's monograph (1929) on psychoanalysis as a method related the technique of psychoanalysis not only to the general issues of introspective knowledge and experimental psychology but also to the then very fresh notions of operational definitions in science (Bridgman, 1927).

Social engagement of a mostly leftist nature was a dominant feature of Hungarian psychoanalysts from the work of Ferenczi on. That originally implied positive aspects, namely, the social commitments of psychoanalysis to the causes of educational reform, to the cause of the poor, to deal with social diseases, like alcoholism and prostitution. Later, this social engagement, however, led to many negative

16 *Disciplinary developments and eclectics*

Figure 1.4 Sándor Ferenczi.
Source: Photo courtesy of the Sándor Ferenczi Society Archives and its president, Judit Mészáros.

experiences both due to the engagement of right-wing critics and due to the works of fellow leftist people. The social aspects of psychoanalysis were used as pretexts for its harsh ideological critic, both from the nationalist and from the communist side. (See Harmat, 1987; Mészáros, 2010, 2017.)

Another important feature of the Hungarian psychoanalysts is their early emphasis on **Ego theory and early infancy**. In a way, Hungarian depth psychologists were object relations theorists decades before the term was coined in psychoanalytic literature in London by Melanie Klein, who also started from Hungary. They all concentrated on the earliest dyadic, mother–child relationship, and on the traumatizing effects of its unsatisfactory nature and of its disruption.

It is remarkable that other followers of Ferenczi, starting from Budapest, Mihály Bálint (1896–1970) and Alice Bálint (1898–1939) (both of them spelled Balint in English) gave a softer interpretation of similar processes. Among the Budapest analysts, there were several who did not agree with Klein's ideas on an infant's inborn primary narcissism, sadism, and aggressive urges. Michael Balint (1965) said that they had arrived at the conclusion in Budapest that the earliest phase of the life of a psyche is not narcissistic. It is directed at objects, and these early object relations are passive. The goal is acquired love, because that is its due as a person: to be loved and satisfied, without being under any obligation to give anything in return. This is passive love/primary love, an archaic relationship between the mother and child; this is the early harmonious experience of the infant with the mother. If it is frustrated, the child has to learn how he/she can satisfy her- or himself. The infant lives from the first minutes on in social relations rather than narcissistic solipsism

(Balint, 1954). The communication **basic faults** on the part of the caring environment in this process would lead to deep pathologies later on (Balint, 1968).

Alice Balint (1954) and Alice Hermann (1895–1975), the wife and coworker of Imre Hermann, made many efforts to propagate psychoanalytic ideas in education, such as the need for love, the libido-directed behavior of teachers leading to maladaptive behaviors in children, and the like. Later studies elaborated these ideas, such as the hospitalism idea by the Austro-Hungarian/American René Spitz (1887–1974), who described the disturbance of development due to hospitalization of infants (Spitz, 1945), and the theory of the Hungarian psychoanalyst Imre Hermann (1943) about the clinging instinct of primate and human infants. This image of early development provided a very easy road and entry of psychoanalysis into everyday life. The receiving environment, that is, the family and education, do not have to become psychoanalysts to see their idea being reinforced: love is important for babies.

A **more accepting and relation-based attitude toward therapy** also characterized the Budapest school. Ferenczi (1932/1995), as shown in his clinical diaries, reinterpreted the Oedipal tension as a confusion of tongues between partners and, in this way, proposed a new recombination of the seduction and infant sexuality interpretations (see Chapter 13 in Volume 1). Alongside this, Ferenczi promoted a more active and, at the same time, more feminine attitude toward therapy.

> The willingness on our part to admit our mistakes and the honest endeavor to avoid them in future, all these go to create in the patient a confidence in the analyst. It is this confidence that establishes the contrast between the present and the unbearable traumatogenic past, the contrast which is absolutely necessary for the patient in order to enable him to reexperience the past no longer as hallucinatory reproduction but as an objective memory.
> (Ferenczi, 1933/1949, pp. 225–226)

This attitude resulted in "an optimal mix of liberalism, respect, and interactive communication," a combination of trust, warmness, liberalism, and still activism in the therapy promoted by Ferenczi.

> Psychoanalysis became a system of multidirectional processes of relational elements between the patient and the analyst. A new psychoanalytic discourse developed. Communication that stressed interpretation and therapy based on teaching was replaced by the need for emotional awareness and a relationship reflective of the unconscious processes of oneself and others, while focusing on the patient's current affective and cognitive capacities.
> (Mészáros, 2014, p. 113)

Object relations theory and Ego psychology

In the 1930s, some of the new substantial changes or extensions of psychoanalytic theory had been related to the finer analysis of infant development and Ego articulation. Freud, with his theory of infantile sexuality, was revolutionary and socially disturbing by attributing desires to preschoolers. One new conceptual development in psychoanalytic theory and practice was the further radical extension of these efforts to understand infant mentality toward still younger ages, with **a more complex interpretation of infancy**. Freudian infantile sexuality gradually became an issue of early relations to the physical and social world. With an interesting change in the notion of narcissism, "object relations" psychoanalysts started to interpret the behavior of very young infants as beings who entertain complex relations to the nurturing and other environmental objects. This shift also implied a gender shift. There was a change from the father-based Oedipal scene toward an ontogenetically earlier mother-centered tender scene. Melanie Klein (1882–1960) was initiated to psychoanalysis by an analysis with Ferenczi in Budapest and then worked in Berlin and London. Based on work, first, on her own children and then using a symbolic play situation to understand the conflicts of children, she promoted a theory according to which infants do form early on representations of the world. Klein followed the road opened up by Freud: she postulated more and more complex psychological mechanisms in younger and younger children. Infants represent the world on the basis of how the world satisfies the needs of the infant (for example, the representation of the nonnutritive breast and mother shall be the basis of the representation of a malignant world). Later organization of experiences shall go according to these earliest representations. The early representations may become distorted projections if the **good enough mother** does not regulate these needs of the infant (Klein, 1921/1975). **Object relations theory** conceived in this way has become part of the general accepted mainstream of psychoanalysis, though in the early periods, Anna Freud (1928) thought it to be a rival to her own approach to children. A constant tension developed between the two approaches in their London emigration, leading to alternative, more classic Freudian (libido-centered) and more object relations–oriented training. As we saw earlier, the Budapest school proposed a general new approach to depth psychology, partly initiating, partly extending the early Ego development debate.

Besides the new theories of infant development, the other key moment of the psychoanalysis of the 1930s was the detailed elaboration of **Ego psychology** for adult life as well. The built-in tension of the psychoanalytic ideas was that an organism that is constantly under the direction of its desires is still adaptable in a biological sense. The starting point was the work of Anna Freud (1895–1982) published in 1936 on the mechanisms of Ego defense. In her classification attempt, she proposed that some of them are in the service of the adaptive Ego. The Vienna-trained psychoanalyst Heinz Hartmann (1894–1970) went a step further in his book published after his American immigration (Hartmann, 1939). The Ego develops not only during desire-related conflicts. There are Ego domains without conflicts that provide for learning and veridical perception. Further, defense mechanisms originally attached to desires may acquire a functional autonomy; thus, sexual exploration, for example, may be the foundation of a general curiosity.

Experimentation and theoretical integration

From the 1930s on, one central aspect of psychoanalysis would be the efforts to overstep the couch situation, that is, to provide for a general psychology in psychoanalytic terms. Series of experiments were taking shape that tried to show the emotional factors in forgetting and the non-conscious emotional determinants of perception (Rosenzweig, 1937; Rapaport, 1942, for a later survey, see Rosenzweig, 1985). Rosenzweig (1907–2004), the later developer of a much used picture frustration test, in his programmatic paper, even claimed that by moving experimental science and psychoanalytic concepts toward each other, psychoanalysis will lose its isolationist character and

> be able to overcome the strong prejudice against it, emerge from the retreat into which it was forced by this prejudice, and flow into its predestined psychological and medical channels. Through *experimental* and practical verification, it will lose it cultist and isolative character.
> (Rosenzweig, 1937, p. 61)

Rapaport (1942), in his detailed survey monograph, showed that emotions in general should be much more broadly conceived than was customary. They should be treated not merely as physiological but also as "presentational" effects. We should forget all simplistic, everyday interpretations of psychoanalysis, like a claim for a tendency to forget bad things, etc.

Psychoanalysts, including Freud himself, were very skeptical about similar efforts. In a paradoxical way, Freud, who started as a naturalist and who is charged to be too biological, believed in the superiority of clinical case-based observations. As Rosenzweig recalled in their exchanges, Sigmund Freud clearly expressed his doubts about experimenting on the unconscious in the 1930s.

> On two occasions, Freud made a similar negative response to any attempts to explore psychoanalytic theory by laboratory methods. This exchange clearly underscored Freud's distrust of, if not opposition to, experimental approaches to the validation of his clinically derived concepts. Freud consistently believed that the clinical validation of his theories, which were based originally and continuously on his self-analysis, left little to be desired from other sources of support.
> (Rosenzweig, 1997, p. 571)

The flourishing of the attitude introduced by Rapaport would come in the "new look" theories of perception in the 1950s and continuing as new look II and III, as Erdélyi (1985, 2006) summarized it. The basic idea underlying many experiments was simple. There is an unnoticed, unconscious, subliminal perceptual effect of desires or sexual connotations of words, accompanied by a repression of conscious recognition. That was highly controversial for many experimentalists (Dixon, 1971).

Parallel to this were efforts to make psychoanalysis into a well-organized theory in the sense of the philosophy of science prevalent in the 1930s. Many psychoanalysts already in the 1930s did not agree with these efforts and considered the couch to be the basic tool for gaining new insights and continued to use case studies and analogical-metaphoric argumentation. The constant optimism toward eliminating the gaps between psychoanalysis and experimental psychology, and between psychoanalysis and learning theory, was a dream for many starting from neobehaviorists, like Hull and Tolman, and for psychoanalysts like the French Daniel Lagache (1949). One key figure in this process was David (Dezső) Rapaport (1911–1960), an American "outgrowth" of the Budapest school. In his early intellectual life, he tried to combine academic psychology training in Budapest (he was tutored by von Schiller Harkai) and psychoanalytic training. His main contribution to psychoanalysis later on during his American career was, in a way, a continuation of this Hungarian start. He widely published on the relationship between experimental and psychoanalytic theories of forgetting (Rapaport, 1942), on the analytic and laboratory studies of thought (1951), and later on, on the conceptual analysis of psychoanalytic systems, the metapsychology of Freud (Rapaport, 1960, see Chapter 13 of Volume 1). He was a devoted proponent of a biologically based Freudian metapsychology.

The extension of instinct theory into fate analysis: Lipót Szondi

Among the major renegade trends in "depth psychology," a biologically minded trend started from Hungary. Leopold (Lipót) Szondi (1893–1986), a medical doctor who specialized in endocrinology, worked until the early 1940s in a laboratory organized as an affiliated part of the *Psychology Institute for the Handicapped*, founded by Paul Ranschburg, and also chartered by the School for Teachers in Special Education in Budapest. During the war, as a persecuted Hungarian Jew, Szondi escaped to Switzerland in rather adventurous ways. In 1969, on the model of Jung, he founded an Institute of Fate Analysis in Zürich.

Szondi was the McDougall of depth psychology. While Jung intended to reform libido theory with an eye on culture and eternal values, and Adler with an eye on social relations, Szondi aimed to replace classical sexual libido theory with a multidimensional biological instinct theory. Szondi started off his career considering endocrinological factors and genetic aspects of constitutionality, by studying reoccurring constitutional diseases in families. This constitutional aspect was replaced in the 1930s by an effort to analyze human choices in marriage and other crucial decisions, like friendships (Szondi, 1937). Why do people remarry persons with a similar constitution as their previous spouse? Underlying diseases and partner **choices**, as Szondi observed, was a constitutional buildup of personality, with unconscious forces in our decisions and diseases. Szondi combined the typological trends in German psychology (Chapter 2) with the instinctual theories taken over from psychoanalysis. In order to account for these choices, Szondi postulated eight human instincts ordered into pairs, like in Table 1.1.

The entire theory remains male-centered. This is both shown by the treatment of male homosexuality as an exaggerated tenderness and by the later development

Table 1.1 The instinct pairs of Szondi, with the corresponding disorders, instincts, desires, and pathological tendencies

Sexual		*Paroxysmal*		*Schizoid*		*Contact*	
H	S	E	H	C	P	M	D
Homosex	Sadism	Epilepsy	Hysteria	Catatony	Paranoia	Mania	Depression

of the Szondi test, which would be a picture choice regarding the sexual instinct circles merely among male portraits.

The instincts are characterized by a peculiar dynamic in the system of Szondi (filling up, dispensation, compensation). Instincts are determining forces in our life in a fateful manner. They are decisive in our pair choices and selections of profession. Szondi (1937) attempted to prove with the genetic analysis of family trees that latent genes, in fact, determine attractions. There is a general "like likes like," *similis simili gaudet* attitude, according to Szondi. We tend to choose partners who fit our hidden, latent genetic factors. "Repressed latent genes in the lineal (inherited) unconscious determine the choice in love, friendship, profession, sickness and death" (Szondi, 1952, p. 1).

After his general twin and genealogy studies, looking for familial aggregation of mental and physical disorders, Szondi developed his test to investigate the multi-instinct theory of choices. The basic assumptions were straightforward, but each of them is questionable in itself.

1. There is a physiognomic affinity relation between types of mental disorders and the face. Thus, he selected portraits of different disordered people, like passive male homosexuals, sadists, catatonic, epileptic people.
2. Diseases are organized in a basic instinctual manner.
3. The choices we make mirror our latent instinctual tendencies.

He postulated that the eight diagnostic syndromes of the test represent basic drives which are hereditarily determined. Both manifest physical appearance and personality are considered to be a function of genetic structure. The pictured patients have a definitely diagnosed psychopathology and, therefore, a known genetic structure and personality. The subject responds to the test pictures in terms of the relations of his own genetically determined basic drives to those of the pictured patients. The picture selections of the subject thus provide a basis for inference about characteristics of his personality.

Regarding the internal consistency and the validity of the Szondi test, a thorough analysis by András Vargha, a Hungarian statistical personality psychologist, provided a disappointing image, based on a decade of profile analysis.

> It has been clearly shown that three factors (e, hy, and k) have no better internal consistency than a randomly composed set of pictures no matter how many times the test was administered. Moreover, the results indicated that

the weak to moderate reliability level of the remaining factors pertains only to cross sectional analyses, since none of the factors had significant longitudinal consistency. This finding also contradicts to Szondi's theory according to which the test is capable to reflect changes in motivational states. The low-level internal consistency of the Szondi factors cannot be attributed to the face selection feature of the test. . . . [I]t is possible to create psychometrically reliable scales that are based on preference judgments of the 48 Szondi-pictures.

(Vargha, 1994, p. 268)

Szondi was not a very popular depth psychologist. In the general psychology literature (PsycINFO), he had high presence only in the 1960s, with 236 mentions. After 1990, he is mentioned merely 21 times. At the same time, in his original home country, Hungary, he was an extremely influential teacher and mentor. Not only is his test still used, but also even his theories of instinctual choice have been subject to a modern evolutionary interpretation. Interestingly, his students in Hungary in the late 1930s became central leading figures of Hungarian psychology after the war. Lajos Kardos, the academic leader of psychology, himself a comparative psychologist, was a Szondi trainee. The same was true of Ferenc Mérei, leader of child development studies and clinical psychology; Imre Molnár, a later industrial psychologist and director of the research institute for child psychology; Flóra Kozmutza, the leader of special education and director of its training school; and finally, István Benedek, a leading psychiatrist in the 1940s and 1950s in Hungary. All contributed toward the development of the Szondi test. Thus, Szondi was certainly an influential figure establishing networks and teaching leadership skills.

Neo-Freudism in Europe and North America: the sociological turn of psychoanalysis

Since the 1930s, several psychoanalytic programs developed that have opened psychoanalysis toward social philosophy and rejected some theses of Freudian psychoanalysis, showing some Adlerian flavor in classical Freudians. At the same time, they usually had a critical stance regarding a "mere medical" approach, and they tend to have a therapeutic attitude, not merely toward the patients, but toward society at large. These attempts are usually referred to as **neo-Freudism** or **neo-Freudianism**. They frequently integrated into psychoanalysis a left-wing, sometimes Marxist, sociology that had as its source the Frankfurt-based critical theory of the 1930s. Later, due to the forced emigration of the Frankfurt school, the ties have become even closer, resulting in joint researches.

Psychoanalysis against fascism: the theory of authoritarian personality

The most characteristic feature of these sociologically, politically, and philosophically motivated innovations were the efforts of some psychoanalysts to search for professional tools in psychology for the case of a democratic credo and the fights against fascism and authoritarianism in general. These efforts were parallel and sometimes similar to efforts of emigrated *Gestalt* psychologists, specifically the Lewin group, and some European social psychologists coming from the circles of Karl Bühler, like Paul Lazarsfeld (1959), and some sociologically minded neobehaviorists, like Miller and Dollard (Dollard et al., 1939).

Already around the time Hitler took power, left-wing interpretations of fascism appeared in Europe that connected the sociological thesis of the *petit bourgeois* origins of fascism with the issue of sexual repressions. Wilhelm Reich (1897–1957), the communist psychoanalyst, was a forerunner of combining psychoanalysis and Marxism in the 1930s. Reich was originally a practicing psychoanalyst in the outpatient center of Freud in Vienna. His theoretical works started by the proposal of a new theory of character. The *Mass psychology of fascism*, published in 1933, claimed that parallel to social exploitation, there was a sexual neglect and an irrelevance of sexuality. The suppression of genital (i.e., healthy) sexuality would lead to an alternation of sadistic/mystical and over-disciplined characters. The racial theory of fascism would be a source for symbolic replacement satisfactions for these people. Reich (1927/1973, 1933/1970) claimed that repression coming from family structure inhibits the proper development of sexuality, resulting in sadomasochistic personality distortions, which are the hotbed of fascism. These could be overcome by a revolutionary liberation of the sexual energies.

The speculative theories and the associated sexual political liberation movement of Reich had a peculiar impact in their own time: both communists and psychoanalysts would bash them. Later, after his immigration to the United States, his peculiar organ theories of disorders were banned as medical malpractice. While he was imprisoned, he had some following among artists and writers rather than psychoanalysts.

A much wider effect was achieved by the combination of the Frankfurt critical Marxist theory, psychoanalysis, and American empirical social science that resulted in the theory of **authoritarian personality**. The conception was elaborated on the philosophical part by the representative of the Frankfurt school of critical theory, Theodor Adorno (1903–1969). Else Frenkel-Brunswik (1908–1958) represented the European social science part, with her qualitative clinical interviews, and Daniel Levinson and Nevitt Sanford represented the Berkeley-based American personality and social psychology part, creating large data sets of questionnaire-based data and a famous *F*(ascism) scale. Adorno himself was mainly responsible for the essayistic summary chapters analyzing the implications of the authoritarian personality regarding social structure and the creation of personality types that were somehow in harmony with a certain social organization. The results of the pioneering "big science psychology project" were published as a summary book of empirical studies (Adorno et al., 1950) of 1,000 pages. The book had a wide audience and effect due to three factors. Through the critical work of Adorno, the European social scientists raised the issue of whether fascism was possible in North America as well, and what the relationship is between the structure of totalitarian institutions like schools and an intolerant personality structure. On the other hand, their work tried to fit into the empirical credo of

American social science. The assumed intolerant personality structure was operationalized in questionnaires and interviews. Finally, these efforts opened the road toward the study of prejudice and ethnocentrism that has become a hot topic during the Cold War times (Gordon Allport, 1954), and the study of personality and socialization patterns within psychology.

The famous book of Adorno and his coworkers (with over 20,000 citations) claimed that with the increased strength of social institutions representing power over the individuals, a socialization practice, and a corresponding personality type, has developed in the Western world, which tends to become the hotbed for fascism and, more broadly, of all totalitarian and intolerant social and political orders. The Adorno group turned to a psychological proposal in explaining the mid-20th-century social tragedies. A strict authoritarian educational style non-responsive to the needs of children, the suppression of instincts and pleasures in the name of obedience and order, as well as an intolerance toward any ambiguities underlies this personality pattern.

The subject achieves his own social adjustment only by taking pleasure in obedience and subordination. This brings into play the sadomasochistic impulse structure both as a condition and as a result of social adjustment.

> The resulting hatred against the father is transformed by reaction-formation into love. This transformation leads to a particular kind of superego.... The Jew frequently becomes a substitute for the hated father, often assuming, on a fantasy level, the very same qualities against which the subject revolted in the father, such as being practical, cold, domineering, and even a sexual rival.
> (Adorno et al., 1950, p. 759)

Notice that all the categories of psychoanalytic rhetoric are taken as evident starting points in this analysis. All issues that make psychoanalytic predictions hard to test are present. For example, the turning of hatred into love. The reader half a century later has the impression that the image of the mind proposed by Freud was taken as proven, and merely its specific tuning by social factors was at issue for social scientists. The other interesting one-sidedness seen later on was that the theory could not handle Asian authoritarian societies.

The F-scale intending to measure tendencies toward authoritarianism and the theory of authoritarian personality has since then followed a rich arborization full of further nuances. It was continuously studied in relation to social class, usually showing that the working class was more authoritarian than the middle classes; it has interesting personality dynamics relating it to dogmatism, and it has varying relations to racial prejudice. Meanwhile, an interesting psychological value issue has also surfaced. Who would suggest that an authoritarian, rigid, and dogmatic personality has the same value as a democratic, open, and flexible person? Due to this democratic and liberal preference, the authoritarianism work of Adorno and his coworkers was partly misread. The authoritarian personality theory has become a symbol of psychology being allied with a tolerant, democratic, flexible image of humans when it shows with an enlightened fever that its opposite also exists and leads elsewhere, toward fascism.

Adorno himself, as a critical theorist, was not entirely happy later on with the liberating interpretation of the relations between psychoanalysis and social structure. He was very well-read in psychoanalytic literature and later applied his critical stance toward psychoanalysis many times. He raised the issue in a conceptual series of papers, for example, if psychoanalytic psychotherapy was socially a welcome development at all. There is a possibility for the critical theorist that all psychotherapies were, in fact, creating and treating a false consciousness, since neurosis and even more serious psychopathologies might very well be signs of social discomfort and alienation.

However, much later theories about the relations between personality and political preferences, sometimes even in a brain lingo, has raised this issue under new lights. Many theories, sometimes based on biased samples, do claim today that conservatives have an intolerant, and liberals a more tolerant information-processing style and political preference. Moreover, religion versus laicity is somehow neutrally coded, not even in their personalities, but in their brains (Haidt, 2013). Meanwhile, the original historical explanatory power, authoritarian personality being an explanation for the psychodynamics underlying fascism, has disappeared. In general, many issues have recently been raised that half a century of social psychology has been dominated directly and indirectly by the "proper democratic liberal values," and this has misled us toward misunderstanding human nature.

Alienation and neurosis: Fromm

Several radical readings emerged in the 1950s that criticized this assumed conservativism of Freud or tried to show that there was a "real Freud," who was not conservative. Erich Fromm (1900–1980), in his works combining the Marxism of the Frankfurt school of left-wing sociology and a reconstruction of psychoanalysis, even went back to the rejection of the childhood abuse theory. According to Fromm, the introduction of childhood sexuality into psychoanalytic theory, the revolutionary breakthrough according to the Freudians, was in fact a concession to Victorian morality. It can be seen as a scientific re-emergence of the puritanical vision that treats children in themselves as being wrong and dirty. A strict education is needed to eradicate this evil from the children. The revolutionary Freud in this reading was the Freud of the seduction theory (Fromm, 1947).

Fromm (1941), in his works done while still in Germany, differentiated the anal-sadistic, authoritarian, and the genital characters, thereby sociologizing Freudism. His later works, published while working in the United States, already show by their titles a combination of the theory of neurosis, the existentialist analysis of freedom and the human condition, and psychoanalysis, flavored with some Marxist overtones, such as *Man for Himself* (Fromm, 1947) and *The art of loving* (Fromm, 1956). According to Fromm, humans, in their efforts to achieve **freedom from something**, forget **freedom for something**. Their human situation becomes external for them as well. This is toppled by peculiar historical alienations. Character structures formed in this way are historically produced. The anal-sadistic character, for example, is the typical character structure of money accumulation in capitalism.

Personality and political stance are related in this vision. The social factors, class position, and character structure do influence and support each other.

> Economic forces are effective, but they must be understood not as psychological motivations but as objective conditions: psychological forces are effective, but must be understood as historically conditioned themselves; ideas are effective, but they must be understood as being rooted in the whole of the character structure of members of a social group.
>
> (Fromm, 1941, p. 250)

Human suffering is due to an inability to really face our situation, from a search of authority to attach to, instead of looking for pleasures. In the slightly utopist image promoted by Fromm, a remedy is to look for a more mother-centered social organization to replace the authority-based, father-centered organization with a cult of love (Fromm, 1956). On a theoretical level, this attitude was similar to the softer, more feminine therapeutic style promoted by Ferenczi. The neurosis of modern humans is the result of repression due to capitalism; the solution is to quit the achievement-centered, alienated culture. In the 1960s, Fromm became, on the one hand, a guru of the new social movements emphasizing the need to leave the alienated society. On the other hand, his approach also fit into those attempts that are self-characterized as humanistic psychology. They offer to replace the healing-through-suffering attitude toward self-knowledge promoted by classical psychoanalysis with a client-centered approach based on acceptance and love.

This sociologizing trend and concentration of love was not without its own critics. **Herbert Marcuse** (1898–1979), also with roots in the Frankfurt radical left, started to claim in California that the Americanization of psychoanalysis tends to forget the original revolutionary message of Freud. There is a necessary opposition between libido and society. Due to this, libido is a forward-moving, revolutionary force in our lives. We do not need pacification and domestication of the libido in the frames of an adaptive conception. Rather, we have to keep the revolutionary message. This made his *One-dimensional man* (Marcuse, 1964) with its critique of the repressive tolerance of modern capitalism a bible of the 1968 revolting youth on both continents. You must keep the revolutionary message of Freud as well: instincts are Romantic liberating factors rather than mere accommodations to reality.

> The Neo-Freudians reverse this inner direction of Freud's theory, shifting the emphasis from the organism to the personality, from the material foundations to the ideal values. Their various revisions are logically consistent: one entails the next. The whole may be summed up as follows: the "cultural orientation" encounters the societal institutions and relationships as finished products, in the form of objective entities – given rather than made facts. Their acceptance in this form demands the shift in psychological emphasis from infancy to maturity. . . . The revisionists do not insist, as Freud did, on the enduring truth value of the instinctual needs which must be 'broken' so

that the human being can function in interpersonal relations. In abandoning this insistence, from which psychoanalytic theory drew all its critical insights, the revisionists yield to the negative features of the very reality principle which they so eloquently criticize.

(Marcuse, 1955, pp. 273–274)

Herbert Marcuse as, one leading left-wing interpreter of the Freudian message, the rival of Fromm, believed on his part that Freud is an inheritor of the German Romantic vision dissatisfied with technological rationality. In the reading of Marcuse (1955), Eros is the constant antagonist of civilization of the *petit bourgeois* sense. According to Marcuse, the opposition of culture and instinct in Freud is not a conservative but a revolutionary idea. The real Freud was abandoned, in fact, by the American neo-Freudians, who emphasize both in theory and in psychoanalytic practice the social adaptation point of view, such as Horney (1937) and Fromm (1947).

The two leaders of the neo-Marxist/neo-Freudian approaches have several further differences. While Fromm emphasized that the seduction theory should be preserved from early Freud, Marcuse was more sympathetic to the infantile sexuality version of interpreting the early dramas.

The conservative-versus-liberating-Freud debate was originally an internal affair of philosophers and psychoanalysts. It became a social issue in the process of the search for roots by the student movements in the 1960s. These student movements, in many places, especially in the United States, also became social movements for pleasure against traditional puritan ethics and against the work-centered way of life. Behind the slogans, they also realized the central intellectual issue: regarding human sexuality, the interpretation of psychoanalysis depends on whether we interpret sexuality in an economic image of limited resources, as a domain of rivalry characterized by antagonisms, or as a sphere of human life that is able to draw people together, especially since it is not exclusively organized according to the shortage economy (think of the cult of love by these movements; Fromm, 1956).

American neo-Freudianism: Horney and Sullivan

Karen Horney (1885–1952), a Berlin-trained psychoanalyst, developed a socially sensitive theory of neuroses in Chicago and New York, where needs for security, self-assertion, and the fight for dominance and power were more important than the unfolding of sexual attractions. In denying penis envy in women, she is also seen as one of the founders of modern feminist psychology. Harry Stack Sullivan (1892–1949) played a central role both in making psychoanalysis more interpersonal and institutional psychiatry more social in America. This medical psychiatrist had two basic inspirations. One was from Freud, the other from the pragmatic philosophical tradition, from comparative anthropology, and the social behaviorism of Georg Herbert Mead. Sullivan was the most important hidden factor in the development of an interpersonal theory, both in his hospital practice and in his talks. His writings mainly appeared posthumously (Sullivan, 1953). Personality was conceived by him as functioning and being formed in interactions. Our interpretations of the world are always validated through the eyes of others. This **consensual validation** has become his most influential concept. Behavior is regulated and modulated by internal representations coming from earlier interactions, resulting in positive and negative self-images. During personality development, ways of thinking and representations develop as well. Sullivan, not unlike Freud, also postulated stages in development, but in his interpretation, the stages were not merely related to biological changes. The oral stage, for example, would be characterized by representations of the mother (good or bad mother in Klein), the period of latency by the development of interpersonal skills, etc.

*

Table 1.2 compares some of the depth psychology trends regarding the points of views of this book.

In the column of *objects*, only the most specific aspect of the given trend is mentioned. Unconscious determination, of course, remains all over the place as a basic issue. Regarding method, the analytic couch is taken for granted in all. They all share the idea of an extended folk psychology. There is mental life with its desires and representations, but these entities are not always available for consciousness. They are related to extrapersonal context, to value systems, and to the representation of the other person.

Table 1.2 Comparison of some trends in depth psychology

Dimension	Object of psychology	Methods	Inner reduction	External reduction
Jung	Values	Cultural patterns	Integration and ascension	Cultural archetypes
Adler	Interpersonal context	Child-rearing patterns	Weakness and compensation	Family situations
Ferenczi	Personal relations	Communication analysis	Symbolization	Evolution
Szondi	Life course and fate	Family trees and a test	Instincts	Genetics
Fromm	Society and instincts	Sociology	Power and tensions	Social factors
Marcuse	Instincts over society	Philosophy	Romantic instincts	Social history
Horney/ Sullivan	Human development	Interaction analysis	Inner social world	Society and adaptation

Tasks

CA

Compare:

Adler and sibling research today.
Collective unconscious and contemporary memetics.
Symbols in Freud and Jung.
Id and the instincts of Szondi.
The Budapest school and object relation theory on infant love.
Attachment theory and psychoanalysis.
Sexuality in Freud and Ferenczi.
Freedom in the theory of Fromm.

DSA

Jung, Adler, Szondi, and Ferenczi in general texts (Google Ngram).
"Collective unconscious" and "archetype" over a century in psychological texts (PsycINFO).
Jung, Adler, and Freud in German, English, and French mind (Google Ngram).
Marcuse and Fromm in psychological texts (PsycINFO).
"Instinct" in psychoanalysis and ethology texts.
"Perceptual defense": history of a concept in psychological texts (PsycINFO).

2 Individuals and types
The victorious march of personality psychology and measurement

One of the central issues of modern psychology is the study of individual differences. These differences were highlighted due to theoretical reasons in evolutionary thought. Functionalist considerations following the logic of finding the "persons needed" translated this into practical issues of testing, as Chapters 7 through 9 in Volume 1 illustrated. On the other hand, psychopathology, and psychiatry, both before and after Freud, clearly indicated that scientific psychology also has to deal with the integrative aspects of personality. Functional disorders and dissolutions of the Self, both in the clinic and in the early 20th-century cultural scene (just think of the new narrative patterns with a disrupted Self in Joyce, Proust, or Musil and Kafka), clearly showed that beyond isolated mental phenomena and their impairments, one has to postulate concepts dealing with personal integrity and identity. This search for integrity in personality theory was in hidden or open tensions with many theoretical trends from Mach on interpreting the disintegration of the modern Self, as well as with the measurement trends decomposing personality into a mosaic of traits. Le Rider (1992) shows that this interpretation issue of the Self was part of the social tensions of Vienna, and Goldstein (1987) shows how it was contextualized in French intellectual history. The topic of personality and the related individual measurement issues gradually developed into a special chapter within academic psychology proper, overlapping but independent of the schools. The tradition we know today as **personality psychology** took shape in the 1920s–1940s. As Gordon Allport (1961), who was trained in both traditions, summarized them, in this process (continental) Europeans were more pattern-oriented, looking for integration, while Anglo-Saxons more piecemeal, looking for decomposition. His comparisons are presented in Table 2.1.

The terms also met their fate. In the early 20th century, the more European preferred word **character** and the more Anglosaxon **personality** competed as central terms. The first and still dominant journal of the field that started in 1932 was originally called *Character and Personality* from 1932 to 1944. It was later known as the *Journal of Personality* from 1945 on. The two terms still do carry diverging connotations. *Character* is more value-laden, full of moral considerations, while *personality* is a more value-free term.

Individuals and types 31

Table 2.1 The European and American traditions of personality psychology according to Allport

Dimension	American	European
Terms	Personality	Character
Preformation	Tabula rasa	Self-actualization
Elements	Elementaristic	Holistic
Mood	Optimism	Anxiety-centered
Society	Social self	Individual self
Methods	Rigorous	Looser
Neuroscience	Brain-based models	Less brain-anchored

Source: Allport (1961).

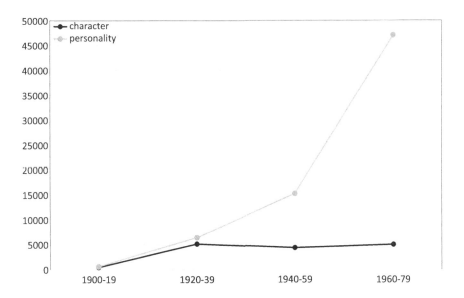

Figure 2.1 **Character** and **personality** as paper titles in the PsycINFO database.

The actual use of them over the 20th century shows both the Americanization of psychology and the moves toward a more descriptive approach to individual differences, as shown on Figure 2.1.

Making personality a central theme: William Stern (1871–1938)

William Stern, an early 20th-century developmental and educational psychologist (Volume 1, Chapters 8–9), was involved both in the measurement and in the integrative research of personality and was responsible in making personality a central topic of modern psychology.

Biography

From eyewitness testimony and the IQ to personalism: William Stern

(Louis) William Stern (Berlin, April 29, 1871–Durham, North Carolina, USA, March 27, 1938) was a German psychologist, philosopher, and professor at Hamburg University between 1916 and 1933. He was crucial in establishing the psychology of personality as a discipline. Stern came from a very educated rabbinate German Jewish family and was a student of Ebbinghaus and Lazarus in Berlin. As Gordon Allport (1968), his student in Hamburg, mentioned, this dual education is responsible for the dual interests of Stern. He felt at home both in the natural science–minded, objective psychology and in the domain of value-centered "mental science" psychology. On the invitation of Ebbinghaus, he was an assistant, and later a full professor, at Breslau (Wrocław, Poland, today). He was, at the same time, from 1906, an organizer of the Applied Psychology Institute and movement in Berlin. Early on, he was characterized both by the idealism of German philosophical thought and by practicism.

On the practical side, already in his time in Breslau, he was involved in progressive education, working for cases such as coeducation of girls and boys in schools, the change of schooling practice more in line with the need of the pupils, and the measurement of intelligence (Chapter 9 in Volume 1). Stern, in many regards, while individualistic, was rather conservative,

Figure 2.2 William Stern.
Source: Wikimedia commons public domain.

denying, for example, infantile sexuality on the basis of his diary studies. Stern claimed that the Freudian "facts" about infantile sexuality are back projections to childhood rather than facts of childhood.

Stern moved to Hamburg in 1916 after Meumann died. He worked in the institute of psychology that was initiated by him and eventually integrated it into the university. It is a characteristic of the German patriotic inspirations of Stern that he involved the institute in humanitarian debates in order to provide an intellectual challenge to the disillusioned masses of young people coming back from a lost war.

The Hamburg Institute was the center of applied psychology and personality studies in the German world at this time. The extent of the Nazis' cruelty can be seen in their persecution of such a patriotic figure. After many troubles, Stern finished his life's work in the United States at Duke University, working on the English version of his personalistic psychology (Stern, 1938).

Stern was an extremely creative and multifaceted author, with a rare combination of theoretical and applied interests. Stern was responsible for transmitting the traditional self and personality issues of psychology into scientific psychology, especially the cult of personality entertained by the Romantic age. He was the first to study the reliability of eyewitness testimony (Stern, 1910). With naturalistic observations, he studied factors of testimony, like suggestibility, the contextual determiners of changes, omissions, and distortions. This work preserved its relevance up to our decade.

Stern was a leading theoretician of early **developmental psychology**. Along with this, in the early 1900s, he was the founding organizer of applied psychology and "psychotechnik," or psychotechnology, in Germany alongside Münsterberg and Lippman, both as a terminology and as an institutional movement. In 1906, he founded a private applied psychology center near Berlin. His most important works are, however, in the field of the psychology of personality.

Stern as a theoretician of development

The polymath researcher and organizer William Stern has a lasting contribution on the formation and methodology of developmental studies. This had several applied aspects, such as introducing the idea of a mental quotient that has become known as the **intelligence quotient** (IQ, Chapter 9 in Volume 1). Stern was very involved in vocational and educational guidance and in the uses of psychology to promote the orientation of new generations in a complex world. As a representative of the German pedology movement, he traveled across Europe, organizing the movement and training seminars about child study.

Stern, together with his wife (Stern & Stern, 1907), was a pioneer researcher of child language. Their book is a systematic diary study. (Note that the wife was the first author.) The Stern couple connected the ideas of German Romantic linguistic philosophy and the ideas of Wilhelm von Humboldt (1836/1999) about language as an unfolding cultural system with the actual development and unfolding of language in children. On the basis of the analysis of diaries, they claimed that when acquiring language, children recreate it, in line with the German Romantic ideas about mental activity. They also formulated ways to identify symptoms of this activity in the error patterns of children. "The child does not reproduce everything said by the adult; she says many things however, never heard from the adult" (Stern & Stern, 1907, p. 135). They differentiated between **immanent errors**, like *goed* instead of *went*, that do not change rules, only apply them to wrong domains, and **transgradient errors**, like *hand-socks* for *gloves*. Modern psycholinguistics took up this challenge when it started to study rule-based performance in the morphology of children (Berko, 1958). Both types of errors imply, from the perspective of present-day psycholinguistics, that children struggle with rules; they do not acquire merely associative habits (Pinker, 1999).

The errors from a wider perspective indicate an interaction between self-development and environmental effects. Stern elaborated this into a general thesis about development, the **convergence theory** (Stern & Stern, 1907; Stern, 1938). The central point of this theory is not merely that our personality is determined by genetic and environmental factors alike but that these factors permanently and mutually presuppose each other and somehow have a converging causal impact on behavioral development. The whole personality is influenced by both genetic and environmental factors, and these are not merely additive; rather, they operate on the same internal structures. In the sixties, David Krech rediscovered Stern while studying environmental and genetic determinants of animal learning performance. Selective breeding and early experience in rodents seem to have the same target: the same cortical cholinergic factors operate under genetic and experiential influence, indicating higher acetylcholine-based synaptic activity in rats selected for smartness and exposed to early rich experience (Krech et al., 1960).

Integration and internal meaning in personality

In harmony with his developmental research, William Stern, from the beginning of the 20th century, tried to develop an ambitious program emphasizing that personality should be the important integrating factor of psychology, as well as a related program about the constructive nature of human development (Lamiell, 2012, 2020; Valsiner, 2005a). In his first synthesis calling for differential psychology, Stern already declared that essentially there are two possible basic approaches to personality psychology. One of them presupposes and analyzes traits and discusses that those "formal regularities that are entailed in the very fact of mental variation" (Stern, 1911, p. 8). A basic Darwinian idea in his approach to personality is the necessary variety of humankind underlying these personality traits. This would be the essential core of **differential psychology**. A second task for this natural science would be to analyze, after examining all the human varieties, **correlations among the traits**.

A similar argumentation showed up in Binet (2010). Binet interpreted "individual psychology" as providing for the two basic topics of later personality research: variation and correlation. (See Chapter 9 in Volume 1.)

One can differentiate two great questions [in individual psychology]:

1. To study how mental processes vary according to individuals, which are the variable properties of these processes, and what is the extent of these variations.
2. To study the relationships between different mental processes in the same individual.

(Binet & Henry, 1896, p. 412)

According to Stern, differential psychology should show a structured image of human individuals. Besides this, differential psychology should reply to classical practical needs, to the requirement that all who work with humans need to know about individual differences and acknowledge them. Stern outlines both the program of what is today **trait analysis** and the study of the whole individual. In both approaches, however, the emphasis is on the features rather than on the individual as such. Another less-nomothetic approach, closer to the followers of Dilthey (1894, 1977), relies on a more ideographic description in dealing with personality. According to Stern (1911), in order to fully understand human personality, we also must approach it starting from the unique and original, that is, from the individual. The two main methods for this latter purpose are **psychography** – a description of individual personal profiles, where biography is compared to individual profiles (that reminds us of contemporary psychohistorical approaches) – and the second is comparative studies, where different particular individuals are compared in their totality.

Figure 2.3 shows the different varieties of differential psychology according to Stern.

Differential psychology as promoted by Stern would use both the nomothetic attitude of natural sciences and the interpretive attitude of the humanities. Compared to most later personality psychology, this image already provides us with ample space for individuality and holism. As Kovács and Pléh (2023) pointed out, this even relates to the issue of intelligence testing. From a present day perspective, the "father of IQ" would in fact favor testing towards an individual profile analysis. But for Stern, there was a need for another level of research on personality. Stern developed a more ambitious conception of integrated personality. He started to publish in 1906 his three volumes of books, *Person und Sache* (Person and thing), that put personhood into the center of his worldview. This system, known as **personalism**, starts off from a conceptual analysis. A definitional feature of all mental phenomena is that they belong to a person; they are personal in this sense. This personalism became an important trend at the turn-of-the-century psychology. In the work of the American psychologist Mary Calkins (1915), this is clearly a new centering on the self, while others, like the French idealist philosopher Charles Renouvier (1815–1903), took an ontological turn and *person* became the basic organizing principle of the world.

36 Disciplinary developments and eclectics

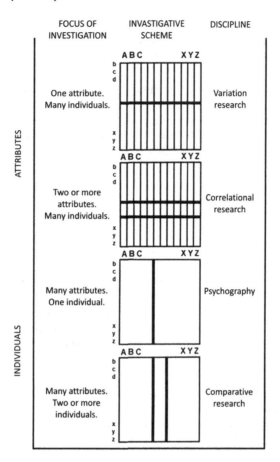

Figure 2.3 The different research strategies of differential psychology according to William Stern. The upper two figures correspond to the nomothetic attitude, while the lower two correspond to the individuum-centered ideographic attitude.

Source: William Stern (1911). Figure redrawn by Kristóf Kovács.

Stern's personalism had a more limited ambition, since in his case even the philosophical interpretation of personhood was seen from the perspective of psychology. According to him, there is no seeing in abstraction, it is always someone who sees. Personality became an integrating factor of an **all-inclusive human science** in the approach proposed by Stern. This reconsideration of personhood happened at the time in the German-speaking world when both the positivism of Mach and the clinical approach of Freud were describing the disintegration of the Self. Stern's approach in this sense was conservative. Most notably, for Stern, *psychology* is the study "of the person having experience or being capable of having experience" (Stern, 1938, p. vii). Though in accordance with his German idealism, he is very value- and culture-oriented, at the same time, the Dilthey–Spranger type of division into two psychologies, one causal, the other "understanding," did not appeal to Stern. He remained a monist in a strange sense. If we look at the "substrate" of the soul, he claims, one has to conclude that:

> The substratum of mind must be something that has existence going beyond or prior to the differentiation into the mental and the physical, thereby certifying personalistics: it is the study of the whole human person. Psychology is a part of this studying the original unity of the individual.
>
> (Stern, 1938, p. 69)

Lamiell (2003), in his interpretation of the personalism, and in his monograph about Stern, shows clearly that Stern repeatedly returned to the challenge made by Windelband of differentiating natural law and individuality-based disciplines. For Stern, it was important to have, besides differential psychology, a personalistic psychology that would correspond to the central idea of persona as opposed to object. He was convinced that there must be a science of personality that treats personality or personhood as an irreducible entity (Lamiell, 2020).

This was still a minority view and aspect, however. Lamiell (2020) shows that about the same time, Thorndike (1911) tried to give the foundations of a differential psychology leading toward the much later "big five" theory. All qualitative differences in this view should be reduced to quantitative differences between the individuals in a limited number of measures. There is no need for quality.

Gordon Allport (1968) took over from Stern the combination of nomothetic and idiographic approach to personality. The Romantic conception of individuum-based research shows up in modern humanistic psychology and is entertained by the Russian neuropsychologist Alexandr Luria (1968, 1979) in his case studies and taken up by Oliver Sacks (1995) as well.

The concept of types and typology in the social sciences and humanities

In the unfolding of a genuine topic of personality psychology, a central role was played by considerations of human types as basic categories. The personalism of Stern certainly had some German idealist overtones. But the tradition of German idealism became specifically tied to the professional psychological study of personality through the turn-of-the-century career of **the concept of types**. Forming types as an aid to organize experiences characterize the development of the humanities at the turn of the century, especially in Germany.

Typologies in different domains: typology against positivism

The notion of types became very popular in the mental history attitude of mid-20th-century humanist scholars. The different cultural and social typologies all tended to emphasize that the unifying force of types was a kind of integrative worldview or vision of life. Types as a network of choices do entail a worldview, as Spranger (1928) spelled out clearly. This bridging, and at the same time value-committed, nomothetic aspect of types was already emphasized by Dilthey and Spranger. Varieties of culture would correspond to variable approaches to reality. Artistic styles, for example, as classical German esthetics portrayed it already, with its opposition between Classicism and Romanticism, in the phrasing of Friedrich Schiller (1759–1805). The duality of Naïve and Sentimental poetry would be realized in mental science psychology as realizations of different human types.

At the end of the 19th century, the very concept of types appeared in the German trends criticizing positivism as a sort of mediating concept between nomothetic natural sciences and ideographic humanities. The concept of types allowed social sciences and the humanities to overcome individuality without being lost in the impersonality of abstract laws. It was meant to be a bridging concept between two scientific attitudes. Types are also able to bridge the gap between value-centered and value-neutral attitudes in the social sciences. Values appear as abstractions going beyond the individual event, as moments that are never literally present, as patterns, as **ideal types**. Several social and humanities typologies appeared at that time, from the theory of social forms through artistic styles to arts of novel writing.

Typological thought in the different social sciences and the humanities from a contemporary perspective was struggling with fuzziness and loose prototype-like organization on the one hand and strict categories and essentialism, combined with values, on the other. While the typologists aimed to cover the entire richness of life using a looser categorization, at the same time, due to the Aristotelian heritage, they would still end up using an essentialist attitude toward their own loose categories. One shortcoming of these attempts was that they lacked a more flexible theory of categories to ground their types in, as promoted much later by Rosch (1978). Not unrelated to this, they were empirically ill-defined, mainly relying on imaginary ideal types. Table 2.2 gives some examples for them.

The "understanding sociology" of Max Weber (1864–1920) claimed that in social events, understanding and explanation do not exclude each other. This was in contrast to the understanding trends emphasizing a clear bifurcation between "understanding" and "explanation." Understanding human behavior is to grasp future-oriented motivations, or to put it in a reverse way, regarding human actions, one has to keep in mind the goal-setting nature of human actions. Understanding

Table 2.2 Typical social science typologies in the beginning of the 20th century

Author	Domain	Characteristic type	Experiential foundation
Lukács	Aesthetics	Heroic and narrow mind in novels (Don Quixote, Sancho Panza)	Analysis of literary experience
Durkheim	Sociology	Organic and mechanical solidarity	Social history, religion
Weber	Sociology	Protestant ethics	History, ideology, economy
Steinthal	Linguistics	Morphological types	Language history
Lévy-Bruhl	Anthropology	Primitive and modern mind	Observation of Aborigines
Frobenius	Ethnography	Etiop and Hamitic	Ways of life

human actions is only possible in an agency-based, hermeneutic way (Weber, 1905, 1913). The notion of **ideal types** was introduced by Weber as part of this analysis. Ideal types are comprehensive patterns. The most famous example of Weber, the ideal type of Protestantism, with its work ethics and concentration on work as service to God, fostered the development of capitalist economy (Weber, 1905). The example shows that ideal types are ideal in the future-directed sense as well.

In linguistics, the idea of **language types** has been around since the linguistic philosophy of Wilhelm von Humboldt (1767–1835). According to him, the multiplicity of languages represents variants of the universal language forming abilities of humanity. The types of languages do show internal patterning and internal coherence (Humboldt, 1836/1999). A characteristic developmental typology was proposed based on the differentiations in grammatical morphology (see about these in Ramat, 2010). Three types of languages were differentiated: isolating languages, such as Chinese, that express each relational notion with separate word; agglutinative types, such as Hungarian, where grammatical relations are attached to the words and each relation is carried by a separate suffix; and inflectional languages, where various morphemes impart grammatical relations. Linguistic typology, both with its early Romantic and Darwinian overtones, clearly raised one of the key issues of all typology: Are we dealing with equal varieties or varieties that have a different value, for example, due to their later development or higher sophistication? In some interpretations, the differences among language types would mirror differences in mental effort: the more grammatical effort, the more developed mind the speakers have. This is by far not an innocent set of claims. Twentieth-century linguistics had a long time to give up the idea that language types were of a different value, both linguistically and regarding the articulation of thought (see Chapter 5). The consensus today is the equality of languages, though there are some striking differences according to their distribution over the planet and the number of their speakers.

Typological thought also appeared in German **ethnography** of the time. Leo Frobenius (1873–1938) published a typology about African cultures in Frobenius (1933/1968), claiming to create a **Gestalt theory of culture**. According to his typology, the earth-digging, farming cultures would be basically mystical in their outlook to life (the Ethiopian type), while hunting and large-animal-cultivating cultures (Hamitic type) would be more rationalistic. In Europe, this duality would put the French and the English on the rational, and the Germans on the mystical pole. The typology of cultures would result in psychological types, similar to the wanderer (German) and hider (Hungarian) types suggested by Lajos Prohászka (1935), a Hungarian speculative typologist.

Classic German typology, with its aims to patterns of lifestyle, certainly had a wide influence in the 1930s. This was evident in the good dozen "mental science"–inspired typologies. The issue of "national characters" was also a typological issue for them. In these soft typologies, however, there was an element of tolerance. They proposed a tolerance based on the recognition of the existence of rival ways of seeing the world in a rather-intolerant time. Typology appeared as an explanation for the irreconcilable oppositions. Even differences in worldview can also be reduced to or interpreted with regard to personality types.

It is an important methodological question whether social science typologies do have anything specific compared to categorization of human thinking in general. In some social typologies, however, there is an idealization made. Types are supposed to be hiding entities that provide self-explanatory reference. Or as in the case of Max Weber, types are offered that create a nomothetic directive function. Robert Winch (1947) classified typologies as either heuristic or empirical. In his analysis, Spranger, Weber, and many other attempts are heuristic typologies, while the empirical ones are measurement-based and amenable to self-correction.

The analytical philosopher Hempel (1965), in his paper on typological thought in the social sciences, showed that many of the specificities of social categorization, such as the notion of ideal types, are mistaken highbrow idealizations themselves. In reality, there is no deep difference between categorization at large and the typologies used by social scientists. "The various uses of type concepts in psychology and the social sciences ... prove to be of basically the same character as the methods of classification, ordering, measurement, empirical correlation, and theory formation used in the natural sciences" (Hempel, 1965, p. 171). The nomothetic aspects of types and the use of the empathic method to understand types are merely pseudo-specificities of the humanist scholar. Hempel certainly was very strictly positivist in this regard. We would see today that the attitude promoted by Weber and the other symbolic typologists was not entirely arbitrary; types are in fact ideal in the sense proposed by prototype theory of category formation today. "Ideal types" would correspond to the prototypes of Rosch (1978). The decrease in cognitive load due to typologization is naturally applied to our fellow humans as well during our everyday life connecting some values to the types which may carry stereotypes or even prejudices.

The royal way of typology within psychology: bodily and purely psychological typologies

With all these positivist reservations, the 1920s and the 1930s brought a great deal of typological thought to European psychology as well. Dozens of typological psychologies were born, many of them with a short afterlife. All were influenced by the general popularity of typological thought in social sciences and the humanities after the war and the German crisis years. Let us take a look at some of their underlying principles. There were extremely speculative but influential proposals for typology coming from the edges.

During the first decades of the 20th century, several speculative attempts were made to connect the idealistic aims of German typology with a concrete psychological message. Ludwig Klages (1873–1956), a German and Swiss speculative psychologist, played a central role in this regard. Klages started to study expressive movements and had become an advocate of graphology. He had made the terms both of *expressivity* and *character research* very popular (Prinzhorn, 1928). According to Klages (1929), human life is an eternal fight between the natural, instinctive tendencies of humans (the Dionysian element in Nietzsche) and spiritual representation (the Apollonian element of Nietzsche). Character is defined by the state of the art of this fight, and this can be grasped in expressive movements, since bodily movements are filled up with thought, with mental content.

Klages had a rather strange, mystical aspect in his life philosophy, including a revival of paganism. His language was also rather obscure, and his attitude is almost a mockery of the looseness of typological thought. Any human feature can be elevated to the rank of a base for typology and then reified as a self-explanatory inner factor, as an essence. This is then translated into further loose talk about bodily movements and graphology, since the body is the expression of the essence of the mind. Klages acted as a speculative bridge between 19th-century German philosophy of life and 20th-century irrationalism. In the mid-20th century, however, he was still rather inspiring to many intellectuals. One of the gurus in the book of the famous Austrian novelist Robert Musil (1930) *The Man Without Qualities* is based on Klages, with a touch of irony.

German characterology in the post–First World War Weimar period, as analyzed by Meskil (2004), was influenced both by a cultural drive toward national revival and a search for national types, but at the same time also by direct instrumental factors of the rearrangement of labor forces. "Psychotechnics," in its German sense, was booming partly because of economic factors of trying to find a best fit between the workforce with its abilities and the needs of industry.

> In the mid-1920s, applied (and theoretical) psychologists in many countries turned from studying elementary abilities to studying character or personality. The turn to charactcrology is seen in terms of German industry's evolving production strategies. As German companies developed a niche in flexible production, they came to value the highly skilled worker, who needed such character qualities as reliability, diligence, and conscientiousness.
>
> (Meskil, 2004, p. 1)

This is also the time of the flourishing of the differential psychology of Stern, himself both committed to non-reductionist personalism and an active promoter of the German psychotechnical movement.

Constitutional theories: body look and personality

The first modern attempts to overcome the everyday use and the classic medical typologies were themselves rather naive. They tended to use analogies and similarity-based reasoning as well. In the physiognomy reintroduced by the Swiss poet and philosopher Lavater (1741–1801), the human differences are interpreted as being the consequences of similarities to animals and their assumed prototypical traits. For example: "He has the eyes of a dog. He has the fidelity of a dog."

Phrenology in the 19th century, with its arbitrary relations between brain areas and dispositions, appeared as a rival to this theory (Chapter 4 in Volume 1). The issue of relations between physical outlook and personality was never given up, however. The Italian psychiatrist Cesare Lombroso (1835–1909) developed his degenerative typology with reference to evolutionary ideas. Like the phrenologists, he dealt with extreme cases, that is, with criminals and extremely talented people. He interpreted criminality as an inherited malformation. Some physical features of the atavistic criminals would be narrow fronts, big ears, expressed zygomaticus, accompanied by a primitive thought and feeling (Lombroso, 1911). This was a theory much challenged by social criminology of his own time already, among others by the French theoretician of imitation Gabriel Tarde. It had one advantage, however, in the very development of criminology. Besides the criminal acts, it directed attention to the personality of the criminal as well. It is also important that his theories were supported by a new medium, photography, that was not available for the earlier physiognomic theories, such as that of Lavater. In this indirect manner, Lombroso played a central role in photography becoming a basic tool of police recordkeeping.

He combined this approach to criminality to an interest toward extraordinary talent and imagined that creative geniuses are basically insane. In his frequently re-edited monography, he analyzed many influences in creativity, such as climate, family, and the like, but in particular emphasized the family resemblance between insanity and talent, analyzing artists and scientists with their bizarre behavior, from Rousseau, Bolyai, and Tasso to Ampère (Lombroso, 1891). He postulated a list of abnormal behaviors in geniuses. Extraordinarily talented people are immature, drink too much, are emotionally unstable, are prudish, are sexually perverted, with a lot of imagination and a usually irregular-shaped brain. All this is far from being a cult of excellence. It is an apotheosis of the average and of normality. Both crime and talent are qualitative, non-normal aberrations. The idea of the average man becoming popular in psychology as well as the birth of social statistics were the driving ideas of Lombroso.

This interest toward extreme personalities as deviations from the norm also implied that the turn-of-the-century typological fever had a widespread social backing. There was a new element related to the German cultural background of modern typology. Modern psychological typology was born in the middle of a latent tension between the need for precise measurement in differential psychology and a general cultural and social science trend toward typological thinking.

A central feature of typologies within psychology proper is whether they try to propose purely psychological types or they start from some assumed similarity between body types and mental types. In this domain, psychological ideas are influenced by the availability heuristics of our naive psychology. In classical personality theorizing, the starting point was not the theory of mind attribution of folk psychology but the naive generalizations based on stereotypes of naive psychology. Body-based constitutional theories have a long past in our culture. Many of them are part of our naive theory of personality. Remember what Caesar says in the drama of Shakespeare about Cassius:

Let me have men about me that are fat; Sleek-headed men and such as sleep o' nights; Yond' Cassius has a lean and hungry look;
   He thinks too much: such men are dangerous.
                               (Shakespeare: *Julius Caesar*, 1.2.192)

The forerunner of many modern biological typologies had been, in fact, Hippocrates and Galen with their conception of **bodily fluids** responsible for temperamental typological differences. This was a greatly honored and highly debated theory of temperament that treated human variability in personality into four types that were supposed to be caused by variations in basic bodily fluids, such as the black and yellow bile, blood, and phlegm (see a summary in Kagan, 1994).

The relations of temperament to differences in bodily fluids were a rather metaphoric image with the equations summarized in Table 2.3.

The modern constitutional typologies starting to be popularized in the 1920s emerged as an extension of the idea of a unity between body–mind and the idea of a genetic determination of individual differences regarding human types. Their direct inspiration was the nascent endocrinology, which portrayed in medicine a new, humoral (fluid based) relationship between bodily functions and mental life. Temperamental differences would correspond to metabolic differences regulated by the endocrine system, and differences in these regulations would differentiate bodily constitutions.

The best-known of the body-based psychological typologies are those of Ernst Kretschmer (1888–1964), a German psychiatrist at Marburg and Tübingen. Kretschmer (1925), in his work on character, started from three postulates. The first one was that there are basic qualitatively different body types, shown in Figure 2.4. The second was that extreme bodily constitutions correspond to typical mental disorders. The third idea uses the continuity between normal and pathological. Differences of personality types can be decomposed according to their similarity to the mental disorders. Pathologies are the extreme values of parametric typological variations. Kretschmer described three basic body types. *The pyknic* body type, with round features and the characteristic mood fluctuations, would correspond to manic-depressive disorders, 67% of this latter clinical group being of the pyknic or plump type. *Leptosome*, fragile, lengthy constitution, would be characterized by abstract thought. The *athletic type* is characterized by strong muscles. Schizophrenics tend to be leptosome and athletic in 67% of cases, with the majority being leptosome.

In his underlying personality and psychopathology theory, Kretschmer believed that mood and sensitivity were the two basic underlying factors. *Mood* would

Table 2.3 The typologies of antiquity with the body fluids

	Phlegmatic	*Sanguine*	*Choleric*	*Melancholic*
Fluid	Phlegm	Blood	Yellow bile	Black bile
Direction	North	East	South	West
Element	Water	Air	Fire	Earth
Season	Winter	Spring	Summer	Autumn

Source: After Kagan (1994, p. 3).

44 *Disciplinary developments and eclectics*

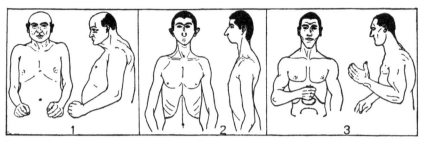

Konstitution: Schemata der drei von E. Kretschmer aufgestellten Körperbautypen: 1 pyknischer, 2 leptosomer, 3 athletischer Typ (aus E. Kretschmer, Körperbau und Charakter).

Figure 2.4 The three basic bodily types proposed by Kretschmer.

Source: "Konstitution" in Der Große Brockhaus, 15. Edition (1931), Vol. 10. p. 417.

correspond to overactivity, dynamicism, mania and slowness, and depression at its two poles. *Sensitivity*, in the schizoid dimension on its positive end, would correspond to idealism, introversion, systematicity, and in its negative extreme form to rootlessness, coldness, and derealization. Kretschmer had a Dilthey-style interest in relating his proposed types to talent. Typological differences show up in cyclothymic and schizoid poets, scientists, and politicians. While Humboldt was a cyclothymic researcher with his rich descriptions, Kant would be a schyzothymic with his systematization.

The assumed genetic affinity between bodily constitution and personality had no clear model for causal mechanism beyond the rather general claim that constitution and temperament are subject to a joint humoral regulation. A methodical move forward was initiated by the American psychologist and medical doctor at both Harvard and Columbia, **William Sheldon** (1899–1977). Being familiar with the work of Kretschmer as well as Jung from his European professional travels, Sheldon made a move both regarding measurement and regarding the mediating causal model. He made the anthropological measurements more precise and extended them to a larger, "average" population, by a large database of nude photos of Ivy League elite students. The connections between bodily constitution and temperament were mediated according to him by embryological factors. The three bodily types were renamed to correspond to the assumed overdevelopment of different tissues in embryonic development. **Endomorph** constitution is characterized by an expressed dominance of bodily cavities, and the corresponding **viscerotonic personality** would prefer eating, sleeping, and comfort. The common factor is the dominance of the endothelium in embryological development. **Ectomorph** constitution and **cerebrotonic personality** would be characterized by the development of ectoderma: lean body and the dominance of the brain. The central nervous system embryologically develops as a series of inward intrusions of the ectoderma that corresponds to the skin. **Mesomorph** constitution is characterized by well-developed muscles and a dominance of the mesoderma. This muscled constitution is accompanied by a **somatotonic**, active body–centered way of life (Sheldon, 1940).

Since he based his typology on embryonic layers, Sheldon could allow for mixed types, assuming that the three thelia can be developed together in harmony. At the same time, while he was continuously refining the constitutional allocations, he did not have any measurements of personality types in the modern sense. He was using qualifier lists to attribute them to his subjects.

Several criticisms of these body-based typologies, especially of Kretschmer, appeared concentrated on three factors. The first is age as a confounding factor. Schizophrenia is characterized by early onset, and at this age, many young people tend to be leptosome. The variation within body types is the second issue. Pyknic constitution appears with all sorts of mental types and disorders. The third issue is the unequal distribution of the disorder. Schizophrenia is the most frequent mental disorder; thus, it is likely to appear with all sorts of constitutions.

Kretschmer thought of all these disorders as constitutional in the sense of being present at birth. That was questioned with reference to several possible modulating factors. The intense later questioning of Kretschmer was also related to him remaining in office during Nazi times and intellectually assisting in the termination of the mentally ill. After the war, Kretschmer navigated to safer domains, and he became a campaigner for psychotherapy among German psychiatrists.

Purely psychological typologies

Parallel to the bodily based typologies appeared the typologies that have mostly ignored the bodily typologies. The very subtitle "purely psychological" itself indicates merely an ideal type. Typologies starting off from psychological considerations started in the early 20th century and continue today to entail biological considerations as well. Their starting point is, however, not bodily functions but the organization of psychological functions. If they deal with biological interpretation, they look for biological equivalents or correspondents for the independently identified psychological types, mainly in higher nervous functions.

There were quite a variety of typologies of this type. I will present two of these. Jaensch is interesting because of a gradual change in his system toward a racist theory, and Jung because of its modern research relevance.

Erich Jaensch and racist typology

Erich Jaensch (1883–1940) was a professor at Marburg. He is the naturalist who had a hard time getting an appointment in Marburg during the naturalism–*Geisteswissenschaft* debates. He started to work on vision and space representation, but from 1927 on, his main topic became typology (Jaensch, 1930). The empirical starting point for his typology was **eidetic imagery**. Eidetic images are extremely detailed memory images. Jaensch spent a decade trying to investigate both the phenomenology of the eidetic images (how perception-like they are), their age distribution, geographical and schooling distribution, and the ability to recall them according to their content or according to the interests of the subjects. Following some ideas promoted by his more physiologically oriented brother Walter Jaensch, Erich Jaensch differentiated between people who could exercise voluntary control over their eidetic images and would be characterized by flexible thinking, the B type (an abbreviation of *Basedow*, but in fact, this would imply cortical control), and T type (tetanic type, subcortical control), who would have uncontrolled eidetic images.

Jaensch, is his later development, gives a good example of how slippery a fast biological interpretation of the supposed "mental science" typology can become. From the first moments of Nazi takeover, Jaensch (1933, 1934) started to claim that psychology has to be at the forefront of the German cultural war for racially pure science, proving Nordic superiority. He combined his typology with a wider race theory during the early Nazi years. He surveyed a lot of mostly speculative studies that tried to show that there is one type of people who are both biologically and psychologically very labile. These people are thus subject to all sorts of external influences (the Jew), and another that is more integrated and directed inward (the Nordic) (Jaensch, 1937, 1939). He generalized these oppositions into a theory of types as opposed to countertypes.

> The "opposite type" [*Gegentypus* in German] of the German national movement is liberalistic, egocentric and individualistic. This is true of its conception of political organization as well as of its perceptions and concepts . . . [and this type] considers the state as an artificial construction rather than a living reality. This "detached" intellect is antagonistic to the German movement. It is most frequent in the following groups: (1) heterogeneous racial mixtures; (2) tubercular and other consumptive patients; (3) underdeveloped individuals; (4) dissociation phases in normal persons (early puberty).
> (Jaensch, 1934, p. 56)

One can see the beginning of anti-Semitic and anti-Southern stereotyping here, which associates the "enemy" with a combination of a biological and a political type. Jaensch even claimed that among farmed animals like chicken, the Nordic animals were more integrated than the Mediterranean ones, showing a racial superiority along the same line you observe in human race psychology (Jaensch, 1939). Thus, the racial differences are not cultural constructions; they are due to environment–genetic biological correspondences. Mediterranean chickens randomly eat, and they can overeat under the influence of environmental contingencies, while Nordic ones are more disciplined and constrained in their feeding habits.

Jaensch was attempting to make his typological fantasies a basis for new German applied psychology. Due to his early death and due to the increasing professionalization of German applied psychology for military selection and industrial psychology in the interest of the German military, his phantasmagoric ideas were rejected together with the early flirtation of Nazism with ideological holism. In the later years of militarized Nazi Germany, the engineering-analytic attitude wiped out the influence of Jaensch (Geuter, 1992).

The typology of Jung

A purely psychological typology is the system of Carl Gustav Jung, already mentioned regarding schools of depth psychology (Chapter 1). Jung initiated the famous extraverted–introverted distinction. In early 2020, there are over 800 mentions of it as a dimension in the PsycINFO database. The extraversion pole is the dominant in the dimension. There are 14,000 mentions of extraversion, while there are 4,700 mentions of introversion. Extraversion–introversion is a general attitude in relating the mind to its objects.

> The introvert's attitude to an object is an abstractive one; at bottom, he is always facing the problem of how libido can be withdrawn from the object. [. . .] The extravert, on the contrary, maintains a positive relation to the object. To such an extent does he affirm its importance that his subjective attitude is continually being orientated by, and related to the object.
> (Jung 1923, p. 3)

The two types even obtain an adaptationist interpretation, almost as evolutionary variants.

> Nature knows two fundamentally different ways of adaptation, which determine the further existence of the living organism. The one is by increased fertility, accompanied by a relatively small degree of defensive power and individual conservation; the other is by individual equipment of manifold means of self-protection, coupled with a relatively insignificant fertility. This biological contrast seems not merely to be the analogue, but also the general foundation of our two psychological modes of adaptation.
> (ibid., p. 3)

Jung proposed further typological subdivisions of these two attitudes. Within both types of basic attitudes, different mental processes may be the dominant ones. In the extraverted "rational or judging types [. . .] their life is, to a large extent, subordinated to reasoning judgment" (ibid., 453). The dominant processes are thinking and search of beautiful and good. At the same time, their unconscious life is irrational. The extraverted irrational types are dominated by sensation and intuition. "Their commissions and omissions are based not upon reasoned judgment but upon the absolute intensity of perception. Their perception is concerned with simple happenings, where no selection has been exercised by the judgment" (p. 469). The introverted thinking type is dominated by subjective ideas.

Jung gave an interesting example here from cultural history.

> Just as Darwin might possibly represent the normal extraverted thinking type, so we might point to Kant as a counter-example of the normal introverted thinking type. The former speaks with facts; the latter appeals to the subjective factor. Darwin ranges over the wide fields of objective facts, while Kant restricts himself to a critique of knowledge in general.
> (p. 484)

Disciplinary developments and eclectics

From psychological types to the typology of nervous system

The typology promoted by Jung was a productive theory, leading to many further developments. The dimension of extraversion–introversion was soon tied to an **empirical method**. It became a typology that was not based on unanchored speculations or questionable theories of expressive movements, like the ideas of Klages, but on rather fixed operations. It relied first on the Rorschach inkblot test, where certain color reactions characterize extraverts, and seeing movement is more typical in introverts.

Half a century later, many questionnaire methods were developed to identify extra-introversion, in line with the decreased interest toward projective methods (Eysenck, 1973). This method includes questionnaire items like "I don't mind being the center of attention," "I feel comfortable around people," "I start conversations" (all implying extraversion).

The typology promoted by Jung, besides its measurement implications, inspired biological interpretations as well. Jung himself sounds permissive here by saying that the two types supposedly have equivalents in the working of the nervous system. This was taken up by Eysenck and by the Pavlovian typologists.

While classical constitutional theories such as Kretschmer proposed a correspondence between an external bodily pattern and a mental internal pattern, the modern synthesis moves the bodily element inward as well. Extraverted behavior, for example, is interpreted as a faster development of inhibitory processes, while introverts would be claimed to learn faster in general (Eysenck, 1973), or else, introverts would be seen as more punishment-sensitive compared to extraverts (see about these Marton, 1972).

From the 1950s on, serious efforts were made to combine the typology of higher nervous activity elaborated in the school of Pavlov in Soviet Russia with the dimension of extra-introversion. This coupling became a central part of mid-20th-century neuroscience typology and behavioral genetics. The Hungarian personality typologist Magda Marton (1972) and the entire book edited by Nebylitsyn and Gray (1972) give a clear example of relating the extraversion dimension both to learning and to the dynamics of cortical activity during learning.

The line of thought initiated by Hans Eysenck (1916–1997) overcomes naivety still in another way. Eysenck, who may be considered to be a neobehavioristic personality psychologist, very consciously tried to overcome all essentialistic thinking in psychology. The basic dimensions of temperament form a continuum according to him, and along this line, you may well be a mixed type. In his initial model, the two basic dimensions proposed were extraversion and neuroticism. Their combinations would provide for the four temperaments of Hippocrates, as shown in Figure 2.5. Eysenck also entertained a dimension-based theory of mental disorder. In order to account for this, in his extended model, besides neuroticism, he also introduced the factor of psychoticism.

With the typology of Jaensch, it was very clear that value issues do show up in psychological typologies. As the CONTROVERSIES section shows, this is a general issue of typologies.

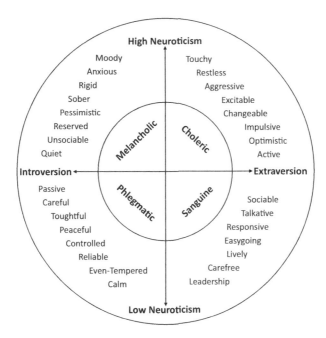

Figure 2.5 The four temperaments and extraversion and neuroticism as basic personality dimensions. The inner circle are the four temperaments, and the outer layer corresponds to the two orthogonal personality dimensions.

Source: Redrawn after Eysenck (1973, p. 187).

Controversies

Value issues in typology

One dilemma inherent in classical typologies is the **value of personality types**. Though most psychologists are committed in a liberal manner to a neutral consideration of varieties of human temperament and character, they are inclined to forget about this commitment to variety in practice. We saw extreme versions of this value-laden nature of typologization in Jaensch. But research on authoritarianism originally conceived in an interpretation of psychoanalysis and neo-Marxist theory, as well as antifascist thought (Adorno et al., 1950, Chapter 1), was also full of values. The **authoritarian personality** was high on the F, fascism scale. If we interpret it as a personality type, the high-authoritarian person certainly was the bad guy, prone to be following all sorts of leaders without hesitation, and full of racial and other prejudices.

The very notion of types as it appeared in the German trends of the late 19th century was intrinsically involved in value issues. It was intended to be a bridging concept between nomothetic sciences and idiographic humanities. Types would allow the humanities to overstep their encasement into singularities, at the same time not being lost in the impersonality of "laws." Types are also available to overcome the tensions between the attitudes that are value-centered and those that consider facts more important than values. The value issue appears in the patterns of ideal types. Second, all the social science, humanities-based, and psychological typologies underline that types are held together due to a peculiar value-laden worldview; types are networks of choices. As a third issue, proponents of given typologies cannot resist to see the varieties corresponding to their own culture (or personality) as being somehow superior to the other varieties. A version is better since it represents higher values on an imaginary scale of values or implies higher differentiation on an evolutionary *scala naturae*. Monotheism is better than polytheism because it is more abstract, and so on.

The extraversion–introversion typology proposed by C. G. Jung tried to avoid evaluation at the onset. Its modern neurophysiological interpretations also avoided the trap of evaluation. They talk about different flexible modes of adaptation without closing any domain of life from either of the assumed types, and they exclude the possibility of using ready-made, ordinary evaluative patterns. Even in their early pathological interpretations, they did not propose one type as the source of pathologies but tried to typologize pathologies themselves as well. Extraversion combined with neuroticism leads to histrionic personality disorders, such as hysteria, while introversion with high neuroticism would lead to anxiety-related disorders.

With these multiplicity commitments allowed, in reality, the overevaluation of introverts and extraverts showed up several times in European culture, depending on the needs of the time. Conservative German thought evaluated the inner-turning introverts more, to be shuffled away by the needs of the German army for more exterior-oriented people during the Second World War.

Can we avoid evaluation? It is certainly rather difficult to avoid the evaluation trap. Are the authoritarian and democratic personality types of equivalent value? Usually, there are explanations put forward for these value choices. One might claim, for example, that openness leads to larger behavioral repertoires and that relative field independence leads to adaptive solutions that are valid for a longer time. There are two issues involved here, however. One is that the researcher cannot easily overcome his everyday commitments. The recently valued "types" (democratic, open, inner control) are only clear in a constantly changing city life. Their positive value is questionable in a stable rural environment. Frozen societies prefer rigid personalities. While we always evaluate, we should analyze our preferences.

> In a cross-sectional manner, we have to be value-free and multidimensional-tolerant. Longitudinally, in a biographical manner, however, we live with our life compasses as values. We wish to create people of some kind. This evaluation is related to our dreams about the society. However, these value commitments may distort research on the long run. At the same time, by proposing multilayered deductions between constitution and observed behavior, they also tend to have an answer to why exactly a given number and set of dimensions is important. These new typologies become motivated in this regard as well, allowing for the inclusion of several other varieties of social behavior typology which originally did not fit in the proposed dimensions.

Types and traits

The traditional notion of types and typology was drastically changed from the mid-20th century on with the advent of the concept of **personality traits**. Certainly, there were many developments in our attempts to classify people. As Gordon Allport and Odbert (1936) showed in their analysis of trait names, our everyday life and the lexicon of our language already provide us with a rich, inbred system of classification of people. Many *ad hoc* typologies were developed from integrative theories, such as using the stages of libido development of psychoanalytic theory to talk about anal and oral personalities and the like. Many research-based motivational concepts obtain a secondary personality psychology flavor as well, like achievement orientation, or inner–outer control.

The underlying "kernel or core" vision of type that would be a hidden explanation for all things, that is, essentialist categorization, coming from idealist German typologies, was replaced by a behavior-based classification. This new attitude is quasi-inductive and starts off from observed regularities of behavior. It contrasts with the classic Aristotelian "all or none" vision of categories. At the same time, the data acquisition methods also did change. Classical personality psychology mainly relied on **projective methods**.

One example is the **Rorschach inkblot interpretation**. The most popular European projective personality test promoted by the Swiss Hermann Rorschach (1884–1922) became associated with Jung's typology. In this inkblot interpretation test (Figure 2.6), reactions tied to the color of the patches would correspond to stimulus-dependent extraversion, while seeing movement would indicate more internal organization of interpretation, thus introversion (Rorschach, 1921/1942). The basic idea in all these projective methods was a combination of **thematic and structural projection**. The topics central to a person show up in interpreting ambiguous situations, and the structure of the responses reflects the structure of personality. That would be a leading idea of relating personality projective methods and depth psychology for the coming half century.

Another classic example for projective methods is the interpretation of social events on photograph-based pictures initiated by the Harvard psychologist Henry

52 *Disciplinary developments and eclectics*

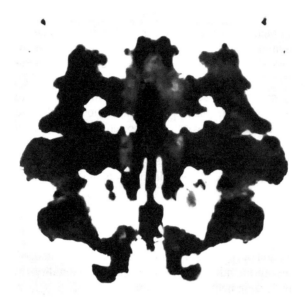

Figure 2.6 An inkblot similar to the inkblots used by the Rorschach test.
Source: Done by an unidentified AI machine.

Murray (1893–1988). The need system of a person is revealed on the basis of stories provided by the subject to eliciting pictures (**thematic apperception test, TAT**). Murray (1938) hoped to reveal the underlying motivational structure of the person from the story-like interpretation of the photo-like pictures.

The quest for objectivity leads far away both from the inner experiences and from the integrity of the personality. Some European countries, including Hungary, have interestingly preserved the use of projective tests, with efforts of standardization and contextualization, even in the middle of the wave of questionnaires. This new trend, for more than half a century by now, uses **questionnaires** to understand personality. Their intended domains are rather varied. Due mostly to the demand of applied psychology, they started to frame methods that intend to characterize the entire personality based on replies to several hundred questions organized into different scales. Most of them were first fit to the needs of clinical practice, the best-known of them being the MMPI (Minnesota Multiphasic Personality Inventory), originally proposed by Hathaway and McKinley (1940) and now being in the revised version of MMPI 2 stage in 2020. The logic of their construction is partly theory-bound and partly empirical. They choose some statements that are supposed to be characteristic to some clinical group with extreme behaviors (e.g., "Frequently, I do not feel like getting up" is likely to be characteristic of depressed patients). Afterward, empirical data collection would clarify which items do really differentiate between average people and the patients. Following this, a client would be characterized by the similarity of his or her profile to groups with a typical behavior. This would be expressed in the form of a **personality profile**. Similar to the *ad hoc* typologies, an entire line of questionnaires was developed toward measuring **specific traits**. A favorite of the behaviorist times was the measurement of **anxiety** theoretically as a measure of generalized drive, practically as a measure based on questions related to worrying, vegetative activation, and nervousness.

Within theoretically oriented personality psychology itself, the questionnaire-based interpretations developed two attitudes regarding the **structure of personality** and the relationships between individual behavioral events and latent personality structure. This is a modern attempt to relate the integrative and decompositional approaches to personality. The first one, represented most characteristically by Raymond B. Cattell (1905–1998), claims that the basis of personality has to be found in a hierarchical organization of characteristics. There is a relatively large number (16) of foundational **root traits** (e.g., emotional stability, suspicion, self-assuredness). These are based on more primitive primary factors. These first-order traits due to their combinations give clusters and provide second-order broader **types**, such as the types of extraversion and anxiety. This approach thus starts from factors that are near to observed behavior and have a narrow scope (Cattell, 1965).

In the other approach, Hans Eysenck (1973) emphasizes broad factors. Extraversion, neuroticism, and psychoticism, together with intelligence, are wide factors intended to characterize personality. In the vision of Eysenck, the overall image is more akin to the classical typology, starting from inward out: the stubbornness and reliability of the introvert are **consequences of introversion**; while Cattell would prefer to say that these features **constitute introversion**. While for Raymond Cattell traits are primary and types emerge out of them through factor analysis, for Hans Eysenck, the starting points are made by the types, and types are assumed to be independent orthogonal "essences."

In the past few decades, the relationship between traits and behavior is seen in a more complex way. Contemporary psychology rediscovered the message of Kurt Lewin (1951): behavior is dependent on personality and the situation. Integrative interpersonal theories relying on new ideas of measurement took shape in the mid-20th century, also analyzing the issue of state–trait interaction. Walter Mischel (1973) challenged the idea that a person's behavior is consistent across situations. Rather than measuring anxiety, they started to measure in what situation the person is indeed anxious. Some are anxious on a date, some in the school.

The contextual dependency of the assumed personality traits has led to several crisis-like interpretation of the concept itself. Usually, five overcrossing traits emerge that later constitute the essence of the big five theory. David Buss (1984) even proposed that the main factors of the new theories of dimensional personality research, the famous big five – extraversion, agreeableness, conscientiousness, neuroticism, and openness – are actually ancient folk tools to help us to orient in the social world of other persons. The five factors should be seen as expressions of even simpler underlying features of adaptation.

Statistics and ability psychology

The intelligence testing movement had a crucial role in the 1910s–1920s in professionalizing American psychology. With the translation of the Binet scale (Terman, 1916; Binet & Simon, 1916), the test itself sold in several hundred thousand copies. The crucial step, however, was the introduction of standardized intelligence testing into the army during the First World War in the form of the famous Army Alpha (reading based) and Army Beta (non-reading based) tests. More than 1.5 million people were measured as part of the military recruitment.

That proved for society at large that psychology was indeed a needed profession, a would-be engineering profession of the mind. In a less-spectacular manner, but through the work of Binet and, later, Toulouse, Piéron, and the educational professional counseling centers in France, and through the work of Stern in Germany, and with their followers in Central and Eastern Europe, intelligence and ability measurement has been central in putting applied psychology on the social scene in Europe as well.

This social spreading of intelligence measurement led to social debates about the functions of intelligence testing already in the 1920s. There was a strong movement toward the multiplicity views of human abilities as contrasted to the unified vision of general intelligence. Soon after testing started to be used, Walter Lippmann (1899–1974), the famous liberal cultural critic and journalist, criticized the testing movement in an article series in a general magazine and raised issues that are essential for later development. For example, he asked questions such as: "How is measured intelligence related to our everyday concepts of intelligence?" "How do you select items for a test?" and "Is it sensible to use mental age to characterize adult intelligence?" (Lippman, 1922). All these became important issues in later development of testing. Interestingly, Thorndike (1920, 1924) already at this time called for a need to measure social and emotional intelligence as well.

Individual variations research does fit into the general issue of conservative and progressive interpretation of variations and of evolutionary theory. The few dimensions of variation, with a clear value attitude, basically go back to the Galtonian paradigm. As we saw in Chapter 7, this attitude treats excellence as a basically unitary construct. This unified intelligence was assumed to be inherited and basically shows a fixed normal distribution. In the 1920s, it also obtained indirect support from the anti-localizationist brain research of Karl Lashley (1929, 1950). The performance of animals after cortical ablation was dependent on the mass of available cortical tissue (**mass action**). Mass action was interpreted at that time as being a brain parallel to g or general intelligence of the psychometricians.

The interpretation of the Darwinian variation issue in the **functionalist psychology** started from an alternative image of society. It entailed a physically changing border, a constantly open and changing world with places for different varieties of people. This corresponded to the image promoting variations along many dimensions. John Dewey (1910) emphasized on several occasions this reading of Darwin. In his tolerant interpretation of individual differences, society moves according to rules of evolutionary progress. Schooling should prepare us for an ever-changing social struggle for life, where in different epochs different qualities may become important. Therefore, the knowledge of individual differences is a crucial key for education, since one cannot define a single quality that is important in social life.

The one-dimensional vision of talent was challenged by several psychometricians. The most remarkable were the efforts of Guilford, who first emphasized in 1950 that creativity has a crucial component, namely, divergent thinking is not measured by traditional tests of intelligence. Later, he developed an entire new theory of human intelligence that is supposed to consist of a multiplicity of over 100 independent components (Guilford, 1967).

As for the structure of intelligence, the more recent theory of multiple intelligences promoted by Howard Gardner (1983, 2000) claims that seven different types of excellence should and could be distinguished: musical, verbal, bodily, mathematical, and the like. Many people claim, however, that these differentiated "intelligences" are in fact personality- and life-history-dependent styles rather than intelligences, and also that they are more specific abilities than intelligences.

Two types of statistics in psychology

Differences between groups and intervention effects

The first issue where statistical argumentation appeared in psychology was the comparison of groups and the impact of interventions. Pearson (1900) published the first χ^2 test that measures the equality of two distributions. It is still the most widely used test (or, rather, class of tests) to look for the distribution of categorical data, like comparing drug use in two genders. Soon after, under the pseudonym of Student (1908), William S. Gonseth (1876–1935), the chemist of the Guinness beer factory in Dublin, published the first test (named t test since then) to compare distribution in two groups based on the standard deviation of the measurements. The use of the pseudonym was related to industrial secrecy. Sir Ronald A. Fisher (1890–1962), the Cambridge mathematician, plant breeder, evolutionary theorist, and founder of population genetics, elaborated the general theory of measurements in the 1930s that had a huge impact in psychology. The design of experiments goes hand in hand with the statistical analysis (Fisher, 1935). You introduce clear-cut orthogonal independent variables that are not tied to each other, like watering, fertilizers, and genetic variation in his plant studies. The analysis of the results is based on the idea that all variations in the dependent variable (crop yield, in this case) are a linear combination of the experimental effect under our control and the random variations. Significance would be measured as a function of the ratio of the experimental effects over the random effects. Fisher's work on the British nature/nurture tradition also followed this line of reasoning. As a continuation of the Galton paradigm, and as chair of the eugenics department at University College, London, he proposed that genetic and environmental effects are also additive, and the genetic issue can also be modeled by an analysis of variance design.

As Gigerenzer (2004) pointed out, the expectation to use this model only spread in the Anglo-Saxon world in the 1950s, probably under the influence of marketing research. The alternatives to the null hypothesis are not always clear, and there is a fishing for p values. Later, the consideration of effect sizes also became a standard part of reporting. The question is not only if girls and boys are different in one mental task but also how great their differences are. Usually, this is done by reporting the amount of variance explained and by the size of the difference expressed in units of standard deviation.

Vectors of the mind: factor analysis

Charles Edward Spearman (1863–1945), after an initial military career, did his PhD in Leipzig with Wundt and then settled at University College, London. Besides devising a rank-based method to measure correlations (Spearman, 1904a, 1907), he became a clear advocate of g, general intelligence, and factor analysis for its foundation. In his famous paper of 1904 (Spearman, 1904b, 1907), he observed in schoolchildren that there were high correlations in their performances. Everyday common sense, school smartness, and sensory discrimination were all correlated. This was practically independent of sex and age. He comes to the conclusion that we have to postulate an underlying general intellectual function. "Whenever branches of intellectual activity are at all dissimilar, then their correlations with one another appear wholly due to their being all variously saturated with some common fundamental Function (or group of Functions)" (Spearman, 1904b, p. 234). Upon comparing different school subjects and the assumed general ability, he came to postulate a general factor, g, and a hierarchy of specific factors responsible for the variations in performance in different school subjects (Spearman, 1927).

This was more or less empirically supported, but still only a hypothesis. Factor analysis is a method to see some order in complex matrices of correlations. It tries to reveal the underlying structure behind the measurements. Spearman's original insights developed in two directions. The g factor theory of human intelligence became more and more elaborate (Jensen, 1998). The followers of Spearman see a kind of a basic brain power underlying it that would mainly be inherited. The statistical notion inherited most of the problems associated with the notion of intelligence, such as differences among ethnic groups and the associated aristocratic social condescending attitude. Most of the later practical applications of intelligence tests (like the Wechsler–Bellevue scale; Wechsler, 1939) assume a general intelligence and some special intelligences, such as verbal- and non-verbal-based (performance-based) intelligences, as components. For practical purposes, these tests, consisting of subscales, try to provide a profile of the person measured.

On the technical side, factor analysis developed into a seemingly neutral technology in the mid-20th century. It became a method of not merely proving the idea of general intellectual ability but also of finding order in all sorts of data, by supposing that the observed variation corresponds to the working of a smaller number of latent variables, referred to as **factors**. Different mathematical solutions are proposed on how to arrive to the latent structure. Due to the geometric interpretation of the factors as supposed axes of the variables, **rotation methods** were also developed to arrive to structures of variables which make more psychological sense, so that the structures may result in total orthogonality of the factors themselves. Factor analysis has become a central method both in personality and in social psychology. From a mere 50 papers with *factor analysis* in their title in the 1930s, it has increased to about a 1,000 in the early 21st century.

Rival schools did emerge in the application of this seemingly neutral method. One of the pioneers of factor analysis, the American Louis L. Thurstone (1887–1955), proposed second-order factors and suggested that there is a large number of primary abilities and *g* emerges only as a second-order factor (Thurstone, 1952). Cattell (1967) shows the broad application of this attitude towards the concept of intelligence. Others, such as J. P. Guilford (1897–1987), proposed that you should not allow oblique rotations of the primary matrix, and this way they keep the independent abilities' image.

As one of the most elaborate attempts to summarize the many decades of factor analytic research into a general theory, John B. Carroll (1916–2003), a leading researcher into primary abilities and language testing, proposed a three-layered "stratum theory" of cognitive abilities. These are defined by him as **narrow**, **broad**, and **general abilities** (Carroll, 1993). This would correspond in practice to the subtests or tasks, the specific intelligence factors, and the general factor or *g*. Carroll suggested that there is a layer or stratum and a speed difference regarding each level. Tasks can test whether someone has the given level (e.g., can he do mental arithmetic?). Here, errors are the most important behavioral measures. The other types of tasks target speed factors. Individuals in these latter tests are distinguished by their fast reactions to the task. Figure 2.7 summarizes Carroll's proposal. The lower layers are the given tasks. The middle layer shows factors like decision speed, retrieval speed, auditory cognition, and the like. The upper layer is general intelligence.

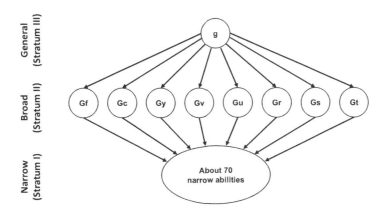

Figure 2.7 The three-layer theory of intellectual abilities proposed by J. B. Carroll.

Regarding the structure of personality, factor analysis does not decide for us whether to look for many or a few dimensions. If you allow correlated factors, you will obtain strong second-order factors, while others would not allow for this. The latter group would obtain more primary traits. This has logically led to a move from factor analysis to the use of experimental data and neurophysiological theory in interpreting personality.

Tasks

CA

Differential psychology in Stern and today.
The concept of personality in Stern and Dilthey.
How introversion became a biological category.
Compare Jaensch and Adorno in their vision of personality.
IQ and emotional intelligence.
Compare "type" and "trait" in personality theory.
Can we measure individuality?

DSA

"Personality," "character," and "temperament" in different languages (Google Ngram).
"Types" and "traits" over a century in psychological texts (PsycINFO).
The popularity of "intelligence" and IQ in the public mind (Google Ngram).
"General intelligence" and "multiple intelligence" today in psychological texts (PsycINFO).
Use of factor analysis in different disciplines.
"Rorschach test" in the public mind (Google Ngram).

3 Motivation and dynamic psychologies

Motivation as the missing link

The issue of motivation, the driving forces of humans, is of course a central issue in all modern psychologies. It is part of our naive folk psychology as well. We tend to ask WHY questions constantly. "WHY doesn't Steve like math?" "WHY is Susan so stubborn in her flirtation?" "WHY will Mr. Smith not stop playing the lottery, no matter his lack of success?" In our folk psychology, the answers refer to causes and reasons, and sometimes to hidden motivations. Someone does not do something because he is afraid of the unforeseen consequences, or she makes something because she has been dreaming for recognition for years. Contemporary philosophy of mind theory follows our folk psychology in attributing a belief–desire system to all human action (Dennett, 1987, 1997a): the actions of others and our own actions as well are explained with reference to existing knowledge (belief) and existing or assumed desires. "She went in because she thought the boy was there." "She went in because she likes the boy."

While our folk psychology works with a dual system of beliefs and desires, classical experimental psychology of the late 19th century, when it concentrated on the issue of representation, seemed to claim that humans can be analyzed merely on the level of beliefs. Attraction, ambition, stamina, and similar everyday issues had not found a place in classical psychology of consciousness. The intentionality theories initiated by Brentano certainly gave an option already in classical German psychology to elaborate a psychology that would start from the centrality of wishes (Chapter 9 in Volume 1). This mainly remained a conceptual inspiration and did not constitute a real strong alternative. The missing link was found starting with psychoanalysis, with the idea of hidden motivations. Psychology again started to be a science of our integral folk psychology. With the topics of hidden intention and non-transparent desires, the psychoanalytic approach positioned the moving forces of humans into the central stage of academic psychology. This aspect of psychoanalysis is so true that, due to intellectual or political constraints, a generation later, "dynamic psychology" started to mean psychoanalysis in its broad sense. In this chapter, I follow a more classic verbiage. I label **dynamic psychology** those trends which originally defined themselves as such.

60 *Disciplinary developments and eclectics*

The move toward a motivational psychology was true for behaviorists as well. From the 1930s on, one of their basic issues was the role of motivation in learning, and the learning of motives (Mowrer, 1947; Miller, 1959). The motivational move was true for Gestalt psychology as well. Chapter 2 already presented the motivation principles of the Lewin school growing out of Gestalt psychology. They referred to their own theory as **personality dynamics** (Lewin, 1935) and **group dynamics** (Lewin, 1951; see also Chapter 6).

In this general changed atmosphere, some psychologists turned to motivation to be the logo of all their work. For them, motivation became a key issue in the search toward the **causes of behavior**. In contrast to classical psychology, representation for them was the trivial issue, and the determining role of desires was the real worthy topic for research. Table 3.1 shows some of these contrasts.

The dynamic psychology of Woodworth

Robert Sessions Woodworth, a professor of psychology at Columbia University in New York, can be accredited for putting motivation and its conceptual machinery into the center of psychological thought. His functionalist approach was a sober, eclectic attitude, unlike the loud voices of the big schools who look for the same principle everywhere, like Freud or Köhler (Chapter 8 in Volume 1). The most important theoretical contribution to psychology of Woodworth was his conception of **dynamic psychology**. His book *Dynamic psychology*, published in 1918, introduced the concept of **drive**. The concept has been a part of mainstream psychology ever since. Drive would replace the rather-popular concept and word of *instinct*

Table 3.1 Some classical psychological theories from the point of view of belief–desire folk psychology

Theory	Belief representation	Desire motivations	Interactions
Wundt	Central	Background	None
Brentano	Two poles	Directedness	None
Freud	They serve desires	Central in all	Desires permeate representations
Woodworth	They exist	Drive is crucial	Drive is basic for any behavior
McDougall	Instinct-driven	Instincts	Social life based on instincts
Early ethology (Heinroth, Craig, Lorenz)	*Umwelt* (Uexküll) Preparatory stage modifiable	Part of all behavior Species-specific fixed	Species-dependent cognition Signal interpretation influenced by needs (Harkai Schiller)
Early humanistic (G. Allport)	They exist, but their individual side is most important	Human-specific motivations are the key issue	Functional autonomy or hierarchy

that, for many, seemed to be too fluid (Figure 3.1). For Woodworth, *drive* included all factors leading to action. Some drives are biological needs (hunger, sexuality); most of them are, however, intentions and preparations formed during the individual's lifetime. These preparations for reactions do not have to become independent beings, since they themselves are derived from earlier behaviors. At the same time, they can gain functional independence. Woodworth, following Sherrington (1906) – with whom he spent a postdoctoral year – differentiated two stages in goal-directed behavior: the preparatory and the consummative stages. Around the same time, the American comparative psychologist Wallace Craig (1876–1954) proposed that all behaviors can be separated into the **appetitive and consummative stages**. This was a more precise delineation than the one proposed by Woodworth. It also includes substages, like satiation and avoidance, and allows more modifiability to the appetitive stages compared to the consummative ones. This implies that behavior is mainly modified during search, when the organism actively looks for specific objects (Craig, 1918). Several decades later – especially thanks to Konrad Lorenz, who had contacts with Craig – the appetitive–consummative pair became a key concept pair for European ethologists. There is a certain continuity in the motivation concepts from classical functionalism to present-day psychology.

Dynamic psychology, as conceived by Woodworth (1927, 1930, 1939, 1948), is motivation-centered in two regards. It looks for the origin of behavioral goals in the life history of the individual and, at the same time, tries to identify the immediate releasing stimuli of motivational states. From the point of adaptation in a functionalist sense, the unit of behavioral analysis for Woodworth is not the stimulus response connection but behavior itself. One has to look for invariances from

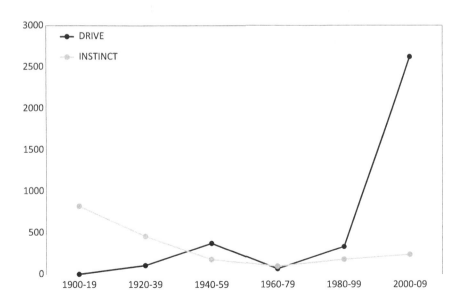

Figure 3.1 The concept of *instinct* and *drive* as titles of papers in the PsycINFO database.

the point of view of the behavior, and we find these invariances in function and need satisfaction. If pressing the pedal with the left or right paw has the same role (brings food to the animal), then from a behavioral perspective, the two movements are equivalent, as both are pedal pressings. This viewpoint would reappear in early ethologists, like Heinroth and Heinroth (1924–1934/1958), and in the theoretical interpretations of Karl Bühler (1927). In the work of Woodworth himself, his idea to introduce the *O*, that is, organismic variables, into his most influential general textbook was an extension of this general attitude regarding the importance of internal factors (Woodworth & Schlossberg, 1954).

Woodworth did not like to make stable "things" out of motives. He was in harsh debates with the teleological motivation psychology of McDougall, claiming that there is no contradiction between causation and goal direction. Human desires become causes.

> Purpose is a real fact of human life. . . . A dynamic psychology must study purpose in its relation to its antecedents and consequences, its causes and effects.
> . . . There can be no contradiction between the purposiveness of a sequence of actions, and its being a causal sequence. A purpose is certainly a cause; if it had no effects it would be without significance.
> (Woodworth, 1927, p. 118)

The hormic psychology of McDougall

The mood of a rival motivation-centered psychology of that time was very different from the sober attitude of Woodworth. William McDougall (1871–1938), who migrated from England to the United States, first to Harvard University (1920–1927), and later to Duke University (1927–1938), promoted a rather speculative theory, sometimes leaning toward mysticism. McDougall, who had a medical background, tried to make the first steps of experimental psychology in Oxford. His real success came with his *Social Psychology*, first published in 1908. He tried to explain social behavior as a result of purpose and goal directedness and a collection of social instincts. Unlike Woodworth, however, McDougall did not consider the teleology of behavior to fit into a causal chain. According to McDougall, behavior is different from physical natural phenomena due to its goal directedness; behavior can be described from the perspective of goals. From the perspective of recent interpretations of folk psychology, McDougall simply took the intentional stance as trivially true. However, McDougall interpreted purpose as the result of a vitalistically interpreted basic driving force, *Horme*, that in Greek mythology was a goddess of driving force of animals and humans. This would go almost like the panpsychism of Fechner. According to McDougall, *Horme* is present in all living creatures and in its traces would show up also in the non-living world. Thus, behind the intentional stance, there is a mystical "physical stance." *Horme* would explain the spontaneous, endogenous aspects of all behavior. On the basis of this central notion, McDougall refers to his own system as **hormic psychology**.

> The creature does not only move in a certain direction, like an inert mass impelled by external force. . . . [W]e can only describe them [these movements] by saying that the creature persistently tends towards an end.
> (McDougall, 1920b, p. 239)

McDougall uses an easy solution in his interpretation: he simply naturalizes the principles explaining behavior by putting a separate instinct behind every type of behavior. As a result of these instincts, in his interpretation, behavior is basically determined by inheritance.

As Figure 3.1 shows it, the sober notion of *drive* as a basic concept has overcome *instinct* only after the Second World War period, by the 1960s.

In the vision of McDougall, instinct is not merely an inherited form of behavior, and it is not merely an inherited drive either; it is an underlying behavioral disposition that shows up in the preference of diverse objects (cognitive side) and in peculiar behaviors with them (effector side). Its essence, its central part, is emotion. Instincts are organized in a hydraulic manner, as in Freud, and later in Konrad Lorenz: their non-satiation leads to replacement activities and vacuum behaviors. McDougall, who underwent therapy with Jung, was a rather sharp critic of Freud. The basic reason for this is the role of sexuality. As Table 3.2 shows, sexuality according to McDougall is merely one of the many instinctual tendencies (reproduction). The modular instinct theory of McDougall is not easy to reconcile with the unifying visions of psychoanalysis, no matter the similarity of their hydraulic visions.

In his social psychology, McDougall interpreted social behavior also as a result of instincts. His examples and arguments are mainly anecdotal. Some of them are summarized in the checklist in Table 3.2. The separable forms of social behavior correspond to separate instincts and their corresponding emotions.

Table 3.2 Correspondence of social instincts and emotions in the hormic system of McDougall

Instinct	*Emotion*
Flight	Fear
Pugnacity	Anger
Curiosity	Wonder
Repulsion	Disgust
Self-assertion	Elation
Self-abasement	Subjection
Parental	Tenderness
Reproduction	Desire, jealousy
Gregarious	Group comfort
Acquisition	Jealousy

As the Hungarian comparative psychologist Paul (Harkai von) Schiller (1948) pointed out, the analytic inventory of the many instincts is a born-again Cartesian approach, this time interpreted regarding the driving forces of humans. The key aspects of his Cartesianism are the neglect of context and situation. Treating the internal determinants of behavior as "objects" underlies these problems. This is the reason that the instinct theory of McDougall is mythological compared to real biological thought. Konrad Lorenz (1965, 1970) criticized him for the substance-like instinct concept but, at the same time, criticized the reflexologists as well for the missing dynamic element in their interpretation of instincts as mere reflex chains.

The other challenging issue is the specificity of social behavior. McDougall created several debates by proposing a biological foundation for social psychology. Early social psychologists did not like the idea of an entire bunch of social instincts. They especially did not like the efforts of McDougall (1920a) to build up a "group mind" as a result of the gregariousness instinct. His impact on social psychology in his second home country was mainly provocative. He has provocatively contributed to the increased conceptual sophistication of American social psychology and its rejection of ungrounded concepts like the group mind. Floyd Allport (1924b) tried to refute McDougall's group mind along with the crowd theories of Le Bon and historical references to group mentality. According to him, the basic fault of all these approaches is "to substitute the group as a whole for the individuals in the group" (p. 691). His brother Gordon Allport (1954) showed decades later the critical importance of rejecting the objectivization of groups for the development of social psychology in America.

Decades later, with the advent of sociobiology and, later, evolutionary psychology, the biological explanation, the naturalization of many social behaviors, came up again. The argumentation changed drastically, however. Contemporary evolutionists try to elaborate an acceptable adaptation history for observed behaviors, like altruism, trying to show its adaptive advantages. Thus, the scale is larger, and the analysis is more careful, and ideally there are no ready-made explanatory principles or concepts like that of instincts for McDougall.

The ideas of McDougall were fermentative in his own time, besides the instinct debates as well. His conception about the teleology of behavior, while in itself was rather speculative, left the issue of goal directedness open for more sober scientists as well. The purposive behaviorism of Tolman (1932, 1959) and Holt (1931) is a typical reaction to this challenge.

Motivation theory continues into early ethology

Motivation psychology as a central topic survived into the 1930s. A new chapter of biology was formed, the study of animal behavior or conduct, with no recourse to the rather mystical instinct-based approach of McDougall.

The biology chapter of animal behavior took shape in the 1920s as **ethology**, from a detailed study of instinct-based forms of behavior. Oskar Heinroth (1871–1945), working with his wife, Magdalena Heinroth, in the Berlin Zoo and Aquarium, initiated the comparative study of behavior in comparing the morphological features and the behavior of several species of ducks and geese (Heinroth & Heinroth, 1924). In this comparative scale, instinct becomes a species-specific behavior. From the mysterious moving force of McDougall, instinct became a descriptive concept: different species are characterized by different species-specific behaviors, nearby relatives by similar behaviors. In its internal organization, instinct for the ethologists is by far not a reflex chain. Some of the hydraulic aspects of the classical instinct concept, such as "filling up," "discharge," and the like, are preserved by the ethologists. A characteristic feature of instinct-based behaviors is "vacuum behavior." There is a built-in need to release certain species-specific types of behavior. Following a long period of deprivation, the animal produces the corresponding acts even in the absence of adequate stimuli and searches for the stimuli (Lorenz, 1942; Tinbergen, 1951). Think of the sexual replacement activities of many domestic pets and even humans. In the psychological interpretation of Paul Harkai Schiller (1948), these observations entail a two-factor theory of animal motivation. Observation on species-specific releasers in early ethology can be fit into the motivational theory of Kurt Lewin (1935) and would correspond to Lewin's **valence of stimuli**.

Ethologists took up an idea popular in German zoology – especially in the writings of Jakob von Uexküll (1864–1944) – that the animal lives in a world articulated by its body and by its nervous system (Figure 3.2), attributing certain meanings to certain elements in the environment. Animals live in a partly constructed *Umwelt* (Uexküll, 1926). "Uexküll thus starts off not from the idea of an objective environment but from a 'subjective external world' given to the living being, selected by its sensory and effector apparatus" (Schiller, 1948, p. 81).

The differentiation between the physical world and the interpreted environment, the *Umwelt*, is echoed by Koffka's (1935) proposal to differentiate between

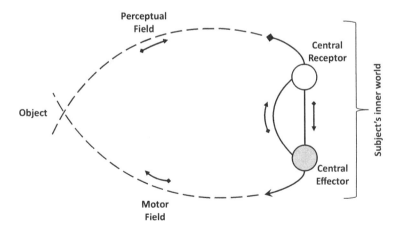

Figure 3.2 The determination of the Umwelt in Jakob von Uexküll. The gray is the interpreted world, and the white is the world out there.

Source: Jakob von Uexküll (1926). Redrawn.

geographical and psychological environments. However, for Koffka, this interpreted vision was important to account for individual and situational differences, while for Uexküll, the species-specific differences were important. Uexküll's vision of animal behavior was Darwinian in the sense that it presupposed that natural selection is valid over forms of behavior and in a certain manner. Uexküll had a wide impact in the philosophy of biology, in German idealism at large, and on the French phenomenological philosopher Merleau-Ponty (1942) as well, through his peculiar holism (Harrington, 1996). He also had an influence on the development of the probabilistic functionalist theory of representation developed by Egon Brunswik (1943; Hammond, 1966), who claimed that each species and each individual organizes the environment according to its statistical history and the reliability of the environmental cues.

The ethologists reduced the idealistic connotations of the *Umwelt* notion. The *Umwelt* for them became a system of species-specific cues; *Umwelt* and "worldview of animals" becomes an issue of **releasing stimuli**. Each species-specific behavior has a corresponding cue; the behavior–stimulus coupling works according to the lock–key metaphor. Experimental manipulations can clarify, for example, that in the feeding behavior of certain duck species, the cue for the ducklings is not the entire beak of the mother duck but a specific patch (visual pattern) on it. If we strengthen this pattern with supernormal stimuli, the ducklings would react even more strongly. In his early enthusiasm for the *Umwelt* concept, Lorenz went as far as to describe the social behavior of birds as creating a social *Umwelt* in his first major paper. "Companions," or social partners, are created in the creation of a social *Umwelt* in the same way as the entire *Umwelt* is created by the preparedness of the species. Lorenz, in his early work, combined the precise behavioral observations he learned from his mentor, Heinroth, with the philosophical inspirations taken from Uexküll. Modern approaches interpret Uexküll's "Umwelt" as everything that sticks out from the background noise and is relevant to the survival of the organism.

Around the same time, the issue of instincts played a central role for behaviorists combining the precise behavioral developmental studies with physiology as well. The 1920s–1930s, especially in America, are characterized by harsh debates regarding the relevance of instincts in psychology. McDougall and Watson engaged in a debate referred to as the battle of behaviorism (Watson & McDougall, 1928). The battle was mainly an exposure of the mentalistic and instinct-centered position and a strictly objectivistic and environmentalist position. There were other players in the instinct debates as well. On the behaviorist side, the environmentalist position was most seriously supported empirically by Zing-Yang Kuo (1898–1970), a Chinese American psychologist who was the most radical in theoretically questioning instincts. He later experimented on mammals in order to show the flexibility of supposedly instinctive behaviors. Kuo had two lines of argument to question the instinct concept. One was methodical: instinct is an empty, ready-made, prefabricated concept. It was even a dangerous concept. "Writers on the psychology of war almost identify the war motive with the herd instinct, the instinct of pugnacity, and other allied instincts" (Kuo, 1921, p. 645). The teleology of early behaviors is only apparent. The individual differences also come out of environmental history rather than inherited differences. All individual psychology is a history of gradual behavioral specialization.

The other line of argument was the empirical lifework of Kuo (1924). He became an early proponent of combining embryology of behavior with psychology. In a way, he was the forerunner of what we call today the evo/devo approach and epigenesis, but assuming much less genetic contribution than we would propose today. In his experimental studies for over 50 years, he showed in animal models that many supposedly innate behaviors in fact result from a complex interaction of organismic development. Rat killing by cats and other supposedly innate behaviors, he claimed, are behaviors under experiential control.

Karl Lashley (1938), nearer to the center of the behaviorist camp and originally a student of Watson, also raised crucial issues regarding the instinct concept, criticizing the psychoanalytically minded notions as well. His conceptual issues are: "What is the adequate stimulus for instinctive behavior?" The supposedly instinctive behaviors in mammalian sexuality, for example, are very flexible.

> An essential first step toward an understanding of the mechanism of instinct is the analysis of the properties of the stimulus situation which are really effective in arousing the behavior. . . . [T]he whole repertoire of learned and reflex movements may be elicited until some definite sensory pattern is produced.
> (Lashley, 1938, p. 468)

For example, in building a nest, "[t]he nest might be built by somewhat random activity, modified until it presents a satisfactory sensory pattern" (p. 450).

The theoretical analysis of instinct by Karl Lashley (1938) does not share the *tabula rasa* program of John Watson. This sentiment is exposed very ardently in *The Battle of Behaviorism* by Watson and McDougall (1928). Lashley concluded that instinctive behavior can be studied without supposing mysterious inner forces as a consequence of the multiple-stimulus dependence and organization of behavior. While instincts cannot be reduced to mere reflex chains, they certainly can be brought to scientific study as multicomponent behaviors. Compared to European ethology, this American comparative psychology tradition attributed less importance to internal factors in the determination of behavior. They did not, however, deny them. They merely wanted to give them a physiological interpretation. This showed up in the chemoaffinity interpretation of a Nobel Prize–winning Lashley student Roger Sperry (1913–1994) in his studies on the effects of anatomical rearrangement of motor and sensory neural circuits in lower vertebrates (Sperry, 1963).

Ethology as a biological discipline in the 1930s had only just taken off, and its impacts in American psychology only showed up after the 1950s. The papers and books of Lorenz and Tinbergen started to appear in English, and major textbooks like Donald Hebb (1958) started to take ethology into account in psychology as well. By this time, ethology appears not merely as an alternative to study instinctive behavior without any mysticism but also as a non-behaviorist account of the modification of behavior over the individual's life course on learning as well. The first radical difference from behaviorist studies of animal learning would be the interest of ethologists toward what the animal does in its regular environment and not an interest in what the animal can be taught. The starting paradigm for ethologists was the observation of natural behavior, which would be a great challenge to comparative psychologists, who were used to laboratory methods by then. Ethology also highlighted the importance of **sensitive periods of development**. Ethologists showed that birds have a critically sensitive period for learning to follow their mother. This notion of **imprinting** was extended and connected to several notions about the importance of early experience emphasized by psychoanalysts. Emotional attachment, learning, communication, and language all started to have their critical period of development similar to the wide embryological usage of this notion. (Scott, 1962, gave a good early review of these developments.) On the other hand, ethologists also pointed out that for different species, different things are easy to learn, and that learning over the individual lifetime has different importance in different species. The fact that humans are an especially learning-dedicated species in itself the result of a genetic program. There is an open genetic program in certain primate species. Emphasizing the importance of internal factors, ethology became one of the inspirations of the cognitive program of psychology in the 1960s (see Chapter 9). Already in its early stages, it showed interesting relations with those comparative psychologists who emphasized internal parameters of behavior. (These psychologists were a minority in the 1930s and 1940s.) The interesting ramifications and changes in the work of the Nobel Prize–winning Konrad Lorenz are discussed under CONTROVERSIES.

Controversies

Konrad Lorenz and early comparative ethology

The early ideas of Konrad Lorenz (1903–1989) were shaped at Vienna University, in the intellectual circles around Karl Bühler (see Chapter 5 for details). Bühler (1927), when he analyzed the goal-directed nature of animal behavior, followed more the ideas of Jennings (1906) than those of Loeb (1900, 1912). Intentions and signs organize animal behavior as well as human mental life: there is no demarcation line between human mentality and animal mental life.

Lorenz (1965) reports how early comparative psychology and the views of Bühler shaped his views on ethology with its central notions of an evolutionary analysis of behavior, the interpretation of species-specific forms of behavior, the releaser stimuli, and a species-specific articulation of the *Welt* into an *Umwelt*.

Lorenz (1996) accounted for the principles of comparative studies of behavior in a peculiar book written at the end of the 1940s. The book is peculiar since Lorenz, a professor at the German University in Königsberg, wrote it while he was a POW (prisoner of war) in Russia, and the manuscript later was assumed to be lost. It was only found in the 1980s, after Lorenz died. However, Lorenz himself recalled that for about two decades, he discussed the ideas from this book in his major talks. Thus, the book, written between 1944 and 1948 and unpublished for decades, still had an influence on the development of ethology. The intellectual curiosity of the book is that it tries to show in a systematic manner how to put comparative behavioral studies into the center of zoology.

By this time, he became much more critical of the program of Uexküll, which he endorsed in 1935. Lorenz criticized Uexküll for his vitalist support of finalistic causes. One of his issues against Uexküll is that Uexküll never had a clear theory of evolution, and he did not believe in the objectivity of the external world. For Uexküll, the sign-mediated *Umwelts* took the place of the real world.

Regarding the Pavlov heritage, Lorenz pointed out that instincts are not reflex chains. In the work of instincts, endogenous rhythmicity is crucial. Lorenz mainly relied on the works of von Holst (1937/1973) which discussed rhythmicity in the nervous system. Another important support in his interpretation of instinct is the distinction of appetitive and consummative phases proposed by the American zoologist Wallace Craig (1918). Lorenz used this distinction by suggesting that the appetitive stages are more modifiable. The species-supporting nature of all goal-directed behaviors require an individual adaptation to the changing environmental conditions that is made possible by conditioned reflexes, that is, by learning.

Lorenz was less-naturalistic in his observations than the other Nobel Prize–winning ethologist Niko Tinbergen (1907–1988). They received the Nobel Prize in 1973, together with the ethologist Karl von Frisch (1886–1982), who described the color perception, orientation, and "dance language" of bees (1950). As for their methodology differences, while Tinbergen (1951, 1963) used field observation widely, for Lorenz (and von Frisch as well), studying animals kept in quasi-natural conditions was the rule, and field observation was mainly used to check the generalizations. They tried to prove their ethological claims by careful experimentation, using systematic stimulus modifications under quasi-natural circumstances.

In the 1960s, modern ethology became very popular and, at the same time, controversial. One basis for the controversies was the extended use of the instinct concept. The other was the specific extension toward human aggression. Lorenz (1966, 1970) started to claim that human aggression might be related to intraspecific competition, for example, to territoriality. Furthermore, in aggression regulation of many mammalian species, special appeasement signals control attacks. When an attacked dog offers his neck to the attacker, this is functioning as a releaser stimulus to stop the attack, since before the invention of tools of aggression humans were weakly equipped to cause harm. Therefore, no biological appeasement signals to stop aggression were developed. This makes humans especially dangerous with their weapons. This biological theory of human aggression created many discussions in psychology and in social sciences.

A Hungarian biological psychologist of the 1930: Paul Harkai von Schiller (1908–1949)

An example for the early impact of ethology in psychology was the work of the Hungarian psychologist Paul Harkai Schiller. He is known in the Western literature as Paul von Schiller, or simply Schiller. Harkai Schiller was a key person in restarting experimental psychology at the University of Budapest in the 1930s, and during and after the war, he also taught and created a circle of followers in the reopened Kolozsvár (Cluj) Hungarian University in Transylvania. In the meantime, he traveled to Vienna and Berlin. After the war, due to political persecution, and on the invitation of Karl Lashley, he emigrated to the United States, where he died in a ski accident.

In his short life, he organized many interesting comparative studies both in Budapest and at Emory at the Yerkes Primate Laboratories. Harkai Schiller was an excellent experimentalist and, at the same time, a very ambitious theoretician. He tried to combine some very innovative trends of European and American psychology of the 1930s. From Kurt Lewin, he borrowed the idea of the contextual determination of the moving forces of humans. The core of his action theory was the motivation and contextual dependence of all behavior.

His trouble with classical Wundtian psychology and with behaviorism as well was the neglect of the moving forces and thereby the neglect of the environment. The "reformed psychology" would concentrate on the context and the environment. Harkai Schiller referred to the speculative theories of Uexküll and the more observation-based ideas of Lorenz as "psychological biologism." The theory of motivation underlying these comparative works was used as crucial support for his own ideas. Harkai was attracted, in general, to the intentionality theory of Brentano, to Gestalt ideas about configurationality, and to an action theoretic interpretation of complex behavioral phenomena (Harkai Schiller, 1940, 1944; Schiller, 1948), including an integration of Piaget as a theory about the development of configurational changes in the mapping of the environment. This was a rather sophisticated holistic functionalist psychology. It was an empirically and theoretically motivated renewal of Aristotelian functionalism. For Harkai, *the task of psychology* (Schiller, 1948) is to overcome the problem of traditional Cartesian dualism, the abandonment of a "multi-level man," rejecting a vision that supposes the reality of a mental world over the physiological processes. Harkai contrasted with this image a biological view of man, which is in fact the renewal of an Aristotelian thought, by proposing that body and soul, physiology and psychology, are not two different levels. Mental phenomena are a particular organization of human bodily or physiological processes. His peculiar functionalism links him in the history of Catholic psychology to the works of Mercier (1897/1925), a Belgian neo-Thomist "modernizer" who contrasted his view with that of Wundt, who basically defended Cartesian dualism in a modern experimental setting. For Harkai, it was also pivotal that there is a continuity between Cartesian dualism and the ideas of Wundt (1903). Wundt was unable to deal with the problem of "fields" and neglected the environmental forces that determine behavioral and mental processes which were popularized by *Gestalt* psychologists and other action-oriented theories of Harkai's time.

Harkai was an articulated biological functionalist; in this sense, he seems to be a parallel to Gilbert Ryle (1949), oftentimes labelled a philosophical behaviorist. Ryle, when analyzing the categorical errors of Cartesian dualism, tried to create a biological grounding of what we now call philosophy of the mind (of course, at his time, due to the accepted behaviorist idiolect, this was not called philosophy of mind).

Harkai's theory also appeared in actual experimental work. His numerous (partly posthumous) publications concentrate on what we would call today representational phenomena in animals, namely, detour behavior (Schiller, 1950), and figural preferences and drawings by apes (Schiller, 1951). Magda Marton (1996) in Hungary, and Donald Dewsbury (1994) in America, made many efforts to show the relevance of the work of Harkai. He is remembered most of all as a fine comparative psychologist (Dewsbury, 1994).

Classification of human motives

In the 1930s, the attempts to apply the centrality of the motivational notions in personality psychology also reached a stage where a need emerged to extract or distantiate the human motivation system both from the explanatory power of the secondary-drive concept of the behaviorists (Chapter 8) and the reductionist attempts of depth psychologies. The issues underlying these endeavors came up several times from the early critiques of utilitarian shortage economies by John Stuart Mill. The novelty of the 1930s was that the issues were raised again in a sober scientific climate without the moralizing overtones or the idealism of German value trends in Spranger or C. G. Jung.

Gordon Allport (1897–1967) at Harvard University was the first real personality psychologist in the United States. He developed a key motivational notion as part of his personality theory. His general theory of personality was eclectic but, at the same time, flexible. Referring to the "German science *versus* humanities" debates, Allport allowed both for idiographic methods studying individuals and nomothetic approaches looking for general regularities in personality (1961). In studying the psychology of personality, he urged both for the use of projective methods that search for hidden "non-intellectual" forces and for direct methods that look for motives transparent for the person (Allport, 1953). Though Allport was also looking for a dynamic psychology, for him, "dynamic" meant not general dynamics but an account for the individuality of the person. Allport balanced the Ego with his complex theories of multilayered motivations. He compared it to the instincts of psychoanalytically inspired colleagues like Henry Murray, and the Superego of the culturalists. In this process, he was clearly differentiating between general drives, and the motives of the person. The key notion used by Allport in this process of building s systematic theory of motivation was the concept of **functional autonomy.** He listed many behaviors that are repeated with seemingly no reason and motivation from circular smiling to neurotic behaviors. The really interesting cases among these, however, are the ones where practice of an ability leads to interest and pleasure that was originally not there or was irrelevant. This is a key to enriching human motivation and personality. "Actions and objects that earlier in the game were means to an end now become ends in themselves. [. . .] The principle of *functional autonomy* is a declaration of independence for the psychology of personality [. . .] it helps to account not for the subtract motivation of an impersonal and therefore non-existent mind-in-general, but for the concrete, viable motives of each and every mind in particular" (G. W. Allport, 1937, pp. 144, 156). It is very telling that a generation later, this vision was taken up by theories of self-actualization and control over the situation as motivational forces (White, 1959).

Henry Murray (1893–1988), also working at Harvard University about the same time as Gordon Allport, developed a projective system for the assessment of personality where people have to tell stories on the basis of rather-general thematic photographs (Murray, 1938; see Chapter 2). In his projective test method, manifest and deeper desires of a person are revealed by the contents of the story. Murray (1938) elaborated a rather sophisticated structured content analysis system to analyze the stories. A *personology* profile can be made by revealing what lower (e.g., sex, attachment) and what higher (e.g., ambitions, leadership) fantasies dominate the person's projections. The essential attitude of Murray to combine the needs of the researcher and the clinician was continued at Harvard University later on. In the 1950s, studying personality on the basis of motivations became a central method in studying one of the most specific human motivation systems, the **achievement motivation** system, that is so central in modern industrialized societies (McClelland, 1953, 1961).

A very influential specifically human motivation program was the proposal of **Abraham Maslow** (1908–1970) that would develop into a part of humanistic psychology. Maslow, after substantial experimental work on animal motivational processes, proposed a motivation theory that was to be based on human considerations in Maslow (1943). His basic idea was that a mere listing of human motives does not give a theory. One has to assume that there is a system of basic needs and they form a hierarchy. Certain needs have to be satisfied for the others to do their work. His basic needs in a proposed hierarchy were physiological needs, safety, love, esteem, and self-actualization. In later phrasings (Maslow, 1968), the ones lower in the hierarchy would be called **deficiency motives** (hunger, love, sex). The ones higher in the hierarchy deal with **growth motives**, the basic existential aspects of being, with increasing our possibilities, looking for the meaning of life, and self-actualization.

It is very telling that power is missing from both the lower and higher needs in his system. Maslow's seemingly innocent conception to replace the listing of motives with a hierarchy has become a central moving idea in the so-called third road, **humanistic psychologies**, that aimed to break away both from behaviorism and from depth psychology (Chapter 10). Figure 3.3 shows the famous Maslow pyramid for the hierarchical arrangement of human motives. To move up to a higher level, the lower-level motives have to be satisfied.

*

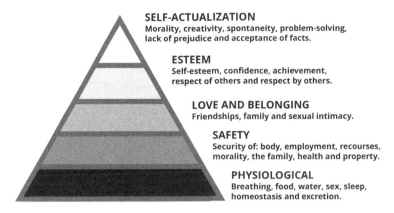

Figure 3.3 The Maslow pyramid of human motives.
Source: Redrawn form many examples.

Table 3.3 Comparison of some early motivation psychologies

Dimension	McDougall	Woodworth	Early ethology	Human motivation
Object of psychology	Action	Action	Species-specific behavior	Higher motives
Method of psychology	Experiment/ speculation	Upbringing habits	Naturalistic observation	Life data, projective tests
Internal reduction	Teleology	Behavioral ends	Behavioral stages	Hierarchy of motives
External reduction	List of instincts	Causal science	Species-specific forms	Values, self-forming

Motivation psychologies in the 1930s both on the biological side (species-specific behaviors) and regarding so-called higher human spheres laid the foundations of some topics of contemporary psychology. Most interestingly, this happened not within the great schools but somehow on the sidelines. This has a message in interpreting history: in the long run, it is not always the most organized and most vociferous who have a lasting intellectual impact.

Table 3.3 shows and compares the action and motivation theories surveyed in this chapter from the point of view of the dimensions of this book.

Tasks

CA

"Instincts" in McDougall and Lorenz.
Multiple instinct in McDougall and the concept of modularity.
How can goals become causes of behavior?
Sensitive periods in animals and humans.
How can Pinker call language an instinct?
"Social instincts" in evolutionary psychology.

DSA

"Drive" and "instinct" in general texts (Google Ngram).
"Drive" and "instinct" in psychology over the past hundred years (PsycINFO).
The popularity of McDougall and Woodworth in psychology (PsycINFO).
Lorenz and Tinbergen in psychology from 1930 to 2000 (PsycINFO).
Maslow in the public mind (Google Ngram).

4 The victorious march of developmental theories

The notion of development and the child itself have been central to modern psychology since the birth of evolutionary functionalism and the birth of the child study (pedology) movement. The dominant new schools also elevated development to a central issue and even an explanatory principle in their psychological thought: both for Watson and Freud, the child is a key to understanding the adult, and for the *Gestaltists*, development is central in the unfolding of structures. Parallel to this, for several important and very influential mid-20th-century psychologists, development became the basic theme of their entire psychology, in line with the social ideas of the century of the child (Key, 1900). Child psychology, which became more and more widespread both in its observations and in its practical applications, would turn into a theoretical psychology for many.

Figure 4.1 shows how the more abstract term, *developmental psychology*, overtook child psychology over the course of the 20th century.

There had been an enormous and growing increase of interest over the century, with a great leap forward in the interwar period. It is also about the time when the primacy of the more general "developmental psychology" term was stabilized over the more descriptive "child psychology."

In this time, along with the unfolding of applied psychology, there were important descriptive developments as well. One of their key figures was Arnold Gesell (1880–1961), a school psychologist and medical doctor at Yale University. He formed a child development clinic there, gathering the developmental profiles of children for several decades. He worked out an entire series of developmental milestones to study infant psychological development (Gesell, 1926) and pioneered the use of naturalistic recordings of development with photos, films, and audio recordings. He wanted to study the pathways of individual differences and overcome or supplement the traditional nature/nurture divide by considering maturation. In the period between 1930 and 1960, he became the reference point for descriptive developmental scales, especially in infant development.

Mainstream American developmental psychology, similar to the spirit of Gesell, in the 1920s and 1930s was mainly descriptive. In the same period, several major European developmental theories of psychology took shape. We discussed some of them in other chapters, and the most central ones in this chapter. Table 4.1 shows

DOI: 10.4324/9781032625805-5

76 *Disciplinary developments and eclectics*

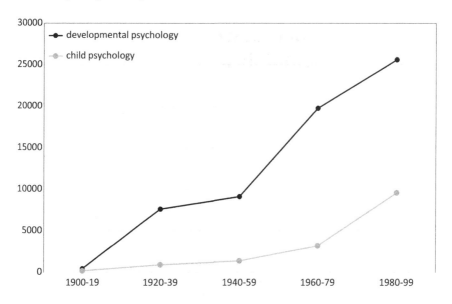

Figure 4.1 The occurrences of the terms "developmental psychology" and "child psychology" in the PsycINFO database over a century.

a survey of the rival developmental theories regarding some basic issues. The last line shows that out of them – in PsycINFO citations until 2020 – Piaget and Vygotsky are by far the most present and cited ones.

We have discussed the developmental theory of Stern in connection with his personality theory (Chapter 2). We will discuss Bühler in Chapter 5, and Vygotsky in Chapter 7.

A German European conception parallel with the Gestalt developmental theory of Koffka, but slightly different from it, was proposed by Heinz Werner (1890–1964). He centers on the overall worldview changes in children, which do change the representation of environmental wholes. A young child and teenager, for example, do see their habitat with diverging geometries (Werner, 1940). In development and the actual genesis of cognition, one has to differentiate the more ancient or primitive movement-affect-iconicity-based and the more mature secondary engineering-objective-geometric representation. The ancient form is present in the adult as well (Werner & Wapner, 1949). This differentiation leads to the formation of a personality typology juxtaposing tonic-elementary, field-dependent, and field-independent types. In his book on symbol formation (Werner & Kaplan, 1963) with Bernard Kaplan, they proposed that development is moving toward a less-embodied, more-distantiated use of symbols, but the origin of symbol formation has to be found in the bodily tendencies evoked by symbols. For a modern evaluation of Werner, see the volume edited by Valsiner (2005b).

Table 4.1 Comparisons of the comprehensive theories of development regarding some key issues

Issues	Piaget	Wallon	Vygotsky	Stern	Bühler	Werner
Central domain	Intellect	Emotions, actions, social	Language/mind	Language	Layers of selection	Perception, personality
Explanation	Biological self-development, constructions	Social and medical	Interactive/social	Interactive, convergence	Biological	Biological/constructionist
Stages	Clear and universal	More flexible	Changeable	??	There are stages	Secondary
Role of language	Secondary	Secondary	Becomes central	Independent world	Independent	Secondary mirrors
Citations	33,000	2,300	26,000	3,900	936	587

From child worldview to operational logics: Jean Piaget

The French Swiss Jean Piaget was the founder of modern theoretical developmental psychology and formed its most comprehensive model, which is very influential even in our new century. From his early age on, Piaget united three attitudes: he was a **biologist** who treated the human mind as a biological product, as a specific tool of adaptation; he was a **philosopher** who looked for a solution to the traditional dilemmas of epistemology and a solution to the empiricism–rationalism debate in the development of the mind; and finally, **Piaget as a psychologist** filled all these biological and philosophical attitudes with empirical substance in the frame of the French functionalist tradition of interest toward children, the tradition of Binet and Claparède. As Hungarian developmental psychologist interpreter Ferenc Mérei said about Piaget, "Piaget is the one who listened to the children."

After the 1920s, in both the Francophone and Russophone worlds (and, after the 1960s, on the British Isles and in America as well), he became the chief theoretician of development, whose ideas motivated generations and whose theories many tried to question and disprove. He was, at the same time, a general theoretician of the position of psychology among the sciences (Piaget, 1979) and the first comprehensive cognitive scientist in the contemporary sense, though in his own time, this self-labeling was not practiced yet. He also had many reservations about the entirely formal approach of the first generation of cognitive science.

Biography

A philosopher disguised as a naturalist: Jean Piaget (1896–1980)

Piaget had a remarkable intellectual course not merely in psychology but in 20th-century science and scholarship at large. With no formal training and no diploma for psychology, he obtained several honorary doctorates while also becoming a theoretician, provoking many fields from biology and psychology to linguistics, logic, and philosophy.

Piaget came from an intellectual family in Neuchâtel. Neuchâtel was at that time a small town center of a watchmaking industrial canton (today it is a high-tech small town with 30,000 inhabitants) with several political and religious divisions, where some factions favored relations between state and religion, and others rejected it. Arthur Piaget, his father, was a local historian and archivist, and his mother, a socially active, sometimes emotionally unstable woman of English descent. His parents became the inspiration for all his future activity. The fatherly side is responsible for the "compulsive need to create order, that will result first in simply catalogization, later classification, going through all of his life and giving it its systematic flavor" (Ducret, 1990). The fatherly structuring pattern was colored by the destabilizing maternal model, with a dynamic need for change. Jean Piaget, during his pre-pubescent years, was already the pride of his small-town high school in Neuchâtel for his zoological work on mollusks. As an early teenager, Piaget was a collector and naturalist who even got into scientific discussions as a teenager, debating with great experts of the field. His studies on the variation of snail populations in different environments raised some of his lifelong issues, such as the role of environmentally conditioned variants and their possible genetic fixation.

This naturalist attitude was followed later by a philosophical, moral, and even theological interest. Fernando Vidal (1994), an assistant and historian of Piaget, even claimed that all the early work of Piaget was in fact, until the 1930s, an attempt to find answers to his moral issues about the tension between good and evil in human nature. Reading the *Creative Evolution* of Bergson was especially puzzling for him all his life. Even as mature scientist, he wrote an entire book criticizing speculative philosophical theories of knowledge, including Bergson (Piaget, 1965). Already as a teenage naturalist, he relied on Bergson to question rigid classifications in biology. In his philosophical reflections, under the impact of Bergsonism, he hesitated whether to allow for a speculative philosophical evolutionary theory or to

Figure 4.2 Jean Piaget.
Source: Wikimedia commons. Public domain.

try to have a scientific foundation for evolution, including the evolution of mind. But Piaget always maintained a progressive, "improvement," and constructivist interpretation of evolution. He arrived at psychology through his search for certainty of knowledge, and the foundations of faith, to allow for a combination of his philosophical and scientific interests. Along this line, he also developed a peculiar holistic version of the organization of knowledge, seeing emerging wholes and constitutive parts rather than pieces at several levels (Ducret, 1990).

His social philosophy expressed in his book *Research* in 1918 is very instructive about his social utopia. For Piaget, cooperation would play a significant role for his entire life. He contrasted the individualist capitalist and the collectivist socialist systems as one-sided and proposed a utopistic cooperation that would preserve individual autonomy.

Piaget studied biology, not spending too much time in classes, and received a PhD in zoology (based on a dissertation on classification of snails) in 1918 from the small university of his hometown, Neuchâtel. Later, in Zurich, he visited the psychiatry courses of Bleuler and Jung and became acquainted with psychoanalysis through Pfister. Later, he even had a very intensive and instructive psychoanalysis with Sabina Spielrein (Vidal, 2001).

In 1919, he took classes from philosophers (Lalande, Brunschvicg) and clinical training at the Saint-Anne hospital with G. Dumas in Paris. While in Paris, Théodore Simon opened the doors of the Binet Lab for him, where in the process of adapting tests created by Cyril Burt to children, Piaget started to see how important it was to understand the reasons children gave to justify their answers. He was invited by Claparède and the functionalist educator and Christian reformer Pierre Bovet to Geneva, to the new Rousseau Institute, established in 1912. From 1921, Piaget obtained a position in the institute, sharing the general liberal Protestant vision and the interest toward children's thought by Claparède. In 1925, he also became a philosophy and sociology professor at Neuchâtel, teaching mainly child psychology. From 1932 to 1971, he was a sociology and later psychology professor at the University of Geneva. His lab there and at the Rousseau Institute became the center for his research involving several dozen international coworkers. Between 1952 and 1963, he was the child psychology professor of the Sorbonne as well, following Merleau-Ponty, who taught philosophical psychology. In his weekly commute from Geneva to Paris, Piaget did not only give classes but also directed a new generation of researchers as well. He always taught his own system but was very receptive to the interests of the students, which can be showcased, for example, when he lectured on the request of the students a semester on the relations of intelligence and affectivity (Piaget, 1954).

In 1955, with support from the Rockefeller Foundation, Piaget established the **Center for Genetic Epistemology** in Geneva, following his vision of science organization and about the structure of knowledge. This was among the first declaratively interdisciplinary centers involving psychology, where epistemological and biological research were all converging toward psychology. The main interests of Piaget (1972, 1977) were to find logical structures in the different disciplines and to find structural parallels between history of science and the unfolding of knowledge in individual children.

Piaget was an extremely productive scholar. He has published over 40 books, 700 papers, and his manuscript heritage in his former institute is assumed to be between 70,000 and 100,000 pages. Piaget became a leading 20th-century theoretician of developmental psychology and of a natural science interpretation of epistemology. He combined a child-centered approach that aimed to interpret children and their world, looking for answers of logic and epistemology, with a theory-centered attitude based on the observations on children. Many publications summarize and honor his achievements. Much of his own works are available at the site of the Piaget Foundation. The edited volume of Houdé and Meljac (2000) gives good international panorama, and the Piaget companion edited by Müller et al. (2009) is a rich source.

Piaget the epistemologist was a central debater of French intellectual life who took part with entire books on discussions regarding the claims of phenomenological, armchair philosophical psychology and structuralism as well. During the last decade of his rich life, he became a debating partner for the new overseas nativists Noam Chomsky and Jerry Fodor. They considered Piaget to belong to a clear empiricist trend due to his constructionist engagements that take knowledge to be a result of an interaction between existing schemata and input from the world (see the details later under CONTROVERSIES).

Piaget was also a practical theorist. He became a key advisor for international educational organizations, beginning in the 1920s, and later for UNESCO.

The clinical method and the worldview of children

Talking with young children

The young Piaget, after obtaining some experience on empirical child psychology in the Binet Lab in Paris, decided to make an excursion lasting a few years toward child psychology within the framework of his general biological and epistemological interests. He had a high ambition: to replace speculative epistemology with a theory based on natural science. This endeavor took a lifetime.

Over his lifetime, Piaget developed not only a comprehensive theory but also specific theories on the development of physical causation, objects, number, mental images, logical inferences, and even naive moral reasoning. At a time when there were no easily accessible databases, he used his own collections of data to search for developmental patterns in different areas. Within developmental psychology, Piaget was a Darwinian scholar who combined careful observation with courageous theory building. Yet at the same time, he tried to reveal, through the clinical method, the inner reality of the changes of representations and thinking. His clinical attitude made him an innovator of the early pedological thought (leading to the complex study of children initiated by Stanley Hall.). Piaget respected children, in an inspiration *à la Rousseau*, and so he recognized the alternative ways of thought in childhood.

The young Piaget combined the methods and tasks he learned in the Binet Lab with the methods and approaches he learned in Zurich and Paris from psychiatry and from his own psychoanalysis with Spielrein and from reading Freud (Piaget, 1920). The essence of his clinical method is that when assigning children different tasks and situations, he was interested not merely in the solutions but in the road leading to the solutions and the reasons children provided to justify them. Piaget talks to the children about complex issues (*Why does the sun rise? What do we do when we sleep?*) with an attitude of interest, avoiding suggestions. He wanted to reveal hidden conceptions and implicit theories underlying performance and behavior. The clinical method supported the main developmental frame of Piaget: in the course of the development of childhood intelligence, **real qualitative changes could be observed**. Thus, unlike the behaviorists claim, development would not be a mere quantitative accumulation.

On the basis of his clinical inquiries, Piaget observed that preschoolers could be characterized by a peculiar vision of the world (Piaget, 1927, 1936). The peculiarities are related to different versions of causality, where causes and reasons are messed up, and to relevance is based on local rather than global constraints in explanations. In this regard as well, Piaget observed that children tend to claim that things fall because they "want to fall"; thus, they are **anthropomorphic**. They also claim that clouds are there because someone put them there. Thus, they are **artificialistic** (or **creationists** in today's vernacular); they believe that all existing things were created. Thus, they are using the folk psychology machinery turned into a teleology to explain the physical world. This is radically different from the later separation of the physical and intentional stances. Decades later, Piaget published many speculative works on how the development of children and that of sciences are showing similarities in these matters. We can interpret teleological conceptions as always appearing as primary models that are contrasted to the later emerging causal models. Interestingly, recent developmental psychology would posit the beginning of these teleological models to a much earlier age than Piaget did. With indirect eye movement and fixation data, the teleological model could be shown already in 12-month-old infants (Gergely et al., 1995). This development is not without its own ironies. For half a century, proponents of various social constructionist models challenged Piaget by claiming that the artificial and anthropomorphic nature of children's supposed worldview was implanted from the adult world, whereas now it has been shown that they have pre-verbally built-in features of the human mind that are first extended to the physical world.

The example from a clinical interview of Piaget reveals one of the basic features of the thought of young children, **artificialism**.

L (3 years 2 months) is in bed, but outside it is still clear:

L: Please switch it off!
A: But it not switched on, look (I switch on and off the lamp).
L: But no, it is not night. It is day, look out, it is daylight. Thus, switch it off.
A: But I cannot switch off outside.
L: But yes, you can make night.
A: How?
L: That you switch it off very strongly.

(Piaget, 1945, p. 415)

Piaget, when trying to speak about an underlying theory or worldview in preschool children, was inspired by the claims of Lucien Lévy-Bruhl (1910/1922) about an incoherent, illogical, and animistic mentality in so-called primitive people. In a recapitulative manner, Piaget believed that this mentality was also typical of preschool children.

Egocentrism and the worldview of preschool children

In his early works, Piaget tried to clarify the relationships between **language and thought in preschoolers** based on clinical interviews and careful playtime observations in nurseries. The social and communicative aspects of thought, and its relation to language, were the topic of his first book (Piaget, 1923), *The language and thought in children*.

Piaget observed that young children frequently murmur to themselves with apparently no communicative intent ("Well, this red over there, such, fine"), and even their partner-oriented speech carries relations that are hard to discern for their partners ("And then this has left and gave it to him, and that brought it back"). Piaget borrowed a key notion of his teacher, the Swiss psychiatrist Eugen Bleuler (1857–1939), for the interpretation of these phenomena. Bleuler (1911) described the thought disturbance of schizophrenic patients as a self-enclosed **autism**, characterized by incoherent thought under emotional guidance. Piaget combined the idea of primitive mentality with the idea of autistic thought taken over from Bleuler and his experience with the psychoanalytic thoughts of Spielrein. For Piaget, egocentrism, and autism of early thought in children, was a developmental stage to be overcome by coherence and coordination.

Piaget (1923) started to claim that the thinking of preschoolers, even if it is not autistic, is certainly **egocentric**. Preschoolers have different rules for coherence, not considering the others' point of view. Cooperation and changing or alternating points of view gradually liberate children from these constraints. The conception of decentration remained with Piaget in his later works as well. We gradually become able to take a decentered point of view and take up the point of view of others.

This ability is key for the development of all moral and cognitive developments and served for an entire societal theory of Piaget (see Chapter 5). The organization of the level of the Ego preserves the self-centered vision, while mature personality bases social relations on mutual respect, moral and intellectual cooperation, and perspective switching (Kitchener, 1991).

The egocentric speech theory of Piaget was met with criticism from Wallon to Vygotsky. Piaget tried to accommodate these criticisms into his system later on, as shown under CONTROVERSIES. Specifically, he started to elaborate a detailed theory of the role of symbols in children's thinking. Symbolic processes like imagination, dream, play, mental image, and language shall serve to re-present objects in a delayed manner and manipulate these internal representations (Piaget, 1945). Real symbolic function requires distancing from the present.

Controversies

Debates on egocentric speech: Vygotsky and Piaget

The very notion of **egocentric speech** and the conversational situations analyzed in Piaget's first book had become the center of many attacks. The most notable critique was Vygotsky (1934/1986), whose critical remarks had become widely available only in the 1960s, when his review appeared in English. According to Vygotsky, egocentric speech indicates that speech gradually becomes a medium of self-regulation or a career of thought and planning. Egocentric speech would be a transition point toward inner speech rather than a sign of the aboriginal asociality of children. Egocentrism is a misanalyzed step in the process, where social becomes regulatory. Piaget, in his much later reactions, acknowledged that the term *egocentric* was not too successful. He also admitted that, as a matter of fact, the use of egocentric speech in social conversations in preschoolers was a function of many contextual factors that were highlighted by Vygotsky.

In his own approach of the relations of language and thought (see in detail in Chapter 7), Vygotsky proposed a semiotic and interiorization change theory of human development. Thought is an event that occurs between people. For the individualistic Piaget, external physical actions gradually become internal actions; for Vygotsky, external speech becomes internal speech. Speech through inner speech develops from a tool of communication and interaction into a tool of internal communication.

A generation later, A. R. Luria (1961; see Chapters 5 and 7) elaborated in detail how external social direction by speech can become the means of directing behavior through inner speech – inner speech becomes kind of a cognitive Superego. Kohlberg et al. (1968) made an empirical comparisons of the claims of Piaget, Vygotsky, and G.H. Mead, showing that egocentric speech was in fact an intermediate step in external communication becoming internal regulation.

Vygotsky also proposed a general phylogenetic and ontogenetic theory about the relations between language and thought. Vygotsky claimed that both in apes (he had in mind the observations of Köhler, 1921/1925) and in children, thinking and communication are independent to begin with, and the great human event is joining them together. Vygotsky could be interpreted in a way where the abilities are modular to start with, and they become gradually integrated. A key step in this integration would be that language, as an agent of social mediation, would become a tool of this unification.

The very notion of egocentric speech followed to play a continuous role in linguistic studies and in child development research regarding the **changing discourse organization of the speech of children**. Piaget (1923) himself described what he called the egocentric elements in sociocentric speech; he noticed that the use of pronouns was situational and showed signs of centration on the self. Kindergarten children, when involved in social play, would use expressions like "Give me this!" or "You see that." The noun phrases are left unspecified by the child with the use of pronouns. This happens because they rely on speech in a deictic setting. Later studies of this phenomenon showed that the transmission from egocentric speech to sociocentric speech on the level of language use requires the formation of discourses that become dissociated from the nonlinguistic situation. Annette Karmiloff-Smith (1981), at that time working in Geneva with Piaget, showed that the secondary, discourse-related use of pronouns like *it* and determiners like *the boy* requires a cognitive restructuring of the already-available linguistic signs – a move away from the situation to the text.

Development of cognition and logical systems

In looking for the organization of thinking, Piaget started to analyze the **formation of cognitive architectures in children**. How do object concepts, permanence functions, and later propositional organization develop? These are architectures – **schemas** in the terminology of Piaget, since they provide the frames, that is, the schemata, for the articulation of specific pieces of knowledge. What was a necessary requirement for a logical system in his vision, and how was it taking shape in his studies for over half a century? This question is illustrated in Table 4.2.

Piaget always concentrated on the operations on objects. All categories and logical structures and operations come from the activity of the human agent. Coordination of actions and reversibility are key conditions for the development of human thought.

In his empirical work on the development of cognition, there are two basic aspects. The first aspect is how objects and systems of the world are represented

86   *Disciplinary developments and eclectics*

Table 4.2 Some of the issues of logical organization in the vision of Piaget, and corresponding developmental research

Logical level	Developmental research
Identity	Object permanence
Conservation	Quantity and number conservation
Propositions	Representation and symbol development
Inference/reasoning	The INRC of logical thought; causality

Note: INRC: the laws of classical propositional logics. Inversion, negation, reciprocity, and the exclusion of third.

Table 4.3 The stages of intellectual development according to the mature system of Piaget

Stage	Time frame	Features	Typical study	Issues
Sensorimotor	Infancy ≤ 2.0	Learning through object manipulation	Object permanence	Some achievements earlier
Preoperative	2–7	Symbols, distantiation, make-believe, ToM	Conservation of quantity pretense games	Role of language
Concrete operations	7–11	Knowledge accumulation Authority	Moral reasoning centration	Language and logics
Formal operations	11–12 ...	Formal and hypothetical thought	Logical reasoning experimentation	Is it true in all domains and all cultures?

in the mind at different ages, that is, the representation of objects, numbers, space, time, and laws of physical reality, about movements, inertia, etc. Second is the development of logical organization itself.

The development of the achievements indicated in Table 4.2 is an unfolding in qualitatively different stages summarized in Table 4.3.

Sensorimotor intelligence is stabilized by the end of infancy. Piaget started from the observations of perceptual psychologists in the *Gestalt* tradition regarding constancies of color, shape, size but went beyond perceptual features to object permanence. During early sensorimotor development, children have to form **object permanence** (Piaget, 1936). Objects disappearing behind a blanket or a screen still exist, and if they come out at the other side with, for example, a different color or disappear, the 1-year-old baby is surprised. The classical arrangements are shown on Figure 4.3

The next stage in the preschool years is characterized by the formation of even more abstract constancies that will form the basis of **preoperative thinking**. While in characterizing the sensorimotor stage Piaget started from object permanence, for the preoperative stage, he analyzed the **conservation of parameters of objects**. These are the preconditions of later acquisition of mathematical and physical

The victorious march of developmental theories 87

Figure 4.3 A classical arrangement to study of object permanence.

abstractions. The formation of quantity and number constancies is a great achievement at the onset of school; 3-year-olds make errors, such as thinking that water poured from a wide barrel to a narrow one (resulting in a higher column) becomes more in quantity, or that tokens on the table widely dispersed are "more" than the tightly arranged ones. The arrangements used are illustrated in Figure 4.4. Quantity and number constancy develop in a gradual manner, and the child's own actions play *a* crucial role in their formation. The source of constancies, the basic stabilities of the representation of the world, is **reversible action**: I would consider the liquid to be identical quantity in the two containers, because I can and I did pour them back and forth.

Quantity conservation situation: After the b situation, are the liquids in the two jars in c of the same amount?
Number constancy situation: Are the two rows the same amount?

After the categories are stabilized, a stage of **concrete operational thinking** takes shape between 6 and 11–12 years of age, or until the onset of puberty. The child is more and more able to think abstractly about the categories. This is replaced by **formal thinking** from 12 years on. The latter is characterized by

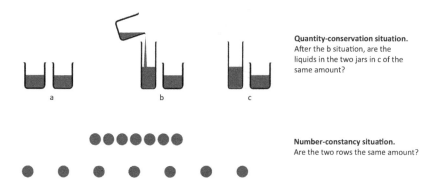

Figure 4.4 Typical Piaget situations for the study of quantity and number constancy.

full-fledged symbolic logic, entirely based on formal entailment relations, with the use of hypotheses and an experimental spirit regarding contingencies. A child in this stage, if asked to equalize the swinging two pendulums, would systematically experiment with length of the ropes and the weights. In the development of thinking, together with decentration, there is a complementary process of interiorization. External movements gradually become internalized; the adolescent is able to solve tasks in the head.

The key for human intelligence for Piaget (1947) is **operations**, starting from infants to the logic of science. In contrast with traditional and behavioristic associative models, which only see associated elements, Piaget sees logical organization everywhere. In contrast to the Frege (1892) initiated language-centered logic, which models logical organization in a sentence-like organization, Piaget claims an operational logic, which bases its abstractions on the operations of the knowing subject (Piaget, 1960).

During the unfolding of operational thinking, children's **social concepts** also change. Being conscious of rules and the development of morality passes several stages. First, there is an authority-based, arbitrary system, followed by a more decentered but absolute rule, a rigid and absolute moral system. "We do not steal because mom said so" of kindergarten age is replaced around 10 years of age by a more rational, convention-based, and flexible system of "We do not steal because stealing is a sin." Along these changes, the perception of action responsibility also changes. For young children, if someone has lost his lunch sandwich, the consequences are the same if he deliberately threw it out. The consideration of intention in assigning blame is a later development (Piaget, 1932). The book on moral development showed most clearly the preservation of the religious and philosophical issues of the young Piaget. The movement from heteronomous to autonomous morality has normative overtones. It led to further developments of empirical moral development (Kohlberg, 1971, 1981–1984). The social aspect of Piaget's theories, his notion of decentration, and the move from authority toward the comparison of points of views and autonomy are central to recent social cognitive theories, and even for theories of moral philosophy as well (Habermas, 1983).

Accommodation and assimilation as explanatory concepts

In the 1960s, Piaget, together with his associates, especially Bärbel Inhelder (1913–1997), elaborated detailed theories of perception, memory, and imagination, both regarding their structure and regarding their unfolding in children (see as an example on the book of Piaget et al., 1948, on the unfolding of space conceptions in children). The basic organization was the same in all domains. In the conception of Piaget, development is always to be interpreted with two key notions taken over from biology that already showed up in his 1947 book on intelligence: **assimilation and accommodation**. All development and all mental processes are two-sided. We assimilate incoming data to the already-existing internal system, and at the same time, since the schemata of this internal system are not immutable either, the schemata themselves accommodate to the incoming experience. The two fulfill the **process of adaptation and equilibration**, in line with the biological functionalism of Piaget. This duality is true from genetic regulation to the unfolding of thought in children (Piaget, 1972, 1978). Learning in this system is more than fixing incoming information; it also involves changes in the learning system itself.

Development has universal features that are valid over cultural contexts, since it is basically self-development and self-organization. The social milieu can foster and assist it, but the organizations and the structure develop from inward to outward. This universalism was strongly criticized by left-wing culturalist approaches who were more constructionist than Piaget.

The impact of Piaget in psychology and cognitive science

Piaget as a psychologist has continued to be successful for over three generations. His laboratory in Geneva was a pilgrimage point for European psychologists in the 1930s. Piaget represented the real, existing pedology program, the idea to make education based on the knowledge of children. Many people obtained their training from all layers of psychology as early as the 1930s, the most famous one, the Polish Alina Szeminska (1907–1986), working on number and space concepts in Geneva with Piaget (Piaget et al., 1956). There were even two Hungarian examples, Dezső Várkonyi Hildebrand (1888–1971), a Catholic priest from Szeged, and Tihamér Kiss (1905–2005), a Protestant minister form Debrecen. They both popularized the approach of Piaget to understand children and had a great impact in Hungarian teacher training in the 1930s.

Piaget, who started from a partnership conception and a vision of thought in children, had already been criticized in the 1930s by Wallon (1942) in the French context, by Vygotsky (1934/1986) in the Russian context, and by many in the Anglo-Saxon world in the 1960s. They criticized him for proposing a self-enclosed individuality. Piaget certainly believed that the development of human thought is a process driven internally by the recognition of results of our actions on objects.

90 *Disciplinary developments and eclectics*

Some critics even claimed that some of his observations even on quantity concepts were in fact a result of his misunderstanding the conversational attitude of children, and the concepts. What is the meaning of *more* for a child of 4?

As Piaget's conception of decentration and his ideas on moral development showed, he was less individualistic than his opponents in many of the dominant "schools" in the 1930s believed him to be. He certainly was not interested in the forces driving development, but in the structural changes during development. Regarding the role of imitation and symbol formation, as well as the relationships between cognitive and emotional development, Piaget accommodated the criticisms of Wallon (1942) in his later work on symbols (Piaget, 1962) and emotions (Piaget, 1954).

The qualitative thinking, the dominance of observation over experimentation, the lack of statistical data, and the somewhat-easygoing attitude toward his own observational practices all became obstacles for Piaget in coming through to an American audience. His time beyond the French-speaking, Central, and Eastern European worlds occurred in the 1960s. A survey by John Flavell (1963) and new translations popularized Piaget across the Atlantic. The new cognitive psychology started to see him as a European forerunner.

According to the Google Ngram system, English and French books about him culminated around 1980, and as Figure 4.5 shows, he was most talked about in the professional psychological literature in the 1970s and 1980s.

Piaget is still with us, and not at all as a merely historical figure. Self-development *versus* instruction, thinking *versus* language, universal course *versus* cultural and individual varieties, continuity *versus* sharp stages – all these debates started with the participation and contribution of Piaget.

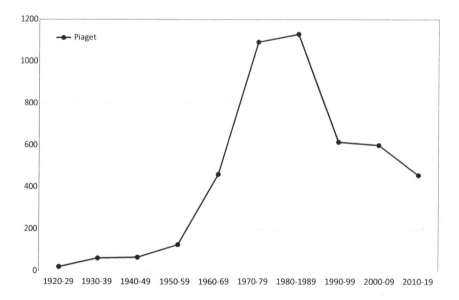

Figure 4.5 Number of papers mentioning Piaget according the PsycINFO database.

The Swiss "giant of the nurseries" has become central to subsequent generations of psychologists and cognitive scientists as well. The centrality of Piaget is shown by the long list of his adversaries and enemies, from Vygotsky and Wallon in the 1920s to Bruner in the 1960s and Chomsky in the 1970s. Even in contemporary developmental theory, anything should somehow be Piaget-revisionist or counter-Piaget, which is a clear sign of the centrality of Piaget.

Piaget has specific affinities to **cognitive science**. In the early years of modern theories of cognitive development, the theoretical stance of Piaget became a leading topic of discussion. From the early cognitive years on, Soviet Russian theories thought his stages to be too fixed, and development should be speeded up. Americans tried to reconstruct the issue of stages as subsequent changes of representational formats. Jerome Bruner (1915–2016), from his Harvard Cognitive Center, was an important figure in these debates. The group of Bruner raised two new aspects. The first one was a sign-based, rather than action-based, theory. According to the now-classical theory of Bruner (Bruner et al., 1966), indexical (action-based), iconic (image-based), and symbolic (linguistic) representations follow each other in cognitive development. The entire domain of cognitive development obtains a communicative interpretation. In discussing relationships between representation and communication, Bruner raised a second, almost-traditional issue, namely, whether representational systems arise from social-communicative interactions, particularly in instructional settings. There are many doubts regarding a strictly communication-based view of the representational system. It is clear enough in the case of sentences and images, where the visual and linguistic environment, the outside world, may be taken as a mere occasion to develop a pre-wired human representational system.

Contemporary research on infant cognition usually tries to criticize Piaget and show how his ideas became obsolete. Many studies using modern eye-tracking and electrophysiological methods show, for example, that Piaget underrepresented the cognitive capacities of very young children in many regards. These efforts usually go together with the assumption of stronger innate components.

While Piaget was looking for logical structure and invariants, looking with a nomothetic attitude to universals, Vygotsky, on his part, was interested not only in the optimistic changeability of the mind but also in its contextual determination and the personal meaning created in situations, in narrative, and in human agent-centered organization (Bruner, 1997).

From the 1950s on, Piaget (1950, 1977) framed his program of **genetic epistemology** in a way that went well beyond developmental psychology proper. This extension and reinterpretation have trivial parallels with modern cognitive science (Kitchener, 1986) and even with evolutionary epistemologies (Kesserling, 1994). Piaget never agreed with a simple empiricist "mirror of the world" or with a nativist Platonian internal self-reflection. The actions of the knowing subject change the representations; this is what he means by "there is no knowledge without a knower." In this sense, his attitude is thoroughly constructionist.

He can be seen as a forerunner and early representative of the program of contemporary cognitive science, with his aims to relate history of science, child development, logic, and psychology. This approach, however, has some characteristic divergences from mainstream cognitive science. Piaget, as a starting point, deals with the relations between perception and cognition, an issue which is ignored by many later cognitivists. For Piaget, **perception** is probabilistic and unreliable, while **thought** is the world of real knowledge and certainty, and it reflects essential relations in a decentered manner. **Representation**, one of the central concepts of cognitive disciplines, had a very specific meaning for Piaget. Representations are not all sorts of internal mappings but only those that can become objects of internal operations. The definitional feature of *representation* is a liberation from stimulus-boundedness, which he showed very clearly in his 1945 book on symbol formation.

Another difference compared to some modern cognitive theories is the fact that Piaget would never have considered mental representations to be by necessity of a propositional nature. Symbols have content to start with, since they merely arrive after several stages of sensorimotor development in the context of situational decoupling.

Piaget, while fighting philosophers, always talked about the primacy of data. In reality, he selected among data and was looking for data that have a theoretical meaning or importance. Piaget saw his own cognitive conception as a synthesis of the two epistemology traditions, being on the footsteps of a modernized and science-based Kantianism. The most challenging aspect of his theory for modern rationalists is his non-Darwinian account of evolution. Piaget believed in a softened form of Lamarckism from early on, where experience could have some effect on the genome. He had a similarly interactionist take on the unfolding of individual knowledge. Knowledge is never given, never ready-made; it always develops through the activity of the subject (and this is the central point of his theory of evolution as well).

Piaget, despite his debates with Chomsky (see under CONTROVERSIES), continued to be a crucial motivator for child language research in a direct and indirect way. Piaget played an inspirational role for actual empirical research of child language from the 1970s on. There were two types of inspirations. Some studies looked for early word combinations from the perspective of sensorimotor development, claiming that early grammatical categories such as AGENT, INSTRUMENT, and GOAL go back to differentiations in object categories. Other researchers worked in the frame of a "softened cognitive hypothesis" with older children, which basically claims that cognitive factors are preconditions for the acquisition of certain grammatical structures. For example, in order to acquire the expressions for *ON* and *IN* relations, children have to distinguish these cognitively, but the peculiarities of the linguistic forms in a given language also contribute to the ease or difficulty of the acquisition of the form. The details of these issues are still part of contemporary psycholinguistics. What demonstrates the ingenious nature of some of Piaget's proposals for the historian is the fact that his ideas motivate research for almost a hundred years.

His debates with the Chomsky followers about general cognition, epigenesis, and modular and innate organization that are part of history now are summarized under CONTROVERSIES.

Controversies

The Piaget–Chomsky debate and the constructionism of Piaget

The discussion regarding the biological, epistemological, and psychological constructionism of Piaget was most clearly directly shown in the debate between Chomsky and Piaget and their followers. It was a great intellectual event, where the 80-year-old senior master and the representatives of the new cognitive innatism (in their 40s and 50s) met at a former monastery in Royaumont, France, in 1975 (Piattelli-Palmarini, 1980). Two camps with two charismatic leaders met there, and their debate created a symbolic bridge between the 1930s and the 1970s. Piaget made his message very clear himself. As Piattelli-Palmarini (1994) summarized almost a generation later with a fresh look, Piaget presented his mentalism, anti-empiricism, rationalism, and rule-centered approach as an olive branch toward the young Turks. Chomsky and his followers raised two basic concerns. In their view, Piaget did not propose (modular) systems that are specific enough and assigned too small of a role to innate components in the development of thought. Piaget and Inhelder replied that they do believe in innate components; however, these are not language-specific but general innate principles.

Regarding innatism at the Chomsky-Piaget debate, the two American philosophers not committed to Chomsky, Putnam and Toulmin, agreed: there are innate principles, but they are, by far, not as specific as Chomsky believed. The French neuroscientist Changeux emphasized that the multistep unfolding of neuronal circuits represented a compromise between innatism and the constructivism of Piaget.

Piaget tried to present his peculiar biological arguments for his constructionism – without much success. From the biological reasoning of Piaget, the selectionist theory of development was missing, especially the idea of pruning, that environmental influences may simplify and streamline emerging networks by eliminating the connections that do not respond frequently to environmental inputs (Changeux & Danchin, 1976; Changeux & Dehaene, 1989).

At the same time, Piaget needed mechanisms to speed up biological evolution. He introduced the notion of **phenocopy** as a radical interpretation of the Baldwin effect. "A new characteristic appears in its phenotypical form and then . . . this same characteristic, or at least a 'copy' of it, becomes a feature of the stable genotype" (Piaget, in Piattelli-Palmarini, 1980, p. 87). The key question is of course how this can happen without Lamarckism. In informal conversations, Piaget claimed that the external environment, the phenotype, and the genome are incomplete without taking into consideration the internal environment, the *milieu intérieur*. If a disequilibrium emerges between the genotype and the internal environment, "new and new variations are produced and these variations are selected by the internal environment, which is modified by the phenotype. This process is still selection within the internal environment, but not in the broad context of survival."

In recent theories of auto-poetic development, a central role is given for chaos and chance, both of which were alien for Piaget. Annett Karmiloff-Smith (1992), who was even a student of Piaget, tried later to present a new interpretation of the relations between Piaget and modern cognitive theory in her widely discussed book a generation ago. In a certain way, after the debate, she tried to combine ideas of the two debaters, Piaget and Fodor. In her framing, our cognitive system has many innate predispositions, tendencies. These are not ready-made and self-enclosed, innate processing modules as conceived by Fodor (1983). They are prepared for an expected environment, and they are innate in this regard, but they become fully operational only through interaction with the environment. This is the reason that she speaks of **modularization** and not of modules. Unlike the generalist vision of Piaget, however, she regards these starting predispositions to be specific to given cognitive domains. Nevertheless, Karmiloff-Smith took over some aspects of the constructivism of Piaget. If something is constructed in development, it is not a mere unfolding of an existing system. Karmiloff-Smith believes that at around 4–6 years of age, the time of the concrete operations of Piaget, there is a "metacognitive shift" of representational re-descriptions. Representations of the world themselves become objects of cognition and formation, which leads, for example, to a much more formalized and sophisticated grammatical system than the first sentence-coordinating patterns.

Karmiloff-Smith continues the approach initiated by Piaget in other ways as well. She interprets the child as a theoretician, as one who makes general theories about the world: the child as a physicist, a linguist, a mathematician, a psychologist, and as a note-maker. In a way, like Karmiloff-Smith, Spelke (2000) postulates five content-specific innate organizations in her core knowledge theory: the system of objects, actions, numbers, space, and social actions. These provide preconditions for further development.

These new frameworks thus question the "general cognition" approach of Piaget. They do postulate innate principles, but specific to certain cognitive areas in development. At the same time, they clearly share with Piaget the constructive role of the knowing subject in the developmental unfolding of cognitive systems.

Henri Wallon: A Marxist theory of development

Henri Wallon (1879–1962) was an eternal rival of Piaget in Francophone developmental psychology. He was an influential professor of developmental psychology at the Sorbonne and at Collège de France with a medical degree (following the French tradition). At the same time, he was a humanistic mentor of the French system of professional orientation and an active child guidance advisor. His work combined the French medical psychology tradition, the French sociological psychology tradition with its social responsibilities for the poor children, the left-wing democratic commitment, and the engagement with pro-Russian (practically pro-Soviet) circles within French political life. All these were combined into a peculiar medical and socially minded child development theory: he emphasized the medical and the social aspects in a combined theory about the development of children (Wallon, 1934).

Wallon, unlike Piaget, was mostly interested as a clinician in the individual differences of children rather than their universal developmental tracks. From the 1920s to the 1950s, he organized a "psychobiological child center" laboratory where, besides the research work, he organized weekly outpatient guidance consultations. He tried to put applied psychology into the service of social progress (Wallon, 1934).

At the same time, Wallon was a highly engaged and rather political social scientist. For him, as he recalls in his life interview (Wallon, 1968), social sensitivity, political engagement, and psychological interest went hand in hand. In the thirties, he supported the Spanish republican cause and, during the German occupation of France, had become a member of the French Communist Party, as a direct consequence of the execution of George Politzer, his former student, and some other of his resistance associates. He took an active part in the resistance movement. Wallon (1942) published one of his important left-wing psychological works during the German occupation and was banned from teaching by the pro-German Vichy French government. He was not an easygoing person, and he disobeyed clandestinity instructions several times. After the war, he became the French Minister of Education for a short period of time and published the famous left-wing social project for the reform of education, the Langevin–Wallon project (Wallon, 1947). In the project of a more democratic schooling, Wallon campaigned for more action-based educational practices and the introduction of professional orientation and streaming children toward different school tracks during middle school years.

His left-wing inclinations went together with a strong sensitivity both to ideological issues and to the social applications of psychology. While he was interested in individual differences and worked in a vocational guidance reference center as well, he was against the use of test methods.

> There is a temptation to homogenize the individual. . . . With the tests one makes means and correlations: the individual is abolished, and what attributed to him is only a creation of means, of statistics. . . . This is a dictionary psychology, and not a psychology of persons.
> (Wallon, 1968, p. 28)

Such an engagement, especially at the height of the Cold War in the 1950s, meant an attempt to communicate the ideological/political message in psychology. Without too much self-reflection, Wallon wrote against what he labeled as "the bourgeois thinking in psychology," and in a rather opportunistic way, he praised what was created by Pavlovism (Wallon, 1955/1963). He is a good example for the often-overstressed ideologization and party line discipline of engaged French intellectuals, even within psychology. This feature did not always help the impact of Wallon outside of France.

The polemic Wallon is not without his own interests, however. In his encyclopedic introduction (Wallon, 1938), for example, he presented an interesting critique of Bergson and Blondel. His main trouble with Bergson was the overly simplistic proposal to replace the introspection of psychologists with his own intuition. According to Wallon, Bergson had a correct starting point, namely, the critique of the easy and shorthand identification of verbal schemata – of a social origin – with real mental content. Thus far, it is a welcome criticism of the theory-laden nature of introspection.

> Introspection is simply the workings of ideological and verbal forms that have an interpersonal origin and usage. Introspections are like coins. They can only mean what is shared in each of our relations with all the others, and all of us with reality.
> (Wallon, 1938, p. 138)

The main mistake of Bergson was believing in the ability to provide a non-conceptual access to, and survey of, internal life, which would be intuition.

Emotions and sociality in development

The developmental theory of Wallon is dialectical in the sense that he believes that development is always under the influence of internal endogenous and external environmental factors. Second, development is always a result of conflicts and tensions between rivaling forces. Third, development is always characterized by a Hegelian, spiral-like ascension. Earlier stages are negated by new developments to allow later for a synthesis. Wallon's image of the child is intimately related to his political idea of progress: similar to social life, there is progress in mental development as well. That is why he sees the child differently from Freud, who always sees return to the original, and that is also why Wallon is critical of seeing any recapitulation between the primitive thought analyzed by Lévy-Bruhl (his high school teacher) and that of children.

The developmental system of Wallon (1934, 1942), outlined in his two books, starts with **syncretism**: thinking moves from analyzed wholes toward part–whole relations that emerge from the context. He also suggests that all development take place within the development of the integrity of the personality. Personality itself has a social genesis. He goes back to James Baldwin (1894a), who proposed that the Ego and the Alter are formed as supplementary or correlative notions. In this regard, Wallon criticized the initial egocentrism and autism theory of Piaget, as well as the Ego-centered instincts of Freud. A social being is constructed from the original undifferentiated chaos. "The individual, if it recognizes itself as such, is essentially social. Social not due to external circumstances, but as an intimate necessity. It is genetically social" (Wallon, 1959, p. 285). The social-psychological child psychology of Wallon transmits and translates the sociologism of the French tradition, where the issue was relationships between the mentality of larger social groups and individual thought, into the micro-social dyads of individual life. This social moment is present in the biology of child development – emotions with a vegetative and motor component have a crucial role in the birth of the two poles of the social system. Wallon (1934, 1942) attributed a central role to motor development and emotions in the unfolding of the personality. As he emphasized from his first publications on, posture was a crucial element in the social representation of infants. Posture, and, in this way, body image, was the integration point of biological determination, emotions, and the social configuration of personality.

While the conception of Wallon is basically organicist and biological, it still does not entail the opposition of Ego and society as a starting point. The rationalist Wallon, with his focus on emotions and movements, is able to distance himself from the Cartesian tradition. Relying many times on Marx, he posited language, morality, and planning as the essential human components of development, compared to animals. With all these differences, he had a long, interesting debate with Piaget concerning the determinants of development as shown in CONTROVERSIES.

Controversies

Wallon and Piaget

Wallon (1942, 1990), in his open polemical attitude, easily recognized in Piaget a Rousseau follower who had an individualistic, "bourgeois mentality" which is revolting for a community-oriented communist. The social and emotional components of Ego development put him in opposition with Piaget in more technical issues as well.

Regarding the matters of egocentric and autistic thought, Wallon pointed out that Piaget sometimes uses the word *egocentric* in the sense of lack of cooperation, and sometimes in the sense of messing up the object with the knowing subject. Wallon also emphasized that there is more than one primary type of cooperation – today we would say that besides the Piaget type of theory of mind attribution, Wallon was claiming an emotion-based, empathy-related cooperation. Cooperation is not necessarily reflective thought. And there are different sorts of sociabilities: "I would reverse the order. Rather than supposing that our logic appears in children as the result of an increased sociability, I would deduce the forms of sociability from the development of these intellectual abilities." Piaget replied that the ambiguities are not his, and that they are inherent to the behavior of children, regarding the relations between intellectual and social development. At the moment, we can only claim correspondence rather than causality.

They also entertained different ideas about the mechanisms of change. Emphasizing dialectical cyclicity, Wallon (1990) considered internal tensions to be the basis of developmental change. Such a spiral-like development is most clearly seen in the relations between emotional and strictly intellectual factors. This is the point where he is most clearly opposed to Piaget, who only sees a movement toward a "real" valid representation in development. This dialectical attitude is a key aspect that was emphasized by Wallon's student, the French René Zazzo, and the Hungarian Ferenc Mérei when they pointed out that even though Piaget emphasized equilibrium in development, the approach of Wallon conceived development always to be open.

Regarding the details of development, Wallon (1934, 1942) attributed a key role to **imitation**, especially delayed imitation during the second year of life. Piaget (1945), in his later work, not just acknowledged but reflected on it when he began to attribute a larger role for symbolic functions and imitation. Nevertheless, the initiative role and the merit are certainly Wallon's. For Piaget, the operational aspect of intelligence was crucial, while for Wallon the representational was central. It is certainly true that Piaget's efforts to deal with the issues of representation from 1945 on appear as a reaction to Wallon's criticisms.

Considering later stages of development, they diverge mainly regarding the sources of discursive thought. The operational intelligence conception of Piaget does not see a real jump here (the logic of actions turns into a logic of operations and then, eventually, propositions). Wallon sees a deeper fault between action-based and discursive, logical thought and ties the latter more to the social sphere.

The impact of Wallon remained in the shadow of Piaget. Their mid-century coexistence in French psychology resulted in development becoming an independent topic, including the search for developmental laws (stages, self-organization versus external determination). From an American perspective, they seem to have much more in common than they have differences. They are observers rather than experimenters, they do not care about statistics, and they consider development to be a qualitative change rather than mere accumulation. Piaget was the "logician," and Wallon the "clinician." Piaget was committed to continuity, while Wallon represented the belief in qualitative change. His interpretation is related to Piaget emphasizing equilibrium, while Wallon stresses contradictions. Voyat (1984b) edited an available critical English reader of Wallon and has a good introduction (Voyat, 1984a). Zazzo's (1984) presentation in this volume is particularly relevant. Piaget was the one in the Anglo-Saxon world who was always presented as a developmental psychologist committed to stages and contrasted to behaviorists emphasizing behavioral habits, and Zazzo shows this features in the work of Wallon as well.

Tasks

CA

Autism in Bleuler, Piaget, and today.
The concept of egocentric speech. Formal features.
Modern methods in studying the sensorimotor stage.
Compare perceptual constancies and conservation phenomena in Piaget.
Emotion in Wallon and Piaget.
Can we measure Piaget's stages?
The clinical method in development and in clinical practice.

DSA

"Egocentric speech" and "egocentric thinking" in psychological texts.
"Clinical method" over a century in psychological texts (PsycINFO).
Piaget, Wallon, and Vygotsky in the public mind in different languages (Google Ngram).
Cooccurrences of Chomsky and Piaget in psychological texts (PsycINFO).
Imitation in texts on child development.

5 Social theories of the mind

> We are victims of an illusion that makes us believe that we ourselves produced what has been imposed upon us externally.
> (Durkheim: *The rules of sociological method*. 1894/1982, p. 53)

Human social life and the organization of mental phenomena

Social psychology is certainly a most influential and most successful subdiscipline of modern psychology that started to take shape as a strong separate chapter already in the interwar period. The following two chapters survey these developments. Chapter 5 concentrates on general social explanatory models that created the idea of a social mind and therefore have a relevance for psychology. Many of them, however, are treated traditionally neither as social psychology nor sometimes even as psychology. Chapter 6 will concentrate on the history of mainstream social psychology.

Social psychology as a concept and term reached its peak in the English-language general literature in the 1970s–1980s, according to Google Ngram, but it already had a first peak in the 1930s, as shown on Figure 5.1.

In the professional psychology literature, as Figure 5.2 also shows, social psychology becomes a more important topic than experimental psychology from the 1920s on; however, its peak was from the 1950s, perhaps as an aftereffect of the World War II.

The essential aspect of the figure is not the precise relations between experimental and social psychology – since the experimentalists are covered under many different labels (comparative, cognitive) – but the advent of social psychology initially in the 1930s, and then its continued prevalence from the 1950s on.

Parallel to the emergence of social psychology, less-visible efforts also appeared in Europe in the first half of the 20th century that tried to interpret the human mind as inadvertently social and tried to elevate the social or societal element into an organizing and integrating principle of psychology. The early theories of **societal psychology** demonstrate most clearly one possible external reduction of modern psychology, namely, **sociologism**, or in their more modest versions, taking social life as a model for the mind. They break with the traditional "lonely man" *à la Robinson* image of psychology, which deduced social processes from the individual, as in classical empiricism and rationalism (Chapters 2 to 4 of Volume 1, and again

DOI: 10.4324/9781032625805-6

Social theories of the mind 101

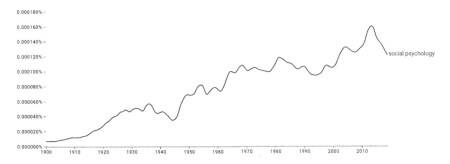

Figure 5.1 The presence of social psychology in the general literature was dominant in the 1970–1980s according to Google Ngram.

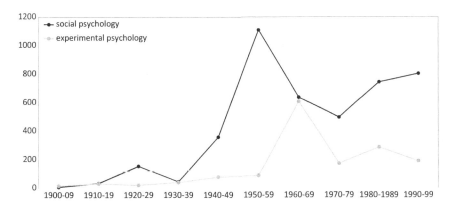

Figure 5.2 Papers by subject area in the PsycINFO database showing the importance of social psychology in the 1960s.

in Chapter 10 of this volume, in contemporary evolutionary psychology). Instead, they deduce the mental processes of the individual mind from relationships and/ or from the dominant social forces or structures. Many of these early conceptions of social determination presented here are referred to by their present-day radical critics as the **standard social science model (SSSM)**. The term as a concept to be criticized was introduced by Tooby and Cosmides (1992) and popularized by Pinker (1997, 2002).

This attitude resulted in three features summarized by Pinker (1997) that are of interest to the history of psychology:

1. The human mind is an unbound general-purpose learning machine with no (biological) constraints.
2. Cultures can differ radically from one another.
3. Cultural differences and varieties do shape the formation of individual mental architecture.

This was clearly spelled out in American anthropology by Boas (1911) but also characterizes those French sociologistic schools of thought presented here that are usually not targets for the modern criticism of the SSSM view. The chapter will show many of these radical sociological reductionist approaches to the human mind. In the work of Bartlett and Bühler, however, I will present more modest interpretations of the inherently social mind that are more in line with contemporary evolutionary and cultural interpretations of the social nature of the human mind.

The French sociological school in psychology

In the French-speaking world, there were various efforts made from the late 19th century on to align the matter of social sciences with psychology. The newly forming science of sociology was trying to extend its competence and coverage to the issues claimed by the newly forming science of psychology, while psychology was trying to come to terms with social aspects of human behavior: mechanisms of the spreading of social practices in the form of imitation (Tarde), disturbances of social behavior and selfhood in clinical cases (Charcot, Janet), and social stratification, which is related to educational success (Binet). As Chapter 9 in Volume 1 showed it, this clinical attitude was motivated by and interest towards helping the disordered people, but also of classifying them as Goldstein (1987) pointed out. Contacts as well as rivalries developed through these mutual efforts.

This tendency started already with the famous **milieu theory** of the French historian and literary scholar Taine (1876b; see in Chapter 9, Volume 1). This view became a favorite topic of French intellectuals over the following century. Richard (2013) analyzed in detail how Taine tried to explain historical events by three factors: race, milieu, and the moment. By *race* Taine basically meant what later has become "mentality": it is a general feeling and a social memory of the group, an inherited intellectual temperament, that differentiates, for example, the French revolutionaries from other nation(al)s. In this vision, art, historical and social events, all express the internal psychology of the actors. Social groups develop typical mentalities shaped by the life of the group, and historical events can be viewed as symptoms of these mentalities.

A generation after Taine, in the late 19th century, sociology and psychology were fighting to find new places in the competitive French university system. The rivalry was for the proper study of the mind. Sociology of the Durkheim type followed the model of Comte: "ultimate principles of human behavior lay in the social, not the individual realm." This approach has one profound difference from the Anglo-Saxon SSSM: it tends to interpret society as a mentally cohesive reality with a structured mentality rather than a mere bunch of habits. This mentality is what Bourdieu (1977), the French sociologist, called a century later **habitus**. Society prescribes its members certain ways of how to dress, speak, use their body, and approach the world. This culturalist social determination of the human mind has provided for the most important variations of French psychological culturalism and sociologism. The proposed solutions are rather provocative because they question the sacrosanct Cartesian rationality, individualism, and universality over cultures.

The different French versions of the "downward moving" societal psychology of the first half of the 20th century are outlined in Table 5.1. They vary with regard to the strength of the postulated societal pressure exerted on the individual and whether they take a mere cross-sectional, or rather, a historical perspective.

In most of their versions, the causal mechanisms were not interpreted in detail. They merely assumed a sociological reduction, without going into the details of the mechanisms. They were even critical of the interactionist theories that tried to account for the effects of society through direct interpersonal means. Most of these efforts dealt with the impact of "present-day society" on individual mentality. However, they started to have historical excursions early on, continuing the attitude of Taine about the role of milieu and mentality. Social change was either interpreted as the changing milieu changing the mentalities.

Pierre Janet and his psychology of conduct

Janet was a multifaceted intellectual and author whose name already came up in Volume 1, regarding functionalism (Chapter 8) and the formation of psychopathology (Chapter 13). Pierre Janet (1859–1947), with a degree in both philosophy and medicine, started his academic career in the footsteps of his mentor, Charcot, as

Table 5.1 Basic varieties of Francophone culturalism/sociologism

Representative	Theses	Impact of society on the individual	PsycINFO
Durkheim: sociologism	Social representations	Shape the individual, but there is still individuality	1,256
Janet: psychology of conduct	Hierarchical system of tendencies to act	Social narratives create the internal world	407
Blondel: collective psychology	Lower and higher forms, the latter social	Is folding and shaping the individual minds	120
Halbwachs: radical sociologism	The social frames of cognition and feelings are dominant	Society infiltrates the forms and contents in the mind	90
Lévy-Bruhl: primitive mentality	Coherent vs. illogical, magical, incoherent mentalities	Society determines mentality	114
Meyerson: historical psychology	The mind is expressed in its works	Sign-based psychology	16
Piaget: genesis of rationality in interaction	Thinking is always coherent, but coherence is based on authority or argument	Harmony between human relations and mentalities	68 (sociology)

the head of the laboratory at the Salpêtrière Hospital. Between 1902 and 1936, he was also a professor of Collège de France. His theory about human behavior used the French word *conduite*, "conduct," rather than *comportement*, "behavior," since he proposed to supplement behavior with consciousness and inner life through the mediation of language. In these efforts, he differentiated between lower and higher levels of behavior.

> One must regard the phenomenon of consciousness as specialized conduct, a complication of the act which is superimposed on the elementary conduct. A second condition is that in this description of conduct one must necessarily be preoccupied with the higher forms of conduct, beliefs, reflection, and experiences. . . . This psychology may be designated by the name **psychology of conduct** in order to indicate that it is concerned with a broader and higher form than behaviorism.
>
> (Janet, 1930, p. 131)

In his general vision, language is the critical instrument that makes us conscious human beings. "Belief, judgement, concept are mental events of a higher order, which fit into the lower movements by the mediation of the characteristically and exclusively human action, namely language." From external and social behavior, language becomes internal "special acts like keeping a secret or telling lies develop this inner speech and turn it into thought" (Janet, 1937, pp. 811–812). The forms of conduct are ordered in a peculiar hierarchy. Goal-directedness is a basic feature of the forms of conduct from the elementary ones on. Moving upward, toward social forms, their degree of freedom increases, however. The arrangement is similar to what Ribot (1890, 1899) claimed a generation earlier in his motor theory of the mind, namely, that all internal mental events can be interpreted as **behavioral dispositions**. Janet's classification in line with his evolutionary-functionalist convictions mirrors a peculiar developmental organization.

> The desire to classify all psychological facts under action *and* conduct has forced me to introduce a new analysis of *consciousness, belief, memory, thought,* and above all *emotions.* . . . Thought is inner language; belief becomes a special combination of language and action; memory is above all a system of recounting; emotions are regulations of action, and reactions of the individual to his own actions. The psychology of conduct adapts itself very readily to our former conception of psychological tensions, which places one tendency above another according to its degree of complexity, perfection, and order of acquisition. . . . The most useful psychology of the future will be a practical psychology of conduct, which will be dynamic and at the same time will study the physiological production of energy and its distribution.
>
> (Janet, 1930, pp. 132–133)

The hierarchy of conducts provided the key to an explanatory system of psychopathology. It is a psychological extension of the concept of evolutionary neurology proposed by Hughlings Jackson (1884), connected to a special motivational theory with the key concept of **tension** (Janet, 1923). Tendencies or behavioral dispositions on a lower evolutionary level have a higher tension, and they have a higher likelihood of "discharge." If, in pathological states, weakness causes a decrease of general tension, self-enclosed, alienated clinical images do appear. If the strength of the dissociative pathologies perseveres, behavior and personality do fall apart, accompanied by a discharge of stronger tendencies (Janet, 1920). In this respect, the Ego fulfills its integrative role by a choice between the regulation of tension or the emerging "tendencies" (Janet, 1923). Carroy and Plas (2000) show in their analysis how important the pathological studies were for Janet to preserve or save the Cartesian integrative Self so central for French intellectual history.

The theory of memory by Janet (1936), outlined in his later writings, was a radical social theory of the higher mental layers. According to Janet, there is no such thing as memory in an isolated individual.

> A single man has no memory and has no need for it. . . . The *souvenirs* for an isolated man are useless, and Robinson on his island has no need to make a diary. If he makes a diary this is because he hopes to reintegrate among people. Memory is a *sui generis* social function.
> (Janet, 1928, p. 184)

Memory in the human sense developed together with social life. Memory first was limited to events shared with the group, and it has gradually become a social function of sharing distant events. In order to accomplish this, social memory is functionally organized in a narrative manner. This social narrative, the stories we tell others, becomes, gradually, **storytelling** for others, which results in seemingly individual memories.

> The basic phenomenon of memory is narration. If we recall a period of our life, we tell it ourselves as if it was an audience; we are making stories and the good memories are showing signs of a sort of literary talent, narrative talent. It is evident that when we teach a child to tell what he was doing when he was playing on the Champs-Elysées, he acquires how to make a story. A literary narration.
> (Janet, 1928, pp. 283–284)

An integration across narratives also develops from this selection process. Our personality is built up as a biography, and as a combination and connection of these self-told stories, with some other narratives that others tell about us.

His student, Jean Delay (1942), combining the neurological and psychological traditions, proposed a tripartite system of memory disturbances: disturbances of sensorimotor aspects of memory (neurology), psychiatric amnesias (disturbances of social memory), and autistic memories. The three are distributed among the respective disciplines of neurology, psychiatry, and psychoanalysis. In his analysis of "psychiatric amnesias," he referred to the psychosociological works of Janet, Halbwachs, and Blondel and claimed that they are basically "pathologies of the 'narrative conduct', that could be called *social memory*" (Delay, 1942, p. 27). The psychiatric memory disorder loses the social constraints of socially validated logical organization.

Janet became a central figure of French intellectual life, both due to his clinical work, his dynamic theory of psychopathology, but also due to his interpretation of the social mind, or the social aspects of inner mental life. His proposal for a social memory was a reference point in French culture, but he also had a strong influence on the social theory of mind proposed by Vygotsky both regarding the central role of language in the genesis of the social mind and in his proposal of lower and higher mental functions. Janet's theory of narrated social memory also had an influence on another early Soviet theorist and researcher of memory, Pavel Blonski (1935, 1977), who was influenced by Janet just as much as by Bartlett (1932).

The sociological school of French psychology: the role of Durkheim

Regarding the issue of social determinism, Janet represents a structural view, where language and social life create internal mental life. In the French intellectual life of the first part of the 20th century, and in psychology, a more radical social point of view emerged as well, which tended to reduce all psychology to a play of social representations.

The inspirations for this trend came from the sociological system of Émile Durkheim (1858–1917). Durkheim, after starting in Bordeaux, was a professor of education, and later social sciences at the Sorbonne, and the French founder of a new science, the methodical study of society, sociology. A central role in this institutionalization of sociology was a yearbook established by him, *L'Année Sociologique*, which was a conceptual and intellectual publication outlet with many theoretical and review papers fostering the formation of the discipline. He campaigned for the independence of sociology, for its separation from philosophy, and for its separation from psychology as well. The social force and interest toward establishing sociology were driven by the need to understand social integration in the new liberal capitalist society. In a varied society, where the common triviality of social life disappeared, the task was to understand cohesion in the life of independent individual actors. Durkheim proposed to develop a pattern-based interpretation of facts about human life. Social facts emerge out of social patterns of individual mental events. Social events are "thing-like" in several senses of this expression. They cannot be changed arbitrarily. "A thing is in effect all that is given, all that is offered, or rather forces itself upon our observation. To treat phenomena as things is to treat them as data, and this constitutes the starting point for science" (Durkheim, 1894/1982, p. 69).

Durkheim (1886), who was very familiar with the works of Wundt, even visited Wundt in Leipzig at the time the idea of *Völkerpsychologie* was forged. He started to work within the framework of a group mind or group consciousness to account for social facts.

> By aggregating together, by interpenetrating, by fusing together, individuals give birth to a being, psychical if you will, but one which constitutes a psychical individuality of a new kind. . . . The group thinks, feels and acts entirely differently from the way its members would if they were isolated.
> (Durkheim, 1894/1982, p. 7)

Society exercises an obligatory force toward the individual. In the same way as we are not aware of the exact workings of our individual minds, we are not aware of these social forces either. Seemingly individual decisions prompt us to follow rules, but they are external relative to ourselves. While Durkheim interpreted the thing-like hard facts of sociology to be of a mental nature on the long run, he considered academic psychology of his own time too decontextualized. Sociology would deal with a concrete, contextualized mental realm, introducing history into the treatment of society.

In the works of the mature Durkheim, the issue of **collective representations** (religions, morals) became more and more central, with group consciousness or group mind fading in the background. Durkheim (1898/1965) developed these parallels in a famous paper (cited about 2,000 times) titled "Individual and collective representations." Representations, according to their 300-year-old European epistemology metatheory, were individual perceptions, images, and thoughts tied to the individual. Durkheim proposed that there are collective representations that carry their epistemic value due to a social frame supporting them. The individual mental representations have their independent life that is not explained by their neural origin. In an analog manner, collective representations act toward the individual as external forces, having their own way of existence. They are symbols and systems of symbols like language, religion, legal prescriptions. The idea of social representations was always difficult to interpret regarding their way of existence. In our European epistemology and folk psychology tradition, ideas, sensations, and thoughts always belong to someone, and in the causal chain, they are connected to an individual nervous system. Thus, collective representations, even if the promoters denied this, suggested a collective career, or a group mind, that is missing as an entity in a rational analysis. The Hungarian sociologist Dénes Némedi (1995) provided a concise summary of the conceptual system of Durkheim.

Durkheim considered social determination to be a central factor in human life. Human behavior has a dual determination: it is the result of supraindividual social trends and individual tendencies at the same time, but social factors play the leading role. **Anomy**, a characteristic dissolution of rule-obeying behavior, appears when collective representations lose their power and individual representations take over. The social aspect is present in categorial behavior as well. Even categorizations and conceptual systems have their origin in classifying people, especially kins or relatives. Durkheim and Mauss (1903), when summarizing the work of ethnologists, started from so-called primitive forms of classification. The starting point of natural classifications is not individual sensory experience but society, and nature is carved out based on the analogy of society.

> The first logical categories were social categories; the first classes of things were classes of men, into which these things were integrated. [. . .] It is because human groups fit one into another – the sub-clan into the clan, the clan into the moiety, the moiety into the tribe – that groups of things are ordered in the same way.
> (Durkheim & Mauss, 1903/2009, pp. 44–45)

Followers of Durkheim developed the issue of the relations between psychology and sociology to a further extent. Marcel Mauss (1872–1950), the nephew and follower of Durkheim, extended the modern positive sociology of his uncle further toward studying so-called primitive societies. His most-known work, *The Gift*, published in Mauss (1925/1966), showed that the different types of gifts and potluck rituals are extremely important glues in the organization of all societies. Humans are not purely economic calculators. Gift for them is a crucial element in the moral, human, and economic integration of society – and the complexity of all these aspects calls for a holistic approach to society.

Mauss, who became a professor of sociology at Collège de France in 1931, winning in the second round of votes against Halbwachs, had more-specific messages about the relations between psychology and sociology. As the president of the French Psychological Society, he gave a talk in 1924 to characterize the relationship of sociology and psychology. His attitude is lax. We have two mature independent disciplines here that should not be jealous of each other. At the same time, the naive "group mind" theory of McDougall that would treat sociology merely as a chapter of psychology should be abandoned. Sociology studies group consciousness according to their morphological aspects and not merely as phenomena of consciousness. There is a certain division of labor between the two disciplines. Sociology adopts many categories from psychology, while psychology has to recognize and take into account the statistical regularities and the historicity claimed by sociology. Sociology also assigns a task to psychology: it should deal with the complete, total person (Mauss, 1924, 1938/1985 in English in the volume of Mauss, 1979.) With all its centrality to French social sciences, the popularity of the sociology of Durkheim was decreasing in France in the 1930s (Karady1976). At the same time, radical psychological interpretations of Durkheim took center stage.

Radical Durkheim followers: sociologism in psychology

The standard SSSM conception, like L. S. Vygotsky, H. Wallon, and G. H. Mead, emphasize socialization practices in the social determination of thinking (Middleton & Edwards, 1990). The radical Durkheimians of the 1930s followed another path: for them, the foundational stone of social epistemology was not the socialization of children but the phenomenological analysis of the individual mind and the analysis of the constructive processes as historical phenomena. Social categories determine individual thought by their mere existence.

Two key actors strongly held to this primacy of the social at the newly reintegrated French University of Strasbourg after the First World War. An interesting rivalry developed between Blondel, on the part of psychology, and Halbwachs, on the part of sociology. The two actors provide a particularly clear example of a rivalry for a single common domain: at the intersection of sociology and psychology the proper domain of **collective psychology** (see about the rivalry in Muchielli, 1999). The two lives are parallel as well. Both were influenced by Durkheim and Bergson, both graduated from the École Normale, and both started to flourish academically in Strasbourg. The specific rivalry developed between them after the publication of their respective works on collective psychology and the interpretation of suicide. Halbwachs was mainly dissatisfied with biological theories, while Blondel with strictly social theories. Halbwachs (1939) criticized Blondel specifically for postulating a level of individual psychology between psychophysiology and collective psychology. According to Halbwachs, there is no place and no need for such an individuum-centered psychology. Blondel (1933) proposed a new theory of suicide that rivalled Durkheim (1897/1951), claiming that suicide was mainly caused by what we would call today depressive psychological conditions. Halbwachs (1930), on his part, claimed that suicide has several causes and several different angles, both viewpoints of individual psychology and sociology, but the concept of anomia should be preserved. He specifically claimed that the differentiation of objective causes and subjective reasons proposed by Durkheim should be forgotten. Social determination is always causal.

Charles Blondel: collective psychology combined with neuropsychology

Charles Blondel (1876–1939) started as a typical "new generation" French psychologist. He combined clinical work and theoretical psychology and obtained philosophy and medical degrees. However, he gradually moved toward a rather radical social interpretation of mental life in his Strasbourg years. Blondel was a very productive writer. His original interests, before he moved to Strasbourg and eventually back to the Sorbonne in Paris, were clinical dissociation. He pursued the clinical dissociation tradition (Blondel, 1914) and also wrote early French reviews and a monograph on Freud (Blondel, 1924). Blondel, as a clinician, unlike Janet (or, for that matter, unlike Freud) claimed qualitative differences between the normal and the pathological. He was particularly interested in the pathological dissolutions of the traditional, stable Ego. The presence or absence of the Cartesian theater was the main clinical issue for him.

Blondel was a very complex humanistic psychologist who concentrated his entire life on keeping psychology independent of, or above, the physiological component and, at the same time, did not forget that the mind was not exclusively socially determined. He extended pure physiology with "pure psychology." While he let physiologists take care of the organic conditions of mental life, Blondel personally was inclined to explore "their social causes. . . . He imagined their effects to be so direct and deep that sometimes he seems to be putting them on the same level as the physiological action" (Wallon, 1968, p. 108).

His small textbook of collective psychology tried to present collective psychology as a study of the social determinants of our most intimate inner life (Blondel, 1928). Blondel also provided a reconstruction of the Durkheimian position, starting directly from Durkheim and Mauss (1903). The organizing principles of rationality emerge from social representations. Blondel was rather radical in his book.

> The ideal towards which a collective psychology shall aim is constructing an objective history of the human mind. . . . Collective psychology is far from being an appendix of psychology. Conceived this novel way it shall rather become the center and core of psychology. . . . It will be convenient to bring a large part of what is referred to by the label of psychology of intelligence under the empire of collective psychology.
> (Blondel, 1928, pp. 205, 201–202)

Social psychology conceived this way, as an analysis of mentalities, together with uncovering the social ways of thought, takes many issues away from sociology and psychology as well.

Blondel suggested that the posterior parts of the brain, whose damage is responsible for aphasia, are under dual control. They are partly under the influence of the social and physical external world, and they also have a widespread visceral afferentation that belongs only to the individual. The social point of view emphasizes the intellectual and action sides, while primary individuality relies on the representation of the person's own body. Some social aspects, through the use of language and interactions, for example, due to selective model following, in fact become a tool for emphasizing our individuality.

The social frames of memory: Maurice Halbwachs

The French philosopher, sociologist, and theoretical psychologist Maurice Halbwachs elaborated the most detailed theory of a radical sociologism with his analysis of **the social frames of memory**. "Raw memories" always go through a social filter that causes remembering to be tied to our social roles as agents of memory. When I am at a high school reunion, for example, my stream of thought will bring up events, places, and persons of a generation ago, with recall being contextually determined. Our memory is collective also in the sense that the memory and the way of remembering group members create a norm, and their reconstruction of the past converges as a function of interaction. Group belongingness is responsible for the continuity of memories. According to Halbwachs, both chronological and conceptual (today we would say semantic, in the sense of Tulving, 1972) organization in memory comes from group belongingness and from the organization of group activities.

Before we evaluate his psychological works, let us take a closer look at his rather complex and rich life.

Biography

On the borders of sociology, history, and psychology: Maurice Halbwachs

Maurice Halbwachs (1877–1945) was an influential sociologist trained in philosophy who worked on highly complex phenomena in social science. On the one hand, he was a crucial actor in continuing the positivist tradition of Durkheim in extensive works concerning land price statistics and suicide. Besides the objectivist statistical trend in his work, he also followed up on the ideas of collective representation when he developed his theories of collective memory.

He combined two intellectual trends and two early influences on his intellectual life: the speculative holism of Bergson and the idea of social representations proposed by Durkheim. Halbwachs, from a displaced Alsatian family, was a student of Bergson at the prestigious Lycée Henry IV in Paris and later followed Bergson's classes at the Collège de France. His mentor's influence, especially the idea of a dual memory system, clearly shows up in his main work.

During his university years, he found a second mentor: he became a student and follower of the mature Durkheim. Halbwachs's entire theory of social memory could be characterized as a social interpretation of the duality proposed by Bergson (1896). He picked up the dissatisfaction with

Figure 5.3 Maurice Halbwachs.
Source: Wikimedia commons, public domain.

early reductionist elementaristic psychology from Bergson, but then he turned this dissatisfaction into a general, non-individualistic view of the mind and to an overall social reduction of psychology through an extension of the notion of social representation that he took from Durkheim (Halbwachs, 1918).

As a follower of Durkheim, he contributed to research on social classes and on suicide (Halbwachs, 1912, 1930). He read most of modern German sociology, especially Max Weber and Karl Mannheim, and he traveled to Chicago for a semester to study American urban sociology.

Halbwachs seems to have extended into the mental realm of Durkheim's idea that social phenomena are "things". For Halbwachs, mental facts are, in accordance with the notion of social representation of Durkheim, also social, and in this regard "thing-like." His approach is an intermediate step between the social objectivism of the Durkheim school and the social representation claims entertained by Moscovici (1984, 1988) half a century later.

Halbwachs acquired a leading role due to his social mentality approach during his time in Strasbourg. The French university there was re-established after the defeat of Germany in 1918. In Strasbourg, in contrast to Paris, there was more cooperation between departments, and professors even visited each other's courses. Cooperation with mathematicians lead to books on probability theory in social science, for example. Halbwachs was not an easygoing cooperator. He tried to promote sociology as the way forward in integrating social and human sciences. He had followers and sustained tensions among the psychologists of Strasbourg. The alternative school of social psychology developed by Blondel (1928) was too psychological for Halbwachs. While Blondel wanted to socialize psychology, Halbwachs wanted to mentalize sociology but still believed sociology to be the key science.

Strasbourg was also the birthplace of modern history writing as a history of mentalities, the famous French *Annales* school, initiated by March Bloch (1886–1944). Halbwachs was a member of the editorial board of the famous journal for a while during his time in Strasbourg (1919–1935) but still kept his beliefs about the superiority of sociology, even above history writing. For Halbwachs, the mentality theory practiced by historians in Strasbourg was too positivistic and too lenient with the notion of historical causality.

His social memory theory was the most interesting aspect for the history of psychology from Halbwachs's Strasbourg years. His changing scientific interests and outlook in the 1920s went hand in hand with tensions in the political and particularly the science policy domains. After the death of the mentor, the Durkheim school lost its impetus, and the French Left also lost its unity, with the creation of the French Communist Party. There was a search for continuity and search for intellectual community that were expressed in his theory of collective memory.

Halbwachs moved to the Sorbonne in 1935 and applied for the chair of sociology at the Collège de France. He continued to work on his theory of collective memory, but the new developments he brought in appeared only in a posthumous, reconstructed book on collective memory (Halbwachs, 1950). After he was elected to the Collège in 1944, he was never able to start his courses on collective representations that mirror the facts of society.

His son was executed by the Nazis as a resistance fighter in Southern France. After that, his Jewish in-laws were arrested and later executed. Halbwachs tried to intervene in Lyon, but he was also arrested. As a left-wing non-Jew, he died in the Buchenwald concentration camp. He was taken to Buchenwald by the last train of German prisoners. Several resistance leaders tried to stop the train in various ways, to no avail. His figure is commemorated by a fellow prisoner, the Spanish writer and left-wing politician Jorge Semprun (1994), who reported the last days of the humanist sociologist.

The notion of collective memory

Halbwachs represents a radical stance of social reductionism within psychology: the individual is a carrier of the social aspects and is nothing but an intersection of social representations and adherence to rules. Halbwachs was influenced by the dual-memory proposal of Bergson and by the vision of Durkheim that psychology and sociology are complementary disciplines of mental representation. Halbwachs takes over from Bergson the dissatisfaction with the early elementaristic reductionism of experimental psychology. However, he does not extend his dissatisfaction toward postulating a supramaterial individuality, as Bergson did, but toward a social reductionism of the entire psychology. Halbwachs reinterpreted Bergson in another way as well. In his view, there are no "raw memories," as the habit memories in Bergson: all memories are, by necessity, interpreted, and this interpretation is socially determined. Halbwachs was more radical than Bergson and even more radical than Durkheim himself.

As his sister Jeanne Alexandre (1948) characterized the attitude of Halbwachs: while originally he was influenced by Bergson, he tried to overcome this influence all his life. The immediate facts of consciousness proposed by Bergson became immediate facts of social consciousness in his social morphology. As his sister concluded:

> For Halbwachs, the task of sociology is to study consciousness as it is found in and by sociality, and the description of this specific society and its conditions (i.e., its language, institutions, the human presence and traditions) that make the consciousness of each member possible. One can only think of himself through others and for the others.
> (Alexandre, 1949, p. 6)

Durkheim believed that individual representations somehow combine with social representations to form the individual's mind. This idea was rather radical compared to the trivial psychologism and individualism of most of his contemporaries. Halbwachs wanted to be even more radical. He claimed more than the primacy of social representations: according to Halbwachs, the social moment penetrates all aspects of the mental. Our mind would be empty or at least disorganized if left to itself.

Regarding the genesis of social memory studies, Halbwachs belongs to a line chartered by the names of Bergson, Freud, Proust, and the Trieste writer Italo Svevo, who became interested specifically in issues of memory due to the radical social and ethnic changes of their time, in prewar and, later, in interwar Europe. The basic innovative idea of Halbwachs was to interpret memory as a socially constructed cultural process. Among these cultural memory idols, Halbwachs was not merely motivated by an interest toward a forgotten past. He intended the conception of collective memory, among other things, to be a theory to help the strengthening of the group consciousness of the working class. This might be the reason he is using the phrase **mémoire collective,** "collective memory," which has a much stronger emotional load in French (and in English as well) than "group memory." The use of *collective* instead of *social* with this emotional surplus meaning is characteristic for all of French sociologism. The important aspect for him was not a return to an assumed "original community," as Nyíri (1992) interpreted him, but a return to the immediate past, the unity of the working-class movement before the broken sense of temporal continuity due to the formation of the French Communist Party in 1920. The other crucial social setting of his new mentality research concerned the **issue of location**. He came from and then lived in Alsace, a region that was returned to France from Germany as a consequence of the Great War after, spending almost half a century within the German world. In addition, he worked at a university that suddenly turned from a prestigious German institution into a French one, and the institution was meant to build quickly a new French prestige.

The structure of collective memory

Halbwachs (1925, 1992), in his original book on social frames, attempted to prove the primacy of the social through the analysis of the adult mind, unlike the socialization-based social theories. Basically, he wanted to prove that both the frames (*cadres*) and the content of memory were social. A crucial moment in this argumentation is to show that the seemingly most personal moments of our life, like our dreams, also have a social character. His methodical stance is very meager. He wants to replace introspective, first-person psychology with social consideration.

> It is necessary to take [mental events] by replacing them in their own frame of reference, i.e., by placing them relative to the social realities of which they are a part of, in order to restore the true nature of collective psychic states, a larger and more consistent picture than introspective psychology has shown us.
> (Halbwachs, 1938, p. 623)

Collective psychology for Halbwachs is available for observation, in a way, externally, in our institutions and "in the products of the group, like science, language, art, and technology" (Halbwachs, 1939, p. 815).

This is a rather arbitrary solution, projecting a psychological interpretation into social facts. It was easier to prove the social nature of the substance of memory, claiming that even our most intimate memories are about **social contents**. Even our dreams – here he takes issue with Freud – emerge in a social setting. Our dreams, just as our daydreams, are full of social peers and interpersonal situations. Halbwachs criticizes the memory conception of his rival psychologist at Strasbourg, Charles Blondel (1928). According to Blondel, the material, or the "residuum," of our memory would be individual, and only its frames would be social. According to Halbwachs, however, in its intentionality the material of remembering is also social. This social intentionality, inspired by Husserl (1911/1965) gave a chance for Halbwachs to overcome a "group mind" type of solution. The collective moment is the "intentional object" of our cognition, and it is not on a separate level. "Though collective memory obtains its force and content from the fact that it is a multitude of humans who support it, it is still only individuals who remember, as members of groups" (Halbwachs, 1968, p. 33).

Halbwachs used an anecdotal and impressionistic methodology for his collective psychology besides the conceptual analysis of institutions. He mainly used an intuitive analysis of his own recollections. This is all the more surprising because in his other writings, Halbwachs was a statistical sociologist. This sort of intuitionism, as well as the use of aphasias in a social theory, shows the enduring impact of his teacher, Henry Bergson.

In the interpretation of Halbwachs, our acts of remembering are always **reconstructions** that correspond to our actual social situation; they are contextually determined. Remembering is always from the perspective of the recent social group. Consequently, aphasic disturbances are not simply disturbances due to a lack of word forms, as Wernicke (1874) proposed, but disturbances of exteriorization.

> It is not the memories that are missing in aphasics, but the ability to put them into a frame. This frame is what enables the person to reply in an impersonal, and more or less objective manner to a question posed by the social milieu. . . . In order to step out of ourselves and to put ourselves in to the place of someone else for a moment, one has to have distinct ideas of oneself, the others, and the relation between us and them: it is a first order, symbolic and at the same time social representation. . . . The loss of words . . . is merely a specific manifestation of a broader incapacity: all the conventional symbolicity, which is the necessary foundation of social intelligence, has become more or less strange for the patient.
>
> (Halbwachs, 1925, pp. 76–77)

Were we ever left on our own, we would only experience a buzzing-booming confusion. Rationality itself has its sources in the direct social moments (such as the influence of our group belonging on recall) and in societal factors, like language. In the moment and situation of recall, the group is present: we recall events in accordance with our activated group membership. "Reason is opposed to tradition as a broader society to a narrower society" (Halbwachs, 1925, p. 291).

Halbwachs also analyzes memory in various groups rather than in the individual. He has several classificatory chapters on family memory, memory in religious groups, memory in social classes, and the like. We would characterize this effort today as an attempt to analyze the role of the practice of collective (joint) memory recall in the constant recreation of group identities. Halbwachs claims that the originally episodic memories become semantic ones in the process of tradition formation and thus get decontextualized. Social frames entail "containers" and "contents" (concepts and images) at the same time and have both a conceptual and a chronological organization.

The position of Halbwachs developed in the 20 years he was interested in collective memory. His monographer, Namer (1987, p. 65), differentiated four stages in the writings of Halbwachs:

1. Collective memory, experienced memory of a group.
2. Social memory that extends in time and space and corresponds to "*courants de la pensée*," that is, fashions of thought, and to cultural memory.
3. More abstraction: oral history and traditions.
4. History. "In general, history starts, where tradition is finished, when the social memory extinguishes or decomposes . . . when the memory of a sequence of events is no more supported by a group . . . the only way to save these memories is to fix them in writing" (Halbwachs, 1950, p. 66).

A further important development of the later works of Halbwachs is the attempt to speculate about the way individual behaviors interact in the group to create collective memories (see Namer, 1999).

1. Globalization, uniting several events into one representation (like "the Christmas" in families).
2. Symbolization, one event symbolizes many.
3. Allusions, such as the uses of nicknames and the like.
4. Repetition.
5. Commemoration.

Halbwachs also tied collective memories to **spaces or locations** (Halbwachs, 1941). Due to rivalling groups, "there are as many ways to represent the space as may groups there are" (Halbwachs, 1950, p. 166). This became evident for him in the treatment of the Holy Land spaces by rival religious groups, which can still be seen in the daily news today. Places and the constant social construction of places in Halbwachs's account are the central, primary, and material bases of collective memory.

Evaluation and rediscovery of Halbwachs

There is a crucial difference between Halbwachs and the better-known social constructivism of G. H. Mead, L. S. Vygotsky, and others. The most known cultural relativists base social determination on the notion of interaction, and they are interested in socialization as an explanation of the adult mind. For Halbwachs, however, the crucial aspect is the impact and the workings of representations – and social representations have their effect somehow in and by themselves in the adult mind. Although during recall he refers to the "presence of the group," he rarely gives an interactive interpretation or explanation for this phenomenon.

The rediscovery of Halbwachs in the late 20th century had two basic motivations. The first one has to do with issues of social memory and the history debates. The other reason is more general. The interest toward social explanatory theories in psychology reappeared, together with an increasing interest toward the social mind, in the second half of the 20th century (Humphrey, 1976). In his framework, the phenomenological analysis of the individual mind is a possible road to discover its social embedding. The volume edited by Jaisson et al. (1999) puts the embedding of this rediscovery into the French context of dealing with mid-20th-century French social theories. There are two basic issues with the radicalism found in Halbwachs for the relations between the individual and the social. The first is the total loss of individuality and the **disappearance of the person**. Roger Bastide (1898–1974), a field anthropologist who studied the survival and coexistence of different religions traditions in Brazil and West Africa and was influenced by Halbwachs before moving to Brazil, characterized Halbwachs as someone for whom the individual is merely a place of cross section of groups, a meeting point of groups. Individuality should be preserved somehow even in social science settings. Unlike the way Halbwachs proposed,

> [t]he individuum is not merely a meeting point of the groups, the group is also an exchange place between persons. Everyone is characterized by activities, as the neural net of Bergson, by receiving stimuli from others expecting replies from them, which causes these activities to form a complementary network.
> (Bastide, 1970, p. 95)

The second critical issue is the danger of the reification of collective memory as an equivalent of **group mind**. It was problematic already for the contemporaries of Halbwachs. The British psychologist Bartlett (1932) saw him as near to be a proponent of the idea of a "group mind," the belief in the reality of supraindividual mental phenomena. Halbwachs tried to avoid the group mind idea. When talking to an American audience on collective psychology, he claimed:

> The collective thought is not a metaphysical entity, which must be sought in a world apart, in a world equally metaphysical. It exists and it is realized only in individual consciousness. It is, in short, only a certain order of arrangements or relationships between individual minds; it is the states of consciousness of a greater or lesser number of individuals comprising the group. For this reason, it cannot be understood at all if it is confined within the individual mind; and it is necessary, in order to reach it and study it, to seek it in the manifestations and expressions of the entire group, taken as a whole.
> (Halbwachs, 1939, p. 818)

The self-defenses of Halbwachs were merely on an abstract level. The missing point in the theory of Halbwachs was his lack of an idea for the procedures of the interactions leading to collective memory.

As Wertsch and Roediger (2008), who are both cultural and cognitive psychologists, pointed out, the entire notion of collective memory exists today in three types of oppositions: contents of collective memory versus acts of collective remembering, collective memory versus history (see the CONTROVERSIES), and collective versus individual memory processes. These oppositions partly touch upon the relevance of Halbwachs for the history debates, but they also have a general significance for cognitive psychology as well.

Wertsch (2008) provided a very careful cognitive and interactive analysis of Halbwachs's notion of collective memory from a present-day perspective. We should see more structure to collective memory compared to Halbwachs, for whom the cherished social determination went together with arbitrariness, in line with the SSSM thinking. In the interpretation of Wertsch, collective memory should always be interpreted as distributed memory over a network. The structure of this distributed memory is embedded into narrative patterns. He postulates two kinds of narrative patterns for social memory, along the lines proposed by Jerome Bruner (1990, 1991). One frame is the individual's episodic narrative pattern, which acts as scaffolding for our autobiographical memory; the other, however, is a narrative template for social expectation.

> [T]he study of collective memory requires taking into account a second level of narrative organization, one concerned with general patterns rather than specific events and actors. This level of narrative organization is grounded in what I call "schematic narrative templates." . . . In contrast to specific narratives, these templates do not deal with just one concrete episode from the past. Instead, each takes the form of a generalized schema that is in evidence when talking about any one of several episodes.
> (Wertsch, 2008, p. 123)

Besides philosophy, history, and cognitive science, Halbwachs showed up in modern French social sciences as well. Gurvitch (1966) in his theoretical sociology has taken up from Halbwachs the concept of frames (cadres) to analyze social relations. Namer (1994) not only reinterpreted the theory of collective memory in detail but also applied it in a novel manner as well. He made case studies of the Communist and the Gaullist cultivation of Second World War losses as a rivalry of collective memories: sometimes not unconscious differences but planned, carefully designed interventions also go into the stabilization of a collective memory. The handbook of collective representation edited by Lo Monaco et al. (2016) details in several chapters that the heritage of Halbwachs is crucial regarding the interpretation of rival social group memories in the present day. This aspect makes his work relevant for the recent memory debates shown in the CONTROVERSIES section.

Controversies

Halbwachs in recent history debates

Halbwachs has become central and much discussed in modern history writing that, in a way, has discovered the affinities between the issues of memory and the issues of history. As Zawadzki (2004) claims in one of the new French Halbwachs commemorative volumes, the re-emerging interest toward his work has to do with the social memory crisis of modern Western societies. There is a parallel between the memory crises of the time of Halbwachs (collapses in social integration between the wars) with that of our own times. The recent re-emergence of interest toward collective memory has obtained two social relevancies.

The first is the recognition of collective memory regarding the birth and existence of groups. Such "memories of origin" treat memory as the foundation of group identity, where "the present is only understandable in the light of the past." This developed regarding the crisis of social memory following the Second World War. Remembering became a moral obligation, and remembering practices have an exemplary nature. This kind of memory practice can be found not only in remembering the Holocaust but also in the cultic city memorial sites that spell out the names of the deceased, or in marches on battle sites.

This multiple articulation of dualities gives Halbwachs a relevance not only in contemporary psychological research regarding constructive aspects of memory but also for the study of the relationship between memory and history, which was the main topic of his later works (Halbwachs, 1941, 1950, 1992). Halbwachs himself was careful when relating collective memory to history. For him, collective memory concentrated on the similarities between the past and the present, while history on the dissimilarities between them.

> Halbwachs articulated three propositions. The past is not preserved, it is *reconstructed* from the present. Since the isolated individual is a fiction, a memory of the past is possible only due to the social frames of memory, or, by reverting the point of view, the individual memory has a reality only to the extent it participates in collective memory. As a consequence, the definition of collective memory continues to oscillate between a conception that emphasizes the group as group and a conception which, on the contrary, emphasizes the individuals who make up the group, and realize collective memory.
>
> (Lavabre, 2000, p. 54)

New French interest toward Halbwachs is related not only to the new "places of memory" movement (Nora, 1989) but also to the new theories of narratively based identities that originate from Ricoeur (1965/1970, 2004). The latter point reveals an important novelty. Halbwachs had a rather unsophisticated theory of memory representation, as most of the time he portrayed memory as a flow of unconnected memory images, organized by social consensus. Contemporary theories of social memory, on their part, propose a structure to social memories. This structure is basically a narrative organization of a human agent's action sequences, which provides a foundation for our identity, as Wertsch pointed out, from the psychological side. In this search for identity, "it is no longer genesis that we seek but instead the decipherment of who we are in the light of who we are not any longer" (Nora, 1989, p. 19).

Comparing collective memory and scientific history, the difference between their epistemological status should not be forgotten.

> [C]ollective remembering inevitably involves some identity project – remembering in the service of constructing what kind of people we are – and hence it is resistant to change even in the face of contradictory evidence. In collective remembering, the past is tied interpretatively to the present, and if necessary, a part of an account of the past may be deleted or distorted in the service of present needs. Historians routinely warn against practices of inventing, reinventing, and reconstructing the past in the service of the present, but this is precisely what is encouraged – indeed celebrated – in the case of collective remembering.
> (Wertsch & Roediger, 2008, p. 320)

And we should add, these distortions are studied by psychologists from the time of Bartlett (1932). An important phenomenological difference between collective memory and history is that in collective memory, there is always a "we" experience and a relationship to identity.

> This suggests that the difference between memory and history is not so much its content, but its perspective: what distinguishes memory from its historical analogue is its first-person character. If the goal of history is that it should be written in the third person, memory is always written in the first person. Just as an individual memory is "my" story, or perhaps it is "yours", a collective memory is "our" story, or perhaps it is "theirs". In each case, the personal pronoun designates the individual or group who finds its identity in terms of that memory.
> (Poole, 2008, p. 159)

To build a reference frame for the world of memories, modern constructionist historical theories do not postulate fixed markers of history as recorded by the mind but presume that memories are constructed via the act of recalling and by the social medium, and the group is the site of remembering. A central issue of these discussions is the problem of the epistemology of history as a discipline and the relationships between narrative models and forgetting. Gábor Gyáni, the Hungarian theoretician of history writing, surveyed the relevance of Halbwachs in these debates clearly. According to Gyáni (2012), Halbwachs – with regards to history writing – reiterated the claims of the classical Prussian German school of history writing that differentiated between memory and history regarding their undisrupted and disrupted nature.

> By stating that history begins only when tradition fades away, Halbwachs did no more than repeat the deep-rooted assumption held by the Prussian (German) historians, who wholeheartedly committed themselves to historicist convictions, according to which the historical past transmitted by tradition should urgently be replaced by a more rational way of recognition. . . . Thus, the fundamental difference between collective memory and historical consciousness manifests itself mostly in their special relation to continuity and discontinuity.
>
> (Gyáni, 2012, p. 130)

The same constructive processes that Halbwachs (1941) identified in the creation of sacred places in the Holy Land during the Crusades seem to operate on the international scene today. The creators of memorial places strive to invest the place with as much historical meaning as possible, even if this contradicts professional history writing (Gyáni, 2012). Historians should not shy away from reflecting on this situation. While they should not criticize people who seek holy places and wish to tailor their memories to these places, they should also avoid thinking that this practice could ever find its positivist scientific justification.

> The only (or maybe the best) option for a historian today is to accept that he is but one among the story-tellers entitled to talk about the past and that he cannot expropriate or monopolize any more the role of telling the truth about history then the others. This situation makes the duty of drawing a line between myths (national historical myth also implied here) and the more scholarly "truths" particularly important, which are revealed and narrated by historians who regularly pursue their work under the aegis of an institutionalized craftsmanship.
>
> (Gyáni, 2012, p. 140)

Confino (1997) showed in detail that for many in the present-day history debates, there is one central inspiration of the collective memory notion of Halbwachs: the postulation and analysis of conflicting memories. The rival group memories somehow contribute to an emerging memory of the broader community. The historian should not give up his task by allowing rival memories.

> It is obviously important to avoid essentialism and to reject arguments that impose cultural homogeneity on a heterogeneous society. Conflicts over memory exist. Differences are real. People are sometimes ready to die for their vision of the past, and nations sometimes break because of memory conflicts. But all this only begs the question: how, then, in spite of all these differences and difficulties, do nations hold together? What were the common denominators that bound French men and women across the dividing lines that separated them?
> (Confino, 1997, p. 1,400)

In this process, the historians have to consider the theoretical issue as well: when and how people themselves use memory to account for their past. "When and why did memory become a habit of mind shared by people to give meaning to the past?" (Confino, 1997, p. 1,403).

Wertsch and Roediger provide an entire set of comparisons to show the epistemic and value/moral differences between collective memory and historical interpretation, from the point of view of modern cognitive psychology. It is summarized in Table 5.2.

Besides these theoretical discussions regarding the rediscovered Halbwachs, Jan Assmann (1992, 2008, 2012), the historical Egyptologist, proposed a detailed theory of cultural memory as a continuation of the collective memory theory of Halbwachs. While Halbwachs concentrated on contemporary collective memories, Assmann connected this issue to

Table 5.2 Differences between collective memory and history writing according to Wertsch and Roediger

Collective memory	*Formal history*
Identity project (heroism, golden age, victimhood)	Objective account of past, regardless of consequences for identity
Impatient with ambiguity	Complexity and ambiguity
Ignores counter-evidence	Revise existing narratives in light of new evidence
Implicit theories, schemas, scripts to simplify the past	Constrained by archival materials
Conservative resistance to change	Can change in response to new information

Source: Wertsch and Roediger (2008, p. 321).

ancient history. As a starting point, he differentiated communicative memory from cultural memory. **Communicative memory**, the result of actual interactions between people, mainly corresponds to what Halbwachs considered to be collective memory. It is based on a relatively short time span and on actual interaction between actual people. **Cultural memory**, on the other hand, is related to more distant and more abstract events and has a wider temporal scale.

> The concept of cultural memory comprises of the body of reusable texts, images, and rituals specific to each society in each epoch, whose 'cultivation' serves to stabilize and convey the self-image of those societies. For the most part (even if not exclusively) each group bases its awareness of unity and particularity on such collective knowledge of the past.
> (Assmann, 2008, p. 132)

Assmann, through his typology of cultural memory systems, considers in detail the impact of writing on memory organization. According to Assmann, more is at stake in the movement between memory systems and writing than a mere opposition between historical, cultural on the one hand, and natural prehistoric on the other. Assmann (1992, 2012) differentiates between three types of memory economies with the advent of writing. These are not levels of cultural evolution of a kind but "strategies of memory politics that are available in all ages." In the Egyptian type (cultural) memory is directed to the repetitive; it is semantic/categorical and organized non-narratively. Both Jewish and classical Greek cultures, on the other hand, cultivate a memory economy directed by human stories. In Jewish culture, the sacred texts are accompanied by a memory organized around stories and, at the same time, require the transportability of culture to have its directing patterns always present due to the presence of the sacred texts. In Greek culture, the narratives are not related to sacred texts but to human possibilities. Individuality plays a central role here. It results in intertextuality and arguing communities. The essential point is not merely writing but plurality: competing stories of a competitive society that go together with a specific kind of identity creation based on literacy. "Cold cultures," such as Egyptian culture, consider repetition to be important for their memory.

> The sense retained in memory here is to be found in the repeatedly returning events, in continuity rather than discontinuity.... [The Jewish and Greek] hot variety of the unique and special, of growth and evolution, or even of fall and disintegration have a meaning and importance, and are worthy to be committed to memory.
> (Assmann, 2012, p. 57)

Primitive mentality and the relativity of thought

The issue of the history of mentalities had taken a specific relativistic form by the early 20th century. This development can be viewed as the result of two tendencies: an extension of social evolutionism toward human history, which showed up in the late 19th century social Darwinism (Chapter 7, in Volume 1), and an application of the colonialist attitude to differences found between groups of people. Patterns of thought and, accordingly, groups of humans form a kind of evolutionary scale, with European logic on the top, as proposed by Haeckel already. The most important representative of this line of thought was Lucien Lévy-Bruhl (1857–1939), the French philosopher and ethnographer. Lévy-Bruhl started a philosophy career mainly with historical interests, writing monographies on Comte and J. S. Mill. At the turn of the century, his interest moved toward anthropology. He had organized the available data on so-called "natural populations" into the conception of **primitive mentality**. He wanted to combine cultural relativity with the observations of French psychopathology. He wanted to do something more than the British anthropologists of the time. The theory of Lévy-Bruhl, due to its qualitative nature, even with criticism regarding its colonial overtones, has played a general inspirational role in the development of modern psychology. It was certainly a productive theory. As a matter of fact, it was the first univocally **relativistic stance** in the history of cultural comparative psychology in the domain of cross-cultural research. Even though it merely used the data and descriptions of others, researchers were already out there on the field. British researchers W. Rivers (1864–1922), C. Myers (1873–1947), and the ubiquitous W. McDougall joined an expedition already in 1898 to the islands of the Torres Straits between Australia and New Guinea and utilized the entire available apparatus of experimental psychology (sensory measurements, reaction times, memory tests). They were unable to show any striking differences between Aboriginals and Britons in the elementary cognitive aspects that were studied (Chapter 7 in Volume 1). The topic of whether mental processes were universal or culture-dependent stayed on the agenda. The universalistic claims of psychoanalysis and Jungian psychology also called for comparative research, as evidenced, for example, by the Australian explorations of the Hungarian ethnographer and psychoanalyst Géza Róheim (1930, 1974, 1992) and, later, others as well. The inspirations regarding relativism came mainly from anthropology and linguistics, but the widely discussed theory of Vygotsky and Luria, inspired by Lévy-Bruhl, came from psychology.

The aim of Lévy-Bruhl was to show qualitative differences. Lévy-Bruhl (1910) contrasted, on the one hand, a primitive, emotion-based, prelogical, and incoherent mentality and a developed, intellectual, coherent, and logical thinking on the other. He carefully avoided calling this mentality simply illogical.

> The mentality of the inferior types of societies what I call prelogical ... is not antilogical and it is not alogical either. By calling it prelogical I only wish to say that in contrast to our thinking, it is not trying to abstain from contradictions above all. It mainly obeys the law of participation.
>
> (Lévy-Bruhl, 1910/1922, p. 79)

Primitive mental attitude consists of broken fragments of mythical content that are organized in an associative rather than strictly semantic manner. Its explanatory principles are magical, which are not under the control of experience and rationality, and they do not follow logical inference rules. Similarity and mythic participation are everywhere, and they direct the way of thought.

The lack of coherence is a pervasive feature. "These representations will very often prove irreconcilable; we know that emotions enter them to a great degree, that primitive mentality troubles very little about logical coherence, and finally, nowhere we find any collections of representations that constitute a system" (Lévy-Bruhl, 1910/1922, p. 79).

Lévy-Bruhl himself never carried out firsthand anthropological fieldwork. He took the notion of collective representations from Durkheim, and he used selected ethnographic examples to illustrate the collective representations in primitive mentality. The features he identified are summarized in Table 5.3. It is important to observe his careful wording in the right column of the table. Lévy-Bruhl never talked about the "Western mind." He tried to avoid a gradualist or scaling attitude of ranking Western people above the supposed primitives. For him, religion and metaphysics belonged to "primitive mentality" in our culture as well due to their mystical and speculative nature. His attempt to avoid making an impression of cultural superiority did not really work out. His contemporaries and later social scientists interpreted his theory as an interpretation or even justification for Western superiority.

Primitive mentality also leads to questioning of the Cartesian Ego:

> In the midst of this confusion of mystic participations and exclusions, the impressions that the individual has about himself, whether living or dead, and of the group to which he 'belongs' have only a far-off resemblance to ideas or concepts proper. They are felt and lived, rather than thought of. Neither their content nor their connections are strictly submitted to the law of contradiction. Consequently, neither the personal ego, nor the social group, nor the surrounding world, seen and unseen, appear to be definite yet.
> (Lévy-Bruhl, 1910/1922, p. 447)

In a turn-of-the-century world, where modern questionings of the coherence of self appeared, Lévy-Bruhl pointed out that this coherence itself (which we are starting to lose) was a late result of human development.

Table 5.3 A comparison of primitive and rational thought in the conception of Lévy-Bruhl

Primitive mentality	*Modern science*
Mystical	Rational
Concrete	Abstract
Supernatural causes	Immanent causes
Incoherent	Coherent
Tolerance for contradictions	No contradictions

Source: Lévy-Bruhl (1910/1922).

Lévy-Bruhl saw the many issues that his primitive mentality ideas raised between 1910 and the 1930s. He even attempted to modify his position and kept as essential the idea of mystic participation. Participation is mainly emotion-based. Emotional coherence replaces what was originally characterized as prelogical: you can be both a Crow and a Human at the same time (Lévy-Bruhl, 1949).

French anthropology two generations later produced a universalistic attitude as well. According to this structuralist position, typically held in the 1950s and 1960s, human thinking always takes place in the frame of binary oppositions that are related to the world of exchange. Claude Lévi-Strauss (1908–2009), the professor of Collège de France and the most active field researcher and theoretician of this approach, maintained that culture is in fact a combination of three exchange systems: exchange of news, goods, and women (Lévi-Strauss, 1949, 1966). All these systems are based on binary oppositions, and human thought has an inherent logic through these systems of oppositions. Variations of culture would relate to the content of these oppositions. "Raw" and "cooked" are a different contrast compared to "animate" and "inanimate," but the basic structure is always a binary opposition, with no third option. Culture in this regard would always be a peculiar system of classification, communication, and practice, using rigid categories rather than fuzzy prototypes. Categorization is a broad basic feature of the human mind.

Later historical transformations of mentality: the historical psychology of Ignace Meyerson

Ignace Meyerson (1888–1983), the laboratory chief at the École Pratique in Paris and a longtime editor of one of the central French psychology journals, *Journal de Psychologie*, wrote an elaborate treatise on historical psychology (Meyerson, 1948). He emphasized the constructive role of language and the historical relativity of the mind and had also tried to give an interpretation of Lévy-Bruhl. Meyerson showed that most of the presumed primitive features are part of a more general effort: the "participation" aspects of rites of passage, for example, can be interpreted along the more general psychological principles of identification.

In his historical psychology, Meyerson, who was originally a revolutionary Polish Jewish émigré from the Tsarist empire with a German education, tried to revitalize the "mental science psychology" in France, outlined half a century earlier by Dilthey (1894). The approach of Meyerson stresses that humans should be understood in their historical reality and movement. Instead of a laboratory experimental psychology, a historical psychology is needed that would concentrate on the "achievements" or creations of humans (*oeuvres*) and should aim to reconstruct the psychological processes underlying these *oeuvres*. This historical psychology would treat the human mind within its historically changing mentalities. When emphasizing mentalities, Meyerson showed many similarities with, and even had an influence on, the French *Annales* school of history writing, which emphasized the study of mentalities as a key issue in history.

The issue of the origins, primitive mentality to be specific, was less relevant for him than the **changes in mentality over historical times** and how these changes are revealed by the "oeuvres," the output of people. He tried to outline his vision of a specifically human historical psychology. Being an experienced primatologist, he took off from comparing animal and human mental functions. Animals are always driven by primary biological drives. They are characterized by a non-mediated mental organization (with the exception of higher primates), they do not use tools or instruments, they do not change nature, they follow universal laws, and they do not have a complex system of sign-based communication. Humans, on the other hand, are driven by extra-biological or non-biological driving forces, they use instruments, they show contextually and historically variable behavior, and they use complex sign systems.

Based on these basic oppositions, Meyerson listed some of the basic features of humans as historical beings: they are producing objects, they work, they are active, experimenting beings, who constitute "works" (*oeuvres* in French). With the development of their "works," their life is characterized by constant changes, and in this process, their culture is segmented into different layers, like religion, art, literature, science, and so on.

> Humans are bathing in the world of "works": languages, religions, laws, sciences, arts. They are modeled by them. . . . Thus, the psychologist adds a new domain to the history of the forms of civilizations, which will have an increasing importance: the history of their deep psychological content, and the history of those functions that create these works.
> (Meyerson, 1952, pp. 8–9)

The analysis of mind proposed by Meyerson (1948, 1987) was based on a few central proposals: the objectivation idea, that is, mental processes, appear in oeuvres, in actual physical manifestations; the idea of psychological functions, basic processes that are manifested in different signs; and finally, historicity, the constant change of the meaning of categories, and even of the functions themselves (Pizzarroso, 2013, 2018).

The ambitious project mainly remained a program, with hardly any examples of actual historical psychological interpretations. His basic tension was how to derive the psychological functions without supposing a folk psychology of psychological functions. As Pizzarroso (2013) has shown, the fundamental tension between Meyerson and his experimental psychology critics in his application for higher positions was the unwillingness of Meyerson to accept a set of initial psychological categories, any kind of rigid "human nature." For example, he was not interested in the process of how memory changes through history but rather in how memory can be understood at all from historical oeuvres. Thus, he revolted against all stable and fixed elements.

It is interesting to see how Meyerson is different from the more famous version of historical psychology proposed by Dilthey (1894, 1977). For Dilthey, the key feature was that the individual always develops; this development goes toward the unfolding of more and more elaborate values. In an important way, what was *Geist* for Dilthey became culture both in its external sense that it is something objective and independent of the knower. Literature was implied to be a rich source for an understanding psychology. Interestingly, that would be the case for Meyerson as well. Meyerson did not pay too much attention to Dilthey in his proposal for a historical psychology, but by far not out of ignorance. According to Meyerson, Dilthey also shared the belief in a basic universal human nature. Meyerson claimed that the human condition should be interpreted as constant change and dynamics (Parot, 2000; Pizarroso, 2018).

Bruner (2004, p. 403) interpreted Meyerson as an early cultural psychologist. Most of human conduct, in contrast to animal behavior, is not directly necessary for the individual or the species.

> Law, art, religion, war, magic, technology – none is indispensable for life, or only very indirectly so; indeed, these activities sometimes work against biological adaptation. Yet these are the things that man most highly values in life. Second, man not only makes tools and instruments, adapting them to local conditions as necessary, but he takes collective measures to assure that the knowledge needed to do so is conserved and transmitted. It is this basic fact that makes "civilization" possible. Human conduct, third, is virtually unlimited in its variability, only loosely tied to the species genome. . . . Fourth, man uses a communally organized system of signs not only for communicating but also for translating experience into symbolic forms.

Another lasting message of Meyerson, his works toward the cultural interpretation of the **notion of the person**. "The uniformity observed in some human conducts [. . .] is a secondary, social uniformity, out of implicit conventions and not a primary biological uniformity. -Man is variety, and this variety is an aspect of its richness" (Meyerson, 1952, p. 11). He and his students, like Vernant (1991), the latter working on Greek thought, showed the varieties of the notion of person and personality in different cultures. One can see the unfolding of personality in the Indian beginnings, a duality in classical Greek times (social relations and individuality) and how it started a new turn in Christian identity issues. Meyerson and his followers analyzed the person in the worldview presented by later cultural changes as well, in particular, in modern novels of Flaubert, Joyce, and Proust – and Pirandello. The crucial element in these changes was the decomposition of personality as a social process in the 20th century, as shown earliest by literature and analyzed in depth by Meyerson (Pizarroso, 2013, 2018).

This is the actual message of this version of historical psychology. The approach of Meyerson regarding the genesis of the modern self has interesting parallels in new literary theory. Similar to the historical psychology proposal of Meyerson (1952, 1954), modern literary theory also believes that the Western humanistic concept of independent individual self is not universal, not given for eternity, and valid for all ages and places but is rather a historical and cultural product. This does not necessarily suggest, however, that it is an outdated idea. Many things valued in civilized life depend on it. We also have to realize that individual self is not a fixed and stabile entity but is constantly being created and modified in our consciousness, during interaction with others (Lodge, 2002).

Primitive mentality and child development

The idea proposed by Lévy-Bruhl that there are qualitatively different ways of organizing our thought was and remains very provocative. The most interesting and constructive uses of the theory of Lévy-Bruhl appeared in studies of child development. While Lévy-Bruhl can be considered to be patronizing and even racist today, in his own time, he was widely influential. As Henry Wallon (1968), the French left-wing developmentalist, evaluated him in a life interview, the three merits of Lévy-Bruhl were the dethroning of the belief in a universal mind (the dethroning of Cartesian universality), the emphasis on emotionality in primitive mentality, and the recognition of the fundamental role of similarity-based reasoning. His limitation was, according to Wallon, not having realized the social transformations needed to overcome these features.

Lévy-Bruhl had an influence both on Piaget and on Vygotsky. As Moscovici (1998), the French social psychologist pointed out, for both authors the main issue was the genesis of the modern mind, in society and in children. How does logical and coherent thinking develop out of an incoherent and illogical organization? While Piaget was motivated by Lévy-Bruhl in his search for logical coordination, he found his model in Durkheim; Vygotsky remained more relativistic and more of a believer in qualitative changes and qualitative differences in thought, which would correspond to dramatic social changes experienced in his Soviet Russia.

Piaget's universalism: from authority to cooperation

Piaget was one of the main interpreters of the idea of primitive mentality. When he tried to characterize the mentality of preschool children, Piaget – besides the clinical ideas borrowed from Bleuler – took an inspiration from the proposals regarding primitive mentality. While Piaget was inspired by Lévy-Bruhl (1910/1922), he already in 1928 claimed that the differences between pre-logical and logical are to be sought for in the nature of the integration of the individual and the social. Piaget tried to show that during development, there is a hand-to-hand relation between certain changes in social organization and certain types of coherence in mental organization. Prelogical thought is characterized by integration based on conformity and authority, while logical thought supposes the comparison of perspectives and argumentation. It also implies a differentiation between Ego and personality. The organization at the level of the Ego preserves the self-centered vision, while personality "is constructed by overcoming the Ego thanks to a special type of social relationship, which is based on mutual respect: on the moral and intellectual cooperation of people who treat each other as having equal rights" (Xypas, 2001, p. 110).

Piaget developed a rather complex theory of social development, where individual minds were supposed to develop rationality through specific types of coherence construction. This was mainly a theoretical reinterpretation, to which he returned several times (Kitchener, 1991).

> Whatever Piaget studies, he always finds identical evolutionary tendencies. The development is always from egocentrism, subjectivity, concrete reasoning, conformism and transcendence towards socialized reasoning, objectivity, abstract thought, autonomy and immanence. These tendencies define progress, from the point of view of the child and of social history as well.
> (Vidal, 2000, p. 34)

This shift from primitive prelogical toward logical was a key for Piaget concerning the development of all moral and cognitive changes. He had two inspirations when comparing the thought of children and the thought of primitives. One was Durkheim and his analysis of the role of cooperation, and the other was Lévy-Bruhl and his focus on qualitative changes. According to Piaget, the qualitative change is not form chaos to order but involves the move from authority and subordination toward cooperation and logical coherence. Regarding primitive mentality, Piaget talks about different types of coherence rather than about a move from incoherence toward coherence.

> We believe that the primitives, just like us, are searching for coherence ... regarding structures, Lévy-Bruhl is entirely well founded to talk about prelogic, in the sense that what seems to be coherent for the primitives, seems incoherent for us, and vice versa.
> (Piaget, 1928, p. 177)

In primitive cultures, prelogic is based on authority and, in the children of our times, on their autism. Cooperation leads the child away from prelogic.

> We call cooperation all contacts between two or n individuals who are equal or believe that they are equal, thus all social contacts where no element of authority or prestige plays a role. ... Keeping this in mind, we believe that only cooperation constitutes a process that generates reason, and autism and social constraint are only convenient for the prelogic in its different forms.
> (ibid., p. 191)

Piaget is against the interpretations that, together with classical theories of socialization, we would see an opposition between individual reason and social life.

> There is neither society nor individuals in themselves. There are interindividual relations, some of which do not make any changes to the mental structure of the individual, but there are others, which transform the individual mind and the group simultaneously. ... With Lévy-Bruhl, we prefer to distinguish a prelogic and a logic, according to the social processes

dominant in a given collectivity. It may sound paradoxical as a conclusion, but the primitive mentality seems to be less socialized than our own. The social constraint is only one step towards socialization. It is only cooperation that brings the mental equilibrium, willing to differentiate the factual status of psychological operations and the normative status of rational ideas.

(ibid., pp. 204–205)

Piaget (1975) made historical speculations as well here. According to his historical speculations, the decentration needed for logic was born as part of the development in Greek culture by the comparison of rivaling cultural points of views, and a similar process goes on in children as a gradual weighing of evidences and points of views. Piaget, as in much of his later works, seeks parallels between individual development and assumed cultural and historical development. In Piaget's highlighting the importance of the Greek market of ideas for the development of logical thought, there is still, of course, a remainder of European centrism. What happened to the possibility of logical coordination based on exchanging points of views in other cultures? And does meeting of cultures always lead to reciprocity and higher-order coordination? Our contemporary experience challenges this optimistic image.

The conception of Piaget the sociologist and social psychologist was forgotten for quite some time. However, after the publication of his collected sociological works and his earlier studies on moral development in French in 1965, Piaget started to play a crucial role in modern social science theory. Lawrence Kohlberg (1927–1987), a Harvard developmental psychologist, was among the first ones who started to reconsider the stages of moral development proposed by Piaget (1932). Kohlberg (1971, 1981–1984) suggested that there are multiple developed stages of morality, including the post-conventional stages, which also involve the possibility of changing moral rules. This line was followed by the German philosopher Jürgen Habermas (1983), who also took up the ideas of Piaget, which relate moral development to cooperation and "a democracy of thought." Jahoda (2000) showed from the point of view of a historian of social psychology the inspiration and distance of Piaget toward Lévy-Bruhl.

As a Geneva sociologist, Moessinger, pointed out, there is an interesting issue of analogy felt between intrapsychological and interpersonal equilibrations professed by Piaget.

In the context of sociology, the central assumption of Piaget is that the laws of *intrapersonal coordination* of values (the intellectual operations of reasoning and evaluating) are also found at the *interpersonal* level. There is an analogy between the equilibration of cognitive structures and the equilibration of interpersonal cooperation. "To cooperate, it is to operate in common" he says. . . . [S]ynchronic equilibria – which do not depend very much on circumstances – are rather general and vary little from one society to another.

(Moessinger, 2000, p. 174)

The cultural relativism of Vygotsky and Luria

Regarding primitive thought, Piaget, as revealed by all his later work, can certainly be taken as a representative of the universalistic trend, who tended to transform the issue of primitive versus rational thought into evolving bases for coherence. He can be contrasted to the conception of the Vygotsky school, who tried to find experimental evidence for a social relativistic vision of the human mind.

A series of studies was started in Uzbekistan in the general political waves of integrating the Central Asian mainly Muslim countries into the Soviet Union. The studies in the late 1920s up to the early 1930s tried to fit the peculiar vision of the mind promoted by Vygotsky (1927, 1997) into the discussion on primitive thought. According to Vygotsky (see the details in Chapter 8), the so-called **higher mental functions** – voluntary attention, voluntary memory, thinking, and so on – are not universally given. There is some general unfolding of some abilities, but they are specific historical achievements. History, and especially the conscious formation of society, is what changes human thought. As Luria, who by then was a world-famous neuropsychologist, summarized their reasoning three decades later, in their conception:

> "Higher psychological functions" ought to have their own origin, but this origin should not be sought in the depths of the soul or in the hidden properties of nervous tissue; it should be sought outside the organism of the individual person, in objectively existing social history, which is independent of the individual. . . . Development on the basis of social work and speech, the higher psychic functions permit man to shift to a new level of organization in his own activity [arrives to levels if organization] which never existed in the animal world, and which in no manner represent initial characteristics of the soul.
>
> (Luria, 1965, p. 388)

The Luria group basically tried to establish an experimental operationalization for the claims regarding primitive mentality and tested the accordingly constructed notions during fieldwork in Uzbekistan. Luria (1933) and his group showed, for example, that when classifying pictures, the Uzbek peasants, when presented with a *shovel*, an *axe*, and a *saw*, created scenarios instead of abstracting the concept of an *instrument*: they attached a log of wood to the saw and the axe, claiming that the wood can be sawn and then further cut with the axe. Thus, according to the analysis of Luria, abstraction was missing, and their categorical organization remained situation-bound. In the sense of Bruner (1990, 1991), they were using the narrative frame instead of the conceptual-descriptive scientific frame. Regarding the situation-bound thought, Luria wrote in an early paper:

> The main function of this thinking is not the formation of abstract connection and relationship between symbols, but reproduction of whole situations, whole complexes closely connected with specific life experiences; . . . with

the change of economic conditions this situational or complicated thinking very quickly changes, giving place to other more complex forms of thought.

(Luria, 1933, p. 192)

Similar results were obtained with syllogistic reasoning. In one type, the Uzbek peasants were presented with syllogisms that were related in content to their daily experience:

Where the climate is warm and humid, cotton can grow.
"N" place is warm and humid.
Will cotton grow there or not?

This type of syllogism did not cause any difficulties. *Of course, it is warm in place N; thus, cotton will grow, but only if there are no mountains nearby*, and sometimes they added, *I know this, I have seen it*. Thus, in the seemingly logical reasoning, the practical knowledge of the person did play a role; the reasoning was not formal.

The other, more abstract syllogisms unrelated to their daily life were like:

In the far North, where there is snow, all bears are white.
Novaia Zemlya is in the far North.
What color are the bears in Novaia Zemlya?

With the abstract inferences, experience did not help. The syllogism was sort of rejected. *I don't know. I've seen a black bear. I've never seen any others. Each locality has its own animals: if it's white, they will be white; if it's yellow, they will be yellow. But what kind of bears are there in Novaya Zemlya? We always speak only of what we see; we don't talk about what we haven't seen.*

There were limitations either referring to a lack of evidential experience or to factual impossibilities. If presented with the syllogism:

In Moscow all males are bold.
Ivan lives in Moscow.
Therefore . . . ?

They replied by negating the major premise, on the basis of experience, *It is not possible that everyone is bold*.

The conclusions of the Vygotsky–Luria group supported qualitative differences and the presence of a "primitive mentality" even in 20th-century illiterate peasant populations. At the same time, in line with a Marxist meta-theory, and along the ideas of the Stalinist social reorganization and introduction of farming collectives (kolkhoz), they also claimed that due to schooling and a general change of the historical context, a primitive mentality can be moved toward decontextualized abstract thought and can be transformed very fast. This idea was in line with the Marxist theory of history claiming that social circumstances have a determining value over mentalities. One can observe "historically determined" changes in individual mechanisms, even in the very structure of thinking.

As Luria summed up what happens after schooling is introduced:

> We found that changes in the practical forms of activity, and especially the reorganization of activity based on formal schooling, produced qualitative changes in the thought processes of the individuals studied. Moreover, we were able to establish that basic changes in the organization of thinking can occur in a relatively short time when there are sufficiently sharp changes in social-historical circumstances, such as those that occurred following the 1917 Revolution.
>
> (Luria, 1979, p. 79–80)

With all the praising of Soviet social changes, these results were still very provocative at that time. Luria was accused of being a racist for his finding cultural differences and removed from his position. The detailed reports of the studies only appeared in the 1970s.

During the half century, following their original expedition, this cultural-relativistic research moved toward universalism and has become tied to the issues of literacy, manners of discourse, and conversational conventions. Michael Cole, a cultural psychologist of the University of California, San Diego, was a student and follower of Luria. He initiated several series of studies in differently educated people in Liberia (Cole & Scribner, 1974; Scribner, 1997; Scribner & Cole, 1981). On the basis of their studies, Cole and Scribner claim that cognitive resources are universal in each culture, and in this regard, there is no cultural relativity. There is relativity in another sense, however. Some cultures emphasize the use of our cognitive resources, like categorical memory, in all contexts. According to Walter Ong (1982), the historian and anthropologist of orality, oral cultures are characterized by additive cognition, by contextuality, subjectivity, and empathy, rather than impersonal analysis. According to Cole and Scribner, the qualitative change caused by literacy would be decontextualization: the use of our cognitive resources in every context. To take the example of syllogism, syllogistic reasoning is based exclusively on the form of the premises, and this would appear as an effect of the decontextualization of thought brought by reading.

Scribner (1997) did several studies in Africa and in Mexico, with people of different levels of schooling. She showed that unschooled people tended to follow either a strategy of concretization and claim a lack of experience ("I have never been to Novaia Zemlia") or of stating the impossibility of conclusions, based on their experience ("It is not possible that all men are bold"). Scribner interpreted the inabilities as issues with discourse conventions. People with no formal schooling always try to react to questions on an experiential basis. This is a seemingly minor change compared to Luria, who also emphasized situation-boundedness. It has become, however, an issue of language practices. Formal practices, which are so frequent in modern schooling, liberate us from experiential bias and make us able to react in similar situations based merely on forms.

The interpretation of primitive mentality raised a century ago has gradually become connected to the use of cultural codes. According to Donald (1991) and Nyíri (1992), cultural media – language, writing, printing, and today, the Internet – fundamentally shape and, at the time of their introduction, change the order of mental processes. Writing and printing, as special cases of such changes, brought about new organizations of memory. There have been two kinds of memories ever since books appeared: an inner (biological) one and an external one, stored in books. Accordingly, we ourselves think differently about the structure of knowledge and memory and use our inner memory in an altered manner. We have grown more Platonistic and suppose that truth is somewhere out there, in the world of books; at the same time, we have become more practical. We can resort to reading and writing to aid our memory. Therefore, a new symbolic space is created, which we refer to in special ways and depend on for the organization of our mental phenomena.

Linguistic relativity: Sapir and Whorf

A peculiar version of cultural relativity is **linguistic relativity**, which also emerged in the social sciences during the interwar period. It is partially related to talks about historically "lower cultures," and it is partially a synchronic talk regarding our present cultural diversity about the impact of different languages on thought at a given time. It was developed in American linguistics by Edward Sapir (1884–1939), an anthropological linguist (Sapir, 1921), trained by Franz Boas, and Benjamin Lee Whorf (1897–1941), an amateur linguist of Native American languages. They represented the mentalistic tradition within American linguistics. The behavioristic description of North American aboriginal languages by Leonard Bloomfield (1926) and his followers at that time was based on the great linguistic and social distance between Indo-European and Amero-Indian languages. Since we do not understand the language and culture of the natives, we can only rely on an objective description of their cultural and linguistic systems, as it is revealed by usage practices, with no reference to shared semantics.

Instead of following this behavioristic metatheory, Sapir (1921, who was also a noted systematizer of these languages into families) and Whorf (1956) refreshed a tradition from the 19th century, which claimed that language was an inner mental reality that has a sort of internal impact on all our cognition. As Wilhelm von Humboldt (1836/1999) formulated it, language determines thought, which shows up in the effects of grammar and the lexicon on various aspects of human cognition.

In the interwar period, the very idea of whether language has a fundamental influence on perception and cognition remained very loosely articulated, similar to the ideas about primitive mentality of Lévy-Bruhl (largely based on anecdotal evidence without any real data collection). A generation later, the issue became a question of more refined interest, leading to behavioral hypotheses and more exact behavioral measures. From the 1950s onward, there have been two types of research efforts to interpret the Whorfian claim in an operationalized, behavioral manner. Some were looking for lexical influences, like the impact of color terms on color memory (for a considerate analysis of many dozen studies, see Rosch, 1978), while others for impacts of grammatical organization on thought, like that of grammatical coding of shape of objects via verbal conjugation in the Hopi language. This was observed in shape-based object classifications in non-linguistic tasks (Carroll & Casagrande, 1958).

After the 1950s, different research outlooks have taken shape regarding the impact of language on cognition. These outlooks also have broader historical interest, as their sequence shows general research meta-theoretical changes from 1950s to the turn of the century.

1. In the 1950s, in line with the dominant American behaviorist SSSM outlook, many researchers claimed that there are large differences in mental capacities, as language differences result in an overall relativity of thought. **Language determines the way we perceive the world.**
2. In the 1960s, together with the advent of inner models of the mind (the cognitive turn), and partly under the influence of the universalistic trend initiated by Chomsky (1965, 1968), relativity was replaced by universalistic ideas. In this view, researchers were looking for biologically founded, universal models of cognition. At the same time, some of these new cognitive trends argued for the independence of language, perception, and thought as well, pointing toward modular organization. **Language and perception/thought are independent domains, each following a universal biological** pattern in this vision.
3. This period was later followed by **more organized typological studies** that were looking for typological effects of language types on cognition in specific areas, instead of looking for cognitive differences of speakers of randomly selected languages (Slobin, 2003, 2004). An example is the program of Levinson (1996) investigating spatial cognition and the coding of space in languages. On the basis of their thorough review of the new experimental literature, Wolf and Holmes (2002) claim for a limited relativity, where language has an attention-directing influence, rather than a limiting impact.

> We did not find empirical support for the view, that language determines the basic categories of thought, or that it "closes doors." Once people are able to make a particular conceptual distinction, this ability is retained, even if it is not explicitly encoded in one's language. . . . There is evidence, however, that while language may not close doors, it may fling others wide open. For example, language makes certain distinctions difficult to avoid when it meddles in the process of color discrimination or renders one way of construing space more natural than another. Lastly, language can sometimes build new doors. For example, language may underlie our ability to represent exact numbers and entertain false beliefs. Thus, language may not replace, but

instead may put in place, representational systems that make certain kinds of thinking possible.

(Wolf & Holmes, 2002, p. 261)

This conclusion is in a way similar to the conclusion of studying the primitive mind: humans have universal cognitive resources, but the use of these resources is sensitively fine-tuned by social and cultural contexts (Hunt & Agnoti, 1991).

Bartlett: schema theories of the social mind to overcome associationism

Invoking Bartlett in the present chapter has some arbitrariness to it. His main works made him a leading proponent of schema theories that overcome elementarism and, as a consequence, an important godfather figure of cognitive psychology in the generation after him. His anti-elementaristic move was, however, always **contextualist** in that it claimed a contextual determination for cognition, including social contexts. The most basic methodical feature of the psychology of Bartlett is the need to move away from the laboratory and abstractions toward everyday life and meaningfulness. Bartlett remained a naturalist in psychology, a scientist who expected research to reveal the studied phenomena in an immediate manner with examples and details of protocols. The naturalistic attitude explains his choice of topics and methods. He experimented, but in a rather casual and impressionistic manner, but still collecting an enormous amount of data. In the midst of the dominance fight of the great schools of psychology (in the mid-1930s), he expressed his *ars psychologica*, which was a praise of eclecticism. "The comprehensive systems and schemata of psychological explanation constitute the greatest obstacles to progress." And "Cambridge psychology of the laboratory type has never committed itself to any hard and fast and settled scheme of psychological explanation. I hope it never will" (Bartlett, 1936, pp. 50–51, 40).

Bartlett represented a rather broad, loose, functionalist attitude that considered psychology to be a biological discipline studying the human "responses," their origins, history, determinants, and functions in mental life. He treated the mind as an active agent, and in this sense, he was a constructivist. He was the psychologist who reminded the biologist about phenomena not yet explained or not easy to explain by the current biological conceptual apparatus (Johnston, 2001). Moreover, in all his work, he remained a committed **social thinker**. For him, the laboratory was a supplement to social life and not a place for isolation and decontextualization.

The laboratory should be a place to work in, not to live in. I am a firm believer in the great value of dumping a student into a social group that he is not familiar with, for I think that this stimulates observation of genuine human life reactions more than anything else. Further what I learned in social contacts at first hand I would try to bring into the laboratory and test under more exact conditions.

(Bartlett, 1936, p. 51)

Disciplinary developments and eclectics

Figure 5.4 Sir Frederick Bartlett.
Source: Copyright British Psychological Society.

Biography

How did you become a psychologist in Cambridge? Sir Frederic Bartlett

Sir Frederick Bartlett was born in Stow-on-the-Wold, England, on October 20, 1886, and died on September 30, 1969, in Cambridge. He became one of the leaders of British experimental and applied psychology in the mid-20th century and remained the main representative of graduate training in psychology in England for decades: he was an instructor and chair of experimental psychology in Cambridge from 1922 until 1952. He took the place that was left vacant after Myers and Rivers took work elsewhere after they both returned from WWI. The university created a chair of experimental psychology in 1931, and Bartlett took the position. Bartlett was elected to the Royal Society in 1932 as the first experimental psychologist there and was knighted for his work with the Royal Air Force in 1948. He also received seven honorary doctoral degrees. As Sir Frederic Bartlett, for a long time, he was the only psychologist knighted.

Bartlett was a boy who came from a rather humble background, with recurring illnesses and a mostly informal secondary education. Bartlett had a varied education in London and Cambridge, combining a preparation in philosophy, anthropology, and sociology, culminating in an apprenticeship of anthropology with Rivers, and another in experimental psychology with Myers at Cambridge. His original intention was to become an anthropologist. This was characteristic of the progressive youth, in contrast to the bookish, philosophical heritage. Bartlett's unique attitude toward psychology was formed in Cambridge. His mentor, Charles Samuel Myers, together with W. H. Rivers, introduced the experimental method to this citadel of knowledge, where James Ward tried in vain to establish a laboratory of experimental psychology in 1877, and further attempts failed in 1879, 1886, and 1888.

Bartlett had to find a place for experimental psychology in an academic world that had basically refuted the direct accessibility of mental content, which was the starting point of German experimental psychology. The peculiarity of Bartlett was that in a context provided by the philosophies of Russell, Moore, Wittgenstein, and Ryle, he promoted and represented a psychology that did not look inward yet, at the same time, was not behavioristic either. In the beginning, he wrote some papers along the British analytic philosophical style, but after his graduate thesis work, he promoted an experimental psychology that was unique in its life-like data gathering and new concepts. It was not based on introspection and concentrated on complex mental phenomena.

Besides introducing experimentation, which implied taking a peculiar role in the context of life at the university, his teachers provided Bartlett with two further legacies. Both Myers and Rivers took part in the famous anthropological expedition to the Torres Strait Islands in 1898, studying the elementary sensation, reaction time, and other laboratory-ready aspects of the mental life of Aboriginals. The results of these studies were not too interesting: they found very few differences. But the very idea that issues of culture and anthropology were relevant to experimental psychology gave a "human flavor" to Cambridge psychology (Bartlett, 1936). At the same time, both Rivers and Myers were medical doctors (that is why they were enlisted during World War I) who kept an interest toward neurology throughout their careers. The English tradition, starting from Hughlings Jackson, to combine levels of mental functioning with levels of the nervous system had led Bartlett to look for support for his memory distortion studies in the schema theories of Sir Henry Head (1920), in order to account for schematizations in memory.

After becoming a noted experimentalist, during World War II, Bartlett contributed largely to the war effort. His vitriolic booklet on German war propaganda (Bartlett, 1940) revealed that the essence of the "miracle of German propaganda" was spreading lies in a consistent manner. (Think of fake news on the INTERNET today.) More importantly, he started to work on the organization of complex skills in aircraft flying and the role of practice and fatigue in complex, guided activities (Bartlett, 1940, 1951). In this particular work, his main support came from Kenneth Craik (1914–1945), a talented young associate who introduced the idea of cybernetic control in understating complex human actions and noted the importance of displays in guiding human performance (Craik, 1943). Craik and Bartlett established the Medical Research Council (MRC) unit of experimental psychology together, studying human performance in war. The unit was first led by Craik, who died in a car accident very early on. The group was crucial in promoting complex experimental psychological studies during warfare and in transmitting findings to peacetime as well, as a coupling of early experimental cognitive psychology and work psychology or ergonomics (Broadbent, 1958). Jet flying, radar, and radio control were crucial in establishing the later new paradigm of cognitive psychology. Bartlett (1951) himself also allowed that "human relations" might be important in industrialized organizations; still, the most important contribution of psychology is to help understand the organization of skilled actions and the coordination of signal guidance in modern work contexts. The students and followers of Bartlett during the next generation would transmit this message of Cambridge psychology: the use of experimental methods to understand information processing of humans, in everyday life and in complex modern work conditions.

The best source for his complex life and work is Wagoner (2017a), who is responsible for the Bartlett heritage at Cambridge.

Besides his famous theory of remembering, Bartlett also contributed to a loosely conceived social theory of human cognition. One of his eternal topics was **cross-cultural psychology**, following the footsteps of his Cambridge predecessors, Myers and Rivers. His first work of note presented the issue of primitive culture on the basis of his African experiences with tribal societies. He was aware of the work of Lévy-Bruhl but believed that he was misled, due to his ignorance of the contexts, by proposing a "primitive mentality."

> The savage attempts explanations, rationalizations, as we do. More than that he proceeds in the same way, by connecting specific events with something else, and generally with something wider than that which he desires to account for. . . . Once times of unusual stress appear, the observational explanation may be lost, and rationalizations may be advanced, which transcend the findings of ordinary observation.
>
> (Bartlett, 1923, p. 285)

Bartlett claimed that we ourselves are as magical as the "primitives" in many mundane matters, and there is no jump between primitives and modern people. Considering his later book, *Remembering*, it is not surprising that most of his early cross-cultural work is on folk tales, their formative influences, and the process of cultural transactions (Bartlett, 1920). His message is rather clear: the real task is to apply universal laws of social psychology to explain the observed organization of mental phenomena in a given culture.

> We need not, then, speak of primitive imagining, belief, thinking, and so on, as if these, considered as psychological responses were any different in the primitive as contrasted with the modern mind. But what we must do is to study how imagining, thinking, believing, or other typical human responses, may vary in the position of dominance, which they occupy at different stages of culture. Moreover, we must try to show precisely what follows from this varying exercise of different outstanding psychological reactions.
>
> (Bartlett, 1923, p. 23)

Bartlett also fought against "group mind" and other mystical phenomena and rebuffed any irrationalism. At the same time, he realized that relationships between groups and members are becoming more complex in modern societies, exactly due to the fact that we are members of many more groups than the so-called primitives. With modern life comes "the increasing differentiation of groups, and, to an even greater extent, to that development of means of communication which places the social individual in a considerable number of different groups all, or many, of which may be in close working relationship" (Bartlett, 1923, p. 257).

Two conceptions of memory and the schemata of Bartlett

The real international fame for Bartlett came through his book *Remembering*, published in 1932. This book questioned several accepted wisdoms of mainstream psychology. Bartlett gave up the tradition of treating all processes, including remembering, in strictly controlled laboratory settings and using extremely simple materials, such as meaningless syllables. In the classification of research styles in psychology proposed by Danziger (1990, 2010), Bartlett combined the experimental method initiated by Wundt with working in a street-interaction-like manner initiated by Galton. This combination resulted in **interactive experiments**. He investigated the recall of complicated materials, like fairy tales, newspaper clips about the ongoing war events or about cricket games, complex pictures, under rather natural circumstances.

One typical situation was repeated recall after unannounced intervals. In another innovative situation, his subjects had to transfer the material in a serial reproduction situation to each other. As he recalled in his account of this work, the idea of serial recalls or reproduction came from his talks with a young Russell student mathematician, Norbert Wiener, who later became a founding father of cybernetics. Figure 5.5 shows a famous example from his book on the transformation of a figure in serial recall.

142 *Disciplinary developments and eclectics*

Figure 5.5 Transformation of a figure during repeated serial reproduction.
Source: Bartlett (1932, p. 180).

Even before the publication of his famous book, Bartlett explored issues of memory in his work toward a psychology of folktales (Bartlett, 1920). He first criticized the Freudian wish-fulfillment theories of tales as being rather unreliable and contrasted them with sociological theories. The latter ones also have an underlying psychological content: they realize that most content and symbolism of folk tales are derived from specific aspects of real life. Then, he moved on to his real proposal: the essence of a psychological study of folktales should be relating the individual selection mechanisms to the social functions. Regarding content, one finds trivial social issues, such as dominance, submission, cheating, and the like; and regarding form, "two impulses which are immediately brought into operation are the tendency to produce laughter, and the tendency to create astonishment and wonder, or to secure dramatic effects" (Bartlett, 1920, p. 289).

In the experimental psychology of memory, the mainstream model and paradigm, even at the time of Bartlett, as we saw in Chapter 9 of Volume 1, was the **Ebbinghaus paradigm**, reducing everything to a few quantitative aspects, using basic principles and quantification. Bartlett used another possible attitude, which claims that psychology should use experiments to study complex phenomena in their integrity rather than reducing them to their components.

I discarded nonsense material because, among other difficulties, its use almost always weights the evidence in favor of mere rote recapitulation, and for the most part I used exactly the type of material that we have to deal with in daily life. In the many thousands of cases of remembering which I collected, a considerable number of which I have recorded here, literal recall was very rare.

(Bartlett, 1932, p. 204)

In his studies of greatest importance, examining the remembering to strange folk tales, as the famous *War of the ghosts*, Bartlett identified several tendencies in memory formation. The material always undergoes **constructive modifications**. Some parts are left out, some are added, and there is always a construction toward a rational, interpretable storyline. Walter Kintsch (1978, p. 75), a modern cognitive memory researcher, put the issue in present-day terms most clearly: "recall is reproductive, constructive, and reconstructive at the same time, and an important problem is to determine under what conditions one or the other of these aspects predominate." This attitude was far away from the stimulus–response attitude; thus, as Roediger (2000) pointed out, the rediscovery of Bartlett came with modern cognitive psychology. This also went together with the general recognition of the several metaphors entering memory research as analyzed by Draaisma (2000) on a general cultural level and by Danziger (2008) on a more technical level.

This rediscovery is a real phenomenon. If we compare him with Halbwachs, our other hero of memory research, in the PsycINFO database, Halbwachs figures 20 times until the 1980s, and 32 times during his rediscovery. Bartlett, on the other hand, has 172 mentions between 1920 and 1950, 271 between 1950 and 80, and almost 1,200 mentions between 1980 and 2010.

The rediscovery comes in the middle of tensions. Is Bartlett too constructive, and can his schemata be accommodated to more disciplined experimentation? This is discussed under CONTROVERSIES.

Controversies

Memory schematization, constructionism, and the issue of memory traces

The key to the success of Bartlett was to give a new interpretation for the recall of his subjects. When European subjects recalled this folktale of North American natives, full of strange shifts for them, they produced many rationalizations and distortions. The complex fairy tale was recalled sometimes in a concise, sometimes in a more elaborate manner, and always in accordance with the logic of the subjects' own interpretation of the story plot. Remembering was always under the control of the subjects' *"effort after meaning."* Bartlett (1916) introduced this rather loose expression in his earlier studies of elementary picture recognition. He observed that people always try to make some sense of the seemingly meaningless, which creates a non-conscious tension or search. "The fact that when interpretation is hindered in one direction, but it will work out in another, helps to justify the use of the term 'effort after meaning'" (Bartlett, 1916, p. 232).

Bartlett's attitude challenged the notion of memory accuracy and memory trace particularly strongly. "Remembering is not the re-excitation of innumerable, fixed, lifeless, and fragmentary traces. . . . It is an imaginative reconstruction, or construction built out of the relation of our attitude towards a mass of organized past reactions or experiences" (Bartlett, 1932, p. 213). The elements that look like traces in recall are also dynamically determined. "Though we may still talk of traces, there is no reason in the world for regarding these as made complete at one moment, stored up somewhere, and then re-excited at some much later moment" (ibid., pp. 211–212).

Recall is not a repetition of traces but rather a reconstruction based on a **schema** extracted during understanding. Bartlett took over the crucial notion of schema from Sir Henry Head (1861–1940), a proponent of the Jackson-type British evolutionary neurology at Cambridge. For Head (1920), schema forms a stable but, at the same time, dynamic basis of reference in the nervous system that allows the evaluation of body movement – the body schema provides a holistic representation of our own body, in a holistic representation of its momentary position. Bartlett, while showing his holistic biological inspiration, extended and modified this neurological notion. Schemata have a dual meaning in this altered interpretation given to them by Bartlett. They are episodic scaffoldings extracted from the material, which direct the further fate of it (e.g., its recall), but they also correspond to the very process of this extraction of scaffoldings, during which the process of schematization of all our past, and all our personality, interacts with the material at hand.

The meaningful units of human remembering – like any higher cognitive process – are not mosaic-like, meaningless elements that do not refer to anything specific that could be recalled in an all-or-none manner. The "effort for meaning" causes recall to be non-veridical and transformed. Bartlett positioned this vision clearly into his general social attitude regarding mental phenomena. Social patterns and mental schemata go hand in hand. "[Bartlett] took remembering out of the head and situated it at the enfolding relation between the organism and its environment" (Wagoner, 2017a, p. 8).

Interestingly, the analogy of (image) schematization and cultural diffusion was already present in a frequently cited paper of Jean Philippe (1897, p. 497).

It is not only our images that are transformed. . . . [W]e find the same thing regarding our ideas and judgments. With a constant application of the law of economy the useless details fell out and disappeared to make more part for wat is needed for the whole. All normal life develops like this, these transformations represent in small what happens at large in humanity. Through centuries, ideas are born, live and die as the works expressing them, the images supporting them. In this way they reproduce widely of what the transformation of our mental images is but a particular case.

The 80 years that elapsed since the publication of *Remembering* showed clearly the dual nature, that is, the ambiguity of this postulated schematization. Oldfield (1954) presented early on an analysis of the ancestry of schematization. While he concentrated on the possible processes, in later work, the interpretation issue has become the validity of memory schemata (Wagoner, 2013, and the handbook edited by Wagoner, 2017b). Some interpreters of Bartlett highlight its positive aspects, looking for the "gist" in materials and the creation of connections in originally unconnected materials. Others criticize him for over-emphasizing the subjective, transformative, and non-veridical nature of human remembering. Some even claimed that Bartlett had factually over-emphasized the distortions. Roediger (2000) mentioned that the distortive aspects revealed in the rather anecdotal studies of Bartlett have become very important subjects of much later, precise studies on memory distortions. Bartlett gave an experimental flavor to the mundane and philosophical dissatisfaction with the classic psychological memory research by stepping out of the model. He was not like G. E. Müller (Müller & Pilzecker, 1900), or even Binet and Henry (1894), who tried to remedy the Ebbinghaus approach. Bartlett designed and represented a new attitude reinterpreting the entire issue of remembering.

Table 5.4 summarizes some of its enduring features contrasted with another paradigm associated with the name of Ebbinghaus (Chapter 9 in Volume 1).

Table 5.4 Some contrasts of the Ebbinghaus and Bartlett paradigms of memory research

Memory research tradition	Ebbinghaus paradigm	Bartlett paradigm
Typical material	Nonsense, mosaic-like	Meaningful, connected
Research setting	Laboratory, instruments	Real life, interactions
Explanatory principles	Association of elements	Schemata and constructions
Data processing	Quantitative	Qualitative
Attitude of subjects	Elementaristic	Search for meaning

Bartlett also performed the jump that, according to himself, is crucial for the creativity of experimental scientists: he attached distant domains to each other (Bartlett, 1958). In his interpretation of schematization, he turned to processes in neurology, such as body image and skill organization, that we rarely connect with issues of human memory for stories, for example. He also connected experimentation with his anthropological ideas. This connection of fields also assures for Bartlett that the specifically human schematic remembering will not become a Bergsonian organization floating over brains but a function that is *in principio* biological.

Bartlett did not associate with his contemporary parallels. *Gestalt* psychology was too speculative in its physiology for him. The French sociological school, the works of Janet and especially that of Halbwachs, were too near to notions like "group mind" for him.

During the rediscovery of Bartlett from the 1970s on the concept of schema became crucial. The discussion about his legacy has been going on ever since. Is his notion of schema an argument for the overall importance of top-down processes? Are distortions and transformations typical in all situations? Do they increase with repetitions? The critical study of Gauld and Stephenson (1967) partially based skepticism about the mnemonic nature of distortive schematization on arguments of individual differences. Importations and distortions in the works of Bartlett and his followers are frequent only because their subjects showed a lenient, liberal attitude to recall. If we warn them to recall only what is really in the story, their recall will be characterized much more by omissions than by distortions. Especially those subjects who describe themselves as more scrupulous tend to produce fewer additions in recall. Anderson and Bower (1973) generalized on the basis of these studies that the entire process of schematization, that is, processes beyond encoding and storing individual propositions, might well be interpreted as the result of a coherence-producing editorial work during recall. When statistics in experimental design replaced the Bartlett-style qualitative analysis, changes in cognitive psychology "coincided with a reinterpretation of 'reconstruction' to mean that memory was prone to error. As such it became negatively valued, whereas for Bartlett it was linked with flexibility and creativity" (Wagoner, 2017a, p. 76). Bartlett was not interested in the truth value of remembering but in its function.

Several careful studies have put the results of Bartlett to more careful tests than the criticism of Gauld and Stephenson a generation earlier. Bergman and Roediger (1999) showed that with motivated subjects and university-related materials, there is less forgetting, but still, over six months, the recall performance went down to 20% from 60. However, the proportions of major distortions did not increase with repeated recalls. Most interestingly, Roediger et al. (2014; see also in Roediger, 2010) compared serial recall and repeated recall, and they found supportive evidence for the basic ideas of Bartlett. On over four occasions, separated by about four-minute breaks, performance was 50% in repeated recall but dropped to 20% in serial recall. Thus, transmission is a basic cause of transformations and distortions.

While experimental psychologists criticized Bartlett for too much construction, social scientists criticized him for not being sufficiently life-like. Neisser (1982), in one of the trend-setting volumes on the new "ecological theories of memory," claimed that Bartlett was too narrow and still too laboratory-based. Edwards and Middleton (1987), as part of a general argument for a conversation-related extension of Bartlett, criticized that Bartlett was too rigorous and did not allow for free conversation between partners and used the transmission of written recalls. The French anthropologist Morin (2016) pointed out in a more systematic argument that laboratory serial recall cannot be literally taken as a model of cultural transmission for at least two reasons. In typical cultural transmissions, there is always a chance for feedback, and there are always multiple serial channels. Gossip reaches us through different channels. Intrinsic interest, psychological biases, alternative routes, and feedback loops make for the stabilization of real traditions. A stabilization of which Bartlett (1923) was aware early on. Wagoner and Gillespie (2014) also pointed out this wider cultural setting issue regarding the social schematizations observed by Bartlett.

We clearly see today that the processes of remembering cannot be viewed either from the perspective of a sky-walker Don Quixote or from an earthbound Sancho Panza: both directions have to be presupposed. The rather loose concept of schemata allows to interpret them as the inner parts of the perceptual cycle and to cover a two-way, bottom-up, and top-down interpretation cycle, as Neisser (1976) argued.

Some of these standardizing schematizations come from storytelling practices. The key for the simplicity of stories, the special schema that we have been searching for (the schema that is easy, appears early in life, and is universal), should be looked for in the **naive social psychology of human action**. In understanding stories, we mobilize our naive social psychology about the structure of human action and about the usual motives for action. Coherence is found by the hearer-reader through the projection of these motivated action schemata to the story. The specificity of traditional simple stories lies in the fact that due to the prototypical motivations in a given culture and due to the simple and transparent narrative perspective, the action organization can be recovered easily and unequivocally by the listener. Complicated events of real life, and the stories narrating them, are made coherent and understandable by relying on a system of expectations using a model of human action (László, 2004, 2008; Pléh, 2003, 2019). This is in line with the ideas Bartlett (1920, 1923) proposed for the underlying organization of the folk tales.

Bartlett, thus, has become an important inspiratory figure of **constructive memory conceptions** at large. Representatives of this social science constructive movement, Middleton and Crook (1996) happily demonstrate this affinity with a Bartlett quote: "In a world of constantly changing environment, literal recall is extraordinarily unimportant" (Bartlett, 1932, p. 204). For them, Bartlett has become the theoretical support for social constructionism at large. The historian and theoretician of psychoanalysis Erdélyi (2006) claimed similarities in this regard even between Bartlett and the constructive processes emphasized by psychoanalysts.

> The laboratory and the clinic have converged on a simple but fundamental insight: Cognition, from perception to memory, is pervasively constructive. We structure our fragmentary reality by omitting from and elaborating on our meager scraps of information. We try to make sense of our reality, intellectually as well as emotionally.
> (Erdélyi, 2006, p. 511)

Edwards and Middleton (1987) argued that concepts like attitude, emotional direction of recall, the "turn round of our schema," and the reported conversations between the experimenter and his subjects all show that Bartlett, in fact, tried to have a dynamic, metacognition- and reflection-based interpretation of his results.

Social aspects of schematization: Bartlett as a social psychologist

Bartlett did not use the phrase *social psychology* in the subtitle of his two main books loosely. His message was that one should unite experimental and social psychology. That is a rare feature even today. When the memory researcher Roediger (2010) recalled his own education, he realized that even in graduate school, similar series of facts were separately taught as parts of social and as parts of experimental psychology. Bartlett claimed that culture was an interpretative system when he gave an account of story understanding across cultures. Culture as the acquired property of the individual is a system directing understanding and recall. The experimenter can only figure out what his subjects have done if he considers the entire cultural background. Cultural patterns are not a disturbing factor to be reduced in his vision but should be used and studied in understanding memory and thinking. In this regard, Bartlett is a respected ancestor both of contemporary cultural and environmental psychology.

The fitting of ethnography, anthropology, and social psychology, which was a topic of one of his research seminars for a decade, together with the liberal and dynamic interpretation of the cultural embeddedness of thought, was neglected for decades and came up in mainstream social psychology after the 1980s. Rosa (1996) and Middleton and Crook (1996) had done much to rediscover this message of cultural psychology and the attempt to combine anthropology and psychology.

This was the real legacy of Bartlett, not simply the introduction of schemas and other notions that are so important for cognitive psychologists.

> Bartlett's early program points to an intriguing way forward. It was both social and cultural, and points to a dynamic integration of the two, a kind of psychology that takes a social system, cultural practices, and temporal dynamics seriously. The recognition of these three facets of early Bartlett not only leads to a new reading of Bartlett's work, but also points to a possibility for developing a truly "culturally grounded social psychology."
> (Kashima, 2000, p. 384)

At the same time, constructive processes have an explanatory value for cultural studies. Cultural transmission of traditions is similar to the schematizations studied on the individual level, and in a way, as Kashima claims, Bartlett's work can be seen as "a useful launch pad for cultural dynamics research." There is always variation according to Bartlett. This variation always goes together with stabilization. "Stabilization has two basic sources: mechanisms of social control, such as conformity, and the working of certain modular systems that have cognitive preferences. The propagation, stabilization and evolution of cultural representations clearly have a variety of causes" (Sperber & Hirschfeld, 2004, p. 45).

The other well-known work of Bartlett is about thinking (Bartlett, 1958) that fits the image of the complex integrative scientist. Even their titles are parallel: *Thinking: An experimental and social study*. Bartlett's book has some chapters that show original ideas. He charactcrized thinking in open systems based on the works of experimental scientists. The discovery of microorganisms, the history of reaction time research, and the formation of his own memory experiments are presented as historical case studies. Bartlett's message is straightforward and rather provocative: good experimenters are looking for occasions, and they try several dead ends before finding the real sources of analogy. Analogy is a crucial point here. The originality of the experimental scientist lies in finding connections between domains that have never been connected before. Helmholtz saw analogies between the world of sounds and waves of metals, for example.

Contemporary sociologists and historians of science show repeatedly that in contrast to the image of method-centered hierarchical organization of science, real scientific discovery is often flexible and more haphazardly organized (Latour, 1987, 2005; Shapin, 1996). The work of Bartlett gives a very sensitive and educative psychological analysis of this process. He liberates the experimenters from any guilty feelings coming with eclecticism and, at the same time, shows that empirical scientists have always been more flexible regarding their science than theoreticians of science. It is very telling that Bartlett was deliberately using process expressions rather than simple nouns.

> It has to be noted that he consistently uses the gerund (perceiv*ing*, imag*ing*, remember*ing*), and practically never nouns, such as perception, imagery, or thought. I think this use was intentional, serving the purpose of emphasizing

150   *Disciplinary developments and eclectics*

the active character of psychological processes, which results from his functionalist approach.

(Rosa, 1996, p. 365)

Modern cognitive psychology discovered an ancestor in Bartlett, who looked for the complex structures of the mind not in introspections but in life-like experiments. At the same time, his affinity to social psychology has a broader message as well: issues of human tradition, culture, self, and memory are intimately related.

The semiotic conception of Karl Bühler

Due to his extremely varied and rich professional profile, it is very hard to classify the work of Karl Bühler (1879–1963), even in the frames of a history of psychology book. He was a pioneer of experimental psychology investigating thought processes, an early synthesizer of child psychology, a theoretician of language structure and function, placing the renewal of psychology on a complex vision of language, and an early theoretician of the multiple variation–selection cycles. Still, he fits into this chapter very organically, as he was emphasizing the importance of social life within psychology with his signal-based articulation of mental life.

Bühler had a medical education as well as a philosophy degree, but he was attracted to psychology early on. As one of the leading researchers of the Würzburg school of thought processes (working there with Külpe), he became a proponent for the psychological reality of abstract thoughts (Bühler, 1908; see Chapter 9 in Volume 1). He was also among the first theoretician of Gestalt phenomena (Bühler, 1913), though his approach was treated as "too analytic" by the Berlin gestalt group. As abstract as this research seems to be, during this work, Bühler introduced the concept of **Aha experience** (*Aha Erlebnis*) to describe the sudden recognition of new insights and connections between ideas. Similarly, as one of his other "brand words," in fact, criticizing Sigmund Freud's supposed wish-fulfilment image of man, Bühler proposed the notion of **functional pleasure** (*Funktionslust*): the recognition that functions are practiced because their practice itself is a source of pleasure (Bühler, 1922). He described it to be very crucial in child development but also in several aspects of human culture.

In his elaborate system, Bühler proposes a triad of fundamental "drives" or motivation systems, stemming from three variations of the experience of pleasure: (a) pleasure coming from the satisfaction of need; (b) pleasure coming from activity, from functioning; and (c) pleasure coming from creative work.

(Bugental et al., 1966, p. 198)

These complex motivations have become central in modern motivation theories from Gordon Allport and others.

After serving in the war as a medical doctor, and following Külpe to Bonn and Munich, Bühler became a professor at the Dresden Technical University, and then

Social theories of the mind 151

Figure 5.6 Karl Bühler.
Source: Wikimedia commons, public domain.

from 1922 to 1938 at the Institute of Psychology at Vienna University. Working together with his wife, Charlotte Bühler, he turned this institute into one of the main centers of psychology in the German-speaking world between the two wars (Ash, 1980, 1988). Bühler and his wife were also leaders of the Austrian pedology movement. Technically, Karl Bühler fulfilled two functions: one as a university professor, and another as an adjunct leader at the Pedagogy Institute of the city of Vienna. The university life was the scene of the more theoretical and experimental works, together with people like Egon Brunswik, Lajos Kardos, and Paul Lazarsfeld. While the Pedagogy Institute was responsible for fostering a socialist-inspired educational reform, both in teaching and in test development, with moves toward a less authority-based and a more child-oriented education. Charlotte Bühler went to the United States for a year as a Rockefeller scholar and developed a taste for observation-based psychological tests of young children, which she standardized and published (Bühler & Hetzer, 1932). Charlotte Bühler (1933) also published

152 *Disciplinary developments and eclectics*

on puberty and its signs in journals of adolescents, on the matter of using personal documents in psychological assessment, and on the adult life course as a psychological problem. These topics continued in her work that she carried out as part of the humanistic psychology movement in the United States (see chapter 11).

Karl Bühler (1922) himself had a crucial role in working out the theoretical framework for child development studies in Vienna, with five German and three English editions of his developmental psychology textbook. His book, besides its general Darwinian outlook, is a basic textbook mainly about the preschool years. Compared to similar textbooks, it has a number of interesting peculiarities: the constant use of comparative psychology examples and analogies in interpreting the instinct, habit, and intellect triad of children, the important role attributed to language and drawing, and an excellent portrayal of infant social behavior.

The institute led by Karl Bühler had an outstanding collection of students and assistants and made contacts with many circles outside psychology as well, including the Vienna Circle of philosophers, and the city agents for progressive education. The institute was visited by many foreign scholars, including Americans, like Tolman, and Karl Bühler had good contact even with US founding agencies, such as the Rockefeller Foundation, supporting the empirical work of the institute and the postdoctoral scholarships of his students. The *Anschluss*, practically the Nazi invasion of Austria, ended this flourishing institute. Bühler was arrested, most likely for his openly expressed liberal political views, and when released, he immigrated to the United States through Norway, together with his wife. In the United States, Charlotte Bühler (1893–1974) followed a successful career as a clinical psychologist and became a central actor of the newly formed "third force," that is, the humanistic psychology movement. Karl Bühler, however, was not so successful. In the behavioristic and positivistic framework of psychological science in the United States, Karl Bühler had lost his impact. He held some college teaching jobs and worked also as a clinical psychologist, but his life and work in the United States was of a frustrated great European man in a strange social setting. In 1960, he was the honorary president of the international psychology conference in Bonn, receiving the highest price of the German psychological association, and later, he was also decorated by Vienna University.

I will present three central and interconnected aspects of the multifaceted work of Karl Bühler: his approach to the assumed crisis of psychology, his theory about the functions of language, and his general ideas about production and selection cycles in the interpretation of the mind. In all three areas, Bühler had an interesting combination of functionalism (which he developed even toward anti-Cartesian historical remarks), an evolutionary interpretation of the mind, and a social theory of mind.

Bühler on the divisions of psychology and the primacy of meaningful organization

As a professor in Dresden, and later, for almost two decades, in Vienna, Karl Bühler (1927) elaborated a sign-based theory of mental organization and a communication-based, semiotic theory of the mind. The features of his rich oeuvre can be summarized as a series of foundational theses, all colored with a strong evolutionary commitment. The evolutionary aspects are highlighted with bold letter type.

1. **All behavior is regulated by signs.**
2. Human behavior is oriented to supraindividual meanings. **All human behavior has three aspects: experience, behavior, and reference to the world (including the symbolic world).**
3. All behavior is characterized by holistic organization aimed at species-specific signals. **Structure, meaning, and goals characterize all behaviors.**

These three main principles unite comparative psychology and the value-oriented cultural psychology as well. Bühler (1927) outlined his mature theoretical position in an influential book on the supposed crisis of psychology. Bühler started from the behaviorist, the *Gestalt*-based, and the *Geistwissenschatfliches* critique of classical experimental psychology. Bühler abstracted three basic parameters of the assumed crisis of psychology: (1) the problem of mechanistic explanation, (2) the indirect study of hidden processes, and (3) the subjectivity–objectivity issue. Bühler tried to overcome the controversies among the internalist, the behavioral, and the culturalist approaches to the human mind and the task of psychology in the 1920s and 1930s. He belonged to the class of those Central European scholars who were looking for a meaningful unity in their science while being aware of the divisive naturalistic and spiritualistic trends. The following quote shows how relevant his attitude is even for contemporary debates of the study of the human mind.

> When someone raises a new topic, why does he have to look down scientifically on his neighbor? In the large house of psychology there is room for everyone; one could direct his spectacles on the skyline of values from the attic, others could at least claim for themselves the basement of psychophysics, while the walls are intended to put the entire enterprise into the causal chain of events.
>
> (Bühler, 1927, p. 142)

Contrary to the postulation of a split within psychology between natural science and human science, proposed by the followers of Dilthey (1894), such as Spranger (1926), Bühler postulated meaningful organization as a characteristic of all behavior and not a specificity of the human mind. Behavior should also be interpreted in new ways. It is always a self-initiated activity, never simply reactive, as most behaviorists would like it to be. Not even animals – and certainly not humans – can be regarded as merely reactive creatures, as mere automata. Organisms always attempt to construct a model of their environment. In this modeling activity, the role of Darwinian selection and its broader interpretation is pivotal for Bühler (1922, 1936).

Early ethologists, such as Heinroth, Uexküll, and Konrad Lorenz, clearly described factors in the unraveling of animal behavior (see Lorenz, 1965, for a review): species-specific behavioral patterns, releasing stimuli, and critical experiences. Karl Bühler tried to unify psychology by relying on these early ethological principles. The key element in this unification account was the idea that all behavior – from the simplest animal behavior to human culture–creating behaviors – is assumed to be meaningful.

He based his argument on a quasi-syllogistic form regarding psychology and the structure and function of human language. In a theory of language, one has to deal with three functions (expression, direction, reference). Language is central for psychology as well; thus, the three aspects must play a crucial, obligatory, and complementary role in psychology as well (Bühler, 1927).

Bühler was not the first to talk about a crisis in psychology. As Mülberger (2012) and Sturm and Mülberger (2012) analyzed it, there were discussions of crisis already in the late 19th century, insisting that psychology had become too varied and disunited. This was followed by works like that of Kostyleff (1911) and continued by Driesch (1925). Bühler did not deny the existence of a crisis, nor did he claim that everything has to be started again from scratch, as Kostyleff (1911) suggested, for example, by proposing a reflexology-based psychology. Bühler wanted to show that it is a structural crisis that can be solved by a conceptual reanalysis. "Bühler's concept of crisis is not bound to the assumption that a crisis is typically solved by a revolution that replaces one paradigm by another one. Rather, different approaches can and should be integrated" (Sturm, 2012, pp. 470–471.) Many treated this as eclecticism, and many disliked the fact that Bühler saw a linguistically based solution to the crisis, by using the three facets of language as a model for a reconstruction of the entirety of psychology.

The three functions theory of language

Bühler developed his three aspects theory of mental life as an extension of his general theory of language. He arrived at this vision through studying sentence understanding and the German case system and published an elaborated general framework for the system of language in 1934, which was published in English in 1990, and in French in 2009 (Bühler, 1990, 2009). Thus, its message (over 10,000 citations) is still valid. His theory is a self-proclaimed **organon model**, referring to the logical theory of Aristotle. It is a conceptual framework, starting from "axioms" that treat language not in an abstract way but as an instrument of communication. Human language has, by necessity, three functions: (a) it has an experiential, inner, first-person reference, thus is an **expression** (*Ausdruck*); (b) it has a relation to other people's behavior, that is, it has a **directive function** (*Appel*); and (c) most specifically, it **represents something** from the external world, thus is a symbol (*Darstellung*), as shown in Figure 5.7.

Each aspect is always present in every use of linguistic signs. In this regard, the model of Bühler, which he calls axiomatic, is indeed more axiomatic then the later, communication- and information theory–based model proposed by Roman Jakobson (1960). Jakobson openly relies on Bühler's ideas and Shannon and Weaver's

Social theories of the mind 155

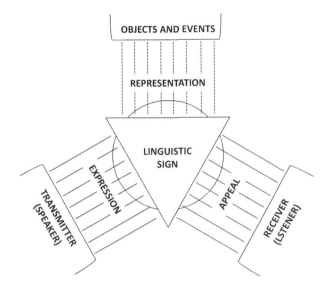

Figure 5.7 Adapted from the three functions of linguistic signs according to Bühler.
Source: Bühler (1934).

(1949) mathematical communication theory, where they propose a model of communication based on partners, contexts, channels, codes, and messages, with a function attached to each. Jakobson proposed that each communicative act is dominated by one message function rather than the obligatory three functions as outlined by Bühler.

The theory of language presented by Bühler in 1934 combined his *Gestalt* engagements with the structural principles of modern linguistics and the theory of the use of language embedded into its relation to the extralinguistic situation and the social relations of the partners. With the extralinguistic embeddings, Bühler created links to the logical aspects of language (reference, deixis, etc.) and to modern speech act theory and even theory of mind. The essence of all sign systems was social coordination for Bühler. In order to understand the semantics of signs, we have to start off from the community of sign producers and sign receivers: "the origin of semantics has to be looked for not in the individuum, but in the community" (Bühler, 1927, p. 38). The referential function has a specific aspect in human language: linguistic signs refer to objects and states of affairs (events) through mobilizing a supraindividual world of coordination and meaning. In this respect, Bühler incorporates into his language theory the message he learned from Külpe (1912) in Würzburg, and from Husserl (1900/2010). Signs of human language obtain their object reference through a supraindividual logical intentionality. In human language, there is a hierarchy among the three functions. The descriptive and intellectual function is always the leading one, like the representative function of mental entities in Brentano. We can express emotions mainly by naming things, and the same holds for the directive functions. At the same time, Bühler was not insensitive to what we would call today the "expressive aspects of speech." He claimed that while the referential function is the basic and defining function of human language, tone of speech, interjections, and other elementary features of our speech channel are also used to express emotions.

The supraindividual semantic is the foundation of the existence of a human sphere of thoughts. Regarding the social aspect, two moments are worth emphasizing. First, in line with his biological ideas, Bühler does not consider social life to be exclusively human; it appears in animal societies as well. Bühler used two elements in his criticism of simplifying physicalist theories of behavior. One is the social element, which is shown in his *Crisis* book (Bühler, 1927) via the analysis of social intentionality in dogfights and in many other examples. The social aspect in humans is not a secondary external regulation but a constitutive moment. He puts it rather clearly: social life needs coordination, and in this regard, semantics is always social. By developing the descriptive function, animal signal systems increase their efficiency of social coordination.

1. Where there is real social life, there is a need to coordinate meaningful behaviors of the members of the community. Since the reference points of this coordination are not given in a common perception, they have to be provided with a higher order contact, specifically with semantic dispositions.
2. Individual needs or dispositions have to be manifested somehow and these manifestations have to be noticed in order for them to be validated in the joint enterprise.
3. By coordinating signs with objects and states of affairs, they do obtain a new semantic dimension. And due to this process, their communicative efficiency increases importantly.

(Bühler, 1927, pp. 50–51).

For Bühler, the central issue in the study of language use was the role of grammar, or linguistic organization at large. He claimed the **structure dependence of the value of individual items**. He combined linguistic structuralism with his commitment to Gestalts in the organization of all psychology. Bühler believed that each linguistic sign obtains its function only with reference to the entire system of signs. On the other hand, signs in combinations form new units, often by rounding up meanings.

Karl Bühler's concentration on the "descriptive function of language" was accompanied by a hypothesis of constant joint social work and coordination between speakers and hearers. While the representational function is crucial, it does not passively determine our vision of the world through language. Bühler treats the representational function in a mediating way: symbolic language drives representation in a dynamic way, much like an instruction system for the hearer to look for things in the real world. This idea is spelled out in detail in his theories of deixis, anaphora, and the relation between the perceptual–deictic and the symbolic fields.

His framework is a complex foundation both for linguistics and for the psychology of language, which treats language as a sophisticated biological and social system, where the biological and social are not in contrast or opposition. One point is missing from the theory, and this is very interesting regarding the history of psycholinguistics. Bühler, just like the other great synthesizer of language and psychology a generation earlier, Wilhelm Wundt, did not intend to connect and confirm his axiomatic and theoretical approach to language with his experimental inspiration. Psycholinguistics remained for Bühler a theoretical chapter within psychology. There were most likely two aspects missing to turn psycholinguistics into an experimental chapter. The lack of technical means to easily manipulate and register language stimuli, which came with magnetic sound recording and analysis systems. Bühler and his generation were also missing language statistics and information theory that later allowed researchers to characterize linguistic stimuli, words, and sounds, and even sentences, as independent variables, with numbers.

Extension of evolutionary ideas to the development of behavior

Bühler tried to identify qualitative changes using Darwinian principles both in the evolution of behavior and in child development. During the 1920s and 1930s, he continued the Darwinian tradition both of Ernst Mach and of James Baldwin. He differentiated levels of instinct, habit, and intelligence both in child development and in animal behavior, which corresponds to his general attitude of trying to establish biological foundations for psychology. Bühler proposed an evolutionary organization for behavior complete with superposed levels of selection. In interpreting the Darwinian message to psychology, he postulated a universal metatheory of selection, with three levels. The selectionist metatheory came as a way to integrate the different attitudes within his works. As part of incorporating selectionist explanations to different domains, Bühler (1922) also extended Mach's (1905) idea of seeing hypotheses and trial and error everywhere. He proposed a continuity between instinct, trial-and-error learning, and intellect and the domain of selection being, respectively, the organism, behavior, and ideas. Thorndike (1898) had already interpreted trial-and-error learning with a selectionist terminology. The third level also appears in the famous experiments of Köhler (1921) on chimpanzees, where insight comes as a selection of "ideas," as an entirely internal process, with no visible solution attempts. "For me, the concept of play field in Darwinism seems to be productive. Darwin has known basically only one such play field, while I point to three of them. . . . These three play fields are: instinct, habit and intellect" (Bühler, 1922, p. VIII). The main point about the relationship between the three levels – as expressed rather definitively by Karl Popper, a disciple of Bühler (Popper, 1972) – is that instead of risking survival as in Darwinian evolution, we are only risking our ideas in intellectual selection.

The three systems (Table 5.5) of instinct, habit, and intelligence always strive to construct a model of their environment. All behavioral organization is characterized by an early stage, where a rich and redundant inventory of behavior is formed,

158 *Disciplinary developments and eclectics*

Table 5.5 Three levels and pools of selection according to Bühler

Features	Instinct	Habit	Intellect
Pool of selection	Individuals	Behaviors	Thoughts
Roads to selection	Darwinian selection	Reinforcement	Insight
Proofs	Species-specific behavior	Associations, new combinations	Detour
Representative author	Volkelt, Driesch	Thorndike	Köhler
Organization	"Naturplan"	Associative net	Mental order

with an excessive number of elements and associations, and a later, selective stage, where certain patterns are chosen on the basis of environmental feedback.

Karl Bühler made these principles and levels central to his idea about child development as well. The three levels appear in children in a gradual manner. As his interpreters underlined it:

> The process of humanization is structured into three "stages" (a) that of the dominance of instinct during the first weeks after birth; (b) that of "training" (*Dressur*); and (c) that of the beginning of an intellectual life, which is distinguished by the use of tools. It is hypothesized by Bühler that these different stages are determined by the maturation of different brain areas, especially that of the brain stem and the cortex with its various functional units.
> (Bugental et al., 1966, p. 197)

Most interestingly, he connected his theory of motivation as well to the three proposed levels. Trial and error are possible due to functional pleasure, and human intelligence is possible due to creative drives.

The influence of Karl Bühler on psychology

The intention-based, teleological, and holistic organization and the unity between the world of biology and that of the mind were very attractive features of the "Vienna school." The Vienna Psychology Institute and the teacher training center were central in training a new brand of psychologists who were biologically minded, rejecting the division between experimental and understanding psychology. They also tried to elaborate some aspects of the framework provided by Bühler. Vienna was also a center in the sense that psychologists from other schools also showed up here, like Tolman, and the progressive Bühler had students recruited from other disciplines as well (Eschbach, 1984). Even Wittgenstein most likely took classes with him for his teaching license, and Karl Popper had his PhD with Bühler. One of the founders of modern ethology, Konrad Lorenz, was also associated with the Institute, and it is easy to recognize in his vision some ideas that originated from Bühler, such as the goal-directedness of behavior and selection regarding behavior. Table 5.6 shows a summary of the followers of Bühler in his time.

Table 5.6 Students and followers of Karl Bühler and some of their ideas

Topic	Student, follower	Continued topic
Gestalten	Ludwig Kardos, Egon Brunswik	Constancies, sign theory of perception
Animal behavior	Konrad Lorenz, Paul (Harkai) Schiller	Releasers, behavior evolution
Language functions	Popper, Lorenz, Kardos, Jakobson	Anthropogenesis, culture, representations
Selection in development	Lorenz, Popper, F. Hayek, Harkai	Selectionist theory of knowledge, competition of ideas

The table presents the breadth of his impact on 20th-century intellectual life. Bühler's work had two characteristic features that are in good harmony with the later development of the work of his students. The first notable idea was the integration of early ethology into the natural foundations of psychology, and the second was his emphasis on a functionalist biological view, that is, the focus on the organization of behavior rather than its simple psychophysiological description. There is no saltation in behavioral development; rather, it is gradualism and the organizing force of selection all over the place that characterize it.

The philosopher Karl Popper was a student of Bühler for quite a long time and wrote his dissertation on the experimental psychology of thought under the supervision of Bühler. Popper (1934), in his philosophy of science, became the most important follower of Bühler during and after his years in Vienna. One central aspect of the influence of Bühler on Popper is Popper's (1972, 1976) idea of a disembodied world 3, which relies on the representative function of language, as initially outlined by Bühler (1934). Popper (1972, 1976) extended the theory of language functions proposed by Bühler to postulate a fourth function, the argumentative function of language, that would be the key to the development of science.

Popper also extended the ideas of Bühler about selectionist models of development. First, Popper (1972) reinterpreted the development of science as a Darwinian selection mechanism: theories are proposed, and the research community selects among them. In his Spencer lectures, Popper characterized the analogy between thinking and natural selection in the following way: "the growth of our knowledge is the result of a process closely resembling what Darwin called 'natural selection'; that is *the natural selection of hypotheses*" (Popper, 1972, p. 261).

During the 1970s, Popper articulated a comprehensive theory, **evolutionary epistemology**, as it came to be cited. His proposal worked out the selectionist vision in great detail (see Chapter 7 in Volume 1 and Chapter 10 in Volume 2). All changes follow a problem-solving strategy, where a first stage is characterized by a proliferation of proposals, and later, an independent cycle selects among them. In the consecutive selection cycles, the criteria of selection are different, but the organizing principle is the same: abundance followed by selection. Ter Hark (2007) shows in a historical reconstruction how this is related to the work of young Popper on the analysis of problem solving.

There are, of course, several concerns with this proposal, especially regarding the production–selection duality. As the Hungarian-Belgian philosopher Nánay (2011) analyzed in detail, the issue is whether all "hypotheses phases" remain random and "mutationist" or if there are any Lamarckian feedback loops. Another controversial aspect of this model, however, is anti-inductionism. Popper tried to reunite epistemology and psychology via a criticism of naive inductionism. There is no knowledge without hypotheses; there is nothing that we could call "an innocent eye." In line with his critique of induction, all knowledge starts from questions – and in this respect, he recognized an interesting parallel between everyday knowledge processes of "ordinary beings" and matters of science. In Popper's evolutionary epistemology, whatever he says of science and of "ordinary knowers," of their psychology and biology, are united in a way not unlike at the beginnings of modernity.

The issue of induction in science, claims the mature Popper, can be resolved by reminding ourselves that in general, there is no uninstructed, empty organism. All acquisition (learning) starts off from a hypothesis. In simple cases, the hypotheses are provided by the evolutionary genetic heritage (Popper, 1972, p. 259). In the most complicated cases of modern science, they are provided by scientific tradition, by a "state of the art."

Donald Campbell (1959, 1974), the excellent methodologist and social psychologist, and himself a follower of Popper, gave the most exhaustive list of what was available as levels of behavior and levels of selection before the onset of modern cognitive science (see Chapter 7 in Volume 1).

Following the footsteps of Bühler, Popper (1972) and Campbell (1974) see an emergent evolutionary relationship between these levels: they are not only homologues but are also assumed to have a common causal history. This "forgotten Viennese tradition" has been reassessed lately through the work of Popper and turned into the self-reflection of present-day cognitive science. Bühler's three levels roughly correspond to what Dennett (1994, 1997a) calls the tower of selection, in other words, the embeddedness and hierarchy of Darwinian, Skinnerian, and Popperian creatures. Kesserling (1994) even shows that this Darwinian epistemology has similarities to the developmental epistemology promoted by Piaget.

Bühler, as recalled on the occasion of his 80th birthday, had a deep influence on many aspects of American social science, though his personal fate was far from being a success. The Vienna style of departmental organization, with many interdisciplinary contacts and a parallel interest toward development, both in children and adults, and the complex analysis of behavior both form a motivational and a value point of view were his broad effects taken over by his former Vienna students (Lazarsfeld, 1959). From the 1960s on, both in psychology and in linguistics, many authors claimed that Karl Bühler was unduly forgotten. In the last few decades, on the other hand, several linguists claimed that it was time to reconsider his importance, and it was time to realize the contemporary relevance of the theory of language he proposed. It is worth balancing this pessimism and enthusiasm and take a look at the existing impact of Bühler.

Early social models of the mind: a summary

The mid-20th-century social models of the human mind discussed in this chapter are rather varied in what they take as a new reference point for psychology. They all share the discontent of the dominant great schools – behaviorism, Gestalt, psychoanalysis – with classical psychology. However, they saw the different solutions by looking for reference frames mostly in other areas of social life or in other scientific disciplines. They do not form a coherent cohort, but it is still interesting and relevant to try to summarize them. Figure 5.8 shows them arranged in a manner highlighting the disciplinary resources they relied on.

The interdisciplinary relations between different fields talking about the social mind mainly commuted the researchers – themselves coming outside psychology many times but having psychological claims – to propose clear (or sometimes opaque) causal claims. Most of the time, they entertained some centrifugal image, where the broader social factors would account for the structure or even the content of the individual mind. Figure 5.9 presents these causal claims.

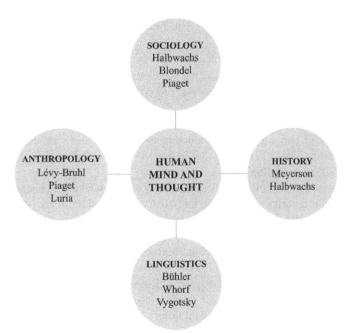

Figure 5.8 The interdisciplinary relations proposed by the different psycho-social theories of the mind.

162 *Disciplinary developments and eclectics*

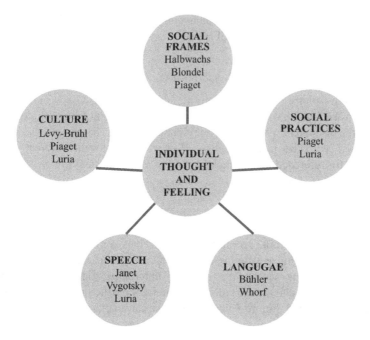

Figure 5.9 Assumed causal relations between individual thought and the "external" social determinants.

When evaluating these theories as the products of social factors of their times, it is worth remembering that social theories of knowledge appeared in three domains during the interwar period:

- In child development as a continuation of the interactive frame introduced by Baldwin (1894, 1911) and Mead (1934) and in the works of Vygotsky (1934/1986) and Wallon (1934).
- In the social theories of individual psychology, reviewed in this chapter.
- In the social theories of scientific knowledge proposed by Fleck (1935), Mannheim (1936, 1952), and Polanyi (1946/1964).

As for the intriguing issue of relations between social frames, culture, and the individual mind, the anthropologist Dan Sperber (1985, 1996) proposed a sober and balanced theory that might be good to keep in mind in our historical judgment as well. His central idea is the **epidemiological model**. According to him, representations are carried in individual minds, but in the social realms, these representations show certain patterns of spreading. The relationship between cultural practices and individual thinking is the same as between internal medicine and epidemiology.

I believe that neither reductionism nor anti-reductionism make much sense in this case, and that the epidemiological analogy provides a more plausible approach.... What I want to suggest with the epidemiological analogy is that psychology is necessary but not sufficient for the characterization and explanation of cultural phenomena. Cultural phenomena are ecological patterns of psychological phenomena. They do not pertain to an autonomous level of reality, as anti-reductionists would have it; nor do they merely belong to psychology as reductionists would have it.

(Sperber, 1996, pp. 59–60)

Tasks

CA

"Primitive thought" in Lévy-Bruhl, Piaget, and Luria.
The concept of "collective memory" and "collective representation" today.
Compare linguistic relativity and cultural relativity.
The concept of "schema" in Bartlett and Piaget.
The effects of contemporary ICT on social relations.
Emotions and the language functions of Bühler.
The memory cultivation today and the concept of collective memory.
Relations between evolutionary and cultural selection.

DSA

"Memory cultivation" and "memory wars" in common discourse (Google Ngram).
Halbwachs, Lévy-Bruhl, Bühler, and Bartlett over a hundred years in public discourse (Google Ngram).
Halbwachs, Lévy-Bruhl, Bühler, and Bartlett over a hundred years in psychology (PsycINFO).
Co-occurrences of Bartlett and Ebbinghaus in psychological texts (PsycINFO).
The concept of "functions of language" in psychology (PsycINFO).

6 The formation of modern social psychology

Formation of social psychology as a central chapter

In Chapter 5, we dealt with theories of the development of the social mind, theories that emphasize the representation of social content in the mind, and the impact of societal forces on the mind. In this chapter, we concentrate on theories that deal with the interaction processes and their reflection in the mind. Social relations and their role in framing the individual habits, success, and mood have always been a central interest to humans. When modern social sciences started to take shape in the second half of the 19th century, several new efforts concentrated on **social groups** and on **human interactions**, the two cornerstones of later social psychology. There is an interesting historical reconstruction issue here: in searching for our past, who do we treat as **ancestors** and who do we treat as actual **founders** of social psychology? Auguste Comte, John Stuart Mill, and Karl Marx were certainly ancestors and not founders, while, for example, Wundt or Baldwin were certainly important toward the future social psychology but still did not have a clear empirical following to be considered as founders (Farr, 1996). Jahoda (2007), in his essayistic textbook on the history of social psychology, has a chapter on 18th-century Enlightenment precursors of social psychology and a long chapter on 19th-century gestation. This latter chapter includes the speculative Herbartian "social psychology," early empirical statistical and economic work, speculations on universality and particularity in relating humans to their culture by J. S. Mill and Comte, and of course, *Völkerpsychologie* and crowd psychology. These are all ancestors. In this chapter, I will mainly consider those ancestors that went parallel to the articulation of individuum-based empirical psychology in late 19th century and then turn on to real founders from the Allport brothers to Kurt Lewin.

There are interesting historical relations between articulation of the different social disciplines and the actual social practices and historical events. Social sciences in general developed in relation to great cultural changes. For example, anthropology came about through the meeting with "the other" as a result of travels and colonialization. Similarly, there is no economy without market economics, no linguistics without writing systems, and no modern literary scholarship without the spread of literacy. Social sciences developed as metacognitive chapters reflecting on existing social practices, at times and when the given social practices became central issues in the given society and when particular natural sciences were taking shape. We may consider that social psychology was also a "meta turn," a reflection on the existing interindividual and intergroup processes. Two special forces were responsible for the birth of modern social psychology. On the one hand, the rise of nationalism in 19th-century Europe and the creation of **modern political movements**, including working-class movements and the accompanying mass events in big cities. As van Ginneken (1992) showed in his analysis of the genesis of mass psychology, working-class movements played a role in the first historical treatment of crowds by Taine and in the speculative theory of mass psychology of Le Bon, with the experience of the Commune of Paris, May Day demonstrations, and the rise of new military Bonapartist movements. This led to theoretical considerations of the foundation of national integration processes, the issue of national differences, the analysis of the rise of group mentalities, and crowd processes. Another possible factor was the increased **social interaction among strangers** in the everyday life of big cities, the rise of secondary and constantly changing social groups. This was related to compulsory schooling and military service, to the advent of big factories with their issues of work organization and leadership. This was followed by the effects of mass media with the advent of radio and television and earlier daily journalism. This resulted in theories of communication and persuasion. These factors may have contributed to the increased consciousness of understanding regulations in our social behavior. Several historical accounts also showed the importance of wars (the American Civil War, both world wars, and later, the Vietnam War) and dramatic social events, like the Great Depression in the 1930s, in the birth of professional social psychology.

There is a feedback issue here as well, as pointed out by Kruglanski and Stroebe (2012) in their handbook on the history of social psychology. The emerging new social sciences, among them social psychology, did influence social life on their part. The existence of opinion polls changed party politics as well as our attitudes about conformist behaviors. The work of Kinsey and his coworkers (1948, 1953) or Masters and Johnson (1966) also changed our opinions about and practices of sex. All the obedience studies in the 1960s–1970s (Milgram, 1963, 1974; Zimbardo, 1973) changed our views about humans as autonomous agents.

On the intellectual and substantial side, the topics that created what we consider modern social psychology evolved most transparently from American social pragmatism, from the studies of work efficiency, from the first interest in group processes and interactions, and from an analysis of childhood development from a social perspective. These initiatives, by the 1930s, formed what continue to be successful chapters of modern psychology.

An account of the history of social psychology is made complicated by the variability of the issues dealt with within social psychology. Group processes, attitudes, and socialization all do have their own history, their own micro theories and schools, and they are not equally promoted by different comprehensive movements of social psychology. In some stages over 100 years, group processes (and, at other times, attitude dynamics and social cognition) played a central role, while socialization was sometimes centered and sometimes neglected. With the pendulums shifting, these differences led to many debates on the history and focal point of the field. A second issue is the intricate relations between general schools of psychology, such as behaviorism, psychoanalysis, *Gestalt*, or cognitive psychology, and their impact and influence on social psychology. Changing social conditions did raise the issue of alternative theories. All these factors lead to alternative accounts of history, which are illustrated under CONTROVERSIES.

Controversies

Alternative histories of social psychology

Gordon Allport (1954/1985), the then "dean of American social psychology," published a now-classic and highly debated handbook chapter which surveyed these developments, as a kind of court history, with a thoroughly discussed concentration on Comte as forerunner. It also bashed and neglected much of the German beginnings, especially the *Völkerpsychologie* of Wundt. This was all the more surprising since Allport had a thorough education in matters of German social sciences. As all surveys go, it was reprinted in several times, and as Lubek (1993) showed, sufficient attention was given to the double origins of social psychology in psychology proper and in social science/sociology at large. From 1968 on, in a rather presentist manner, almost exclusive attention was paid to the birth of experimental social psychology, moving away from sociology toward exclusively psychology and toward experimentation. Moscovici (1925–2014), the French critical social psychologist, who introduced social representation and minority influence into the mainframe discourse of social psychology, stated in a short historical witty note that social psychology from a historical perspective suffered from two basis issues. First, whether it had to go along with social science or with psychology, an issue that extends throughout its history.

> Social psychology was originally conceived as a place where two disciplines (sociology and psychology) could meet and interact. In the course of time however, an exclusive relationship was established with psychology, of which it became something like a secondary branch. . . . If we were reduced to psychology alone, how could we explain whatever general principle we have, and how we have so painstakingly elaborated the established facts? And as we cease more and more to be a bridge between the fields of reality, to act as a mediator or as a matchmaker between the two ways of thinking, we lose all our importance for both.
>
> (Moscovici, 1993, p. 27)

The second issue is to decide who is doing it: the protagonists themselves (as is the case of most medical history) or professional historians (like in the history of mathematics). Social psychology chose the first option, which also means that since history is written mostly by major participants, there is substantial metahistory criticizing the historians themselves. Moscovici (1993) also remarked that there was a threefold division. Gourmand usage presents the full menu, gourmet usage shows forgotten heroes and traditions, and there is an exotic one that juxtaposes different traditions with no communication between themselves. He himself was calling for a gourmand history, presenting the entire menu. This is the intention of this chapter, together with Chapter 5, too, with some gourmet excursions toward neglected key concepts and players.

There were many events along this line, resulting in different versions of critical and emancipatory social psychology. Morawski (2012), in her handbook chapter, gives a sober new emphasis on trying to relate social history to social psychology. There are three issues in her account: historical effects on data, on methods, and on theories. Why were there, for example, so many interpretations of reflexivity in social psychology and on the status of the experiment from the 1970s on? These were related to the social tensions in America during the 1960s–1970s and its social transformations (civil rights, emancipation, feminist movements) as well as the wars. Were our experiments really relevant to these pressing social issues? Ironically, while this self-analysis went on, the entire social psychology has become even more scientific by the cognitive and neuroscience moves.

Mainstream social psychology compared to its beginning has become gradually depoliticized in the 1970s. See the handbooks edited by Lindzey (1954), Maccoby et al. (1958), and by Lindzey and Aaronson (1968). It has lost its original impetus of providing a basis for social sciences and social policies between the 1930s and 1960s. This depoliticization, probably as a disappointment over the Vietnam War, was mainly true for the 1970s–1990s. It is no longer true for the last two decades, as the critical psychology movement and the arrival of political psychology has renewed this interest again.

While Gordon Allport, in his classical chapter of 1954, and modern European presentations like Farr (1996) showed the relevance both of the representational trends in early French sociology and the early interactionists like Tarde and Baldwin, many new American treatments largely glossed over in these early developments. Le Bon as well as *Völkerpsychologie* lost their historical interest because they were neither experimental nor statistical. This is an unfortunate neglect, since the issue of relating representation to interaction is a key to contemporary social psychology, and this was crucial, for example, in their visions of imitation in their own, even in the first American textbook of Ross (1908). For James Baldwin (1894), the social aspect was the center of individual psychology, and this aspect related psychology to social sciences at large. That was also true, as pointed out by Robert Farr (1936–2013) of the London School of Economics, for the Chicago school and especially for G. H. Mead time (Farr, 1990, 1991). In a way, social psychology has gradually become a discipline that has treated all old-style societal approaches as prehistory, and in this regard, from 1968 on, a clear American European division emerged. With Moscovici, Tajfel, Farr, and even those in Eastern Europe, like Ferenc Erős (2017) and János László (László & Wagner, 2003), European social psychology has been regaining its societal vocation, while American social psychology remained individuum-centered.

The issue about the primacy of interest toward the history of the experimental approaches, and neglecting the societal elements, has continued since. The issue of alternative historical reconstructions touches upon the contacts and boundaries of psychology and sociology. It also depends on what kind of sociology we relate to psychology. Some sociologies deal with social macro phenomena. In this case, the competencies of psychology are clearly differentiated from those of sociology. In those schools of sociology that concentrate on roles, it is difficult to see a clear, logical demarcation between microsociology and social psychology. In many cases, it has been a historical accident who is considered to be a sociologist and who is a social psychologist. In the late 20th century, rule-based interactional theories of sociology, such as Goffman (1959, 1974) or Garfinkel (1967), also analyze everyday interaction phenomena, the same way as psychologists do. This entirely new interactionist move questions the boundary issues. With all the historical relativity of the sociology/social psychology distinction, there was still a chapter that was labeled to be sociological social psychology in function of thematic preferences rather than issues of finding boundaries.

Preparing the setting I: the role and stages of *Völkerpsychologie*

In the half century preceding the establishment of professionalized social psychology in the 1920s, there were several attempts to form a specific chapter for dealing with social behavior. Sociology, with its programs promoted by Durkheim and Max Weber, tried to deal with all social processes. Cultural anthropology mainly tried to work on the so-called primitive people, specifically their social customs. Ethnography worked on the oral cultural habits of our Western societies, and cultural psychology in the sense of Dilthey was interested in the cultural practices of literate cultures. Social psychology had to find its place among these rivaling neighbors to be born among the cousins that started to be formed from the 1870s on. The first, mainly speculative social psychologies, ***Völkerpsychologie* in Germany** and **crowd psychology in France**, were extending the relevance of psychology, sometimes on a biological foundation, sometimes on the basis of a specifically cultural psychology. As extensive intruders, they were criticized in their own time by the rival humanities and the newly formed social sciences: "they want to steal history," "they are not experts on anthropology," and so on. At the same time, they were also criticized by their experimental psychology counterparts, the already-professionalized colleagues as well, since they were not following a proper, that is, experimental, methodology.

There were two attitudes typical in these early representation-based approaches, both related to issues of nationhood.

1. **Comparing European nations.** *Völkerpsychologie*, using notions like **national character** to compare, for example, French and German mentalities, was a reaction to early biological comparisons using physical anthropology by influential people as Broca (1861) in France and Wirchow (1872) in Germany, both claiming craniometric differences among European nations and both being anti-Darwinians. As naive and ethnocentric the "national character"–like notions may sound as of today, they represented a step forward in contrast to comparing skulls and brains of ethnic or national groups.
2. **Progressivists.** They proposed to compare "primitives" and "us." They assumed some kind of universal social evolution and progress, comparing primitives and European people, proposing an evolutionary or cultural hierarchy of development. This would start from Wundt (1888) and Ribot (1899) and lead to Lévy-Bruhl (1910/1922) and his ideas about primitive mentalities (see Chapter 5).

In both regards, there were, in the late 19th century, simple racist attitudes comparing groups of humans as being diffcrent in an inherited manner. Broca (1861) even sided with human multigenesis theories. Later, they were replaced in many cases by some sort of culturalism, where the nascent social science consciousness replaced inherited racial differences with stabilized cultural differences. As the modern reanalysis in several papers in the volume edited by Kail and Vermè (1999) showed, the cultural differences in many later versions were also substantialized, seeing culture as an obstacle to change, as race was originally conceived by biologists. Regarding the relations between human biological diversity and history, both multigenesis and monogenesis theories were easily developed into theories of cultural superiority of White Indo-Europeans. In multigenesis theories, qualitative differences between human races were assumed. Monogenesis theories assumed a continuity between biological evolution and social history. All cultures have to come through the same stages, and again, the "White people" are ahead on the same scale. Jahoda (1993) has given a very detailed analysis of the social use of monogenetic and polygenetic theories. He also showed that the universalistic ideas in modern psychology had their origins in Christian faith, and also in universalistic enlightenment theories. These later theories implied a Spencer-kind interpretation of evolution. This image was very much challenged a hundred years later, in two regards. Karl Popper (1972, 1994), among others, started to claim clearly that there is no progress in evolution. We have to imagine the "tree of life" in a horizontal manner of differentiation. As an addition, we should be careful not to look for simple continuities between biological evolution and social history.

170 Disciplinary developments and eclectics

During the last third of the 19th century, different speculations on national and large human group differences contributed to the birth of social sciences in general. Usually, they tended to interpret differences to be more issues of culture and habit, thus results of cultural heredity rather than of biological heredity.

Figure 6.1 shows their main trends toward the first wave of speculative social psychology.

In the German tradition, these ideas were formed as a supplement to experimental psychology, another psychology that was formulated in the form of a *Völkerpsychologie* program. Klautke (2013) analyzed in detail the three phases of this program:

- The Berlin *Völkerpsychologie* of Lazarus and Steinthal (1860–1890)
- The Leipzig *Völkerpsychologie* of Wundt (1870–1920)
- *Völkerpsychologie* in Hitler's Germany (1935–1950)

Lazarus and Steinthal

The idea of *Völkerpsychologie* was present in the German milieu since the 1860s. For many humanistic scholars, it was used as a self-explanatory thought pattern to interpret the individual mind and its relations to the larger social community, the *Volk*, "people." The conception of a *Volksgeist*, "people's mind," had strong roots in German idealism. Rather than speaking of a *Volkseele*, "folk soul," they were referring to a more abstract entity, *Geist*, "mind," that was related to the philosophy

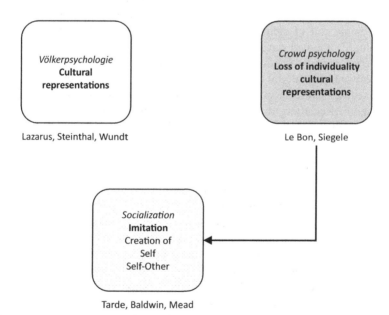

Figure 6.1 The first speculative approaches to the social mind.

of Hegel, where the central term was *Geist*. *Völkerpsychologie*, coming out of these considerations, was a conceptual study of cultural representations, mainly mythology, folklore, and language.

In the 1860s–1890s period, two Berlin-based and Berlin-educated German Jewish scholars, the philosopher Moritz Lazarus (1824–1903) and the linguist Heymann Steinthal (1823–1899), constructed out of these general cultural feelings the first program of German *Völkerpsychologie*. Besides Wilhelm von Humboldt and early comparative linguistics, their two inspirations were Hegelian philosophy and Herbartian psychology, with some touches of the Romantic vision of nations proposed by the followers of Herder. Lazarus and Steinthal combined Hegel and Herbart in order to have a "naturalized" interpretation for the objective spirit postulated by Hegel. As emancipated Jews in new imperial Germany, Lazarus and Steinthal had a political program as well. For them, nation was the crucial interpretation domain of *Volk*. The use of plural is also very telling. *Völker*, "peoples," rather than *Volk*, shows a commitment to human variety. The French reader edited by Trautmann-Waller (2004) shows the interaction of disciplines and social and scientific interests underlying the interest toward the *Volk* in imperial Berlin.

There certainly was a flavor of nationalism in these disciplinary efforts, as a continuation of the 1848 national liberalist revolutions in Germany, especially around the times of the Franco-Prussian War. The ideological relevance was the core idea that a nation, especially the German nation – before 1870, it was still a politically divided nation, with half a dozen states – is united in its mentality, even if it was politically divided. The national mentality would be a primary reason and justification for unifying Germany in this interpretation. This postulated unifying principle was explicitly supposed to be a cultural, "spiritual" unity and by far not racial/biological.

The program of *Völkerpsychologie* in Germany was realized by the journal *Zeitschrift für Völkerpsychologie und Sprachwissenschaft*, launched in 1860 (Lazarus & Steinthal, 1860) and published until 1890 by Lazarus and Steinthal. The aim was to understand the moving spirit underlying historical changes of people. That shows how the *Volksgeist*, the "folk mind," moves toward progress in civilizations. They studied cultural change and aimed to contribute to its progress. The very word "progress" is all over in the folk psychology tradition. While Lazarus tended to be entirely mechanistic and Herbartian in his outlook, Steinthal was more holistic, with an emphasis of a language-like organic form in mental life. Psychology, in its *Völkerpsychologie* variety, would explain cultural phenomena, while for Wundt these same cultural phenomena were used as main evidence for larger-scale psychological organizations.

Völkerpsychologie claimed that individual psychology had to be supplemented by the psychology of collectivities, of which the *Volk* was supposed to be the basic one, more general than family, class, or other social organizations. While they were trying to overcome limitations of individual psychology, for most representatives of early *Völkerpsychologie*, this mainly meant the application of classical Herbartian philosophical psychology for the interpretation of the postulated *Volksgeist*. They were not even touched by the new experimental psychology of their contemporaries, Wundt, Ebbinghaus, or G. E. Müller. Methodically, while they claimed to be empirical, they were rather speculative. They mainly relied on occasional observations and anecdotal social essays. When they talked about the *Volk*, they did treat it as a cultural voluntaristic unity. Due to this early "social constructionism," they were influential. The French social writer and historian Ernest Renan's (1882/2018) famous "voluntaristic" definition of the nation, for instance, was based on a notion that was very similar to Lazarus's definition of the "folk." Simmel's (1895/1982, 1917) pioneering works on cultural sociology were based around central concepts of the folk psychology of his teachers Lazarus and Steinthal, as well as evolutionary selectionist theory; central pillars of Durkheim's sociology – "social facts" and "collective representations" – owed much to his reading of Wundt's *Völkerpsychologie*. The founder of American anthropology, Franz Boas (1911), was a student of Steinthal, and he adopted the arguments against biological anthropology and treating culture as a symbol-based unity from his German teachers. Through Potebnja, an early linguist follower from Russia, Lazarus and Steinthal had an influence that even extended to Mikhail Bakhtin (1986) in the late 20th century.

They had some negative reactions within German-language culture as well. The linguistic philosopher Mauthner and the historical linguist Hermann Paul criticized them in the name of an individualized epistemology. They claimed that there cannot be anything like group mind. "All psychic processes take place within the individual mind and nowhere else" (Paul, 1888, p. 11). The alternative to *Völkerpsychologie* proposed by Paul was an unspecified cultural science. Other German humanities scholars, such as Windelband and Dilthey, did not like the Berlin Völkerpsychologie colleagues for their imitation of natural science, and for "stealing" the place of real history writing (Lessing, 2004). It is very telling that they did not have any reaction to the later, more elaborate *Völkerpsychologie* of Wundt, their influential rival, either. The ignorance was mutual, as far as *Völkerpsychologie* is concerned. Ebbinghaus (1896) did criticize the *Geisteswissenschaftliches* psychology, but they never realized their methodical similarity to *Völkerpsychologie*. "Mental science" approach interpreted "folk psychology" as being too naturalistic.

In Austria, *Völkerpsychologie* had an early but alternative follower, Gustav Adolf Lindner (1828–1887), who was an influential textbook author. Interestingly, for the social embedding of the traditions of *Völkerpsychologie*, for Lazarus and Steinthal, *Volk* corresponded to nation, whereas for their Austrian counterpart, who was working within a multiethnic empire, *Volk* was interpreted as equivalent to state. Lindner (1871) proposed a more interaction-based vision of *Völkerpsychologie*.

> The task of social psychology is the description and explanation of phenomena which depend on the interaction of individuals and on which rests the whole mental life of society. . . . Lindner claimed that society did not exist independently of the individuals: the "mental life" of society could only be found in the individual consciousness of its members. Hence, Lindner

concluded, social psychology could borrow its principles from individual psychology.

(Klautke, 2013, p. 38)

Incidentally, this is the first use of the very term *social psychology*, from 1871, besides a more obscure Italian reference from 1864 (Jahoda, 2007).

The folk psychological program of Wundt

Wundt, as usually noted in histories, started to publish his ten-volume *Völkerpsychologie* from 1900 on and worked on it for the last 20 years of his life. However, he was interested in the topic much earlier. He talked about two psychologies complementing each other – one experimental, and the other cultural – already in his earliest books (Wundt, 1863). In the 1880s, he held classes of *Völkerpsychologie* with many hundreds of students (including Durkheim) in the lecture halls in Leipzig. Leipzig was, for social reasons, an ideal place compared to more compartmentalized Berlin for such an interdisciplinary enterprise. Leipzig in the late 19th century had a very strong faculty community combining natural science and the humanities. From the tradition of Fechner to the neogrammarians of Hermann Paul and even further on to the new geographers and new historians, there was a fresh interaction between traditions and circles, even with Friday coffeehouse meetings to discuss relations between sciences and the humanities (Espagne, 2009). But this Leipzig circle was positivistic, in contrast to the more spiritualistic, idealist Berlin circles.

In this interdisciplinary cavalcade, Wundt was careful even in choosing his terms when outlining his program for studying the social mind. As he summarized in his later mature summary of his *Völkerpsychologie*:

> A term such as "folk psychology" must be formulated with reference to the most important conception with which it has to deal. Moreover, scarcely any of the proposed emendations are practicable. "Gemeinschaftspsychologie" (community psychology) may easily give rise to the misconception that we are concerned primarily with such communities as differ from the folk community; "Sozialpsychologie" (social psychology) at once reminds us of modern sociology, which, even in its psychological phases, usually deals exclusively with questions of modern cultural life. . . . The "folk" embraces families, classes, clans, and groups. These various communities are not excluded from the concept "folk" but are included within it. The term "folk psychology" singles out precisely the folk as the decisive factor underlying the fundamental creations of the community.
>
> (Wundt, 1916, p. 12)

The early *Völkerpsychologie* of Lazarus and Steinthal had two features Wundt tried to overwrite. He had shown this first in a polemical paper he wrote in 1888 against the critic of the linguist Hermann Paul on Lazarus and Steinthal. Wundt protected the very idea of a supraindividual psychology against the outright individualism of Paul. He pointed out that talking about "folk mind" is not a "reification," as Paul has charged; it is parallel to the attitude of individual psychology which deals with mental phenomena, without referring to the individual soul (Wundt, 1888, 1912). Wundt considered that his Berlin colleagues promoted a wrong psychology. The first issue was that the advocates of *Völkerpsychologie*, along with the tradition of German idealism, tried to interpret some phenomena of collective psychology as manifestations of some supraindividual *Volk* mind. The organization of this *Volk* mind was assumed to be in line with the association psychology of Herbart. Thus, the Hegelian conceptual system relying on Humboldt and applying the notion of *Geist* as proposed by Steinthal is supplemented by Lazarus with a Herbartian psychological mechanics. As Wundt wittily mentioned, the Herbartian atomistic vision of the mind can be mixed with the Hegelian *Volksgeist* like water and fire. The Herbartian mechanistic psychology belonged to the past and had to be replaced with Wundt's own voluntaristic approach.

The way Wundt (1888) himself approached *Völkerpsychologie* from his earliest attempts on could be seen in two contexts: the context of his own time, and the context of his own work.

1. Context within psychology. Experimental ⇒ Limitations of introspection ⇒ *Völkerpsychologie*.
   Völkerpsychologie has to find a clear relation to experimental psychology, and it has to bring in the comparative methods where experimental psychology is unable to use its experimental methods (see in Chapter 6 in Volume 1).
2. Context within humanities. Group mind notions ⇒ Ontological reservations about group mind ⇒ **Völkerpsychologie product–centered.**

The social representations like language are all collective achievements that cannot be studied as accidental events in the individual mind. But they do not constitute a new folk mind; they are merely social patterns. Regarding the larger German context, Wundt was to become an opponent of the reification of the group mind. For him, *Seele* and *Geist* – soul as used in old psychology, and *mind* as used in the social studies – cannot be differentiated. Individual soul is studied only in its processes; the group mind or mentality has to be studied through its objectivations, through its products. There is no need for a hypothesized soul-like entity in Völkerpsychologie. Phenomena of Völkerpsychologie are studied by Wundt in their objective manifestations: the group mind evaporates.

Within psychology, *Völkerpsychologie*, for Wundt, represented a new domain where the non-cumulative, emergent aspects of the mind could be studied or revealed. There were certainly some ambiguities in this program. While Wundt tried to avoid postulation of a group mind by emphasizing the relative stability of social representations, like language, he found himself in a difficult balancing situation. The key notion of the mature Wundt creative synthesis implies an agent behind the construction, some sort of a group mind.

Völkerpsychologie *as a universal science of laws of change*

The way Wundt conceived *Völkerpsychologie* had a conceptually different message as well. First of all, he emphasized that the "main problem of psychology is the question of mental development" (Wundt, 1888, p. 17), and that should be at the center of *Völkerpsychologie* as well, together with the integrative role of volition that is missing both from Lazarus and Steinthal and from Hermann Paul. "Development" in both senses of the word – unfolding of more complex out of simpler in individual mental acts, as the theory of apperception claims, and historical mental development, that is, change of mentalities – should both be central to the study of the social mind. The efforts to show the difference between his approach and his rivals' and predecessors' resulted in some neat conceptual distinctions in Wundt. Wundt differentiated between social acts that have an individual reference, such as emotional expressions, and socially organized intentional acts that have the partners, the socius, in the forefront (Danziger, 1983). In a similarly interesting claim, Wundt believed that in the same way as the individual mental life is subject to general laws of psychology, there are general developmental laws of the "folk mind" as well (Wundt, 1888, p. 23).

Wundt was a universalist. He did not see any structural changes of the mind by history. The most serious obstacle for Wundt in developing his *Völkerpsychologie* further was, first of all, his lack of firsthand knowledge of the anthropological data he was talking about and the lack of data on human interactions. The systematic reliance on the analysis of interactions – together with the new technologies, like magnetic recording and filming – would broaden social psychology in the mid-20th century. In a way, it was the nascent and, most of the time, rival neogrammarian historical linguistics school that showed using positivist philology, one may have real historical data to chart the real course of changes. In this continuous change, however, universal laws could be observed. In this regard, Wundt and Paul agreed.

Methodically, Wundt did not surpass his predecessors. Wundt practiced folk psychology as an armchair scholar and used the materials collected by others. The *Völkerpsychologie* of Wundt looks more like anthropology for the present-day reader rather than psychology. It was a soft German version of cultural evolutionism. The comparative perspective remains in Wundt, but it is much less a comparison of national mentalities, as the Lazarus–Steinthal program imagined it; rather, it is a comparison of stages of mental development on a universal cultural evolutionary scale. There are many reminiscences of Haeckel (1892) and similarities to Stanley Hall (1911) with their belief in stages of mental development, even extended to historical times. Darwin was still rather clearly present in Wundt's lectures on psychology from a comparative perspective, especially regarding the instincts in humans (Wundt, 1863). In *Völkerpsychologie* proper, Darwin disappeared, as well as the entire evolutionary narrative of mental development. One can only speculate about the reasons for this, but most likely, it is related to the emergentist views Wundt was entertaining regarding mental development in his theories of volition.

The task of folk psychology is the study of supraindividual organizations.

A language can never be created by an individual. It is the product of peoples, and, generally speaking, there are as many different languages as there are originally distinct peoples. The same is true of the beginnings of art, of mythology, and of custom.

(Wundt, 1916, p. 1)

This attitude survived. This will be the stance of Saussure (1922) in his positioning of language as a social system, and of Wittgenstein (1953) in his critic of the idea of a "private language."

Wundt proposed the equivalence of basic psychological processes and culture in the following manner.

Representation ⇒ language
Emotion ⇒ mythology
Volition ⇒ habits, morals

The emphasis on laws of genesis intended to resolve the discrepancy between the universalistic aims of Wundt and his seemingly relativist claims about development. As the human mind develops and changes, the very laws of their change revealed by *Völkerpsychologie* are universal. "Qualitative differences in psychological principles and processes associated with different cultures and historical periods reflected different stages of sociocultural development: qualitative differences in stages were thus held to be consistent with the postulation of a universal developmental process" (Greenwood, 2003, p. 64, note 32):

The relations of the *Völkerpsychologie* of Wundt to later, modern psychology are rather intriguing. As Greenwood (2003) presents it, there is a mistaken interpretation and a partly mistaken revisionism here. This mistaken perception sees in Wundt a clear divider of psychology along methodical lines: social phenomena are important, but they cannot be studied with experimental methods. Modern social psychology, however, would be born out of a need to use the experimental method. On the other hand, for the revisionist claims, Wundt was actually practicing social psychology, but without the use of experimental methods.

Greenwood clearly illustrates that for Wundt the use of comparative rather than experimental methods in his *Völkerpsychologie* mainly had to do with his interests. The social psychology conceived by Wundt mainly treated diachronic phenomena and the psychology of genesis; therefore, there was a need for the comparative method. In addition, the debates regarding mental sciences which were highly characteristic of the age are missing from *Völkerpsychologie* altogether. Wundt would never even mention Dilthey in this context. Wundt, with all his interpretation efforts, would still go for an objectivistic, causal interpretation of the mind.

While Wundt was "stages minded," this was mainly rooted in classical German idealism rather than phrased in evolutionary terms. Wundt aligned himself with those who identified the *Volk* issue with a mentality rather than race. This was in line with the Lazarus–Steinthal tradition of *Völkerpsychologie*. At the same time, however, he was not interested in ethnic mentality differences. He was a clearly universalistic author, for whom *Völkerpsychologie* was relevant due to the possibilities it offers to study the unfolding of the mind.

Völkerpsychologie *and language*

Völkerpsychologie had the largest impact for decades to come regarding language. The best-known volume of Wundt's ten-volume series of *Völkerpsychologie* was the first one, about language. Wundt had these interesting proposals: one on sentence structure, another on the psychological mechanism of language change, and a third on the gestural origin of language.

It is very interesting historically that Wundt only saw a conceptual and a historical attitude to language and did not realize that language can be studied experimentally. This had to wait until the 1960s, when experimental psycholinguistics was born. Even Karl Bühler, who was an opponent of Wundt in claiming experimental methods for higher thought processes, would still never consider experimenting on language. Even for the next generation of Bühler (1934), language was the domain of psychological theory and observation and not of experimentation, as in his diary studies on child language. Half a century later, modern psycholinguistics would be born with reverting this limitation. Though language is a social construct, it does shape the individual mind, and this can be studied with experimenting on specific language-related events of the individual mind.

Wundt's theory of sentence was rather elaborate, and since it was a basically holistic model, it obtained modern reinterpretations as well. According to Wundt (1900), the sentence is a clear example of a complex, simultaneous idea being decomposed into its component parts during production, and of sequential elements forming a simultaneous reality in understanding. The sentence is an example for the general dynamics of apperception, the movement between parts and wholes, between simultaneity and sequentially. Blumenthal (1970), around the birth of American generative linguistics, in his rather presentist reader, overemphasized the similarities between generative grammar and the conception of Wundt. This was also the reading at get me of Wundt. Zoltán Gombocz (1903, p. 49), a Hungarian historical linguist, summarized the importance of these ideas in terms similar to Blumenthal's:

> Thus, from a psychological point of view, a sentence is a simultaneous and a successive whole at the same time: it is simultaneous since at any moment of its genesis it is present in our consciousness with its entire content; it is successive, since the state of the entire consciousness changes form moment to moment accruing to the specific ideas moving in a sequence before the point of view of consciousness.

Blumenthal (1970, 1987) went as far as to claim to find in Wundt a precursor of the notion of deep and surface structure as proposed by Chomsky (1965). Blumenthal (1987) and Levelt (2013) also pointed out that regarding language processes, Wundt has remained critical of the entirely mechanistic image promoted by his contemporaries, like the historical linguist Hermann Paul). Bühler (1918, 1934), then upcoming new psycholinguist, was dissatisfied with Wundt for two main reasons. Wundt was not structural enough in his theory of sentence, combining simultaneity and sequentiality, and his approach did not deal with the multiple functions of language. Wundt only dealt with representations, while a more pragmatic attitude should be used when dealing with language as a sign system used for communication.

The *Völkerpsychologie* of Wundt was cultivated and proposed in the middle of radical changes in linguistic theory. His ideas about **change of meaning** and the like led to many debates between the linguistic psychologism leader Hermann Paul and Wundt, where the essence of the tension was a tension between Herbartian (Paul) and more voluntaristic (Wundt) psychology. In analyzing change of meaning, Wundt, the psychologist, curiously juxtaposed a logical model against the psychological associative model of the neogrammarian linguistic school (Gombocz, 1903). In this process, he could not always follow the principle of treating cultural phenomena as the objective reference point of *Völkerpsychologie*. Wundt challenged the practice of applying simple associative machinery to language to explain language change. In his view, the essence of meaning change would not be associative change but, rather, conceptual differentiation (think of the two meanings of a word like *chair*). At the same time, if we look further toward explanations for language change, it is revealed that the clear psychological versus logical explanation controversy is really about a narrow and a broad view of association. Wundt used a broader notion of association, not relying exclusively on contingency and similarity, but allowing for internal, that is, logical, associative relations.

The pragmatic attitude was found to be missing in Wundt by another of his commentators, George Herbart Mead (1934). While Mead was inspired by the ideas of **Wundt regarding the origin of language** and the importance of gestures in this process, at the same time, he considered that a more special social psychology would be better to treat language. **Gestures** had two roles for the system of Wundt. Gestures were crucial both for the genesis of language and for an elementary sociality. They had shown a drive-based, almost-automatic social integration that was a real topic of the folk psychology of Wundt, in contrast to the second, more elaborate and decision-based system. Wundt (1973) saw aborted acts in gestures, analyzed in detail the roots of their symbolization, and claimed that gestures elicit in the interpreter the traces of the original eliciting context and emotion.

According to Mead (1934), the essential problem with Wundt is the initial supposition of an interpretive Ego or consciousness, while in fact it is their genesis that should be explained, for example, through the role of gestures. Individual mind is antecedent to social life in Wundt, while according to Mead, who represented a pragmatic communicative point of view, it is the other way around: social life is antecedent to individual minds. *Völkerpsychologie* was a science of representations and not of interactions and communication, and that is what the modern science of social life should be.

The fate of Völkerpsychologie

While Wundt had not had any serious followers in Weimar or Nazi Germany, there were later nationalist interpretations of *Völkerpsychologie* (Hellpach, 1938). However, in the new postwar Germany, all *Volk* psychology soon became dead. This was partly a dissociation with the past, but partly also Americanization.

> The 1950s and 1960s German psychology was finally, but slowly, turned into a social science based on quantitative, empirical methods. The traditional "hermeneutic" approach of folk psychology . . . did not fit into this reconceptualization of psychology. The transformation of psychology into a modern, "Americanized" discipline reflected the eagerness of younger German scholars to integrate their discipline into Western traditions; it also cut the ties with the traditional topics of folk psychology – language, myth, religion and customs – which were now delegated to disciplines other than psychology, insofar as they could not be conceptualized with quantitative, statistical methods.
>
> (Klautke, 2013, p. 151)

Dahrendorf (1967), a sociologist of the following generation, published a devastating critique of all concepts of **national character** and included the folk psychology tradition under this banner. While the new generation criticized folk notions, they smuggled them back.

> Dahrendorf's text became a major point of reference for a generation of German historians and social scientists whose main aim was to end this "special path" and integrate Germany firmly into Western traditions. Their view of German history, of German traditions and of the German mind included a form of inverted folk psychology: while highly critical of anything deemed typically German – from militarism to authoritarianism, from anti-Semitism to anti-Americanism – this worldview still depended on the notion of a unique German character.
>
> (Klautke, 2013, p. 155)

Interestingly, as Klautke also pointed out, the holistic group-related notions continue to be around in social sciences. For example, in the French *Annales* tradition, some ideas of folk psychology also survive, as issues of "mentalités." We may add that these notions also survive as national identities in the identity research tradition, in cultural psychology, and even in the notion of *habitus* proposed by Bourdieu (1977), or the entire program of research on social representations initiated by Moscovici (1961, 1984, 1988). Thus, the conceptual heritage of *Völkerpsychologie* is still present. Social representations, however, are different in one crucial regard from the collective representations of the classics, especially of Durkheim. While collective representations were supposed to be shared in a community, social representations are more distributed and correspond more to an individualized image (Moscovici, 1984).

Preparing the setting II: crowd psychology

Relations between individual behavior and large social groups became a special topic in Europe at the turn of the last century, under the influence of the great mass movements. As many historical analysts remarked, the interest in crowds was, in a way, a second reflection of the crisis image of the French Revolution, already proposed by Taine (1876b) a generation earlier. It was also a direct reflection of the experience of the Paris Commune of 1870 and the mass working-class and later feminist movements, marches that characterized modern industrial towns in Europe. Crowds appeared in the popular mind as disorganized "feminine," dangerous elements in the modern city life. Taine, in his original positivist enthusiasm to combine history, psychology, and biology in his theory of race, milieu, and personality, was shocked by the events of the Commune. From then on, new revisionist rewriting of the history of the French Revolution interpreted the revolution as a pathological lowered level of functioning in the crowds and as a regression leading to anarchy. Other historians questioned this account both on ideological and on philological grounds, questioning both the role of the crowds and the assumed disorganized behavior during the revolution. What is important, however, is that the new vision of French history thematized the topic of crowds in nascent new social sciences. Regarding a favorite late-19th-century topic, **dissociation**, French researchers of hypnosis were seeing parallels between laboratory suggestibility to the suggestibility in crowds (Carroy, 1993; Lindholm, 1992).The misogynic attitude attributing all lower-level functioning to the feminine social and mental elements was rather prevalent at that time; it was not specific at all to crowd psychologists but appeared as well in the hypnosis debates. The assumed femininity, proneness to crimes, and in general "social mud-like" nature of crowds were present throughout 19th-century French intellectual life and history. The crowd psychology movement was a new way to make conservative liberal politics. It was a discussion of the relations between the individual and the new mass society. It was the other side of the crisis of the Self we saw about turn-of-the-century intellectual life in Chapter 10 of Volume 1. In modern art and science, the dissolution of the traditional Self was the road to new artistic expression and a clearer understanding of ourselves. For social worriers watching the crowds, the loss of Selfhood was a threat toward bourgeois order. As the monography of Nye (1975) summarized it, the interest towards crowd psychology was related to the tensions of mass democracy in Western society.

At the turn of the 19th century, there were several attempts to envision a crowd psychology in French intellectual life, all starting from these historical experiences. It is a further interesting background factor that all representatives of the crowd psychology, like Sighele, Le Bon, or Tarde, had some contacts either with criminology or with clinical psychiatry. Crowd behavior somehow was seen with the eyes of a pathologist or a criminal examiner. The crowd was insane or criminal in the eye of a stabilized bourgeois society.

The crowd psychology of Le Bon

Gustave Le Bon (1841–1931) became the popular advocate of crowd psychology, with several books on political processes and mass behavior (Le Bon, 1894, 1903). Writing in an anecdotal manner, he basically proposed that disorganized social groups have a diminished rationality and disorganized and uncritical behavior.

Le Bon was an intriguing figure in the history of social science. He was a successful "externist" who always remained outside academia, but at the same time, he was socially always successful. By 2020, his English-language crowd book alone has over 6,000 citations. The Google Ngram (Figure 6.2) shows that Le Bon was very popular in the 1910s–1920s, with his popularity having since come back starting from the 1990s, both in English and in French general texts.

Le Bon certainly was not integrated to the university academic life. He had a dubious medical training, with no real medical degree, and he moved between different circles of scientific societies and publications. In addition to medicine, he had experience in geography, ethnogenesis, hippology, and education. While being outside academia, he was still very much integrated to French intellectual high society from his first works on. He was a writer in the prestigious journal of Ribot, *Revue philosophique de la France et de l'étranger*; organized a salon with Ribot; and held weekly coffeehouse meetings in Paris. At the turn of the century, he became editor of an influential series of books of the publisher Flammarion. The series was called *Bibliothèque de Philosophie scientifique*, "Library of scientific philosophy," and during the 30 years Le Bon edited it, leading intellectuals with their popular writings appeared in the series, including Poincaré, Mach, Oswald, Bergson, Binet, Claparède, and Dewey. The series even included a dozen volumes by Le Bon. By social standards, Le Bon was a successful man. His books sold over 350,000 copies, of which the crowd book alone in about 40,000 copies. His edited book series was also a success; in some years, around 20,000 copies sold from the series.

Thus, Le Bon, rather than being peripheral, was a socially and financially successful man, a science popularizer in contemporary sense. This is important to remember since his crowd publications give an amateurish impression. In his first books on psychology and in all his works, Le Bon (1894) was originally a rather racist speculative popular psychologist. As Mucchielli (1998) characterized him a

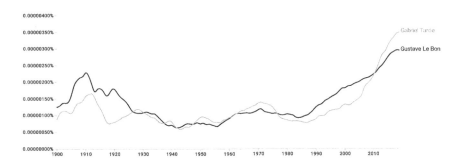

Figure 6.2 The popularity of Le Bon and Tarde in the English-language general literature.

century later, Le Bon proclaimed racial essentialism and hereditarianism. Among the races, there is a clear hierarchy, where the Japanese and Chinese are in the medium range, and the Indo-Europeans are of the superior kind. The primitives are unable to reason, while in the White man, reasoning and critical thought are much more developed. The racism of Le Bon was related to his elitist theory of the crowd. Racism and social Darwinism made for the objectification of group characteristics, and crowd theory, in a way, showed that there is no way to avoid this racial hierarchy. The crowd even in our society moves us toward the lower prototypes.

As the edited volume of Kail and Vermè (1999) showed, between 1870 and 1910, rather naive writing on "national character" was generally popular in France. Besides Le Bon, many other people were also writing specific monographs on national character. However, that was also true of many European countries, in contrast to the universalism of the *Völkerpsychologie* of Wundt. Hunyady (2001, 2006) showed how national character ideas were present, for example, in early speculative social science in Hungary in the late 19th to mid-20th century.

Le Bon dealt with the issue of crowds in a society in transition, locally as a result of the crisis of the Third Republic. He was preceded by Scipio Sighele (1868–1913), an Italian criminologist with his book on criminal crowds that would have a lower-level social organization (Sighele, 1891). Sighele (1903), due to his left-wing political alignments, including his involvement in the Dreyfus affair, later abandoned the idea of the irresponsibility of crowds and also published about the intelligence of crowds. These facts created primacy tensions at that time, with Tarde claiming more than once that Le Bon was, in fact, taking over ideas from Sighele.

Primacy issues notwithstanding, Le Bon was the success of crowd psychology. For Le Bon, the essence of the crisis of the France of his time was the loss of individuality that was most striking in crowd behavior. People in crowds are psychologically different. The essential message of his crowd psychology books is straightforward. People in crowds think qualitatively differently, there is loss of Ego functions, and super-individual entities are formed that are based on emotional integration.

> The sentiments and ideas of all the persons in the gathering take one and the same direction, and their conscious personality vanishes. A collective mind is formed, doubtless transitory, but presenting very clearly defined characteristics. . . . It forms a single being, and is subjected to the law of the mental unity of crowds.
> (Le Bon, 1903, p. 13)

In crowds, the conscious personality disappears. This is responsible for the coordination of behavior in crowds.

> Crowds, doubtless, are always unconscious, but this very unconsciousness is perhaps one of the secrets of their strength. . . . The part played by the unconscious in all our acts is immense, and that played by reason very small.
> (ibid p. 4)

This "collective mind" idea is rather similar to the "folk mind" of early *Völkerpsychologie*, and to the latter group mind of McDougall. Image and emotion control people in the crowd, and the leaders use them in their illogical state of mind. This corresponds to a fleeting associative organization of thought.

> Characteristics of the reasoning of crowds are the association of dissimilar things possessing a merely apparent connection between each other, and the immediate generalization of particular cases. It is arguments of this kind that are always presented to crowds by those who know how to manage them. . . . Contagion is so powerful that it forces upon individuals not only certain opinions, but certain modes of feeling as well. . . . The opinions and beliefs of crowds are specially propagated by contagion, but never by reasoning.
>
> (ibid., 51)

One could say that Le Bon's book on crowd psychology was a pop psychology book at that time. He was an elitist and not someone who would stand for a cult of the crowd. Le Bon was politically a disenchanted liberal who wanted to gain back somehow the individual rationality that seemed to be last in the group processes. The word "groups" is relevant here, since Le Bon often talked about "group processes." He interpreted most groups as having a tendency to become crowds. He included under the name of crowds even instructional organizations, like churches and the military. He even went into details of organized and unorganized crowds. Some organized crowds are in fact social events, like jury sessions.

Le Bon was proposing a nonstandard theory of social influence, where all social groups tended toward losing rationality. Le Bon did not see any positive, constructive aspects of social life. There was an important difference in this regard between the German and the French visions of collective mind. For the early *Völkerpsychologie* thinkers, along with their Herbartian tradition, "group mind" was a positive notion, as well as later for Wundt. It represented something like a "collective knowledge source"; it is in a way a higher-level functioning, as the example of language showed it. For Le Bon, however, the "collective mind" existed in contrast to critical individual thought; it was the site of a lower-level functioning. Le Bon was in clear contrast with his contemporary French sociologist Durkheim and early and later constructivist sociology as well. Durkheim, with his ideas about collective representations, treated society as a carrier of thoughts rather than a depersonalized mass.

Le Bon was afraid of losing traditional French Cartesian individuality. For Le Bon, the individual was a central issue that was in a crisis from two respects. Individuality had to be born during a long historical process; thus, some people and races did not yet develop individuality. At the same time, this development of individuality was threatened by the new social crowds. In a way, at the turn of the century, both folk psychology and crowd psychology were pointing out the changing, flexible nature of human self, which they felt was in danger.

The fate of crowd psychology

Le Bon soon became a popular writer, not only in the number of his readers, but also in being used as a point of reference. During the Dreyfus affair, the most divisive social affair of turn-of-the-century France, both the pro-Dreyfus and the anti-Semitic anti-Dreyfus and pro-army reactions referred to his crowd psychology. While the anti-Semites were marching in real crowds, the Dreyfusards were interpreting the conservative Le Bon in their own manner: they saw a threat of modernity in the crowds, with a good amount of misogyny, and re-emphasized virility. Rioux and Sirinelli (1998, p. 124), in their general historical presentation of 20th-century cultural history, showed not only the relevance of the revolutions and class movements for the rise of crowds but also the role of the printed press in creating crowd moods and the artistic revolutions' being against the crowd moods played in the elevation of crowds into a real factor in the social mind. All this called for practices of manipulating the crowds.

> Le Bon's psychology was leading towards a to be invented technic of manipulating the crowds. The hatred of crowds at the end of century, and the entire pseudo-scientificity of these bizarre doctors have led to the demagogueries and confabulations of modern politics, with the many bad dreams of the democratic space.

In his own time, Le Bon had a cold reception in French academia but a warm public and, later, political reception. Psychoanalysis, however, took the impact of crowds very seriously, with its assumed relationship to the functioning of the psychological apparatus. For Freud, the changes in crowds are no surprise. They relate to the diminished inhibitions and the activation of unconscious instincts. "The apparently new characteristics which he then displays are in fact the manifestations of this unconscious, in which all that is evil in the human mind is contained as a predisposition" (Freud, 1921, p. 73). Freud went on to show how the contagion in groups corresponds to hypnosis and that all these group phenomena are related to the primal horde, to the role of the father there, and the issue of identification with the father. "The leader of the group is still the dreaded primal father; the group still wishes to be governed by unrestricted force; it has an extreme passion for authority; in Le Bon's phrase, it has a thirst for obedience" (ibid., 127). This line of thought was followed by a century of psychoanalytic group theories that always tended to relate group processes to decreased mental control. In a crucial regard, psychoanalytic group psychology is in harmony with Le Bon: they do not see the constructive nature of sociality, only its destructive effects.

With later political developments, Le Bon's ideas about the crowd somehow seemed for many to predict the depersonalized revolutionary crowds in Russia, the feminist marches, or the later depersonalized crowds of fascist rallies. The real impact of Le Bon in this regard is discussed under CONTROVERSIES.

Controversies

Relations of crowd psychology to authoritarian politics

There were many facts and rumors that, from Mussolini to Mao, he was an inspiration of many later leaders of the crowds. Among French leaders, Foch and Joffre, and other French military leaders of the First World War certainly read Le Bon, as well as the politicians Clemenceau, Theodore Roosevelt, and Churchill.

Was Le Bon so influential later on Mussolini and Hitler? Was his work an early warning about our mass society, or is this, in fact, another myth, this time about Le Bon that is rightfully ignored by later mainstream psychology? There are issues of value and value protection involved here. We have to differentiate between Le Bon himself and his later assumed uses. Le Bon himself, as an elitist, was not a proponent for the use of crowds in modern politics. This later idea was a feature promoted by the leadership of political movements. Le Bon was afraid of the deindividualizing aspects of all group processes.

The authoritarian uses of crowds had a different vision. They aimed to base their authoritarian rule on the assumed force of the crowd and on the need of crowds for charismatic leaders (Lindholm, 1992). For the new leaders of mass movements, crowds were no more weak feminine agencies, as for Le Bon. They were presented as threats to the enemies and foundations for "our power." In reality, the new authoritarian leaders were mainly trying to use and manipulate the crowds.

Le Bon and the issues of crowd also figured in the collective reflexology proposed by the Russian neuroscientist Vladimir Bekhterev (1921). He proposed 21 natural science–sounding laws for the behavior of communities, including crowds. These are laws like "law of relativity" or "law of periodicity." Bekhterev takes many examples from the history of Russian revolutions for his laws. "Relativity" is exemplified by the abolishment of capital punishment and its re-establishment after the cruelties in the army. "Periodicity" is illustrated by the return of the rejected Tsarist officers into the Red Army. Thus, these laws are not any better than the descriptions provided by Le Bon, but they come from the book of an accomplished naturalist.

Anecdotes continue on the Left as well, claiming, for example, that Lenin was a reader of Le Bon, and that he was a Machiavellian leadership advocate. Most likely, there are some mythologies here as well. But the Russian Communists had a symbolic usage for crowds. The crowd in Soviet art, in contrast to early avant-garde art, appeared as a positive factor, as a moving force of history. Geldern (1993) even documented that the very symbolic revolutionary event, the storming of the Winter Palace in St. Petersburgh, was re-enacted three years later in 1920 as a theatrical show on the very site, with 10,000 participants. This demonstrates a top-down organized crowd. Later on, Eisenstein's *October*, released in 1928, also contributed to this image. I call it "image" since, in fact, the revolution and the very storming of the Winter

Palace were not a real mass event, as only a few hundred soldiers took part in it. Art entered the story early on to make sure that the masses were playing a central role. There was a convincing story of a real "popular uprising." In a similar manner, also in fascist propaganda movies by Leni Riefenstahl, like the *Triumph of the Will* in 1935, the crowd is presented as an organized source of power. Susan Sontag (1975) analyzed how this adoration of crowds was characteristic both of early Soviet and of German fascist movies.

The Nobel Prize–winning writer Elias Canetti (1962) wrote a synthesis of 20th-century crowd phenomena from an opposite point of view from Le Bon and Freud. For Canetti, crowds are most interesting because they obey leaders. They provide participants with a feeling of security; thus, they are not destructive. They are flights from freedom, flights from facing the unknown.

Through all these uses of the crowds, the idea of crowd has gradually become a mythical idea in our societies over the last century. It is becoming a fictive major actor of our fears. Bosc (2010) presented convincingly, for example, that from the 1970s on, Le Bon has become an idol for the extreme right wing. European extremists formed a society to republish and popularize Le Bon's works, from France to Holland. As the Hungarian social psychologist Ferenc Pataki (1998) showed, the cultural pessimism related to crowds was very widespread in the writings of the Spanish philosopher Ortega and other cultural philosophers in the mid-twenties. They have, in many regards, gone beyond the crowd issues of Le Bon. They treated crowd people in an aristocratic manner as the new uneducated mass society looking for power, and later looking for immediate consumption. Mass society was more than a mere appearance of crowds; it was a new organizing principle of social life.

Interestingly, as also summarized by Pataki, the 1940s–1970s also showed a combination of experimental social psychology with the relations of crowd to opinion and to leaders, starting with the study of Cantril on the virtual integration caused by a radio show on the "invasion from Mars," to the study of Festinger et al. (1964) analyzing the reactions to sects to the fact that the world has not ended, though the end was predicted.

Serge Moscovici (1985), the French social psychologist, tried to revitalize Le Bon in professional context, by putting him into a sequence not only with Tarde and Freud but also with Max Weber. This is certainly an interesting turn, where the issue of leadership is treated together with the issue of the crowd. Moscovici, in many regards, was convinced of the idea that Le Bon was really an inspiration of authoritarian crowd manipulators, which is now questioned by many.

Besides these political and philosophical issues, one interesting heritage of the crowd psychology issue is the integration of opinions and behaviors in large human groups. This is very challenging today, when virtual crowds are formed with new media. Yet it is also a classical issue from the late 19th century, where the crowd problems had become connected to the interactionist beginnings of social psychology in the work of Tarde.

Imitation theory and social interaction: Tarde

A contemporary of Le Bon, Gabriel Tarde (1843–1904) had a better academic career than Le Bon had. As a legal scholar, Tarde was a judge, later a state prosecutor. He was a legal and social writer, and on issues of criminology, he was the great opponent of the biological degeneration theory of crime promoted by Cesare Lombroso. He was elected to the Collège de France in 1900, beating Bergson, for a chair of philosophy (Bergson was compensated a year later), where Tarde mainly taught sociology and psychology. Tarde promoted a kind of sociology that was much criticized by Durkheim, who was also a contender for the position at the Collège de France. While Tarde concentrated on the processes integrating society, Durkheim treated society in a ready-made dominant role.

In his most famous book, **imitation** is put into a general frame of repetition in nature (Tarde, 1890/1903). Imitation is responsible for uniformity in social groups.

> In social life, it is imitation that is the main responsible for similarities. The social being, in the degree that he is social, is essentially imitative, and that imitation plays a role in societies analogous to that of heredity in organic life or to that of vibration among inorganic bodies. . . . All resemblances of social origin in society are the direct or indirect fruit of the various forms of imitation, custom-imitation or fashion-imitation, sympathy-imitation or obedience-imitation, precept-imitation or education imitation; naive imitation, deliberate imitation, etc.
>
> (Tarde, 1890/1903, pp. 11, 14)

Tarde elaborated a two-way sophisticated social theory of the role of imitation. Belief would spread based on credibility, leading to truth, while desire would spread through docility, leading to social values. Both cognition and motivation would be thus based on social imitation processes.

In actual social life, there are always tensions between different rival waves of imitation, and imitation and invention compete in social life.

Tarde tried to speculate and illustrate with examples from language and history how the tensions between imitation and innovation drive social life. In innovations, there are accidental factors, while imitation is a general tendency, with many social forces acting against imitation at the same time. Imitation is often balanced, for example, by our fear of being imitators.

Tarde (1903) extended the issue of imitation into what he claimed to be interpsychic research. **Interpsychology** was a key notion for Tarde in his later work. This was, in a way, a realization for a need to support his theory of representational spreading with an interaction-based model. In his outline, he pointed out a thesis that is the source of his essential contradictions with the Durkheimians (Tarde, 1903, p. 74). "What is society? I have answered: Society is imitation. We have still to ask: What is imitation? Here the sociologist should yield to the psychologist." The terms of social psychology and collective psychology all suppose that there is a society out there to which the individuals adapt. The child is raised through interactions of two, four, five persons toward society. There is an interactive development toward larger groups and toward society. Tarde developed an entire classification of possible influences between individuals and groups, in ideas, in communicative rhetoric, in emotion contagion, and so on. For Tarde, the interpsychological interactions were crucial in explaining social life, rather than the collective representations of the Durkheim school. Vargas et al. (2008) provide a modern account for the relevance of this debate. The possibility of tension between academic psychology and sociology in explaining social phenomena was present at the turn of the century. This tension appeared in a famous debate between Durkheim and Gabriel Tarde on the proper relations between the two disciplines in 1903 at one of the prestigious new schools for social research. They were already engaged in fierce discussions regarding the interpretation of the individual and social factors in the explanation of suicide. In the open debate, Tarde argued that the laws of imitation are basic general psychological phenomena of an individual kind, that are able to explain the spreading of habit, while the collective representations of Durkheim were somehow ungrounded. Tarde even claimed that they were "pseudorealistic entities."

> In the study of social facts only acts coming from intermental psychology can be relevant. Thus, one has to turn to this interpsychology to explain social facts. . . . There are two types of social categories to be studied: 1. Groups of persons acting intermentally (families, classes, nations). 2. Action groups (languages, morals, institutions). It would be desirable for the social sciences to constantly remember this distinction instead of self-feeding from vain entities. Intermental psychology is elementary sociology.
> (Tarde in Durkheim & Tarde, 1904, pp. 83–4)

Durkheim, for his part, emphasized that the essential issue is that sociology should remain a theoretical philosophy of society. It has to study the most general laws of sociality.

> All the facts studied by the distinct social sciences would have a common feature, since they are social, and sociology would have as its object of study the social fact in its abstraction. Comparing social facts, one would see what elements are found in all of them, and what are the general signs of sociality.
> (Durkheim in Durkheim & Tarde, 1904, p. 5)

Durkheim argued that the social determination and the social patterns can never be deduced from individual psychology. Tarde went so far as to claim in the debate that he was representing a nominalist vision, while Durkheim was a realist in the sense of proposing the existence of social representations. The two approaches were not as diametrically opposed as the participants felt. Both supposed that society is made up of individuals. Neither of them was really denying individuality. They had alternative theories, however, about the ways the individual agent is constrained. Tarde emphasized interaction, while Durkheim proposed abstract constraints. Due to the sudden death of Tarde, the debate did not directly continue. Later on, in the 1920s, further debates developed, mainly conceptual in nature, along the radical interpretation of Durkheim – there is no individuality, merely social facts, and the rest is physiology. The substance and implications of the debates were very interesting: Where do social phenomena belong, and what is the proper relation between individual, social, and societal? (We saw this in Chapter 5 as the Blondel–Halbwachs debate.)

The substantial issue is still with us. It comes back in the debates about individuality and social life, in the "interpsychic" theories of recent approaches to the social mind, and in concerns about the ontological status of social factors, that is, from the world 3 ideas of Popper (1972, 1976) to the social representation theory of Moscovici (1984).

Tarde (1901) was aware of some of these issues when he took up the challenge of crowd psychology as well. His most important contribution in this regard was to oppose crowd to publics. **Publics** arise in modern times as distant communities, readerships of a journal, and so on, something like what later is going to be called **public opinion**.

> The *public* . . . is a dispersed crowd, where the effect of minds on each other is a distance action. The *opinion* that results from these distant or contact actions if for the crowds and publics is somewhat what the thought is to the bodies. And if we look for what is the most general and constant of these actions of which it is a result, we shall find *conversation* which is totally ignored by the sociologists.
>
> (Tarde, 1901, p. 7)

The other important element in the theory of Tarde was his idea of emphasizing that imitation corresponds to a "modeler–model follower" image, where the social hierarchy of what later was to be called **opinion leaders** is crucial.

In this regard, it is interesting for a historical consideration how much the theory of Tarde, but in fact the crowd theories, and folk psychology as well were technically missing data for their enterprise. It is easy to criticize them for their naive or anecdotal attitude. Most of the time, unfortunately, they were missing data. Tarde himself, the professional criminologist, was well aware of the new social statistics. He proposed, however, that in the domain of cultural integration, these hard data are missing. How could they obtain data on the distribution of social practices?

The basic idea of imitation as proposed by Tarde and Baldwin came back in the mid-20th century in several waves. First, the neobehaviorists rediscovered imitation as a basic mechanism of social learning, from Neal Miller and Dollard to Bandura (Chapter 8). Later, the radicals of the cognitive movement, especially Chomsky, seriously questioned the explanatory power of imitation (Chapter 9). As a still later move, imitation has become a basic mechanism and, indeed, even a rational mechanism (Gergely et al., 2002; Gergely & Csibra, 2006). Imitation is more and more interpreted in contemporary theories of development as a tool of cultural integration and socialization.

Timeline of main events in the genesis of social psychology

Social psychology has gradually emerged by leaving speculations regarding the "group mind," national differences, and crowds alone. In the 1920s, both in Germany and in the United States, it became a respected chapter of psychology with its own data gathering methods. It was interpreting humans as social agents and also offered practical help for societies with multiple social tensions.

The crucial and moving issues in the structure of social psychology have an influence over its historical reconstruction. House (1977) showed that by the mid-20th century, there was a differentiation between an individuum-based psychological social psychology, mainly using experimental methods (and assuming a universal human subject), an interaction-based mainly observational symbolic interactionism, and a sociological social psychology (House labels the latter one as psychological sociology) that deals with the effects of large societal structures on human behavior and personality.

The new handbook edited by DeLamater and Ward presents a more substance-oriented classification instead of a discipline and method-oriented classification (DeLamater, 2013, pp. vi–vii):

- The impact of one individual on another
- The impact of a group on its individual members
- The impact of individuals on the groups in which they participate
- The impact of one group on another

This interaction-based approach is a bit cheap with the representation-based approaches; thus, I propose a slightly richer agenda, also indicated in Figure 6.3.

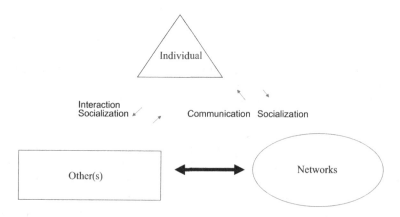

Figure 6.3 Main topics of social psychology.

Classified roughly, the main parts of social psychology deal with the following issues:

The socius, the general other. Issues of person perception, factors of attraction, socialization, imitation and modeling, the role of others in self-development, attributing human agency, theory of mind. Personality and social psychology.

Group processes. Group structure, leadership, group decisions, spontaneous and institutional groups. From crowd psychology to group dynamics.

Society and the mind. Social rules and morality, social systems (language, family, etc.) and the mind, attitudes and their dynamics, categorization, stereotypes, prejudice.

Socialization. Role theory and the development of ToM and Self.

Social representations and the mind. From *Völkerpsychologie* to social representations. Networks of persons and of the mind.

Interaction, communication, and mental processes. Language and body language. Persuasion and psychological rhetoric. Mass communication.

In the general outline of the new history of social psychology handbook edited by Kruglanski and Stroebe (2012), they present the fate of social psychology over 150 years in the making with two crucial issues, and this usage shows already a clear American self-image: the rise of experiments and the appearance of textbooks. Following their ideas, I propose a slightly enriched timeline.

1890: Around 1890, **group effects over individual performance** were first seriously studied, almost the same time as the interest toward crowd behavior was raised. Experimentation was started by looking for the impact of peers, the presence of social groups, and competitive settings on performance.

1920s: Attitudes and public opinion became central, with measurement efforts and the formation of a neutralized non-essentialist equivalent to the group mind, "public opinion."

1925: Field notions and groups in Germany. An alternative experimental social psychology was developed in the frames of Gestalt psychology in Berlin, around Kurt Lewin (1926). Lewin introduced dynamic methods into experimental social psychology by creating situations where, for example, success and failure were experienced as results of manipulated feedbacks.

1930s: Elementary phenomena under social influence. During the next decade, many elementary phenomena were shown to be under social influence. Sherif (1936), in his famous studies, showed that even the autokinetic effect is influenced by the group frame when the subjects are in a group decision situation.

1930s: Lewin in the USA. Lewin's influence in America was twofold. His pervasive influence was both practical and experimental. In this process, the Lewinian input became individualized. What is psychological field and space for Lewin becomes internal balancing for Heider and Festinger.

1940s–1950s: learning theory, imitation, and psychoanalytic concepts. The Yale group and others, Dollard, Miller, Mowrer, Bandura. Aggression and imitation.

1950s–1960s: Attribution and dissonance theories, theories of communication and persuasion (Heider, Festinger), and the development of **cognitive social psychology.**

1950s–1960s: "Cold War social psychology." Studies on the issues of authority, obedience, cruelty, prejudice. Based on experiences during hot wars in Europe and Asia and the Cold War between the Western world and the Soviet Union and its bloc.

1970s: Europe starts its own efforts from the late 1960s on. A European association was founded in 1966, and a *European Journal of Social Psychology* was started in 1971. Conferences and workshops were trying to integrate social psychologists on a European level, and alternatives toward experimental social psychology were articulated. The Americanization was widely criticized, concentrating on minority issues and the new concept of social representation. This later issue has led to general new reconsideration of the differences between micro-social and societal social psychology.

During the articulation of social psychology, the classic experimentalists have become citation classics. Table 6.1 shows some examples from the first 30 years.

Social psychology developed its own journals. The two main American journals, in an interesting way, approached social psychology with human personality. They were more with the socialization type of social psychology promoted in the prehistory by Baldwin (1897) than with the spirit of victorious experimentation. From 1921 to 1965, the top journal was *Journal of Abnormal and Social Psychology*, and from 1965 on, *Journal of Personality and Social Psychology*.

According to the historical survey of Jahoda (2007), Darwinian social psychology was initially strong in America. William James, Baldwin, G. H. Mead, and Cooley belonged to this group. Imitation and the social function of language were

Table 6.1 Presence of classical social psychologists of the experimental trends according to Google Scholar citations.

From the 1930s	Lewin	82,000
	Sherif	35,000
	Moreno	10,000
From the 1950s	Festinger	74,000
	Cartwright	37,000
	Heider	32,000
	Asch	19,000
From the 1960s	Bandura	317,000
	Kelley	49,000
	Zajonc	34,000
	Milgram	30,000
	Schachter	25,000

Note: Using Harzing (2011) method.

crucial for these people. In an interesting twist, both the cultural and the Darwinian flavor of early American social psychology was lost when social behavior was started to be treated by the neobehaviorists as a learning issue and by the Lewin followers as an issue of group dynamics. Social psychology has become a more and more detailed study of present-day White middle-class socialization and social integration processes.

Social becomes individualized and experimental: the American move of establishing social psychology

The professionalization of social psychology took great steps after the First World War. As we have seen on Figure 5.1, that was the first time "social psychology" as a topic became popular in the professional psychology literature. In the general literature also, its first popularity is to be found in the 1930s, according to Google Ngram plots. Two aspects were crucial in this process, which are two sides of the same movement. Especially in American psychology, in different forms of behaviorism, there was a further reinforcement of empiricism, as well as the proliferation of mass psychological data collection in the study of intelligence and personality. With the moves toward data, it became clear that even if we are talking about social aspects of human behavior, it can only be measured in the individual reactions. In the methodology, this meant trying to operationalize "social effects" in actual experimental settings. Alongside this move, a conceptual reinterpretation appeared that was looking with more and more suspicion to notions of "collective consciousness," "group mind," and the like. This has resulted in a radical reinterpretation of the place of social psychology. Rather than being a study of group representations, it has become more and more a study of **actual interactions among actual people** and the mental representation and behavioral effect of these interactions.

The rise of experimentation

As Kurt Danziger (2000) summarized it, the social psychological experiment was stabilized in three consecutive waves between 1920 and 1970.

1. The 1920s, Floyd Allport (1924a, 1924b). **Only individual behavior is measurable.**
2. Lewin. **Experiments are holistic.** They depend on the entire situation, along with *Gestalt* ideas about a structured environment (Lewin 1931, 1935, 1951). Experiments are illustrations. They are pure cases, but they do not exhaust the phenomenon studied, and they always presuppose a theory to which they do fit. All group dynamics, and all researches using contextual manipulation, go back to the introduction of the whole situation and, as a part of it, the use of false feedback into the laboratories, into schools, factories, and so on to manipulate the situation.
3. **Treating individuals as coming from populations, not from real groups.** Experimentation in social psychology also started to use in the 1950s the

analysis of variance models. This attitude usually picks participants in group experiments on a random basis and ignores existing real groups and, as Danziger presents it, treats subjects as anomic individuals who drift from this interaction to another.

> Before they became subjects in a social psychological experiment individuals would be involved in all kinds of social relationships [. . .] In the now dominant paradigm all this would be controlled for by their random assignment to various experimental groups. [. . .] that was true only of multi-individual formations that had no internal structure, that is, *populations*. [. . .] In the case of social formations structured by inter-individual and inter-group relations, for example, kinship groups, economic organizations, or administrative bureaucracies, a sampling theory based on the random selection of *individuals* would be inapplicable. An experimental practice based on the randomized assignment of individuals to treatment groups has an implicit social ontology, one that operates with populations rather than societal formations.
> (Danziger, 2000, p. 344)

We have to remember, however, that the criticism of Danziger is only partially true. In modern city life, it is actually true that many of our interactions go on with strangers. While the random assignment model does not represent well processes involving families, work groups, interest groups, and the like, it does represent interaction between strangers in modern life. It is a great issue for future social science to relate these two aspects of human relations. Even the semantics are changing with the advent of new virtual communities. We talk less of groups and more of networks today.

Individualism

Floyd Allport (1890–1978), the older brother of Gordon Allport, was trained at Harvard by social behaviorists like John Holt and Perry, as well as by Münsterberg. The behaviorists made Allport sensitive to interpret social interaction in a stimulus–reaction framework, and Münsterberg made him aware of the early German work on social facilitation. McDougall, with his instinct theories, was more of an alienating factor in his Harvard years. Floyd Allport started to do experimental work on group effects, and that is what has led him to be a leader of the experimental spirit and individualization in American social psychology. Floyd Allport was crucial, with his brother, in connecting social psychology to the issue of personality, with a groundbreaking study of a later key notion of personality research, **personality traits** (Allport & Allport, 1921). This was a crucial move toward an operationalization of personality research. They also worked alternately as associate editors of the *Journal of Abnormal and Social Psychology*. Their association was not ideal after a while. Gordon Allport wanted to develop a separate chapter of personality psychology, while his older brother, Floyd, believed that personality should be entirely studied in its social setting. The attitude of Floyd Allport was a middle-of-the-road behaviorism that treats behavior to be a central notion for psychology, including social psychology as well, while Gordon Allport was more "mentalistic" in all domains.

Floyd Allport was crucial in making the individualizing move central to American social psychology. There was an interesting affiliation between the general individualism and its rise and the individualist methodologies of social psychology started and promoted by Floyd Allport. Individualism had a long history from the Renaissance through the impact of printing to economic individualism. In the early 20th century, it became a motivation and an underlying ideology of individualist methodologies in contrast to collectivistic ideologies that underlay the collectivist theories of Durkheim and McDougall and Karl Marx in the background. Floyd Allport was, in fact, analyzing the category errors in his argument for individualization. The essence of the category error was that psychological, mental predicates can only be assigned to individual human agents. A category error was seen when people were talking about things like "the nation remembers your sacrifice," "Austria wants revenge," "England is upset." Allport supported the category mistake by a substantial claim as well: there is no body-like organization corresponding to the "group mind," while for individual thought, we have a corresponding bodily continuity of the tissues

Social sciences believe they can explain things by relying on properties of the groups. These errors Allport calls the "group fallacy."

> This fallacy may be defined as the error of substituting the group as a whole as a principle of explanation in place of the individuals in the group.... We do not need a super-mind hypothesis to explain mob action, if we but take the trouble to study the individual in the mob and observe how he is responding to the stimuli afforded by the behavior of his fellows. This neglected field of study is being brought to the foreground by a modern social psychology whose data comprise the social behavior of the individual.
> (Allport, 1924b, p. 689, 690)

His textbook started from the same individualistic metatheory.

> Social psychology is the science which studies the behavior of the individual in so far as his behavior stimulates other individuals, or is itself a reaction to their behavior; and which describes the consciousness of the individual in so far as it is a consciousness of social objects arid social reactions. More briefly stated, social psychology is the study of the social behavior and the social consciousness of the individual.
> (Allport, 1924a, p. 12)

The textbook outlined his program in detail. Besides presenting his studies in social facilitation, Allport also gave a detailed criticism of crowd psychology. Rather than talking about undifferentiated crowds, he outlined a comprehensive taxonomy of group types and their effects on individual behavior. Unorganized group effects are fashion and fade, convention, public opinion, and the likes. Organized, controlled group effects come with church, state, and education.

Decades later, F. Allport (1937), in his clear individualistic stance against any kind of group mind ideas, even criticized the notion of public opinion. He warned American social scientists that they often treated the public as a personalized agent, committing many errors in demonizing it. He reminded his colleagues that the group phenomena has a new twist actually in modern urban societies, with less integration than in the rural communities.

> We are not denying the possibility that a superior product of group interaction may exist. . . . Writers who have stressed them have perhaps been thinking of small, totally inclusive rural or pioneer communities where adjustment to nature and to one's fellow men is direct, and where the common, integrated opinion is practically synonymous with the common life. . . . In our modern vast and growing urban populations, complex in composition and organization, where face-to-face contacts of whole personalities are giving way to occupational and other groupings, it is doubtful how much real integrative effect does take place in an individual's ideas through discussion with others.
> (F. Allport, 1937, pp. 11–12)

Here is the argument for studying social behavior with strangers.

There was a dialectical development here. Following Allport, all social phenomena were to be studied on the individual level. By using this methodical strategy, they had to realize the centrality of the social element in the individual cognition later on. There are aspects of human life, such as language, that are inextricably social. In sharing meanings, meanings are not constructed by individuals; they are somehow inherent into social usage, such as language. Floyd Allport, the methodical individualist, is presented as responsible for the loss of the social (Danziger, 2000). This is a simplification, however. While Floyd Allport was a methodical individualist, he claimed that thinking is, by its very nature, social.

> *The Social Character of the Individual's Thinking.* The stability of human society is best appreciated when we realize that thought itself has its origin in social contacts. Concepts, or symbol reactions, the essential tools of thinking, have evolved through language and have therefore a social origin. A word had its original use as a means of representing an object to *another* and *controlling another's behavior* with reference to that object. . . . This fact gives to meaning itself a fundamental social significance.
> (Allport, 1924a, p. 468)

Individualism has taken a new, less-methodical, and more-substantial turn in the last generation. The new approaches for the interpretation of social life that break away from the SSSM framework claim that elementary sociality is embedded into the individual mind and has some primary individualized biological bases. Thus, in the long run, the individualist move initiated by Floyd Allport is with us under new evolutionary guises. But one has to add that, with the new possibilities of depersonalized data mining, opportunities emerged where data on social behavior can be collected without studying or asking the individuals producing them.

The individualization around the 1920s had interesting evaluative dimensions about the role of communities and individuals in life at large. In Europe, around the turn of the last century, the shaken individual has become important for many representatives of the nascent social sciences as a protection against deindividuation in modern life and against the threats appearing in modern crowds. A bourgeois/citizen individuality was to be preserved. This was a defense of the Cartesian Ego by authors so different as Bergson or Le Bon, Marcel Mauss, and the personalism movement in the psychology of W. Stern. In America, the individual was to be protected not as a Cartesian Ego but as a self-organizing autonomous economic agent. Protection of individuality here had some anti-religious, secular overtones, as a protection against the dominance of the church community. Socially, it was an agentive individuality and not a cognitive epistemic one that was to be protected. In psychology, the American defense of individuality was based on methodical individuality and not an individuality reconstructing an internal cognitive self.

Group processes

Group psychology and crowd psychology became popular around the same time in the general mind. A Google Ngram search shows their parallel popularity in the 1920s–1930s, but then in the 1960s, group psychology wins in the common mind as well as in academia. The concept of group would allow for an integration of the individualistic methodology and the issues of the social influence in a pragmatic way: social influences on individual behavior appear in group settings. Further, the groups have a characteristic structure that is related to issues of group ambiance, leadership, and societal structures. Groups studied by psychologists can be related to large social groups studied by sociologists. Finally, group relations are seen by the individuals; individuals do represent their contacts that are going to be the bases for a network-like image of human relations.

Regarding the structure of disciplines, group psychology as the key chapter of social psychology takes shape in the 1920s, by the time sociology is more or less established. Thus, the individualistic study of the social life of people takes place in settings of their immediate social life that is studied as a component of society by sociology. Through the involvement in studying groups, the entire danger of losing the social, as emphasized half a century later, was less-threatening.

There was a macro social aspect to the interest toward groups. By the early 20th century, due to the development of industry, the compulsory schooling system, and military service, the experience and adaptation to newer and newer groups was a fact of everyday life. Social psychology tried to model these events.

Group influences on individual behavior

The study of the influence of actual group presence was started early on. On cycling speed and motor speed in general, social facilitation was found in the first works summarized by Floyd Allport (1920), but depending on the subjects – sometimes young teenagers were used – they also found some slowing down of the good performers and speeding up of the weak ones (Moede, 1920). The group effects in German educational settings were also observed very early on by Meumann (1913) in the comparison between homework and schoolwork. Moede, with his monograph, was a systematizer of this early tradition of group effects. These German efforts were transmitted to Floyd Allport by his adviser at Harvard, Münsterberg. Moede did not have too much effect in Germany. He called his own work crowd psychology (*Massenpsychologie*), which was a dubious term. Floyd Allport (1924a), in contrast, generalized the effects found to groups at large in his textbook. Issues of group have become issues of group influence on behavior in the experimental spirit. Allport also proposed general ideas about rule following in social settings, claiming a so-called inverted J effect: most people would follow the rule, for example, in an actual traffic regulation behavioral observation study, with a small fraction of deviations.

In the mid-1930s, Muzafer Sherif (1906–1988), a Turkish American psychologist, showed that even seemingly simple perceptual phenomena, such as the autokinetic effect (seeing stable projected lights as moving), do follow social norms. In a group situation, a social norm is formed to which the subjects accommodate. There is an increasing conformity after people in groups of three listen to the announcements of others. If they were put into a group situation after they established an individual norm, there was still a group convergence, but to a lesser degree. Sherif (1936) outlined a comprehensive theory of social norm formation and the way the social norms were crucial for the development of the Ego. In this regard, he combined psychoanalytic consideration with his own studies of norms. That was the way he approached the individuality challenge proposed for social psychology by Floyd Allport. Sherif continued his pioneering works on group processes later on. In a frequently cited study (Sherif et al., 1954), he combined experimental work with real-life observation. He created groups of 12-year-old boys unknown to each other in a summer camp and introduced situations of competition for scarce resources. He showed the genesis of intergroup prejudices and conflictful behaviors, but he had also shown the possibility of reconciliation.

The study of group effects on performance, the exact parameters, and contextual determinants goes continuously ever since. Group processes became crucial for democratic decision-making in the Lewin tradition. In this matter, a highly debated rethinking was introduced by the notion of **groupthink** proposed by Janis (1972). He basically claimed that if there is a high level of group cohesion, an increased need for assumed conformism, and if the group is isolated from outside influence and the group is under high stress, group performance may become irrational. His famous case studies involved the Bay of Pigs invasion of Cuba, the continuation of the Vietnam War, and similar real political fiascos directed by socially isolated think tanks. The general effect is that if the ingroup is very integrated and isolated from the world, there is more danger of groupthink. The proposal has been subjected to many case studies and laboratory studies. The essential point is that the tension between invention, or rationality, and following the group that was identified by Tarde (1903) is still with us.

Lewin and group dynamics: the ideologist of democracy

Kurt Lewin (1890–1947) and his students in America, both in Iowa and at MIT, performed several studies that turned his personality system developed in the German *Gestalt* frame (Chapter 12 in Volume 1) into a theory about the person moving in a social field (Lewin, 1951). Lewin was an activist researcher – also in contact with the Frankfurt group of neo-Marxists – for whom the fight against Nazi ideology was a central issue of his science as well. Lewin, as part of the fight against authoritarianism, also meant to prove the superiority of democracy in quasi-experimental settings. His famous experiments in group climate made him a classic of social psychology, while the motivation for his research was of an actual political nature. One study had to do with the effects of frustration. Lewin, Lippitt, and White (1939) showed that children undergoing frustration regressed to a lower, developmentally more primitive level of behavior. Human aggression – we are in a world preparing for another war – is not a biological fate of man but one possible reaction to frustration, regression and stereotype formation being the other two. With this research, the Lewin group fit well into the New Deal American image of showing social science evidence for the role of frustration in the development

Figure 6.4 Kurt Lewin.
Source: Wikimedia commons. Public domain.

of negative social behaviors, especially aggression, as shown in animal and child models by Dollard, Doob, Miller, Mowrer, and Sears (1939).

The same study of the Lewin group showed the impact of **leadership style** on mood and efficiency in groups. Lewin, Lippitt, and White (1939) showed with children that democratic leadership style (with bargaining allowed for members, but with a disciplined execution of joint decisions) led to better mood, less aggression, and in some cases, improved performance, as contrasted to authoritatively directed groups. Under democracy, there is more mutual trust, less free riding, and less superficial obedience. With these works, Lewin clearly aligned himself with the Roosevelt-style American political liberalism.

This theory and this study were a mirror of the large social system differences on the level of mid-20th-century society. In a way, it was the psychological equivalent of the theories proposed by Popper (1945) on open society and Arendt (1951) on the totalitarian systems, criticizing both fascist and communist authoritarianism. According to the optimistic image promoted by Lewin, groups are dynamic, open systems fitting into the larger society. Groups can become important tools to fight prejudice, change of behavior, and efficient fast social change. Under the initiative of Lewin, this led to the development of practical group work from the 1950s on in many areas of psychology, from clinical groups to managerial, military, or teacher training groups.

Lewin was also a crucial person in shaping the methodology of modern American social psychology. He was responsible for training people in how to manipulate the setting and the feedback to increase the likelihood of certain feelings and reactions. For Lewin, this was a tool to study the effects of internal factors, especially the level of aspiration on performance and the experience of success and failure done by Tamara Dembo and summarized in Lewin (1935, 1951). These were the bases for personality or internal factors–based theories of achievement and forerunners of the intrinsic motivation ideas. At the same time, the context manipulation experiments obtained a wider impact in America. They were responsible for all the false feedback and stooge studies from Asch and Schachter to Milgram. An originally phenomenologically motivated idea of how to manipulate the internal factors of situation interpretation has become a tool to study the agent and "double agent" situations during the Cold War.

There certainly was much naivety in the campaign of psychologists for a democratic society, both regarding the data and the theoretical analysis given "The leadership studies have been simplified into a moral fable, in which democracy was shown to be 'good' and autocracy 'bad'. . . . To use Lewin's terminology, these scientific stories are told using moral concepts that are Aristotelian, not Galileian" (Billig, 2015, p. 452). This simplification had several messages. The social-political simplification and the cross talk between the social commitments of generations of researchers simplify the issues. That was true for several cultural settings, even for French textbooks, or the use of Lewin references in the 1970s in communist-governed Hungary, where Lewin became a reference for a dream of a free and democratic society. This kind of simplification is seen today causing much of social science to be engaged in political issues, which in turn cause severe political tribalism, wherein arguments and facts of the rival group are patently ignored (Clark &

Winegard, 2020). Further, the famous motto of Lewin – *there is no more practical than a good theory* – showed the powers of theory in all this history. Third, the important conceptual tools of Lewin, like his topological drawings with their complicated environmental value giving diagrams, were entirely dissociated from his empirical studies. The American followers of Lewin took up the experimentation, including cheating the subjects, as well as the practical interest action research, but they were not really interested in the sophisticated theory about the reality of groups (Danziger, 2000). Lewin's theory may have been undervalued in America, but his research style was valued and had a central impact on social psychology around the entire world. He is duly interpreted as the founder of the idea of "democratic social engineering." The lasting effect of Lewin is shown also by the prestige of the Kurt Lewin Memorial price for American social psychologists.

Sociometry

Jacob Lévy Moreno (1892–1974), the Romanian-born, Austrian-educated psychiatrist, social therapist and movement organizer, spent most of his active life from 1925 in the USA, partly as a teacher at Columbia University and the New School, but mainly propagating through private foundations his new approaches to group psychology and group therapy, which also had applications in criminology. Moreno had a social utopist message. He was also a constant dynamic improvisationist, having some allures of a surrealist happening organizer. Moreno positioned himself between social theorists like Marx, individual psychologists like Freud, naive crowd psychologists, and hypnosis theorists, as he recalled in his memoir (Moreno, 1985). His aim was to show that the human species is specifically social and that is what distinguishes us in the animal kingdom. To understand human personality and disorders, and cure the latter ones, we have to concentrate on social relations. This message was outlined in his program book titled *Who Shall Survive?* (Moreno, 1934).

In order to understand human relations in groups and personality, he introduced some surprising new concepts. In his interpretation, social networks are formed from elementary relations that Moreno calls **social atoms**.

> Social Atoms [are] the smallest constellation of psychological relations which can be said to make up the individual cells in the social universe. It consists of the psychological relations of one individual to those other individuals to whom he is attracted or repelled and their relation to him all in respect to a specific criterion (as living in proximity).
> (Moreno, 1934, p. 476)

The relations between the individuals are based on tele, that is, distance, attractions. **Tele** for Moreno is a basic attraction between people; it is like sexual attraction.

> A feeling is directed from one individual towards another. It has to be projected into distance. Just as we use the words tele-perceptor, telencephalon,

tele-phone, etc., to express action at distance, so to express the simplest unit of feeling transmitted from one individual towards another we use the term tele, distant.

(ibid., 159)

The distribution of these attractions and repulsions was studied by questionnaires tapping the sympathy relations between the individuals. For example: "Choose five girls from the whole community whom you would like best of all as coworkers and name them in order of preference, first choice, second choice, third, fourth, and fifth" (ibid., 109).

The method reveals the internal structure of the groups. Figure 6.5 shows an example from Moreno himself.

Moreno tried to classify the groups as being well- or less-organized, vertical or horizontal, and the individuals as leaders, subordinates, isolates, and so on. In all this process, "the basis of sociometric classification is not a psyche which is bound

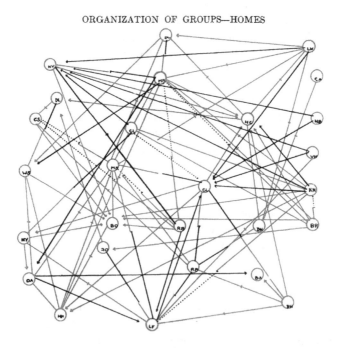

ORGANIZATION OF GROUPS—HOMES

STRUCTURE OF A COTTAGE FAMILY—C13
27 individuals; isolated 5; pairs 23; mutual rejections 1; incompatible 1; chains 2; triangles 5; squares 1; stars 3.
Distribution, 74% Attractions, 26% Rejections.
Type of organization, highly introverted.

Figure 6.5 The sociometric structure of a family living together.

Source: Moreno (1934, p. 128).

up within an individual organism, but an individual organism moving around in space in relation to things or other subjects also moving around him in space" (ibid., 377).

Besides his elaborating the method of sociometric group measurements, Moreno (1946) developed his method of group psychotherapy that aimed to heal through role-playing in group situations. This method has become a successful combination of the spontaneous drama tradition and the "role consciousness" of group-based dynamic psychotherapies. The long success of group intervention methods in psychology has started with psychodrama. The goal-oriented groups, as well as the groups aiming "merely" to enrich personality, have become supplements or even substitutes of family and community relations in modern humans. In his psychodrama practice, where he acted together with his wife, and in his movement, Jacob Moreno felt he was the organizer, and his wife, Zelka Moreno, the spontaneous part.

Sociometry became extremely popular in the 1950s–1960s since it also had a central place in the handbooks of social psychology at large, and of group processes in particular, and psychotherapy (see, for an overview after half a century, Borgatta, 2007). Moreno's method is still with us; it is becoming connected to new methods of network research. In 1937, Moreno founded the journal *Sociometry*, which existed under this name for 40 years and later turned into a general social psychology journal of the American sociologists. As Figure 6.6 shows, in popularity, both psychodrama and sociometry figured high in the 1950s, and while sociometry declined, psychodrama had two further increases in the 1970s and during the late 1990s.

Sociometry continues to be a widely used method, even today. Let me show this by taking the example of Hungarian sociometry. The leader of its innovative usage was Ferenc Mérei (see Chapter 5). In his first social psychology works, he tried to find social influences in elementary psychological phenomena. He pointed out an "experiential surplus" in group situations that is different from the mere sum of the individual experiences. He observed in children's groups that there was an intricate interplay between the leaders and the group. The new-coming leader always tried to accommodate to the value system of the group. The experienced "group surplus"

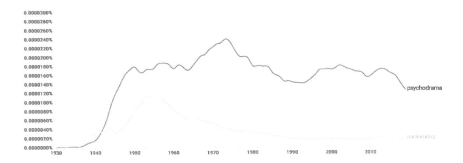

Figure 6.6 The mention of *sociometry* and *psychodrama* in the general literature.
Source: Google Ngram data.

is not some mysterious effect but a tradition carried by the individuals, who are strengthened by it (Mérei, 1949). Later, Mérei (1997) had shown these effects in the community enforcing allusions of adults.

Around the same time, Mérei developed the method of sociometry into a multidimensional procedure (Mérei, 1971). Besides attraction, he has also asked for functional abilities (who would be the best drawer, best group organizer, and so on). Mérei, who myself was imprisoned for his participation in the 1956 revolution, with the personal qualities of a network guru, found the place of real human groups in a centralized authoritarian society (Hungary in the 1960s) that concentrated on institutional socialization and institutional networks and communities with all its official weight. The superiority of the spontaneous and emotion- or attraction-based groupings versus the formal ones was claimed in an authoritarian society, where the official ideology paid an enormous amount of lip service to "communal organization," and to the idea of an abstract predominance of the social over the individual. At the same time, the *de facto* society was based on strong hierarchies, and societal organization in communist Hungary was bureaucratic. Mérei (1994) worked as a committed social scientist even when in prison. Analyzing his dreams he had shown the dominance of actual social contacts in manifest dream content.

Group interventions have also proven to be important in industrial interventions. The famous Hawthorne studies on an American electric plant have shown, for example, in the work of Elton Mayo (1880–1949) of the Harvard Business School, that caring for the workers has more effects on work efficiency than improving the physical plant. The **human factors** and, among them, group organization and leadership style have become leading slogans of new management. With the work of Mayo (1933), social psychology entered industry.

Interestingly, group psychology has been on the decline since the 1970s. There are several factors contributing to this effect. There is a lack of an integration of small group research results into a general theory of society, the moving interest of sociology also toward issues of culture rather than groups, and finally, the shift toward networks in society instead of groups. A crucial factor within psychology was the victory of cognitive social psychology, which started to treat humans as social information processors. One aspect of group research, however, has come up during the last few decades. With the advent of the general network and social relationship theory promoted by the British anthropologist Robin Dunbar (1998, 2003, 2021), empirical research started to study human relation networks rather than groups. They showed, for example, that the spread of mood, smoking, and even diseases can be interpreted in a framework of network theory. Networks take over the place of groups in early 21st-century social sciences, along with the fact that parallel to this intellectual interest, swiftly changing and many times virtual networks have begun to dominate everyday life.

Attitudes and prejudices: the psychology of social evaluation

The other key notion besides groups for the new empirical social psychology from the 1930s would be **attitudes**. This notion introduced to psychology the idea of an individual evaluation of social partners or socially relevant others. Thomas and Znaniecki (1927) used this notion in large-scale sociology in Chicago in their work on Polish peasants. They treated attitudes as being equivalent of general social and cultural values directing social behavior. Psychologists translated this into the issue of evaluation of particular objects, persons, and situations and tried to find a measurement method for them.

Thurstone (1928), who was a leader in psychological measurement at that time, extended his psychophysical efforts toward the measurements of social attitudes, by listing different possible opinions. He tried to show that one can have an ordinal scale of measurement for social attitudes about a given object. Likert (1932) wrote an entire monograph on the measurement of attitude, starting from the non-trivial relations between behavioral dispositions and verbal expressions of them. The general consensus was "that attitudes are dispositions towards overt action; second, that they are verbal substitutes for overt action" (Likert, 1932, p. 9). He developed a series of response variations from yes–no to a five-point agreement, used for evaluating a long series of value-implying statements. The statements themselves were about international relations (Should the United States recognize the Soviet Union?) and race relations (White people should only buy from White farmers). Technically, he showed that the five-point agreement–disagreement scales provide a stable measurement; there is no need for considering the standard deviations and no need for experts. As for the substance, clear general attitudes for internationalism and racial equality (he called this pro-Negro attitude) could be observed, and they had a clear correlation and a clear social class–related distribution. The measured political attitudes are determined by social and cultural factors rather than by individual biology, and their interrelationships (e.g., positive correlation between racial equality and internationalism) may point toward a general radicalism-conservativism attitude.

The methods of attitude measurement continued to develop, with many marketing and other practical implications. This was later developed into finer methods, including the study of emotional meanings by the semantic differential of Osgood (1952, 1960). The concept was applied by many to the explanation of intergroup tensions, until the time Gordon Allport (1954) has taken it over to the detailed analysis of prejudice.

There was a clear social and political background underlying the career of the notion of attitudes. Attitude has become a crucial concept in explaining the possibilities and obstacles for social change, since attitude research went together with research on social stereotypes and prejudices. Attitude research has been a constant topic of liberally committed social psychology in its fight against prejudices and in its dreams about a more equal and fair society. "Look at the prejudices we have, and fight against them" was the liberal message. There was much idealism in these efforts, since they all implied that by changing the perception of people, their actual chances would also change. Gradually, a three-level theory was developed with three components in the technical concept of attitude: cognitive evaluation of attitude objects, emotional evaluation of attitude objects, and behavior. LaPiere (1934) showed in a classic study that attitudes and behavior do not necessarily go together.

While in the 1930s over 90% of American hotel managers showed anti-Chinese attitudes, basically all of them accepted real Chinese guests. We observe deviations in the other directions as well during the 20th century. Accepting verbal attitudes may go together with *de facto* discriminating practices. The century of research on attitude components showed that the emotional and the cognitive components do show an independent coherence, and the emotional aspects are more important in determining behavior than the cognitive components.

Work on attitudes was involved from its onset on in socially and politically sensitive issues. The novelty of new attitude research is related to the cognitive turn, thereby becoming more and more elaborate in trying to see what was already raised by Likert: How do attitudes to different objects interact in the mind?

Cold War social psychology: authoritarianism, conformism, and obedience

The increasing inter-country political and military tensions, together with the influx of persecuted continental European social psychologists and social scientists to America, created a peculiar atmosphere for a genesis of what one can label today with hindsight as **Cold War social psychology**. The label is misleading in one regard. It was mainly Western social psychology showing the impact of the political Cold War, and countries in the Soviet-dominated bloc were mainly involved by Western efforts to export their ideas into Eastern Europe.

In the 1950s–1980s, politics had a direct effect during the Cold War, for example, in the model experiments of the prisoner's dilemma, in research on social and sensory isolation. However, a more intricate issue was the indirect effect of the overall social atmosphere on social psychology. There were several aspects to this, some of them related to personality and society, some others, however, to basic social mechanisms of adaptation. Several essayistic sociological works showed in the mid-20th century that American society had generally become more consumer- and less work-oriented, and with the development of urban mass culture, it had lost its traditional moral stance of community integration and strong democratic commitments, as the success of the book of Harvard sociologist David Riesman (1908–2002) *The Lonely Crowd* pointed out in Riesman (1950). While a generation earlier the fear was the loss of individuality, now the fear was the dominance of social pressures in wealthy suburban America. Social psychology contributed to the understanding of the inner dynamics of these dramatic social changes. A central feature of mid-20th-century Anglo-Saxon social psychology was the constant emphasis on **anti-authoritarian attitudes** and on the importance of **democratic group leadership**. Both authoritarianism and centralized control were assumed to be, at that time, features of Fascist and Communist opponents of the (assumed) open society of mainly American capitalism. While the Lewin- and Adorno-inspired (and mediated) notions retained their original antifascist meaning, they transmitted a more general anti-authoritarianism at the same time (see Erős, 1991, for an Eastern European interpretation). They carried an implication (though openly not spelled out but tacitly assumed) that Western society also showed signs of the illness of authoritarianism and cannot really face democratic leadership practices on any level. The combination of social criticism, the analysis of Western social superiority, and the real tensions during the Cold War led to typical social psychology researches at that time.

1. **Authoritarianism.** Immigrant psychoanalysts and Marxist philosophers of the Frankfurt school started a large-scale American investigation and theoretical work into the origins of fascism. The Frankfurt school, in the 1920s, expressed alternative interpretations of Marxist social theory. While later its representatives distanced themselves from Marxism, they always stood for a critical social science. In their vision, the task of psychology is to also help change modern society. Part of this was questioning the belief in a value-free objective scientific truth. In the American context, they tried to contribute to the understanding of how German fascism had been possible, that is, what were the human, psychological factors involved? Their basic idea was that the power of Hitler was based on a sexually repressed personality development conditioned by the oppressive German socialization patterns. Under the theoretical leadership of Adorno, they developed a questionnaire method that was to identify people high on the F(ascism) scale. It included items like:

   Obedience and respect for authority are the most important virtues children should learn.
   What the youth needs most is strict discipline.
   There is going to be always war and conflict, due to human nature.

   This attitude of combining psychoanalytic interpretation and social commitment (see Chapter 1) was in principled harmony with the approaches of Popper (1945) and Arendt (1951) on showing how both fascist and communist political authoritarianism was threatening to democratic values. It had a crucial role in laying the foundation for research on conservativism as a socially central personality variable as well. At the University of Michigan, Milton Rokeach (1918–1988) successfully extended this issue into a general concept of dogmatism and into a contrast between open and closed mind as a basis of human value systems (Rokeach, 1960, 1973).

2. **Conformism.** Experimental social psychology started to find a clearer way to demonstrate what was claimed to be the negative side of human social life by crowd psychology. They designed situations where, by the use of stooges, there was a tension between group-based opinions and the real factual situation. Solomon Asch (1907–1996) showed that people can sometimes believe the group rather than their own eyes in seemingly simple perceptual decisions (Asch, 1952). However, some people could resist group pressure, and still some others were counterformists. They went against the group even if the group was right (Krech et al., 1962). The studies on group pressure and conformity set the tone for a social psychology always reminding us of the fallibility of the social being to social pressures.

3. **Obedience.** The most dramatic studies about the fallibility of humans to social pressures and its relationship to cruelty came from studies of obedience. Stanly Milgram (1933–1984) at Yale University asked people to administer electric

shocks of differing strength to fellow students if they were underperforming in a learning task. The subjects complied rather well. Milgram (1963) can be interpreted on two levels. Even Americans could be induced to act like obedient servants of the Holocaust. But one can look at the studies from the perspective of the (stooge) victims as well. They project a strongman image as a social setting of postwar American masculinity: for example, I am strong; I can take shocks. Philip Zimbardo (1973), who was a high school classmate of Milgram, at Stanford showed in his infamous prison experiment that if students were assigned to be guards in an experimental prison, they started to exhibit signs of cruelty without specific instruction in this direction.

These studies raised our self-awareness about the "dark sides" of human nature, leading to many value discussions. The studies also raised issues regarding the ethics and practical value of deception-based social psychology research.

4. **Decision theory with its "prisoners dilemma."** Even the cognitive "world model idea" was born in the atmosphere of the Cold War. An entire class of decision situations was developed, with detailed studies of the effects on decisions, issues of rational choice, and emotions. Their model was a Cold War imagined situation: as a prisoner, you have to calibrate of the fellow prisoners to tell the truth or try to hide it.
5. **Brainwashing and sensory deprivation.** While decision theory was motivated by imaginary prison dilemmas, another trend analyzed actual accounts of prison experiences. Due to the accounts of prisoners' treatments in the Korean War in the 1950s, an entire combination of experimental studies and social science research was looking for the possible effects of mere sensory isolation (Heron, 1957) and the supposed re-education called brainwashing.

There were many further aspects of the Cold War. As analyzed by Farr (1996), even the American social relations and the need to decrease social tensions, respecting workers unions, for example, were related to Cold War competition. The need to decrease social tensions as a key to survival was articulated by politicians and by social scientists as well. Gordon Allport raised the idea that social engineering was an important element in the moves toward social peace already during the Second World War.

National character, political culture, and similar group-related ideas were also (re)integrated into the understanding of international relations and to understand the third world and the process of decolonialization. Even David McClelland (1961), with his achievement motivation construct sponsored by the US government, promulgated these ideas in order to try to encourage preindustrial societies to adopt capitalism by developing their cultures toward achievement motivation.

Social psychology goes cognitive: attitude dynamics and attribution theory

By the 1960s, with the weakening of psychoanalytic social psychology and sociology, a cognitive move was taking place in experimental psychology. All this gave a new perspective to revisit the *Gestalt* tradition and also to propose formal theories. *Gestalt*-inspired contributions started to move toward what has later become cognitive social psychology in the 1960s. In a way, "[t]he migration of the *Gestalt* psychologists from Austria and Germany to America was the principal source of inspiration for the cognitive social psychology which is such a distinctive feature of social psychology throughout the modern area" (Farr, 1996, p. 7).

Much of this was initiated decades earlier. Fritz Heider (1896–1988), an Austrian German émigré to the United States, showed in a few experiments the unavoidable social nature of our interpretations of movements of cartoon figures (Heider, 1944; Heider & Simmel, 1944). In seeing small geometric cartoons, people tend to interpret the movement in attributional terms, projecting intentions, and even personality features to the moving drawings (the angry circle chasing the small triangle.) Heider combined the experimental tradition of apparent movement research in the *Gestalt* tradition with an effort to see for social interpretation causation, like *chasing, fleeing* (Heider, 1958, 1983). This research technology became the inspiration for studies done half a century later. They showed that infants already tend to see human agency in moving patterns (Gergely et al., 1995). Heider was thus integrated into the new individualistic frames of biologically based social interpretive models.

In his own time, Heider developed his insights into a general theory of social influence in a book that has over 25,000 citations (Heider, 1958). He proposed a basic theory of tension and balance between beliefs and attitudes. Our situations are always socially evaluated, where we are trying to search for a balance between background knowledge and the incoming stimulation. This work was a bit abstract, but it had become influential through Kelley (1967, 1992) and others developing a more transparent **attribution theory**. Some principles are promoted according to which we tend to attribute some of our failures to chance, while our successes to our own competence. We commit the fundamental attributional error: explain behavior in terms of internal dispositions and tend to neglect situational factors (Ross, 1977). Further, we interpret the behavior of others as being based on wills, while our own behavior finds excuses in the situations, and so on. Festinger (1957), with his very successful theory of cognitive dissonance, showed how practical we are in reconciling our opinions if there are tensions between components (cognition and emotion) or between opinion and reality.

The cognitive mood changed the style of attitude research. Self-identification as "cognitive" appeared even earlier in social psychology than it did in general experimental psychology. Attitudes became internal representations. They started to be interpreted as becoming integrated with other internal representations, thus creating an entire internalist "social worldview." This cognitive trend of attitude research moved them closer to later theories of social representations promoted by European social psychologists, especially Moscovici (1961, 1984). Another factor that has led attitude dynamics close to cognitive psychology was the recognition of how close concepts of stereotypes so central to attitude psychology were to issues like schemata which are so pivotal to general cognitive psychology. Schank and Abelson (1977) and Rumelhart (1980) clearly showed this continuity of stereotype research and cognitive schemata research (Chapter 9 gives more details on this). This went together with the integration of the rediscovered schema theory of Bartlett (1932) to social psychology.

Social psychology and alternative social movements

American social psychology from the 1930s was full of social reforms. The belief in democratic leadership on the group level, the belief in reducing social tensions by reducing frustration, the commitment to interpret interethnic tension as issues of prejudice were all related to the New Deal ideas of social engineering. Following these ideals, social psychology became a central discipline in many countries in an alliance with conflict managing social policies. From the 1970s on, this attitude has been criticized as a reformist social science by the new emancipatory social movements. The mainly left-wing new alternatives did not start from the idea to search for adaptive, tension-reducing social solutions, but rather, they began with a need to uncover injustices and inequalities by means of social science, including social psychology, and make social science an integral part of movements intending to radically change society. The silent majority, however, continues to believe in connecting social psychology to a soft liberal attitude in social policy and in politics.

In a famous paper, Kenneth Gergen (1973) raised the issue that social psychology should be seen more in connection with the historical conditions of its birth and practices and in a stronger alliance with other social sciences and humanities. This perspective shift would, for example, make social psychologists realize not only that they deal with a specific subject pool, the WEIRD, as this group was later called (Western, educated, industrialized, rich, democratic), but also that it has some clear preferences or prejudices toward assumed progress, something like an increased sophistication as a goal of personal development. In this Western middle-class ideal, conformism, authoritarianism, field dependence, and the like are all described as lower-level qualities. In fact, most of the research traditions relating to them come out of a given social situation – from postwar America – and its worry about fascism and communism related to authority and obedience. The new proposal emphasized that we should work toward a psychology that aims more to sensitize people to injustice rather than to predict and control.

Gergen's message has become influential due to his raising the value issue. But as pointed out by Jost and Kruglanski (2002), it lead for a further separation of the experimental and the historical-constructionist traditions within social psychology. Another factor for its influence was to raise the metatheoretical issue of methods. Did not all the laboratory tradition of social psychology depend on culture? Starting from the simple fact of asking subjects to quietly sit in a laboratory, without leaving the session, to their obedience to the authority of the experimenter. Around the same time, behavioral studies on animals, and social studies in school settings by Rosenthal (1966; Rosenthal & Jacobson, 1968), showed how prone behavioral research is to artifacts. They showed that subjects, even animal subjects, were sensitive to the expectations of the researcher. This suggested a general role of the demand characteristics of the psychological experiment as a socially instituted status situation.

The dissatisfaction with the WEIRD people, the dissatisfaction with only doing research on White educated student populations, was translated into real cross-cultural research by Nisbett (Nisbett et al., 2001; Nisbett, 2003) and others, claiming a **holistic–localistic difference** between Asians and Europeans. Nisbett (2003) proposed this series of oppositions as a divergence of worldviews. Eastern people are assumed to be more context-sensitive, including social contexts, and thereby socially more authority-oriented. In contrast, Westerners pay more attention to items and categories. They are therefore less sensitive to contexts, including social contexts, and are cognitively more analytic and socially more individualistic. The opposition also entails some crucial cognitive consequences. In Nisbett's presentation, culture basically has an impact on the primary cognitive processes by directing our attention. So attention is directed more to contexts and relations in Easterners, and it is more directed to elements and ignores context in Westerners (Nisbett & Miyamoto, 2005). This theory is often discussed regarding its factual validity and superficial treatment of East and West. It has one important advantage. While it claims quantitative differences, it no longer has the colonialist overtones like the theories of Lévy-Bruhl (1910) almost a century earlier.

European emancipation

An interesting new consciousness was created in the self-reflection of social psychology after 1968. This year was decisive in several regards for the fate of several social sciences. First, it was hallmarked with the radical and alternative student movements in France, Germany, and the United States. In the same year, radical left-wing movements popped up all over the West, resulting in even terrorism in Germany and Italy. The Prague spring and its Soviet crackdown all initiated a consciousness rising in social science. For the left-wing social scientists, this suggested a need toward **critical theory**, looking for alternative narratives and practices, and a need also arrived to be more historically sensitive for the mainstream social psychologists. Further, a strong local consciousness, a critique of discrimination, self-colonialization, and a changing feeling toward international cooperation were emerging, partly for a more equal US–Europe balance, but partly also to integrate Eastern European social scientists.

Moscovici (1993), in his witty analysis of the epistemological issues involved in the history of social psychology, raised the issue of **relative colonialization**.

After the Second World War, social psychology was taken to most of Western Europe, especially Germany and France, as an American gift. This (self-)colonialization had two consequences, according to Moscovici. First, Europe is not present in American textbooks. Further, even our own past seems to be forgotten by Europeans, and if considered at all, it is considered from an American perspective. This import model of America being the importer is criticized by Moscovici as relying on Durkheim and French crowd psychology as early models of social psychology.

There were many particular events along the line of European emancipation. Europe started its own efforts from the late 1960s on. A European association was founded in 1966, and a *European Journal of Social Psychology* was started in 1971. Conferences and workshops tried to integrate social psychologists on a European level, and alternatives toward experimental social psychology were articulated. The Americanization was widely criticized, concentrating on minority issues and the central concept of social representation. This later issue led to a general new reconsideration of the differences between micro-social and societal social psychology.

Hilde Himmelweit (1918–1989), the German-born social psychologist at the London School of Economics, pointed out that the neglect of societal psychology is a result of a neglect of contexts in all senses. One clear example is the issue of attitude research. Classic examples on opinion leaders and reference groups showed that a more societal approach is needed to understand even the impact of mass media and propaganda, where the role of intermediate reference points is crucial to understand the relations between societal agents and individual behavior (Himmelweit, 1980).

The European efforts were oftentimes also framed as efforts toward a new critical psychology. Many new critical psychologists presented themselves as descendants and agents of the revival of the critical Marxist social theory of the Frankfurt school of the 1960s. They tried to campaign for a psychology that would try to align itself with emancipatory efforts in present-day society and also try to change society (Erős, 1991, 1992).

As the historical book edited by Moscovici and Marková (2006) showed, there were many peculiar American and European social psychological perspectives by the late 1960s on. In these comparisons, Americans were seen to be more static, more factual, while European social psychologists were seen as more dynamic and socially critical, more theory-oriented. A further crucial point was that, for the most part, the same actors who campaigned for a more self-conscious European social psychology also campaigned for a reintegration of Eastern Europeans to world psychology from the 1970s on. They had several meetings across the Iron Curtain. These meetings represented "exciting, though somewhat bizarre encounter between established and self-confident Western scholars, old-fashioned East European Marxist intellectuals and younger social psychologists from behind the 'iron curtain' who showed much eagerness to establish contacts with West European and American researchers" (Erős, 2010, p. 533).

During the emancipatory process, social psychology became realigned with major social changes in the Western world. The new alignment was between different minority movements and social psychology. From the 1970s on, this reconsideration was also put into the frame of gender issues. This implied a dissatisfaction for many with the subordination image of women accepted by mainstream social psychology. The rising feminist movements, with their critique of the study and cultivation of traditional gender roles by social sciences, and the discussion of inequalities became central motivating forces of innovative research perspectives during the last generation. Many of these issues were raised even in connection with mainstream social psychology and mainstream American politics. Many upcoming minority issues were raised in a new manner after school integration following the *Brown v. Board of Education* decisions (Farr, 1996).

Social and societal

The individualization of social psychology and all social science from the 1920s on also resulted in a gradual loss of the social in (mostly American) social psychology with the individualization of social psychology and all social science (Greenwood, 2004; Farr, 1990). That is why in the 1960s you will have new subdisciplines emerging, like **cultural psychology**, **environmental psychology**, and the like, because social psychology itself was largely assigned to individual-behavior level. At the same time, in sociological social psychology, the psychologists emphasize the individual to save it from the over-socialized image (Farr, 1996). Do we need new social psychologies?

Sociological social psychology has two main sources today (Farr, 1996). One is the symbolic interactionism following G. H. Mead. The other background for new societal psychologies was the French social representation movement following Moscovici (1961, 1984). This new approach has been very fruitful. It arose out of a certain distributed organization of attitudes and shared values that are partly organized in a manner similar to the primitive mentality proposed by Lévy-Bruhl. It is different from ideologies in the sense that ideologies, compared to social representations, are elitist, living in communication from elites to other elites, while social representations exist in everyday realities in a bottom-up manner (Moscovici, 1988, 1993).

They are crucial in modern social psychology also since they represent the societal aspect of mental organization. As Sandra Jovchelovitch, the British social psychologist, summarized for the Anglo-American tradition the underlying message, they represent the distribution of ideas in a society. At the same time, they also represent a commitment to certain genesis of these coordinated ideas. She also pointed a way out of the constraining image of society entertained by classical theories of social life.

> The acknowledgement of the social as a whole, which accounts for the genesis of social representations, should not prevent a clear characterization of the social and of its relationship to individual agency. . . . The interplay between subjective and objective, and between agency and reproduction, which constitutes the social fabric is at the very heart of how social representations are formed.
> (Jovchelovitch, 1996, p. 124)

Feminism, critical discourse, and narrative research challenge the traditional separation between small-scale social and large-scale societal. There may well be a pragmatic compromise that would recognize the multifaceted nature of the social mind.

We have to remember that, for over more than a century, the three fields of individual psychology, social psychology, and sociology took their demarcation lines gradually, and it is a mistake to think that these boundaries were somehow fixed to begin with. The two determinations and embeddings are not identical, indeed. Real interactive relations and their entire system constitute the foundations of social determination and embedding. The distinctions are forgotten in ambitious theories. Piaget (1965/19715), for example, talks about social but means *societal*.

Halbwachs (1924, 1950) intended to talk about societal while, in his actual examples, shows social in a small scale, ignoring interaction at the same time.

One can arrive to a dual perspective from sociology, inviting theories like reference group theory that relates society, groups, and individuals (Merton, 1957). Biologically anchored approaches to social life also tend to claim that social embedding is not identical with societal. According to the new biologistic theories, social nature is a crucial characteristic of primates, but this does not entail society. For them, social frame does not necessarily mean a constraining social frame like in SSMS but a constructive one as well, as entertained by many new theories of socialization. A trouble with now-traditional social constructionism is the neglect of this distinction between social and societal.

As we have seen in Chapter 5, many approaches in modern social science treat social and societal in a control function or as a formator of any arbitrary representation. There are several considerations, however, that the biological system of individuals, including the socially anchored biology, constrain social and societal arbitrariness, and social interaction might be a source of representations, not merely a controller. Individualization shows up under a new cover: as a biology of sociality.

Tasks

CA

Compare *Völkerpsychologie* with modern folk psychology.
Völkerpsychologie of Wundt and language history.
Arguments of F. Allport for an individuum-based social psychology.
Compare sociometry with network research today.
Political liberalism and social psychology in different ages.
Prejudice in social life and in social psychology.
The effects of contemporary ICT on group formation.
Virtual reality and society.
Ethical issues in obedience studies.
Validity issues in conformity research.

DSA

"Attitudes" and "prejudices" in common discourse (Google Ngram).
Asch, Milgram, and Zimbardo in psychological texts (PsycINFO).
Floyd and Gordon Allport over a hundred years in psychology (PsycINFO).
Kurt Lewin and "democracy" co-occurrences in psychological texts (PsycINFO).
The "prison experiment" in public discourse (Google Ngram).

7 Soviet/Russian psychology

> In studying what the child is capable of doing independently, we study yesterday's development. Studying what the child is capable of doing cooperatively, we ascertain tomorrow's development.
>
> (Vygotsky, 1934/1986: 203–204)

Political, social, and philosophical background: why a separate chapter?

Why do I treat Soviet psychology in a separate chapter while the national aspects have become gradually moved to the background in my presentation? There are several reasons for this treatment. The first class of reasons is political and sociological. During the decades following the October Bolshevik Revolution in 1917, Soviet Russian psychology was characterized by a development separated in relation to international psychology.[1] Soviet psychology in its early decades was very open to Western influences, but for half a century, between the 1930s and 1980s, Soviet science developed in an autarchic manner. During the Stalinist autarchies, this separation was valid in both ways from 1935 to 1960, to be followed by decades of Cold War "peaceful coexistence" that only allowed for a limited exchange of ideas and people. There was a much more limited access to Western ideas, and there was always a Cold War flavor to international exchanges, with expected criticism of any Western ideas, well into the 1980s.

This created an intellectual style that was isolationist and, at the same time, looking to substantiate Soviet superiority. The vast country was characterized by constantly re-emerging **critical fronts**. Due to the political authoritarianism which was a traditional Russian feature reinforced by the Communist Party and the association of the party with a dominant, and later singular, Marxist philosophy, there was a constant need to evaluate all ideas in the light of the official (single) party line. The tensions between schools and directions in international psychology were translated into local polarizations. There was a repeated re-emergence of a critical stance against either idealistic spiritualistic or mechanistic materialistic tendencies within psychology. Due to these social and political conditions, Soviet psychology was always much more theoretical compared to Western psychology, full of pseudo-methodological principles and theoretical generalizations. This went together with a need to connect psychology to building a new society (Kozulin, 1984).

DOI: 10.4324/9781032625805-8

The centralized social and ideological situation entitles us to present Soviet developments as being different from Western developments. The centralized ideological interventions and the relations between the needs of a changing society and the possibilities of psychology make the history of Soviet psychology a case study of the general issue of science–society relations in the fate of psychology.

Two dualities of the Russian tradition: community and mysticism, hero worship and radicalism

Soviet Russian social and intellectual changes were, in several regards, a modernized continuation of centuries of Russian social and intellectual development. These peculiarities were a special combination of late feudalism, the continuity of serfdom. Peasant society was organized differently from the Western world. The group land ownership and the communal land cultivation, the so-called *zemstvo* system of Russian feudalism, favored deindividualized social practices based on mechanical solidarity and a cultivation of the community combined with authoritarian threats. This went together in Russia with a state religion and the spiritual and ideological authority of the Orthodox Church. In the late 19th century, Russia, with industrialization and increasing Western influence, developed an internal tension with respect to individuality and collectivism within the Russian intelligentsia. This was mainly expressed as a tension between individualistic Westerners and collectivistic *narodniks*, "nationalists." In the western part of Europe, the revolution of individuality started with Reformation and was reinforced by the Enlightenment and industrialization. Eastern Orthodox Christianity was missing its reformed church challenges. As a result of this, in Russia, there was no clear separation of theology, philosophy, and science even at the end of the 19th century.

The official national ideology in Russia, both intellectually and emotionally, favored a mentality that treated (and, in some regards, still treats) community as being of primary value. The community-based attitude was even true of dominant 19th-century Russian literature (Tolstoy) and philosophies as well. Capital-based ownership and citizen individualization were a late achievement in Russian social and intellectual life.

All this had a dual effect that characterized both the content of intellectual trends and their connections to group organizations. There were two reactions to this community-based and theologically driven social life. Revolutionary radicals appeared with reductionist scienticism on the one hand and the preservation of authoritarian, conservative, and mystic traditions continued in spiritualistic innovations on the other hand (McLeish, 1975). The Russian writer of mid-19th century Turgenev (1861/1948) vividly characterized the tension of radical scientific and traditional values in his novel *Fathers and sons*.

Radicalism. When ideas relating to an individualized bourgeois life appeared in Russia from the middle of the 19th century, they tended to remain out of officialdom. They usually remained as an intellectual opposition, sometimes even subject to state exclusion. The lack of organic gradual development, with the backdrop of the alliance of church and spiritual conservativism with political oppression, resulted in radical new secular philosophies. Already, the so-called revolutionary democrats had a dual message. They were fighting for the rights of the individuals and toward a radical reorganization of society from the bottom up, and at the same time, they also treated humans as unified psychophysical beings.

With this intellectual and social background, modern Russian psychology did not start with an ontologically neutral play of mental images but with materialistic programs proposed by the friend of the revolutionary democrats, by Sechenov (1863). This modernizing materialist trend constituted the **radical natural science pole** of an attitude toward psychology along the adaptation evolutionist model (Chapter 7) in Volume 1. Yaroshevsky (1968), a then official Soviet historian of psychology, summarized a radically objectivistic Sechenov. The notion of inhibition and muscle sense played a crucial role in Sechenov in his extension of the reflex principle to all internal life phenomena. There is a certain amount of simplification and glorification when, later, a Sechenov-Bekhterev-Pavlov line is presented as the Russian materialist heritage. This reconstruction was criticized by Joravsky (1989). Sirotkina and Smith (2016) pointed out that for a large portion of Russian intellectuals, psychology was not conceived according to this naturalistic vision. One crucial issue debated for decades between materialists and old- and new-style spiritualists was the issue of the freedom of the will. In these debates, the Sechenov-style naturalists were standing on the deterministic side that was challenged both by followers of the Orthodox Church and by modern idealists. The issue was also important because freedom and initiative were central for the liberal and scientific thinkers as well (Sirotkina & Smith, 2012).

Mysticism. The radicalism of these visions was not only questioned by interventions of political power. Religious and modern idealist and mystical visions of humans did bloom and were articulated in official science, and they were fighting against the radicals. Religious faith, divine truth, and collective intuition have become part of Russian scientific discourse in the second half of the 19th century and during the Silver Age. This spiritualistic and community-related dissatisfaction would be reduced after the revolutions. Later, however, the mentality would reappear as a dialectical pole assuring the overcoming of determination and the self-actualization of humans, even in versions of Stalinist doctrine.

A **hero worship** went together both with radical materialism and with the emotion- and soul-centered conservative visions. The belief in a religion-based mission and unselfish sacrifice stands as one type of heroism, while the other typical hero was the revolutionary who overcomes all difficulties, especially his weaknesses, who tolerates all strains without the wink of an eye to become a professional revolutionary. Neither the principle of community nor individualism excludes the hero cult. This had, among other things, direct scientific consequences. Both emotionally and organizationally, the cult of leaders or rulers led to professional structures, schools, and organizations of a much tighter structure compared to other cultural settings.

Russian psychology before the revolutions of 1917

At the time of the February and October revolutions of 1917, both the materialistic and spiritualistic trends had a characteristic institutional and intellectual representation in Russian life. In the early 20th century, the "spiritualistic" trend took two forms relevant for psychology. It was present in innovative idealistic Romantic philosophies of spirit. The turn-of-the-century Russian Silver Age culture was very much under the influence of Nietzsche concentrating on issues of death and eternal return. This was a culture where many idealistic trends played a central role. The novelist and philosopher Dmitry Merezhkovsky (1866–1941) and the Russian religious existentialism of Nikolai Berdyaev (1878–1948) were typical of these intellectual trends. There were impressionistic typologies like the duality of Dionysian and Apollonian cultures proposed by Nietzsche. These typologies were also cultivated by poet Vyacheslav Ivanov. There was also the cultivation of the typology notions proposed by Jung as idealistic images or the mythical visions of Rudolf Steiner (Etkind, 1994, 1997/2020).

Along with the development of industrialization, conditions for a secular, Western-style **laboratory psychology** were also formed. In 1885, the neurologist Bekhterev formed the first Russian psychology laboratory in Kazan, and this was followed by a series of laboratories founded partly by neuropathologists, partly by philosopher psychologists in Kiev, Moscow, Kharkov, Odessa, St. Petersburg (Sirotkina, 2007). Early Russian experimental psychologists also became part of the international network of psychologists. Nikolay Lange (1858–1921), working in Odessa, brought his preparation and his topic from the laboratory of Wundt. He studied fluctuating of attention as a function of motor preparatory attitude. Early Russian empirical psychologists also proposed some methodical innovations. Among them, A. F. Lazurskiy (1874–1917) was the first proponent of naturalistic experiments.

In the Russian environment, humanist scholars and artists as well as the centralizing political powers did not like "experimenting on the soul." Psychology laboratories had an easier role in the neuropsychiatry departments compared to philosophy departments (Sirotkina, 2007). This is not a trivial issue in Eastern Europe. Sometimes the reverse was true. In Hungary, for example, medical faculties were divided. The one in Budapest did not welcome "experimenting on the soul" and gave a hard time for Ranschburg, the first experimentalist, while the medical school in Kolozsvár/Cluj, in Transylvania, welcomed it. At the same time, philosophy departments in Budapest and Pozsony/Bratislava welcomed modern experimental psychology at the turn of the century, with Géza Révész.

In 1914, a well-equipped and soon-to-be-huge Institute of Psychology was organized at Moscow University, with the financial aid of a wealthy merchant (Kozulin, 1985). The four-story building still serves psychology. It is the site of the Psychology Research Institute of the Russian Academy of Education. The institute is named after the original financial supporter, Sergei Shchukin (1854–1936), a Russian merchant who was a great art collector and supporter of post-impressionist French art. Chelpanov, the later director, travelled two summers in Germany and America to get the best advice of how to build a modern department and laboratory. In the mid-1910s, the laboratory was strong and attractive, with the best equipment in Europe.

The new Institute was run under the leadership of Georgy I. Chelpanov (1862–1936), who came to Moscow from Kiev in 1907. He was trained in Odessa's Novo-Rossijsk University and also in Moscow but had a mentor relationship with Wundt. His program was clear: real psychology has to combine philosophical ideas, introspection, and experimentation and promote psychophysical parallelism (Kozulin, 1985). This psychology in the Russian environment had a clearer labeling and a difficult ideological fate. The German scholars tried to avoid the blame of materialism with claiming psychophysical parallelism, while in Russia, this kind of subjective experimental psychology obtained an idealist connotation and sometimes even self-labeling. Chelpanov himself, in his very successful book *Brain and soul* (which was based on his lectures at Kiev University), stood for a dualistic conception, which was interpreted by later Marxist evaluators as a clear idealism. The "idealistic interpretation" of experimental psychology in late Tsarist Russia was a self-defense, allowing to enter modern psychology at all into the humanities faculties. Chelpanov ran the laboratory in a liberal manner, both intellectually and politically, allowing his young associates to become political radicals and behaviorists.

Parallel to experimental psychology in humanities faculties, **objective psychologies** were advertised in the 1910s in the two parallel schools of Pavlov and Bekhterev in medical institutions in St. Petersburg. They stood for an objective psychology that was to be able to fit the integrity of mental phenomena into the world of reflex processes. When Chelpanov and his associates spoke about introspection, they had polemics with reflexological notions, and when they spoke about subjective psychology, they contrasted this mainly to the highly controversial objectivism of Bekhterev.

Versions of the New Man and psychology

In order to understand what happened after the Bolshevik Revolution that totally changed the social outlook of psychology, one has to consider the stages in the formation of the key concept of **New Man** so central to Soviet social thought. The conception of the New Man that was so central in Soviet psychology was not entirely new as a Soviet brand. It manifested itself in the writings of mid-19th-century Russian radical democrats. In 1860, Nikolaj Chernyshevsky (1828–1889) even named the prototype as a New Man. This New Man would be unselfish, community- and abstract-value-oriented.

The stages of Soviet social development and Stalinization were intimately related to changing conceptions of how to form this New Man in the new society. Bauer (1952) differentiated several stages of Communist Party strategy and ideology regarding psychology and its relation of creating a new social man. The stages were identified not only according to the direct nature of political intervention but also on the basis of how the substance of the image of man projected in them was changing. As Tucker (1956) and Bauer analyzed, there were different stages of Bolshevik rule. These drastic changes were related to the changes of how to interpret "in a proper Marxist materialist manner" the determination of human mind and what is the role of human efforts in a deterministic worldview. These changes were crucial for the interpretation of psychology.

Stage 1. **Man, and the human mind, is determined by natural laws.** Early 1920s.
Massive determinism comes from a materialist as a heritage from Marxist

philosophy. This attitude was socially optimistic and naively believed that with changing social conditions, humans would also change. This attitude favored behavior-based and naturalistic approaches to psychology, such as Pavlov followers, Bekhterev, the reactology of Kornilov, the developmental psychoanalysts, the mass measurement psychotechnicians, and the pedologists. These approaches still had some internal debates about the proper place of internal life in a behavior-based approach and the relations of physiology to behavioral laws. At the same time, they mostly ignored folk psychology or put it into brackets. They were continuing the radicalist Russian heritage and concentrated on behavior and no particular interest in inner life. This also implied a distantiation from traditional community feelings and a cultivation of individuality. In this regard, they were similar to the radical abstract Russian revolutionary art and to the form-based literary theories. All the three tried to overthrow the intimate meaningfulness of traditional life and art.

Stage 2. **Humans must be active and change themselves.** Mid-1930s to 1947. Together with the creation of the centralized planned economy (the five-year plan), the image of a more activist, voluntaristic image of man was promoted in the more and more centralized party state in the early 1930s. **Transformism** is the label often used by followers of Stalin for this process as a new banner (Tucker, 1956). The New Man of the 1930s is optimistic, self-determined, inner driven, and responsible, characterized with high ambitions (Bauer, 1952; McLeish, 1975). People should not merely wait for social change but actively have to change themselves. In the political vision, human life is not simply determined by external circumstances; it must change its own environment. Class "consciousness" in these conceptions would become the slogan of Communist Party–directed voluntarism: anything is possible with proper efforts of the working classes. Humans are no longer slaves of their conditions. There was a shift from the deterministic image of man toward a more Romantic self-shaping. For psychology, this had radical consequences. Simple behavior-based psychology was treated as too passive, and individual-difference-based school psychology, alongside its testing practices, was banned. In its slogans, as recalled by later Soviet historiography in a positive manner, this meant a change toward a psychology of consciousness and theories of activity. Regarding traditions, this meant a reconstruction of folk psychology, and a concentration on intimate meanings, and a reconstruction of community feelings, this time in the name a socialist community. "Consciousness" became the psychological buzzword for Stalinist "five-year plan efforts." This new attitude, in the middle of harsh political purges in psychology as well, implied a concentration on optimistic school and learning topics, like organization of voluntary learning done in the 1930s, in the works of A. N. Leontiev (1932), Blonski (1935, 1977), and Zinchenko (1939). It also initiated many studies of "volitional" mental organizations, which became a Soviet Russian way to talk about human motivation. The very theoretical nature of later Soviet psychology is, in a rather direct manner, related to the idea of a planned economy, where research is no more an issue of isolated individuals making some research efforts but researchers accomplishing a PLAN (McLeish, 1975).

Stage 3. **New recombination of determinism with inner efforts.** From 1947 to early 1960s. After WW2, Soviet people started to have motivational problems again. They become lazy, in the eye of the politicians. The New Man delivered no more after the War.

> The most difficult problem faced by the Stalin regime in the postwar years was the profound passivity of the Soviet populace, its failure to respond positively to the goals set before it. . . . [There] was widespread apathy, resignation, spiritual disengagement from the goals of the Stalin government.
> (Tucker, 1956, p. 463)

Something had to be done. Transformism in this third stage was recombined with an image of mechanistic causation and externalism. This was the time of the Lysenko type of transformationist biology. In this vision, even genetic makeup can be changed by planned human interventions. Regarding psychology, this was the combination of a deterministic image following an enforced Pavlov interpretation and an increased party rule on the political agenda. Humans are determined by natural science laws of brain-determined learning mechanisms, but careful planning intervenes in how to use this determinism. This required a reconstruction of all of psychology along Pavlovian lines.

Stage 4. **Relative independence of psychology.** From the 1960s on. As Rubinstein (1957/1965, p. 8), one of the surviving theoretical psychologists, stated the autonomy slogan for this stage: "outer causes act through inner conditions." Psychology in this new stage would be a central science studying those inner conditions. This implied a concentration on personality as a research topic and a gradual embedding into the Western models of psychology.

The genesis of a new psychology: moves toward objectivism

After the Russian revolutions of 1917, there was an urgent need to have a new start in all areas of social and intellectual life, with the aims of a destruction and reconstruction – to build something new out of scratch. For the arts, this implied the cultivation of an absolute new start in the form of a revolutionary avant-garde art. In the social sciences, including psychology, the drive toward novelty resulted in objectivist, behavior-related trends corresponding to a materialist approach to the mind, along with new ideas about the underlying moving forces of people, including even a short-lived cultivation of psychoanalysis. This was accompanied by the needs of a new understanding of work organization, with needs toward a new industrial psychology in Soviet Russia, which came to be called psychotechnics.

For psychology, the initially liberal attitude of the cultural minister between 1917 and 1929 Lunacharsky meant the survival of the established centers of "subjective psychology." This proved to be a loophole for Chelpanov and his followers in Moscow, as their positions were soon weakened in the early 1920s by the expulsion and forced emigration of an entire generation of intellectuals by Lenin, among them many psychologists. These were people who were charged with cultivating new varieties of bourgeois idealist visions of the world and ways of life. The chair of the Moscow Psychological Society, who was also the organizer of the journal of philosophy and psychology, L. M. Lopatin (1855–1920), was also persecuted. These tragic purges provided a clearer table for the new initiatives toward a new objectivistic psychology.

The first Marxist attempts: the principle of behavior in the works of Blonsky and Kornilov

The innovation mood brought about by the revolutions soon found its ways to psychology.

Psychological life in the first decade after the revolution was the decade of young Turks. Their challenge toward traditional psychology appeared in three domains.

- In the academic world, they challenged the psychology of consciousness as promoted by Chelpanov and his Moscow institute. The challengers were usually young people employed there and started to undermine classical psychology in the name of entirely new psychologies following **behavioristic principles**, thought to be in line with Marxism. At the same time, they were usually fighting against neural reductionism claimed by physiologists and neurologists. Umrihin (1989) provided an interesting account of these early Soviet behaviorists at the time of the end of the Soviet era.
- Another new move came from the reconsideration of the **psychology of work** in the new socialist society, based in its political, ethical, and philosophical principles of work. In their vision, the new psychology should be a new psychology of work and adaptation of individuals to work conditions.
- A third early move tried to reconcile the needs for a **Marxist theory with psychoanalysis**, looking for a new science of human moving forces.

In the fast-changing revolutionary times, the debates and fast social and political changes entailing huge personal and institutional consequences followed each other with great speed and were more and more under the direction of central Communist Party organizing forces. In the academic domain, the first generation of challengers were direct students of the mentors they challenged. It was partly a question of fighting for limited funds, as it happens frequently in the history of science (Sirotkina, 2006; Sirotkina & Smith, 2012), but it was also an Oedipal revolt against fathers. Marxists and the Communist Party soon after provided the young people with the resources of the relatively wealthy institutes, especially in Moscow. On the intellectual side, the Young Turks believed that "dialectical materialism" would help them navigate between old-style introspective psychology and the threatening reflexological visions coming from the north, from St. Petersburg.

Pavel Petrovich Blonsky (1884–1941) was the first challenger. The life of Blonsky (sometimes also spelled as Blonski) illustrates the typical path of progressive Russian intellectuals (Kozulin, 1982). He was a well-educated historian of philosophy who started to combine his interest in philosophy with his education commitments and political activities early on, already in Kiev as a student of Chelpanov. In Moscow, Blonsky was one of the founders of the Russian psychoanalytic association, was a promoter of sex education (Blonski, 1930) applied psychological testing, and argued for a work-based school movement. The politically rather active Blonsky had different political positions, especially on education boards. He was one of the leaders of the Soviet pedology movement in the 1920s, also supporting it with successful textbooks (Blonski, 1925). He believed that the change of schools should be based on the study of children, and the change of schools was a key to changing society. This child-based progressivism was similar to the one promoted by John Dewey. In his educational efforts, Blonsky (1928) was an ally of Nadezhda Krupskaja (1869–1939), wife of the Communist movement leader Lenin, who was herself one of the leaders of the reorganization of education, with her Academy of Communist Education, a new partisan school of higher learning separated from traditional universities. In Blonsky's pedological vision, anthropometric, physiological, and psychological characterizations together provide a basis for a comprehensive analysis of the personality of children, showing the child in each age as an integrated whole. For them, this should be the starting point of education.

Luria characterized the importance of the pedology conception of Blonski and his book for Western developmental psychologists at that time.

> It is the first time that pedology has been regarded not as child psychology and not as experimental pedagogy but as a genetic science of the growth of the child. In this book every phase of the child's development is considered from three different angles: growth, constitutional peculiarities, and behavior.
> (Luria, 1928, p. 351)

With all his practical efforts, Blonsky was a committed theoretician as well. After the revolution, working at the Moscow Institute of Psychology led by Chelpanov, he was the first one to campaign for a Marxist psychology, centered on **behavior** and **historicity**. Blonsky called for a rebuilding of psychology on the basis of objective criteria of natural science. His first work along these lines was his methodical book (Blonski, 1920), *Reform of science*. He proposed that in contrast to a psychology based on self-observation, there has to be a biological psychology using natural science methods to precisely unravel the exact laws of behavior. In 1921, he concretized this program in his *Outlines of a scientific psychology*. He tried to combine his enthusiasm toward the mechanical Descartes, the eager search for mechanistic explanations, a behavior-based vision of psychology, and Marxism. Humans must be looked for in an evolutionary frame as behaving beings. This was complemented, however, with the principle of **social embedding**. Cooperation, instrument use, and work are the keys to understand the specificities of the human mind.

> *Sociality.* The life process is a social process from the beginning, it always presupposes interaction of individual organisms.... Human society is merely the higher form of animal societies, and social life in animals is the forerunner

of human sociality. The foundations of the later on are the same life instincts (or reflexes), the instincts of feeding, self-protection, and reproduction.

(Blonsky, 1921/1962, p. 89)

Blonsky, in his later works, developed the details of his conception of sociality and development. His speculative book in 1927 presented the evolutionary development of behavior. The evolution of behavior is a constant fight between the primitive disintegrated state and awareness, a constant tension between sleep and wakefulness.

Blonsky, with his pedological role, was subject to harsh criticism but managed to survive the purges of pedology and testing in the 1930s, where even his books were banned. He continued to work in the Institute of Psychology in Moscow, but his work thereafter clearly shows a psychology dominated by education. He started empirical studies of the development of memory and thinking in children (Blonski, 1935). In these new works, Blonsky studied rather traditional teaching materials and methods, such as textbook-based learning. The educational progressivist thus disappeared. In Blonsky's view, it is a basic feature of human development that thinking penetrates memory. In this process – and here he relied on works by Janet and Bartlett – a crucial role is played by **story memory** created under social conditions by transforming our experiences into socially coded stories. This would be responsible for the schematizations so characteristic of human memory. Blonsky polemicized with Vygotsky. For Blonsky, the turning point of the development of thinking was in adolescence, with the birth of strict logical thought.

K. N. Kornilov (1879–1957) was the key person in introducing Marxism with a behaviorist flavor to Soviet psychology, both in the institutional and in the intellectual sense. He was a bold campaigner and, at the same time, a good organizer. He was often ridiculed in Soviet and post-Soviet histories as a country boy, an outsider who came up to Moscow from the Altai region in South-Western Siberia. In this regard, he was like John Watson. Both were country boys moving to the big city, being able to rely for orientation only on the behavior of people, and in research on their childhood experience with animals. Kornilov was a protégé of Chelpanov, and his first assistant, interested in the nature of motor reactions to begin with. He showed his teeth early on, however. He unexpectedly published his book on reactology in Kornilov (1921), where he put behavior at the center of the new psychology. Blonsky concentrated on concepts and substance, while Kornilov engaged in fierce polemics. Kornilov's main prerogative was to finish with the psychology of consciousness of his master, Chelpanov. This revolt against the intellectual fathers is rather frequent. Kornilov, at the same time, endeavored to avoid making psychology entirely the territory of the Petrograd reflexologists, especially Bekhterev, as part of physiology. "Let us protect the independence of psychology, but let us become objective ourselves!" The strategy had two outcomes. It certainly led to more behavior-based psychologies. As a side effect, however, the tensions created by Kornilov caused psychology to lose its freshly gained independence from philosophy. From this point, it became administratively connected to Marxist philosophy and, especially, Communist Party protection and direction for quite some time. Due to the debates, psychology became interesting for Communist Party leadership, which was supportive for a while but later became restrictive. In its deterministic phase, it supported reactology, but 10 years later, the transformist program looked for conscious effort–based psychologies. Kornilov was partly responsible for this unfortunate move threatening the independence of psychology. Kornilov's first attempt to outline a Marxist (behavioral) psychology occurred in his talk at the first psychoneurology conference (1923). It was published in the first issue of the newly created Communist Party central ideology journal, *Under the Banner of Marxism (Pod Znamenem Marxisma)*. The fate of psychology was thus becoming tied to the Communist Party, which meant not only an increased role of personal favors and disfavors but also occasional disciplinary measures by the Communist Party toward psychology and psychologists. This also meant interventions into the substance of psychological theory and especially psychological practice.

In Kornilov's reactology, behavior was the central, but not the exclusive, topic of psychology. The new psychology used a dialectic method, which was a synthesis of subjective and objective, that is, behavioral, approaches. This was a compromise, but where was Marxism? Kornilov stood on the deterministic pole of interpreting Marxism. He read into Marx and Engels that they allowed for a material nature of mental phenomena without a commitment to physiological reductionism. The other aspect was sociological. Reactions are complex biosocial phenomena. Marxism reminded the psychologists that in interpreting these reactions, a constant attention has to be paid to the social aspects of our mental life and personality.

Kornilov attracted many young researchers, among them Vygotsky and Luria. At the same time, the Moscow psychology institute had become a center for the new pedology work on child development and the psycho-technological applied psychology research as well, organized by Isaac Spielrein (1891–1937), brother of the psychoanalyst Sabina Spielrein. The role of Isaac Spielrein was central in the establishment, methodical development, and international presence of Soviet psychotechnology, with hopes of having 3,000 actionists around the country. "You have to go out to the field, and study for example, the reaction patterns of 'genuine Moscow proletars'" was the brand logo. Psychotechnics itself had a foundation along its own logic, in line with the process of industrialization. Several laboratories were established in industrial centers. One of the key social issues for the new psychology was the ergonomic measurement of the work process, including a comparison of the work style of women and men, along with a politically flavored optimization of the work process, absorbing and, at the same time, criticizing the capitalist rationalization of work introduced by Taylor (1911). Spielrein organized in 1931 in Moscow an international conference of applied psychology, mainly centered on psychotechnics (Spielrein, 1933). The entire psychotechnology was later purged in the name of the new transformist Stalinist social policy, and Spielrein himself was arrested and executed.

Alternative reflexological conceptions

The behavior-centered objectivistic psychology promoted by Blonsky and Kornilov was not a simply hegemonistic trend. It was victorious in the Moscow

University Institute of Psychology, but other trends mainly concentrated in Petrograd (Leningrad from 1924 to 1991, now, and earlier St. Petersburgh) also claimed to found new objective psychologies. These ideas mainly came from the clinic and from the animal physiology laboratory. There was a harsh rivalry between the two Petrograd-based schools of reflexology: that of Bekhterev and that of Pavlov. There were also clear political differences between them. Pavlov was more or less apolitical in Soviet times, presenting an "ivory tower" image, while Bekhterev was much more involved in personal relations with the communist leaders. This resulted, in a paradoxical manner, in a more difficult fate for the school of Bekhterev. Pavlov also had some contacts with the political leaders, but always from the position of an independent academic leader (Todes, 2014).

They also had clear scientific differences. Their first methodical difference was that while Bekhterev had a clinical starting point and observed humans, Pavlov continued to believe in the primacy of the animal model. The other substantial difference was that Pavlov intended to discover a general mechanism with the aid of conditioned reflexes, while the neurologist Bekhterev (1923, 1925a) was more "modularist." He tried to explain learned conditioned reflexes from the workings of the so-called associative cortical areas. During their controversies, it became crucial for Pavlov to show with extirpation studies that there were no separate "centers of association," merely connections made between different analyzers, that is, specialized cortical centers.

While Pavlov, Bekhterev, and the reactologists dominated the objectivist intellectual scene, there was also solid comparative psychological and biological work done in Russia, as analyzed in detail by Joravsky (1992). **Vladimir Wagner** (1849–1934), the comparative psychologist, was involved in constant tensions over his Darwinist beliefs before the revolutions. Boris Kotin's [1895–1950] major work was devoted to the study of imitation in animals.

> He was interested in instinctive (inborn) behavior, which in its simplest form is manifested in one individual following another: a child following its mother, a member of a herd following the leader or another member. . . . Having adopted Wagner's evolutionary approach to the working out of psychological problems, Kotin turned to the study of imitation in the phylogenesis and ontogenesis of vertebrates. Hence the amazing diversity of the species he used for his experiments: fish (wild carp), birds (doves, hens), and mammals (rats, cats, dogs, wolves, sheep, reindeer, monkeys), studying young animals as well as adults.
>
> (Joravsky, 1992, p. 57)

The reflexology of Bekhterev

The **reflexology school**, led by Vladimir Mikhailovich Bekhterev (1857–1927), had an especially dynamic role in becoming the leader of a behavioristic psychology. Bekhterev was a very successful neurologist and, at the same time, a promoter of psychology. As a young graduate of the St. Petersburg medical school, he travelled to German laboratories and French clinics. In the 1880s, he established the first Russian laboratory of experimental psychology at the University of Kazan, where he also became a noted neurologist. As a neuropathologist, Bekhterev became world-famous. He has seven reflexes, several procedures, and a disease of chronic rheumatic inflammation named after him. He also promoted early ideas about the role of hippocampus in memory. In 1893, he was a central organizer of neuropathology in the clinic and in an association established by him in St. Petersburg. He also started a journal that had "experimental psychology" in its title.

Alongside his clinical work, Bekhterev also became a promoter for a general reflex-based vision of the human mind. Accommodating reflex theory with learning was an essential issue for him, like for Pavlov as well. Unlike the mostly vegetative reactions – salivation and digestive fluids – of the Pavlov group, he studied the movements of legs becoming associated to a warning stimulus with the use of a mild electric shock. These associated reflexes could easily be studied in humans as well. His efforts toward an objective psychology made his name well-known both in Russia and in the Western world (Bekhterev, 1913). Later, with the help of the Soviet power, he founded his *Brain Institute* in St. Petersburg. The Institute has been several times reorganized and "re-founded," but it is still active in combining basic neuroscience and clinical work.

Bekhterev basically believed that

> objective psychology studies the same things [as classical psychology] but from another point of view by treating them as neural processes taking place in brain centers. . . . And those who want to make an objective psychology should exclusively use the objective method, avoiding scrupulously all subjective terms and all subjective interpretation of neuro-psychological activity.
> (Bekhterev, 1909, p. 482)

The radical neuroreductionism of Bekhterev is a prime example of eliminating folk psychology and the intentional stance. He characterized his objective attitude to psychology in a straightforward manner in his 1913 French book.

> On the final analysis every neuro-psychological act can be reduced to a reflex schema, where the excitation, reaching the cerebral cortex activates the traces of earlier reactions and finds in them a factor that determines the process of discharge. . . .
> . . . The development of personal experience is not connected to anatomical modifications, but to functional modifications of the brain. . . . This means that the Ego of the individual has no anatomical substrate and it is merely the sum of the reflexes which have pathways with traces in the nervous system.
> (Bekhterev, 1913, pp. 12, 473)

In the conception of Bekhterev, reflexology was apt to deal with social and societal phenomena as well. In his **collective reflexology**, published originally in 1915 but republished in other languages later on, Bekhterev (1921/2001) deals with social aspects of human life in a rather-courageous manner. Social psychology would be the study of reflexes under a social environmental setting. "The object of collective reflexology is the development and activity of human groups" (Bekhterev, 1921/1957, p. 22). While he criticized social organism notions as well as social consciousness, he himself proposed that: "On my part, I propose to define society as a collective personality" (ibid., 45).

He went on to outline some basic phenomena, like the role of imitation, social instincts, and the like, and then proposed a general energetic vision of social life. Twenty-one chapters outlined so-called laws of social life. These were *ad hoc* generalizations supported by individual historical facts. Laws of the conservation of energy, repulsion, law of historical development, law of periodicity, and the like. The entire book is a naive historical speculation with trivialities, such as: "All revolutionary movements have a tendency due to the law of inertia to go beyond their goals reverting not only those that oppose them but also what could have been conserved" (ibid., 193). And then he gave as examples the futurist and cubist art movements.

In the 1920s, Bekhterev also published the results of many experiments done on group effects in working quantity and quality, with and without group discussion. The works fit well into the early experiments on group influences, of which Bekhterev had knowledge. He was optimistic about the relations of community and personality and group standardization. "Collective work . . . [is] improving the weak ones, and not from bottom up, in the sense of weakening the strong ones" (Bekhterev, 1921/2001, p. 337).

Both the behaviorist psychologies and the provocative neuroreductionism of Bekhterev, and some extremist interpretation coming from the Pavlov school, created many internal Soviet discussions in the 1920s, presented under CONTROVERSIES.

Controversies

The reflexology debates

Over the span of a decade, there were three debates involving the issue of behavioral psychology in the Soviet world.

1923: Reactology debate. Kornilov against Chelpanov.
1929: Reflexology debate. Kornilov against the Bekhterev school.
1930–1931: Marxists against Kornilov.

The critical issues in all these debates were double: preserve or forget the folk psychological vision of an inner life, and allow or question in this process a total neuroreductionism. Since traditional "idealist" philosophy was out, defenders of all positions claimed that theirs was the properly materialist and Marxist position. But in the meantime, Russian mainstream Marxism moved from determinism towards voluntaristic transformism.

1 The reactology debate

There was a two-year intrigue in the early 1920s, following the talk of Kornilov about the reactology program, that was made public in the government newspaper. Chelpanov tried to prove that Kornilov was ignorant of Marxism. He published his own pamphlet, claiming more place for the independent study of thought processes. It was a short pamphlet of 27 pages (Chelpanov, 1924). The German-educated Chelpanov mainly used Marx, Engels, and Feuerbach citations to show that the classics of Marxism did, in fact, allow for the relative independent organization of mental life while claiming its brain bases.

The Chelpanov pamphlet was easily ridiculed by Kornilov in further intrigues, and he came out as a winner. The end result was that Kornilov emerged as the new director of the Moscow Psychology Institute. While his reactology, concentrating on the form of the speed and strength of movements, was rather mechanistic, he hired new associates, among them Luria and Vygotsky, all adjoining first to a reactological way of speech but, in fact, smuggling in psychoanalytic and new developmental and pedological research to Moscow.

Kornilov (1930), while in power, presented his approach to the Western audience as well. He emphasized the objectivity of the reactology school but dissociated his approach from that of the reflexologists. Following Engels, Kornilov claimed that there is a dialectical non-reductive relation between thinking and the brain, where quantity becomes quality.

We are not at all inclined to associate ourselves with the adherents of the extreme objective school of psychology, which either flatly denies the existence of the human consciousness or identifies it with the mechanical movement of matter. . . . [From] the extreme objective and the subjective schools of psychology neither of them actually studies the individual as a united whole, in which objective and subjective manifestations are fused organically.

. . . This is why we regard psychology as a social science rather than as a branch of natural science.

> We regard the conception of reactions as the basis of the analytical study of psychology, and we prefer it to the purely physiological conception, deprived of every subjective content of reflexes.
> (Kornilov, 1930, p. 268)

In the vision of Kornilov, reactions are movements with a goal-directedness, which is not true for reflexes. Thus, the issue of the intentional stance of folk psychology is smuggled back again. For a while, reactology seemed to be the winner of the show. The traditional Soviet historiographic account treated Kornilov as being a victorious researcher over the old school.

2 The reflexology debate

The position of Bekhterev (1923, 1925a, 1925b) was provocative in his own time not merely due to the social ambitions of his theory but also because it made psychology futile. That made psychologists sensitive to it, both for intellectual and for existential reasons. The Bekhterev school was, in the mid-1920s, the most dominant of Russian behavioral directions. Reflexology was propagated at that time in public schools and, as it was popular in the party leadership, among people like Bukharin and Trotsky. Bekhterev (1925a) himself referred to his approach as being Marxist. As they presented themselves to the Western audience, they were more objective than Kornilov and more flexible than Pavlov.

But Kornilov also used a victorious rhetoric. The polemics of Kornilov led in 1929 to the so-called **reflexology debate**, where followers of Bekhterev, who himself was already dead for two years, were forced to have some self-criticism. The essence of the self-critique was that reflexology had lost its radicalism by recognizing the specific issues related to consciousness.

Kornilov seemed to be a winner with his reactology, both against Chelpanov and against the reflexologists. By the end of the 1920s, reflexology came under sharp attack and was regarded as a vulgar-mechanical materialism. The Second All-Union Conference of Marxist–Leninist Research Institutes concluded that reflexology deviated from the true Marxist position. There were also local voices against reflexology. In Leningrad, other young people, especially Ananiev in his early 20s, started to campaign mainly against the reflexology represented by Bekhterev, and thereby the entire tradition of the Leningrad Brain Institute was changed. Ananiev claimed that "[i]n psychology there has to be no schools except a unitary school based on the classics of Marxism" (Ananiev, 1931, p. 32). In 1930, the first national conference on behavior-based psychology was held, and everything seemed to be on the right track toward a behavioral psychology. Soon, however, the Communist Party initiated campaigns against the mechanistic aspects of his reactology.

3 The second reactology debate

Along with new activist, transformist line of Stalin concentrating on conscious efforts, administrative decisions were made that had a lasting effect on the assessment of people touched by the decisions. First, internal party meetings with a talk by a military psychologist declared reactology was behaviorism and essentially a school in the service of American capitalism. Kornilov and reactology were declared to be too mechanistic, not caring about the conscious efforts of people, and Kornilov, Vygotsky, and others were removed from their positions. The Vygotsky school started a more activity-, initiative-, and consciousness-based approach. As the presentation of Teplov (1947) showed on the 30th anniversary of the revolution, the new debate on human behavior corresponded to a reintroduction of the long deceased party leader Lenin (1870–1924) into the psychological discussion (Lenin, 1909/1972, 1929/1976) and the general criticism of bourgeois science. It also corresponded to the need for a socialist applied psychology that was gradually associated with anti-testing campaigns. As the official party history by Teplov showed, this practically meant a critique of reactology, as well as a critique of the mental history school of Vygotsky as well.

Kornilov himself, with all the Soviet political purges, remained the eternal survivor in Soviet Russia. In 1943, he was elected vice president of the newly created Russian Pedagogy Academy. In 1955, after the great Pavlovization debates, he came back in the first issue of the new journal *Questions of Psychology*, claiming that psychology in the Soviet Union is in a backward state. Publications lagged or were nonexistent. Institutional impediments were many. Most of Soviet psychology was concentrated in the area of child and pedagogical psychology, and much of this, being unconnected with more general problems, is of little value for the broad theoretical development of Soviet psychology. There is no industrial psychology to speak of; comparative psychology just about managed to survive; general psychology pleaded for attention; and "liquidation of psychology, as an independent discipline," by misguided Pavlovian enthusiasts, is constantly threatened, since, in basing the psyche on a physiological substratum, they identify the former with the latter. Soviet psychology lacks a psychology of personality, especially one of the Soviet man. Such a psychology must go beyond Pavlovian theory (Kornilov, 1955).

Pavlov and his school

The other star, the Bekhterev rival of the St. Petersburg–Leningrad reflexology scene, was Pavlov. He had an ambiguous and rather tumultuous relationship with Soviet political power, with the intrigues within Soviet psychology, and with the discipline of psychology as well.

Pavlov did not himself participate in the local, Russian, and Soviet debates on the relations of psychology and physiology, in the reactology debates. At the same time, on the level of his massive work, his entire work opened the ways toward a neural reductionism. Pavlov had a message for psychology and psychiatry. On the one hand, he emphasized openly that he was studying "higher nervous activity", that is, brain functions (relying on non-observable events happening in the brain), and not psychology. At the same time, in a hidden way:

> Pavlov believed that one can make the foundation of psychology as a scientific discipline on the basis of his theory, as well as psychiatry as a medical specialty. He ignored his contemporary psychologists, with the exception of G. I. Chelpanov to whom he wrote a letter of congratulation when the institute of Chelpanov was opened.
> (Sirotkina & Smith, 2016, p. 34)

Biography

The Nobel Prize–winning physiologist and psychology

Pavlov, Ivan Petrovich (Ryazan, September 14, 1849–Leningrad, February 27, 1936), was a successful physiologist during Tsarist and Soviet times who received the Nobel Prize in medicine (physiology) in 1904 for his research on digestion and its regulation. It is rather interesting how he arrived there and how he continued.

A life devoted to science

Soviet descriptions of the life of Pavlov by his own associates usually presented the maestro with a two-way distortion. They presented him as a lifelong materialist, a continuator of the Sechenov tradition, and as a theoretician of a materialistic but not sufficiently dialectical approach to the mind (Asratian, 1953). The recent detailed and evaluative biography of the American medical historian Todes (2014) – the culmination of two decades of study devoted to Pavlov – shows a different picture based on newly available archival materials.

The basic stages of the intellectual life of Pavlov of a theoretical interest are:

Studying for priesthood
Medical school and postgraduate training
Work on the digestive system in St. Petersburg
Research on higher nervous activity on dogs
Successful Soviet scientist: generalized theory of the human mind and behavior

Following a family pattern, Pavlov studied to become a priest in his hometown in central Russia, the Ryazan seminary. Two factors diverted Pavlov from this choice. The first was a son's desire to revolt against the model set by his elders. The second was the intellectual, social, and political revolutionary model and ambiance of Russia in the 1860s. The liberalism that inspired Pavlov followed the model set by the imprisoned nihilist liberal writer Dimitry Pisarev. Pavlov repeatedly returned to the inspiration of the 1860s, which held a dual message for him. In this vision, the key to a new modern life, especially in science, was **liberty**. This freedom, the independence of thought emphasized by Pisarev, had to be tied to a commitment to **Russian national ideals**. In the midst of many shakeups and transformations, national liberalism always remained the guiding principle for Pavlov. Pavlov skipped the ecclesiastic comprehensive exams and started to study natural science in St. Petersburg. Professional and existential considerations led him to pursue a dual degree: one at the science faculty, and one at the medical school.

Pavlov, as a junior physiologist who became a skilled surgeon at the clinic of Sergei Botkin (1832–1889), had a hard time finding a job. After a few years in Germany, he was not even accepted at the newly opened medical school of Tomsk in Siberia. He managed to get his first real "tenured" job at around 40. But this time, Pavlov obtained two parallel jobs that he kept most of his life, adding a third job later when he was elected to the Academy of Sciences in 1907. In 1890s, Pavlov became professor of pharmacology, and later of physiology, at the Military Medical Academy in St Petersburg. Pavlov taught at this institution for decades and stepped down only in the 1920s, when communist students kept provoking him during his lectures and accusing him of mechanical materialism using the then new Stalinist logos.

The position that truly allowed Pavlov to create a laboratory materialized in his other job, at a new and rather specific institution. Prince Alexander Oldenburg (1844–1932), a member of the Tsar's family, a devoted philanthropist, under the influence of Pasteur and Koch, created a huge center of epidemiology in St. Petersburg with the primary aim of curing rabies, tuberculosis, and syphilis. In his new *Institute of Experimental Medicine*, in order to widen the profile, Oldenburg, in 1891, asked Pavlov to create a "laboratory factory" of surgery and physiology. This would become the environment where Pavlov conducted the pioneering research which eventually led to his Nobel Prize. In addition, it became the increasingly articulated center of "Pavlovism," which was coupled with experiments with an even greater number of dogs, an increasing number of graduate students and postdocs, and an increasing number of better and better labs.

Work on the digestive system in Saint Petersburg. Pavlov's physiology factory, as Todes (2012) named it, represented a peculiar research practice together with a peculiar research metaphor. He followed the practice of 19th-century German chemists and physiologists. Spending two postdoc years in Germany, in Leipzig and Breslau, where he developed his surgical techniques, Pavlov was familiar with German science organization. Thus, he organized his research group as a factory, where dozens of PhD students worked in research cabins with research scaffoldings for the animals. Pavlov started to organize a real factory where his collaborators were set up to work on a common project. They studied the digestive fluids of dogs for over a

Figure 7.1 Pavlov in his laboratory factory, 1913.
Source: Wikipedia commons.

decade, and the supposed dynamics of the cerebral cortex for three decades. The "factory" is also a conceptual factory, because in Pavlov's interpretation, digestive secretion shows signs of a factory-like working style. Its direction is governed basically by the nervous system, like a factory where production is directed by a manager. Pavlov first underlined the role of the *vagus*, and later that of the **cerebral cortex**, in regulating digestion. **Regulation** was a core idea throughout all of Pavlov's work. He followed Claude Bernard (1878) in looking everywhere for a factory-like precise arrangement.

Pavlov was a Darwinist and, at the same time, a follower of the ideas of Claude Bernard about physiological regulation. For Pavlov, adaptation was a key notion. He remained very close to the idea of always looking for the functions rather than details of executive mechanisms. His aims were pursued by making in vivo animal preparations allowing the neural regulation of digestive fluids. Most of the important discoveries were made on a few or a dozen dogs available for many years in the same experimental settings. Besides being distant from considerations of precise histology, statistics also remained alien to Pavlov all his life, even in his later excursions into personality typology. Pavlov kept trying to draw sharp curves with no standard deviations, only temporal functions.

Pavlov summarized the work of his lab in the late 1890s, in German- (Pavlov, 1898), French- (Pavlov, 1901), and English- (Pavlov, 1902) translated books. This resulted in the Nobel Prize for physiology and medicine awarded to Pavlov in 1904. Analyzing salivation, gastric and pancreatic juice production, Pavlov already emphasized the importance of neuronal control. That is the source of **nervism**, the origin of which Pavlov has dutifully attributed to Sergei Petrovich Botkin (1832–1889), his Russian mentor, and that also became a key notion in the later Pavlov cult. Everything in physiology and in the etiology of diseases is regulated by the nervous system. For Pavlov, however, this was accompanied with an unwillingness to follow developments in modern biochemistry and the proposals for hormonal regulations for digestion. This was a limitation used as a charge against Pavlov in the Nobel deliberations.

Research on higher nervous activity in dogs. In the process of studying digestive fluid secretion, Pavlov, and especially his students, noticed that there was a learned salivation evoked, for example, by the approaching steps of the experimental assistant. At the 14th International Medical Congress, in Madrid, Spain, held between April 23 and 30, 1903, Pavlov presented a talk titled *The Experimental Psychology and Psychopathology of Animals* (Pavlov, 1928, pp. 48–60). This talk was the first public proposal to differentiate between unconditional and conditional reflexes, on the basis of the complexity of determining factors. Pavlov also clearly positioned his studies into the debates of mechanical causation and vitalistic explanation. He showed that by extending the domain of physiology, he could obtain an explanation of psychic salivation with no recourse to the soul.

> For the naturalist everything is in the method, in the chances of attaining a steadfast, lasting truth, and solely from this point of view (obligatory for him) is the soul, as a naturalistic principle, not only unnecessary for him, but even injurious to his work, vainly limiting his courage and the depth of his analysis.
> (Pavlov, 1928, p. 60)

Thus, Pavlov started with a rejection of folk psychology and a search for explanations of behavior in the mechanical stance. In his laboratory, a decision was made to renounce psychological terms in reference to the phenomena under investigation – no anthropomorphism. In later years, a laboratory fine was imposed on the "unlawful" use of such terms.

Pavlov, in his Madrid talk of 1903, that is published in English in his 1928 volume, outlined that there was a move here from the psychical to the objective.

> The so-called psychical phenomena, although observed objectively in animals, are distinguished from the purely physiological, though only in degree of complexity. What can be the importance of how they are designated – "psychical" or "complicated nervous" – in distinction from the simple physiological, once it is recognized that the duty of the naturalist is to approach them only from the objective side.
> (Pavlov, 1928, pp. 59–60)

Pavlov arrived to accommodate the neuroscience research into his physiology factory style and proper physiology after several shifts of terminology. Experimental animal learning psychology becomes the study of **higher nervous activity**. In the two decades of work at the St. Petersburg laboratory, Pavlov developed the methods to use modification of visceral activities (salivation, gastric and pancreatic secretion, circulation) to unravel the most basic laws of learning. Basic phenomena, like **generalization** (responses to similar stimuli), **discrimination** (selective reinforcement leads to the animal only reacting to a single stimulus), and **extinction** (neutral stimulus without food leads to disappearance of reaction), were described. All this has become part of the core material of associative learning processes, especially due to behaviorists throughout the entire world from the 1940s on. The textbook of Hilgardand Marquis (1940) played a crucial role here; for an example from another culture see Le Ny (1961). The type of reactive learning described by him is contrasted with the other, more active type of conditioning, and Pavlov remains a central anchoring point even in the most elaborate neuroscience theories of basic types of learning (Kandel, 2001, 2009; Kandel & Squire, 2009). In the theoretical sense, he remains the basic reference for all connectionist models of learning. In the famous Rescorla and Wagner (1972) model, Pavlovian conditioning even becomes a cognitive model for all expectation-based learning phenomena. Thus, Pavlov, as a theoretician of learning, is still with us. For Pavlov, all these learning phenomena were expressions of cortical dynamics. From this perspective, Pavlov's self-proclaimed message and the message living within psychology are rather different.

Table 7.1 summarizes the stages of the activity of Pavlov from a psychological point of view and related to the science policy interpretation of his work.

Table 7.1 The stages in the work of Pavlov

Stage	Topic, method	Results	Research and politics
1890–1903	Digestive regulation, surgery	Digestive fluids under neural control	Military institute, Nobel prize
1903–1920	Higher nervous activity	Excitation—inhibition dynamics learning and cortical connections	Independent, tension with Bolsheviks
1920–1936	Extensions to clinics and humans	Second signaling system typology Neural disease theory	Criticized as reductionist Accepted by power
1936–1949	Pavlov labs continue	Generalized cortical learning theory	Criticized and sidetracked
1949–1970	Extension all over the country	All-encompassing Pavlov theory	Central figure in Stalinist new determinism

Pavlov and psychology: a generalized neural theory of the human mind

In the 1920s, the internal logics and the organization of the Pavlov laboratories became more and more expansive, entailing more and more psychological issues as belonging under the study of higher nervous activity. The facilities were extended, and besides the university laboratory, an academy research institute and a new biological station in Koltushi were also under the leadership of Pavlov. Already in 1910, Pavlov conceived the nervous system as a telephone switchboard in which conduction and connection between centers was the crucial aspect. As for the centers themselves, Pavlov had a clear vision of the system: there are lower and higher centers. In the higher centers, "inner processing" is more important than in the lower centers. Pavlov had many debates with Bekhterev and other contemporary reflexologists who posited the existence of specific connection making associative centers. For Pavlov, these centers did not exist; all connections in the nervous system were made by the cortical analyzers in the sensory and motor centers. His students also attempted synthetic works at the time, Ivanov-Smolensky (1933) is a typical medium level synthesis of the empirical methods, and the results of conditioning, both on animals and on human subjects.

In his 1927 synthesis book, Pavlov, along with his entire philosophy of science, tried to reduce everything to a few principles. The basic notions are excitation and inhibition, coupled with irradiation and concentration that is supplemented with the idea of analyzers and the opening and closing of neuronal pathways during learning. The aging Pavlov allowed for interpretations of the human brain as a more active, in some sense self-organizing, system corresponding to the image of the five-year plans (Bauer, 1952). This was an important self-defense as well that corresponded to the new, more activist Stalinism. A communist member of his laboratory Maiorov (1948, 1951) tried several times an ideologically fill proof synthesis.

In the 1920s, Pavlov extended his research toward psychology. The two notions that became central in later Pavlovism in the Soviet world, the idea of **personality typology** and **second signaling system**, emerged in Pavlov's last years. One aspect of this psychological extension was his theory about the signaling functions of the neuronal system. Elementary events in the neuronal system were interpreted as signs due to the work of the analyzers. The signal theory of the analyzers that goes back to Helmholtz was supplemented by Pavlov's cursory remarks on language. The **second signaling system** was originally a mere side remark about hysteric patients who are unable to express themselves with words. From this remark, Pavlov jumps during a seminar to postulate that the working of the analyzers creates a system of signs – and in humans, words are the expressions of these signs – as secondary signs. Pavlov ascertained a psychological interpretation of a traditional sensualistic theory of language (meanings of words are internal images). The introduction of verbal materials with human subjects into the Pavlovian heritage became the starting point for an entire movement of research in the 1950s analyzing lexical phenomena and for the acquisition of words by methodologies related to conditioned reflexes, Luria and Vinogradova (1959) being high-quality examples of this type of approach to language. Chapter 8 shows how these ideas spread over from Russia.

Regarding **personality**, based on a few dog observations, Pavlov refreshed classical **typology**. Pavlov started to propose typologies based on postulated basic neuronal processes. Personality types would be the result of three dimensions of cortical activity: strength of neuronal responses, dominance of excitation and inhibition, and the speed of learning. (See more in Chapter 2.)

The typology was not a negligible detour. The relations between inherited and acquired were at the center of this issue. For the psychologists, Pavlovian typology led to the study of individuality. Here, in fact, the individual life path, which is a social path, would explain real differences. The biological determinist approach was emphasizing the genetic aspects and the additive relations between experience and genetics, nature and nurture.

The **theory of pathology** proposed by Pavlov is related to his rather simplistic typological considerations. The balance of excitation and inhibition is the key to pathology, the basic pathological processes being a consequence of their disturbed balance. This is true for hypnotic processes, which are generalizations of cortical inhibitions, but it is also true of neurotic processes that can be seen as the contrast of excitation and inhibition to the same stimulus. The clinical work of Pavlov was also extended in the Soviet times. Studies on experimental neurosis in dogs were done in the lab. Differentiation between a gradually more and more similar ellipsis and circle would result in neurotic behaviors in dogs, to overexcitation or inhibition. The neurotic tension of the clinical cases would be explained as failures of discrimination between situations.

Pavlov connected neurosis as an imbalance issue with his typology as well. Neurosis appeared as a learning disturbance in situations where an opposite reaction is needed compared to the dominant reaction mode of the given person (Pavlov, 1928). As a further clinical extension, Pavlov, and especially his students, among them Konstantin Mikhailovich Bykov (1886–1959), created experimental analogies of several organic disorders. Peptic ulcers, hypertonia, and other allegedly psychosomatic disorders came to be interpreted as results of learning disturbances related to higher nervous activity (Bykov, 1959). This line of relating interoceptive organizational disorders to the literature on interoceptive self-regulation was continued in modern times, among others by the Hungarian psychophysiologist György Ádám (1922–2013), who was also a student of Bykov, in his books on interception and its role in consciousness and behavior (Ádám, 1967, 1998).

Pavlov and the communist power

Socialist biographies schematically showed Pavlov as an initially anti-Bolshevik intellectual who moved to the side of Bolshevism because of Lenin's support for his lab (Asratian, 1953). In reality, until the late 1920s, Pavlov had a tense relationship with the new power. Pavlov criticized them openly in his lectures, in 1919. He interpreted the revolution as being a behavior free from all inhibition. The way to normal functioning is a proper balance between *excitation* and *inhibition*. The Bolshevik Revolution unleashed excitatory processes and, without any control and inhibition, created a crazy system ruled by the law of the streets. These talks of his in 1918 were revealed only a 100 years later (Pavlov, 2014). Later, in the established Soviet system, during a Stalinist autocracy that developed and introduced an established system of inhibitions, Pavlov changed his target. He stood up against the system in the name of freedom and, specifically, freedom of science.

He stood against the communist climate of social life as a general intellectual as well. Pavlov was very critical of Stalin and Stalinism, especially during the reorganization of the academy and the forced election of new members, such as Bukharin.

At the same time, Pavlov was a determined protector of the interest of science and scientists. When something had to be done, he used his good connections to high-ranking individuals like Leningrad party secretary Kirov and central committee leaders such as Molotov and Bukharin. Pavlov's reconciliation with the Soviet system only came during the last years of his life. Yet even during those years, Pavlov opposed the new authoritarian system but acknowledged the special support of science in the new system.

Pavlov's situation was peculiar due to the changes outlined by the classic study of Bauer (1952) and Tucker (1956) regarding the shifts of communist ideas and their relations to psychology. In the first post-revolutionary years, in the early 1920s, Pavlov was popular in philosophy and psychology, as being in line with the deterministic materialist image of man and the removal of folk psychology from official discourse. That is the time where only a minority criticized Pavlov for being a mechanical materialist. Later, with the advent of activist Stalinism, mechanical types of materialism were highly criticized, and a requirement for people to be responsible for their own fate was introduced. This time the deterministic image of Pavlov made him an inadequate model of man. That is where Pavlov and his followers, detecting the traps, highlighted the more synthetic aspects of Pavlov's work, the role of language, etc.

Pavlov was, after a few victorious years, practically excluded from Soviet psychology by the early 1930s. This was one result of the series of reactology debates. However, his time came in 1949, when his heritage returned as the national Stalinist solution to many disciplines, from medicine to education and with psychology in the middle. Pavlov was reinterpreted as being in line with the new Stalinist activism combining transformism with the leading deterministic role of the Communist Party.

Marxist Freudians

Among the early efforts to look for a proper Marxist psychology, the one sailing under the flag of **psychoanalysis** was also important for a short time. Many young psychologists in the early Soviet times (e.g., Alexander Luria, Pavel Blonsky), while cultivating other trends as well, believed Freudian theory to be a possible kernel of a monist psychology. This proposal appeared on the one hand because it treated biological and social determinism together; it entertained a holistic vision of the person and the mind. Luria, already in 1923 (Luria, 2003), saw the advantages of psychoanalysis in its holism, specifically in the fact that it dealt with personality as a whole. Luria, the very young Russian pioneer organizer of a psychoanalytic circle in Kazan, expressed this opinion rather clearly in a volume on Marxist psychology published in 1925: "In contrast to scholastic, atomizing psychology, psychoanalysis starts out with the problems of the whole person; it proposes to study the person as a whole, and the processes and mechanisms that shape behavior" (Luria, 1925, p. 34). In a similar way, psychoanalysis, by its study of unconscious processes, also gets away from the old soul-based folk psychology.

> Unconscious mental activity becomes the entire focal point, whose symptoms are easier to ascertain objectively than to perceive in oneself by means of introspection, which places them on a level with other processes in the organism from which they are functionally, but not fundamentally, distinct.
> (ibid., 35)

All the new enthusiasm was colored by the ambivalent reception of Freud in pre-revolutionary Russia.

Psychoanalysis in pre-revolutionary Russia

Ovcharenko (1999) gave a general periodization of Russian and Soviet reactions to psychoanalysis.

Periods in the history of Russian psychoanalysis

- The educational, 1904–1910
- The adaptive, 1910–1914
- The disintegrative, 1914–1922
- The institutional, 1922–1932
- The latent, 1932–1956
- The bilateral, 1956–1989
- The integrative, 1989–to date

There was an affinity in the early years of psychoanalysis due to the Russian patients of Freud and the common Jewish Yiddish cultural background between the Viennese psychoanalysts and many Russian intellectuals of Jewish descent, including psychologists. Etkind (1997/2020) pointed out that in the Russian context, the sexual moment played a much lesser role, and in the analytic work, the issues of transference were transformed and became related to issues of power and riot. In cultural desexualization, the Nietzsche-inspired Russian symbolic poet Vjacheslav Ivanov (1866–1949) played a central role. Instead of libido, Ivanov concentrated on impersonal abstracts, symbolic ideas, and combined this with an anti-intellectualistic and anti-rationalistic attitude.

The turn-of-the-century Russian Silver Age, the idealistic modernism, both in its religious and its Nietzsche following varieties, had reservations about the body, and the rapprochement of human sexual life and the mental realm in psychoanalysis was considered as "pansexuality." Furthermore, the idea of unconscious determination would be contrasted with the self-shaping consciousness of humans, a kind of elevated consciousness both by spiritualists and by later communist leaders.

Soviet/Russian psychology 241

In this turn-of-the-century Russian setting, psychoanalysis was a provocative minority culture in opposition both to the religious and to the artistic revolutionary symbolic trends. In a way, psychoanalysis as an imported Western novelty was both alien for the basically anti-psychological Russian traditional mystical spirit and for the new symbolic movements with their renewed spirituality (Etkind, 1994, 1997/2020). Thus, after the revolutions, Russian psychoanalysis was naturally tied to the new revolutionary social and philosophical trends.

Trends in early Soviet psychoanalysis

Psychoanalysis in the early Soviet times was interpreted by an upcoming new generation as a new, more materialistic attitude compared to the pre-revolutionary anti-psychologism. Alexander Luria (1925/1977), the later neuropsychologist, was a theoretical organizer in this new stage in his early 20s. In his rather lengthy essay in a volume edited by Kornilov on relations between psychology and Marxism, Luria, who had just arrived in Moscow from his local Kazan psychanalytic society, tried to relate psychoanalysis mainly to the unity of science monistic ideas expressed by Engels. Marxism was mainly treated by Luria as a materialistic anthropology of the body/mind unity of humans. Psychoanalysis is first presented in a historical manner, as a distantiation from the earlier subjectivistic psychologies of consciousness. Instead, psychoanalysis is holistic in the sense that it treats humans as unified beings, with no separation of body and mind. On the other hand, in the interpretation of Luria, monistic psychoanalysis is also dynamic.

For him, Freudian metapsychology, in its bodily materialistic image, is central. In the psychoanalysis related work of Luria, besides his theoretical efforts, there was a practical affinity as well. He was an organizing talent in bringing psychoanalysis to Soviet Russia with his psychoanalytic society in Kazan, and later acting as a secretary of the Moscow-based Russian Psychoanalytic Association. He also tried to have an experimental combination of reflexology and psychoanalysis by creating a method to study conflicts where he measured vascular, motoric, and verbal reactions to critical word stimuli. Unconscious conflicts in criminal investigations, for example, can be shown by a careful analysis of associative and vascular reactions to critical words. He was greatly inspired by the notion of complexes introduced by the association method of Jung (1906). Luria published this earliest use of lie detectors in 1928 in Russian (Luria, 2003, is a new edition). The book version published in the United States (Luria, 1932) was very successful in its own time (it has about 1,000 references) as an early attempt to relate experimental, behavioral psychology and psychoanalysis in a pioneering lie detection exercise.

Clinical work was started in a state institute that continued into the Soviet era. In the 1920s and early 1930s, the *Russian Psychoanalytic Society* (1922–1930), the *State Psychoanalytic Institute* (1923–1925), the *"International Solidarity" Experimental Home for Children* (1921–1925), and the outpatient unit were all established under the Soviet Ministry of Education, officially recognized in the Soviet sense. Psychoanalysis as an applied child psychology played an important role in the first decade of Soviet power. The Russian followers of Freud interpreted the Viennese expert as an unequivocally liberal or even revolutionary social thinker. They believed that psychoanalysis would be an important support for a more liberated education with coeducation, sexual enlightenment of the youth, and even sexual liberties. Psychoanalysis was used as one source of the renovation of education, as a support or chapter of pedology in dealing with the pressing social issues of homeless youth. In this reasoning, psychoanalysis points out the parallels between oppression and repression: one form of oppression that leads to mental troubles is sexual oppression. Trotsky, the later ostracized communist leader, most likely intervened from time to time in the workings of the Moscow Psychoanalytic Orphanage of Children.

In the early 1920s, psychoanalysis and pedology developed intensively and extensively, to be replaced later by the community education principles of Makarenko. New centers, laboratories, and experimental schools were set up. From 1922 until 1929, Ivan Ermakov (1875–1942), the Moscow psychiatry professor, published a series of books titled the "Psychological and Psychoanalytical Library." Between 1919 and 1930, 19 more books by Freud, Anna Freud, and other famous psychoanalysts were translated and published. This went parallel with the institutional developments (Vasilieva, 2010).

The psychoanalytically minded nursery led by Vera Schmidt (1869–1937) gradually become a shelter for the children of party bureaucracy – even the son of Stalin was kept there for a while.

> The Detski Dom [House of Children] was funded partly by the State, and partly by the share in profits from Freud's publications in Russian, partly by international support from a German Trade Union. In 1923, 18 educators were busy with 12 children from 2 to 4 years old. . . . It was an elite institution supported by the officials to keep their children in hard times. Luria recalled orally that among these children was the son of Stalin (Vasilii, born in 1921).
>
> (Etkind, 1997/2000, p. 12)

It increasingly became a foster home and less and less a psychoanalytic child center. After it was closed in 1925, the writer Gorky lived in this elegant villa, and after his death, the son of Stalin returned there.

A special place in this process of child-centered psychoanalysis was played by **Sabina Spielrein** (1885–1942). She was a student and allegedly an intimate confidant of both Jung and Freud. She became one of the central figures of Russian psychoanalysis after a more or less successful Swiss and German psychoanalytic start. In Spielrein's relations with Jung, in line with the Russian Silver Age, the symbolic aspects, Wagnerism, Siegfried, and the dream for a spiritual child were central for her. Hesitant between Freud and Jung, she proposed a dual-component theory of the reproductive instincts, claiming that sexuality entails a creating and a destructive component as well (Spielrein, 1912). She was among the first successful female psychoanalytic practitioners, with young Piaget as one of her clients in Geneva. Spielrein and Piaget mainly had a research type of psychoanalytic session every day for eight months. Spielrein (1923) even reflected on their similarities in a paper, where her analysis of infant speech as mainly emotion-based is parallel to Piaget's vision of early egocentric speech. They both went in their own intellectual ways afterward, still learning a lot from the experience.

Afterward, Spielrein went back to Moscow, got involved in Russian psychoanalysis and in the working of the Moscow child psychoanalytic orphanage. Sabina Spielrein was one of the central mediating figures of psychoanalysis in Soviet Russia, and for a while, she was a central figure in the clinical movement there. Later, she was involved in general child psychiatric care, until the German occupying forces killed her in her hometown.

Ideology and Soviet psychoanalysis

There were alterative interpretations of the relations of psychoanalysis and Marxism in Russia (but that was true for the wider world as well). Some claimed that the clinical message and the social theory should be separated; others believed that the liberating message of psychoanalysis will only come to bear fruits with the cessation of the oppressive circumstances of bourgeois society, in socialism. The theoretical interpretation of psychoanalysis was not an exclusive issue of the psychologists in early Soviet Union. Philosophers and literary people were also involved in it. In the 1920s, the literary scholar Mikhail Mikhailovich **Bakhtin** (1895–1975) and his students wrote extensively on psychoanalysis, alongside Bakhtin's general dialogical approach to literature. They presented a remarkable cultural interpretation of the Freudian image of man and, in a way, continued the Russian cultural animosity toward psychoanalysis in a more modern flavor. The Bakhtin circle proposed that, due to their linguistic anchorage, psychological conflicts are always "ideologically laden," that is, are not natural science– or biology-based but are society-related. The conflicts and fights within the mind are fights between official and non-official culture. The "unconscious" is sign of an unofficial culture (Bakhtin, 1986; Volosinov, 1927/1976). The linguistic conception of unconscious promoted by Bakhtin and his circle was rediscovered by the linguistic and sign-based innovators of psychoanalysis in the 1970s. Bakhtin and his followers proposed that the social nature is an irreducible aspect of human life that cannot be reduced to human psychophysiology. The non-naturalistic image of the world and of humans was based on the dialogical principle. This was against natural science reductionism and centralized social reductionism as well. In this respect, Bakhtin's critic of psychoanalysis was one part of his general critique of all assumed stable entities (Etkind, 1997).

The Bakhtin reaction to naturalized psychoanalysis was a soft intellectual episode. In the period until the late 1920s, there were repeated tensions between ideology and psychoanalysis coming from the party circles. Luria and Vygotsky, in 1925, even claimed that the social elements of Freudianism are represented in the libido projecting into the happy socialist future. Soon it was realized that the marriage of communist utopism and psychoanalysis was a short-lived flirtation, and psychoanalysis became suspect both ideologically and politically. A young Bolshevik party philosopher, Bernard Bykhovsky, published in a party outlet a critique of Freud, basically criticizing Freud for overstating the role of sexuality and unconscious life and his disregard for social determinism. With the victory of Stalinism, Soviet society stopped to look for more freedom and openness regarding everyday human relations. A special factor was that the final evil, Trotsky, had a positive attitude toward psychoanalysis, already from his time in Austria. Trotsky tried to promote a combination of Freud for the substance of the human mind with Pavlov regarding its mechanism.

Soviet psychoanalysis received blow after blow, along the lines initiated by Bykhovsky, and coinciding with Trotsky's political eclipse.

> In 1926 the Psychoanalytical Institute was defunded by the state and thus killed. In 1927 Moshe Wulff, one of the leading Soviet psychoanalysts, defected to the West. In the same year, Luria resigned as secretary of the Russian Psychoanalytic Society (which would be defunct by 1930); this was in part a political decision in response to the growing anti-psychoanalytic chorus at the *Institute of Psychology* where he worked.
> (Miller, 1998, p. 88)

From the 1930s on, psychoanalysis as a psychiatric practice also disappeared, especially due to a general political fight against non-conscious determining forces. This was in line with the new voluntaristic interpretation of the Stalinist New Man. The New Man is a conscious planner, mobilizing the forces in a voluntary manner. Even the motivational concepts of the textbook of Rubinstein (1940) were criticized as being too Freudian in their acceptance on non-conscious driving forces. That contrasted with the new planning vision of humans and human societies.

In the late 1920s, all these fine-tunings became obsolete. Psychoanalysis stopped being interpreted as a special science and emerged as a result of the discussions as a bourgeois ideology, with its own representatives condemning it and removing themselves from the scene, or entirely change course, like Alexander Luria. In these discussions, both political leaders and party ideologists took part. Both psychoanalysis and Marxism were extremely unifying ideas. Either everything is class struggle or tension over the libido – there is no middle-of-the-road position tenable.

A further factor of their differences was concentrating on the past versus concentrating on the future. There was much concentration on the individual and evolutionary past by the psychoanalysts. The New Man should live in and for the future. The Bolshevik authorities under Stalin were committed to the principle that the post-revolutionary socialist society should have no individualized past. Their past was one of economic systems, forms of political authority, and sets of values.

Zalkind, a former supporter of Freud, gave the killing blow in the midst of Stalinist purges. He was also very critical of industrial psychology, reactology, and Vygotsky, himself being later fired from all his positions in the Stalinist purges. Zalkind asked:

> Does the "Freudian man" meet the demands of the task of socialist construction? The obvious negative answer to this identity-defining question, we should recall, was not applicable to psychoanalysis alone. The entire

profession of psychology was in turmoil and under attack at this moment. What had begun in the early 1920s as a vibrant and pluralistic debate on the intersecting links between methodology and ideology had evolved into a rigid monolith. The criticism was savage and the attempt at resolution proved to be more of a dogmatic political doctrine than a scientifically demonstrated theory.

(Miller, 1998, p. 886)

The combination of Marxism and psychoanalysis, and ideological tensions related to this, was true for other East European contexts as well, beside the well-known excursions of the Frankfurt school (see Chapter 1). The Hungarian historians of the left-wing psychoanalytic movements, Ferenc Erős (1983) and later István Kapás (2020) showed by detailed textual analysis that in the 1930s the issue of the relations between Marxism, left-wing social movements, and the psychoanalytic theory of unconscious life and sexuality were central in left-wing Hungarian literary and philosophy circles, both in Hungary and in Romania.

There was a similarity in the later discreditation as well. In Soviet Russia by the time Freud was roundly denounced at the 1930 Congress on Human Behavior, he had no defenders. As the 1930s went on, denunciations of psychoanalysis increasingly associated it with Trotskyism. The oppression of psychoanalysis was true of most Eastern European countries under Soviet dominance from the late 1940s on. Between 1949 and the 1980s in Hungary – the country of Ferenczi, Alexander, Hermann, and Balint – the psychoanalytic association was banned, and no books of Freud appeared, except for an accidental re-edition of *The Psychopathology of Everyday Life* in 1958, in the cultural rearrangements following the 1956 Hungarian Revolution (Mészáros, 2010, 2012). This is all the more telling since, at the same time, Hungarian psychology as such was more and more Western-oriented. Freud's writings scarcely appeared in collections, but the dream analysis was republished only in 1985.

The second Marxist wave: the Vygotsky school and Rubinstein

By the end of the 1920s, new and more sophisticated attempts were raised within Soviet psychology toward a synthesis of the teachings of Marx and modern psychology. They were more thoroughly bred in the intellectual traditions and innovations of modern psychology, familiar with behaviorism, *Gestalt* psychology, and psychoanalysis as well. They were less committed toward a simple equation of objectivity with behaviorism, and they also had a more subtle understanding and interpretation of the message of Karl Marx. The two basic forms were the historical genetic method of Vygotsky and the new interpretation of the unity of action and consciousness of Sergei Rubinstein. For the coming decades, until the 1970s, there were two rival metatheories of a proper Marxist psychology within the Soviet world. Both were rooted in the analysis of German psychology and its eternal crisis, or reformulations, supplemented by some impact of Francophone psychology, especially influenced by Janet and Piaget. Their other critical reference point was behaviorism and the Russian reflexology tradition. They both proposed a combination of a theoretical materialist approach to the mind with a recognition of a need toward integrating consciousness into a monistic theory. That led them to propose an activity-based approach. The concentration on activity and consciousness corresponded to an ideological demand, to the need for self-initiative emphasized by the second stage of Stalinism in the 1930s on (Bauer, 1952; Tucker, 1956). This implied activity with motivation rather than reactive behavior as the metatheory of psychology. Interestingly, the third stage of Stalinism that combined ironclad laws and determinism with internal motivation was also accommodated by psychologists, in the theory of Rubinstein (1957/1965, 1958), about external factors being determinant through the intervention of internal conditions.

The historico-genetic instrumental method and the Vygotsky school

Vygotsky (1927), in his analysis of the emerging new trends in psychology, believed that the truth was missed somewhere both by the behaviorists and by the "mental science" spiritualists. Humans have mental phenomena that can be interpreted in a combination of natural science and history. The **higher mental functions** do build on these foundations. (Notice the lexical similarity with the **higher neural functions** terminology promoted by Pavlov around the same time.) Higher mental functions are not given by nature; they are of a historical origin, and they are formed during social interactions in the individual. This also implied that brain representations of higher cognitive processes are more plastic and historically determined.

Biography

The Mozart of psychology

Vygotsky is an extremely popular psychologist, even in recent times. He has over 280,000 citations in Google Scholar in 2023, out of which about 140,000 are his *Mind in society* collection and over 50,000 are citations of *Thought and Language* (Vygotsky, 1978, 1934/1986). Stephen Toulmin (1978), the American philosopher and historian of science, called Lev Semjonovich Vygotsky (November 5, 1896–June 11, 1934, Moscow) **the Mozart of psychology**. The comparison is well-founded. Vygotsky was also a countryside *Wunderkind*, wonder child, like Mozart, who had already performed something substantial in literary scholarship when he was barely 17. This was a dissertation on *Hamlet* that became the core of his psychology of art in 1925. Like Mozart, Vygotsky also died very young of tuberculosis and, worse yet, was often neglected as a scholar, even by his students. Like Mozart, with the Habsburg emperor Joseph II, Vygotsky also had very intricate shifting relationships with the high powers of communist Soviet Union.

He was involved in the radical social reforms of science, being a teacher at the Krupskaja Communist Academy, together with Luria and Leontiev, but with the hardening of Stalinism, he became much too child-centered and too cosmopolitan. Like Mozart, he had his own less talented Salieries, like Kornilov, at least according to Vygotsky hagiography, but also according to the notes of Vygotsky. Vygotsky created foundations in several fields that are still valid and motivate modern cognitive, social, and educational researches.

Vygotsky had a lot of home tutoring in Gomel, where he was raised. The city was the center of Jewish life in Western Tsarist Russia (today Belarus) along an enlightened Jewish tradition. Spinoza played an especially central role in his intellectual upbringing. In his Moscow student years, where formally he was a student of law, he was far from being a committed materialist to start with. Rather, he was a spiritualist who was interested in the articulation of culture most of all. He returned to Gomel without finishing his degree. He published theater critiques, read philosophy, and was an active literary critical theorist. They were summarized in his *Psychology of Art*. At that time in Soviet Russia, formalism dominated art theory. Vygotsky was familiar with the debates and the works of art psychologists and Russian formalists like Shklovsky, Eichenbaum, Tinanov, and others. At the same time, he did not become a committed formalist. Vygotsky believed that the peculiar relation between form and content are the central issues in art. Instead of the creator, as the psychoanalysts would do, or the experience, as the cultural psychologists would do, Vygotsky tried to concentrate on issues like how **the structure of the work of art** led to certain types of emotional reactions that lead to catharsis. The analysis of tales, classical short stories, and *Hamlet* all became case studies of emotional reactions evoked by the art. His collection of art writings was accepted as a dissertation for a degree and appeared posthumously as his psychology of art.

Regarding the tragically short psychological period of Vygotsky between 1924 and 1934, one can still identify stages.

1. **Fight against reflexology and behaviorism**, but partially also identifying with reflexology as his educational psychology showed (mid–late 1920s).
2. The second stage would be the attempts to **overcome the duality of objective and subjective psychologies with the instrumental method**, involvement in pedology (1927–1929).
3. Searching for the **real units of analysis in psychology**, and a more activist theory of consciousness, and a return to Spinoza (1930–1934).

Vygotsky entered the Soviet psychological arena with full preparation. In the 2nd Psychoneurology Conference held at Leningrad in 1924, he had a presentation about the relations between psychological and reflexological method (Vygotsky, 1926). He basically proposed that there should be an objective study of the internal world, without identifying the objective method with the reflexological one. On the basis of this successful talk, Kornilov, the new director, supposedly through the mediation of Luria, invited the unknown country college teacher to the Institute of Psychology in Moscow.

His early theoretical works in the 1920s tried to clarify the whys and hows of consciousness in a behavioral psychology (Vygotsky, 1925, 1927). Marxist psychology should not be conceived as supplementing an existing psychological trend with Marxism but by an elaborate introduction of Marxist methodology into psychology. The solution was a combination of the Marxist analysis of work with his instrumental method in psychology.

Young scholars at the Moscow Institute constituted a group around Vygotsky, associates who were already there with A. R. Luria and A. N. Leontiev creating a troika, and an entire bunch of new people joined, like Bozhovich, Zaporožec, Sakharov, Elkonin, Galperin. The theory under formation had two cornerstones. One was the historical-genetic interpretation of higher psychological functions, with an emphasis on higher human specific functions and on consciousness. The second cornerstone was the **mediated nature** of these functions, where signs shall be instruments, tools for a division of labor between participants in mental organization (Galperin, 1938/2009).

Vygotsky also had a central institutional role. Besides working in the Institute of Moscow University, he taught at the Academy of Communist Education, run by the widow of Lenin, Krupsakaja, and founded the Experimental Defectology Institute. He also worked out close ties with neurology clinics.

Vygotsky combined theoretical work with his works as a committed practical psychologist. He became part of the Soviet pedology movement, making many efforts to make child study methods scientific and for the introduction of psychology into education. A test for the theory according to him is the impact of modifications based on the theory. He was the prototypical example for a socially engaged psychologist who, in all areas of practice, from testing to special education, campaigned for possibilities of helping and remediation, rather than ironclad laws of development.

His pedological works were criticized soon after his death as deviations from proper educational theory. It was this practical embedding and their political associations that caused the rejection and even oppression of the Vygotsky school from the mid-1930s and especially after the party decision against pedology. The challenge against them was threefold. Vygotsky and his coworkers were too associated with the names of Trotsky and Bukharin, even citing the two communist leaders sacked by Stalin. They were too child- and less institution-centered, and they were too cosmopolitan. All this led toward a discreditation of their theories a decade later and even led to the removal of their books from libraries. The intellectual revival of Vygotsky in the Soviet Union waited until 1956, which was followed by his Western fame. This contributed to the image of Vygotsky as the "muffled deity" of Soviet psychology, as Joravsky (1987) ironically characterized this process.

This account is questioned by the new Vygotsky studies movement that relies on more archival materials and in-depth studies of interviews and biographic notes of participants, as well as a careful study of publications. There is an entire revisionist Vygotsky study movement lab led as such by Yasnitsky (2011) and represented by a volume collected by Yasnitsky and van der Veer (2015). The first reinterpretation concerns the sources of Vygotsky. Some authors do claim that his Marxism was the central turning point in his activity, while others maintain that Vygotsky had multiple inspirations, an interpretation of Spinoza and the enlightened Jewish tradition, and the affective theories of Shpet, an idealist philosophy teacher of his in Moscow. Gustav Shpet (1879–1937), with Husserlian inspirations, promoted in Moscow a rather idealistic theory of culture, based on the independence of culture. In the intellectual outlook of Vygotsky, these culturalist influences had a greater

Figure 7.2 Lev Vygotsky (1896–1934).
Source: Wikimedia commons. Public domain.

role than traditionally proposed. Marxism was one among these influences on the one hand, but on the other hand, it was the possibility for a synthesis of materialistic and human science inspirations in Vygotsky (Veresov, 1999).

The other revisionist aspect concerns the neglect of Vygotsky. Fraser and Yasnitsky (2015) pointed out that part of the victimization was created by his followers Leontiev and Luria in the 1960s as part of their carrier moves. In the middle of the Stalinist purges, Vygotsky died in peace and went on to be buried in the most prestigious Moscow cemetery, where many intellectuals are buried. While his pedological work was certainly criticized, he was not really forgotten. Rubinstein (1940) cites him 40 times in his textbook. The silence about Vygotsky only came between 1949 and 1954, in some of the harshest times of the Cold War. The publication of the collected works of Vygotsky was delayed mostly due to hesitations by Leontiev. Thus, his followers were partly responsible in creating an image of the entire school being ostracized. As a third aspect of the new Vygotsky studies, several divergencies and tensions within the troika are also revealed.

His family compiled a very instructive account of his short life and published many upublished writings of Vygotsky (Vygodskaia & Lifanova, 1996), and many of his writings are available in new English translations (Vygotsky, 1996–1999) and some in the Digital Vygotsky Archives.

The analysis of the mind by Vygotsky

In his systematic psychology, Vygotsky tried to separate natural and cultural and explain a move between them as a move from lower to higher levels of mental organization. The three basic ideas to interpret the move from natural to cultural for Vygotsky were:

1. The instrumental organization of the mind, and the role of tools in mental organization.
2. The role of language and (adult) social mediation in mental organization.
3. The ontogenetic and historical development of mental organization from non-logic to logic.

His statements regarding the **instrumental method** about the organization of mental life, and the proper way to study psychology, as expressed first at a talk at the communist academy are central to understand his general theory.

> In the behavior of man, we encounter quite a number of artificial devices for mastering his own mental processes. By analogy with technical devices these devices can justifiably and conventionally be called psychological tools or instruments.... The following may serve as examples of psychological tools and their complex systems: language, different forms of numeration and counting,

Soviet/Russian psychology 251

mnemotechnic techniques, algebraic symbolism, works of art, writing, schemes, diagrams, maps, blueprints, all sorts of conventional signs, etc. . . .

The relation between instrumental and natural processes can be clarified with the following scheme – a triangle.

In natural memory a direct associative (conditional reflex) connection A→B is established between two stimuli A and B. In artificial, mnemotechnic memory of the same impression, by means of a psychological tool X (a knot in a handkerchief, a mnemonic scheme) instead of the direct connection A→B two new ones are established: A→X and X→B.

. . . [I]n the instrumental act we see activity toward oneself, and not toward the object.

(Vygotsky, 1930/1997, p. 1)

The implications of the instrumental method were taken up by several later trends in modern cognitive studies. One example is the Hungarian-American scholar Vera John-Steiner (1997) who elaborated the instrumental conception towards a general theory about the role of external notes, drawing, charts in organizing not only our memory but our creative processes as well.

The further development of the Vygotsky approach was related to the idea of development, speculations on the relations of **ontogenetic development, evolution**, and **cultural unfolding**. In his *Thought and Language* book (1934/1986), which was published as a summary of his ideas, and while he was again fighting tuberculosis, Vygotsky promoted four basic ideas of consequence for later developmental and theoretical psychologies.

1. **Language and thought**, and communication and representation, have different sources both in evolution and in child development, and they do **unite only gradually**. For their evolutionary independence, Vygotsky relied in the observations of Köhler (1921/1925) on chimpanzee insightful problem-solving, where no communication and observational learning seemed to be present. In children, Vygotsky claimed that the early Piaget (1923) studies, in fact, showed that communication at the beginning did not play a role in the mental development of the child (see Chapter 4).
2. A central role in humans is played by **inner speech**. Language, through this mechanism, gradually becomes an actual mediating tool for cultural unfolding. Inner speech and regulation through speech have become a central proposal to

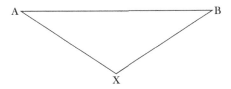

Figure 7.2 a Mediation processes according to Vygotsky.

understand socialization in developing children. These ideas were developed in detail by Luria (1961).
3. **The process of interiorization.** "Every function in the child's ... development appears twice: first, on the social level, and later, on the individual level; first between people (interpsychological), and then inside the child (intrapsychological)" (Vygotsky, 1978, p. 57). In this way, cultural determinism overcomes natural determinism.
4. The possibilities of development. Here, Vygotsky introduced the notion of **the zone of proximal development**. This concept was elaborated in light of the mental testing movement and the importance of two factors there. Vygotsky questioned the importance of mental age as a clear-cut factor and proposed that instead of independent individual solutions, the children's ability to use adult models should be studied. If the child is aided, the reactions of the child were to be seen in situations of adult aid, whether the wrong solutions were discontinued. A dynamic learning-based proposal for testing was initiated. What should be measured is not a static condition but how far the child can arrive. "In studying what the child is capable of doing independently, we study yesterday's development. Studying what the child is capable of doing cooperatively, we ascertain tomorrow's development" (Vygotsky, 1934/1986, pp. 203–204). Vygotsky's theory about the mentor and guide role of teachers is rather similar to the guiding role of the Communist Party regarding the development of class consciousness in the working classes.

Regarding the **historical determination of mental functions**, the Vygotsky group took very seriously the implications of the historical determination suggested by the historicity of the Dilthey-style mental science psychology and the French sociogenic attitudes, especially the conception of Janet and Lévy-Bruhl about primitive mentality. They inferred from these inspirations a general idea for a **historical psychology**. They claimed a general historical relativism and a historical psychology similar to the one developed by Meyerson (1948, Chapter 5). They elaborated and tested a psychological anthropogenesis idea. Luria and Vygotsky (1930/1992), in their studies done in the early 1930s in Uzbekistan (see Chapter 5), believed to have proved that illiterate primitive peasant communities do not have a logical organization of thought, whereas schooling and collective farming, the creation of kolkhoz, drastically changed the situation. This work was subject to harsh criticism in Soviet Russia in their own time. They were interpreted as being too bourgeois in their general educational theory but especially wrong in conducting conversation-based studies among peasants. It was even labeled as an anti-Marxist theory that claims that Soviet people cannot think logically.

Further developments in the Vygotsky school

Vygotsky, together with Luria and Leontiev in the early 1930s, formed the famous troika of the Vygotsky historical cultural activity school. From a present-day perspective, their weights are different. Vygotsky is all around the place, appears 3,800 times in PsycINFO, while Luria 2,200 times. The third of the troika, A. N. Leontiev, however, figures only 116 times.

In the early 1930s, the troika was often separated. Vygotsky was teaching in Leningrad, Luria was working in Moscow, and Leontiev was establishing a new group in Kharkov. There certainly was a separation due to practical reasons. As a reaction to the repercussions against psychology starting from the early 1930s, associates of the Moscow group fled Moscow, moved to safer cities. There were some theoretical divergencies as well. A. N. Leontiev moved toward an activity theory instead of the mediation theory of Vygotsky. In Leontiev's (2005) account, this was a dramatic bifurcation. Vygotsky became more and more interested in the affective components of mental life, which explains his return to Spinoza. At the same time, Leontiev himself was more interested in the organization of practical activity.

Rebirth of the Vygotsky school from the 1960s

The Vygotsky school survived the war years mainly by working in military rehabilitation hospitals that included not only the later well-known neuropsychologist Luria but A. N. Leontiev, Galperin, and Zaporozhets as well. **Bluma Zeigarnik** (1900–1988), who had just returned to Soviet Russia from Germany in the 1930s, and being a follower of Lewin (Zeigarnik, 1927), soon became another advocate of the Vygotsky school. She formed a double commitment, both to her mentor Kurt Lewin and to Vygotsky. During the rebirth of the Vygotsky school, she remained a committed Vygotsky and Lewin student of psychopathology. She combined the meaning-centered approach of the Vygotsky school with the task and ambition (aspiration level) ideas of her mentor, Lewin, in creating a new experimental psychopathology (Zeigarnik, 1972).

After the war, the main core group of Vygotsky's former students participated in the Pavlov discussion, but with a low profile. From the late 1950s, they reassembled at Moscow State University, where Leontiev, Luria, and Galperin recreated a new Vygotskian troika. Leontiev was the official leader. At that time, he was doing general experimental psychology of perception and personality psychology there. Luria was working out the functional localization theory about historically developing cultural organs in the brain, becoming an international expert of neuropsychology. Galperin elaborated the developmental theory into a general educational theory on the role of work organization in teaching. Many others joined their ranks at Moscow State, like the neuroscientist **Evgenij Nikolajevich Sokolov** (1920–2008), who became a leading researcher of the neurobiology of the orienting reflex (Sokolov, 1960, 1975), and the developmental psychologist Elkonin (1972, 2016), who was at the Pedagogy Academy Research Institute of Psychology. The activity theory conception of Alexei Nikolayevich Leontiev as dean of a gradually created psychology faculty at Moscow State University played a central, integrative role.

Alexei Nikolajevich Leontiev (1904–1979), the later leader of a Marxist developmental and educational psychology, especially in the 1960s and 1970s, started

Figure 7.3 A. N. Leontiev.
Source: Photo courtesy of his grandson D. Leontiev.

early on in his research on mediated memory. In this work, he gave children a list of words to remember with a series of pictures as mediating aids. The mediating stimuli helped recall (Leontiev, 1932). Vygotsky tended to assume that mediated forms of memory would reduce natural memory, while Leontiev was hesitant in accepting this.

In the 1930s–1950s, Leontiev was working extensively on elaborating the evolutionary message of the Vygotsky school, by working in comparative psychology, in different institutions, after he moved back to Moscow. However, his main base was the Institute of Psychology in Moscow, which changed hands between the university and the newly formed Russian Academy of Pedagogy in 1943. Leontiev stayed at the university, turning his base into a faculty of psychology in the 1960s. As a researcher, A. N. Leontiev was mainly active in three domains during the renaissance of Soviet psychology in the 1960s. He elaborated the developmental theory of the Vygotsky school into **a general theory of both phylogenetic and ontogenetic development** (Leontiev, 1958). In this view, human mental development essentially turns natural mental phenomena into socially mediated ones through language and tool use. Phylogenetic forms of mental organization were analyzed by him with reference to the way of life of animals. This interesting view mainly relied on classical zoology and zoo psychology, with some embedding into the German debates of the 1930s, at the same time ignoring modern ethology. Regarding human evolution and culture, Leontiev presented a continuity vision from the tool use of apes to the beginning of instrumental mediations in cultural memory organization. In modern child development, the crucial moments are the genesis of mediated mental organization. At the same time, there are crucial motivational and ecological changes in development as well. Development is always characterized by tensions between old and new forms and by dominant forms of activity in each developmental time frame. Play is the central activity in preschoolers, learning in school years.

His other topic that became central in the 1960s was the experimental elaboration of his **activity theory of perception**. In this regard, the work of their group became part of the new cognitive theories of active perception worldwide. His associates developed detailed methods and theories about the role of eye movements in vision relying on the methodology of Yarbus (1967). Eye movements, according to their theories, would play a constructive role in pattern vision, thereby representing the active nature of perception (Zinchenko & Vergiles, 1972).

Finally, in his last works, Leontiev elaborated a **Marxist theory of motivation and personality**, uniting it with his theory of activity. Leontiev elaborated the speculations of the Vygotsky school regarding the proper units of mental life into a general theory of action. The teleological element, goal setting, was centralized by him as underlying human actions, in contrast to a deterministic, reflex-like vision of action. In the later, full-fledged development of this theory in the 1970s (Leontiev, 1978), he would differentiate three levels of action organization: evoked reflex actions, goal-oriented activities (*dejatelnost* in Russian), and performing actions relegated to the goal directed action.

> Actions are not separate things that are included in activity. Human activity exists as action or a chain of actions. When we consider the unfolding of a specific process – external or internal – from the angle of the motive, it appears as human activity, but when considered as a goal-oriented process, it appears as an action or a system, a chain of actions.
> (Leontiev, 1978, pp. 103–104)

His action theory reintroduces the folk psychology vision of human action with a special modification. Human actions both have a teleology (a goal) and an intentional starting point (a motive). There is a cross hearing between the design and the intentional stance of Dennett (1987).

Personality interestingly became central to several trends in modern Soviet psychology, probably also as a reaction to the biological personality theory embedded inti Pavlovian typology.

Personality for Leontiev is the result of social development.

> One is not born a personality; one becomes a personality. For this reason, we do not speak either of a personality of a newborn or of a personality of an

infant although traits of individuality appear at early stages of ontogenesis no less sharply than at much later stages of growth. Personality is a relatively late product of social-historical and ontogenetic development of man.

(Leontiev, 1978, p. 151)

Leontiev contrasted this approach with traditional and Pavlov-inspired typologies.

Traits characterizing one unity (individual) do not simply enter into the characteristics of another unity, another formation (personality).... Although the functioning of the nervous system is, of course, an indispensable prerequisite for the development of personality, yet its type does not all appear to be this "skeleton" on which personality is "constructed."

(ibid., 156)

This self-transforming personality as an ideal of life development was basically an optimistic Stalinian image of self-transforming individuals. This was combined with a self-actualizing flavor of humanistic psychology. As one of his followers, Alexei Asmolov (1997) emphasized, the fate of psychology, genetics, and some other sciences during the Stalinist period was undermined through a centralized system of utility, rather than merit and meaning. In his analysis, the real novelty in the re-emergence of the Vygotsky school was the elaboration of a motivational theory and the analysis of meaning-centered relations in the human mind.

Alexander Romanovich Luria (1902–1977) was the third member of the troika. During the criticism of psychology in the 1930s, he obtained a medical education as well and was constantly working, besides Moscow University, at the Burdenko Institute of Neurosurgery and moved in two directions in the interpretation of the Vygotsky heritage from the 1950s on. He elaborated a detailed theory of the instrumental vision of the mind into a communicative theory of the mind. In his vision, mediation was indeed accomplished by the role of speech interiorization. Speech has become an organizer of our own behavior in a stepwise manner. First, the adult gives directives, then the children give the directives to themselves, and finally the directives become internalized as inner speech (Luria & Yudovich, 1959; Luria, 1961). The main impact of Luria and his international fame came by his elaborating a *neuropsychology* based on the detailed study of many brain-damaged patients, combined with the attitude of Vygotsky regarding higher mental functions.

Luria (1966a), in his mature **neuropsychology**, differentiated three basic systems of brain activity:

- The unit for regulating posture and waking, limbic and reticular systems.
- The unit for obtaining, processing, and storing information (most of cortex).
- The unit for programming, regulation, and verifying mental activity and prefrontal brain areas. These areas represent the goal system and the regulatory role of speech in mental development.

His basic idea was that for higher mental function, neither strict, narrow localization nor holism in the style of Kurt Goldstein (1940) was correct. Higher functions like language, voluntary memory, or planned action follow a culturally systematic pattern. For writing, for example, in an alphabetic language, one needs phonemic analysis, knowledge of lexicon and grammar, fine motor organization, and relating intention and movement. Thus, there is no single writing center in the brain. Rather, there is a functional organization – a **functional organ**, as Vygotsky had already named it – that corresponds to this culturally conditioned functional system.

> Social history ties those knots which form definite cortical zones in new relations with each other, and if the use of language evokes new functional relations . . . then this is a product of historical development, depending on "extra-cerebral ties" and new "functional organs" formed in the cortex.
>
> (Luria, 1965, p. 391)

This cultural formation of functional organs is similar to the contemporary idea of Dehaene and Cohen (2007) about the cultural recycling of neuronal circuits. Luria and his hundreds of students from many countries developed a battery of tests for the diagnosis of various types of brain damage, as the Luria–Nebraska Neuropsychological Battery (Golden, 2004). Their rehabilitation principles were based on the idea of developing a possibly equivalent functional system on the basis of remaining brain functions. With his famous case studies of a memory expert (Luria, 1968) and the disturbed identity of a brain-damaged soldier (Luria, 1987), Luria has become a modern representative of what Oliver Sacks (1995) calls Romantic medicine – what Luria saw as a patient-centered neuroscience (Luria, 1979/2010). For a more personal account, his autobiography, especially the rewritten version, is a good source. As a neuropsychologist, he was the only Eastern European psychologist who became a member of the American Academy of Sciences, until the Hungarian Gergely Csibra of Central European University was elected in 2017.

Piotr Galperin (1902–1988), working in the Kharkov group of Leontiev, started a further, newer theory of orientation activity. This was related to another change in the outlook of the work of Leontiev in the 1930s. He systematically started to analyze different psychological phenomena in an **action theoretical** context. Leontiev concentrated on the organization of action rather than sign mediation. There was some sort of separation because of the interpretation of mediation itself. Galperin started from a criticism of Pavlov, as a basically stimulus–reaction theorist, and a need to overcome physiological reductionism. His thesis at that time was among the first to propose the analysis of tools as the basis of a new psychology. Tools become specific carriers of certain functions, and for Galperin, the mediating role of language was less important here. The central issue was the specific **human practical activity** organization. A spoon, for example, carries in it a human meaning about a specifically organized eating activity. In this regard, he deviated both from Vygotsky and from Leontiev. The essential difference was the concentration of Galperin (1938/2009) on "meaningful activity." In his later view, the object of psychology

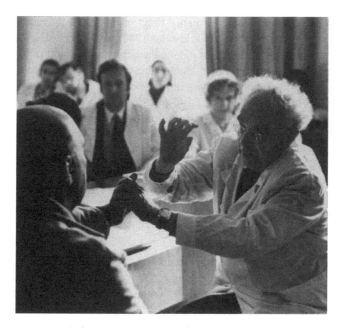

Figure 7.4 A. R. Luria examining a patient.
Source: http://luria.ucsd.edu/Luria_Pics/Pages/Image2.html.

became **orienting activity**. Human activity is organized on several layers, and the essential moment is orientation. Meaningful activity for Galperin became personalized activity, and this, in turn, became orienting activity. Orientation became a guiding principle in his theory of differentiating psychology from neuroscience. Psychology studies the orienting activity of the mind (Galperin, 1976). In his later works, he played a central role in designing new methods of teaching. Methodically, his claim was, "No more observation, only formation." Stepwise formation of mental activities is needed in schools, with actual manual activity, followed by external speech, later to be replaced by internal speech (Galperin, 1969).

The psychological Marx interpretation of Rubinstein

Sergei Leonidovich Rubinstein (Odessa, June 6, 1889–Moscow, January 11, 1960) became the opinion leader after Vygotsky in the fight for a proper interpretation of Marx toward the new psychology. Rubinstein had a German education mainly of neo-Kantian philosophy and defended a PhD in Marburg on philosophical issues of methodology. On the invitation of Nikolaj Lange, he first became an assistant professor, and later a full professor and a chief librarian, at Odessa Novorossiysk University, after the revolution until 1930. From 1930 to 1942, he became a central figure as the head of the department of psychology in the Herzen State Pedagogical University of Russia in Leningrad. Many important psychologists defended their state theses there, like Boris Ananiev, Boris Teplov, and A. N. Leontiev. The two outliers, who came to Leningrad from elsewhere to get their degrees, Teplov and Leontiev never created a mentor or sponsor relation with Rubinstein, though they were a decade younger than Rubinstein, and later become harshly disillusioned with him. Rubinstein was one of the organizers of the university evacuation during the German siege of Leningrad, and from 1942, he was appointed chair of the psychology department at Lomonosov Moscow State University until 1949. In 1942, he was elected member of the Soviet Academy of Sciences and received a Stalin price (the highest state price) for his book on general psychology. In both regards, he was the first psychologist with these distinctions. From 1945 on, also in Moscow, he organized a psychology group in the Institute of Philosophy of the Soviet Academy, where he was a leader until 1949, and then from 1956 to 1960.

Rubinstein was a well-read philosophical psychologist, with a mainly German background from neo-Kantianism. As a longtime librarian – in Odessa, that was his main university function – he always preserved his bookish German style. He elaborated a rather-philosophical theory about the unity of consciousness and activity. In this framework, mind and consciousness can only be studied through activities, and activity gives the basis for mentality. Rubinstein connected this general framework to Marxism with the then newly published writings of the young Marx (1932) in a locally very influential paper *The problems of psychology in the works of Karl Marx*. The paper, published in 1934, first outlined his approach to consciousness. Rubinstein started from a critique of the psychological debates about consciousness on the one hand and, on the other, from an analysis of the early works of Marx, such as the *German ideology* and the *Economic-Philosophical Manuscripts*, that became available through the Moscow Marx–Engels Institute in the 1930s. Rubinstein claimed to reveal a hidden psychology from the works of Marx. This psychology was different from traditional introspective psychology, but it was also different from behaviorism and from French-style social constructionism. It was "naturalistic," but not in the way reflexologists and behaviorists would talk about naturalistic psychology. It was naturalistic in the sense that it would treat **work as the key human activity**, as a relation between humans and nature, and saw the essence of consciousness as being established in real human activities.

In his criticism of the spiritualistic and the behavioristic position, Rubinstein announced a two-front battle that was a "must" of the age, in line with the Stalinian two-front battles in politics and in ideology.

> The basic approach has to be not a "synthesis" but a "fight on two fronts", in order to eliminate rather than combine errors accumulated by different schools. The error of introspectionism did not lie in taking consciousness as its object, but in how it did this; and, behaviorism's concentration on behavior was not false but wrongly done. Therefore, the solution lies in ignoring neither the psyche nor behavior, but in radically reconstructing the understanding of both human consciousness and human conduct in their inseparable continuity. This, we claim, is exactly the path that can be clearly inferred

from Marx's statements. He provides us with the opportunity to construct Marxist-Leninist psychology as a really contentfull and actual science.
(Rubinstein, 1934/1987, p. 114)

He also interpreted the Marxian theses about the changes of the mind as a result of historical changes as literal suggestions for psychology regarding mental changes.

If the psychological nature of man is dependent on twisted social relations, then the latter have to be changed. In place of the frequent bourgeois notion of unchanging social structure based on unchanging human nature, we have the notion of the changing nature of all. . . . Only in actual socially reconstructive practice in labor are found the internal contradictions which incite human consciousness to develop all the politically necessary changes.
(ibid., 122)

The Vygotsky school that was and is rather theoretical for most Westerners was in Russia the experimentalist pole of interpreting Marx, in contrast to Rubinstein. The rather meager empirical work of Rubinstein was mainly on meaningful memory and textbook learning with his students in the Herzen College, and later on thought processes in the 1950s (Rubinstein, 1958).

His real influence came through his textbook. The definitive textbook on general psychology, which numbers over 1,000 pages, offered a synthesis along Marxist lines of modern Western and Soviet psychology as seen in the late 1930s. Rubinstein combined a deterministic vision with the principles of monism, individual development, and historic determination.

This psychology treated consciousness in an action-embedded manner. At the same time, this psychology treated the human mind in a socially embedded manner as well.

Consciousness is not the narrow personal possession of the individual, locked up within his own inner world; it is a social formation. . . . Marx's formula concerning consciousness and language implies that the practical form of consciousness which is real for others and therefore real for myself, expresses not only the common origin of consciousness and language, but also their common structure. Man's consciousness is cloaked in words; it is conditioned by social relations and serves a cognitive purpose.
(Rubinstein, 1945, p. 256)

During the first troubled decade of psychology, in the 1930s and early 1940s, he became very well respected, but in the late 1940s, he was sharply criticized. The open charge was his cosmopolitism (also implying him being a multilingual Jew), and the seemingly professional issue was that he neglected the reflection theory of Lenin (1909/1972) and the role of activity. For example, he ignored the mirroring role of emotions. He concentrated too much on internal factors in his vision for emotions, and in this regard, he was charged to be too Freudian. These charges, together with the Pavlov debates coming within a year of each other, resulted in the

Figure 7.5 S. L. Rubinstein.
Source: Wikimedia commons. Public domain.

removal of Rubinstein from his academy and university positions. From 1955 on, however, he participated in the renewal of psychology. Most of his positions were reinstated, except that of Moscow University, where, at that time, the Vygotsky line of Leontiev took over.

At the same time, the style of Rubinstein, after his return in the late 1950s, is disappointing for a modern Western reader. Compared to the definitive, straightforward style of his textbook, in the late 1950s, we observe a self-defending scientist who escaped into scholastic verbalisms in his own defense and in the defense of his science.

The two rival theories of activity in Soviet psychology of the 1960s were the one proposed by Leontiev and the earlier one proposed by Rubinstein. The two, after a time, while working at the same place in Moscow, became not only rivals but also intellectual antagonists.

But there is an interesting parallelism. In their own manner, they both positioned personality as the central concept to save independent psychology and individuality both from Pavlovian naturalization and from ideological dogma. **Personality** was a Russian way for the reemergence of individuality under the dominance of a communal concept of humans. It was already a way out of the tensions between party constructive determininism and Pavlovian typology for the old school Kornilov

(1957), but for Rubinstein and Leontiev as well. Personality became a key word to salvage psychology proper.

> Rubinstein and Leontiev disagreed on the nature of psychic phenomena and personality. Rubinstein used to say that personality structure can be understood as an explication of inner drives and needs: "The outer is the incarnation of the inner", Leontiev argued that personality structure should be considered as the internalization of outward activity: "The inner is the incarnation of the outer".
>
> (Mironenko, 2013a, p. 384)

Discreditation of psychology: psychology in the Stalinist times

Soviet psychology had a difficult fate between 1930 and 1955. The increasing authoritarian centralization and Russification of Soviet science, together with the political tensions over the visions of a New Man in a new society, created sometimes-harsh conditions for psychology, as well as for other social sciences as well. Some of the repercussions against psychology, and the very fate of psychology, could be seen in the broader context of the two stages of transformism. The impact of Stalinist centralization and dogmatic authority is oftentimes presented in a simplified manner as a unified anti-psychological stance that lasted for 30 years, from the early 1930s until the early 1960s. There were several partly overlapping steps in the Stalinization of psychology, as shown in Table 7.2. As the *time* column shows, certain political moves had a more lasting effect than others.

The first transformist Stalinist moves: messages of the reactology debate

From the beginning of the 1930s, the rather varied Soviet psychology became the subject of several waves of ideology-based campaigns. Regarding the party-enforced rhetoric, at the time when "ideological purification" of psychology was raised, psychology entered the domains of ideological debates on two fronts (against mechanization and against idealism), and a cycle of critique and forced self-critique began. This led to the discreditation, existential annihilation, and sometimes even execution of many types of activities, institutions, and people.

Table 7.2 Stages in the Stalinist questioning of Soviet psychology

Times	Issues
1930–1936	Deterministic questioning; Ananiev et al.
1936–1970	Pedology decisions; anti-test moves
1939–1947	War years, military service, education
1947–1949	Against cosmopolitism, Russian psychology
1949–1960	Pavlovization of psychology
1955–1964	Rehabilitation of modern psychology

During the reactology debate in 1931, as we have seen earlier, the leading role of Kornilov in Moscow was questioned. The political and ideological charge against him, as against many later psychologists, was eclecticism, an insufficient integration of Marxism into psychology, especially the reflection theory of Lenin (1909/1972, 1929/1976), and most specifically a mechanistic interpretation of humans.

The (second) reactology debate was the first Stalinist move against psychology. There were several issues involved in the 1931 decisions against reactology.

1. The first aspect was **the party context**. Within the ideology of the Communist Party, Stalin started a campaign both against the mechanistic materialists and the so-called "dialecticians" represented by Deborin (1881–1963). These later were labeled as idealists of a Menshevik kind. "Menshevik" originally, in 1903, meant the literally "minority" socialist party faction of the pre-revolutionary times. Stalin started to use this label against anyone charged to have idealistic tendencies.
2. The debates within the Russian Communist Party were generalized into two general frames by Stalin. The class struggle intensified, he claimed, and there was to be found a **hidden class struggle in all areas of culture**, including science. The official Stalinist doctrine became dialectical materialism. In all matters, there was supposed to be a fight on two fronts, one being mechanistic, the other idealistic. All this, furthermore, was to go together with a **general criticism of Western culture** and Western science. Regarding psychology, the two front battles meant a criticism both of old-style subjective psychology, as being idealistic, and a need to criticize the new behavioral trends as well, as being mechanistic.
3. **Institutional contexts.** The former young Turks of the psychology field, including the research institute in Moscow, generated a generation of still younger Turks who wanted to overthrow the establishment. The moves of Stalin created a **transformist image of humans** (Bauer, 1952; Tucker, 1955, 1956). In the reshaped Stalinist movement, this traditional Russian criticism was clearly directed against local authority in the name of a centralized authority. The destruction of the behavioral heritage went on two fronts. One was at the Moscow institute, where the reactology of Kornilov was the main target. Reactology became a variety of behaviorism, and behaviorism is essentially a school in the service of American capitalism. It is a psychology of man as an automaton permitting more ruthless exploitation and more deceitful decoying of the working class (sic!), as Talankin (1932) described reactology. Talankin (1931/2000) was also attacking the Vygotsky group. Luria, at the same session, was trying to defend psychology, proposing that it must preserve its experimental attitude, without mechanistic tendencies. The way to overcome mechanistic experimentation was to realize that the experimental subject is a social being, and experimentation should be supplemented with the study of verbal aspects of behavior. A decision by the local party unit condemned the assumed idealistic and mechanistic trends and removed Kornilov from his position. The former psychoanalyst and pedologist

Zalkind, criticizing Vygotsky as well, was nominated as new director, and the military psychologist Talankin was responsible for human resources. Talankin joined the campaign against the Vygotsky group as well (see Towsey, 2009). Neither of them lasted for too long; Aron Zalkind (1988–1936) died in a heart attacque, in 1931, and Talankin (1898–1937), after an interlude in the Leningrad Bekhterev institute, was executed for counterrevolutionary activities.

In Leningrad, another young Turk, Boris Ananiev, started to campaign mainly against the reflexology represented by Bekhterev, and thereby the entire tradition of the Leningrad Brain Institute was changed. **Boris Gerasimovich Ananiev** (1907–1972), a later leader of the Leningrad group of psychologists, emphasized that psychology in its Marxist fervor should not forget about its own past and should not pretend to do everything entirely out of scratch in the reflexology and reactology debates (Ananiev, 1931). The main enemy at that time of the reflexology debate was mechanicism. In the mid-1930s, the scope of the party decisions has become broader.

The pedological decision and the fight of three words: **pedology, psychology, pedagogy**

A further, more thorough campaign started with the questioning of different applied psychological domains. In 1931, the widespread industrial psychology and its associated psychometric and testology works were questioned. Industrial psychology in Russia was born together with the Bolshevik ideas of organizing applied research. The leading figure of establishing industrial psychology in the Moscow Psychology Institute was I. N. Spielrein (1891–1937), brother of the psychoanalyst Sabina Spielrein. He was mainly formulating a trend in psychotechnology that was intended to work with the aim of developing testing-based industrial selection. He was so successful that in 1930, the international industrial psychology congress was held in Moscow. At the same time, his rival, A. B. Zalkind (1888–1936), preached about the total plasticity of the human nervous system in the communist's training academy (Sirotkina & Smith, 2016, p. 21). He was critical of the testing movement and preferred optimization of work as a main aspect of socialist industrial psychology. Zalkind was a typical man of the time. He worked in central educational institutions, in managerial positions, and meanwhile moved from psychoanalysis to pedology, then to psychotechnics, but remained a full-time party official the entire time. The self-criticism enforced by the Communist Party led to a total questioning of industrial psychology as not fit to the tasks of massive industrialization. **Psychotechnicians**, as they called themselves, started to blame themselves in waves of self-criticism. They do not have sufficient contacts with theoretical developments, they take over Western test methods in a rigid, non-interpreted manner, and they do not consider the features of the Marxist theory of work and the new conditions of socialist work (self-consciousness, workplace competitions, the issue of socialist work being a question of pride and honor). There were some objective factors behind the repercussions against applied psychology. First of all, the underdevelopment in forced industrialization did not really welcome selection methods. Regarding schools also, pedology was indeed used many times for selectionist purposes, with some elitist overtones, and certainly with non-egalitarian consequences.

The initial, seemingly routine self-criticism turned in the second half of the 1930s, in the wave of Stalinist purges and the victory of the transformist ideology, into a total extirpation of industrial psychology and its connected test usage in Russia: the journal *Soviet Psychotechnics* ceased to be published, the industrial psychology section of the Institute of Psychology ceased to exist, their society was abolished, Spielrein was arrested and executed, Zalkind dies of a heart attack in the middle of criticism, and the use of tests and a selectionist logic became taboos in the Soviet Union until the 1970s.

An even harsher and more expansive blow came, by a strike against **pedology**, and practically against all the school use of psychology. In the early thirties, Soviet psychology was full of pedological efforts, both on the theoretical and on the practical levels. Child development had its own regularities, and schools had to adopt to children, rather than the other way around. Many psychoanalysts, as well as Blonsky and Vygotsky, identified themselves as pedologists, while their conceptions, emphasizing the interiorization of culture and social determination, went well beyond the traditional pedological visions. A leading proponent of Soviet pedology was M. J. Basov (1892–1931), who argued for different levels of mental organization and a joint role of heredity and environment. This later moment would be sufficient to ostracize him, while in reality, Basov (1932) was claiming for the primacy of environmental factors. But in the Soviet reality of the time, the mere mention of the role of heredity was becoming a sin. Minkova (2013) gives a datelaied description of the Russian and Soviet pedology movement.

The reactology debate was started by a local Communist Party move in the given Moscow institute. With pedology, however, the decision came from the top. Its starting point was a decision by the central committee – the main decision body – of the Communist Party on July 4, 1936. The decision was immediately released in the central Soviet daily *Pravda*. Compared to the earlier, not always executed decisions, the new decree, to be executed within one month, decided that pedological activities in schools and, in general, the application of testing methods to reveal individual differences should be stopped. On the level of professional power relations of disciplines, the pedological decree meant a reconstruction of the **power of pedagogy**. The main sin of pedology, according to the party decision, was a deterministic fatalism in dealing with the fate of learning-impaired children, an insensitive transfer of children toward institutes of special education.

> The so-called "scientific" bio-sociological point of view of contemporary pedology was applied in these investigations to disclose the hereditary and social factors that impeded the student's progress . . . to find a maximum of negative influences and pathological disturbances in the student, his family, relatives, environment.
>
> (Pedological distortions, 1936, p. 243)

266 *Disciplinary developments and eclectics*

The rights of pedagogy and pedagogists had to be reconstructed, and pedologists had to be fired from schools. In addition, this specialty could not be taught in colleges, and their books had to be destroyed.

The campaign was public across the entire nation. It did not name any bad guys; thus, it could be used against many psychologists. Figure 7.6 shows a Russian cartoon at that time mocking the labeling practices of pedologists in the testing efforts.

There certainly might have been some arrogance in the school-practicing pedologists (today we would call them school psychologists) and some fetishization of tests methods used by them, as mocked on Figure 7.6. Many incompetent people were working in the schools as pedologists who had neither the theoretical nor the methodical preparations needed for such a guidance work. The decree functioned as a harsh political and administrative decision. As a practical consequence, traditional psychodiagnostic methods disappeared from the entire Soviet psychology for two coming generations. Besides that, everyone who was associated with the label of *pedology* became undesirable and uncitable. Institutionally, psychology inclined toward pedological distortions went under the tutelage of pedagogy. The activist claims and the wide scope of the anti-pedology campaign were against spontaneity in all forms.

At the same time, while it had a hard time, through the war years, psychology did not cease to exist. From 1943 on, however, all psychological research had to be done under the direction of the newly formed *Academy of Pedagogical Sciences*, and this tutelage was by far not merely formal. All psychological questions had to

Figure 7.6 A 1930s Soviet cartoon mocking the assumed stigmatizing practice of pedologists.

be raised within the frames of educational psychology, with an emphasis on the plastic malleability of human nature. The end of the 1930s is the time when Blonsky and Rubinstein turn toward studying school textbook learning.

The psychology journals ceased to be published – *Psychology* and *Soviet Pedology* in 1932, *Soviet Psychotechnics* in 1934. Journal publications in psychology restarted only 20 years later, in 1955, with the publication of *Voprosi Psihologii, Questions of Psychology*, with the military psychology veteran Boris Teplov as founding editor.

The malleability of humans

In a way, the 1936–1955 period can be characterized as a fight and tension between three words: *pedology*, *psychology*, and *pedagogy*. With the fight against pedology, a strong case was made against psychology at the same time: both are too static, unlike pedagogy, which was assumed to be committed to voluntaristic change. With the two campaigns against psychology, there was a move toward pedagogization of psychology, and also toward a new cultivation of personality and the will system. This went together with an image of man that went beyond the transformism factors analyzed by Bauer (1952) and also became characterized by isolationism and xenophobia, with a hatred of all foreign influence, and an increasing Russocentrism in matters of science as well.

At the same time, there was a constant change of terminology in the human sciences, newer and newer fabricated theories becoming more and more central. The conception of New Man represented by party propaganda and by the Stalinist president of the Soviet Union, Mikhail Kalinin (1875–1946), revived the anti-individualistic Russian tradition that diluted individuality in the community, combining this with the heroic features of vocational commitment and sacrifice. The dissolution of individuality into the community is active sacrifice taking. The Russian hero cult re-emerges in the New Man, who is community-oriented. For him, work is a source of pride. He is optimistic and relates to anything based on an ideological stance, following a party commitment (McLeish, 1975). The leading science about humans would be pedagogy, since it promised to realize this New Man, who, as a Munchausen, would able to elevate himself from the mud of Russian reality. Along this line, the major tasks of psychology would be to carefully study the process of education without providing a universal panacea. The early pedology movement and psychoanalysis were two rival and sometimes cooperative movements for shaping modern individuals. This was overcome by the community education principles of Makarenko (1888–1939).

Why was psychology such an undesirable science and profession for Stalinist management? Psychology, as imagined by early Russian behaviorists, at the time of a deterministic communist ideology, could also become an "engineer of mind," an obedient technical servant of social manipulation. The dislike of psychology went together with the new transformist versions of Stalinist communism. Rapid industrialization and farm collectivization went on in a backward, non-modernized peasant environment. All social scientific conceptions, including most of earlier

Marxism that emphasize the determining role of the environment, be it physical, economic, and social, would be seen as "reactionary" by emphasizing the obstacles toward modernization. In the world of emerging heavy industry, with the peasant crowds moving to industry, there was hardly a need for an industrial psychology concentrating on selection, since the new proletary had no choices, and human beings are, in any case, replaceable "screws" (Stalin's own expression). Emphasizing existing parameters of human individuals represented constraints and obstacles toward development and progress. Similarly, any psychology starting from the characteristics of children presented parameters difficult to overcome, obstacles to the process of educational tasks and preaches. Psychology and pedology would teach us, for example, that development has its own laws, and that changes are slow. The messianistic voluntarism of Stalinist transformism wanted to change nature in a single stroke, over a single generation, and, as part of this program, believed in the **transformability of human nature** as well. The other typical subject of Stalinist voluntarism alongside psychology was modern genetics. The fixed parameters in Mendelian genetics were towering obstacles toward the needed dramatic changes in agriculture; therefore, a cultivation of the transformist theories of Lysenko about the Lamarckian claim of the inheritance of acquired characteristics was started.

Most of the psychologists of the middle-aged and young generation had to use enormous efforts of individual resistance and persistence, applying much creative ingenuity, working under different covers to preserve their lives and knowledge for 20 years. The destruction of pedology and industrial psychology did not erase all psychology in the Soviet Union of the late 1930s. Chronologically, the middle and late 1930s were the starting years of the formation of the schools of S. L. Rubinstein and A. N. Leontiev.

During the war years, Rubinstein and Teplov were responsible (alongside Leontiev) for the survival of psychology, which was not a negligible achievement. Besides the post-trauma rehabilitation and similar army-related works, academic topics increased in volume and variety in an interesting manner. In 1937, there were 49 psychological research topics in the entire education system, which was 16% of the entire educational palette. In 1941, 148 psychological topics showed up, which made up 32.5% of the entire educational research effort. Thus, psychology in the difficult wartimes was not neglected. It changed substantially, however. As shown both by the summary of Ananiev (1948) and Teplov (1947), it took a fundamentally educational outlook. Ananiev emphasizes the large quantity of research endeavors on school-based research on teaching materials and understanding, while Teplov focused on the postwar rehabilitation efforts and studies of reading, arithmetic, and the like again in schools. Thus, they tried to fit psychology into the new human malleability image. At the same time, they criticized both earlier spiritualistic and mechanical behavioristic approaches and, most of all, the Western orientation of early Soviet psychology. Interestingly, especially Teplov (1947, pp. 29–30), they criticized the social history school of Vygotsky, but they did not ignore him, as later accounts would suggest. The criticism was mainly based on the fact that the cultural historical school was making a few observations on instrumental reorganization of mental processes into the basis of all mentality. Both Rubinstein and

Leontiev became subjects of several critical discussions in the late 1940s. They were even contrasted, showing Leontiev to be better and more holistic. The belief that there is a real Soviet psychology that is superior to any others was even continued by the later school of Leontiev.

Pavlovization of psychology

The generation-long vicissitude of Soviet psychology did not end with a subjection to ideology with pedagogy as its executor. At the turn of the 1950s, Soviet psychology became the victim of another forceful science policy move: it would be reclassified under the study of **higher nervous activity**. This meant a Pavlovization of psychology. There were reflexological moves and reductionism fights within Soviet psychology in the 1920s–1930s. In the post–Second World War years of the Stalinist search for new dynamicity and the search for Russian models of science, a new aggressive move took shape, idolizing Pavlov. The new invasion came as a result of a debate organized in 1950 by the Soviet Academy of Sciences and the Medical Academy, the so-called **Pavlov Session**.

On the 100th anniversary of Pavlov's birth in 1949, Stalin and Zhdanov, his cultural commissar, expressed their dissatisfaction with the cosmopolitan and non-Pavlovian leadership of the Pavlov research empire. A decision was made to criticize them in a high-profile public session. In the Soviet science policy of the 1930s, individual party agents posing as scientists initiated the criticism, and the results were criminal charges. In the 1950s, there was a new rhetoric. There had to be a public pseudo-debate, with resolutions, and the bad guys had to practice self-criticism. They were removed from their academic positions, but they were not imprisoned or executed. The Pavlov session took place after Stalin himself intervened in the discussion of linguistics, and after the success of pseudo-genetics by Lysenko. Stalin personally intervened into the preparations of the Pavlov session, listing possible scapegoats. The session was nominally organized by the science and the medical academies. Administratively, it was managed by the Communist Party secretary for human resources, later prime minister (1953–55), Georgy Malenkov (Pavlov session, 1950). Georgy Malenkov (1901–1988) made his name as a science political commissar in rocket technology, including the movement of over a thousand German experts to Soviet Russia.

The session was not merely a commemoration of Pavlov but a real debate as well. Part of the discussion was going on within neurophysiology, but with a strong ideological element to it. There were 81 talks and over 200 interventions. It was an over-ideologized debate, with typical sequences of criticism followed by self-criticism. Participants labeled each other as mechanists and idealists (very bad words at that time), and during all these labelings, the stakes were high. Those labeled as being deviant from the main Pavlov line were going to be intellectually and existentially discredited.

The Stalinist idea behind moving Pavlov into the center was the need for **a unification of science,** like the unification of the Communist Party (see about this affinity Joravsky, 1977). This was accompanied by strong postwar nationalism.

Genuinely Russian and holistic scientific theories had to be promoted. In the case of Pavlov, that view brought up not only a body–mind unity but also the interpretation of conditioned reflexes in the context of the regulatory functions of the whole organism. The uniqueness of Pavlov was overemphasized, even by those coworkers of the Pavlov empire who were forced to have some self-criticism. **Pavlovism,** as sanctified 15 years after the death of the scientist, was intended to become an integrative theory of physiology, medicine, biology, psychology, and pedagogy. The other aspect of this holistic integration was the **flexibility** idea. Pavlov was to be promoted as a scientific foundation and explanation of the malleability of humans. The 1950s cult of Pavlov was related to the needs of the new transformist vision of society. It was related to a need "for formulas by which reality could be transformed and remolded to the dictates of the Soviet regime" (Tucker, 1955, p. 4). The parallel with Lysenkoism was that pseudo-geneticist Lysenko also denied the existence of internal forces. The new Pavlovism would be presented as a way to deny internal, *sui generis*, self-related and motivational forces to humans. Humans were interpreted as reflective mirrors of the communicative environment around them. In this regard, the late stage of Stalinism is a peculiar combination of determinism and transformism.

> The principle of the conditioned reflex was made the basis of a new Soviet concept of man. According to this concept, man is a reactive mechanism whose behavior, including all the higher mental processes, can be exhaustively understood through a knowledge of the laws of conditioning, and can be controlled through application of this knowledge. . . . [T]he motivating springs of this movement were not scientific but political According to Academician K. Bykov, who played a part in the Pavlovian revolution similar to that of Lysenko in genetics, the whole development took place 'under the directing influence of the Party.
>
> (Tucker, 1955, p. 144)

The Pavlovian image toward social sciences was a variation of the Stalinist new transformism. Strict laws determine a flexible behavior. Those former Pavlov students, now institutional leaders and contenders who considered themselves to be the carriers of the real message, such as Konstantin Bykov (1886–1959) and Anatoly Ivanov-Smolenskij (1895–1982) preached a rather mechanical system at the session. They concentrated on cortical organization responsible for all functions and some basic mechanisms of assumed conditioned reflex formation, with a deterministic flavor. They criticized the works of I. S. Beritov-Beritasvili (1885–1974), a Georgian who was studying memory traces, and P. K. Anokhin (1898–1974), who tried to combine the Pavlovian heritage with ideas of regulation and internal functional systems. (For a much later synthesis of his views see Anokhin, 1974.) They were specifically critical of the work of Lev Orbeli (1882–1958), an Armenian Pavlov student and director of the Pavlov Institute at that time. The Pavlovian orthodoxy interpreted the work of these more dynamic neurophysiologists as being subjective distortions of the Pavlovian heritage. Jerzy Konorski (1903–1973), at that time working in the Soviet Union as a war refugee, was also seen as an enemy since he tried to combine the Pavlov and the Sherrington heritage and integrated the micro neural mechanisms of learning and representation with the Pavlov theory of conditioned reflexes (Konorski, 1948). He was interpreted as not being sufficiently holistic, dealing too much with neuronal histology. In the image of Pavlovian orthodoxy, the study of higher nervous activity should be based on the study of acquired simple reflexes in dogs tied to a laboratory podium. Those who believed in spontaneous neural activity and internal neuronal modeling were interpreted to be idealists. Furthermore, in the orthodoxy, there was no need seen for a direct study of the nervous system.

The Pavlovian orthodoxy was victorious at that time. Orbeli was removed from his functions, Bykov was nominated as his successor, and Ivanov-Smolensky (1954) became the director of a newly established Brain Institute in Moscow that was under the tutelage of a Pavlov Commission working until 1955 at the Academy. Orbeli, the fallen director of the Pavlov institute, was allowed to form a new research group in his seventies that was transformed in 1956 into a *Sechenov Institute of Evolutionary Physiology and Biochemistry*.

There were only two psychologists allowed to talk at the session, Rubinstein and Teplov. The situation of both of them was rather delicate, since earlier, in the 1940s, they both spoke against the senseless generalization of Pavlovian physiology into psychology. They provided self-criticism and criticism of the other as well. Teplov (1896–1965) interpreted his role that he had to take on the task to become a leader of psychology along Pavlovian lines. In fact, out of this resolution, the Teplov (1956–1967) school of Russian typology emerged in Pavlov style. Teplov was to become a favored psychologist in the postwar years because Stalin personally appreciated the military psychology leadership brochure of Teplov (1941), who was originally a military psychologist specializing in camouflage.

During the debates, there were several rather loose general remarks about the relations of subjective and objective aspects and if there was a need at all for psychology. Some concrete advice toward psychologists was also aired: the work on the second signaling system (language) as a human-specific organization and the elaboration of a human Pavlovian typology were proposed as tasks toward a new psychology. This advice was taken seriously. A bulk of empirical research started along these lines.

From all the second signaling system talk, the regulatory function of language promoted by Luria (1961) became the most influential. Signals that relate humans to each other turn into internal social control. The naive form of the New Man with its internal determination is replaced by an outer directed type "whose behavior is guided by signals from outside. Thus, the New Man now has no wishes, instincts, emotion drives, or impulses, no reservoir of energies of his own" (Tucker, 1955, p. 62).

Psychologists dared to interpret Pavlov more flexibly, less as a physiological determinist during a special psychology Pavlov session. The psychology Pavlov session in 1952 led not a to a weakening of psychology but to its strengthening (Anonymous, 1953). As the Soviet central journal *Questions of philosophy* summarized, they invited consciousness and inner experience back to psychology. As Tucker (1955, p. 57) interpreted the declarations of one of the key agents, the Pedagogy Academy Psychology Institute director, Smirnov: "Far from facing liquidation, psychology was destined to occupy a position of crucial importance among the sciences. By employing the theory of Pavlov, it would open up the subjective world of man to the objective study and the theory to regulation."

After Stalin's death, in the newly started psychology journal *Voprosi Psihologii*, Rubinstein re-launched the idea that there is no direct external determinism regarding human behavior. As a reply to the critiques, Rubinstein presented a spelled-out conception of determinism. In his 1957 book *Being and consciousness*, he aimed toward a definite presentation of the deterministic conception in psychology. Its essence seems to be rather dry: **external influences take effect always through internal conditions and actions**. This is a post-Stalinian articulation of the postwar new Stalinist policy that tried to combine self-initiated commitment and external determinism or combine fatalism about the imminent victory of communism with the devoted contributions of the agents themselves. Rubinstein pointed out that there is a personality in between the environment and the effects of an external, state-directed man.

> The model of the state-directed man presupposes a one-to-one correspondence between the verbal propaganda stimulus and the individual's reflex response. . . .
> The central link here is the "psychology of personality." This is the point of departure and the point of arrival for an adequate theory of motivation.
> (Tucker 1956, p. 480)

The Stalinist Pavlovization of psychology was not restricted to Soviet psychologists. The Soviet power even produced new foreign volumes of Pavlov like the English selected works (Pavlov, 1955). In the mid-1950s, excellent left-wing researchers, like Henri Wallon or even Michel Foucault, acknowledged Pavlov. Wallon also saw the relevance of Pavlovism: finding a compromise between biological, material foundations of the mind and human flexibility. "The conclusions of the experiments of Pavlov fit exactly into the frames of dialectical materialism, that supposes simultaneously a fundamental unity of reality, and its evolution towards more and more differentiated forms of being" (Wallon, 1955/1963, p. 79).

The dual impact of Pavlovism in Eastern Europe. Though the Pavlov session within psychiatry and the neurosciences at large had an ideological stance in denying the international nature of science, and moving toward a Russian model, the Pavlovization soon became a liberating factor in some parts of Eastern European psychology. After their own session on Pavlov, even Soviet psychologists started to initiate research that was no longer subjugated to education and pedagogy but (rebuilt) psychology with a natural science orientation.

There was a limitation and opening in the effect of Pavlovism on Eastern Europe. The limitation was that everything should be phrased as an issue of conditioning, generalization, and the like. Since explanations were readily given in Pavlovian terminology, there was no need for innovation in neuroscience.

By the mid-fifties, Eastern European psychologists realized in an ironical manner that it was better to be a butler of neurophysiology than being a maid of the ideologically oriented and transpired Soviet-style education theory. The renaissance of psychology under a Pavlov exegesis was a difficult time and used a clumsy terminology, but it was a way toward factual objective psychology. What started as a strike due to the political embeddedness, through the political changes under Khrushchev, turned into a starting point of the return of genuine psychology.

Those changes that were taking place in Soviet psychology from 1930 to the 1960s – thus over an entire generation – were packed up into a single decade in most of Soviet-dominated Eastern Europe. Between 1948 and 1949 and in the mid-sixties, the educational subordination of psychology and the Pavlovization were appearing almost simultaneously, in a way as rival communist interpretations of the possibilities of psychology.

Let us take the example of Hungarian psychology. After the fascist atrocities during the war, a relative liberal re-emergence of modern psychology characterized the period between 1945 and 1947. Several schools of depth psychology and psychoanalysis were reactivated, and there was a *Gestalt*-based experimental tradition at the university of Budapest. Most importantly, however, there was a strong child study movement combining Wallon and Piaget with a Moreno- and Lewin-inspired social psychology interest led by Ferenc Mérei, an ambitious young French-educated communist psychologist (See Chapter 4 and 6). There was a first crackdown on psychology related to successes of the pedologist Mérei (1948) who even published a book entitled pedology. After being a star of education and psychology for two years, he was ostracized. The campaign to discredit Mérei was led by irrelevant party apparatchiks. All psychological activity was being blamed as unscientific, and the professional associations were disbanded. Psychology came under the dominance of education even in the scientific degree system. This lasted in many regards until the early 1960s. At the same time, however, in 1951, as a consequence of the Soviet Pavlovization moves, a Pavlov Commission was created at the Hungarian Academy of Sciences. It was under medical leadership and mainly dealt with issues like how to interpret internal medicinal problems such as hypertension or peptic ulcers under the light of Pavlovism. In a way, psychology also came under the tutelage of this Pavlov commission. There were three types of interesting consequences of this after the death of Stalin.

Technical combination of Pavlovism with experimental psychology. This came up with the new experimental typologies practiced by Magda Marton (1972; Marton & Urbán, 1971) similar to the Teplov line in Soviet Russia. In another line, some of the experimental psychologists were trying to live with Pavlov by showing that it was possible to reconcile Pavlov with experimental (*horribile dictu*, American behaviorist) psychology (Kardos, 1960).

Institutionally, in an interesting manner, among vivid tensions for leadership and against the ambitions of the educational authorities, the Pavlov committee helped save the entire psychological research enterprise that was threatened to be swallowed by education. The committee stood up against reorganizing a small institute of child study and psychology existing from the early 1900s into a chapter of an education institute.

Passive organism versus activity. Activity became a central issue in central Eastern Europe during the 1960s, and the interpretation of the Pavlov heritage became integrated into this broader philosophical issue. A fuzzy, "cloud-like" opposition set up between two approaches to behavior and mind. They corresponded to two views on human nature and to two visions of social organization. The non-orthodox, that is, non-Marxist, and non–party line visions of human behavior were united in a feeling of looking for more activity and initiative in humans and criticized automatic, mechanical, old-style determinism. In the debates about active and passive views of perception, regarding the importance of instrumental and Pavlovian conditioning and the like, this became a hidden underlying social issue. Pavlov and Pavlovism in central Eastern Europe, by the 1960s, became a symbol of passivity and inertia. How far were we, as subjects of the Big Brother, indeed, merely instances of large-scale social laws, or were we ourselves agents, with intentions and an active self-determination? The open-minded psychologists in the 1960s of Eastern Europe were looking for more "agency."

One of the most clear-cut oppositions was between Pavlovian and instrumental learning, as summarized in Table 7.3. The good guys stood for instrumental learning. Pavlov's dogs are constrained on the experimental podium. They are tied with scratches. The animal cannot move; typically, its only possible action is to modify its digestive fluid like salivation. (Or to move its one untied leg.) The instrumental learning situation, on the other hand, was seen as using freely acting animals, and the opposition was seen on a trivial symbolic level, as Russian versus American. There is, however, a further, semantically richer symbolic opposition as well. The animal in a Skinner box seems to have much more initiative. "Cats in the puzzle box," to use Thorndike's (1898) expression, try several movements, and one is selected due to the consequences. Thus, in instrumental conditioning, there is a role for chance.

There is a social implication that can be easily projected to these two images: on one image, one needs to make people interested in what they do; in the other image, one does not need immediate rewards for any social activity. In the instrumental view of knowledge and in instrumental learning, you need direct motivation and also the self-initiated activity of the animal.

All these features made for a peculiar "ideological position" of instrumental learning in a strictly restrictive society. The same Skinnerian model of learning,

Table 7.3 Some contrasts of the two views of learning

Classical conditioning	Instrumental conditioning
Constrained animal	Freely moving animal
Learning by association	Learning from consequences
Motivation not required	Motivation essential
Essential determinist	Chance essential

which became in the late 1960s the symbol of control, manipulation, and a lack of freedom, became a symbol of the overambitious reductionism of Skinner (Chomsky, 1959). In Eastern Europe, the Skinnerian model became a symbol for activity and freedom, as contrasted to Pavlov's dogs, who were merely subjected to interventions and were undergoing learning without doing too much.

The small textbook by Barkóczi and Putnoky (1968) and the neurophysiological theory of reinforcement elaborated by Endre Grastyán (Grastyán et al., 1967; Grastyán & Buzsáky, 1979) from the early sixties on, and presented to broader audiences as well (Grastyán, 1967), were clear examples of this interpretation in Hungary (Pléh, 2008).

The end of the exile: Soviet psychology from 1960 to 1990

The roughly two decades of subordination of Soviet psychology to direct party leadership was finished in the late 1950s. There were visible institutional signs to this. From 1955 onward, the Moscow Psychology Institute of the Educational Sciences Academy started a new journal, *Voprosi Psihologii* (Questions of Psychology). The journal was the central outlet of psychology in Soviet Union for an entire generation. Psychological book publications started in 1957, and the Russian Psychological Association was re-established (today it is called *Russian Psychological Society*, http://www.psyrus.ru/en/about/). Teaching of professional psychology was restarted, and in 1966, under A. N. Leontiev as dean, an independent Psychology Faculty was organized at Moscow State University. Under his guidance, with much support of the international fame of the neuropsychologist Luria, Soviet psychology came back to the international scene. Leontiev became the vice president of the *International Union of Psychological Science*, and a large East–West meeting, the 18th International Conference of Psychology was organized in Moscow in 1966, under the chairmanship of Leontiev (Luria, 1966b). In 1971, a research institute of psychology by the Soviet Academy of Sciences was launched, under the leadership of Boris Lomov (1927–1989). Lomov tried to develop a united Soviet psychology based on system analysis and campaigned for it on the international arena.

There were many signs that Soviet psychology started to be reintegrated into international psychology. An interesting sign of this age and stage is the reader of translated papers edited by Cole and Maltzmann (1969). This rebirth, however, should not be interpreted as a sudden denial of earlier developments. Soviet psychology in the 1960s–1980s continued to be theory-oriented (touching on the speculative), critical of Western psychology (that continued to be referred to as "foreign psychology") and kept its Marxist labels. It continued to preach such broad ideas as the "unity of activity and consciousness" as methodical principles. In applied psychology, test methods and psychotherapy were missing for a long time, and for a long time, in all practical matters, the lip service to normativity and education remained in the center.

With all peculiarities, an essential aspect of the renaissance in the academic field was the renewed contacts with international psychology. Isolation and total autarchy were stopped. While the stars of Soviet psychology in the 1970s were critical of world psychology, stars such as Piaget (Elkonin, 1972) or Chomsky (Luria, 1974), they took over the results and technologies of world psychology at the same time. There were fluctuations in this openness and activity. Science continued to be under Marxist ideological control, some logos continued to be needed, and internal science intrigues, such as rivalries between Moscow- and Leningrad-based researchers, had an influence on individual life paths. Fluctuations notwithstanding, from the early 1960s on, psychology could not be questioned on an institutional level.

The fomer official historian Yarosevsky (1989) also edited an interesting book of repressed science in the Soviet Union with many psychogical revalations. Due to the new, more organic developments, it would be difficult to characterize the generation of Soviet psychologists from the 1960s to the 1990s in a comprehensive manner. Most of their works are referred to in the chapters dealing with the second half of the 20th century. There are three important features of this renaissance of Soviet psychology.

One was the strength of nominally Pavlov-based **psychophysiological thinking**. The new generation became much more micro mechanism–oriented than Pavlov and his followers ever were. The studies of E. N. Sokolov (1960, 1963, 1975) developed detailed behavioral and neuroscience methods to study the orienting reaction postulated by Pavlov and, analyzing habituation responses, argued for a more activity-oriented image of the workings of the brain. The cortical systems were supposed to develop a neuronal model of stimulus configurations, and that was to become the basis for neuronal memory representations. Modern cognitive psychology also started to flourish, many times in Russian-Western exportations like in the work of Boris Velichkovsky (1982, 1988) on visual attention.

Another feature of the renaissance in the 1960s was the **return of the forgotten past**. We know today that the postulation of the forgotten past itself was a partly social mechanism. Still, at that time, it seemed to be that a really forgotten Marxist tradition from the 1930s was coming back. This was especially true of the new cultivation of the Vygotsky school. This was not merely an issue of establishing historical truth but a source of continuous inspiration. The freer atmosphere had become so evident that even during the difficult decades, empirical and theoretical work along the principles set by Vygotsky was continued. Further, Vygotsky continued from the 1960s on to be a continuous foundation of theoretical inspirations, regarding culture/mind relations, holism, and socialization theories of the mind. Vygotsky's local success and international fame from the 1960s were based on three factors. Vygotsky, in fact, moved into the center of his theory a reconstructed Marxist historical image of humans with the conceptual analysis of work and an instrumental proposal for modern psychology. Vygotsky also tried to create a theoretical psychology that was based on a critical assimilation of international psychology. A further factor of the success of Vygotsky was that he was able to combine his theory in an organic manner to actual empirical research.

These factors made him an important reference to the developmental theories of cognitive psychology promoted in the Anglo world, especially by Jerome Bruner

(1984, 1997). He became a central reference to all meaning-based approaches of new psychology that concentrate on historicity, social embeddedness, and meaning in directing mental life (Harré, 1990). Vygotsky has a very wide-ranging inspirational role in contemporary cultural theories. He is the starting point for the relativistic cultural psychology of Michael Cole (1996), but he is also the source of the word-object-partner developmental triangles in the evolutionary theory of culture promoted by Michael Tomasello (1999, 2014).

What happens later as a consequence of the fall of communism was a **spreading of the field** and a birth of the psychological society (Sirotkina & Smith, 2010; Vasilieva, 2010).

> In 2003 there were about 300 institutions of higher education in psychology in Russia and about 5000 students graduated annually. You can guess that these universities were very different from the old. Now they were making money not on fundamental research, but on "educational services."
>
> (Mironenko, 2013b, p. 157)

Mironenko (2013b) presented in several papers how one can characterize the theoretical outlook of present-day Russian psychology. In an interesting manner, in the political liberation in many areas, pre-scientific cults of spirituality, community, and internal intimacy also came back.

She identifies three groups as of today: "Westerners," "Slavophiles," and activity theorists, also ackowledging that some of these lead to separation form the West again (Mironenko, 2014).

> Representatives of these groups are easy to identify on the basis of reference lists in their papers. . . . The group which we have designated here as "Slavophiles" is rapidly growing since the beginning of the XXI century Christian Orthodox, Spiritual or Philosophical psychology, develops the traditions, rooted in the pre-Soviet period of Russian psychology. This is an entirely authentic trend, closely related to Russian culture, focused in practices on a vast Russian market, based on Russian authors and appealing to the Russian mentality. Representatives of this group show no globalist tendencies, counter globalist tendencies are strong.
>
> (Mironenko, 2013b, p. 158–159)

Tasks

CA

Compare Russian and early American behaviorists.
Neuroreductionism in Bekhterev and today.
Psychoanalysis and social optimism in Soviet Russia.
Compare Russian pedology with the pedagogy of Makarenko.
"Higher nervous activity" in Pavlov and "higher mental functions" in Vygotsky.

The analysis of human action in Rubinstein and Leontiev.
Soviet typology and Western typologies.
The instrumental view of the mind and comparative psychology today.
Compare "functional organs" of Luria with "neuronal recruitment" of Dehaene.

DSA

"Soviet psychology" and "pedology" in common discourse (Google Ngram).
Pavlov, Bekhterev, and Vygotsky over a hundred years in public discourse (Google Ngram).
Blonsky and Kornilov over a hundred years in psychology (PsycINFO).
Co-occurrences of Vygotsky and Piaget in psychological texts (PsycINFO).
"Marxism" and "psychoanalysis" over a hundred years in public discourse (Google Ngram).
"Marxism" and "Soviet psychoanalysis" in the psychological literature.
Sabine Spielrein over 100 years in the psychological literature (PsycINFO).
Compare Leontiev and Rubinstein in the psychological literature (PsycINFO).

Note

1 I treat Soviet and Russian psychology together. For most of 20th century, that was valid due to the Russian dominance in Soviet times, between 1917 and 1990. But the Soviet/Russian qualification is sometimes misleading from the present-day perspective of national identity formation. Certainly, several key players for the Pavlov empire as Orbeli, Beritov, and Asratyan were ethnic Georgians and Armenians. Chelpanov or Blonskij were from Kiev, Ukraine, Vygotsky came from a Belorussian small town, and Rubinstein from Odessa, Ukraine. But their career moves attached them to Russian developments. Regarding spelling of place-names, I also use the standard Russian version, like Kiev (though today this would be properly spelled as Kyiv).

Part II
On the road toward contemporary psychology

This part of the book attempts to show how our science and our profession developed during the last 80 years. I will first show the theoretical developments. In this area, in an unconventional manner, and in line with a general Americanization of modern psychology, a continuity between neobehaviorism (Chapter 8) and cognitive psychology (Chapter 9) is presented. The concluding chapters (Chapters 10 and 11) present two further issues: How did the controversies and tensions around cognitive psychology evolve into general issues of relations between the image of humans and psychological research, and how did a combination of evolutionary, neuroscience, and social explanatory models develop in coordination? This leads naturally to an analysis of the way applied psychology developed into different directions (Chapter 11).

The general attitude of the concluding chapters is partly paradoxical and partly ironical. What my generation lived through as present has gradually become past. It is natural that from the point of view of the 1940s, the turn of the 19th century is history. The same is true, however, for the relation between the 2020s and the 1980s.

8 Psychology as learning theory
Neobehaviorism

All behavior, individual and social, moral and immoral, normal and psychopathic, is generated from the same primary laws.

(Hull, 1943, p v.)

An interesting combination: strict norms and liberalization

From the 1930s on, American behaviorism, with an ever-widening international impact, has gone through a methodical and conceptual liberalization in what has later been called **neobehaviorism**. On the one hand, several challenges appeared from the laboratory. Phenomena like latent learning questioned the piecemeal vision of all learning being associative. Similarly, data on the perception of *Gestalts* questioned the simple physical characterization of stimuli in a stimulus–reaction way of thought. *Gestalt* psychologists also raised the issue of sudden insightful types of learning. These internal issues all pointed toward a liberalization of behaviorist principles and toward a variety of behavioral approaches. Parallel to these internal developments, a new generation of behaviorists started to have connections with new philosophies. The principle of behavior came to be connected to a neopositivist philosophy of science and to **operationalism**.

During this process, the concept of behaviorism started to have three conceptual interpretations. According to **ontological behaviorism**, or as Woodworth (1931) liked to call it, **conceptual behaviorism**, there is no mental life; only behavior exists. This was the conception of the founding father, John Watson. For most of the "new behaviorists," with the possible exception of Skinner, this attitude belonged to the past. According to most representatives of the new generation, we do have an inner life, but it is difficult to study. **Logical behaviorism** (that characterized an entire class of philosophers, Gilbert Ryle, 1949, among others) reduced "inner processes" to behavioral dispositions. Many of the British logical behaviorists have become part of the **linguistic turn** of modern philosophy. They tried to interpret mental phenomena in a linguistic manner, by using "dispositional language." "Liking" or "being afraid of" in this regard means a disposition toward certain types of behaviors, like approaching or avoiding someone.

The experimental psychologists themselves mostly represented from the 1930s on the third variety: **methodical behaviorism** (Woodworth, 1931). Science must use public data, and that holds for psychology as well – it cannot be a science of the first person. In psychology, one can directly study only behavior; one can, however, assume internal processes underlying behavior, provided behavioral consequences do correspond to them. In a theoretical sense, the anti-behaviorist cognitive psychologists also share assumptions of a methodical behaviorism (Chapter 9).

Together with this methodical liberalization, the topics of neobehaviorism have become wider in scope. Besides studying elementary learning mechanisms, the study of language, thought, motivation dynamics, personality, and psychopathological phenomena has become accepted as well into the cathedral of behavioral interpretations, sometimes replacing the animal model with human subjects. One could say that neobehaviorists are usually more liberal, finding little back doors for those internal mental processes (memories, desires) which were scrupulously excluded in the classical program.

The neobehaviorists hardly referred to themselves as neobehaviorists. Usually following a *pars pro toto* principle, they referred to their own school(s) as **learning theory**. This can be captured in the effective terminologies. In the *PsycINFO* database, *neobehaviorism* figures only about 69 times between 1920 and 2020, while *learning theory* appears over 10,000 times. The most frequent uses of "learning theory" are from 1960 to 1990, with 3,200 cases. However, "learning theory" remained both as a referential self-label for neobehaviorists even after the advent of cognitive psychology and is increasingly tied to many specific theories of behavioral change.

Within the neobehaviorist world, there was much variation, but all directions concentrated on the issue of learning, continuing Watson's heritage. With the centrality of learning and objectivity, neobehaviorism has become a rather assimilative and accommodating direction in modern psychology. It tried to include into the behavioral idiom all of what it considered to be relevant from psychoanalysis and *Gestalt* psychology. This move went on in the opposite direction as well. *Gestaltists* forced to move to America started to talk more and more about behavior, and many of the immigrant psychoanalysts also started to talk about behavioral adaptations. Behaviorism has become learning theory, and learning theory, in the eye of its representatives, covered the whole of psychology, as the history reader of Marx and Hillix (1963) showed most clearly during the victorious times of neobehaviorism.

The impact of science theory: neopositivism and psychology

The relationship between neobehaviorism and neopositivist philosophy of science was seemingly simple. Both wanted objectivity. In reality, their relations were rather complex. There was a temporal complexity. The early behaviorism of Watson played a role in the formation of a restrictive and constrained theory of mind proposed early on by Bertrand Russell (1921). Compared to our naive folk psychology, this was a restrictive theory of mind, since it treated several trivial inner mental phenomena at least with reservations. Here is an example from Russell (1921, p. 46): "Desire, like force in mechanics, is of the nature of a convenient fiction for describing shortly certain laws of behavior. A hungry animal is restless until it finds food; then it becomes quiescent."

In the 1920s, this attitude developed into a general restrictive framework for the use of terms in scientific discourse in Vienna and Berlin, mainly in the so-called Vienna Circle of neopositivist philosophy and its Berlin chapter. Ideally, only terms that have a clear reference in the external world would be allowed to be used in science. As a second step, this attitude was reapplied to psychology by followers of the Vienna Circle, basically claiming that there was nothing specific to psychology. If someone has a toothache, this internal state is to be accepted on the basis of behavioral evidence, like facial expressions, sounds, etc. All folk psychology can be chased away from science. The second twist, however, has been more liberal toward psychology. Psychologists may speak of the internal world without ontological commitments, but they have a price to pay. They have to obey the rules of formalization. This is like sexuality being sanctioned by marriage.

Operationalism in psychology and the measurement theory of Stevens

Neopositivism and its continuation in analytic philosophy were a complex series of movements. A table summarizing its chronology is 70 pages long. I only highlight some moments of this complex series that had a clear impact on psychology. Neobehaviorism was a Janus-faced trend in psychology. While it aimed to be neutral and objective, it tried to contain the whole of psychology using a few methodical principles. Psychologists oftentimes try to be more "objective" than natural sciences. Let us make psychology more objective; let us fit into the leading natural science, into physics and its general methodology; let us separate clearly the scientific propositions about facts (e.g., visual acuity increases over infancy) from statements that merely clarify the internal relations of our concepts (e.g., visual acuity increases the sharpness of perception); let us build scientific theories starting in a bottom-up manner, from observations, going in a stepwise manner. This was the way the eternal scientific goals sounded for the new generation of behaviorists. This was usually supplemented with a dislike for any "folk psychology" that may, if at all, only be used as a heuristic starting point, but the best is not even to talk about it. This repression of folk psychology hardly ever worked.

Psychology was most influenced by the new theory of **operationalism**. This term goes back to the argument of the Nobel Prize winner American physicist and philosopher Percy Bridgman (1882–1961). Bridgman (1927) claimed that science can only use terms that have a corresponding measuring operation, and these operations (arguably) exhaust the meaning of abstract terms. The notion of distance is exhausted, for example, by the operations we apply in measuring distance. This was extended towards a general theory of translating all categories used in scientific talk to measurement operations (Hempel, 1954).

In its first applications to psychology, this seemed to suggest a cynical renouncement from solid conceptual analysis. The Titchener student, and later leading historian of psychology, Edwin Boring (1886–1968) played a central role in making notions of classical psychology still acceptable in the American context by the use of operationalism (Boring, 1945). For the general public, for example, in the middle of the debates about intelligence testing, armed with experience of army testing during the war, he proposed a seemingly circular definition of intelligence. "Intelligence is what the tests test.... It would be better if the psychologists could have used some other and more technical term, since the ordinary connotation of intelligence is much broader" (Boring, 1923, p. 35).

The prophet of the operational principles was working on the treasure of first-person psychology, in psychophysics, also at Harvard, S. Smith Stevens (1906–1973). The interests of this well-known researcher, later textbook organizer (Stevens, 1951), were far from the interests of the behaviorists. Stevens developed the modern methods of psychoacoustics research. He replaced the Fechner-type absolute judgments (are two stimuli the same?) with new measurement situations (e.g., make the sound twice as strong). According to results obtained in this manner, in quantitative dimensions (e.g., loudness), the proper psychophysical function is not logarithmic but exponential (Stevens, 1957, 1975/1986). This is still debated in psychophysics, but how does it connect to operationalism?

Stevens extended psychophysics into a general theory of psychological measurement. In all research, including psychological research, we do apply measurement operations to assign numbers to values of variables (Stevens, 1935). These operations attribute numbers to the variables following different constraints, thereby resulting in measurement scales of different rigorousness. "Rigor" here means the mapping relations between the measuring scales and the measured variables. There are nominal scales based on mere category allocation (such as sex or gender), and ordinal scales (e.g., school grades), where transposition does hold (A > B and B > C, then A > C is valid, but it does not follow that the differences between A and B and B and C are the same). Interval scales, on the other hand, keep the equality of distances (e.g., traditional temperature scales or IQ). Finally, ratio scales that have a natural zero point preserve the constancy of ratios (e.g., Kelvin absolute temperature). With these clarifications, Stevens (1946) provided the frames of psychological measurement as shown in Table 8.1. For a generation, the ambition of psychologists was to upgrade their actual measurements from ordinal to interval levels. The theory underlying them was a combination of psychological measurement with mathematical considerations.

Table 8.1 The scaling theory of psychological measurement

Scale type	Measure properties	Math operations	Advanced operations	Central tendency	Example
Nominal	Classification	=, ≠	Grouping	Mode	Gender
Ordinal	Comparison, level	>, <	Sorting	Median	School grade
Interval	Difference, affinity	+, −	Yardstick	Mean, SD	IQ
Ratio	Magnitude	*, /	Ratio	Geometric mean	Kelvin temperature

Source: Stevens (1946).

Dealing with issues of psychophysical measurement, Stevens has become a propagator of operationalism in psychological measurement. These were restrictive, excluded "private" moments but at the same time allowed to reintroduce inner processes into psychology by making them public. The crucial moment was sensory discrimination. You can only agree on something if you can differentiate it.

Operationalism is a guarantee of "second-person versus first-person" psychology, thus the public nature of science; but at the same time, it does create a community based on agreement about principles of measurement. There were interesting examples for this wide use of operational definitions besides the psychophysics of Stevens. Imre Hermann (1929), the Hungarian psychoanalyst, claimed early on in his methodical book that the operational analysis *á la* Bridgman gives the solid foundations even of psychoanalytic concepts.

The operational principle implied a liberation from the strict ontological constraints of classical behaviorism. Through the analysis provided by Tolman (1932), this "liberating interpretation of operationalism" has become dominant in neobehaviorist psychology. Introspection and folk psychology may be used as heuristic tools, but the decisions are in the hand of the behavioral observers.

> It is of course true that human organisms report verbally their "demands", "hypotheses", etc. . . . Personally, however, I am suspicious of such verbal reports. I prefer, for the present, to try to work out psychology with the aid of only the more gross forms of behavior. My motto for the present is: "Rats, not men. Gross behavior, not verbal reports".
>
> (Tolman, 1936, pp. 390–391)

Tolman was a mentalist compared to what he called "muscle twitch" behaviorists, like Watson, but at the same time did not allow for uncertain introspections in science.

In its concrete form within the behaviorist camp, operationalism appeared in two forms. It existed in a sober and practical form which could be referred to as **substantial operationalism**. We can talk about an animal being hungry if it was not fed for n hours. This route will re-enter the "internal world" of traditional folk psychology into objective psychology. Operationalism did exist within behaviorism in a more formal manner as well in the descriptive behaviorism of Skinner. **Operationalism in the formal manner** was used in talking about behavior with no ontological reference. Concepts were defined merely with reference to each other.

> The only way to tell whether a given event is reinforcing to a given organism under given conditions is to make a direct test. We observe the frequency of a selected response, then make an event contingent upon it and observe any change in frequency. If there is a change, we classify the event as reinforcing to the organism under the existing conditions. There is nothing circular about classifying events in terms of their effects.
>
> (Skinner, 1953, p. 73)

At the same time, a response is what can become under the control of reinforcement. This functional definition of reinforcement would include anything from food to verbal praise. In a way, no matter what Skinner said, operational analysis in descriptive behaviorism has become circular (see his exposition in Skinner, 1945).

There were many discussions of operationalism. As a contemporary historian, Green, summarized these debates:

> Although operational definitions might have a role to play in piloting nascent thought about a given phenomenon, they cannot ultimately replace the fruits of hard, rigorous thought. In the words of Immanuel Kant (1781), "thoughts without content are empty, [sensory] intuitions without concepts are blind."
> (Green, 1992, p. 317)

Operationalism still had a very progressive role in the history of psychology. As Feest (2005, p. 145) argued in a less-critical and more broad treatment, it was merely a historical coincidence that within psychology the issue of operationalism coincided with the rise of neobehaviorism. Operational anchoring is an issue for all empirical psychology (think again of Stevens); thus, it is theory-neutral.

All empirical psychologists have to operationalize their concepts. And all empirical psychologists have to argue for their results by laying open both their conceptual presuppositions and their empirical data. Viewed this way, the issue seems to be whether psychology can be an empirical science at all.

The concept of intervening variables

The immediate relative "liberalizing" influence of neopositivistic science theory for behavioristic psychology was the introduction and carrier of **intervening variable** in the interpretation and explanation of behavior. Behavior was no longer described as an immediate function of external conditions but through mediation of auxiliary concepts. These are postulated to be in between the behavior and the external environment, with the stimuli, and therefore they are called "intervening." One may want to take them to correspond to the mentalistic concepts of traditional psychology, but they are not identical with them. They themselves have to be defined with the objective terms of behavior and environment.

The concept and term were introduced by the Berkeley psychologist Edward Chace Tolman (1936). His account of intervening variables (IV) in his "operational behaviorism" is a list of commitments that IVs have to become part of equations about independent variables and the behavior.

In its full-fledged form, the intervening variables proposed by Tolman constitute a complicated system themselves. There are some that are nearer to independent variables, such as hunger, and there are some that are of higher level, secondary functions of "lower-level" intervening variables (e.g., learned expectancies as the function of learning and the motivational system). The origin of the concepts seems to be good old folk psychology, or traditional mentalistic psychology. Intervening variables are mainly needed to make subjective concepts scientific. The kind of intervening variables postulated by behaviorists is a function of the rather "subjective" folk psychological theories.

The conception of intervening variables introduced by Tolman (1951a) had a long life. For about three decades until the 1960s, it has become one of the *passe par tous* notions of most of American experimental psychologists. Only Skinner (1938, 1953) tried to avoid using them in a consequential manner.

Some conceptual restrictions were also introduced in the time this notion was in vogue. MacCorquodale and Meehl (1948) emphasized that in the middle of the increasing popularity of the notion of intervening variables, on the one hand, we have the original, strict intervening variables, which are logically **dispositional concepts**. The concept of habit or drive is like, for example, resistance or conductance in physics. Using this concept, certain behaviors can be predicted after certain interventions. On the other hand, **hypothetical constructs** are not directly amenable into the language of directly observable events; they refer to some entities that are not yet amenable to operationalization (e.g., anxiety, libido).

> These latter ones are not to be purged from psychology. The researcher just has to be aware that they are theoretically laden hypothetical entities. Examples of such constructs are . . . "anxiety" as used by Mowrer, Miller, and Dollard and others of the Yale-derived group, and most theoretical constructs in psychoanalytic theory.
> (MacCorquodale & Meehl, 1948, p. 104)

The new theories of science promoted in the 1960s (Chapter 9) will emphasize that all scientific data gathering and concept formation is theory-dependent, and even those intervening variables that seem to be most descriptive are also of a hypothetical nature: they entail models of reality that are by far not innocent and trivial.

Besides proposing intervening variables, Tolman also introduced a differentiation between **molecular and molar types of behaviorism**.

> Whereas the molecular behaviorist – that is, the behaviorist with physiological bent – seeks to state the nature of these intervening variables in terms of such concepts as chemical or other physical action in the sense organs . . ., the molar behaviorist seeks to state the intervening variables as specific types of behavior-readiness or, in more common sense terms, as objectively definable "demands", "intentions", "expectations" and "attainments".
> (Tolman, 1935, p. 366)

Thus, molar behaviorism reintroduces the intentional levee folk psychology.

Clark Hull, the leader of the Yale neobehaviorist group, took over the concept of intervening variables. Hull was the most ambitious of the behaviorists in tying psychology to the quasi-axiomatic language of modern physics. Hull (1935) started with a need to list all the important engagements of a science, basically claiming that definitions and postulates should lead to "specific statements of the outcome of concrete experiments or observations [and the generalizations] . . . must be submitted to carefully controlled experiments" (Hull, 1935, p. 496).

His system is illustrated in a concise manner in Figure 8.1.

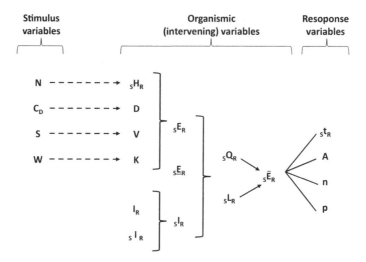

Figure 8.1 The essence of the determination of behavior with intervening.
Source: Variables in the system proposed by Hull (1952).

Statistics and ecological functionalism: Egon Brunswik

The general outlook and inspiration of science theory toward psychology in the 1930s was physicalism. The Austro-Hungarian, and later American, psychologist Egon Brunswik (1903–1955) was an exception. While he was directly exposed to the Vienna school physicalism, he gave a more statistical and biological interpretation of the message of neopositivism toward psychology. He was a student of Karl Bühler, with a training in engineering and a degree in physics and math. Brunswik took seriously the challenge of science theory but combined it with a probabilistic twist. As Gigerenzer (2000), the contemporary researcher of probabilistic decision-making, described it, this attitude and the famous probabilistic attitude of the Wednesday Vienna Bühler seminars (Chapter 5) were in contrast to all-or-none attitude of the Thursday seminar of Vienna Circle people.

> The intellectual tension between Wednesday and Thursday evenings was vibrant. The logical positivist doctrine of the Vienna Circle posited that the relation between scientific language and its sense-data referents should and could be unambiguous. Bühler, in contrast, had shown that the relation between perceptual cues and their objects, as well as between words and their objects, was irreducibly ambiguous. Brunswik sided with Bühler. He did try, though, to resolve the tension by adopting the position of Hans Reichenbach, the leader of the Berlin school of logical positivism, who argued that all knowledge is probabilistic.
>
> (Gigerenzer, 2000, p. 45)

Brunswik (1955) proposed that instead of physicalism, the model for psychology should instead be economy or meteorology. While physics claimed nomothetic universal laws, the determination of behavior is much more probabilistic. Brunswik took American behaviorism seriously and expressed an alternative to it as a probabilistic functional psychology.

> Nomothetic behaviorism overexpands physicalism beyond the necessary observational and procedural core and includes unessential borrowings from the specific theme of physics. A functionally oriented objective psychology, on the other hand, dealing as it does with organism-environment relationships at the more complex level of adjustment, may be seen as falling in line with a more searching interpretation of the historical mission of psychology.
> (Brunswik, 1955, p. 193)

The actual relationships between objects and stimuli are itself probabilistic; organisms form a **probabilistic mapping of the world**. Referring to Holt (1915), Brunswik pointed out that in experimental research, one has to separate variables that are tied together. In the example of Holt, the issue was whether birds fly over a green field or whether they fly southward. The experimental psychologist has to separate variables that are sometimes covariants. The second validity issue is that the actual experimental setting has to represent the real ecological circumstances. Stimuli used in the laboratory have to represent something about the world. Brunswik proposed an **ecological psychology**. We do have to work with independent variations of stimulus dimensions, but the situations and the stimuli have to capture real stimulus concordances (Tolman & Brunswik, 1935). In his actual studies on size constancy, or face preferences, Brunswik used this attitude both on the representative sampling of stimuli and in creating naturalistic settings, taking size constancy out of the laboratory to the open field (Brunswik, 1934). Constancies were proved to be compromises between the retinal image and the real size, serving a probabilistic accommodation of behavior to the real size in real life settings.

Brunswik organized his conception into the so-called **lens model**. The model underlies the "one to many" relations between stimuli and objects, and the "one to many" relations between intentions and goals.

In this model, the organism, and the mind, is seen as a double convex lens, both in input and output. It is focusing either on the organism or on the far environment. "Imperfections of achievement may in part be ascribable to the 'lens' itself, that is, to the organism as an imperfect machine" (Brunswik, 1952, p. 23). "In the light of this model all 'constant' or rather, quasi-constant function, be it 'intuitive' or explicit, can be explicated as a statistical reasoning process remindful of Helmholtz's 'unconscious inference,' albeit without its introspectionistic and perfectionistic overtones." (Brunswik, 1955, p. 9).

The very idea of ecological, or at least ecologically relevant, psychology, and the program for a representative design of experiments, was not too popular for a long time. In the PsycINFO database, Brunswik only showed up 5 times between

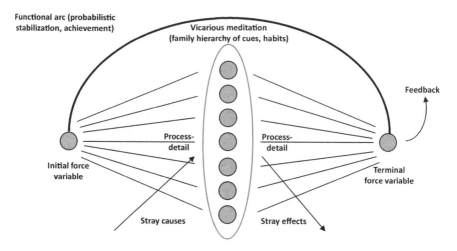

Figure 8.2 The lens model of perception and action proposed by Egon Brunswik
Source: Redrawn on the basis of Brunswik (1955).

1960 and 1990, but 30 times between 1990 and 2010. His time has come with the rediscovery of probability models in psychology. The mathematized vision of psychology promoted by Brunswik was to re-emerge in modern cognitive psychology.

The age of learning theories

Neobehaviorists shared two aspects with the enthusiastic optimist of the originator of the movement, John Watson. **All psychological topics are issues of learning.** The goal of psychology remains the discovery of the laws of learning to allow the formation, the social shaping, of behavior. This is supplemented with the not directly proven belief in the within-species and cross-species **universality of the laws of learning**. The within-species generality and cross-disciplinary validity of behavioral laws are well expressed by Clark Hull (1943, p. v) in his preface to his major book. "All behavior, individual and social, moral and immoral, normal and psychopathic, is generated from the same primary laws. . . . Consequently, the present work may be regarded as a general introduction to the theory of all the behavioral (social) sciences." The cross-species aspect allowed the use of animal studies to figure out regularities that are relevant for humans. The radicals would apply Morgan's Canon (1894), even to humans: try to explain human behavior in the simplest way. A vivid example for this cross-species generality belief was that Tolman (1932) dedicated his innovative work to MNA, that is, *mus norvegicus albinus*, the laboratory white rat. Skinner shows this animal preference as a summary of decades of research work.

> We study the behavior of animals because it is simpler. Basic processes are revealed more easily and can be recorded over longer periods of time. Our

observations are not complicated by the social relation between subject and experimenter. Conditions may be better controlled. We may arrange genetic histories to control certain variables and special life histories to control others. . . . We are also able to control current circumstances to an extent not easily realized in human behavior – for example, we can vary states of deprivation over wide ranges. These are advantages which should not be dismissed on the a priori contention that human behavior is inevitably set apart as a separate field.

(Skinner, 1953, pp. 38–39)

Hull even considered the possible criticism and the issue of "innate" within and between species differences. The laws of behavior are universal, but some of the parameters in these laws can vary.

The *forms* of the equations representing the behavioral laws of both individuals and species are identical, and that the differences between individuals and species will be found in the empirical constants which are essential components of such equations. . . . If this should occur it would mark a genuine junction between pure and applied psychology, which of late have seemed to be drifting farther and farther apart.

(Hull, 1945, p. 60)

Regarding the role of intervening variables and their structure, three influential positions were articulated in neobehaviorism. One class of neobehaviorists filled the mind, starting from the stimulus side, moving up from perception to the mind. They talked about **sign Gestalts mental images, maps, and expectations** (Tolman, 1932). This was classical folk psychology rephrased in operationalized terms. The other class, mainly active at Yale University, filled the mind moving from the response side in. They talked about shortened behavior, motor fragments, and "response-produced cues." The followers of Clark Hull (1937) reinterpreted motor theories of the mind in a behavior terminology, with no commitment to folk psychology. Both groups were, at the same time, inspired by their European contemporaries, be them friends or rivals, that is, to say by *Gestalt* psychology and by psychoanalysis. The third group, the radical behaviorists following Skinner at Indiana University, and later at Harvard, did not propose any internal or mental language. They extended the new operant learning paradigm to all aspects of life, entirely rejecting folk psychology.

Since they had lived as parts of the great social programs of the post-Depression years, and much later in the Great Society of America in the 1960s, the social optimism of these years had given a social inspiration for all of them to build up a new social science based on behavioristic psychology. They wanted to propose a behavioral science that was responsive to the actual needs of the society. They were progressives. It is an interesting aspect of their social commitments that no matter their differences, most of the famous neobehaviorists had had problems with religion as young scholars or earlier, already as students, including, Hull, Skinner, Mowrer, and Tolman as well, causing them to become committed to the cause of a secular science of human behavior.

Conditioning as a basic phenomenon

Neobehaviorism in American psychology was also the age of discovering Pavlov. Due to the publication of the major works of Pavlov (1927) in English and of some survey publications like Yerkes and Morgulis (1909) and Morgulis (1914), from the 1920s on, the metatheoretical idea that **all learning is connection formation** started to be promoted. In the theoretical book of Hull (1943), Pavlov is referred to 82 times – he is by far the most-quoted reference. John Watson, the founder of behaviorism, has a mere five references in the same book. Classical conditioning, as it has come to be called in its basic form, created a connection between a neutral stimulus and a biologically relevant reaction. Most behaviorists believed that the more complicated learning situations used by them (e.g., maze learning, discrimination learning), and the seemingly higher-order human learnings (e.g., learning a list of words), are also amenable to the formation of a series of elementary connections. The contribution of Pavlov to behaviorist theory was not only the idea of connection formation. Basic notions of his system (discrimination, generalization, etc.) have become unquestionable natural laws of behavioral analysis, oftentimes without coupling them with the physiological doctrine of Pavlov about cortical dynamics. In Skinner (1938), the word *brain* appears only twice in an entire book. Moreover, in rather negative contexts, one should not speculate about the brain, especially about brain waves. Hull (1943), in his book, talked about the brain, but merely regarding sensation, and cortical dynamics as a basis of learning only appears in Pavlov citations. It is characteristic for the feeling of innovation that in the comprehensive intentions of the book of Hull, all the Loeb–Jennings debate about animal intentionality is entirely missing, as well as classical memory research, like Ebbinghaus.

Two types of conditioning

The analysis of behavior relying on conditioned reflexes obtained a peculiar new flavor due to the discoveries of Skinner (1938). The young Skinner (he was 20 years younger than Hull or Tolman) was originally trying to defend a deterministic notion of reflex in psychology, working on the exact movement characterization of animals. Studying a single runway behavior, in an accidental manner, as he recalled it (Skinner, 1956), he noticed that when animals went back to the start box after receiving food in the goal box, there was variation in their waiting times. Skinner simplified his apparatus to study the waiting times, and from then on, the study of this phenomenon is done in the famous **Skinner box**, shown on Figure 8.3. The hungry animal moves around in a box. During its random movements, the rat steps on the lever in the cage, and it gets a food pellet; the frequency of level pressing would increase in a probabilistic manner. In this model situation, one can study many classic features of reflex behavior, such as discrimination and generalization, by introducing specific stimuli, reinforcement and extinction, and so on. Most importantly for Skinner, the recording makes a cumulative chart of the bar pressings as a function of time, and the effects of all possible interventions.

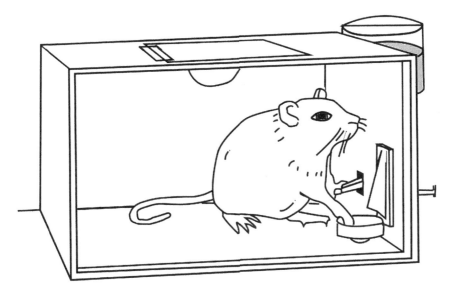

Figure 8.3 The Skinner box arrangement.

Skinner realized the similarity between his box and the Thorndike (1898) situation. Behavior is shaped by its consequences, and the eliciting stimuli are not too relevant. The behavior in the beginning is "spontaneous" and becomes gradually reflex-like. The research of the Polish Konorski and Miller (1937) modifying the ideas of Pavlov came to a similar conclusion. If one leg of the dog in the Pavlov chamber was freed, and preceding the electric shock as a negative stimulus, the experimenter lifted the leg of the dog; after a while, the dog lifted its leg "spontaneously" to avoid the shock. Skinner, when commenting on them, claimed his originality.

The new type of reflex had been running under several names, which all express the basic features of this type of learning. It is called **operant learning**, since the organism acquires an action, an **operation** on its environment. It is called **instrumental conditioning**, since behavior here is an instrument of obtaining the reward, while in the Pavlov situation, the dog obtains the food even if it does not salivate to the CS. Finally, it is referred to already by Skinner as **R type of conditioning**, since here the behavior, or the response, is modified in contrast to the Pavlovian situation, where a new stimulus value is obtained (**S type of conditioning**).

Instrumental learning was important in shaping the theoretical interpretation for all learning. As Miller and Dollard (1941) spelled out the consequences in their book on social learning, there are four conditions that must be met in order to learn a new response.

- DRIVE (or motivation): a person must want something. A drive may be innate, as with hunger, or learned, as fear or the desire for money.
- CUE (or stimulus): a person must notice something.

- RESPONSE: a person must do something. A response may be an overt act or a central nervous system event, such as a thought, a perception, or paying attention.
- REWARD (or reinforcement): a person must get something that is wanted.

In the 1930s, when psychologists were talking about conditioning, they had Pavlov in mind. Most theories of learning (Hilgard, 1948) started from a detailed presentation of Pavlov. The fronting of Skinner on equal footing with Pavlov was mainly due to the textbook of Hilgard and Marquis (1940) on conditioning and learning, and later the neuroscience-based theories of Donald Hebb (1949). From the mid-1950s on, in the search to find the most universal laws of learning, some efforts were made to unify the two types of learning into a comprehensive behaviorist theory of learning. This had a methodological aspect. Neobehaviorists believed in economy in science, in modeling the most of behavior with the least number of processes. Mowrer (1947, 1960) attempted this unification on a psychological level. Classical (Pavlovian) conditioning would form the basis of learning motives for actions. On the basis of Pavlovian learning, we would associate **hope or fear** to a situation, while learning new behaviors tied to these motives would follow the principles of instrumental conditioning and would be under the control of consequences. Regarding their physiological unifying principles, Neal Miller (1969) showed results to the effect that even visceral reactions like blood pressure or heart rate could be drawn under the control of feedback. That has led on the practical level to the popularity of biofeedback models. On the theoretical level, it suggested at the same time that response discrimination is available both in lever pressing and in heart rate; thus, the two learnings may not be as different as assumed. The instrumental visceral conditioning in the animal models did not prove to be a reliable effect, but the feedback-based human visceral conditioning worked well.

Skinner, with his indeterminate and flexible type of learning, introduced a duality into his own **social message**. All his life, until the 1980s, he would have two attitudes. On the one hand, he would be the representative of the deterministic vision of humans, with reflex-like determination. On the other hand, due to the built-in indeterminacy in the operant and the shift toward a probabilistic determination, Skinner himself believed from the mid-1940s on that he was showing a more indeterministic trend in the course of behavior. In his late writing (Skinner, 1984), he gave a Darwinian selectionist interpretation of instrumental learning, allowing to put the original random behavior to be out into a general hypothesis testing scheme by people like Dennett (1997a).

The determinism–indeterminism duality continued to show up in the social implications of Skinner. The Skinnerian model of learning became the symbol of control, manipulation, and a lack of freedom, a deterministic view of man in American society, and in the high intellectual circles, a symbol of the overambitious reductionism of Skinner (Chomsky, 1959). It is of some interest to meditate on how it became the issue of classical versus instrumental conditioning so hot in the sixties in Eastern Europe. There were two aspects of Skinner himself that made this approach relevant for freedom issues in Eastern Europe, where the operant learning became a symbol of initiative and freedom (see Chapter 7).

Mental maps: the purposive modeling behaviorism of Tolman

Edward Chace Tolman (1886–1959), a professor of psychology at Berkeley starting in the 1920s, saw the leading proponent of a filling up of the mind from the stimulus side, and in this regard, he can be seen as the **cognitivist of the neobehaviorist movement**. Tolman was a student of John Holt, who, as a theoretical psychologist and philosopher, interpreted behavioral causation and teleology (Chapter 11 in Volume 1). Tolman started off from a combination of the purposive behaviorism of Holt and the ideas of neopositivist philosophers to arrive at the concept of intervening variables. Tolman had very wide interests and travelled a lot to Europe and was much more cosmopolitan than most of the American psychologists of his generation. He spent a sabbatical year in Vienna, in 1933–1934, getting closely acquainted with the work of the Vienna Circle, Egon Brunswik, and Karl Bühler, as well as with psychoanalysts. He even visited the hearing researcher physicist Békésy in Budapest. Tolman, besides having been influenced by behaviorism and by neopositivism, was also influenced by the ideas of *Gestalt* psychology (especially Kurt Lewin), by the sign theory of Karl Bühler, by the probabilistic ideas of Egon Brunswik, and by psychoanalysis as well.

Starting with the example of "purpose," Tolman (1932) tried to turn the entire conceptual apparatus of classical mentalistic psychology and folk psychology into a system of intervening variables related directly to behavior. Some of those would be event-like in his analysis (e.g., perception of something, recalling an event), and some would be of a dispositional character (e.g., personality traits). Their introduction would be grounded in representative experiments that varied a defining feature (e.g., keeping everything constant, we observe the relations between behavioral activity and the time without food). The two basic features of Tolman are a view of multiple

Figure 8.4 Edward Chace Tolman.
Source: Wikimedia commons. Public domain.

determination of behavior and the need to move from the periphery to more central explanatory concepts, as he summarized it at the end of his life (Tolman, 1959).

Tolman highlighted many peculiarities of animal learning in the favorite maze learning situation. One such peculiarity was **latent learning**. Animals learned faster if they were allowed before the learning trials merely to wander in the maze, as first shown by Blodgett (1929) in the Tolman laboratory. The second aspect was **orientation**. When rats are blocked by walls in the maze, they seem to be still oriented toward the goal. These facts suggested for Tolman that, even in simple learning situations, rats make a model of the situation; they are not merely learning a set of turns attached to given choice points. In learning a maze, the animal learns **sign Gestalts**. This is a combination of perceptual organization and learning new values. "The 'figure on grounds,' etc., of *Gestalt* psychology are always caught up into some larger whole i.e., sign-gestalts and means-end relations" (Tolman, 1951b, p. 78). The summary of these expectancies forms a **cognitive map** that directs the behavior of the animal (Tolman, 1948). Tolman concentrated on large molar units of behavior that have a biological function (e.g., finding food, escaping from the box, etc.). This attitude, as already shown even by the title of his 1932 book, attributed a central role to motivation and purpose. The cognitive maps directing the organism have differently valued regions. Our movements in the real world are movements to approach positive regions and avoid repelling ones. This process is exemplified with sketches of fields reminding of Kurt Lewin (1935, 1951) and reconstructing the belief–desire folk psychology. Tolman also tried to give an interpretation in behavioristic terms of several psychoanalytic notions. In his case, however, this attitude did not lead to new empirical work, like in the case of the students of Hull, only to the theoretical interpretation of notions like identification, regression, and the like.

Tolman did not form his own school in his own time. He did, however, have colleagues like Egon Brunswik and students like Isadore Krechevsky (1932). Krechevsky claimed the renegade vision that rats do learn by forming and checking hypotheses. This was highly debated as anthropomorphism at that time. But in fact, it corresponded to the idea that all variation-based change, including trial-and-error learning, is in an abstract sense testing hypotheses. Later, with a changed name, as David Krech (1909–1977), he became a well-known left-wing social psychologist, working on conformism and writing textbooks (Chapter 6). Interestingly, at the same time, he remained a devoted researcher of learning, combining methods of biochemistry with early deprivation and environmental enrichment (Krech et al., 1960).

Tolman was also a symbolic political liberal in American academia. During the McCarthy times of the anti-communist purification campaigns on American university campuses, he refused to sign a loyalty oath and led a movement about this, winning a court case against the state. By this act, he was in fact protecting some of his extreme left-wing colleagues, like David Krech. Berkeley University named the psychology building after Tolman in 1963 as Tolman Hall. In 2018, the building was demolished due to earthquake safety reasons.

Tolman was a great name in his time, and his debates with the followers of Hull on place versus response learning in mazes were central to theories of learning. This seemingly outdated debate is still relevant. For the cognitivists, it is related to the issue whether we are entitled to postulate animal representation systems. The cognitive approach to learning represented by Tolman became popular again in psychology in the 1970s. Cognitive maps in cognitive psychology are no longer outlandish, extravagant notions but trivialities. The mentalistic linguist Chomsky (1968), in his Berkeley talks, presented Tolman as a forerunner of his own mentalistic modelling. Tolman is also presented by many as a forerunner of the image-based representation systems opposed to the propositional ones (Kosslyn, 1994). Tolman will be a reference point for many modern semantic theories, especially regarding space orientation and spatial language. Cognitive maps showed up in neuroscience as well, in the studies that later led to a Nobel Prize, and showed space-sensitive cells in the hippocampus (**the hippocampus as a cognitive map**; O'Keefe, 1976; O'Keefe & Nadel, 1978). Tolman had an influence on Hungarian psychology as well (*map*). The theoretical model of the Hungarian comparative psychologist Lajos Kardos (1988) on **animal memory** proposed that spatial memory in rodents is related to their locomotor way of life (Kardos et al., 1978). Kardos, however, treated the internal representations not as maps but as sensory remnants. Paul Harkai Schiller (1944; von Schiller, 1948) another Hungarian comparative psychologist took over the other engagement of Tolman, the study of purposeful aspects of behavior.

Regarding the lasting message of Tolman, it is very ironic that one very successful student of Tolman, Donald Campbell (1977, 1988), complained in the 1970s that the message of his mentor was lost, and the followers of Hull, especially Kenneth Spence, took the lead through their influence on personality theory in the heritage of American neobehaviorism. Times, however, do change fast. Figure 8.5 shows that, regarding the fate of some of the neobehaviorist stars, this trend was

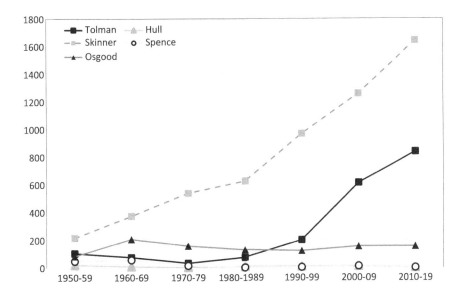

Figure 8.5 References to leading neobehaviorists over half a century in the PsycINFO database.

very much reversed. Skinner and Charles Osgood are constantly very important due to their social theories and radical social messages (Skinner) and due to the semantic differential methodology (Osgood). From the 1990s, the relevance of Tolman rose again, and he is cited much more in the cognitive areas than any of the neobehaviorist schools.

Movements as mediators for mental life: the system of Clark Hull

The other type of neobehaviorism working with intervening variables was the group of researchers around Clark Hull (1884–1952) at Yale University. They tried to reduce internal (mental) processes to interpret internal fractions of overt behavior, and later, they are usually referred to as **mediation theories**. At the same time, they connected behavior theory to wider issues of social science and society, fitting the neobehaviorist approach to the demands of modern industrial society and its social tensions.

Clark Leonard Hull had a difficult training, marred by serious illnesses, like polio, but he kept his interest both in theoretical mathematics and in psychology for his entire life. He started by making a pioneer study of artificial concept formation (Hull, 1920), followed by an experimental analysis of hypnotic phenomena, and a presentation of human eyelid conditioned reflexes. Hull became a real system maker as a professor at Yale University in the 1930s.

Like Tolman, Hull also believed that the study of behavior must be refreshed by the use of intervening variables. Their positions radically diverged, however, in three regards. Hull was a molecular behaviorist. He believed in breaking down complex behaviors into simple S–R connections. On the other hand, in line with his love for mathematics, Hull was aiming to follow the ideal of a **hypothetico-deductive method** when talking about behavior. For him, this aspect was the most important from the neopositivist inspiration. Hull intended to build a theoretical psychology that interpreted specific behavioral processes in the light of the most general **postulates** and provided a logical order for intervening variables. Finally, Hull and his followers built the "internal system" starting not from the stimulus but from the response side, deducing the most crucial intervening variables from movements.

Hull's system is basically an associative system, where all forms of behavior are built up from elementary S–R connections. All stimuli are always followed by a response. This was a syntactic approach to behaviorism. The S–R rule had to be followed even if there was a seemingly distant relation between stimulus and reaction. In these cases, internal reactions were postulated that served on their part as stimuli for observable external reactions. This syntactic expectation was the linguistic turn in neobehaviorism, and in a way, the formal stimulus–reaction expectation was equivalent to the formal syntax of scientific language in the science theory of Carnap (1934).

These efforts toward a formal syntax of behavioral language were not a simple task for Hull. In all his theory, there is a peculiar contradiction between two attitudes. He is committed to a very broad general and supposedly axiomatic system of behavioral science, using generalizations based on model experiments. At the

Figure 8.6 Clark Leonard Hull.
Source: Wikimedia commons. Public domain.

same time, however, both in his model experiments and in the phenomena he was studying, he was entirely elementaristic. He wanted to start and build up all his system from conditioning phenomena and, in humans, from rote learning of nonsense syllables.

Hull developed a peculiar notifying convention of how to talk about intervening variables. Every intervening variable had to have an $_S$IV$_R$ structure. The *S* and *R* subscripts remind us that the intervening variables are inserted between stimulus and reaction, and they always have to be anchored in stimulus and response variables. Intervening variables corresponding to internal processes are also portrayed as internal stimulus–response chains in harmony with the syntactic convention. Learning processes are characterized by universal laws. The generalizations appear in the form of postulates. His system looks like a series of rather clumsy equations (Hull, 1943). Behavior likelihood (excitatory potential) is a function of learning (habit strength), general drive level, stimulus intensity (*V*), and how attractive the stimulus is (*K*).

$$_sE_R = {_sH_R} \times D \times V \times K$$

This would be refined later (Hull, 1952) by thresholds (*L*) and fluctuations (*O*) and inhibitions (*I*) to arrive at a formula like this:

$$_sE_R = V \times K \times {_sD_R} \times {_sH_R} - {_sI_R} - {_sO_R} - {_sL_R}$$

Hull not merely proposed these universal postulates but parametrized them as well.

Postulate IV: the law of habit formation ($_sH_r$)

The habit strength changes as a function of reinforcements in the following manner:

$$SH_R = 1 - 10^{-.0305 N}$$

Due to the negative exponent, if N is large enough, habit strength will be the maximum, that is, 1.

The pompous system of Hull did not have to be accepted to realize its substantial importance. One principle of his system that had a large consequence was the **drive reduction postulate**: habits leading to decrease of needs lead to an increase in these habits. The principle was one of the leading ideas of psychology of that time and has been ever since: motivation is needed for learning. Later, this principle, as the principle of drive reduction, has become the leading issue in the physiology of learning. What are the discrete physiological mechanisms corresponding to drive reduction and to the connection-reinforcing nature of them (Miller, 1957, 1959)? Hull (1943) already saw that the consequences are not necessarily based on a reduction of the physiological need itself. Some of his contemporaries, like Guthrie (1935) and connectionists from the 1980s (Rumelhart et al., 1986), conceived that in some cases mere coincidence was sufficient for learning. There is pure cognitive-associative learning.

The other concept of Hull that had a long and successful career was **anticipated goal reactions** or **fractioned goal reactions**. The concept started from maze learning, where observations showed that animals produced particular movements characteristic in the goal box already before arriving to the goal box. Hull generalized the validity of this observation and started to claim that the proprioceptive stimulation coming from internal fractions of goal movements become motivated stimuli for actual movements. Anticipated goal reactions were model situations for the mediating role of internalized movements in higher achievements. In followers of Hull (mostly Osgood, 1957), these internal mediation responses would not only be derived from overt behavior but would also represent overt behavior and become explanatory principles of higher human cognition.

Hull's group was very active in the direct social extensions of the principles of behavioral science during the years following the American Great Depression and during the war.

Is there a need for reinforcement for all learning? Guthrie

The majority of neobehaviorists from the value matrix of Tolman to operant conditioning of Skinner, and drive reduction of Hull, have emphasized that all learning requires some vital interests; thus, there is no pure cognitive learning. There was a dissident voice at that time, however. E. R. Guthrie (1886–1959), a professor at Washington University, defended two principles throughout the course of his life (Guthrie, 1935, 1959). In his vision, the basis of learning is a **mere contiguity** between stimulus and reactions, or contiguity of two stimuli. In typical situations, the animal always repeats the last movement. Furthermore, according to his second principle, all contiguity results in learning on a **single trial**. Not many people liked this. It did, however, help elevate the prestige of Guthrie, so much so that even Pavlov (1932) criticized him in detail.

How could one uphold such a counterintuitive theory? Guthrie did face the challenges. Stimulus situations do change at every single trial, and multiple presentations bring forward joint features. On the other hand, during repetition, only performance or execution improved and not the connection that was already formed. The role of reward and punishment in this vision was not reinforcement but changing the stimulus situation. In a Thorndike cage, the food changes the situation. Reward has an effect, but not by reinforcing already-formed connections, but by preventing interference.

Everyone was against Guthrie, except early mathematical theoreticians of psychology (Estes, 1950, 1959), as Guthrie was also a good mathematician. The parallel distributed processing model of Rumelhart et al. (1986) a generation later using the same name, **connectionism**, partly returned to Guthrie's conception. Learning is based on contiguity, with a unit increase of connection strength in each trial.

Descriptive behaviorism: Skinner

Skinner against the tide

Burrhus Frederic Skinner (1904–1990) was a compulsive naturalist who introduced what is now called **descriptive behaviorism**. At the same time, he was a radical social philosopher all his life, and a very talented and successful writer. Skinner originally intended to be a writer but was not moving fast enough with his writing. He came across some books of Russell on behaviorism, then went on to read Watson and then Jacques Loeb, as well as the then new English book of Pavlov. Russell remained an inspiration for Skinner all his life. In his widely discussed *Verbal behavior* book, Russell is by far the most-quoted philosopher. Skinner pursued graduate studies at Harvard, hoping to become a behaviorist, which he did, but not in psychology, where the mentalists with Boring prevailed at that time, but in physiology. His mentor was William Crozier (1892–1955), a follower of the mechanistic ideas of Loeb and a noted researcher on chemoreception. Most importantly, Crozier, originally a zoologist, campaigned for a "general physiology of the human body" rather than speculations about the inner workings of the nervous system. This positivistic attitude and the Loeb-style mechanistic vision (using the physical stance regarding behavior) were crucial influences for Skinner. He made his PhD on reflexes, and after a short time in Minnesota, he established the first department of the experimental analysis of behavior, at Indiana University, Bloomington. In the meantime, he became famous due to his book in 1938 and his radical attitude and was invited back to Harvard, first to give a William James lecture series, and then to become a professor from 1948 until 1974.

The seemingly simple discovery of operant behavior, or instrumental conditioning, combined with his social rhetoric and his organizing skills in creating social movements, made Skinner the most influential psychologist of the 20th century in many regards. This claim can be substantiated by a survey conducted by

Figure 8.7 Burrhus Frederic Skinner.
Source: Wikimedia commons. Public domain.

Haggbloom et al. (2002) in which he combined measurements of textbook and journal citations as well as ratings from leading American professors in psychology. Freud is only more influential than Skinner in textbook citations.

By studying in detail the contingencies of reinforcement, he showed the dependence of operant behavior on consequences (Skinner & Ferster, 1969). Animals behave more reliably with intermittent reinforcement, when not each and very peck gives a reward. The fixed-ratio schedules (e.g., each fifth response gets a food pellet) produced high response rates, while fixed interval schedules (there is food every 30 second) show a temporarily varying rate. Skinner and the committed members of the experimental analysis of behavior society revealed everything about the functional dependency of learned behaviors on the environmental conditions for three decades. The method of operant learning has become the most standard method of studying animal behavior in neuroscience and pharmacology, today using touchscreen methods with animals as well, and for the designers of slot machines. Skinner himself, after a while, experimented with pigeons, since the beak pecking had a reliable high response rate.

Skinner deliberately stayed outside the grandiose theory building and speculation of what was characteristic of the "intervening variable" behaviorists all his life. In 1950, at the height of the different learning theories proposed by his colleagues, he defended his positivist attitude. The most rapid progress toward an understanding of learning is made by research that is not designed to test theories. "An acceptable scientific program is to collect data of this sort and to relate them to manipulable variables, selected for study through a common-sense exploration of the field" (Skinner, 1950, p. 215).

There are four divertissements, escapes from the laboratory. Escapes to real men (to folk psychology), mathematical men, inner men, and everyday men (folk psychology again). Skinner wants to stay in the laboratory, with its total disinterest, and desanthropomorphization.

The radical positivist scientist treated physiological thought as empty speculation as well. In this regard, he was following on the footsteps of Loeb. The description of behavior should concentrate on the entire organism in its behavior and should think of a conceptual rather than an actual nervous system.

> The concepts and laws of reflex physiology at this level differ from those of behavior principally in the local reference implied in the term synapse. . . . [T]he traditional "C. N. S." might be said to stand for the Conceptual Nervous System. . . . I venture to assert that no fact of the nervous system has as yet ever told anyone anything new about behavior.
> (Skinner, 1938, pp. 421, 425)

In some of his last writings, Skinner, who seemed to be an ontological behaviorist and criticized two decades earlier the easy application of ethology, arrived at a multilevel theory of selection not unlike the one proposed by Bühler (1922/1930, 1936) half a century earlier. Skinner came to acknowledge the similarities of different selections. He suggested that selections based on consequences were in fact building up in different layers.

> Selection by consequences is a causal mode found only in living things, or in machines made by living things. It was first recognized in natural selection, but it also accounts for the shaping and maintenance of the behavior of the individual and the evolution of cultures. In all three of these fields, it replaces explanations based on the causal modes of classical mechanics. The replacement is strongly resisted. Natural selection has now made its case, but similar delays in recognizing the role of selection in the other fields could deprive us of valuable help in solving the problems which confront us.
> (Skinner, 1981, p. 501)

For Daniel Dennett (1994, 1997a), when he proposed the towers of selection metaphor with Darwinian, Skinnerian, and Popperian beings, this was to become a positive elaboration of the worldview message of Skinner.

The social utopia of Skinner

The antitheoretical Skinner had, at the same time, a strong underlying theory about society. Society with all its institutions allocates reinforcements, and thereby shaping behavior. Its problems all relate to the mismanagement of reinforcement schedules. This program may sound very plain and juiceless. Its radical messages surfaced when, in the 1950s, it started to become a foundation for intervention programs. Followers of Skinner would start working on behavioral therapies and behavioral organizations in closed totalitarian systems, like prisons, based on careful administration of rewards, in the frames of the so-called **token economy**, where small rewards can be exchanged for bigger ones. Skinner (1968) was also a theoretical and practical advocate to promote **programmed learning**. The to-be-learned material in this conception was "dissected" into small learnable parts, and the movement of the student in the material was dependent upon the student handling all the preceding parts. Skinner also moved toward a social utopia ripping off any "prejudices" regarding internal mental life and replacing punishments with carefully administered positive reinforcements.

Skinner did not pay too much attention to the softer social science excursions of his mostly Yale-based colleagues toward imitation, aggression, and the like. Even when he talks about issues like this, Skinner never mentioned Neal Miller, Mowrer, or Bandura. He gradually developed his one-level theory of social behavior. His radicalism can be summarized in a simple statement. **All human behavior is operant behavior**, which can be analyzed regarding the ways it is under the control of the social environment. Consequently – and that is where his utopia enters – for social amelioration, the best road is to change the environmental conditions. Skinner expressed his vision of "higher behavior" for the scientific community for the first time in his provocative book *Verbal behavior* published in 1957. This book has created many CONTROVERSIES.

Controversies

Skinner and Chomsky on language

Skinner spelled out his general utopian perspective for a social use of the science of behavior.

> There is no reason why scientific methods cannot now be applied to the study of man himself – to practical problems of society and, above all, to the behavior of the individual. We must not turn back because the prospect suddenly becomes frightening. . . . "Personal freedom" and "responsibility" will make way for other bywords which, as is the nature of bywords, will probably prove satisfying enough.
> (Skinner, 1957, pp. 498–499)

Regarding verbal behavior and language itself, Skinner claimed that language was a peculiar response system full of self-reinforcing capabilities. Skinner preferred to talk about "verbal behavior" rather than language, for very clear individualistic reasons. "The term 'verbal behavior' has much to recommend. . . . [I]t emphasizes the individual speaker and, whether recognized by the user or not, specifies behavior shaped and maintained by mediated consequence" (Skinner, 1957, p. 35).

There are two general comprehensive images in the book to make language fit into the overall system of behavior. The first is **determinism**. Verbal behavior, what we say, is dependent on the stimulus situations and on the reinforcement history. If we know these two, we will predict what one says. The second image is that of the child. **The mastery of language by children follows general principles of operant behavior formation.** Principles learned in the animal laboratory can be directly extended to language acquisition.

> In teaching the young child to talk, the formal specifications upon which reinforcement is contingent are at first greatly relaxed. Any response which vaguely resembles the standard behavior of the community is reinforced. When these begin to appear frequently, a closer approximation is insisted upon. In this manner very complex verbal forms may be reached.
>
> (Skinner, 1957, p. 63)

This is particularly shown for word learning, with verbal reinforcers. "A child is taught the names of objects, colors, and so on when some generalized reinforcement (for example, the approval carried by the verbal stimulus *Right!*) is made contingent upon a response which bears an appropriate relation to a current stimulus" (Skinner, 1957, p. 118).

Three types of language functional units are specific to Skinner's analysis that are worth considering. They try to elucidate the way Skinner believed in relations of language to the behavior of others (MAND), to the eliciting situation (TACT), and to the specific reinforcing conditions of verbal behavior (AUTOCLITIC).

MAND (from *demand, command*, etc.). Basically, the language units that require something from the partner. "A 'Mand is' therefore under the functional control of relevant conditions of deprivation or aversive stimulation" (Skinner, 1957, p. 69).

TACT. Makes *contact*, reference to something, etc. "A tact may be defined as a verbal operant in which a response of given form is evoked (or at least Strengthened) by a particular object or event or property of an object or event." (p. 116). This corresponds to certain words being evoked by certain objects.

AUTOCLITIC. Self-referential operands. The term "autoclitic" is intended to suggest behavior which is based upon or depends upon other verbal behavior. Grammar is not a separate sphere but a type of autoclitic.

> The sentence *The boy runs a store* is under the control of an extremely complex stimulus situation, most features of which may be important to the listener. The relational autoclitic of order in English carries a

> heavy burden: roughly speaking, it must be clear that it is the boy who does the running and the store which is run.
>
> (p. 373)

From the perspective of modern cognitive theory, some of the autoclitics correspond to propositional attitude expressions, while others to metalinguistic statements.

Skinner did not do much with regard to the empirical support of his radical vision of language. The real interesting follow-ups came from applications of verbal operant principles to psychotherapy, with empirical applications or proofs of the dependency of verbal behavior on reinforcement consequences. Some studies showed that consequential social reinforcement (nodding, yes saying, etc.) can be used to increase features of "verbal operants," such as the use of singular or plural nouns. Speech thus can be drawn under the influence of reinforcement (Greenspoon, 1955; Krasner, 1958). Cognitive research in the coming decades questioned the unnoticed or uncontrolled and unconscious nature of the effects. According to Brewer (1974), in all these cases, there is a conscious realization of the contingencies used in the experiments before the change in behavior.

Skinner's book has become a center of attention in the clash between the behaviorists and the new upcoming cognitive trends in psychology. Skinner's theory was a grandiose thought experiment with no efforts to really prove it. This was mainly related to a review written by Noam Chomsky (1959), a junior colleague of Skinner (a whole generation younger) at Harvard for a while. This review had a great impact in social sense, with over 2,000 references to it. It has shaken the belief of many would-be Skinner followers and encouraged the new generation of cognitive psychologists within the same context at Cambridge, Harvard University (see Chapter 9). The long review of Chomsky clearly showed the tension between radical behaviorists and the new generation of radical cognitivists.

1. The **use of stimulus, response, and reinforcement is circular** in Skinner, especially regarding higher behaviors.

   > Skinner's claim that all verbal behavior is acquired and maintained in "strength" through reinforcement is quite empty, because his notion of reinforcement has no clear content, functioning only as a cover term for any factor, detectable or not, related to acquisition or maintenance of verbal behavior.
   >
   > (Chomsky, 1959, p. 38)

   Chomsky here criticizes the formal operationalism of Skinner.

2. **Human behavior is relatively stimulus-independent** and is a function of the "specific 'contribution of the organism' to learning and performance" (ibid., p. 27). Chomsky lists many studies about the role of curiosity in animal learning that question the image of a merely reacting organism. The most important external support for Chomsky's ideas came from ethology.
3. **The acquisition of language is not possible in terms of conditioning and reinforcement.** "The fact that all normal children acquire essentially comparable grammars of great complexity with remarkable rapidity suggests that human beings are somehow specially designed to do this, with data-handling or 'hypothesis-formulating' ability of unknown character and complexity" (p. 57).
4. **There has to be some mental organization, basically a grammar.** One could postulate of innate factors:

> [T]he remarkable capacity of the child to generalize, hypothesize, and "process information" in a variety of very special and apparently highly complex ways which we cannot yet describe or begin to understand, and which may be largely innate, or may develop through some sort of learning or through maturation of the nervous system.
> (p. 43)

This famous and harsh critique had its own life. The open clash of two research cultures has become evident both for the followers of Skinner and for the mentalistic cognitive youth. There was basically a tension between a functionalist (Skinner) and a structural approach (Chomsky) to language. The tension is shown that MacCorquodale (1970), a Skinner follower, published a reply only a decade later. One key issue was the status of mentalistic concepts; Skinner himself pointed out a crucial issue about the "mental reality" of grammar. What is the sufficient evidence to claim a mental reality for the "formal description of behavior" (such as grammar)?

> To make grammar have a "psychological reality" is a category error for strict behaviorists – it is an ontological error. To say that "the child who learns a language has in some sense constructed the grammar for himself" (Chomsky, 1959) is as misleading as to say that a dog which has learned to catch a ball has in some sense constructed the relevant part of the science of mechanics. Rules can be extracted from the reinforcing contingencies in both cases, and once in existence they may be used as guides. The direct effect of the contingencies is of a different nature.
> (Skinner, 1963, p. 514)

Skinner did not give up his social speculations. In the 1970s, he expressed his vision of society in a much-discussed, new provocative book. His social utopia book came at a much-tensed time in American social history: a few years after the student unrests, in the middle of the civil rights movement, the Vietnam War, and partially overlapping in its effect with the Watergate scandal. With all these events, American society was in the middle of great changes and ready for drastic reinterpretations. In 1949, in his novel *Walden Two*, Skinner already proposed a contingent reinforcement-based new social engineering. Furthermore, he pointed out repeatedly that humans are free agents in that they depend on the environmental reinforcements. The mature Skinner tried to be non-utopian and published an essay on his vision of society and morality, with the provocative title *Beyond freedom and dignity* (Skinner, 1971). In this essayistic book, analyzing Socrates, Rousseau, Dewey, and Dostoevsky, Skinner formulated a dual provocative message. First, the science of behavior analysis can form the foundation of social practices. Second, we should forget about our prejudices relating to human dignity in the process.

Human society, in his vision, is basically a system of rewards and sanctions.

> A culture is like the experimental space used in the study of behavior. It is a set of contingencies of reinforcement, a concept which has only recently begun to be understood. The technology of behavior which emerges is ethically neutral, but when applied to the design of a culture, the survival of the culture functions as a value.
>
> (p. 178)

The basic problem of modern social practices is their punitive nature.

> Governmental sanctions remain almost entirely punitive, and the unfortunate by-products are sufficiently indicated by the extent of domestic disorder and international conflict. It is a serious problem that we remain almost continuously at war with other nations. . . . [W]hat must be changed are the circumstances under which men and nations make war.
>
> (p. 154)

The individualism as a result of punitive technologies is found as a final refuge of the existing order.

> The traditional concept of man . . . was designed to build up the individual as an instrument of counter control, and it did so effectively but in such a way as to limit progress. . . . [I]t is not difficult to demonstrate a connection between the unlimited right of the individual to pursue happiness and the catastrophes threatened by unchecked breeding, the unrestrained affluence which exhausts resources and pollutes the environment, and the imminence of nuclear war.
>
> (p. 208)

In religion and psychoanalysis, external punishing agents are introjected. The solution is to **change the environment, not the mind**. The image where rewarding the good behavior is more efficient than punishing bad behaviors was very central to the social message of Skinner.

Skinner's book created many ardent philosophical and social criticisms. Skinner was criticized due to his efforts to unravel the vanity of individualism and the vain efforts toward human dignity and morality both by traditionalists and by libertarians. From the conservative side, Spiro Agnew, then vice president to Richard Nixon, saw an attack on the American ideas of individuality in Skinner and other behavioral proposals.

> In his book, Skinner attacks the very precepts on which our society is based. . . .
> To the behaviorist, man is not an individual; he is one in a herd, a particle in a mass of humanity who does not know what is good for him, and who needs to be saved from himself by a superior elite using intellectual cattle prods.
> (Agnew, 1971, pp. 31, 48)

A US Senate subcommittee started to study behavior modification in the middle of this social mood, at the end of which stricter regulations have been articulated for research involving human subjects.

Some liberal critics of the social vision of Skinner criticized him as a proponent of strict behavioral order in society, while in his words, at least, Skinner was campaigning for a more reward-based social system. But the real libertarian criticism came again from Noam Chomsky (1972a). Chomsky, by this time, was in the middle of developing his version of libertarian philosophy of mind connected to a philosophy of human freedom. The traditional version, which connected human freedom to the image of a basically empty and totally flexible human mind – the standard social science model – must be forgotten. Innate structures of the human mind make it free. Language is specifically important for Chomsky since it has built-in structural features of indetermination and limitless capabilities that, in a way, are assurances for freedom. They make it sure that limitations of our expressive system will not limit our freedom of thought. The frames of thought themselves come as innate preparations of knowing. Due to this commitment toward innatism, Chomsky's first issue with Skinner was Skinner's image of human flexibility that is connected to the issue of social control over thought.

> In his speculations on human behavior . . . B. F. Skinner offers a particular version of the theory of human malleability. . . . There is little doubt that a theory of human malleability might be put to the service of totalitarian doctrine. If, indeed, freedom and dignity are merely the relic of outdated mystical beliefs, then what objection can there be to narrow and effective controls instituted to ensure "the survival of a culture."
> (Chomsky, 1972a, pp. 12–13)

Chomsky did not accept the positive reinforcement–based optimistic image for the future of society promoted by Skinner either.

> In the delightful culture we have just designed, there should be no aversive consequences. . . . [A]ll behavior would be automatically "good", as required. There would be no punishment. Everyone would be reinforced – differentially, of course, in accordance with ability to obey the rules. Within Skinner's scheme there is no objection to this social order. Rather, it seems close to ideal.
> (Chomsky, 1972a, p. 31)

Daniel Dennett, in a less socially critical manner, also criticized Skinner regarding his two errors: Skinner's rather frivolous extrapolation of laboratory results as analogies to social explanations, and his fear of cognitive theories.

> Skinner is playing the same game with his speculations as the cognitivist who speculates about internal representations of information. Skinner is simply relying on a more cumbersome vocabulary. Skinner has failed to show that psychology without mentalism is either possible or – in his own work – actual, and so he has failed to explode the myths of freedom and dignity.
> (Dennett, 1978a, p. 90)

The most visible success of Skinner's social program was apparent in **behavior therapy**. Pathological and destructive behaviors are to be changed using a consequential reinforcement plan. First, one has to analyze pathological behavior, for example, if you are on a smoking prevention or reduction program and discover when you are most likely to light a cigarette and what the things you are unlikely to do while smoking. After this analysis, the reinforcing bad behavior (lighting a cigarette) should be replaced by another innocent reinforcing behavior (e.g., chewing gum, listening to music). The easiest ones have to be replaced first, and then gradually, one can move on to the most difficult ones, following the principles of shaping. This applied behavioral analysis was to be used in all behavioral and social pathologies. As an alternative to psychoanalytic theories looking for "deep" causes, they represent behavioral therapy as immediate intervention. The charge they had and have to face was that they were treating humans as externally directed beings, and they were only treating symptoms, not the underlying disease. They do not realize that there are "internal" troubles and internal forces as well. This charge is certainly tenable. These factors, however, do not exist in the worldview of Skinner. Their mention is merely a flight to the nonscientific "inner man." Interestingly, the critique of behavior modification was soon to arrive in popular culture. Kubrick's *A Clockwork Orange* in 1971, thus before Skinner's scandalous book, showed how political control uses behavior modification to control criminality (with not too much success). Due to these social representations, behavioral control in the eyes of many was seen in the 1970s as a new authoritarian technology.

As part of the full picture, it is interesting to see that from the 1980s on, cognitive behavioral intervention therapies developed. They are not trying to mix fire and water. They claim to try to change behavior, but on the basis of a more flexible image of man that allows for humans making complex models of their environment.

Toward contemporary experimental psychology: neobehaviorism in the 1950s–1960s

The 1950s were characterized by great changes in European and American society and in the general approaches of psychology as well. On the social level, a general increase in the standards of life and a general "consumerism" with an increased individualism would become typical in Western societies following the Second World War. This overall social change increased the chances of psychology at large and, among other things, the interest toward social engineering. That included the increasing use of psychotherapy and in general social sciences labelled in the American model as behavioral sciences as a key participant in this process. The very term **behavioral science** was coined by James Grier Miller (1916–2002), a clinical psychologist who, after serving as an organizer of clinical psychology services during the Second World War, was a key organizer in many areas of American science policy and worked toward the integration of life sciences and social sciences. Part of this was the new term *behavioral science*, which he shaped and then implemented at the University of Chicago, and on several US national committees, also initiating the journal *Behavioral Science* (see for its system theoretic attitude Miller, 1965) that existed until 1996. The term **behavior science** itself wanted to avoid the bad connotations of the word "social" in the Cold War and wanted to move biological and social sciences nearer to each other. From the 1950s on, as part of this concentration on the psychological mechanisms of social integration, it became central to behaviorist psychology as well to deal with the specificities of social learning. As a continuation of the early work of Neal Miller and Dollard (1941), this went on with Bandura (1962, 1963), who has presented model following imitation as a crucial new mechanism of learning.

All these effects led to new socially relevant proposals of neobehaviorists on the societal side and to a spread, liberalization, and gradual dissolution of neobehaviorism itself. The neobehaviorist way of talk spread to more and more chapters of psychology, and in this process, it had become merely a way of talk, without any ontological commitments. Interestingly, many of the new players were identical with the ones who started their career in the 1930s; thus, names will reappear here. This approach would turn into informal behaviorism, ending with a softened proposal that psychology was an objective science as well. It gradually lost its face, had become a series of chapters, and within experimental psychology, neobehaviorism gradually gave its place to cognitive psychology.

Formalizing learning theory

In the 1950s, the tradition initiated by Hull started to diverge, in line with the two internal factors of the system of Hull himself: one is formal theory formation, and the other is the peculiar liberalizing considerations extending learning theory toward social and personality phenomena. In the 1950s, psychologists also realized the possibilities in the formal apparatus of mathematics for psychology. Hull had a hypothetico-deductive learning theory that had its continuation in **mathematical theories of learning**. William Estes (1919–2011) played a central role in this process. Estes (1950, 1959) and others, in the *Handbook of Mathematical Psychology*, edited by Luce, Bush, and Galanter (1963), tried to generate overall models for different typical learning situations (paired associate training, operant learning, discrimination learning) and tried to fit empirical curves to the derived learning functions. The parametrized postulates of Hull became issues of curb fitting for them. The basic model of Estes (1950, 1959) is a probabilistic sampling. On each occasion, or learning trial, one stimulus aspect is chosen, and thereby learning proceeds because responses are always attached to a different aspect of the stimulus. As the analysis by Gordon Bower (1994) showed half a century later, in a historical regard, Estes, as a student of Skinner, tried to be very general and precise. At the same time, the entire substance of his theory is more similar to Guthrie rather than to Hull or Skinner. In his own time, this attitude was not too popular; it was functional in paving the way for later mentalistic mathematical models in cognitive psychology. Junior people like Richard Atkinson and Richard Shiffrin (1968) and John Anderson and Gordon Bower (1973) in this Estes-type modeling tradition would become central players of cognitive theory from the 1970s on.

The formalization efforts of Hull were continued in a less-extreme manner by Kenneth W. Spence (1907–1967). He was a direct student of Hull and tried to work toward developing a general theory of behavior and learning. His two most important empirical contributions are the analysis of discrimination learning and the elaboration of methods to study human conditioning with the eyelid reaction (Spence, 1956). This later method allowed him and his followers to study the effects of general tension, or as later he and his wife, Janet Taylor-Spence (1923–2015), called it, anxiety effects on learning (Taylor, 1956). Janet Taylor-Spence later became the president both of APA and APS and a leading researcher of gender identity. The attitude of Taylor (at that time an active clinical psychologist as well) and Spence to interpret anxiety as the general drive state of the organism was different from other neobehaviorists like Mowrer (1936, 1950) who derived anxiety from specific fears.

Following the interpretation of D as equivalent to a general tension, or anxiety, with the leadership of Janet Taylor (1956), an entire tradition of studying relations between general tension and human learning developed. Self-reporting questionnaire methods were developed to study the learning effects of anxiety as tension. Then, first in eyelid conditioning situations, then later in more complicated learning and performance situations, they moved toward a learning theory–based typology later followed by Hans Eysenck. This became a second opening for neobehaviorism toward personality psychology, namely, the systematic studies of individual differences in learning as corresponding to typological differences of personality. In a theoretical regard, this step related the two traditions of scientific psychology, the psychometric and the experimental tradition, as contrasted by Cronbach (1957).

The British typology school, led by Eysenck, and the Soviet Pavlovian typologists tried to identify the most important typological differences in parameters of learning; thus, in this regard, they also belong to neobehaviorism, though not to the Hullian type.

Conflicts and personality in learning theory: Neal Miller and Mowrer

The early generation of neobehaviorists in the 1930s lived under two further important external impacts. Due to their travels – as in the case of Tolman – as well as due to their readings, and due to the impact of the European emigrants chased away from Europe by Hitler and his cronies (the later famous identity theorist Erikson was an associate of Hull, for example), they mapped their efforts of learning models for the mind onto personality and individual differences as well. Alongside this, they were also attracted to the entire issue of how to provide a behavioristic account of social phenomena, like prejudice, social group effects, and the like, in the frames of the great social changes taking place in America and the world. In their vision, behavioristic principles could provide quasi-deterministic and developmental explanations for issues studied by clinicians and social psychologists using conceptual frames like the frustration–aggression principle, imitation-based learning, or the transfer and generalization of emotional tensions. The utopian visions of Skinner were only one road to look for social relevance. The Yale people were trying to intervene into social life with actual relevant research.

Though the social engineering aspect was most characteristic of the students of Hull, it was widespread in the liberal commitment of the Tolman circle as well. As in the introduction to his collected papers, his followers describe their ideas as a way to find social pathways, using the cognitive map metaphor:

> All of us in Europe as well as in America, in the Orient as well as in the Occident, must be made calm enough and well-fed enough to be able to develop truly comprehensive maps, or, as Freud would have put it, to be able to learn to live according to the Reality Principle rather than according to the too narrow and too immediate Pleasure Principle. . . . We must, in short, subject our children and ourselves (as the kindly experimenter would his rats) to the optimal conditions of moderate motivation and of an absence of unnecessary frustrations, whenever we put them and ourselves before that great God-given maze which is our human world.
>
> (Tolman, 1951b, pp. vi, xii)

This extension of behavioral principles to everyday life and everyday social phenomena provided a great social weight to the neobehaviorists. Their general efforts were twofold. One can create animal models for general psychodynamic processes, like aggression, identification, and so on, thereby fitting them into a general science of behavior. Second, by analyzing social phenomena, they could really help reduce social tensions.

The Yale Institute of Human Relations

A crucial role was played in this process by the famous Monday-night seminars of Clark Hull at Yale University on the interpretation of psychoanalytic concepts, and especially by the interdisciplinary research center at the same university, the **Institute of Human Relations**. The center was established in the late 1920s. The president of Yale University, Ronald Angell (1929), a champion of functionalism a generation earlier, had a crucial role in its inception. The institute aimed to relate the different humanities, law, sociology, medicine, and psychology for a better understanding of human social matters. A functionalist heritage was also represented by its first organizer, Robert Yerkes. The institute was loosely organized for almost a decade, until Clark Hull took the initiative to reorganize it and to introduce some leadership structure to it. The research initiated by Hull stood for human malleability and the understanding of the effects of social context. Together with the efforts of Kurt Lewin and Gordon Allport, these psychologists campaigned for the use of human relations technology toward the efforts of Rooseveltian **New Deal**, and later for the superiority of democratic society over authoritarian and dictatorial systems like Hitler or Stalin. While the institute originally was to combine efforts of humanities and behavioral sciences, on the final run, psychologists remained its main researchers in organized teams due to the efforts mainly of Clark Hull looking for general explanatory rules of human behavior. The IHR researchers, like many others, relied on mundane knowledge about social organization. Their anchoring point was individual behavior, along with the general individualist commitment of most American social science.

The entire institute was related to the American idea of **progressivism**. Most American social scientists in the 1930–1960s believed in progress. They even treated evolution as progress that can be facilitated by education. Interestingly, as pointed out in detail by an analysis made by Nadine Weidman (1996, 1999), there were some central exceptions to this. Karl Lashley, an important reference figure of the time, was against moving from the laboratory toward social issues, and he was specifically against progressive efforts. He engaged in discussions about this with Hull, but he also campaigned against easy applications of behavioral attitudes at his Harvard home university, specifically against the flirting of scientific psychology with psychoanalysis, and especially against Henry Murray (1938). Lashley saw in all these applications a hidden religious commitment, an idea of volitional spiritual development underlying the American progressivist movements, both in neuroscience and in psychology. Lashley (1923) remained a methodical behaviorist; he allowed for a neural study of consciousness, but he was against anything spiritual and remained ardently anti-religious.

Psychoanalytic thought played a crucial role in the fitting of academic psychology and social issues for two reasons. Psychoanalytic concepts that seemed rather abstract and mystical for behaviorists, such as anxiety, identification, projection, meant an intellectual challenge for the behaviorists. If we can give them a learning theory interpretation based on the individual's life history, then facts highlighted by psychoanalysts may be integrated into a general behavioral theory. The further point was the search for reasons of human destructiveness. As an alternative to the Freudian *death instinct*, something should be found that would not see aggression as an inevitable fate but rather as a result of life history.

One key junior coworker of the Institute was O. H. Mowrer (1907–1982). Mowrer came to Yale after being trained by a radical behaviorist of German origin, Adolf Meyer (see Chapter 11 in Volume 1), and found his interest in social factors in behavior. Mowrer, analyzing the concept of anxiety, arrived at the very central notion of secondary drives.

> In contrast to the older view, which held that anxiety (fear) was an instinctive reaction to phylogenetically predetermined objects or situations, the position here taken is that anxiety is a learned response, occurring to "signals" (conditioned stimuli) that are premonitory of (i.e., have in the past been followed by) situations of injury or pain (unconditioned stimuli). Anxiety is thus basically anticipatory in nature and has great biological utility in that it adaptively motivates living organisms to deal with (prepare for or flee from) traumatic events in advance of their actual occurrence, thereby diminishing their harmful effects. . . . [H]uman beings in particular, show tendencies to behave "irrationally" [regarding anxiety]. . . . Such a "disproportionality of affect" may come about for a variety of reasons, and the analysis of these reasons throws light upon such diverse phenomena as magic, superstition, social exploitation, and the psychoneuroses.
> (Mowrer, 1936, p. 564)

One may see that the concept of *angst* (anxiety) as used by philosophers from Kierkegaard on, and later by clinicians, like Janet (1923), which includes objectless fears, is rather much simplified here. Later, even behavioristic theories would deal with the concept of anxiety in a subtler manner. They believe, however, in finding a life history reduction to anxiety and thereby fit it into the general model of learning theory. The role of Mowrer (1960) over two decades in the formation of experimental psychopathology was crucial in following these early promises.

A similar fate would befall the notion of **aggression** in the hand of the behaviorists. John Dollard (1900–1980), a sociologist and anthropologist with psychoanalytic training from the Berlin Institute, and his many coworkers in their **frustration–aggression hypothesis** based on animal experiments and conceptual analysis, stated that obstacles lead to aggression. "Aggression is always a consequence of frustration. (a) The occurrence of aggressive behavior always presupposes the existence of frustration" and (b) "the existence of frustration always leads to some form of aggression" (Dollard et al., 1939).

Several ramifications followed this over three decades, as Berkowitz (1969) summarized them. Frustration only leads to aggression if the frustration can be interpreted as deliberate, and other reactions to frustration may also come up, like regression, childish behaviors, and fixation of rigid behavior patterns. The theoretical conception in its original form had a clear social policy implication. By reducing the frustration of underprivileged social groups, and by teaching constructive solutions in education, we can reduce social aggression. All this appears at a time when instinctive theories of aggression emphasized the inevitability of aggression and, on the final run, the inevitability of wars.

The social reformer overtone can be heard in the **social learning theory** promoted by Neal Miller and Dollard as well. The psychologist Neal Miller (1909–2002), an associate of Hull at the Institute, and later a leading professor at Yale and Rockefeller Universities, was elected to the American National Academy of Sciences in 1958 for his research on learning from the social mechanisms to the brain and received the highest American science merit order from President Johnson. In the 1930s, Miller started with a behavioristic interpretation of psychoanalytic concepts (Miller, 1941, 1944, 1948). He even spent a year in Vienna on a short training analysis with Heinz Hartman. As he recalled, he could not afford Freud, who was charging 20 dollars per session. Working with the sociologist John Dollard, they analyzed **imitation**. Unlike the traditional conceptions following the mainly instinctual automatic imitation theory promoted by Tarde (1890/1903), they proposed a learning account. They interpreted imitation-like behaviors in rats as being based on secondary rewards from matching with the behavior of the partner. We increase our imitation because "match-dependent behaviors" were reinforced. The book of Miller and Dollard (1941) also presented a social case study of a lynching in the American South, thereby showing a direct link between social behavior theory and social life at large.

Socialization and learning theory

Due to all these efforts on the theoretical level and diligent laboratory work lasting until the 1960s, a huge amount of work accumulated regarding the fine structure of the assumed processes of socialization by the neobehaviorist camp. This analysis of social learning initiated a tradition that connects them historically to the Chicago social behaviorists, like George Herbert Mead, and to the later analysis of social learning in actual social situations in the work of Bandura (1973, 1977) on delayed model imitation in children, and its role in the spreading of aggressive patterns of behavior. This would open the road to many modern studies on imitation.

The two directions initiated in the Yale group by Neal Miller, the study of aggression and imitation, were joined in the imitation studies of Albert Bandura (1925–2021) of Stanford University. His frequently cited studies (Bandura, 1963, 1973, with 4,000 citations) with movie watching and playing dolls showed that children show delayed imitation of the aggressive models. The aggressive hero, if reinforced, becomes a model for children. Hundreds of studies since then elucidate the precise parameters (role of the time, the reinforcement of the model, the peculiarity of actions, etc.). The first theoretical advantage of this study for neobehaviorist theory was a clarification of the explanatory value of imitation. It also stepped over the earlier neobehaviorist interpretation that took imitation merely as an issue of secondary reinforcement. The partner as a model started to play a crucial role. Delayed imitation shall also become an experimental model for the psychoanalytic concept of **identification**.

Regarding the causes of aggression, these studies go beyond frustration and secondary rewards. The issue of symbolic modeling rewards also shows up, where mere imitation would have a reward value for the imitator. This conception raised a new social consciousness. Behavioral research raises the stakes not merely of the parents but of the broader social environment as well. Model following is a powerful source of reward learning. Bandura saw these consequences, and he became involved in trying to revise mass media for decades but later developed a much-cited theory for self-efficacy (Bandura, 1977). This theory basically claims that we may learn to be responsible for our fate. That is, in fact, one of the main goals of psychotherapy according to Bandura: not merely reduce anxiety but increase the feeling of mastery over situations.

Learning theory and psychopathology

Neal Miller (originally with Dollard, later with others) continued his efforts after the war to investigate social processes, personality, and psychopathology with learning theory concepts and methods. Miller (1948) published papers interpreting psychoanalytic concepts, using his ideas about approach–avoidance conflicts. Similarity he was responsible to the generalization of approach and avoidance, replacing approach to situations similar to the ambiguous ones, but less-threatening.

Miller also started to elaborate animal models of conflict phenomena, partly inspired by Lewin (1935). He made precise studies of animal approach avoidance conflicts, with rewarding and punishing the animal in the same place, for example. In a handbook chapter, Miller (1959) gave an entire typology of conflicts and their possible negative effects. The most trivial are the approach–avoidance conflicts (the girls are attractive to the teenage boys, but the boys are also afraid of the girls ridiculing them); there are approach–approach conflicts (choose between going to the movies or to a party), and the most difficult ones are the avoidance–avoidance, no-win situations (e.g., being afraid of a dangerous slope and fearing the mocking by your peers for chickening out). Neurosis in this approach would be interpreted as the result of conflicts and faulty learning of conflict resolution.

For Neal Miller, the early studies on imitation were also related to his psychopathology project. Dollard and Miller (1950) later elaborated one of the founding texts for a behavior-based approach to psychotherapy as well. It is usually typical of the American context that even psychoanalytic theories are reformulated as **disturbances of adaptation**. Smaller behavioral disturbances would gain their explanation in enduring and unmanageable conflict situations, while neurosis as a pathology would be an inability of relearning. The person is unable to relearn new modes of behavior to replace the adaptations acquired in early socialization. This is related to the neurotic paradox. If the patient follows the avoidance behaviors corresponding to early fears in a consequential manner, then the patient will never realize that the fears underlying the avoidance have now become unfounded. In this interpretation, psychotherapy would be a difficult and long process of relearning. Both in the treatment of disorders and in their overcoming, symbolic fears have a central role. Fear is not only a strong secondary acquired drive, but its reduction also functions as reward, and due to this, it can become the foundation of complex learnings.

Dollard and Miller, and Mowrer (1960), worked out this reasoning in more detail. Mowrer paid special attention to the temporal arrangement of rival reinforcements. Maladaptive behaviors may come by unaccepted forms of behavior bringing immediate tension reduction to the person; think of biting your fingernails, or drinking. Later, Mowrer (1961) left the behavioral explanation of psychoanalytic concepts and started with his wife his own school of psychotherapy, called **integrative therapy**. Its essential idea is that the psychoanalytic approach basically explained many neurotic paradoxes by an overly powerful working of inhibition provided by the Superego. In his new approach, Mowrer (1972) started to claim that the causes of anxiety were the neglect of social prohibitions and a feeble working of the superego. His integrative therapy developed a guilt vision of anxiety. People are anxious for what they committed, and their Superego should be strengthened in group work. This, in fact, moved Mowrer close to religious interpretations of mental health.

Besides the animal models of psychoanalytic concepts, the Yale group also took up another feature of the psychoanalytic message. They initiated longitudinal studies on a group of families of the assumed psychanalytic developmental models. Robert Sears (1908–1989), who also participated in the frustration studies and, in 1943, gave a summary of the Yale and other experimental studies of psychoanalytic concepts, later initiated a systematic family study of patterns of child-rearing (Sears et al., 1957), with peculiar attention to the process of identification (Sears, 1959; Sears et al., 1957). Sears was the first to introduce observation of child–parent dyads into the laboratory, which was a key for many later developments in counseling. These studies showing, for example, a preference for mother dolls in girls and a faster development of sex typing in girls, have been very important, if not in testing psychoanalytic concepts – their role in this regard is questioned – then in furthering future research into the determinants of gender behavior differences – done at Stanford (where Sears had moved), mainly by Eleanor Maccoby (1917–2018) (Maccoby & Jacklin, 1974). At Stanford, Sears also became the responsible leader of the longitudinal research on the Terman talented group of longitudinal cohorts.

There is a central principle in these personality and clinical extensions. They start from the necessity to motivate learning, where all **intervention is basically a motivational change**. Its other characteristic is the wide liberalization of concepts of behavior. Stimuli include symbolic stimuli; responses can be central ones (like fear or anxiety). They extend behaviorism toward studying more and more complex environmental determinants, such as conflicts, and at the same time move from the periphery toward postulated internal responses. Miller, in his own work on drive reduction and the nature of reinforcement, moved toward the precise physiological and hormonal mechanisms of these processes. Regarding the complex environmental determination, mediation theories appeared.

Signs and language: specificities of language in neobehaviorism

In the 1920s, there was an alliance between linguistics and behaviorism. This cooperation stopped later with the advent of structural linguistics with its concentration on form. This is paradoxical in the sense that Bloomfield (1926), the initiator of American structural linguistics in his methodical commitments, was a full-fledged behaviorist, seeing linguistic stimuli in a behavioral chain in a social setting. Alongside this, the distributional analysis initiated by him tried to reveal formal structure with no reference to meaning or any subjective aspect. In the renewed interest of some behaviorists toward language, they did not go back to the 1920s early heritage. They mostly started off from a vision of language without too much formal structure, concentrated on meaning along the efforts to widen the behaviorist horizon.

In the 1950s, the interest of behaviorists toward language mainly was individuum-centered. They tried to elaborate constructs that dealt with language on several levels, and basically four different approaches were formed:

- Language as the special issue for learning theories: the verbal learning tradition
- Language as a special kind of operant behavior: Skinner and his followers
- Language and classical conditioning: words and semantic generalization
- Mediation theories of meaning: meaning as internal behavior

The study of verbal learning: a typical empirical extension

One characteristic feature of American experimental psychology in the 1950s was the extension of the behavioristic approach due to its associative commitments to **human verbal learning**. This has become a leading topic, producing thousands of papers over a few decades. The leading researchers did not belong to any neobehaviorist camp. They were sober positivists tied to behaviorist learning theories, and they were studying general rules of learning that were supposed to be valid even over language materials. In fact, they were connecting the classical Ebbinghaus pattern of rote memory research with a behavioristic terminology.

Thorndike (1931, 1932) made efforts in this direction as early as the 1930s. When he tried to find scientific foundations for education, he concentrated on verbal learning, which is what he considered to be the most crucial in school settings. After the war, there were some people with a theoretical bend toward a general interpretation of language in behavioristic terms as verbal behavior. The most radical was, in this regard, Skinner (1957), who tried to develop a fully fledged account of language and its use in operant terms, as seen earlier. There were less-radical people as well. They were behavioral, but without a specific behavior-analytic background. From the 1940s on, in the empirical domain, the behavioristic associationism worked in two directions in the verbal domain.

The study of the formation of associations. The researchers tried to uncover the formation of individual associations in simpler and simpler situations and more and more precisely, the interaction between learnings, and its temporal unfolding.

The paired association method formed half a century earlier by Mary Calkins (1896) and Müller and Pilzecker (1900) was their basic method. The rediscovered advantage of paired associations was its practical similarity to stimulus–response animal learning. When I learn a pair like 6–ZUV or GOAT–LAMP, the first of the pair can be treated as stimulus, and the second verbal element as response. Cofer (Cofer & Musgrave, 1961), James Deese (1965), and many others tried to understand the exact nature of the formation of associations. The issue of similarity in positive and negative transfer was reinterpreted by proposing a multidimensional transfer surface (Osgood, 1949, 1953). The results have become part of the core material of experimental psychology.

At the same time, the simple associationist theoretical presuppositions were gradually questioned. The very researchers who were studying rote learning realized that verbal learning is not legally interpreted as mere "external connection formation." As James Gibson (1960) pointed out in a famous paper, the stimulus is not a nominal category in psychology. In learning a nonsense pair like *zit–lar*, the person learns the pair by relating the syllables to real words, like *sit* and *large*. Subjects both with nonsense and with meaningful materials used self-initiated **mediations** to learn the pairs. They may look for common associates (*bread–KNIFE–scissor*), they may try to form sentences from the words (*dog–CHASED AWAY THE–snake*), or they may try to form a joint mental image corresponding to the word referents (*The dog PISSED on the brick*). Furthermore, as shown first by Bousfield (1953), longer lists are not randomly recalled. The subjects spontaneously categorize the words and put them into categories (*furniture, animals, plants*). Thus, instead of a simple cumulative formation of associations in the studies of verbal learning, **coding** (Melton & Martin, 1972), **mediation** (Jensen & Rohwer, 1963), and **organization** (Mandler, 1967) became key concepts, by which the study of verbal learning turned into the study of memory.

Study of existing verbal associations. The neobehaviorism of the 1950s rediscovered the study of already-existing verbal associations, framed as well with a terminology of (verbal) stimuli and responses. They use mass data not to reveal and interpret individual complexes as Jung and Luria did decades earlier but tried to find structural regularities underlying the statistics of data. Many descriptive works are made on age norms (Palermo & Jenkins, 1964), the statistical parameters of association hierarchies (e.g., rare words are rarely given as answers, frequent words elicit stereotyped responses, and the like; see Deese, 1965). Even new concepts, like information uncertainty, in the sense of Shannon (1948), were introduced. As Laffal (1955) showed in a clinical context, the entropy of associative responses (how varied the reactions are in a population) to a stimulus word correlated with reaction times and with reaction errors. Traditional ideas, like clinical conflicts with a stimulus word, started to have a more statistical foundation.

Two factors have promoted these efforts into new directions, moving beyond the frames of stimulus response psychology. Several efforts were made to provide a **semantic interpretation of associative relations**, even within the behaviorist camp. First, Noble (1952) tried to characterize the meaning of words in a way as the amount of meaningful context they evoke. He developed a measure called meaningfulness that characterized how many words you recall for a given word in one-minute periods. The more contexts recalled, the more meaningful is the target word. Deese (1965) started to study the overlap of associations between words to characterize their meaning similarity. Based on overlap matrices, they started to use multivariate methods to reveal overlap structures in associative fields and, in this way, to arrive at an analysis of underlying semantic structures.

Another approach was the introduction of **linguistic concepts to analyze associative structures**. In the linguistic lore, from the time of Saussure (1922) on, there is a difference between syntagmatic relations that relate words in a sentence, like *boy–walks*, and paradigmatic relations that relate word forms in a grammatical paradigm (*learn, learns, learned*). The Russian American linguist Roman Jakobson (1960) extended these ideas into a broader vision of language with two axes. The axis of selection, the paradigmatic axis, would correspond to meaning relations and in stylistics to metaphor (*John is a pig*), while the syntagmatic axis of combination would correspond to sentence construction and in stylistics to metonymy (*John is a great head*). These ideas were applied to the existing data on word associations. Susan Ervin (1927–2018), at Berkeley (Ervin, 1961), showed that one can analyze the category superordinate associations as paradigmatic ones *(dog–animal)*. Roger Brown and Jean Berko (1960) proposed that, in fact, the move from syntagmatic associations (*cat → sits*) to paradigmatic ones (*cat → dog*) is a movement representing a reorganization of grammar in children. Sentence structure starts with contingent associations and a good memory for strings. As the strings become more numerous, a reorganization into categories follows. Grammar from 4–5 years of age is based on form classes or categories and is no longer a list of strings. In a similar spirit, Palermo and Jenkins (1963, 1964) analyzed the dependency of associations on word class (noun–noun associations are more frequent than verb–verb), and age (older children show more within word class associations). This can, of course, also be given a more semantic and cognitive interpretation as well (Nelson, 1977). The important point is that association that used to be a primitive contingency-based explanatory concept had gradually become not an issue of contingency but more and more a cognitive mirror of semantic and grammatical factors. There are many ramifications, or modulating factors – dependence on age, word class, and so on – but the original simplicity of associations was lost.

The details make part of present-day psychology of human memory organization and psycholinguistics. Association for many stopped to be an explanatory concept. It was becoming merely an important phenomenon and method that, in fact, mirrors complex processes of human memory organization and the mental representation of language. The weight in all the verbal learning tradition moves toward human memory and memory organization. It is very telling that in 1961, they founded a journal for the verbal learning trend, *Journal of Verbal Learning and Verbal Behavior*, as a result of many efforts spanning over a decade long in different national agencies (Committee on Linguistics and Psychology of the Social Science Research Council, the Office of Naval Research, etc., as described by Cofer, 1978). After two decades of its publication, this same journal became the *Journal of Memory and Language* in 1985. This change within one journal's self-identification expresses the move toward cognitive modeling. Neobehaviorist verbal learning gradually became cognitive memory organization.

Mediation theories

All these efforts were characterized by a non-social vision of language. Besides this fact, they were also characterized by a feature that would become crucial in their discussion with the next generation, with the upcoming cognitive psychologists. They were almost exclusively word-centered. Sentence and pure formal syntactic (grammatically based) organization were not important for them. The role of syntax would be the crucial issue in most of their discussions with the next generation.

Mowrer, in his later works, as professor at Harvard and later at the University of Illinois, went further along the inspiration he received in the Yale group and from Hull. He proposed that, in more complex serial behaviors, anticipation of the final goal-related behavior might be an important internal stimulation for the regulation of behavior. Mowrer (1947, 1960), in his two-factor theory of learning, already claimed an important class of mediators. In a situation, we learn to associate **hope** or **fear** to the situation, and by the principles of instrumental learning, we connect approach or avoidance behaviors to these internal tensions. In this two-step system, the use of signs has a central role. Images – he is the first among behaviorists to talk about images (Mowrer, 1960) – and words are tools for a delayed and also for an anticipated direction of behavior. They allow for displacement. They allow the human organism not to be a prisoner of immediate environmental conditions. In talking about language as a communicative system, Mowrer concentrated on the motivational and emotional aspect of language use.

He speculated on how secondary rewards can be based on language structure in children. He proposed to analyze language where emotional values are transmitted from one stimulus to another, as by a very efficient secondary-drive learning device. Even language structure serves in his vision as a very efficient device of classical conditioning. He expressed these visions at a talk presented as president of the American Psychological Association (Mowrer, 1954).

> The sentence is eminently a conditioning device, and its effect is to produce new associations, new learnings as any other paired presentation of stimuli may do. This position is congruent with the traditional notion in line with the traditional linguistic idea that predication is the essence of language.
> (Mowrer, 1954, p. 666)

Conditioning meaning and semantic conditioning

Partly due to the success of Mowrer, but also partly due to indigenous developments, the 1950s–1960s neobehaviorist approaches to language are characterized by several lines of research that aim to study word meaning with learning theory methods. They are mainly in line with the approach of the last years of the work of Pavlov about the second signaling system. Pavlov postulated that the working of the analyzers creates a system of signs, and in humans, words, as signs of these signs, develop a **second signaling system**. This had become the starting point for an entire movement of research analyzing lexical phenomena and the acquisition of words by methodologies related to conditioned reflexes. The Russian-born American psychophysiologist Razran (1939) showed this kind of conditioning early on. He started off with very straightforward studies. He studied his own salivary reactions to the word *saliva* in different languages he spoke. Later, he was projecting words while the subjects were eating and checked the salivation to the associated words, their synonyms and homophones. Razran also reported on the relevant Russian research in detail. Conditioning to a physical stimulus, say, a red lamp, was generalized to the word denoting the stimulus, *red*, and then the salivary or vascular reactions were also transferred between two languages, for example. Luria and Vinogradova (1959) used this type of approach to language in a systematic manner when they showed that conditioned vascular reactions after a weak electric shock to a verbal stimulus, like *violin*, can be shown to generalize to other stimuli, depending on the similarity of their meaning. There was more response generalization from *violin* to *brass* than to *saxophone*. These generalizations based on semantic organization were much stronger than generalizations based on sound similarity (*violin–volition*). The most important point in all these studies was that they did not, in fact, equate the meaning of a word with the reaction conditioned to it; they only suggested that by conditioning techniques, the semantic relations between words can be studied. Levelt (2013) provides a modern evaluation of these studies of semantic conditioning for the interest toward meaning. These studies introduced the idea of a systematic investigation of semantic organization by quantitative measures. This was carried further in the mediation theory proposed by Charles Osgood.

Charles Osgood and the measurement of meaning

Charles Egerton Osgood (1916–1991), the very influential professor of Illinois University, continued the mediation ideas toward a more elaborate system and tied it to a very successful method to study meanings. Osgood was a student of Hull at Yale and a follower of his system at Illinois University. As a young assistant at Yale, he had already had important tasks during the war – to teach instead of contribute to the war effort, as some of his colleagues had been doing. His textbook based on his teachings and published in 1953 became a bible for the Hullian trend. He organized all the material as material about the science of behavior organization on different levels. He was a very successful scholar and was elected to the National Academy of Sciences in 1972.

According to his later elaborated theory (1957), behavioral organization has three levels. On the **projection level** (the name came from the primary sensory projection areas of the nervous system), simple associative learning, conditioning, goes on. On the **integration level**, larger perceptual units are formed (Osgood allocated *Gestalt* organization to this level, too, but even sentences and syntax belong here), and complex skill formation goes on. Prediction-based organization would characterize this level. The peculiar level for human behavior is the **representational level**. Stimuli obtain meaning on this level, and regulation goes on through signs and through considering the behavior of others. At this level, the fractional goal reaction proposed by Hull comes in. The meanings of signs on the representational level will be those fractions of movements that are most specific to the referential stimuli corresponding to the sign. Thus, for the word *ball,* the fractions of kicking and throwing movements that are associated with real balls will be crucial. This conception is summarized on Figure 8.8.

There were two interesting consequences of this vision of behavioral organization for the psychological interpretation of language. The first one was more theoretical, the second one more practical, with many follow-ups. The sentence-like organization of language that, by the early 1960s, had become crucial for the new cognitive movement in psychology was treated by Osgood as belonging to the integrative level. He treated sequential organization basically as a predictive skill, like probabilistic structuring (Osgood, 1963). This proposal was rather negatively interpreted by the then new mentalistic and grammar-centered cognitive movements which, along the lines of the planning conception proposed by Miller et al. (1960), saw in sentences the basic form of a structure-based holistic planning rather than "mere prediction." Osgood even created sentence elicitation protocols, where he tried to prove that sentence organization is, in fact, much more dependent on the eliciting contexts than expected by purely grammatical theories. He claimed provocatively for the new generation of cognitive psycholinguists that syntax is

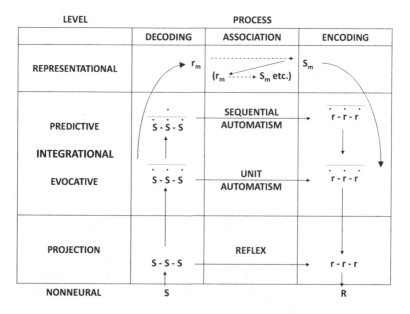

Figure 8.8 The three levels of behavioral organization in the vision of Osgood.
Source: Redrawn based on Osgood (1963 Figure 4, p. 740).

not central but rather peripheral to language. You have to care about elicitation of sentences and their meaning.

The other idea was the extension of the "pure stimulus acts" proposed by Hull into an elaborate theory of **representative mediation**. In his vision, words as signs obtain their meaning by these representative movements. In Illinois, Osgood was heavily involved with the newly formed communication research, and he tried to combine his behavioral mediation theory with developing a universal tool to measure meaning. His basic methodical twist was to interpret meaning in the terms of the American pragmatist Morris (1938) in dispositional terms and find a purely linguistic index for mediation reactions. This was a theoretical difficult *tour de force:* measuring implicit behaviors with the use of words. It meant to characterize the meaning of a word by other words. This is made possible by the fact that many of our words obtain their meaning by taking over parts of the meanings of other words. In this way, we may study the meaning of words with the help of other words. Osgood started to use and refine the scaling techniques already applied in much of social psychology of attitudes by that time. He simplified the scales as pairs of opposed adjectives and assumed that by a metaphorical usage of these adjectival pairs, all concepts or words can be assigned a place in these polar adjective spaces.

From the viewpoint of experimental semantics, this both opens the possibility of measuring meaning in general objectively and specifies factor analysis as the basic methodology. The method he developed came to be known as **semantic differential** (Osgood, Suci, Tannenbaum, 1957). Though Osgood conceived these general scales as being "reflections (in language) of the sensory differentiations made possible by the human nervous system," they turned out to be rather universal emotional components of connotative meaning in fact, which even he acknowledged, claiming it an evaluation of "an affective meaning systems."

```
              DOG
good   : : : : :  : : : bad
strong : : : : :  : : : weak
soft   : : : : :  : : : hard
```

The method, with a large-enough number of adjective pairs and to-be-judged concepts, and subjected to factor analysis, arrived at the conclusion that the (emotional) meaning of words has three basic components, **evaluation (E)**, **potency (P)**, and **activity (A)** (Osgood et al., 1957). Since then, it has become one of the most widespread methods in attitude and marketing research. We can decide if it is *hard* or *soft* about a shaving kit or a politician as well, not only about words. In social psychology, the method has been a central player in the method and theory of congruence between different attitude objects, with a proposition that, in fact, the more polarized attitude objects undergo more change. "Interacting elements are modified in inverse proportion to their intensity or polarization" (Osgood, 1960, p. 356).

Osgood extended the method for cross-cultural studies as well (Osgood et al., 1975). His team showed that these dimensions of emotional evaluation of objects and words are rather universal, though the evaluation of a given object or word varies between cultures, and even between individuals. The three dimensions of emotional meaning more or less correspond to classical theories of emotion dimensions, like already Wundt (1897) proposed. The concepts themselves are then represented in a virtual semantic space, corresponding to the distances of the emotional meanings.

The semantic differential method was very popular from the 1960s to the 1980s, with over 2,000 papers published in two decades; and it is even used in the present day, with 1,000 papers published over the last two decades. (The original book has more than 20,000 references.) Osgood has become a well-respected figure in the mass communication and social policy scenes as well. Besides his work on attitude change, he also presented a Cold War–inspired book on international tensions and their possible reduction strategies (Osgood, 1962). He proposed a trust-based stepping down of nuclear arms that is pretty much what happened half a century later. From the 1960s on – besides his methodical cross-cultural work in the area of language and the forming new psycholinguistics – Osgood defended the neobehaviorist stance against the new generation of cognitivists. He always emphasized that the central matter in language was meaning, rather than syntactic form, as the new generation suggested. Interestingly, recent neurobiology of language partially proved Osgood to be right, and even the proposals of a follower of Osgood, the Hungarian Jenő Putnoky (1979), regarding the action-specific representation of some words. Pulvermüller (2002), using evoked potential and brain imaging data, showed that there was some specificity of the brain representation of meaning related to movement, at least in movement verbs. Words like *throw* involved much more than the motor cortex parts representing the arms, while *kick*-type words were involving more the representation if the legs. While he connects this to the cell assembly theory of Hebb (1949), we can see connections to the motor meaning theory of Osgood. Similarly, regarding the opinion promoted by Osgood (1957, 1963) that syntax belonged to the predictive skill like organization of mental buildup, there are some new theories in psycholinguistics. Ullman (2001) claimed that the sentence-producing machinery is basically skill-like, related to a procedural memory system, and partially to basal ganglia.

The attitude of Osgood to provide broad, across-the-board quantitative measures of meaning had many non-cognitivist followers. Alternative attempts to measure meaning were initiated. The very idea that the words of a language can be arranged along a few dimensions had two inspirations. One was the structural semantics of the linguists and philosophers, with their hierarchical structures (Katz & Fodor, 1963), and the semantic differential technique introduced by Osgood. Allan Paivio (1925–2016) would refresh the image-based approach to meaning. He proposed that words can be characterized by how vividly they remind us of sensory images (**imagery value**). Here again, we have an effort toward quantification. What matters in the approach of Paivio (1971) is not the qualitative nature of the image activated but their "strength." He supported his theory by scaling methods and by memory recall experiments claiming a **dual-coding** approach. Abstract words like *freedom* only have a verbal coding for their meaning, while concrete words would both have a verbal and an imagery coding (Paivio, 1971, 1986, 2007). The Hungarian psycholinguist Jenő Putnoky (1928–1982) in a way combined the approaches of Paivio and Osgood. He returned in a unique way to the original **motoric ideas** implied in the initial theory of Osgood. He asked people to judge the *motority value* (action-evoking value) of words. He pointed out that instead of the rather-empty verbal codes proposed by Paivio, abstract words are accompanied by strong internal movement representations and acoustic images (Putnoky, 1979). It is also remarkable that the image–movement debates started by students of Hull and Tolman would come back in several form in cognitive psychology. Besides the dual coding, the analogue and propositional representation debates between Kosslyn (1994; Kosslyn & Pomerantz, 1977) and Pylyshyn (1973, 1981, 2003) also repeat this original tension. It seems to be that the relations between sensual and abstract come up in all theoretical engagements.

Information theory and psychology: statistical behaviorism

Regarding the intellectual fate of neobehaviorism, a crucial factor was that, during the Second World War, and later, during the Cold War, many American and British experimentalists came into close contact with the issues of complex machine–human interactions and constraints on technological communication in difficult circumstances. The new mathematical chapters and technologies of **information theory and cybernetics** provided the frames for these ergonomic contexts. The essential aspect of the theory proposed by Shannon (1948; Shannon & Weaver, 1949) had a threefold message for psychologists. First, signals can be dealt with merely as signals irrespective of their meanings in a communication system. Second, the notions of a probabilistic approach to psychology, which showed up in the work of Brunswik, would have a more systematic treatment. Many psychological processes of perception and decision, even sensory thresholds, would be interpreted in the frame of this probability-based approach. Information value of individual signals, average value of signals in a system, entropy values in transmission appeared in the characterization of stimuli. Third, the substantial communication model of Shannon would be taken first as a model for the psychology of communication (Osgood & Sebeok, 1954) and later as a model of all internal processes of coding, information transfer, etc.

As MacKay (2003) presented these principles two generations later:

1. A communication *system* requires a sender and a receiver to be in possession of a source code defining the scope of the possible messages that can be transmitted.
2. Communication across the system is not concerned with the *meaning* of messages. In a Shannon system, the receiver *reconstructs* the source message from the received signal by *discriminating* the source message from other possible messages.

The information value of the signs can be characterized by the amount of uncertainty they reduce in the receiver when they arrive. Thus, the information value of an alphabetic letter is higher than that of a numeric character. Another factor is the probability distribution. If the signs have an equal distribution, their average information value is higher compared to the situation when there is a very likely, high probability. Another feature is the internal relations in sequences of signals. A signal coming after another one with high probability has less information value compared to a randomly appearing sign in a sequence. If an English word starts with the letters *pr*, *o* follows with high probability, thus carries little information, while *o* in the middle of words has higher information value, because it is less predictable.

Psychologists soon realized the attractiveness of this seemingly merely technical theory. Already during the war, they initiated researches that were interested in the human ability to tolerate signal distortions (rhythmic interruptions, filtering high or low pitch, etc.) and how one could increase the transmission capabilities of the technical channels (Miller, 1951, summarized these in an influential textbook). A typical further general issue was what the limits of information transmission and storage are. Are they in accord with the quantity of information (statistical predictability) or to some another parameter, like the number of elements, the magical number 7 plus or minus 2 (Miller, 1956)? With new experiments and with a reanalysis of many old data, Hick (1952) observed that reaction time in choice situations was a function of the logarithm of the number of alternatives, thus basically a function of the average information value of each stimulus.

In the United States, in the works of George Miller (1951), and in England, in the new research unit of the medical research council led by Donald Broadbent (1958) and animated by Colin Cherry, a peculiar statistical behaviorism was formed. Miller published a book that summarizes all the new and classic materials of frequency and in general statistical approaches to the perception of linguistic signs. In his preface, he tried to define this statistical behaviorism in a metaphorical manner.

> We are objective but take patterning of stimuli seriously. Psychological interest in patterning is traditionally subjective, but not necessarily so. Discussion of the patterning of symbols and the influences of context run through the manuscript like clotheslines on which the variegated laundry of language and communication is hung out to dry. It is not pleasant to think that these clotheslines must be made from the sand of subjectivity.
> (Miller, 1951, pp. v–vi)

This kind of statistical behaviorism concentrated on the communication metaphor, even for internal processes, and started to treat humans as information-processing systems. Only a single leap from here would be the vision of cognitive psychology, which is a leap that would be made by many, including Miller and Broadbent themselves. Statistical behaviorists did not open yet the black box between input and output; they merely renamed stimulus and response as input and output. The mathematical model was used to characterize the relations between the stimulus situation and behavior, and the upcoming cognitive approach would easily open this black box. Chapter 9 on cognitive psychology shows the persistence of information theoretic notions even in cognitive psychology.

Neurophysiology in neobehaviorism

In the 1950s, it became clear again that the explanations in behavioral psychology must have close ties with development in thoughts about neurophysiology. (Neuroscience as an integrative field and a label only came in the 1960s.) There was a new recognition of a brain–mind unity, if not identity. Psychologists realized that they use a hidden system of presuppositions about the working of the nervous system when they do not state this explicitly. This is referred to by Skinner (1938) slightly ironically, and by Hebb (1949) programmatically, as a **conceptual nervous system**, CNS. New developments regarding the nervous system led to a change in this vision of conceptual nervous system. This had several components:

1. **Development of research technologies over the intact brain.** Watson and, partially, Skinner were right for a while that "brain talk" was merely imaginary. The new technologies changed this situation. Electroencephalography was only started by Hans Berger in 1929, and its brand journal, *J of Electroencephalography and Clinical Neurophysiology* in 1949. EEG now has over 30,000 entries in the PsycINFO database, but it only started to appear in 1938. In the 1950s, there were already a thousand papers about the method. EEG recordings would be supplemented with studies of event-related brain potentials (ERP) and finer movement registrations, like eye movement recordings. These technologies allowed direct observations of the workings of the brain. Thus, the methodical doubts about the speculative nature of central – as opposed to peripheral – theories were becoming unfounded overreactions.
2. **Spontaneous activity.** Activation and active search behavior, and related ideas about optimal stimulation, came up in the 1950s. The 1950s centered on the idea of animals and humans being active beings. This figured in the theories of activation mechanisms started in neurophysiology (Moruzzi & Magoun, 1949). It continued in the theories of curiosity and its role in learning (Berlyne, 1954), as well as the importance of manipulation as a drive (Harlow et al., 1950). Active models of perception also showed up from animal deprivation studies, proving that active movement was crucial for visual development in animals and humans (Held & Hein, 1958, 1963) extended to human speech perception. The non-orthodox visions of human behavior were united in a feeling of looking for **more activity in humans**.

The Canadian psychologist Donald O. Hebb (1904–1985) was central in highlighting the energetic aspect of behavioral regulation. He was, among others, a student of Karl Lashley and Penfield, the famous Canadian neurosurgeon. At McGill University, alongside his students, he built up an approach of theoretical neuropsychology that combined behavioral studies with an interest toward neuronal models and the upcoming ethology. (For an evaluation of his importance see Brown & Milner, 2003.) Both regarding functioning of the mind/brain and regarding development, they centered on the optimal level of stimulation. Stimuli do not only direct the behavior but are also important to assure an optimal level of arousal. Another leading topic would be the issue of activity and tension regulation through optimal developmental stimulation. From sensory deprivation effects to the long-term issue of the importance of environmental and social stimulation in development (Hebb, 1949) and, on the short scale, the optimal tension in efficiency (Hebb, 1955) all showcase that there is a non-trivial regulatory system, not merely particular acquired pieces of behavior.

Regarding the activation continuum, they proposed a theory about the middle-level optimal stimulations. An old recognition, the inverted U-shaped relation between tensions and performance, the so-called Yerkes–Dodson Law (Yerkes & Dodson, 1908), obtained a more physiological interpretation. Through the concept of activation, the notion of attention comes back to behaviorally minded psychology, and the notion of orienting reaction proposed by Pavlov and his followers obtained a new interpretation. Orienting reaction is a phasic change in the activation continuum, and its habituation, its diminishing through repetition, would be interpreted as an indication that a neuronal model of the stimulus was formed. The Soviet Russian E. N. Sokolov (1920–2008) and the Hungarian Endre Grastyán (1924–1988) moved the activation issue into the center of learning and memory. In the interpretation of Sokolov (1960, 1975), the essential aspect of learning is the formation of neuronal model of the stimulus and habituation under repeated stimulation shows this formation in a selective manner. Grastyán (1961) pointed out by neurophysiological electric markers (theta waves in the hippocampus of animals) that the basis of orienting reactions was the non-correspondence between expectations and the present stimulus. Later, he developed a cognitive sign learning theory where the essence of all learning was interpreted as a new orientation in the environment based on signs (Grastyán & Buzsáky, 1979).

Endre Grastyán (1967) pointed out that at some stages of learning, increase of tension leads to learning. Later, people would suggest that this corresponds to orientation and latent learning, all that the 1930s "cognitivists" highlighted. In general, from a psychological and a neuroscience perspective as well, orientation and curiosity, that is, tension-increasing factors, are also central to learning.

Psychologists meanwhile elaborated in detail the ecological stimulus characteristics of **orientation-evoking stimuli**. Daniel Berlyne (1924–1976), working with Hebb in Canada, pointed out that besides novelty, incongruity, ambiguity, and complexity were also important in evoking orientation. He named them **collative variables**. Berlyne (1960) even initiated a new experimental esthetics based on these factors as bases for preference.

This new vision of humans as being oriented toward novelty and increasing tension challenged the dominant drive reductionist vision of the neobehaviorists. It seemed to be that some behaviors are preserved and reinforced exactly because they have a **drive induction** value. Many animal studies also showed that in mammals there is a preference for novelty and a corresponding **exploration drive** that step over the traditional homeostatic image of motivation regulation (Harlow et al., 1950; Montgomery, 1954).

As an extension of this interest toward optimal stimulation, the issue of critical periods of developmental sensitivity, this notion of embryology and ethology shows up in explaining psychological maturational changes as well (Scott, 1962).

3. **Physiology of motivation.** In the 1950s, the starting point for the physiological interpretation of motivation was the **drive reduction principle**. Neuroscientists and psychologists were looking for the possible neurophysiological mechanisms and sites responsible for it. The new technologies of immediate electrical and chemical stimulation, extirpation, and activity recording with implanted electrodes in the hypothalamus and other phylogenetically ancient parts of the brain. This was greatly facilitated by an accidental discovery in 1954 in the laboratory of McGill that, for the direct stimulation of some brain parts, animals are willing to work and learn. This **self-stimulation** (Olds & Milner, 1954) helped clarify many details of the motivation systems in the midbrain. Centers for hunger and satiation were revealed. It was revealed that the neural organization of motivated behavior was also twofold. Experience mainly has an influence on appetitive, preparatory phases, like learning the incentive value of stimuli, while less on the consummative phases. With these interpretations, a connection was made among three conceptions: the classical vision of motivated behavior originating from Wallace Craig (1918), the modern ethological visions promoted by Konrad Lorenz (1965), and psychophysiology of motivation. Physiologically minded interpretations spent a lot of time in trying to interpret the drive reduction concept, to test the role of consumption, to observe reduction of hunger, to analyze their brain centers, and so on (Neal Miller, 1957). The issue that sometimes tension increase has a reinforcing value was also raised (Miller, 1963).

4. **The modeling function of the nervous system.** By the 1950s, neuropsychological models which, while emphasizing the central nervous components of behavior regulation, simultaneously highlighted the regulatory role of neural representations instead of immediate reflex regulation. Karl Lashley was responsible with his extirpation studies for a **mass action** and **equipotentiality** interpretation of the relationships between learning ability and the cerebral cortex: there is no strict localization of functions, and the entire cortex is responsible for animal intelligence (Lashley, 1929, 1950). He presented a very influential talk on serial order claiming that even to explain co-articulation effects or speech errors, one has to postulate neural representations rather than mere reflex chains. Sequential behavior moves too fast and is too finely tuned to the context to be merely regulated by chain reflexes. Chain reflexes could not account, for

example, for anticipatory errors, that is, for the fact that something coming later has an influence on behavior. Behavior in speaking or music is too fast-changing to have a simple sensory feedback control.

Any theory of grammatical form which ascribes it to direct associative linkage of the words of the sentence overlooks the essential structure of speech. The individual items of the temporal series do not in themselves have a temporal "valence" in their associative connections with other elements. The order is imposed by some other agent.

(Lashley, 1951, p. 116)

The issue of syntax is true of all complex movements.

Finger strokes of a musician may reach sixteen per second in passages which call for a definite and changing order of successive finger movements. The succession of movements is too quick even for visual reaction time. . . . Sensory control of movement seems to be ruled out in such acts. They require the postulation of some central nervous mechanism which fires with predetermined intensity and duration or activates different muscles in predetermined order.

(Lashley, 1951, p. 123)

Lashley's presentation at a high-profile neuroscience symposium, the so-called Hixon symposium, had a wide effect. The audience was full of leading computer modeling and neuroscience people, like John von Neumann, Lorente de No, McCulloch, and so on. D. O. Hebb had a more detailed presentation of the neural theory of representation. In his conception first spelled out in his theoretical book in 1949 *The organization of behavior*, he claimed that for cognitive organization, the cortical cell assemblies responsible for them are characterized by working more and more detached from immediate stimulus dependency. These cell assemblies would form the basis of mediating reactions. In the phylogenetic development of mammals, behavior would become more and more dependent on internal representations provided by cortical control (Hebb, 1949, 1958, 1960). Delayed reaction, detour behavior, and other seemingly simple behaviors require the supposition of representational factors in animals as well. Due to these factors, one can talk about the conception of Hebb as a representation-based neurophysiology. With his emphasis on less stimulus dependency in primates and an increase of the role of representations in directing behavior, Hebb prepared the way for many later cognitive psychologists. In his own time, he emphasized looking for a harmony between our conceptual nervous systems and theories of behavior. In learning, for example, they emphasized expectation learning and mental maps. Personality is more and more interpreted as an integral unity of internal models and attached evaluations. In the 1960s, these more flexible behaviorists came into contact with theories of spontaneous behaviors, and with ethology. With the exception of Skinner's followers, the conceptual apparatus of neobehaviorists had become so liberal and sometimes so loose that, after a while, the terminology of cognitive psychology was almost a simplification by the mid-1960s.

Neobehaviorism as a school is more or less finished by now. However, the objectivism introduced by behaviorism, the idea that all our models have to be anchored in behavioral data, has remained with us; furthermore, the idea of having some universal basic types of learning and modification of behavior has also remained with us as stable heritages.

Tasks

CA

Compare imitation in Tarde, Miller, and Bandura!
Neuroreductionism in Skinner and Hebb.
The Skinner–Chomsky controversy.
Psychoanalysis in neobehaviorist interpretation.
Compare the social message of Skinner and the Yale group!
The concept of "meaning" in different neobehaviorists.
What is meant by "descriptive" in Skinner's descriptive behaviorism?
The concept of anxiety in neobehaviorism and psychoanalysis.
Movements in mediation theories.
Compare the statistical ideas of Brunswik with information theory!

DSA

"Learning theory" and "conditioning" in common discourse (Google Ngram).
Skinner, Osgood, and Badura from the 1960s in public discourse (Google Ngram).
Hebb and Lashley from 1950 to 2000 in psychology (PsycINFO).
Cooccurrences of "statistics" and "information" theory in psychological texts (PsycINFO).
"Aggression" and "imitation" over a hundred years in psychology (PsycINFO).
"Instinct and "drive" in neobehaviorist texts.
Hull and Tolman between 1950 and 2000 in the psychological literature (PsycINFO).
Compare Hebb and Osgood in the psychological literature (PsycINFO).

9 The transformations of experimental psychology
Birth and destiny of cognitive psychology

> *We can now imagine . . . a psychology which exhibits quite complex cognitive processes as being constructed from elementary manipulations of symbols.*
> (Fodor, 1985, p. 98)

The cognitive revolution

The generation of American psychologists that matured in the 1950s and 1960s experienced a challenging and non-trivial shift of methodologies and concepts of modern experimental psychology, **the cognitive revolution** (Baars, 1986; Greenwood, 1999). This movement partly overlapped with the blooming of neobehaviorism. These accounts, together with some autobiographical notes (Bruner, 1983; Miller, 2003), showed that the human mind has a real existence, and that there are scientific ways to study the mind without losing the objectivity professed by behaviorism and the then-governing positivist philosophy.

As Gardner (1985) summarized the participants' point of view, the precondition for the cognitive revolution was a disappointment with and a motivated rejection of behaviorism. In the eyes of the protagonists, there was a dramatic shift of interest and terminology between the 1960s and 1980s. The weight of research moved over to studies of so-called higher mental processes in human subjects, such as perception, memory, language, and thought. In this attitude, the basic determinant of behavior was to be the interpretation of the world, the internal model of the environment, rather than a non-interpreted stimulus automatically evoking a response. It always went beyond the information given (Bruner, 1974). Cognitive psychology was felt to be a new scientific paradigm or model – a "revolution," not merely as a series of new chapters or new contents, like perception, attention, and memory.

The essential novelty was the rediscovery of **humans as knowers**. A vision was gradually created according to which **humans can be seen as actively modeling the environment**, and human behavior can only be understood with reference to these models. Most of cognitive psychology did not really question the practical functionalism transpiring in most modern psychology. The internal models should not be interpreted in themselves, but they should be interpreted as serving the functions of adaptation. In a way, this was a reintroduction of folk psychology. However, because of the machine-inspired technological way of talk, folk psychology

DOI: 10.4324/9781032625805-11

was reintroduced by the first generation of cognitivists as if they were using the physical stance rather than the intentional stance.

Events and dates in the self-image of the birth of cognitive psychology

The new theory of mental representations also included the very productive image of treating all laymen, every human being, as a theory builder. Jerome Bruner (1984, p. 5), one of the path breakers in his recollections on the cognitive revolution, also claimed that they

> construct models that stand for or represent some kind of reality – models which in theory are used to construct or stipulate the nature of the world we cannot know directly. These models are not only in the heads of the scientist at work but also in the head of every human being.

Similar ideas were proposed early on in a popularization talk by George Miller (1963, p. 150) at the time of the cognitive shift. "The scientist is Everyman, looking just as you and me. We go and look for the things we want, and when we find them, we find part of ourselves." This parallel of cognition in everyman and the work of scientist recurs in the history of cognitive research. A further "democratization" move would come when cognitive developmental research starts to talk about babies as being scientists (Gopnik et al., 1999).

There are several accounts of the factors and characteristics of the assumed changes and steps in the changes. Segal and Lachman (1972), in an early paper written at the very time of these changes, listed information theory, modern linguistics, changes in the formal sciences like logic and mathematics, and the attraction of computer models as external scientific factors. The repulsive factor was the persistence of obsolete concepts in behaviorist rhetoric, that people were talking about "response produces cues" instead of memory and thinking. Table 9.1 indicates some of the converging influences that encouraged as well as motivated the first generation of cognitivists within psychology to break away from the behaviorist credo.

Table 9.1 Important factors in forming the modeling approach of cognitive psychology

Field	Impact incentive
Behaviorism	Objectivity: input–output analysis
	Softening of theories
	Rejection of clumsy terminology
Perceptual research	New look
	Gestalt theory
Information theory	Quantitative description of communication
Cybernetics	Regulation, feedback, modeling
Mathematics	Algebraic structures, axiomatization
Computer science	Machine analogy: flowcharts
Linguistics	Mentalism: structures and rules
Ethology	Innate modeling, releasers
Radio technology	Information processing, coding

George Miller (2003) considered 1956 to be an *annus mirabilis*. Miller listed many AI conferences, the important book by Bruner et al. (1956) on concept formation, and his own paper on the limitations of human information processing as pointing toward the "cognitive revolution" (Miller, 1956). Miller also gave a special moment of inception as well as the birth date of the cognitive move. According to his account, the moment was a conference in the fall of 1956, on September 11, the second day at a "symposium organized by the 'Special Interest Group in Information Theory' at the Massachusetts Institute of Technology" (Miller, 2003, p. 142). Here, the new cognitive psychologists, such as Miller himself, the linguists represented by Chomsky, and the researchers of the new computer approaches to thought represented by Newell et al. (1958) problem-solving programs met: "1956 could be taken as the critical year for the development of information processing psychology." This account is shared by Gardner (1985) based on interviews with the participants.

The earlier interdisciplinary efforts at Yale and Harvard tried to coordinate psychology with the social sciences in line with proposals promoted by Gordon Allport, Neal Miller, and other social-minded psychologists. The novelty of the new cognitive center at Harvard was its focus on the mind and adoption of methods from the signal technology fields and the formalized humanities, like modern linguistics. Interdisciplinarity meant socially for the psychologists a liberation from power struggles and relations in established departments. Technically, for the psychologists, this meant an assistance from other fields in describing their stimuli (for example, linguistic analysis to describe language stimuli) and incorporating models from other disciplines, for example, models of economic rationality, into the interpretation of their psychological results. For Bruner and Miller, this was a continuation of the interdisciplinary wartime research projects (Cohen-Cole, 2007). In an interesting manner, with all the interdisciplinarity, psychology remained at the center even in the move toward cognitive science (see Chapter 10).

Biography

A most flexible mathematical psychologist: George Armitage Miller (1920–2012)

George Armitage Miller, professor at Harvard at the time of the "cognitive revolution," and later at Princeton, was a key player in the cognitive field. He started working at the Harvard psychoacoustic laboratory for military signal processing. His book (Miller, 1951) was a summary of the inspiration of information theory toward psychology. It shows the continuity between a purely statistical and a mentalistic formalism in the work of Miller, but in the entire cognitive movement as well. In 1955, again at Harvard, he produced his citation classic – 40,000 citations in early 2023 according to Google Scholar – on the "magical number seven" and the limits of human information processing (Miller, 1956). In this survey paper, Miller showed that our capacities are limited both in perceptual units, in short-term memory, and in assigning stimuli to categories. The limits are not related to the amount of information conveyed but to the number of categories and/or chunks. He mockingly mentioned that this goes together with famous sevens in cultural history, like seven sins, seven daughters, seven dwarfs, etc.

Miller, in alliance with Bruner at Harvard, avoided the tensions in experimental psychology between Skinner and Stevens, the descriptive behaviorist, and the human psychophysicist, and as a strategic move they launched the first leading center of cognitive studies. In its frames, Miller published a theoretical book that argued for the postulation of pre-existing PLANS of behavior, starting from simple movements to complex plans of chess playing, or language (Miller et al., 1960). He started to collaborate with Noam Chomsky, the leading linguist of the new generation, on a theoretical foundation of how to move formal grammar into the individual mind (Chomsky & Miller, 1963). At the same time, Miller started the formal grammar-inspired studies of sentence processing while still at Harvard. His students at Harvard were to become central in cognitive research, like Susan Carey, Roger Shepard, Donald Norman, and most importantly, the psycholinguists Tom Bever and Jacques Mehler. These first-generation cognitive students would become the new mainstream generation of theoretical cognitive psychologists and sentence processing psycholinguists. Miller also initiated the earliest studies of artificial grammar learning at Harvard in order to investigate the role of structural constraints in grammar in the learning process. He was not too lucky with the issues of development and children. Both the *Grammarama* project of learning artificial grammars and his later efforts to introduce video recording into the study of child development remained unsuccessful dreams. Miller moved to Princeton University. His interest in Princeton turned toward words – both how children learn them and how they are represented in the mind (Miller, 1991). As part of this interest, Miller was a founder of the WordNet (https://wordnet.princeton.edu/) project of theoretical and applied digital lexicography. This is a computer linguistics enterprise that reflects the internal structures of the lexicon of languages by creating a network of relations between words and underlying conceptual nodes. It has become a source of many practical applications of network-based psycholinguistics and semantic memory research, leading to many search engine developments, dictionaries, and translation projects.

Miller was a well-respected researcher who was elected to the National Academy of Sciences in 1962, received the National Medal of Science (1991), and the lifetime contribution award of the American Psychological Association. As president of the APA, he started the campaign for a new applied psychology that would contribute to human welfare by helping change our self-image (Miller, 1969). The message of the cognitive psychologist was clear, though he never used the word "cognitive" in this famous talk: people should not treat themselves as predetermined beings, and they should realize that they are not merely interpreting the world but interpret themselves as well.

Internal factors in the move toward cognition

The young Turks of the 1960s rejected the preceding generation, but in several ways, they actually built on their work. That was true in many regards for their relations with the behaviorists, but also for other predecessors. This fact is often overlooked by accounts of the "cognitive revolution" that have, for a long time, accepted the idea of a total rupture with the past. There were several important internal reasons in the move of experimental psychology toward the cognitive mode.

Perceptual research

The study of perception was motivated, besides internal intellectual reasons, also by the signal processing and human control issues encountered and investigated during the war. Two issues came up very clearly in the 1950s that went beyond traditional bottom-up psychophysical considerations: the issue of perceptual organization, brought over to mainstream American psychology by *Gestalt* psychologists, and the issue of effects of contextual expectations, values, and other non-local factors on perception. This later issue combined an information-centered talk with notions taken over from the psychoanalytic idiom.

The new look direction of perceptual research in the late 1940s and early 1950s was responsible for the introduction of ideas concerning contextual determination into perceptual research. They pointed out that values and needs play a role in recognition, and there is no clear-cut dividing line between perception and cognition. This created an active vision of perception promoted in the 1950s by Jerome Bruner (1957) and his associates at Harvard. Bruner's summary paper has become a classic, with over 4,000 citations. This research initiated their studies in a manner seemingly fitting into a behaviorist metatheory about the role of learning and experience in perception. At the same time, they promoted a sophisticated contextualism. They pointed out the complicated interactions beyond the local stimulus that are responsible for perception. They also established early contacts between psychologists and linguists. Theories of perception and language processing based on modern linguistics both emphasized the theory- or organism-dependent nature of the very concept of "stimulus" and the top-down effects in processing.

Historically, the interest in perceptual learning was a rejuvenation of the Helmholtzian tradition of treating all perception as hypothesis testing. This active nature of perception was also emphasized by the British perceptual researcher Richard Gregory (1923–2010). Being the last student of Bartlett, Gregory campaigned for a Helmholtzian intelligent eye concept analyzing illusions and perceptual distortions as by-products of the regular, active formation of perceptual representations (Gregory, 1966; Gregory & Gombrich, 1973).

Around the issues of perceptual learning, besides the Helmholtzian intelligence and enrichment version, a new theory of "direct perception" was also developed at Cornell University by James Gibson (1904–1979). Gibson (1950, 1966, 1979), who was a leading expert on army pilot training, developed a theory claiming that perception was in fact "reading out" what was available in the visual display. It is an ecologically adapted system where perceptual learning is basically training attention to the relevant stimulus dimensions.

There was an influx of the new information theory to the analysis of perception as well. Tanner and Swets (1954), in a seminal paper, proposed a new way to analyze incoming information. They treated stimuli as "signals" that were accompanied by a noise, and perception as an issue of reacting to the signal under noise. The sensitivity of the system is characterized by d', the differentiation between noise and signal from noise alone. It is basically a distinction between hit rate and false alarm rates in observers. Hits, misses, and false alarms were precisely differentiated: in certain situations, such as military watch outs or recognizing signs of cancer, misses were riskier, while in other situations, like going home when the alarm system is armed, false alarms were more expensive. Besides the classical notions of signal detection theory, they also introduced decision criteria, and in this way, all perceptual decisions were treated in an elegant mathematical manner of differentiating between noise alone and signal plus noise situations. Since then, this attitude was extended to issues of memory, medical diagnosis, and the like, and also to distinguish between kinds of representations at large.

Thus, partly due to its embedding into early military signal processing work, perceptual research gradually moved closer to issues that became crucial for later cognitive approaches, as the effect of top-down processes, the nature of "active perception," and interpreting the human mind in terms of information flow. These issues were taken into cognitive psychology both on a personal and on an intellectual level. Jerome Bruner was a key person in this continuity.

Biography

A constructionist vision of the human mind: Jerome Bruner (1915–2016)

Jerome Bruner, the other founder of the Harvard Center for Cognitive Studies, was a leading figure both of modern cognitive psychology and of modern educational theory. His rich oeuvre can be divided into four stages that all relate to cognition and to the cognitive revolution, and they were all crucial in forming the image of humans entertained by modern psychology. He has become a giant of modern psychology, with over three and a half million (!) Google hits in 2023, and well over 280,000 citations in Google Scholar as of early 2023.

Bruner had a difficult start in life. He was a second-generation son of Polish Jews in New York. He was born blind with a cataract that was operated when he was 2 years old. (This handicap might be a reason for his interest in learning effects on perception.) Bruner finished his graduate studies at Harvard in 1941 and served in the army studying the social psychology of war situations. His PhD dissertation was on war propaganda. He returned to Harvard and became a professor there in 1952. From 1960 to 1972, he also directed the university's *Center for Cognitive Studies* established by him and George Miller. He left Harvard to become professor of experimental psychology at the *University of Oxford* (1972–1980). He later taught at the *New School for Social Research*, New York, and finally at the *New York University School of Law*.

The **new look theory of perception** was developed by the young Bruner (1945–1957). He showed with many experiments that perception is under the control of values, actual needs, the context, and social expectations (Postman et al., 1948). This led to his view that perception is always a function of the person and the situation (Bruner, 1957, 1974). The perceptual research at Harvard, with its emphasis on continuity between perception, cognition, and value, shaped the foundation of his peculiar constructionism (Bruner, 1983). From the active view of perception, he almost directly stepped over to the study of an active view of cognitive categorization and its development in children.

At the Harvard Cognitive Center, they wanted to build an opposition to the image of behaving humans promoted by Skinner also at Harvard. They aimed to replace it with an image of humans as cognizing and representing agents. Bruner took part in this new endeavor with two contributions of his own. He extended his earlier research on perceptual categorization toward more abstract categories, and he introduced new methods to study conceptual categorization. The novelty was in treating humans as active information seekers who form hypotheses about (even the artificial) categories they create (Bruner et al., 1956).

Bruner soon discovered that to understand cognition, he had to move to **issues of development**. On the level of dissemination, he was crucial in making the work of Vygotsky (1962) translated and known in America. He also started an ambitious project of developmental research on young children. Bruner elaborated a conception that concentrated on changes in the levels of representation. Bruner rediscovered the classical pragmatic semiotic epistemology of Peirce (1883), which differentiated indexical, iconic, and symbolic representations. In the conception of Bruner, children start with an action-based enactive representation (first year), followed by a similarity-based image-like representation (1 to 6 years), ending and becoming stabilized in the third stage with symbolic language–based representation after schooling starts (Bruner et al., 1966). The world of signs and communication is intended to play a central role in this vision, and even the enactive representation is interpreted in communicative terms.

Bruner had already been involved in the **Brown v. Board of Education of Topeka** Supreme Court case, preparing studies about the effects of racial separation on children. As a matter of fact, the court decided partly based on social science evidence produced by Kenneth B. Clark and his wife,

Mamie Clark (Clark & Clark, 1947), indicating self-depreciation of African American children and self-overevaluation in children of Caucasian descent. Kenneth Clark (1988, p. 131), himself a noted African American scholar and consultant psychologist, recalled a generation later the summary of his expert opinion: "Those children who learn the prejudices of our society are also being taught to gain personal status in an unrealistic and non-adaptive way." The court decided to end segregated schooling in the United States. This was a ruling that had consequences for racial discrimination across American society by acknowledging how central schools were to society.

Bruner became an education and science advisor to Presidents John F. Kennedy and Lyndon B. Johnson. Bruner played an active role in the formation of the compensatory education programs of the dreams of Great Society in the Head Start program (Appleton, 2016). Alongside his practical advice, Bruner became one of the developers of modern constructionist educational theories. Children are active in absorbing knowledge, not merely passive receivers of instruction. Bruner's (1960) small book on education that was sold in several hundred thousand copies in over 20 languages campaigned for a cyclic organization of curricula, where science can be taught at any age level with accommodated methods for the preparation of children. Teaching material at every level should be structured and more concept- or theory-oriented than simply based on an inductionist approach to instruction on all levels. Institutions and culture provide **scaffoldings** for building knowledge, but they should not indoctrinate children. In building up his ideas, Bruner discovered ethology that would give a biological support or back-up for the notion of scaffolding and for the role of own activity and play in development.

His move from Harvard to Oxford was partly due to his disappointment with the cognitive movement he initiated. As he himself recalled, the cognitive move seemed to be too mechanistic and algorithmic for his constructionist mind that was always looking for meaning creation.

The ethological inspiration, and the postulation and study of the earliest signs of social mind, characterized his third scientific program at Oxford. Bruner was one of the founders of present-day **competent infant** theories. On the one hand, he started to reinterpret the grammar-based child language theories of the followers of Chomsky with an emphasis on the functions of early child utterances, inspired by the philosophical speech act theory of Austin (1962). This reinterpretation also involved a richer consideration of the contexts of mother–child dialogues that have become central for the more functionalist theories of language acquisition. Early utterances were interpreted in their social contexts in this framework, and their functional analysis was taken to be the key to understanding the development of language (Bruner, 1975). At the same time, Bruner started the first studies based on video and eye movement recordings of the micro-social frames of cognitive achievements, investigating the situation of joint attention. Alison Gopnik,

Figure 9.1 Jerome Bruner.

Source: Picture from the homepage of the Hungarian Academy of Sciences.

Alan Leslie, Andrew Meltzoff, and Annet Ninio emulated these experiments, most of the time with a more biological interpretation of the early signs of sociality, compared to the original "scaffolding" vision of Bruner.

From the 1980s, back in New York, Bruner was one of the key players in cultural psychology, proposing his **narrative theory of knowledge** and its acquisition. He maintained his developmental and educational emphasis. He differentiated two types of attitudes toward knowledge. One is categorical and timeless. This attitude corresponds to classical science. It looks for causal relations between categories. At the same time, we apply a more anthropomorphic attitude early on, the narrative approach. It is characterized by a human action–based organization of events that are put into a sequential order. There is a human intention–based organization to them. They are organized as a world of reasons, not merely causes; they do organize everything into a human story (Bruner, 1990), as spelled out by the Czech-French writer meditating on writing Milan Kundera (1986) as well.

This is the most cited book of Bruner, with over 27,000 citations. They are also taken to be his new proposals for reorganizing education. Narration is taken as the meaning on which our life is based. Bruner also saw a cultural message of narratives. Narratives do make cultural sense out of the chaos of the world and, in this regard, are essential for the socialization of child.

"Cultures could not exist in the constrained harmony they do reach beyond their inherent contradictions, without the intervention of narratives. In fact, narratives provide us the tools to understand what is expected, and at the same time showing their accidental nature" (Bruner, 2006, p. 125).

The narrative turn, at the same time, is not anti-science or "literary," to use Bruner's own words. It is merely part of a movement toward realizing a need for postulating multiple uses of human intellect in the drive to bridge evolution and culture. "Cognitive science should become the repository of our knowledge about *possible* uses of mind" (. Bruner, 1997, p. 289). The narrative approach even shows up in the Self theory promoted by the philosopher and neuroscientist pair of Daniel Dennett and Marcel Kinsbourne (1992) who claim the both our notion of Self and consciousness come from a narrative interpretation of our flow of experience. We create stories and postulate a writer behind these stories.

The life and work of Bruner represented within the cognitive trend a classical pragmatic attitude (the attitude of Dewey) that treats psychology in its goals and in its practices as a means to understand the changing and open human mind as a meeting point of the individual and culture. Bruner's intellectual style was unbeatable and uniquely optimistic. As Steven Pinker once tweeted: "Bruner gave the sense that problems of great antiquity were on the verge of solution by the group there assembled that very afternoon." See about him also the Remembering Bruner (2017).

Gestalt *theory*

Gestalt psychology was a constant challenge for English-speaking experimentalists from the 1930s on. Its claims about organization were taken seriously in perceptual psychology in a straightforward manner (Hochberg, 1962), but its nativistic claims were challenged by the new look researchers with their emphasis on the role of learning in perceptual organization and recognition. The impact of Gestalt theory was partly a chapter in the perceptual tradition. It was also a chapter of connecting the new cognitive moves to a German-language European tradition. Second-generation immigrants such as George Mandler (2002a, 2002b, 2007) tried to bring a reading of German professional literature traditions and to integrate them to the American experimental tradition. This was shown by several translations of *Gestalt* literature at that time (Mandler & Mandler, 1964; George Miller, 1964; Blumenthal, 1970).

Mandler showed three reasons for the limited direct influence of the Gestaltists in behaviorist America. They promised to move forward from visual research toward other cognitive domains, but they rarely accomplished it. Their nativism was also alien in a culture claiming an empiricist metatheory. Finally, *Gestalt* theory was too complex and too theory-oriented for Americans. These reservations changed during the cognitive turn. In the cognitive turn, there was a substantial

German reading and tutoring influence across generations in the United States. Modern American linguists and psycholinguists were influenced by European mentalistic traditions through the mediation of Roman Jakobson (1960), a Russian Jewish immigrant at Harvard. Lenneberg (1967) and Teuber (1966), and as he recalls, Kurt Goldstein (1940) had a great influence on the biological interpretation of cognition through their reading and importing of German neuroscience and early ethology. Mandler and Mandler (1968) evaluated this German influence in a summarizing historical essay.

An additional factor was the discovery of European developmental psychology. Mainstream psychologists would also discover that, in child psychology, there was a century of cognitive studies with no interruptions. The American presentation by Flavell (1963) and the active participation of Piaget in the new cognitive moves were central, as well as the discovery of Vygotsky after his American edition by MIT Press in 1962. Unlike the cumulative image of development promoted by the behaviorists, which treated development as a mere cumulative addition of habits, these European alternatives represented the idea that development always involves internal transformations of the mental apparatus.

Cybernetics and cognition

A good decade before the 1960s, **early cybernetics and information theory** also paved the way for a peculiar study of cognition. The majestic two-volume book of Margaret Boden (2006), as well as Dupuy (2009), concentrates on this cybernetic prehistory. Dupuy argues that two to three decades before the advent and strengthening of the cognitive movement in the late 1970s, the idea of a computational theory of mind was formulated by the cyberneticians, like Wiener (1948, 1950) and Ashby (1956). With the idea of regulation, and with the theoretical promise of a thinking machine, Wiener and his followers were already proposing one of the leading ideas of the cognitive movement that thinking was nothing but computation.

Early information theory as an associate of the cybernetic approach to cognition has certainly played a central role in a new approach to perception and decision, as a method of providing a content-neutral statistical characterization of stimuli. It also created a synthesis before the victory of the cognitive approach in the book of Fred Attneave (1959), who came to the field, similar to George Miller (1951), from military signal processing work.

SOFTENING OF BEHAVIORISM

Parallel to the inspirations coming from perceptual research and cybernetics, mainstream behaviorism has also been softened. The mediation systems proposed by Osgood (1957), and the multiple-level learning ideas of Kendler and Kendler (1962), used sophisticated conceptual machinery that, in a paradoxical way, has assisted in their own slow attrition (see Chapter 8). The first factor was that they were themselves playing with fire when working on higher processes, like human language, thought, and the like, moving away from universal models based on animal learning. At the same time, their conceptual apparatus has become rather clumsy and almost scholastic. When we talk about stimuli produced by internal movement reactions, as "response-produced cues," this is merely the result of a peculiar syntactic convention of psychological language, where stimuli have to be followed by reaction, reaction requires a stimulus, and that reaction might be a stimulus for another reaction, etc. Would it not be easier to reintroduce folk psychology and talk about "thinking"? As Bruner remarked in his autobiography, originally there was a clandestine behavioristic smuggling back of the mind into psychology.

> The clearest way to espouse mentalism in an age of behaviorism was to conceal it in learning theory . . . that was forcing Clark Hull into such Byzantine absurdities (like "pure stimulus acts" standing for perception) that he finally came down of his cumbersome weight.
>
> (Bruner, 1983, p. 109)

There were some puzzles coming from the animal laboratory as well. Effects like constraints on learning (rats learn tastes, and birds learn colors easier) as well as autoshaping questioned the simplistic universal animal learning models. Based on these dualities, the Canadian psychologist Donald Hebb (1960) even proposed that the original stimulus reaction type of "American revolution" should be supplemented by a new revolution to study cognitive phenomena. The two do not imply an either/or choice, since behavior has an associative and a cognitive organizational mode, according to Hebb.

Social factors in the genesis of cognitive psychology

The changes that started to emerge in experimental psychology went together with many changes in general social life. On the level of science policy and education, the birth of the cognitive movement went together with the age of the **Sputnik shock**. American (and some Western European) politicians were shocked by the strength of Russian space power (including military rocket technology) caused by the launching of the first artificial satellite in 1957. That led to Cold War efforts to revise science funding and science education. This was started in the United States by the establishment of the National Science Foundation in 1950, which doubled its budget under the effect of the Sputnik shock. That was then followed by a multiplication of support to the universities, with an emphasis on natural science and technology. This included a concentration of the development of computing technologies and radical changes in communicative efficiency together with revision plans for science education.

Both aspects were crucial for the birth of cognitive psychology. The new generation of experimental people would use computer technology for the design and administration of their experiments and would also start to treat the human mind in computational terms. The introduction of information technologies started earlier by a strong affinity between computation and military development during the Cold War (Miller, 1951, is a good example for this). After the Sputnik shock, the direct association of psychology and cybernetics, the issue of regulation, as well as computational theory in combining machine and human approaches to communication and thought were more and more typical efforts. The actual changes of human work went together with changes of our conceptions of humans.

The new brand of cognitive psychologists would be involved in the new **science education program**s. Psychologists also took part in suggesting innovative, more theory-based, and mentalistic theories of education like Bruner (1960). In a way, the Sputnik shock set the background and the stage for a technologically motivated study of the mind and education.

The 1960s can also be characterized by great **changes of lifestyle** in the United States and in most of Western Europe. This was the coming of age of the "baby boomer" generation, with a tremendous increase in university enrollment. The new student populations created many new teaching jobs on the faculty level and created a need for curricular changes on the level of content. The wider university student population brought in new ideas for lifestyle also that were creating a quasi-revolutionary atmosphere at the universities. The radical changes in life standards, including the sexual revolution with the "pill" and the rise of purchasing power, allowed a creation of a generation-based culture resulting as the extreme pole in the hippie movement. This was accompanied by social movements and social unrest related to the civil rights and anti-war movements in America and led to the radical social movements of the youth in the spring of 1968 all over Europe, including the rise and fall of leftist hopes of a more "human-faced socialism" in Prague.

All these social changes were related to the birth of cognitive psychology. Cognitive psychology as a new approach to the mind was born in the middle of other, more juicy novel approaches, from neo-Freudism to humanistic psychology. In the full panorama of psychological novelties, cognitive psychology was a more disciplined and more academic novelty compared to the lifestyle-inspired other innovations. They were, however, in agreement over a need of radically changing our vision of humans.

The cognitive paradigm

From the late 1960s into the 1970s, the new generation of psychologists was influenced by new theories of science, among them the two most influential ones being Karl Popper (1959, 1963) with his theories of falsification and Thomas Kuhn (1962, 1970) with the notions of scientific paradigms and scientific revolutions. The theory-based and revolution-oriented conception of science helped the creation of **new identities** in the frames of a group belongingness. The message was simple. There are drastic changes in science. The new cognitive forces may be the agents of one of these drastic changes. Interestingly, unlike philosophers, psychologists were not worried about the relativistic implications of these qualitative changes. The second inspiration of Kuhn was broader and was, in fact, true of many new theories of science. That was the key idea that science is theory-dependent, which was also promoted by Karl Popper. The new generation of cognitive psychologists started to treat not merely science but the individual knower as "theory-dependent," as a being characterized by strong internal theories.

The new attitude that was taking place from the 1960s to the 1970s in psychology had to overcome behaviorism. It criticized the adaptationist limitations of social sciences and used the computer as an inspiration toward a new image of humans. There are several aspects of identifying a paradigm in a given field. Some of those are both intellectual and, at the same time, sociological.

Pretheoretical and theoretical commitments. The first cognitive generation interpreted humans as general-purpose symbol-manipulating machines and modeled human processes in flowcharts and block schemata, relying on the central notion of **representation**. This is usually accompanied by a primary concentration on **formal aspects** both regarding representations and regarding the models of cognition. Cognitive research in the 1960s repeated for general cognition what was initiated by linguistic and literary theories in the 1920s (early linguistic structuralism of Saussure and literary theory of the Russian formalists) and by the several waves of form-centered avant-garde artistic movements also in the 1920s. This element is emphasized by the language-centered people of the cognitive movement around Chomsky in their recollections. This was accompanied by a decompositionist vision which is also familiar from the arts: dissecting complex processes into simple components.

New data gathering methods. The experimental methods of classical cognitive psychology, for a good two decades, used more and more sophisticated and more and more digitally controlled classical instruments, such as tachistoscopes or memory drums, and edited magnetic tapes and voice keys for acoustic presentation. The advent of personal computers radically changed this. From the 1980s on, the computer is not only used for data analysis but also becoming the universal experimental laboratory instrument.

Stimulus preparation has become more and more sophisticated. Technically, this meant filtered and decomposed stimuli. But it also brought new characterization of stimuli. Language materials, for example, were characterized incorporating linguistic and logical analysis into the preparations, for example, active versus passive sentence, true or false sentences. Regarding the reactions measured, cognitive psychologists partly went back to classical experimental psychology. The main data once again became **time and errors**. There are new ways of obtaining the times, but basically, they go back to the Donders (1868/1969) model: any more complex decision would show up in decision times. Trade-offs between time and errors are analyzed and interpreted. This is also usually accompanied by a belief in **mental chronometry**, that is, using temporal data to analyze the internal organization of inner mental processes.

Time is used to differentiate between levels of representation. The famous Posner (1976) experiment asked subjects to decide the identity of pairs of letters, like **A–A**, **A–a**. If the time between the two stimuli is short enough (100 ms), the first decision is faster. Thus, a model was created where a very short-term, iconic, image-like representation, where letter case did matter, was followed by an articulation-based feature representation where the letter case does not matter. Errors were also supposed to reveal the nature of representation. After short presentation times, identification errors based on visual similarity (**C–G**) are typical, but after slightly longer times, errors based on sound (i.e., letter name) similarity (**C–T**) are observed.

The **errors of confusion** in a complex subsystem (e.g., color names vs. speech sounds) can be treated as indicators of a similarity matrix. This matrix then can be analyzed by multivariate methods (cluster analysis, multidimensional scaling), which can reveal the underlying system of basic dimensions. This was first done for confusion of consonants under strong noise but was extended to word meanings. The underlying idea has become the concept of **mental spaces** that characterize internal representations (Shepard, 1978; Shepard & Chipman, 1970; Shepard& Cooper, 1982).

Identification of crucial research areas. The leading thematic commitments of the early cognitive models were so-called higher cognitive processes, like attention, memory, thinking, and language. Most of the cognitive psychologists had a methodically objectivistic attitude, and for the purposes of experimentation, they tried to isolate self-sufficient subsystems even before the advent of "modularist" theories, while we do know now that in natural settings, the subsystems always have a strong interaction.

Human cognitive psychology as a laboratory experimental science has produced many new challenging phenomena and associated "minitheories" with empirical discussions and alternative theories.

Table 9.2 shows some classical examples moving from perception through representational systems to symbol manipulation and thought.

There were a few Nobel Prizes related to cognitive psychology. H. Simon (1978) and D. Kahneman (2002) both won the prize in economics for their research on decision systems, and R. Sperry (1981) won it in medicine and physiology for his research on brain developmental plasticity and interhemispheric differences in processing.

Preference for internal types of explanations and reductions. The early cognitive psychologists looked for a formal theory with an uncommitted functionalism that was uninterested in psychophysiology and avoided traditional reductionisms. Though they also believed that these cognitive processes were realized by the human brain, the level of formal processes provided enough database for the psychologists to deal with the mind without going into any physiological details. Explanations were mainly internal reductions, working within the frames of the intentional stance. Cognitive psychology stood for the autonomy of psychology and did not propose a strong neural reductionism. That would drastically change in the mid-1980s, when neural and evolutionary explanations showed up.

Societies, textbooks, and journals. As for the institutional background, cognitive psychology was first conducted in small laboratories in psychology departments or created small extra-departmental units. There were exceptions, however. The most notable one was the Department of Psychology at the University of California, San Diego. That was a new campus with a new department. The

Table 9.2 Some new experimental discoveries and related theories of modern cognitive psychology in the 1960s–1980s

Phenomenon	First description	Debates	Citation	Σ citation
Perception				
Recognition by templates	Biederman, 1987	Invariance N of geons	5,900	21,000
Attention filters	Broadbent, 1958	Early and late filters	9,500	24,000
Representation				
Iconic storage	Sperling, 1960		4,300	12,000
Recoding of letters	Posner, 1976	Additivity	3,200	114,000
Mental rotation	Shepard & Metzler, 1971	Iconicity of mental images	5500	37,000
Mental images	Kosslyn, 1980		3,400	45,000
Prototype categories	Rosch & Mervis, 1975	Sharp and loose	8,500	46,000
Memory				
Magical number 7	Miller, 1956	Limits chunks	26,000	110,000
STM models	Atkinson & Shiffrin, 1968	How many store times	9,000	44,000
Working memory	Baddeley & Hitch, 1974	Active storage	14,000	118,000
LTM structure	Collins & Quillian, 1969	Types of arrows	4,100	7,000
Semantic memory	Kintsch, 1974	Nodes with slots	3,300	54,000
Decisions				
Thinking decisions	Tversky & Kahneman, 1974	Judgment uncertainty	41,000	182,000
Decision errors	Wason, 1968	Selection errors	2,100	13,000
Theory of mind (ToM)	Premack & Woodruff, 1978	Theory of mind in chimps	6,500	20,000

Note: Citation on the basis of Harzing (2011) rounded to 100s and 1,000s, in 2019. The first citation refers to the given paper, and the second to the (main) author.

management looked for prestigious leaders. They even tried to recruit Skinner and Charles Osgood and finally nominated George Mandler (1924–2016). The department has become a crucial stronghold of all cognitive psychology and, later, cognitive science at large

Regarding scientific associations, the American Psychological Association grouped the cognitive psychologists in the experimental session, without too much distinction. However, the *Psychonomic Society*, established in 1959 by experimental psychologists, has become, with its conferences and journals, like *Memory and Cognition*, a central meeting place for cognitive psychologists in the United States. As Dewsbury and Bolles (1995) described, originally it was a society of all experimentalists, along the tradition of earlier secessions, with a dominance of behavioristic topics. It has gradually become a concentrated effort to bring together people in cognitive psychology and its neighboring disciplines, such as cognitive neuroscience.

The strength of cognitive psychology as a paradigm was demonstrated primarily in the first two decades by specific publication efforts and outlets. Showing its paradigmatic ambitions, **comprehensive textbook**s characterized the cognitive movement early on, such as in American psychology, Ulric Neisser's *Cognitive psychology*(1967) and Lindsay and Norman's *Human information processing*(1977). Ulric Neisser (1928–2012), himself a student of George Miller and of *Gestalt* psychologists like Wolfgang Köhler, played a central role in the American cognitive movement with his first textbook, *Cognitive Psychology*, in 1967. He presented an overview of studies of perception and memory systems in the visual and acoustic fields proposing different memory systems from sensory memory, through short-term memory, to semantic memory. In the textbook, Neisser arranged the complex material in a way that united perception, memory, and thought into the overall process of cognition, differentiating between passive and active processes. The textbook has become a citation classic, with over 11,000 citations in just half a century. It is very telling about the fast-changing models of cognitive psychology that the second successful volume Neisser published a decade later combined the bottom-up flavor of information-processing psychology with the direct information pick-up approach of James Gibson into an active processing model of the human mind, where humans always have to deal with an interpreted environment, and where the existing models play a crucial role in an interpretation cycle with schema-driven processes (Neisser, 1976). He has become a leading proponent of the ecological approach to memory starting from real-life phenomena rather than application of computer models (Neisser, 1982).

Regarding **journals**, there were two distinct steps. First, the establishment of thematic journals indicating separation from the then mainstream experimental psychology. The second step was the takeover of existing journals that implied cognitive psychology itself becoming the mainstream. The movement soon started to establish its own journals. *Cognitive Psychology* was established in 1970 and is already at volume 142 (in 2023). In 1972, the interdisciplinary journal *Cognition* was founded. By now (2023), it has 236 volumes. Several specific cognitive psychology thematic journals were created in the 1960s and 1970s, like *Brain and Language, Brain and Cognition, Journal of Psycholinguistic Research, Vision Research*, and so on.

As for the second step, some leading journals of experimental psychology, such as the *Journal of Experimental Psychology* of the APA, have been "dissected" into several sub-journals along with the cognitive trends in 1975. *Journal of Experimental Psychology: Learning, Memory, and Cognition*; *Journal of Experimental Psychology: Human Perception and Performance*; *Journal of Experimental Psychology: Animal Learning and Cognition*; and *Journal of Experimental Psychology: Applied* were born. In 1995, a new general session was added: *Journal of Experimental Psychology: General*. During this period, other relatively new journals also turned into cognitive ones, like the *Journal of Verbal Learning and Verbal Behavior* becoming *Memory and Language* in 1984.

Moving over to the new camp. The changes certainly followed the logic of paradigm shifts in the demographic sense as well. There was a social generation effect characterizing the emergence of cognitive psychology. The new upcoming cognitive psychologists were of a younger generation, searching for a place in the world. At the time of the assumed great changes in 1956, there was a clear generation difference. The leading behaviorists were researchers in their accomplished mature age.

Skinner, 52
Mowrer, 49
Spence, 49
Osgood, 40

At the same time, the (eventual) cognitive leaders were mainly under 30.

Sperling, 22
Neisser, 28
Chomsky, 28
Broadbent, 30
R. Brown, 31
G. Miller, 36
Bruner, 41

There was a desertion effect well-known from the literature on scientific change. Some of the young promoters of behavioristic psychology of the 1950s moved over to the cognitive camp in the 1960s, including George Miller, Gordon Bower, James Deese, David Palermo, and even Roger Brown, who started as a Skinnerian. Also in France, there was Le Ny (1961, 1979), who started as a Pavlovian and eventually changed into a semantic memory researcher. A relatively late dissident was the excellent primatologist David Premack (1925–2015), who started as a Skinnerian operant conditioning expert. There is even a principle of reinforcement named after him – it is always the more probable behavior that is reinforcing (Premack, 1959). Later, he was among the first to try to teach language to chimpanzees with his wife (Premack & Premack, 1972), and in the Chomsky–Piaget debate, he was the behaviorist present. However, later, with his famous paper on theory of mind in chimpanzees (Premack & Woodruff, 1978), he became a central reference point for the cognitive camp.

The dissidents make a good argument for a paradigm shift. G. Miller openly admitted his change from behaviorism in the mid-1950s.

In 1951, I apparently still hoped to gain scientific respectability by swearing allegiance to behaviorism. Five years later inspired by such colleagues as Noam Chomsky and Jerry Bruner I had stopped pretending to be a behaviorist. So, I date the cognitive revolution in psychology to those years in the early 1950s.

(Miller, 2003, p. 141)

In fact, in the beginning, even the terms were missing for the defectors. Miller et al. (1960, pp. 211–213), in the epilogue of their book on plans of behavior, admit that they became "subjective behaviorists." They used this strange expression because the self-identification as a cognitive psychologist was not yet available.

The cognitive movement soon started to **extend toward Europe**. In the UK, the *Applied Psychology Unit*, founded in 1944 by the *Medical Research Council*, continued to work during the cognitive years under the direction of Donald Broadbent and, later, Alan Baddeley, William Marslen-Wilson, and Susan Cathercole. British psychologists soon rediscovered their own cognitive past in the work of Bartlett (1932) on schemata, and his associate Craik (1943) on the nature of explanation. Craik was presented as the originator of the idea of mental regulation based on representations.

In **France**, the changes happened on several tracks. The benchmarking French periodical *Année Psychologique* became more and more cognitive under the editorship of the experimental psychologist Paul Fraisse and the psycholinguist Juan Séguy. There were many moves toward cognitive psychology at French universities. With its research on perceptual learning and time perception and the interest in language, the psychology institute at the Sorbonne, led by Paul Fraisse (1911–1996), was always rather cognitively oriented with his studies on time perception and psychological time. Another key player, Jean-Francois Le Ny (1924–2006), going from being a strong left-wing, Pavlov-oriented learning researcher (Le Ny, 1961, 1975), gradually developed at different Paris universities to a researcher of the semantic aspects of language processing (Le Ny, 1979; Le Ny & Kintsch, 1982). In the frame of the French national science support scheme (CNRS), a dozen cognitive psychology and general cognitive centers started to be supported from the 1970s on, continuing in the 1990s in a broader frame of cognitive sciences. As Marc Jeannerod (1935–2011), the founding and lead neuroscientist of the Lyon Cognitive Science Institute, recalled, a ministerial decision was made based on advice from a commission under the leadership of the neuroscientist Jean-Pierre Changeux that favored cognitive psychology after a decade-long discussion about the relations between biological, technical, and human science–initiated research on cognition (Jeannerod, 2004). Within psychology, the experimental psychology was reorganized as cognitive psychology and, at the same time, created a new organization opposed to clinical psychology. From 2005 on, Stanislas Dehaene, as a continuation of the earlier neuroscience chair of Changeux, obtained a chair of experimental cognitive psychology at the prestigious Collège de France, which supports high standards and innovative domains with a strong neuroscience emphasis.

In **Germany**, one of the key players of research founding with its network of independent research institutes is the Max Planck Society. In West Germany, and from 1990, in the reunited Germany, it created several institutes, of which six were and are involved in several aspects of cognitive psychology. The Max Planck Society research related to cognitive psychology were crucial in taking an interdisciplinary attitude and combining cognitive psychology, brain researches, and evolution.

In East Germany, especially under the leadership of Friedhart Klix (1927–2004) at Humboldt University, the Berlin psychology department was responsible for introducing cybernetic and information theoretical ideas into East German psychology (Klix, 1971) and establishing a tradition of memory coding research (Klix & Hoffmann, 1980; Klix & Hagendorf, 1985) in line with Western developments.

In 1985, in line with the developments in individual countries, a European Society of Cognitive Psychology (Escop) was founded with the *Journal of European*

Cognitive Psychology (from 2011 simply *Journal of Cognitive Psychology*). ESCOP is now a major integrative force of these European developments.

Soviet Russian psychology soon realized in the 1960s–1970s that many of its commitments were in line with Anglo-American cognitive psychology. The Vygotsky tradition of developmental psychology had a strong resonance with the new interest in cognitive development. There were two developments partly related to this (see Chapter 20). The neuropsychology of Luria (1966, 1968, 1970), with its multicomponent brain-related decomposition of complex cognitive performances, had a clear affinity with new theories of cognition. As a specific issue, research on eye movements tried to relate the Vygotsky-inspired activity approach to human psychology promoted by A. N. Leontiev (1959/1981, 1978). Eye movements in this approach were interpreted as special abbreviated actions that relate action to representation (*reflection* in the Soviet terminology). They aligned themselves with the active perception Western debates of the 1970s, representing a strong motor theory.

With all these self-defining of a cognitive revolution, there are critical voices shown under CONTROVERSIES that question either the fact or the radicality of the revolution.

Controversies

Questioning the "revolution"

The presentation of cognitive psychology as a radical breakaway from behaviorism and a return to the psychology of consciousness two generations earlier is, in some regards, an image created by the protagonists. For most of the participants in cognitive innovation, there seemed to be a revolution, a radical breakaway from behaviorism. Further reflection two generations later suggests that there are several similarities between behaviorism and cognitive trends. Or as Hebb (1960) put it, these are two consecutive revolutions. There is agreement in the two revolutions in the hope for a reductionist account of the mind and a neglect of the use of phenomenological introspection. The appearance of attention, perception, thinking, and language in the psychological laboratory was related to the changes of neobehaviorism (Chapter 8). After WWII, even behaviorists recognized the importance of information, communication, and meaning. They had inherent reasons to concentrate on perception and language in their models, and their study of human learning was turned into issues concerning human memory. Thus, the return of the outlawed, or the return of the ostracized, to borrow from an expression used for imagery research by Holt (1964), was partly a result of organic development and organic changes. Furthermore, and importantly, the rediscovery of the knowing subject was not accompanied by a rehabilitation of introspection as an unquestionable data source. Cognitive psychology remained objectivistic when it tried to build models of internal mental life. In this process, they may use first-person data, but merely as one type of data. Cognitive psychologists treat introspection as self-report and do not rehabilitate its assumed infallibility that was characteristic of the Wundtian pattern. Thus, there is an inherent contradiction between the methodological and the ontological commitments of cognitive researchers.

There was a lot of self-supporting and self-reflective "generation change" ideology and bashing behaviorism. "One of the standard procedures of behavioristic psychology – the assumption that rats could stand in for humans or other organisms as experimental subjects – came under attack as religious dogma" (Cohen-Cole, 2005, p. 115).

As Green (1996, p. 31) pointed out, there are several interesting hidden aspects of the revival of the term "cognitive" in psychology. The very term "cognitive" first became popular in social psychology, in theories of cognitive dissonance, for example. This relates to the fact that cognitive psychologists also tend to study many areas that are not cognitive in the traditional sense, like perception, emotions, consciousness, and the like. Rather than becoming a chapter, they intend to be a new school for the entire domain of psychology. Some further, hidden aspects are related to the methodological issues of the anti-mentalist tradition of the behaviorists. The cognitivists do not go back to traditional mentalism: "as long as the aspects of the mental that are revived are restricted to those that are susceptible to truth-evaluation . . . then the behaviorists' criticisms of mentalism will be stayed" (Green, 1996, p. 37).

There are three aspects in the reinterpretation of the "revolution" rhetoric:

- Questioning the darkness of behaviorist times.
- Questioning the disappearance of behaviorism and the overall victory of the cognitive camp.
- The one-time revolutionaries become mainstream themselves. Did they become winners across the board?

Questioning the darkness of behaviorist times and the abrupt break. A key player, George Mandler (2007), honestly admitted that, for him, the behaviorism–cognitive psychology relation was not a break but a natural development. This participant has seen more continuity, and mostly a natural generational "changing of guard." Even behaviorist times were not as behaviorist as usually conceived. Even the dominance of the animal model was not true in American psychology. From 1917 to 1977, in the central American experimental psychology journal, there was certainly an impact of the animal model. Animal subjects were more than 20% of all experimental subjects in the 1940s and 1950s. For the 1960s and 1970s, the proportion went down to 15 and 10%. Mandler interpreted this as a gradual waning of the behavioristic animal model. We should add that even during the behaviorist high times, most of the experimental psychology never, in fact, moved over toward the use of animal studies, even though the behaviorist theoreticians believed this. In the verbal learning–memory literature, terminology shifted from issues of association to issues of organization, syntax, and meaning, but with an effort not to alienate the "old guard."

Mandler narrated his own personal socialization story as well that does not fit the image of abrupt changes. For him, an Austrian Jewish immigrant, the moves were multiple. Through the teachings of Hempel (1935/1997, 1965), George Mandler was exposed to the Vienna school's scientific reasoning in America, and this was combined with a socialization in the Hull school. That led him to the cognitive camp with no dramatic changes. At the same time, as he shows, the real change within "learning theory" circles in the 1960s was the fading away of the Hull school, not the disappearance of behavioral talk altogether (Mandler, 2007).

Did behaviorism disappear with an overall victory of cognitive psychology?

Roediger (2004, p. 41), as president of APS, answered his own question: What happened to behaviorism?

> The analyses of the early cognitive psychologists (Broadbent et al.) were rigorous, provocative, and opened new intellectual vistas. Many problems that were somewhat outside the purview of behavioristic analyses – perceiving, attending, remembering, imagining, thinking – were approached in a radically new way. In this telling, nothing really "happened" to behaviorism; it was not really shown to be "wrong" in any real sense. . . . [C]ognitive analyses swept the day as being more exciting and interesting in opening new arenas of study.

Some **publication and education statistics** about the changes are interesting to consider. Figure 9.2 compares the presence of **behaviorism** and **cognitive psychology** in the psychology literature. There are three interesting aspects of this figure. First, the "victory" of cognitive psychology as a self-identity only arrived in the 1980s. Behaviorism did not die out, as many of the scientific revolution interpreters tried to claim. It is present as a strong minority even in our time. At the same time, the dominance of cognitive psychology continues well into the present, and by the use of self-labelling, it has an extremely strong identity function.

This same pattern is supported by the analysis of the general and fictional literature for the presence of the words *mind* and *behavior* and, more broadly, *behavioral* and *mental* terms in the general literature done by Virués-Ortega and Pear (2015) over the 20th century. There was a dominance of behavioral

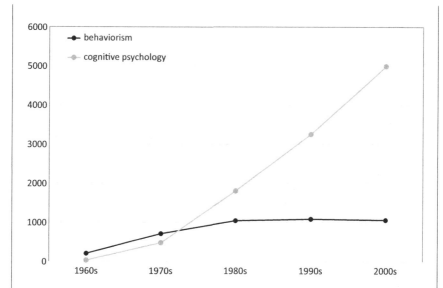

Figure 9.2 The presence of *behaviorism* and *cognitive psychology* in the PsycINFO database over two generations.

terms between the 1950s and the 1990s, after a dominance of cognitive terminology in the first half of the century. They pointed out that the early appearance of the cognitive revolution is a myth regarding the "common mind." The cognitive change, in fact, happened only in the 1970s.

Revolutionaries themselves become the dominant mainstream. It is interesting to note the retraction of theoretical radicalism after victory is assumed. To begin with, in the flirtation between a new theory of science and psychology, psychologists never were interested in the most radical anarchistic vision of science. Some of the key players in the "cognitive revolution," after becoming an assumed majority from being an oppressed minority, started to claim in an anti-relativist flavor that we should forget the radical changes and interpretative flavor of our youth. They specifically disengaged from the disturbing, revolting, and relativizing message of the paradigm notion. Fodor (1983) gives the new interpretation:

> I hate relativism. . . . The idea that cognition saturates perception belongs with . . . the idea in the philosophy of science that one's observations are comprehensively determined by one's culture; with the idea in sociology that one's epistemic commitments including especially one's science are comprehensively determined by one's class affiliations. . . . [What all this] relativism overlooks is the fixed structure of human nature.
>
> (Fodor, 1985, p. 5)

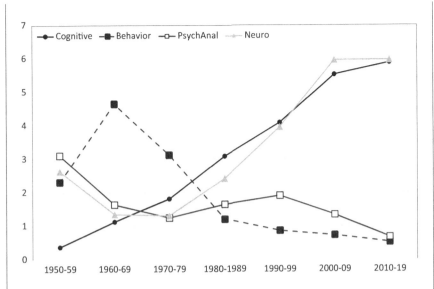

Figure 9.3 Conceptual trends in all psychology journals in the PsycINFO database.
Source: Much simplified on the basis of Spear (2007).

Spear (2007) showed in multiple manners how the intellectual reorientation has taken place in American psychology, and that it was only relative. He used a broader comparison than previous attempts. Most interestingly, he compared all the journals that appear in the PsycINFO database. That database includes not merely American journals but also European journals and a large number of applied journals as well. The journal keywords in this huge representative sample are shown in Figure 9.3.

What you can see here is that psychoanalysis had already lost its importance in the literature in the 1960s, when it was still behaviorism that dominated, and the cognitive victory only appeared in the 1970s, to be taken up by neuroscience in the 1980s. Interestingly enough, the downward course of behaviorism occurred earlier in the entire journal pool than in the main US journals. There is an almost-parallel rise of cognitive- and neuroscience-related ways of talking. Regarding PhDs, he showed that during the last generation, instead of cognitive psychology, it is clinical and consulting psychology that dominates the PhD domain with 50%.

Thus, cognitive psychology is not a great winner in a paradigm shift sense. However, that should not imply looking down on it. "Cognitive psychology is important to modern psychology. It is just that the degree to which it has been revolutionary or prominent within psychology appears to have been intuitively and now empirically overestimated by many" (Spear, 2007, p. 378).

The information processing vision of human cognition

In the early decades of cognitive psychology – from 1960 to the mid-1980s – several central research programs were instrumental in establishing the new cognitive image of humans who represent the world with certain coding steps and levels of representation and make decisions on the basis of these representations, as the textbook of the time summarized it (Lachman et al., 1979). There were two basic issues of the first round of information processing psychology:

- The formation of representations, that is, mirroring the world
- Making decisions on the basis of these representations

That duality was already present in the first synthetic book *Plans and the structure of behavior* by Miller et al. (1960), where they were still talking about behavior, but they claimed that behavior is regulated by images (representations) and plans (decisions) and the two constantly intersect each other.

> Knowledge must be incorporated into the Plan since otherwise it could not provide a basis for guiding behavior. Thus, Images can form part of a Plan. . . . Changes in the Plans can be affected only by information drawn from the Images.
> (Miller et al., 1960, p. 18)

The very idea of making the processing of form – or "shape," as Fodor (1985) prefers to call it – central in information processing existed well before the advent of the machine metaphor and the impact of information theory. It was present in modern structural linguistics and in the philosophy of language as well. This attitude is usually referred to as the **symbol processing metaphor of human cognition**. This was a general unifying idea of all cognitive research by the late 1970s. Here is a summary of its basic tenets (Newell, 1989). It is easy to see a general preference for a linguistic mode of cognition in the characterization and language of the entire vision, as Andy Clark (1989, 1994) noticed.

1. Human cognition can be characterized as a **recoding process** of several steps working over symbols. It turns representations into different formats, the final format being a propositional calculus.
2. Human information processing is like a machine that works in a **sequential linear manner** and has limitations due to this linear organization.
3. There is a **single common human processing limitation** because all operations that require computational resources are translated into the language of a joint resource.
4. Processing requires the cooperation of relatively **small-capacity operative storage systems and large-capacity background stores**. Our knowledge is stored in the background memories, while operative memory represents the activated knowledge and incoming input.
5. Our cognition has but a **single active processing unit** that would correspond to the Cartesian unity of thought and to the CPU of a classical computer with a Neumann architecture.

The representing mind

Donald Broadbent (1926–1993), the British psychologist, published his duly famous book *Perception and communication* (13,000 citations) in 1958 that was the first summary of this attitude. In that year, after working on acoustic projects of military communication, Broadbent promoted this approach as the leader of the MRC Applied Psychology Unit at Cambridge. In the vision promoted by Broadbent, which was like the ideas proposed by Miller (1951) first in behavioral frames, experimental psychology treats humans as information processing systems. He started from technical issues and considerations as well. The basic challenge was the relationship between human information processors and the multichannel information systems of aviation. In a way, this is a rebirth of the 19th-century idea of humans as a weak point in the measurement chain (Canguilhem, 1980). But this time human cognition as the week point is put into a decision chain moving very fast, that is, a supersonic fighter jet. Broadbent introduced into the psychological laboratory, working together with Collin Cherry (1966), a communication engineering professor, the multichannel tape recorder. This made possible the laboratory study of processing competing channels of communication and the ways of selecting among them.

Later, rather than analyzing signs in themselves, such as sound stream coming from left or right, more elaborate cognitive models would concentrate on representations based on stimulus meaning (English or German). With all these refinements, cognitive psychology would use the communication/information metatheory or metaphor, talking about **coding and information transformation or recoding in the mind** for quite a while. Figure 9.4 shows this new vision from Broadbent (1958). The figure illustrates well the non-accidental fact that the step toward a new cognitive model was done by the same people who introduced statistical behaviorism a few years earlier. It also shows a metaphoric feature of early cognitive psychology: the BOX metaphor that stands for different levels of representation as

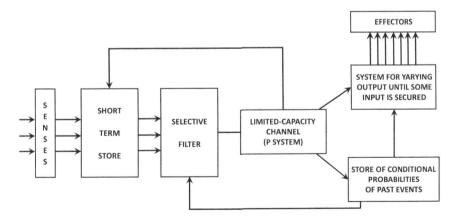

Figure 9.4 Human cognition as information processing in the model of Daniel Broadbent.
Source: Seriously redrawn from Broadbent (1958).

storage boxes. Together with the flowchart models taken over from programming flowcharts, these were the most pervasive metaphors of first-generation cognitive psychology.

Broadbent's followers and his model claimed that we are unable to process simultaneous messages (texts) in parallel. Usually, one is only able to concentrate on one text and we are aware only of the physical features of the unattended message. Parallel processing was presumed at early, "shallow" stages (left side of the figure), followed by a bottleneck and serial processing (form the middle of the figure). A similar system with several stores was also postulated in the influential textbook of Neisser (1967).

In the analysis of the filtering function, for example, the classic issue of whether we can indeed make several things in parallel is reformulated as a model, according to which, in the early stages, preceding recognition, there is indeed parallel processing through multiple channels, but this is followed by filtering in the recognition stage. Recognition would be a strictly sequential process. The corresponding experimental paradigm was the **cocktail party situation**: while you consciously follow one message chain, you overhear your name from an unattended channel.

The initial model, with all its limitations and shortcomings, is still a very important reference point. Short-term store and the information bottleneck corresponding to it would correspond to computing memory store in machines. On the other end, ideas of sequential thought and limited central resources taken from machine analogies would correspond on the human level to sequential language processing and, at the end, the concept of an integrative self.

Some of the later approaches in the study of cognition from the 1980s, including parallel distributed processing, correspond to a revolt against this traditional model by allowing for parallel processing even on semantic levels (Rumelhart et al., 1986). It has also become evident that the **temporal fate of different codes and representations is a flexible process**. The context and the task have a determining influence over the retention of different codes. The physical code in the famous matching experiments of Posner that seemed to disappear after 1 s may be present for longer times, provided that physically identical pairs are much more frequent in the set (Posner, 1976). The working memory conception of Baddeley (1976) also emphasized flexibility in the memory system. Although it presupposes stores, it treats their interrelationships in a functional rather than a preassigned way. It has also become clear that in models of recognition, long-term stored knowledge cannot be assigned to such a late phase in the process, as the original model has suggested. If we want to account for the recall of words after a few seconds (the so-called short-term memory performance), we must postulate a temporary activation of the knowledge store of overlearned items (the long-term store) prior to short-term storage. Thus, in a way contrasting with the initial model, the workings of the "long term box" somehow precede the workings of the "short term box" (Ericsson & Kintsch, 1995).

Another central issue has become the **format of representations** in the long-term storage. Two models were developed: a propositional theory that is in line with the sequential language bias of early cognitive psychology, and an image theory that clams that even long-term storage is like perception. The propositional camp is represented most emphatically by Pylyshyn (1984), and for verbal information by Kintsch (1974, 1998; Kintsch & Mangalath, 2011). The image-centered people, using data from the psychological laboratory, show similarities of mental images to physical images, like size-dependent sensitivity to rotations. They argue that representations have an analogue kind of structure, and they are at least not always of a propositional form (Kosslyn, 1980, 1994).

Decision theory and cognition

In addition to the varied studies on the formation and types of representations, modern cognitive psychology has taken up traditional issues of research on thinking in the form of studying typical **constraints and errors in decision-making**. The first explicit version of this was the general model of cognition proposed by Herbert Simon (1916–2001) and his associates, mainly Alan Newell (1927–1992). Simon was a central figure at Carnegie Mellon University, stretching from psychology through artificial intelligence to economy and sociology. He was the first to analyze human organizations with a framework of decision-making. His theory of **bounded rationality** (Simon, 1977, 1982), for which he received the Nobel Prize in economics, basically stated that in our decisions we are not driving toward optimal solutions but toward slightly improved conditions compared to the recent one. In their work with Alan Newell on artificial problem-solving by machines and the analysis of human problem-solving protocols (Newell, 1989; Simon, 1981, 1982; Simon & Newell, 1972), they proposed that the very same general problem-solving principles show up in every human process. Human cognition applies a so-called production system to repeated problems. Their structure is the same in every problem area. They look for an input of a certain kind, and from there on they arrive at the result because of a chain of reasoning. The neutral language of the human mind is the language of logical calculus: IF PATTERN P, THEN DO X. The train of thought is the same, be it a question of chess playing, sentence understanding, or even typewriting. At the same time, our entire background knowledge system participates in all cognitive processes, so our system in this sense is informationally transparent. In his efforts to relate psychological steps to computer machine steps, Newell even claimed that one could "translate" all cognitive solutions into the language of a simple machine code, using elementary functions like ASSIGN, COPY, WRITE, READ, DO, EXIT, and CONTINUE (Newell, 1980). A rival approach developing from the late 1960s on claimed that human cognition is in fact qualitatively different in different domains, and this evolved into the comprehensive modular approach by Fodor (1983, p. 1), claiming "that many fundamentally different kinds of psychological mechanisms must be postulated in order to explain the facts of mental life." (See more in Chapter 10.)

The next generation of research combined the search for universal features of the human mind with the search for **errors and mistakes of the human mind**. A research program was developed to study human heuristics and the way they lead to successes and errors in judgment. These limitations are well-known from the history of philosophy and natural sciences. Amos Tversky (1937–1996) of Stanford University and Hebrew University, and Daniel Kahneman of Princeton University and Hebrew University, engaged in a systematic program for four decades to reveal the underlying biases in human problem-solving and decision-making (Kahneman, 1973; Kahneman & Tversky, 1973; Tversky & Kahneman, 1974). They identified three underlying mechanisms of human biases: frequent things are ascertained to be more valid, frequency of cooccurrence is interpreted as a basis for correlations, and by highlighting certain striking cases, illusory correlations are formed. We are tempted to make individual cases the base for correlations. "This redhead man was nasty; thus, redheads are nasty." The case-based bias is further colored by semantic similarities or affiliations: for example, fat people are lazy, where the generalization is based somehow on the intuitive similarity between laziness and fatness and the conceived lack of effort. As a further step, based on correlations, we deduce causality. "Red hair causes negative behavior." Moreover, our judgments are often tinted with emotions, leading to hasty generalizations and prejudices, such as, "Russians are dangerous." As the final step, we have difficulties in testing our hypotheses. We tend to look for corroborative cases (in our example, redheads) and ignore the contradictory cases (nasty blondes or brunettes). Karl Popper (1959) showed how difficult it is even in natural science to look for cases which would refute or question our hypotheses. In analyzing the systematic errors rather than the simple singular mistakes that have become interesting, their systematic nature reveals the underlying naive strategies of people in reasoning. Peter Wason (1924–2003), the British cognitive psychologist, designed some simple tasks to study our everyday limitations in reasoning. He basically showed that everyday people have as much difficulty using an indirect proof attitude as scientists do. Cards with letters on one side and numbers on the other side are laid out in front of you with either the numbers or the letters facing you, with a purported rule (Figure 9.5).

The simple and famous Wason (1968) selection task was done on many thousands of subjects for over half a century. People tend to make a systematic error. They claim that one must turn over paired numbers. That is correct, since it is logically informative. They also claim in 90% of trials that one must turn over consonants. This move, however, is logically irrelevant since, according to the rule, consonants could have both even and odd numbers on the other side. Many theories were proposed for this inability to learn from the inversion of our hypotheses, among them evolutionary (Barkow et al., 1992) and pragmatic ones (Mercier & Sperber, 2017).

Figure 9.5 The Wason task. Thesis: All paired numbers are coupled with consonants. Which cards do you have to check (turn over) to decide the validity of the rule? Figure drawn on the basis of description in Wason (1968, p. 275).

The decades of research on decision were summarized by Kahneman (2011) in a general model of **fast and slow processes**. Compared to the contemplative image of human cognition presented by a generation of cognitive researchers concentrating on representations or on systematic transformations of everything into a language of logical calculus, like Herbert Simon, Kahneman (2011) concluded that humans, in fact, do have two systems of direction. The **intuitive system is very fast**. It performs well in many cases, requiring fast decisions, but it has a hard time with situations that call for an actual comparison of huge data sets. The other system is slower, more enumerative, and more considerate. This latter one was the one that was studied mostly by the Herbert Simon type of decision research.

Hundreds of studies in social psychology have shown that the fast, intuitive system, while seemingly stupid and too fast, does not lack intelligence. Semantic priming and repetition effects all happen within this window. This evolutionarily ancient, fast, and intuitive system uses algorithms that pay off many times. For example, we have a tendency for increased sympathy based on mere reappearance that is used a lot by marketing and by politicians. This nonrandom effect is related to our suspicions. For our ancient mind, the very reappearance was a sign in our evolutionary past that something was not dangerous, since we are still here to experience it again. The fast system deals with emotional characteristics. The slower, more calculating system seems to be more reliable, but it may also trap us. Its biases are because we feel ourselves to be experts all the time, even if we are not. We also commit errors of the "law of small number" type. We assume, for example, that probability works in a self-corrective manner. We feel that if event X happened already, due to probability, now it cannot happen again. Kahneman claims that we must balance the two systems. For example, he taught courses for Israeli fighter pilot trainers on motivation and claimed that reward was more efficient than punishment. It was very hard to teach the trainers that their impression of diminished performance following praise was due to messing up random fluctuations of performance with the advantage of reward.

These effects of the "law of small numbers" are in line with the classic observation of Meehl (1954), who claimed that statistical prediction was always better than clinical prediction. Clinical case-based prediction is a case of our usual belief in false expertise. Our slow system should slow down further and be based on statistics, no matter how counterintuitive it may feel. This attitude can be extended to the analysis of human stereotypes. Stereotypes should not be treated as prejudices. Rather, they are mechanisms reflecting the dynamics of the dual system. This decision theory stands out against the overly rational economic theories of the Chicago School of Economics, which is against any central intervention into human affairs. Kahneman believes, in contrast to this, that "enlightened absolutism" should try to manipulate reward systems. Remind people, for example, that their rational decisions may lead to poverty or dependency illnesses. In his Nobel Prize acceptance speech, Kahneman (2003) suggested that one should clearly see the similarities between perception and intuition and how prototypes may help the interaction between the two systems.

How did computers influence cognitive psychology?

Computers had three contributions toward the birth of modern cognitive psychology:

Computers
- Did change scientific psychology.
- Did change everyday life.
- Did change the self-image of humans.

For the first impact, computing machines and the "box mentality" of early cognitive psychology provide each other with powerful metaphors. For changes in academic psychology, the mere knowledge that the machines do exist somewhere was already enough. In academic psychology, the attraction of information processing machines was visible early on from the late 1950s. The Cartesian machine way of thinking prevalent in many earlier psychological theories contributed to this. The new **information processing machines** embodied a challenge and a provocation compared to other machines for the behaviorist way of thought. Computer engineers started to talk about "memory systems" and the like in their machines. Why can't we then talk about human memory? Hebb (1960), in his presidential address, saw this challenge and proposed that psychologists should not be afraid of seeing analogies or even identities between machine states and mental states. In a way, the new generation of cognitive psychologists smuggled back folk psychology, but through the machine metaphor, they pretended they were using the physical stance in the meantime.

As a second step, when psychologists started to take a closer look, they realized that in actual work with computers, they found interesting flowcharts and ways to handle information. There is a certain abstract "ephemeral" attitude in this that called for a search for human analogies. The **abstraction research strategy**, the concept of software, presented information processing machines as new vistas for classical philosophical functionalism. As a recent sociological analysis summarized it:

> [I]f the computer could demonstrate higher thinking, then surely it would not be pure speculation to attribute those thought processes to people. There could, therefore, be a defensible science of thinking. The computer metaphor was also used to make an anti-behaviorist point and emphasize the way in which human nature is creative and (partly) autonomous of the environment.
> (Cohen-Cole, 2005, p. 123)

Flowcharts, like computer algorithm charts, invaded not merely psychology but linguistics and anthropology papers as well. For the psychologists, this machine kind of thinking had an important consequence of making their models explicit: running computer simulations refines our psychological models, as Bruner (1984) noted.

A related notion is the recognition of **multiple levels of functional analysis** on the analogy of machines. The same way as we talk of algorithms, programs, and machine implementations regarding artificial intelligence programs, we can think of cognitive models and the relationships between body and mind on similar levels of abstraction.

Theory-based modern cognitive studies, the works of David Marr on vision and Chomsky on language, made this inspiration toward a more theoretical level in cognitive science, usually referred to as computational theories, modeling human achievement as a computational system. In a similar manner, Jerry Fodor proposed a basic similarity between machines and humans in his proposal for the *Language of Thought*. The **LOT hypothesis** promoted by Fodor (1975) generalized the attitude of cognitive psychology into a philosophical proposal, and it rephrased the Leibnizian topic of *lingua mentis* in the light of the machine age. In actual machines, programming languages translate instructions of a higher order into instructions of a lower order to arrive in the end at a machine code. Similarly, in humans, there is a final language: **mentalese**. Human thought can be interpreted as an organization where some final instances (the propositional organization) correspond to a pre-wired language. The proposal that the language of thought is like a machine code was intended to avoid infinite regress. While all thought is symbol manipulation, that is, translation, there is a language, a form of thought provided by nature herself, or an *a priori* linguistic system of the human mind. This is also postulated to be responsible for the integration of different subsystems of human cognition, as a kind of an internal *lingua franca*.

As a third issue, computers promoted and provided a language-centered **linear view of humans based on sequential processing**. Humans would be compared to their favorite machine: they would be interpreted as having processors, small- and large-capacity storage areas with different temporal constraints, inputs and outputs, and programs. Like machines, they would be supposed to have declarative and procedural knowledge. Overall, humans would be interpreted as systems that have their own **architecture** that implies a physical arrangement as well as a slowly changing, relatively stable system of computation as well (Anderson, 1983; Newell, 1989; Pylyshyn, 1984). One of the leading ideas since the inspiration of the Neumann (1951, 1958) computer was the notion of *architecture*. As applied to humans, *architectures* mean relatively stable, slow organizations of information flow. The special structural constraints in this process are referred to as mental architectures. These are assumed to be constraints in the sense of implying certain data formats on the one hand and structural and temporal aspects of information coding on the other. The notion of architecture covers issues, such as:

- The knowledge types used (propositions, images, models, skills)
- Their temporal parameters
- Their internal organization (sequential or parallel, associative or hierarchical structure)

The particular representations – my recognition of a dog, reading a given sentence of yesterday's message – always happen as unique events (token events) in these structural arrangements. In this regard, architectures contrasted to particular representations correspond to the duality of long-term background and short-term foreground factors, highlighted by Hilgard (1962) as a general duality for all psychology. The different varieties of representational and non-representational approaches, as well as the differences between unified and modular approaches, also imply differences in assumed architecture. During the debates of the camps, the concept of cognitive architecture gained popularity in the psychological literature. It first appeared in 1983 and is mentioned 15 times in the 1980s, then 129 times in the 1990s, and 380 times in the first decade of the new century.

Changes in everyday life after the 1960s were a central driving force toward the advancement of cognitive psychology. Everyday, mundane issues are present in the very abstract-sounding chapters of formal sciences as well. The engineering notion of NOISE always entails the real noise as a starting point, and biological or cognitive regulation always remains related to issues of regulating engines and calculating the trajectory of projectiles of guns. In line with the general vision of Bruno Latour (1993, 2005), the division of science and everyday life was a program, but it never really worked. Hybridization of science and mundanities is a constant addition to our attempts toward their separation.

In the 1950s, mainly in the military domain, and in the 1960s across the board, the nature of industrial work in the Western world changed dramatically. The new industrial revolution introduced machines that have become partners and rivals of humans in information processing. Humans, and gradually machines, must oversee hundreds of sensors, for example, in flying a supersonic jet. New information processing relations characterize actual industrial work, which opened the way to ideas that **humans are also information processing systems**.

It is important to remember that the two-way interaction between machines and humans was true for the relations between mundane, daily calculations and computations and academic cognitive psychology. Psychologists had a role through their ergonomic ideas and works in designing new interfaces. Donald Norman (Lindsay & Norman, 1977), a leading experimental and theoretical cognitive psychologist, with his applied work and with his move to Apple for a while, is a good example for this cross-fertilization (Norman, 1988). Yet psychologists even had an influence with their theories of representation on the computer architectural designers. A representative anecdote about Jerome Bruner is very telling in this regard. Given Bruner's later antipathy toward computers and computational theories of the mind, it is surprising that Bruner was, in fact, an inspiration for the McIntosh–Apple user interface with his theories of embodied cognition.

Computers do foster a change in our self-image. Computers did fit into a rather long as well as intellectual story about the impact of machines on human life. It is a general feature of the modern Western image of man to treat the then available machines as possible analogues to man. This metaphoric mental pattern interpreted the nervous system as a fountain, as a clock, or as telephone switch board. This tendency is supplemented, however, by two further factors. First, the idea is raised that, after all, we humans are not engines of this type. Man cannot be interpreted as determined clockwork; since man is free, man is an initiator of actions. However, due to the nature of the new computing machines, they did create a more organic relationship between humans and machines, both on the instrumental and on the metaphorical levels. We do not consider the steam engine to be a human, though we refer to our emotions as boiling steam in a pot. While we do consider the pencil to enter our life and restructure it, that does not lead us to become pencil-like in our self-imagination at all. Computers are unlike this: they have peripheries similar to sensory organs, they have memories, and we might entertain the idea to compare ourselves to machines of that kind.

Not only do we interpret humans on the analogy of the available machines, but so, too, is the opposite idea raised, according to which humans create and interpret machines on the analogy of humans. Thus, when machines are treated as the measure of man, a full circle of analogies arises: the machine was built on the analogy of humans, and this analogy is re-applied to humans. This has become extremely important when comparing humans to computers, because in the local context of the intellectual information revolution, official academic psychology as well as social science was dominated by a view of humans with a focus on behavior that can happily live without internal processes. Official behaviorist psychology put "folk psychology," or the naive, mentalistic view of humans, into parentheses. Therefore, the machine vision operating with internal information flows and representations has had a liberating influence on psychological thought instead of a restrictive effect. Very "hard" objective matters can be treated with a supposition of internal processes. Modeling does not entail subjectivity (Segal & Lachman, 1972).

Limitations of the computer models in psychology

While the philosophical and everyday issue was if machines can really think, the issue for cognitive psychologists was the reverse one: researchers soon realized that there are limitations to taking the linear computer as a model for human thinking. The general metaphor of the Neumann-type computer in psychology, besides having a positive impact upon research, has introduced or reinforced several limitations of early modern psychological research on cognition.

The comparison between Neumann-type machines and human thinking was a modern equivalent to Boole's mid-19th-century dream of being able to translate all intellectual activity into the language of a logical calculus (Boole, 1854/1958). This attitude had its own early phenomenological critics. Dreyfus (1972) basically claimed that machines by themselves are unable to resolve which setting to use (the frame problem), and Searle (1980) reached similar conclusions in his Chinese room thought experiment. From the fact that we cannot differentiate a machine and a human translation, it does not follow that the machine was really thinking. Real interaction and social as well as perceptual embeddings are needed to decide these questions. Douglas Hofstadter (1979) also criticized the traditional symbol processing attitude of the AI community. He also challenged the metaphorical idea made famous by Herbert Simon that whatever is interesting in cognition happens after 100 ms, since 100 ms is enough to recognize your grandmother. That puts perception in the shadows and somehow outside of mainstream cognitive interests. Hofstadter claimed that "subcognition" is the most interesting part of human mental life. The very fast processes of recognition – recall and the like – and whatever happens before you recognize your grandmother, that is, in the range below 100 ms, are crucial to understanding the mind.

We simplify the human model by using ideas derived from the machine. Later, contradictions are observed between the simplifying model and experimental results. Therefore, the oversimplifying model is refined. However, both steps are fruitful in this process. Simplification and revision are two steps in the endless process of approximating reality, while flirting and disillusionment with the machine are examples of this dyadic process.

1. The overwhelming nature of **sequential processing**. This has become the most controversial issue from the 1980s on, in the parallel models of cognition, though already noticed as an issue by John von Neumann (1959), the Hungarian American founder of computational theory, in his trendsetting book comparing computers, brains, and human thought.
2. The nature of **capacity limitation**s. In the early simple models, our resources were limited in a unified manner, like the central processing unit in a classical computer. The new proposals created an opposition between automatic and controlled processes. In the 1980s, both the idea of parallel processing (e.g., Rumelhart et al., 1986) and that of modularity (Fodor, 1983) challenged the concept of limited capacity as the common denominator in cognition. The capacity limitations are not due to a neutral central processor but to the competition of different tasks for the same executive system, that is, for the control of speech.
3. The idea of **stores with fixed parameters and fixed order**. The linear-sequential metaphor has proven to be of limited validity in memory research as well. In the classical view, a correspondence was suggested between the representational form and the temporal sequencing of stores. Sequencing in this way corresponded to representations going from the physical code toward the more abstract ones, in which form is followed by meaning. This was questioned by data and theories of top-down processing (see following).
4. **Machine and human parsimony.** The starting point was the early machine model that considered memory to be the most expensive ingredient. Thus, all data should be stored only once. This conception had a dual effect on models of semantic memory interpreted for psychology. The paradigmatic example is the knowledge representation and retrieval system proposed by Collins and Quillian (1969). Due to the hierarchy relations between nodes (*canary* → *bird* → *animal*), predicates that are valid over the extension of the superordinate node are only stored by that node (e.g., the canary node has no separate predicate about flying; only the bird one does). Experimental studies to verify this model compared decision times for specific predicates (*The canary is yellow*) with decision times valid over the superordinate node (*The canary can fly*). Early studies supported the theory: specific predicates had faster reaction times (RTs)

than generic ones. Nevertheless, it did not take much time to realize that the real situation was more complicated. There are subordinate concepts that have fast RTs for certain generic predicates (*Eagles can fly*). Also, not all subordinates have the same RTs for a generic predicate (compare *Swans can fly* with *Pigeons can fly*). It seemed safer to propose a dual-parsimony principle for humans. In the human processor, redundancy is avoided, but decision speed plays a role as well. Frequently used information has multiple representations in the network.

Language processing and developmental research in the cognitive mode

Language was a key issue for the new cognitive psychology since psycholinguistics played a central self-defining role for many cognitivists for over two generations, even showing the internal diversifications of the form- and meaning-based models. When he analyzed the birth of the cognitive movement, Jacques Mehler (1969, p. 3), the French psycholinguist, underlined the specific role of language sciences in the changes in science philosophy:

> [T]he decline of behaviorism seems to be related to the birth of modern psycholinguistics. The basic idea underlying the post-behaviorist study of language in psychology was *mentalism*. It involved the basic assumptions of mentalistic linguistics that each speaker carries in her head a grammar of her language and this grammar is used in creating and understanding an infinite number of possible sentences and second that speakers have an 'access' to this hidden language of theirs in forms of linguistic intuitions.

The initial commitment to self-reflection and linguistic intuitions, as claimed in the "mentalism in linguistics program," has gradually become less important. The methodical mentalism was skipped, with the preservation of an ontological mentalism. Even Chomsky (1980) has given up his original belief that grammar is accessible for laypersons in the form of linguistic intuitions. He claimed (after having claimed direct intuitive access for almost two decades): "Our perfect knowledge of the language spoken by us does not give us access to these principles; we cannot even hope to be able to define them 'internally' relying on introspection or reflection" (Chomsky, 1980, p. 231).

The importance of Chomsky

Language is one clear example where the experimental work of new cognitive psychologists went together with a deep theoretical analysis of the domain. The other similar field in the 1970s had been vision. Their approach is referred to as **computational theory**, in an abstract sense. This is a new pattern different from the one proposed by early artificial intelligence researchers. For the early studies, the starting point was the program rather than the structure of the cognitive task. David Marr (1945–1980) was a British-trained mathematician and neuroscientist working at the Psychology Department of MIT and campaigning in several domains for a theoretical and formalizing interest in the workings of the brain and in cognition. The idea of formal analysis brought an abstract level into the structure of the research endeavor as seen by Marr. According to Marr (1982), the first task of the scientist is to make a conceptual analysis into the problem, which is the "computational level" in the logics of research. With respect to vision, this means the analysis of visual scenes, the incoming light into surfaces that constitute volumes. There is a one-to-many relationship between this level and the second level of the algorithms used by humans or machines. In principle, several realizations could be made available for the very same computational theory.

In a similar manner, Miller and Chomsky (1963) emphasized 60 years ago that the theories of performance (e.g., speaking, or the third, implementation level in Marr's terminology) have to embody a grammar, a theory of competence, and a naive model of language that is necessary for the acquisition of language. The machine, rather than setting a limit to the phantasy of the researcher with its physical constraints, stimulated the need for an explicit abstract theory which is a formal kind of inspiration taken from issues of computation.

The work of Chomsky, both in its technical linguistic details and in its general, sometimes ideological message, remained central to the development of cognitive studies, and in particular to cognitive psychology over 50 years. Noam Chomsky, born in 1928, continues to be a central figure in Western intellectual life from the 1960s on. He was a student of linguistics with Zellig Harris (1951) at the University of Pennsylvania, where Harris introduced Chomsky to the methods of structural descriptive linguistics and to left-wing political engagements. Chomsky spent years in the 1950s at Harvard as a fellow, meeting Roman Jakobson, Eric Lenneberg, and Morris Halle, central players of modern linguistics, and his archenemy, Burrhus Skinner, as well. From 1955 on, Chomsky continued to work at MIT until 2017, when he moved to the University of Arizona. His most important work for psychologists is his universal theory of grammar in its different versions. Chomsky's influence as an anarchist political thinker, and as a constant critic of American politics, the distortive strategies of the media, and international anti-liberal trends, also made him a rather central visionary of the image of humans in modern psychology (Chomsky, 1972a, 1972b, 1986, 1988). His views on language and on freedom are related. Chomsky proposes a theory where humans are unboundedly free, and this freedom is related to the central, distinct, human-specific features of human language, which is characterized by unconstrained creativity.

Chomsky is a greatly cited intellectual, with over 400,000 citations in Google Scholar. Chomsky was the key factor in the general and strong appeal of linguistics that attracted a new generation of psychologists in the 1960s (Levelt, 2013).

Roger Brown, one of the leading psycholinguists at Harvard, identified and spelled out this attraction of psychologists who already felt it when getting acquainted with pre-Chomskyan American descriptive linguistics.

> It has taken the psychologists a long time to realize that the linguist means something when he says: Language is a system. Very simply, he means that

when someone knows a language, he knows a set of rules, . . . The most important thing psychology can get from linguistics is the reminder that human behavior includes the response that is novel but appropriate.
(Brown, 1958, p. X–XI)

Chomsky had already shown this abstract affinity to cognitive psychology in 1968 in a programmatic manner in *Language and mind* (12,000 citations), which is based on his talks at Berkeley.

The study of language may very well, as was traditionally supposed, provide a remarkably favorable perspective for the study of human mental processes. The creative aspect of language use when investigated with care and respect for the facts shows that current notions of habit and generalization as determinants of behavior or knowledge are quite inadequate. The abstractness of linguistic structure reinforces this conclusion and it suggests further that in both perception and learning the mind plays an active role in determining the character of the acquired knowledge. . . . It seems to me then that the study of language should occupy a central place in general psychology.
(Chomsky, 1968, p. 84)

In the formal model of language, from the time of his Syntactic structures on (Chomsky, 1957) an essential feature for Chomsky was the onbounded nature of human language. Grammar is allowing for recursive formations where a structure becomes part of another structure, and here are no formal limitations to this recursion. This commitment remains there even after many changes in the internal details of the grammatical theories over half a century (Hauser et al., 2002; Chomsky, 2005, 2016). In the formation of the specific attitudes of psycholinguistics, the concept pairs introduced by Chomsky had a strong influence, as the essence of his computational theory of mind. Initially, they were literally interpreted by psychologists, and later, they provided food for thought for much conceptual clarifications and criticisms. Each of these dichotomies initiated a sort of dialectic between orthodox interpretation and reformulation.

Competence–performance dichotomy refers to the abilities of the ideal speaker contrasted to the actual behavior of fallible human information processors (Chomsky, 1965). Followers of Chomsky reinterpreted these distinctions by claiming that, in fact, psycholinguistics aims to study language in a three-layered way. There are three levels of abstraction – knowledge, algorithm, and implementation – and their relations are postulated as competence, performance, and **performance mechanism** (Bever, 1970), similarly, as it was done later by Marr (1982), for vision. The distinctions would also correspond to the intentional, the design, and the physical stances of Dennett (1987).

Surface and deep structure. The distinction, coming from Chomsky (1965), implied a more elaborate, sentence-structured version of the structure-versus-meaning distinction in classical linguistics, meriting him 45,000 citations. For psycholinguistics, it implied a representational sequence where understanding would go from form to meaning in a rather strict way, and it also implied (mistakenly) a belief that in developmental unfolding also, structure precedes meaning.

These notions of the computational theory of linguistics combined with the developmental theory of innatism and the idea of a "self-unfolding of language" have become important motivating factors for the development of empirical psycholinguistics. There was an experimental adult branch and an observational child branch, but later, even the developmental studies became more and more experimental.

Empirical psycholinguistics of sentence understanding and word recognition

Chomsky had an easy wording: linguistics is a chapter of human psychology. Cognitive psychologists were not satisfied with the abstract identification of linguistics as a chapter of psychology and instead looked to develop a specific chapter of cognitive psychology, developing a modern linguistics-educated **psycholinguistics**. Cognitive psychology in general needed a more careful, non-physical characterization of complex stimuli. As a first step, linguistics helped with a new characterization of complex stimuli. Words were characterized according to their structure (*learn-ed*, "stem + past") and meaning, sentences according to structure and truth value (*5 is not an odd number*, "negation, false"). With all changes in detail, this attitude remained a constant feature of the new psycholinguistics for half a century.

The second step was to look for the **psychological reality of grammatical descriptions and rules**. As an early statement:

> The psychological plausibility of a transformational model of the language user would be strengthened, of course, if it could be shown that our performance on tasks requiring an appreciation of the structure of transformed sentences is some function of the nature, number and *complexity* of the grammatical transformations involved.
> (Miller & Chomsky, 1963, p. 481)

Technical changes toward more online measures. From the 1960s on, experimental psycholinguistics started out with relatively slow processes that revealed more "knowledge" aspects of the language than its processing (Miller, 1962). Typical tasks looked like:

Pair sentences from two lists you are reading!

a. The girl is kissing the boy.
b. The sailor is chasing the dog.
c. The truck hit the cyclist.
d. The nun accompanied the priest.

1. The priest was accompanied by the nun.
2. The cyclist was hit by the truck.
3. The boy was kissed by the girl.
4. The dog was chased by the sailor.

Soon after, **quasi-online methods** followed. One typical method was measuring summary reading times of sentences as a function of their grammatical complexity. The real **online methods** were the most technically challenging ones, requiring much editing and preparation. Researchers were looking for reaction time measures as a function of sentence complexity or lexical difficulties, either in reacting to extra-sentential materials ("Push the button when you hear a click!") or to specific words in the sentence, for example, "Push a button when you hear a word denoting *dog*!" This direction was accompanied by the realization that sentence understanding is extremely fast. Within a 400 ms delay – about two syllables – we are already aware of basic grammatical roles or rudimentary meanings.

Separate modules and module interactions in sentence understanding.
Early models followed the separation and ordering of levels, familiar from linguistics, and suggested that during the process of understanding, following sound, and word recognition, an assignment of phrase structure is typically first step (surface structure parsing), which is followed by a recovery of the underlying semantic relations (deep structure). However, interesting interaction phenomena were discovered soon, which were interpreted as signs of online interaction of different levels of understanding. Marslen-Wilson and Tyler (1980) discovered that, in listening to continuous texts, already after the first syllable, we recognize words based on meaning (*Indicate if you hear a dog name!*) as fast as based on sound (*Indicate if you hear a word sounding like doodle!*) when the actual stimulus word in a sentence was *poodle*, like *There were in the house, alongside the poodle, many cats*. Thus, they proposed a selection strategy for spoken word recognition where, based on first syllables, half a dozen word candidates are activated, out of which usually the context allows for selection. Their conclusion was straightforward:

> The results demonstrate that both types of analysis [formal and semantic] are actively engaged in processing the input from the first word of a sentence onwards, and that there is no sign of any delay relative to the syntactic analysis of the input. Thus, there is no evidence that the global structure of sentence processing is ordered in time in the ways which the autonomy assumption requires.
> (Marslen-Wilson & Tyler, 1980, p. 57)

Later scholars who belonged to the "interactionist camp," such as the connectionists, claimed that we are fast because all our mind is transparent and uses all information in a parallel manner in sentence understanding (Bates & MacWhinney, 1989). The modularity people, in contrast, claimed that, in these situations, the context does not change word recognition but merely softens the acceptance criteria. According to the modularists, we are fast because we have stupid, single-minded components of understanding (Forster, 1999).

With the many sophisticated, time-sensitive behavioral measures, like eye tracking, and neural measures, such as evoked potentials and neural models, even if there is no clear winner in the modular versus interactive modeling approaches to this date (see the final parts of this chapter), we have much finer, multilevel models of sentence processing that relate language to the domain of object perception and social interaction and the timing of brain mechanism during language processing (Friederici, 2002). With sophisticated elicitation settings, the production of speech that seemed to be so elusive also became the subject of experimental studies (Levelt, 1989), even modeling the across-speaker determination of dialogue structure (Pickering & Garrod, 2004).

During its 50-year career, several lines of *explanatory models* also developed in psycholinguistics (Cutler, 2005).

1. **Internalist linguistic-psychological explanation.** The understanding of computations is explanation in itself. Difficulties of sentence processing might be explained by the allocation of working memory resources, for example.
2. **Neural.** Especially due to evoked potential technologies becoming easier to handle and more sensitive (Friederici, 2002) and due to the appearance of functional brain imaging while processing language (Posner & Raichle, 1994), computational explanations started to look for different brain localizations and temporal components of supposed sub-processes, such as early syntax, later syntax, semantics, and pragmatics.
3. **Computational models.** Strong claims have been proposed by postulating powerful general pattern generating statistical procedures. Regarding processing, this is a radical interactionist move, and regarding development, it corresponds to general (statistical) learning mechanisms as contrasted to domain-specific, modular models (Saffran et al., 1996).
4. **Evolutionary.** Distal (final) explanations are sought for phenomena such as the role of human sociality, even in structuring sentences. The "usage-based" pragmatic theory of language processing is supposed to find its evolutionary anchorage (Tomasello, 2003).
5. **Social.** Both processing and development should be interpreted in basically pragmatic frames. These frames are grounded in behavioral and communicative coherence building (Sperber & Wilson, 1995) or in the socialization practices related to intention attribution and naive pedagogy (Csibra & Gergely, 2009).

Child language: observation, experiment, and the issue of grammar building

Child language research has been on the move with fresh powers emanating from the cognitive revolution since the 1960s. The image we can observe here is very different from the speculative theoretical child we saw in the 1950s in the behaviorist camp. Mowrer, Skinner, and Osgood talked about language learning in children, but they never looked at actual children. They merely illustrated their theories on abstract children, making thought experiments on the role of reinforcement, conditioning, or imitation. The data-oriented behaviorists were not interested in data in this domain. In a paradoxical manner, the new, rather theory-oriented cognitive generation was more data-oriented.

The new movement coming to age under the inspiration of Chomsky changed the terminology as well. They started off with the idea that the unfolding of language in children was a qualitatively different achievement compared to other learning processes. Thus, rather than talking about learning a language, they started to talk about **language acquisition**. This term started to appear in the 1960s, and since then, it has about 9,000 entries in the PsycINFO database. (Nevertheless, **language learning** has a more even historical distribution of 14,000 entries.) Acquisition is very fast, follows universal stages, and appears in critical early periods.

The new generation of cognitive child language researchers introduced two sorts of methods that are still used today: observational methods with the aim of grammar writing, and new experimental methods to test language development.

A set of **systematic observational methods** has been introduced, which refreshed the traditional diary method with regular tape-recorded observations of children, usually in typical social settings, like bathing or dinner, and sometimes following an individual child for years. Observations were gradually supplemented with video recordings and rich social interpretations that considered the broader context and the adult interpretations of the interaction. The dream of the new observational research was to describe **the underlying grammar at different ages** in detail and to characterize development as an unfolding of subsequently more and more complex grammars.

The most systematic data gathering and grammar writing was done by **Roger Brown** (1925–1997) at Harvard. Roger Brown was a very influential teacher and a key player in the entire cognitive field. Besides his interest in child language, he was especially interested and very insightful in finding ways to study everyday cognitive phenomena. (Many of his pioneering psycholinguistic papers are collected in Brown, 1970.) He provided the first systematic description for the **tip-of-the-tongue phenomenon** (Brown & McNeill, 1966). This happens when we feel we know a word, are searching for it, but are unable to find it (*compass . . . sixth* when the word looked for is *sextant*). Brown realized that words on the tip of our tongue indicate that we have both a semantic and a form-based aspects of lexical storage and search. Later, he started to study **flashbulb memories**, or the fact that we tend to have almost photographic memories to what happened when some great historical event like a tragedy took place – for example, where you were the day President Kennedy was killed (Brown & Kulik, 1977). In linguistics and sociolinguistics, he was the first to describe the *Tu/Vous* and other pronoun alternations observed in many European languages as a function of changing power relations and solidarity between the speakers (Brown & Gilman, 1960). Roger Brown was also a successful and rather innovative textbook writer in social psychology, which was his central teaching load at Harvard (Brown, 1986).

In psycholinguistics proper, he wrote the first systematic text of the new cognitive trend, emphasizing the interface issues of cognitive categories and lexical choices and the problem of formal choices children need to make, for example, between nouns and verbs (Brown, 1958). These issues also surfaced in his pioneering studies of the language/thought interface issues in color terminology (Brown & Lenneberg, 1954). Not surprisingly, with all these achievements, he was elected to the American National Academy of Sciences in 1972.

The most important work of Roger Brown was the **systematic study of three children over a few years**. He wrote systematic grammars based on the speech of Adam, Eve, and Sarah. In this process, Brown compared the adequacy of grammars based on formal and on semantic relations (Brown, 1973). Brown identified typical stages and analyzed the relations between grammatical complexity and mean utterance length. As Pinker (1998, p. 208) pointed out in his obituary of Brown:

> [T]his masterpiece suggested that children have a very active role in acquiring language, and environmental control has no key role in there. Thus, he saw a picture emerging that supported the ideas put in the air by Chomsky. In Brown's own words all of this of course gives a very "biological" impression almost as if semantic cells of a finite set of types were dividing and combining and then redevising and recombining in ways common to the species.

The model of the corpus-based approach of Brown was picked up by many colleagues. Brian MacWhinney at Carnegie Mellon University, and Catherine Snow at Harvard (MacWhinney & Snow, 1985, 1990), organized these corpus efforts into an international Child Data Exchange System (CHILDES) that has several hundred thousand carefully transcribed and annotated texts, complete video recordings, and all sorts of help functions for individual analysis (http://childes.psy.cmu.edu/).

The scientific family tree Brown created is rather impressive even merely within psycholinguistics. His first-generation students were Ursula Bellugi, Jean Berko, Melissa Bowerman, Courtney Cazden, Richard Cromer, Camille Hanlon, and Dan Slobin. Slobin, for his part, trained Elisabeth Bates, Brian MacWhinney, and all the associates of his huge cross-linguistic project on language development in child language. On the next round, Elisabeth Bates educated Li Ping, Kerry Kilborn, Anna Székely, and many others on the language and psychology interface. Elisabeth Bates (1947–2003) was a founding member of the Cognitive Science Department of UCSD and developed a crucial developmental psychology unit there. She was involved in promoting learning-based developmental theories (Elman et al., 1996) and, at the same time, was central in developing research tools of modern psycholinguistics, such as the international vocabulary project and the early childhood communicative inventory.

Experimental works on the grammatical abilities of children started soon as well. These approaches usually stem from two early types: elicited forms and sentence interpretation. Elicited forms as measures of grammatical abilities were introduced by Jean Berko (1958). The Boston University developmental psychologist invented the famous *wug* test. Figure 9.6 shows an example of the test she used. The idea was to study the proper usage of plural endings for artificial words. She employed plurals, past tenses, and *-ing* verb endings and compared 5-year-olds with first graders. The most important result was that children accepted the task involving nonsense words. This proved that knowing a language is not simply knowing all its words with all their possible forms. It is the active usage of the **rules** that matters. This much-cited study (4,000 citations) has become the model of many studies using artificial words and objects to study the acquisition of grammar. The 92-year-old Berko is still very active at Boston University, and her last textbook (Berko-Gleason & Ratner, 2024) with its tenth edition is a great success.

Experiments on understanding in children. Many other types of experiments also were started by the Brown group. To see understanding of grammatical forms

Figure 9.6 An example from the WUG test.

Source: Figure courtesy of Jean Berko-Gleason (1958), the author.

(such as plural) from children, they asked children to interpret forms by choosing pictures (Fraser et al., 1963). They tested children between 5 and 7 years old in comprehension. Children had to choose between two pictures after hearing a sentence like, *The sheep are jumping*, when one picture depicts a single sheep and the other depicts two sheep jumping. These sorts of picture references for sentences are still in use. In the extensions of Slobin and Bever (1982) and MacWhinney and Bates (1989), picture selection was replaced by enactment, where the child has to interpret the sentences by playing out the actions with toys. These methods were initiated in the move to compare the strategies used in different languages to identify basic grammatical distinctions, such as agent and patient. Today, many eye-tracking and behavioral recordings are used to see grammar-based reactions of surprise, even in preverbal infants.

Grammar building in children. All the new data gathering methods supported the idea that grammar is central to the acquisition of language. This line of language research has also produced supporting evidence for the Chomskyan ideas of the child, starting with some kind of preliminary innate organization and an active role in grammar building. Brown and Bellugi (1964), in an early analysis of some of the data of a longitudinal project, proposed three processes in syntax acquisition. The first two might be related to traditional learning theory notions: **imitation with reduction** (Mom: *There is a red ball there*. Child: *Ball there*.) and **imitation with expansion** (Child: *Eat candy*. Mom: *You are eating the blue candy*.). The third proposed process is, however, more difficult for learning theories: **induction of the latent structure**. This would be responsible for the emergence of the crown jewel of our language: productive syntactic competence. Most importantly, according to Brown and Bellugi, the last one of these processes is by far the most complex and likely to put "a serious strain on any learning theory thus far conceived by psychology" (p. 150).

During the following decades, many debates developed about the proper interpretation of child grammars and regarding the roles of biological preparedness and environmental input. Child language first became a testing ground and, later, a model for new developmental theories. Language is certainly a biologically prepared social system (only humans acquire language) but, at the same time, flexible (in a Chinese setting, the same child acquires Chinese; in a French setting, French; etc.). Slobin (1985) initiated an entire comparative empire around these extensions to other languages.

Regarding the organization of child grammars, three approaches developed: strictly formal ones implying a self-development of grammar, with setting the relevant parameters of the given language early on. More cognitively/semantically based approaches see the child as relying on other cognitive achievements, like knowledge of objects, agency, and space relations, which contribute to solving the puzzle of language. Finally, pragmatics- and social action–based (speech act–based) approaches showed up that assumed early language to be based on social intentions of the child (Bruner, 1975).

They all shared the assumption that children build up internal grammatical systems to deal with language: **children are theory builders**. That was the result of the novelty brought in by Chomsky and the first child language researchers following him, like Roger Brown. Second, all models assumed, and still assume, that during the process, there is a constant internal change of the "grammars," and some even allowed for a change in the organizational principles of grammars.

In the ensuing 50 years, a lot of rivaling data and rivaling models were produced. The community of psychologists has taken literally and seriously one of the Chomskyan innatism claims: the **universality** of the unfolding of language. The parameter setting approach was interpreted by Piatelli-Palmarini (1989) as an example of selectionist acquisition. Out of the many options provided by innate universal grammar, the child would select the relevant parameters on the basis of the input data. There were two further important points regarding later articulations. First, several solutions allowed for children changing their style of grammar on the way. The Soviet Russian neuropsychologist Luria (1974) cited the cognitive-based research as arguments against innatism early on. He claimed that all the new child language research had shown was that the articulation of grammar relies on basic object categories of the world rather than on innate mental realities. Pinker (1989), in his **bootstrapping** proposal, claimed that children first use a semantic cognitive strategy – a "bootstrapper" – to form cognitive-based categories, such as agent. As a second stage, however, they arrive at more formal categories, hiding the bootstrap and landing on the formal notion of grammatical subject.

As another aspect of these procedures, Tomasello (2000, 2003) started to reverse the argumentation. Rather than supposing that children form sentence grammars – which was the claim of Brown half a century earlier – the Tomasello group proposed that children first make schemata based on individual actions in the world and then map them to individual verbs. These **verb islands** would be based on statistical learning, and the grammar of children would move toward sentence-related grammars only later as a secondary reorganization.

The idea of children as theory makers was outlined by Chomsky in several trendsetting papers on innatism. The structure of the argument had implications for all of psychology. Language acquisition itself is a process of theory formation and hypothesis testing, and psychologically speaking, grammar itself is an implicit theory of the given language.

> The [language acquisition] device might proceed to acquire knowledge of a language in the following way: the given schema for grammar specifies the class of possible hypotheses; the method of interpretation permits each hypothesis to be tested against the input data; the evaluation measure selects the highest valued grammar compatible with the data. Once a hypothesis – a particular grammar – is selected the learner knows the language defined by this grammar. . . . [H]is knowledge extends far beyond his experience and is not a "generalization" from his experience in any significant sense of "generalization."
>
> (Chomsky, 1967, p. 8)

The vision of the child as a little linguist was provocative and even seemed to be arrogant when it was first proposed. It has become a widespread motivation for later developmental and cognitive research at large. The move started with infants being interpreted as little linguists, which was then continued by the conjecture that humans entertain theories of the mind – especially ideas about other minds (Leslie, 1987) – and theories about the articulation of the physical world (Spelke, 2000).

Regarding the **mechanisms of language acquisition**, the original, strong, and rather philosophical claims of the Chomskyan stance have been taken seriously by the data-minded cognitive researchers as well. Chomsky thought that the arguments for an innate system underlying language were some of its universal structural features. He contrasted it with animal communication systems and, most importantly, for the psychologists, its **universal and fast acquisition, based on limited and distorted data, and its following a critical period style of development**. It is of historical interest that Chomsky took these ideas from his European mentors. He identified his distant inspirations from Descartes and Port Royal grammar to Humboldt (Chomsky, 1967). He had more local inspirations as well. A most likely key influence was Roman Jakobson, who was teaching at Harvard at the time Chomsky was there. In 1941, Jakobson claimed that there are universal tendencies across languages in the acquisition of the sound system, and the system unfolds in a preprogrammed and universal manner. Another European refugee, Eric Lenneberg (1967), was transmitting all the mid-20th-century German biological and innatist ideas, together with an inspiration to read modern ethology. As he mentioned in several places (Chomsky, 1965, 1968), new neuroscientific discoveries about geometrically sensitive cortical structures (Hubel & Wiesel, 1959), and the ideas of Lorenz (1941), were important immediate motivations for his innatism.

The theoretical innatism of Chomsky has led to two translations in the language sciences. One is the modern child language research that has questioned the innatist program in many ways, particularly regarding the setting of parameters during development. In the 1970s, Jerome Bruner in the 1990s, Annette Karmiloff-Smith (1992, 1998), and recently, Michael Tomasello (2003, 2014) have argued for the formative role of the environment in the unfolding of the linguistic system in children. The poverty of stimulus conception promoted by Chomsky is replaced with a modern, ethologically inspired argumentation where the child and the environment form a combined learning-teaching system together (Csibra & Gergely, 2009). It is the very process of acquisition that is assumed to be innately organized, not the grammar itself.

From cognitive psychology to cognitive science

The **cognitive trend** showed up in other sciences as well. It appeared rather directly in anthropology and sociology, even in the form of self-labeling. Several authors started to view society and the differences between societies as well as animal behavior as modeling issues. Within all these cognitive branches, there are two basic underlying topics relating them with cognitive psychology: (1) **modeling the world** – in the form of representations in humans, it is crucial to the essence of higher forms of life – and (2) **external stimuli can determine behavior only through interpretation by the organism**, and culture can only have an effect through the mental representation of culture.

From the perspective of modern (mostly American) psychology, the cognitive move happened in two waves. First, cognitive psychology was born, and then, with a further step toward abstraction on the one hand and toward natural science on the other hand, cognitive science was also born as a result of a second move (or revolution, if you like). The new cognitive psychology has gradually become connected to other, more formal disciplines dealing with knowledge, such as epistemology, logic, and computer science. On a philosophical level, cognitive psychology and cognitive science could even be a naturalistic interpretation of epistemology, in the sense of Quine (1969). The developing new **philosophy of mind** chapter gives a new synthesis of philosophical issues of ontology and epistemology which serves both as an interpretation task and as a conceptual integration for empirical cognitive researchers (see the handbook edited by Beckermann et al., 2009 and Hatfield, 1995, 2002).

It is no exaggeration to talk here of a second revolution with a further abstraction and interdisciplinary cooperation move. As the book edited by Johnson and Erneling (1997) showed, sometimes mockingly, cognitivists were and are always in a need of newer and newer revolutions. The first move toward this second cognitive revolution was making things even more abstract. Mainstream cognitive psychologists in the 1960s made a courageous move toward a neutral characterization of cognition, abstracting from the biological/neural mechanisms responsible for cognition. The newly emerging cognitive science in its first stages continued this abstraction and deliberately neglected the brain-based interpretation of its models. The cognitivists also consciously put aside the evolutionary issue of what types of beings are responsible for cognition. The ideal level of abstraction for classical cognitive science intended to be a common denominator between machines, humans, and animals. This kind of physical neutralization basically argued for a substance-neutral functionalism. The very same way as we can characterize the work of early computing machines in the form of flowcharts without being interested in issues of electric circuitry (i.e., the hardware), we can do the same thing with human thought (Putnam, 1960).

As for the **dating of these moves**, Figure 9.7 certainly shows how this move or concentration took place in the general literature. The shift appeared around 1995 in American and, slightly later, British English. The very expression of cognitive science, as recounted by Greco (2012), was first used by a British chemist and theoretician of artificial intelligence, Longuet-Higgins, in 1973, and it was made popular by the edited volume of Bobrow and Collins (1975), which treated language representation and understanding both from psychological and from computational aspects. (Incidentally, that was one of the first books using digital-type setting and print formatting.)

An interpretation in line with the idea of two stages in the birth of CogSci dates the (American) birth of CogSci proper to a Sloan Foundation initiative that supported the articulation of the new science from the mid-1970s on. As a follow-up to their efforts to launch neuroscience, Sloan engaged an expert committee to

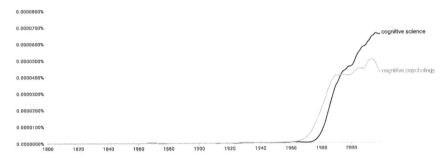

Figure 9.7 The term "cognitive science" overtakes "cognitive psychology" in the mid-1990s.
Source: Google Ngram, from the English-language general literature.

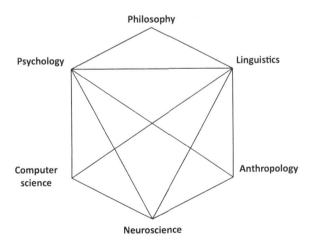

Figure 9.8 The different component disciplines of cognitive science in the Sloan Foundation initiative.

Source: Redrawn on the basis of Miller (2003).

investigate the possibilities for a science of mind. The committee came up with an interdisciplinary cooperation proposal that is shown in the hexagonal figure relating the different neighboring disciplines.

Why was there suddenly a need for a second cognitive revolution? It certainly had sociological reasons. More and more well-rounded youngsters worked with different combinations of expertise in artificial intelligence, engineering, mathematics, philosophy, linguistics, neuroscience, and of course, psychology. Their identity hopes did not exactly correspond to any of the fields. Many psychologists were busy with formal modelling issues, while many AI researchers raised theoretical, and many times philosophical, questions, and more and more people were experimenting on human subjects. The move in names (science) also meant a look toward more natural science, like substantial founding.

Institutional aspects of establishing CogSci

The formation of a new discipline entailed some institutional aspects as well, during the 1970s and 1980s.

- Creation of learned societies, 1979
- Establishing of journals, 1972–1976
- Creation of textbook-like reference works, 1981–1990
- Creation of symbolic places, centers, departments, 1986

Learned societies. Cognitive science as a new disciplinary movement also meant conferences. It also meant founding of a new society, the *Cognitive Science Society*, which was created on the first CogSci conference in La Jolla, California, at the University of California, San Diego campus, in 1979.

University department and programs. In some places, special departments were formed, like at UC San Diego, in 1986, as a secession from psychology after a decade-long cognitive involvement of people there, like D. Norman (1980, 1981, memory and cognitive theory), G. Mandler (1967, 1996, memory thinking), Marta Kutas (1993, on electrophysiology of sentence processing), D. Rumelhart (Rumelhart et al., 1986, modeling), Elisabeth Bates (Bates & MacWhinney, 1989, development), and the dean of the UCSD campus (1980–1995) and president of the **University of California** (1995–2003), Richard Atkinson both a renowned memory model researcher (Atkinson & Shiffrin, 1968) and a successful university administrator. At MIT, the **Department of Psychology** that was established in 1960 by the excellent neuropsychologist H. L. Teuber (1916–1977), was turned into a **Department of Brain and Cognitive Science** in 1986 and moved to the science faculty at MIT. In several places, the cognitive institutional units form more of an umbrella organization (Boulder, Colorado; Rutgers, New Jersey; Indiana University, Bloomington).

There were crucial early European contributions even regarding the institutional aspects. Piaget opened an interdisciplinary center of cognition five years before the one at Harvard, in 1955, though this was not referred as "cognitive science" yet.

Today there are a few dozen departments and a dozen centers or institutes of cognitive science in Europe, sometimes in combinations expressed in their names as well, like cognitive science and linguistics, brain and cognitive science, cognitive science and psychology, and the like. According to the Cognitive Science Society, over 130 institutions were giving graduate degrees in cognitive science as of 2017 (http://www.cognitivesciencesociety.org/studying).

Journals. *Cognition* was the first interdisciplinary journal of the field initiated by two MIT- and Harvard-graduated psycholinguists, Tom Bever and Jacques Mehler. That was started in 1972. Until the early 2000s, Mehler (1936–2020), who worked as a developmental psycholinguist in Paris and in Trieste, was the single editor of this extremely influential journal that has 12 issues annually now.

The **Cognitive Science Society** established its journal, *Cognitive Science*, in 1976. The journal had its 47th volume in 2023 and continues to flourish. Its digest journal *Topics* in 2010 presented a survey of 30 years of CogSci. Out of the analyses given in the new journal, the most telling for psychology is the paper by Gentner (2010). While CogSci started 40 years ago with the promise of becoming a comprehensive, integrative field, it has become more and more a field dominated by laboratory psychologists and in general with the experimental spirit. That is also true of *Cognition*. Another multidisciplinary cognitive journal *Behavioral and Brain Sciences* was launched in 1978 by Stevan Harnad, a Canadian-Hungarian psychologist working at Princeton at the time. BBS remained interdisciplinary with a more biological flavor.

The greatest success story, with the highest impact factor, is an independent journal of the *Trends* group (Cell publishers), *TICS: Trends in Cognitive Sciences*. It is in its 27th volume as of 2023. It publishes short but very readable position papers that are usually solicited by the editors. The editing style is to summarize a small domain (e.g., is there an evolutionary origin to the number sense?), with the author pointing out the touchy issues in the given field and speculating on the future of the research area. In general, the trend toward psychology becoming the victorious disciplinary attitude continues. As Núñez et al. (2019, p. 788) showed in a paper that surveys institutions, degree programs, and journal citations, there is a dominance of psychology to an extent of 65% in all measures. "The field has been essentially absorbed by psychology, and the journal does not directly contribute to advances in brain research, or to many (if any) advances in anthropology or philosophy." The paper was, of course, discussed quite a bit. But the issue is central: cognitive science that was originally a move toward even higher abstractions has gradually developed toward an empirical mode.

The new moves from the 1980s: questioning symbol processing and the non-interpreted vision of the mind

From the point of view of our history of psychology models, near the turn of our century, external reduction programs appeared again as moves of interpreted cognition.

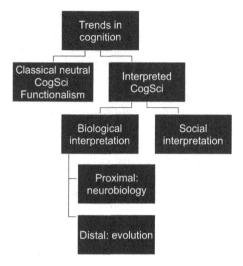

Figure 9.9 The different version of present-day cognitive research regarding interpretation.

The interpreted cognition

The last two decades of cognitive psychology and CogSci show how the internal tensions of classical cognitive research led to conceptual innovations and tensions through variation. A basic differentiating issue has become the original ontological neutrality. In a way, after three decades of Platonist cognition, the three basic forms of reductionism of psychology come back to cognitive research: evolution, neurobiology, and social. The three approaches are summarized in Figure 9.9.

The real novelty of present-day interpreted cognition models is, first of all, that the different types of interpretations and embeddings are not treated as rivals but as complementary to each other (see Pléh and Gurova, 2013). Think of the way mirror neurons were introduced: there is a great neuroscience discovery, followed by cognitive interpretation toward empathy, language learning, and so on (Rizzolatti & Arbib, 1998), that is followed in turn by evolutionary speculations about the role of mirror neurons in the genesis of language and self-representation (Arbib, 2005). In the same way, neuroscientific interpretation of language goes hand in hand with ideas about the evolution of these neural centers and their social function (Bickerton & Szathmáry, 2009).

All the interpretations are accompanied by a developmental attitude. In a way, they move as if fulfilling the dreams of Piaget and Vygotsky: all cognitive science, as they wished for psychology, is basically a developmental science. They propose new, intricate relations between representational and non-representational cognitive systems. Chapter 10 surveys some of these neuroscience reconsiderations, mapping to the entire field of psychology, and showing their affinity to the re-emergence of evolutionary psychology (Chapter 5 shows in detail the rivalries and the fate of the whole of social reductionism in contemporary psychology.

The cognitive enterprise remained multidisciplinary; the contributing disciplines of the hexagon did not disappear, with a dominance of psychology.

Representational and non-representational approaches

Compared to traditional cognitive psychology and philosophy in the 1970s and early 1980s, the study of cognition since 1990 has become a much more varied and divided enterprise. In all these varieties, the issue of representations is still crucial. Psychologists, philosophers, and linguists rioting against behaviorism of the 1960s–1970s were happy to show that there are representations. A few decades later, it has become clear that representations have two conceptually divisive factors. Representations have some sort of "truth relation" to the world they represent; they have semantics. They also have an internal structure, that is, they form a representational system. Due to this, they enrich individual representations with additional knowledge that "comes for free." Logical and language-like representations have an entailment type of semantic organization. If the sentence "A brown dog came in" is true, then it is also true that *a dog came in*. This is a result of the syntactic structure in language. Pictorial representations, on the other hand, have a spatial organization to them. If *the clock is over the table* and *the picture is over the clock*, it follows that *the picture is over the table*. One divisive issue has become the relationship between these two central representational systems, that is, their exclusive or additive nature. A further issue is that our mental world and our cognitive adaptations are not exhausted by representations. Besides emotions and desires, cognitive research has to deal with our *KNOWING HOW*-type competences as well. In relating these alternative directions regarding the representational relations, different schools appeared, as shown in Figure 9.10.

In the early 20th century, followers of the classical sensual ideas as well as later *Gestalt* psychologists claimed that the basic vehicle of human thought would be **images**. Thinking is always image-like, and the sensual content of images is the carrier of meaning rather than propositions. At the same time, the anti-psychologism of Frege (1892) claimed that thinking does not happen through images but rather through propositions. The two theories are still with us as two rival approaches of representational theories that had characteristic debates in several areas.

Propositional theories in modern cognitive theory could be called Frege's return in cognitive psychology: 100 years ago, propositions were weapons of an anti-psychological campaign, but they have now become reintegrated into psychology three generations later. Today, cognitive approaches with a propositional bent are integrating Frege into the empirical sciences, and naturalism is back again with the evolutionary trends. The original linguistic turn a century ago turned completely around to become a biologically interpreted theory of the human mind.

> Frege himself would have been equally surprised to learn that after a century of anti-psychologism and anti-naturalism influenced by his critique, many philosophers who took the "linguistic turn" have taken the naturalistic turn and come back full circle to a position close to that of his colleague [in Jena] Haeckel.
>
> (Engel, 1998, p. 375)

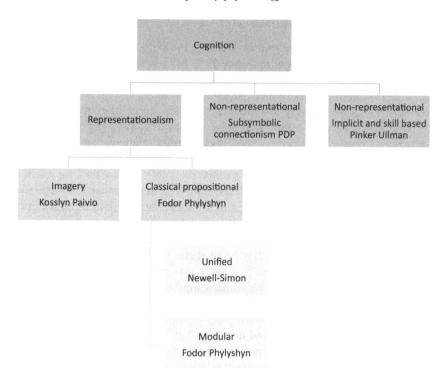

Figure 9.10 Different trends in representational relations.

The connectionist challenge

Both propositional and image-based cognitive architectures proposed between 1960 and 1980 were of the symbol processing kind. The first great challenge to classical symbol processing cognition came from **connectionism** in the 1980s and continues to be a constant challenge, even in the now-popular deep learning AI approaches. Connectionism, extending the ideas of a neural calculus promoted by McCulloch and Pitts (1943) towards large neural networks, was a real breakthrough technically and intellectually as well, both for psychology and for cognitive modeling at large. It challenged the ontological neutrality of classical cognitive approaches by claiming a brain-based approach to cognition, though building on rather simplified abstract neurons. It returned to a triple association of neuro-psycho-computational approaches. At the same time, it challenged the idea of symbolic representation and symbolic processing as well. A famous example for the idea of interfacing computational, psychological, and neural processes was the **hundred steps rule**. Feldman and Ballard (1982) raised the following modeling issue. The individual neurons have transmission times in the magnitude of milliseconds, while psychological reaction times are in the magnitude of 100s of milliseconds. This constitutes a constraint. You cannot propose more than 100 steps following one another in a sequential manner in cognitive modeling, for example, in word recognition. In sequential models, there is a danger of having more than 100 steps. They used this claim to promote the idea of parallel processing.

Connectionism promoted a general and architecturally new model of cognition. It is based on two fundamental ideas. The first one is to start from micro features. Starting or basic entities in the model are taken to be many small features. ANIMATE, for example, is not coded as a primitive feature but emerges out of micro features, like moves, perceives, reacts, etc. (Clark, 1989). The second basic feature is that both knowledge and understanding are interpreted in associative networks of the non-symbolic nodes.

David Rumelhart (1942–2011), a key initiator of the connectionist movement, was a mathematical psychologist. After obtaining a PhD from Stanford University, he was the moving spirit of a language and conceptual processing unit at UCSD from 1967 to 1987. He worked on top-down processing models of language, even working on story structures. After the structured top-down models, he moved to an entirely shallow structured elementarist model, namely, the parallel distributed model developed with many of his associates. In 1987, he moved to Stanford and was elected to the National Academy of Sciences in 1991. He died of a brain tumor. One of the most prestigious prices of cognitive science has been named after him since 2001.

The PDP model for cognition has a very shallow architecture, with little prewired knowledge.

The defining and challenging features of the model are:

1. The model consists of **units and their connections**. Units are interpreted as theoretical neurons. We are back at the conceptual nervous system of Donald Hebb (1949). The theoretical neurons take the weighed sum of activation coming from their environments of other neurons. Connections are positively and negatively weighted "wirings" between units.
2. The basic procedural feature of the architecture is a **massive parallel and interactive organization**. The first famous example was recognition of visually presented words (Rumelhart et al., 1986). All classical models of word recognition, like the logogen model of Morton (1969), while they claimed to be interactive, treated word recognition as a process of activating holistic units corresponding to the word, with this firing being facilitated by associative connections within the lexicon and the levels of letters and words being clearly separated. In the new cascade model of the PDP group, visual word recognition is a result of full interaction on three levels: elementary visual or phonetic features, letters or sounds, and words. In recognizing the word TIME, the unit corresponding to "–" facilitates all the letter units that contain a horizontal dash (A, T, G). Initial T facilitates all the units at the word level beginning with T (TRIP, TAKE, TIME), and these units, on their turn, facilitate the perception of letter T (its corresponding unit) backward and inhibit units representing other letters. Recognition of the target word corresponds to the unit that has the highest activation.
3. **Representations are patterns of activation** over the units in the network in connectionist models, and there is no need for a further central processor.

4. **Processing is the unfolding of activation** over time. There are no separate folders or boxes corresponding to assumed stages.
5. **Learning is the modification in the strengths of connections.** Each activation during processing is an event of learning as well. Both occur according to specified functions of weighing. This is the domain of the so-called Hebbian rule. **Units that fire together wire together.** This was spelled out in detailed mathematical forms.
6. **Knowledge** is a pattern of connections. There is nothing but connections to represent whatever knowledge we have of the world.
7. This is supplemented by an important postulation of **hidden units**. Statistical learning is made powerful by allowing emerging layers between the perceptual and behavioral units that are responsible for generalizations in learning.

The shallow prewiring, together with the learning model, represented a new, simplified empiricism. Thanks to the theoretical "associative counterrevolution" embedded into the learning models, connectionism has become a general inspiration for new empirical studies and theoretical debates.

The last quarter-century saw interesting empirical and theoretical debates starting from the non-representationist challenge of the connectionists. Connectionism was, and continues to be, a challenge for the classical symbol processing models of cognition. This was first contrasted with traditional approaches by Pinker and Prince (1988) and in the volume edited by Pinker and Mehler (1988). Table 9.3 shows a classical comparison of the two approaches to higher cognition.

Fodor and Pylyshin clearly contrasted classical cognitivism with the connectionist challenge a generation ago and claimed that the basic limitation of connectionist models is their lack of structure. "Models based on patterns of (co) excitation cannot differentiate between two concepts being active simultaneously, and them being in a given relation (like IS PART OF etc.)." The associationism of connectionist models situated the human mind at the mercy of the arbitrary unsystematicity of the world: it allows any connections whatsoever. The new approaches of deep learning continue the radical connectionist ideas to the present while allowing for more and more hidden layers and caring less and less for psychological reality.

Table 9.3 The juxtaposition of connectionist and classical cognitive architecture according to Fodor and Pylyshyn (1988)

Connectionists	*Classical view*
Nodes	Descriptions
Only causal relations	Rich relationships
(history of excitation)	(language of thought)
Excitation paths	Rewriting rules
Structure independent units	Structure-dependent entities
(items)	(constituents)

Birth and destiny of cognitive psychology 389

Continuous empirical and conceptual debates have come up regarding the reality of rules that were crucial for classical symbol processing theories, as shown under CONTROVERSIES.

Controversies

The (psychological) reality of rules

One area where connectionism was basically contrasted to the classical attitude was the **reality of rules**. Connectionists started to claim that rules are not part of the system; they are merely secondary abstractions on the basis of the performance of the system. The illusion that human language and human behavior in general follow rules comes from a combination of three factors: fast pattern-matching capacity, good predictive modeling of the environment, and perception of the result of our own manipulations on the environment. The environmental feature in most accounts is a social feedback. It results in a circle where our behavior impacts the system in a form-like inner speech. They explicitly refer to Vygotsky (1978) as an inspiration for this cultural view of thought. This interpretation of rule-like behavior suggested that the individual mind is not rational as such; it becomes rational by the fact that a rationally organized habit system is implemented in the mind by following external social rules. Smolensky (1988) postulated a subsymbolic and a symbolic system for cognition. In this view, the subsymbolic system corresponds to the connections in a network and the symbolic system of a socially conditioned secondary governing system. Cultural knowledge is represented in a transparent, rule-like way in the mind, while intuitive knowledge is embodied in the networks in a non-transparent way that, in itself, does not look like a rule at all.

For three decades, an intense debate emerged regarding the psychological status of rules. The debate concentrated on language, where the testing ground was the system of the English past tense (for a survey, see Pinker & Ullman, 2002). The starting point was the fact that children acquiring English at certain ages do overgeneralize the general rule of *-ed* past tense to irregular, so-called strong verbs. They say *goed* rather than *went*, *comed* rather then *came*. Traditional cognitive accounts claimed that overgeneralization errors observed in children around 3–4 years of age indicate the emergence of rules compared to earlier reliance on elements (Ervin, 1964). As Table 9.4 indicates, this was historically followed by a victory of rules across the board. The new approach introduced by generative grammar concentrated on rules in understanding and the learning of language, as opposed to simple patterns and habits. This was accompanied by the claim for the

Table 9.4 The fate of rules over half a century of cognitive research

Stage features	Main topic about rules	Representatives
Rules win over habits, 1960–1970	All higher behavior rule-governed	Generative grammar child: Berko, Ervin, Slobin
Mental rules direct everything, 1965–1980	Linguistic rules have an inner reality	Miller, Bever, Mehler Fodor, Slobin
Associative counter-reactions from 1980 on: connectionism	Habits and frequencies instead of rules	Rumelhart-McClelland Bates-MacWhinney
Dual models: words and rules, 1990–	Habits and rules for different things; temporal and frontal cortex	Pinker, Marcus, Ullmann
Dissociation of memories: procedural/declarative model	Rules belong to the procedural knowledge system in basal ganglia and Broca's area	Ullmann

mental reality of rules and an explicit denial of the role of habit formation in establishing language competencies. Chomsky and his followers criticized learning theory principles in and via language acquisition. Language acquisition was characterized by them as a self-organization and rule formation on the basis of overregularization phenomena (Marcus et al., 1992). Rumelhart and McClelland, with their connectionist model, proposed that one does not need to postulate rules at all here. A proper statistical learning machine can produce the same errors. Rumelhart et al. (1986; McClelland & Rumelhart, 1986) treated rules not as internal, inherent laws of the mental system but as external characterizations of the products of the mental system. They ran computer programs that reproduced the error pattern of children with simple associative item learning, eliminating the level of rules from the proposed mechanism.

Fierce discussions followed about the technicalities, like whether the software was really missing any linguistic knowledge. After the great controversies of symbol processing versus subsymbolic or connectionist networks, synthetic works by Pinker (1991, 1994, 1999) in the following decade allowed symbolic and rule-based systems for syntax, regular morphology (*learn–learned*), and an associative item-based (connectionist) network for irregularities (*teach–taught*) and for lexical storage words in general. Pinker proposed a dual model, where the duality represents smart, rule-based systems along with probability-based associative subsystems. The rule systems would be related to the anterior, frontal parts of the cortex, while the item-based associative system to the posterior, temporal part, in line with clinical and brain research data. Marcus et al. (1999) as part of these efforts showed that already seven months old human babies can form rules.

Pinker suggested that even approaches that remain strongly committed to the overwhelming importance of structure and rules cannot ignore pattern induction and frequency-based elementaristic factors in human cognitive processes like language. Still later models, such as Ullman's (2004), tend to juxtapose the two systems in a new manner as a procedural system (rules) and a declarative system (words). In this way, the entire symbolic–subsymbolic debate has become a question during a generation of cognitive research of how to put cognition into the explicit/implicit dimension or into Gilbert Ryle's (1949) differentiation between KNOWING WHAT and KNOWING HOW. Classical information processing machines and the corresponding psychology would be criticized for singling out the world of KNOWING WHAT, while the domain of KNOWING HOW, that is, the domain of procedural knowledge, skills, would become critically important and would re-emerge in the third generation of cognitive psychologists, like in the work of Ullman (2001, 2004).

Table 9.4 shows how the rules fared over half a century of psycholinguistics and learning system discussions.

Uniformity and multiplicity in thought: modularity debates within the representationist trends

The re-emergence of multiplicity in thought appeared as the renaissance of an interpretation of classic faculty psychology in the modularity conception of Jerry Fodor (1983). It was a move that combined modules with the language inspiration of a large group of modern cognitive psychologists. Gradually, it has become clear that the cognitive trend was radically divided in this respect, and its division might very well be interpreted as a division of opinion regarding the explanatory power of the unitary symbol-manipulating machine. According to the machine-inspired researchers of human thinking, the central idea was that human cognition follows basically the same principles everywhere. The structure-dependent vision inspired by linguists has become gradually separated from this unified vision of cognition promoted by Simon and Newell (1972).

From the independence of syntax to modularity

Within linguistics, and following in psycholinguistics as well, a peculiar image of language developed that emphasized **the independence of subsystems**. As a first step, early generative grammar in the 1950s proposed that syntax (grammar) was independent of meaning. *Colorless green ideas sleep furiously* may be nonsense, but it is a syntactically well-constructed sentence (Chomsky, 1957). As a next move, an image of language was proposed with independent parts, and syntax, semantics, and phonology were assumed to be organized and working independently of each other, with their only interaction being the aligning of their outputs

(Chomsky, 1965). Parallel with this process, the psychological interpretation of the mind inspired by generative linguistics has gradually become the most straightforward opponent of unitary theories of the Herbert Simon style. The modular conception of mind was an extension of the model of modern linguistics.

The term "modularity" has several different sources and interpretations in the late 20th century, starting from the electronic idea of modules to the concept of neurological modules in the cerebral cortex, as put forward by the Hungarian neuroanatomist János Szentágothai (1975). One of the basic features of this neural modular proposal was the emphasis on a unitizing organization in the cerebral cortex. The units in the cortex serving different functions have basically the same kind of histological organization. They function as a highly interrelated structure of multiple layers with many more internal connections than external ones. They communicate to other modules only the net result of their computations. George Buzsáki (2006), the Hungarian-American neuroscientist, provided a detailed histological and system-related argumentation for the creation of similar cortical modules. When the cerebral cortex becomes huge in mammals, and especially during hominid evolution, a need has emerged for areal specialization. If, in these neural networks, all intercortical relations would be random – everything connected to everything – information flow would be extremely slow. Modularization in the anatomical sense means that there are dense neural connections within a given area with many internal interactions, and these modules would relate to fast output-level fibers.

The **cognitive modularity** conception has adopted the idea of encapsulated computational units from the neuroscientific conception. It has proposed, however, modules of a much broader scope, like a module for face processing or grammatical morphology. At the same time, it has put the emphasis not on the identity of structure but on the qualitative differences in function, which was later referred to as domain specificity.

This conception was most clearly articulated by Jerry Fodor (1935–2017). Fodor, originally a student of Hilary Putnam at Princeton, was a leading philosopher of the innatist group of Chomsky followers at MIT and later at Rutgers University, in New Jersey. He was a key proponent of an extended body–mind functionalism and, most importantly, a proponent of innate architectures of the human mind. His three main philosophical proposals that have a psychological consequence are his idea of a **language of thought**, his thoroughgoing **innatism**, and his proposal for a **modular organization of the mind**. When arguing for modularity, Fodor (1983) had a dual motivation. He claimed to go back to the conception of phrenology, and like Gall's 19th-century model (see Chapter 4 in Volume 1), Fodor proposed a set of innate organs of the mind and brain, which are specialized for certain types of very specific tasks, like musical memory, memory for faces, memory for words, etc. Thus, there is no single basic faculty, like "memory," but several specific memory faculties. Fodor called this interpretation of faculties a **vertical faculty theory**, in contrast to the horizontal theories of general abilities, like memory, vision, and the like.

Fodor started from a critical analysis of a specific shortcoming of the classical "unified" information processing positions. These models are problematic with regard to the specific processes of perception. They simply suppose that the perceptual analysis provides a description of the stimuli in terms of its specific features, but the particularities of features and the process for their extraction are not clearly articulated. For an information processing paradigm, there are no quantitative differences between the treatment of data from vision and from audition, for example. The modularist vision starts from issues of perception, calling all interesting "encapsulated" subsystems **input systems**. Fodor (1983) and Pylyshin (1984) define those supposed neural components as "input systems" which perform the separate tasks of coding incoming information independently of each other in a genetically determined order and which interact with each other only at the level of their outputs. This conception combined the philosophical tradition of the faculty psychology of Gall, the linguistic and language processing approaches with the primacy of form over meaning, and the neurobiological concept of modules (Coltheart, 1999).

Fodor's (1983) idea of input modules is connected in an interesting way to his vision on the language of thought (Fodor, 1975). The outputs of the different input modules are integrated into an abstract propositional format that is the vehicle of any internal thought process. However, this claim is made with no clear position regarding whether this *lingua mentis* is related to actual speech in either its genesis or its workings, like a recoding into inner speech.

The modular micro machines are encapsulated and impenetrable also in the sense that knowledge, in the traditional meaning of this term, cannot influence their workings. Knowledge, expectation, and other contextual factors have an influence only on the output of these computations and never on their inside operations. Fodor was originally relying on data on the knowledge independence of visual illusions and the automatized first-pass interpretation of linguistic ambiguities. This was generalized into an idea that most of our cognition is organized according to the principle of input systems: most of the human mind consists of encapsulated task-specific modules that fulfill their tasks with remarkable speed and in a reflex-like automatic way.

The modular approach is put forward in opposition and as a challenge to the new look view of perception with their ideas that perception depends on several factors beyond the local stimulus: frequency, the actual context, our expectations, and the motivational significance of the signs (Bruner, 1957; Erdélyi, 1985, 2006). The modular conception, on the other hand, treats perception as separable from knowledge. In this sense, it denies continuity between different levels of cognition and between perception and cognition. From the point of view of the machine metaphor, this conception suggests that several task-specific small processors coexist in our mind, and the results of their computations are made available to a general problem solver–like symbol-manipulating system. Thus, little room was left by Fodor for experience-bound general cognition. He did this unwillingly, and the domain of this factor has been gradually narrowed until a new challenge, an even more radical modular conception proposed by evolutionary psychologists, forced Fodor to reconsider.

The module concept was a large success. Fodor's book has over 20,000 citations. The conception created a lot of research in many fields, from language processing to vision and to social cognition, from machine research to developmental studies. It has two provocative aspects. One is the assumed stupidity of many cognitive processes, and the other is the general assumption of innate organization of modules.

Concerning language, for example, the modular thesis claims that context or frequency has no effect on the immediate mechanisms of word recognition. These factors have only a *post hoc* effect, modulating the ease of word use. In a similar vein, there is no interaction between the lexical, syntactic, and semantic components of understanding: all of them operate as self-contained systems. Both "early" and "late" indicate here rather fast processes. In processing ambiguous words like *bank*, according to the modular vision, both meanings are active for about 3–400 ms, while according to the interactionist claims, the relevant meaning is selected in 300 ms.

A new challenge: radical modularity

From the 1990s on, the innatist modular claims of Fodor and his followers met a new challenge. This was the radical modularity proposed by the new evolutionary psychologists. The evolutionary psychology (EP) of the Tooby and Cosmides (1992; Cosmides & Tooby, 1994) and Pinker (1997, 2002) style is based on the "Swiss army knife" model of mental structure. This is a radically modular view which postulates that the human mind is a series of independently evolved and autonomously functioning adaptations. This view has faced many criticisms both on conceptual and on experimental grounds. When these proposals showed up, Fodor emphasized that we have to keep the duality of specialized and general problem-solving modules in order to have a rational animal.

> Eventually the mind has to integrate the results of all those modular computations, and I don't see how there could be a module for doing that. . . . If in short, there is a community of computers living in my head, there had also better be somebody who is in charge; and by God, it had better be me.
> (Fodor, 1998, p. 19)

Fodor continued his battle on two grounds. One was the evolutionary psychology group; the other was new, sophisticated learning theories. As a continuation of connectionist theory, new specific models questioned his version of innatism. Domain-specificity and nativism were criticized by Elman et al. (1996). They also began a reanalysis of the facts that were obtained by people in the nativist camp. They proposed that sufficiently complex connectionist learning models could replace innatism.

Fodor (1998, 2000) also questioned these modularization conceptions that start off from a stepwise formation of modular organization. For Fodor, the essence of innatism is **content innatism**, and for many of the psychologists, this is a bit questionable. This hotly debated issue is basically the crucial dividing line between them.

The issue of mental architecture and modular organization comes up along lines that are similar to the issues of epigenesis and the prehistory of the human mind. Gerry Marcus (2005, 2006) offered a proposal to combine modularity with evolution in a systematic way.

> Descent with modification offers a way out. Although modules are by definition computationally distinct, they need not be genetically unrelated. Although evolutionary pressures can clearly lead distinct physiological structures to diverge and specialize, natural selection tends to be a slow process and many putative modules (e.g., a language faculty) are relatively recent and as such might be expected to derive from common origins. . . . [D]istinct neuro-cognitive modules could overlap considerably in their genetic substrates. If each module were built according to its own set of genes it would be unexplained why there is so much overlap between genes in (say) frontal cortex and the genes in (say) occipital cortex.
> (Marcus, 2006, p. 448)

*

Cognitive psychology in the mid-1950s started off as a rather ontologically neutral enterprise, trying to talk about the experimental proofs of an internal life and its relation to symbol processing. The first decade of cognitive science proper in the 1980s tried to make everything even more abstract and machine-like. This has given way, from the 1990s onward, to a return to the interpretation of the mind. The new trends all tried to have an interpretation of cognition. They either do it in terms of **neuroscience** (proximal biological interpretation), in terms of **evolution** (distal biological interpretation), or in terms of **social embedding**. Table 9.5 summarizes these developments according to the basic parameters of this book.

Table 9.5 The changes of cognitive psychology over half a century

Trend	Classical symbol processing	Connectionism	Interpreted cognition	Modularity and LOT
Object	Mind as representing	Elementary units	Complex mind	Specific, then universal
Method	Experiments, RT, error, simulation	Modeling	Experiment, brain data, modeling, development	History, experiment, brain data
Internal reduction	Basic boxes of architecture	Connections, associations	Core knowledges	Domains and propositions
External reduction	Irrelevant	Theoretical neural nets	Evolution, genes, brain, social relations	Genes (?), brain (?)

Tasks

CA

Compare symbol processing and connectionist models.
Top-down and bottom up in different cognitive models.
Neural processes in connectionism and in modularity.
Relations of neural and evolutionary interpretation of cognition.
Phrenology and modularity.
Innatism and child language development.
Compare visual pregnancy and the centrality of syntax in Chomsky!
What is meant by "computational theory" in Marr?
Rival models for the speed of language processing.

DSA

"Cognition" and "emotion" in common discourse (Google Ngram).
Chomsky, Bruner, and Simon from the 1960s in public discourse (Google Ngram).
Chomsky and Bruner from 1960 to 2000 in psychology (PsycINFO).
Co-occurrences of "syntax" and "meaning" in psychological texts (PsycINFO).
"Connectionism" over a hundred years in psychology (PsycINFO).
Kahneman, Newell, and Simon, 1970 to 2010, in the psychological literature (PsycINFO).
"Competence" and "performance" in the psychological literature (PsycINFO).

10 Roads toward a new psychology at the millennium

> I remain quite serious in suggesting that psychology is today turning the tables on physics and hard science. . . . The former stark, strictly physical, value-empty, and mindless cosmos previously upheld by science becomes infused now with cognitive and subjective qualities, values, and rich emergent macrophenomena of all kinds.
> Roger Sperry (1995, pp. 505–506)

The task of writing history certainly becomes more complex as we approach our times. The historian has the ambiguous task of writing objective, depersonalized histories of those events of which he was also a witness. Personal memories, or as the theoreticians of history writing like Nora (1989) tell it, collective memories and history, sometimes supplement each other, but sometimes they become rivals. I would still like to show the characteristic features of psychology of the last generation and suggest some extrapolations they might allow. Chapter 10 concentrates on theoretical novelties, while Chapter 11 on changes in the profession.

A self-conscious millennium

Psychology at the millennium, both regarding the profession and regarding the science of the mind, is characterized by a multiplicity of methods and a more and more complex embedding into society. This has also been coupled with an integration into the network of other sciences and professions. One could say that the wheel is rolling, and psychology develops in a cumulative road shaped by its intellectual issues and social needs. Our turn-of-the-century feeling is certainly present in psychology. In early 2019, there were about 5,000 entries mentioning 21st century in the PsycINFO database, with 965 containing "21st century" in their titles!

A representative enterprise provided an interesting vision. On the basis of the 27th International Congress of Psychology held in Stockholm, Sweden, in 2000, Bäckman and Holsten (2002) edited a twin volume on the situation of psychology at the millennium. The two volumes over 1,100 pages showed the state of the art based on 22 invited keynote talks and 45 state-of-the-art surveys. The first volume

DOI: 10.4324/9781032625805-12

dealt with theoretical foundations, cognitive psychology, and biological aspects, while the second volume concentrated on applied psychology and the profession. Though the survey had some random features of self-representation and selection, it provided some mirror of our recent past. In the theoretical volume, nine chapters dealt with experimental/cognitive psychology. That certainly showed the continuous strength of the cognitive movement. However, five chapters did deal with emotional processes. This is a sign of the times: affective psychology is indeed coming up. The health chapters dealt as well with emotion-related phenomena, like connections of stress and disease. Nowhere, however, was **any sign of interest toward motivational issues** present, not even in the neuroscience/neuropsychology chapter. In contrast, in the mid-20th century, motivation was at the fore. It was a key issue in the discussions of aggression, the role of drive reduction in learning and dependencies, whether imitation was a learned drive, and the dynamics of life from libido to achievement motivation (Cofer & Appley, 1964). As a consequence, yearly volumes of the *Nebraska Symposium on Motivation* were enthusiastically waited all over the world. The series is continued today, but it concentrates now on applied issues of emotion/motivation, such as anxieties, substance abuse, and similar ailments.

In the developmental/social volume for the millennium, out of the nine developmental chapters, three analyze the genetic determinants of behavior, temperament, and gender roles. Traditional issues are missing from the seven chapters on social psychology. There is no mention of group processes or attitudes in the entire book, and the chapters on "social psychology" concentrate on issues of cultural psychology and intercultural comparisons. This is a clear indicator of globalization. Another sign of the times is that three chapters deal with gender psychology issues. In the PsycINFO database, from 1950 to 1980, there were 350 papers with **gender** in the title, while in the next three decades, from 1980 to 2010, 25,000 similar papers showed up. Between the 1980s and the first decade of the 21st century, that number increased from 3,000 to 15,000.

Thus, the general outlook of these summarizing volumes is a strong cognitive psychology, colored with emotions and combined with neuroscience and genetic determinism, as well as a sensitivity to culture and identity combined with a neglect of motivation, group organization, and classical group-related attitude issues of social psychology.

A detailed scientometric analysis of 500,000 papers between 1995 and 2015, using keywords and internal coherence of the texts, showed the naturalization tendency. "[T]opics related to natural sciences are trending, while their 'counterparts' leaning to humanities are declining in popularity" (Wieczorek et al., 2021, p. 9699). During the 20 years, psychoanalysis was declining, as well as "pure" cognition, but they were still rather dominant topics.

New methods and problems with the data

There are several **methodical components** of the changes in present-day psychology. They basically involve three issues, which are of interest for historical reasons.

1. Finer behavioral methodologies.
2. Using new data gathering methods and public big data.
3. Refining statistical methodologies and realizing a data crisis.

Finer behavioral methodologies. One key issue in the development of psychological methods was the use of increasingly sensitive methods to study intact brains, sometimes on freely moving subjects, with time resolutions down to milliseconds and spatial resolutions down to microns. We can also know more about the psychological consequences or correlates of genetic variations as a corollary of the Human Genome Project. Of particular interest to psychology are the finer and finer behavioral observational methods that were also developed that made it possible to study behavior in natural circumstances. This allowed to supplement the precise timing of stimulation, characteristic of the cognitive movement, with a precise timing of the measurement of minute aspects of behavior that is extended to the observation of infants and children, as well as animals.

Think of one typical change that shows both the development of sensitivity of the methods and their generalization beyond their original target domains, the changes in **eye movement research**. In the 1960s, eye movement research was almost exclusively concerned with the role of eye movements in visual perception, following the tradition of Helmholtz, Sechenov, and Ribot, set up a hundred years earlier. A crucial issue was whether the eye movement patterns themselves are related to figural perception. What is the possible role of eye movements in shape recognition? The much-cited figure made by the Russian biophysicist Yarbus (1967) shows this attitude in Figure 10.1. The saccadic eye movements are

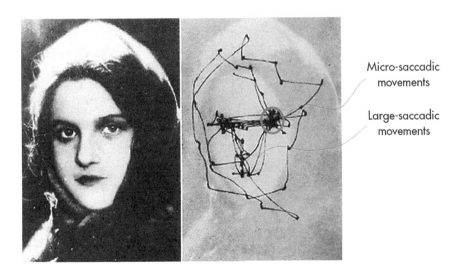

Figure 10.1 Saccadic eye movements while watching a photo.

Source: Yarbus (1967, p. 179). WikiCommons CCA-4.0 Source – Modeling and Simulating Eye Oculomotor Behavior to Support Retina Implant Development.

concentrated on the most informative parts of the face, on the eyes, mouth, and the outer contour.

The studies were made by rather uncomfortable devices, having little reflective prisms attached to the surface of the eye, and the reflection of infrared beamers from the prisms was photographed over a time window of sometimes several seconds. Today, the technologies do not apply mechanical attachments to the eyes. They follow the variant light reflection of the eye from the sclera and the cornea, making the tools available even in research on infants. At the same time, a substantial part of the research using **eye tracking** is no longer interested in the role of eye movements in vision as such but rather in what we can learn about the interest of the subject, for example, from a baby, or from an innocent customer from the direction of gaze. Thus, eye movement recording as a tool has become a new window to the mind, rather than a method merely for studying vision (Figure 10.2).

Using new data gathering methods and public big data. With the spread of the Internet, new options of data gathering, and new data types, appeared in psychology as well from the 1990s on. Both in experimental psychology and in personality and social psychology research, tailored Internet solutions to run experiments or fill questionnaires were initiated. The use of the Internet has become widespread in experimentation, social psychology, and counseling, with over 4,000 entries mentioning *web* in their titles from 1995 to 2019. Later, web-based platforms appeared that allow the collection of data from large samples, such as the *Qualtrics* platform. These approaches have a built-in methodological duality. They do allow for the increase of sample size, thus, to avoid the danger of the limits of generalization due

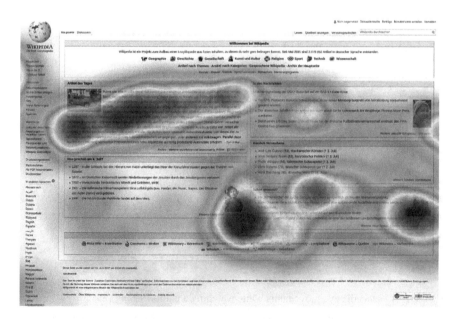

Figure 10.2 Eye movements "heat image" while watching a web page.

to small sample sizes. At the same time, the sample demographics might be skewed – people attached to the Internet would be overrepresented – and data gathering might be also distorted (such as other family members contributing to an attitude survey or a personality test with their opinions).

Still another novelty did appear with the spread of web surfaces. The age of **big data**, using online data from millions of people based on their Internet use, appeared in demographics, marketing research, and sociology. This big data revolution in social sciences basically asks people to do nothing. It merely analyses their manifest behavior on the Internet, such as their log-ins, the sites they visit, the likes and clicks they distribute. As summarized by Kitchin (2014), this new type of data gathering is characterized by three Vs: data **volume**, **velocity**, and **variety** about human users. In an optimistic frame, this is accompanied by a flexible and more fine-grained analysis.

The social science impact of the big data movement soon reached psychology. Studies started to do research both for practical and for theoretical purposes on how much we can learn about someone's future political or buying decisions on the basis of their likes on a social platform like Facebook, or how likely news spread, depending on the shared values of people connected in networks (Brady et al., 2017). These new possibilities promise increasing sample sizes, more variables, and finer temporal analysis for many aspects of behavior interesting for psychology. There are varieties that combine large n, for example, with less variables, and so on. In the meantime, psychologists should not forget that science does not come out of data with no theory. Further, while using large data sets, we still must face that using these data sets implies a general deindividualized philosophy of life.

Refining statistical methodologies and realizing a data crisis in the meantime. All statistical approaches do treat humans and their mental events as depersonalized variables, as well as treating the process of research as hypothesis testing in line with a masculine image of humans domineering the world. However, even within this hypothesis testing framework, there were dramatic changes of sophistication during the last generation. In the 1950s, when statistical comparison became a must, comparisons of two groups with t tests were acceptable, and analysis of variance was sophisticated. Today, due to the easy availability of computer software, multilevel analyses of variance with covariates and factor analysis belong to the repertory of even third-grade researchers. Narrative, that is, verbally and logically arranged reviews of empirical material, has been replaced by strictly and statistically organized meta-analytic protocols that combine the significances and the effect sizes of the studies reviewed.

The statistical refinery of psychology has substantially increased both in the experimental and in the psychometric traditions. Effect size estimates appeared and have become traditional methods besides p values over the last generation. Interestingly, psychologists worried about the idea of significance testing long ago, emphasizing that by rejecting the null hypothesis, many alternative hypotheses are in fact still valid. You can conclude when you compare, for example, girls and boys that they cannot be equal on a measure of grasp strength; thus, you reject the null hypothesis, though it can still be that girls are stronger or boys are stronger. It does not matter; you tend to use *ad hoc* hypotheses for *post hoc* explanations. More recently, Jacob Cohen (1994) insisted that psychologists should look at their data charts, use effect size estimates and replication studies, in order to become more reliable, besides merely using the $p < 0.05$ criterion.

In the last few decades, these issues have become dramatized under the labels of a **data and replication crisis**. For the history of psychology, it is worth remembering that the data crisis went on through three stages over a century, and the new millennium crisis is merely a last step.

1. Firstly, the very **data became uncertain**, as the debate on mental images showed more than a century ago. At the turn of the century, with the debates between image-based and imageless theories of thought, leading laboratories could not agree on what the data were, showing a bias of the laboratories (see Chapter 9 in Volume 1, and Ogden, 1911). This data crisis created two reactions. One was to dismiss these kinds of unreliable first-person data in the name of behaviorism; the other was to increase awareness of distortions, the role of experimenters, and the like.
2. The second crisis came with a realization that **data are influenced by expectations**, which was very heavily discussed in the 1960s and 1970s. This time, the troubles were no longer related to introspection as a weak chain in the research network but realized as distortions in relations to behavior. Experimental psychologists pointed out in carefully controlled experiments that expectations do have a role both in animal studies and in socially important human situations, such as the role of teacher expectations in education, the so-called Pygmalion effect (Rosenthal, 1966; Rosenthal & Jacobson, 1968). This was also the time of the later much-debated, cheating-based social psychology studies of various levels of obedience to authority or social majority, from researchers like Asch, Milgram, and Zimbardo. In the 1970s, these studies on experimenter effects were important for the experimentalists by pointing out the importance of hidden communications in determining behavior. They were also important for the anti-experimental people like Kenneth Gergen (1978), who questioned the entire possibility of experimenting on complex phenomena. This stage of data crisis pointed toward more careful consideration of context and more blind controls for the experimentalists. As a self-posed puzzle: How does one interpret experimental results from now on, since experimental data showed the context sensitivity of experimental data? This context sensitivity has led to many suggestions regarding eyewitness testimony and the restrictions on leading questions (Loftus, 1975), or to the restrictions on labeling students and clients. These debates have led to more awareness in experimental planning even in animal research, where issues like the sex of the human assistant is considered when studying, for example, animal stress hormones.
3. Our recent data crisis is related to the **problem of data and statistics**. There was a shocking realization of the problem following a paper written by a huge consortium of scholars (Open Science Cooperation, 2015) who tried make reproductions of 100 modern psychological studies. To their great surprise, even with

all the identical method controls, only 40% could be replicated. This has led to fierce debates, sometimes with entirely discouraging connotations, supporting anti-scientific feelings.

A very influential anonymous writer, Neuroskeptic (2012), on the basis of these tensions, created an entire list of the social dangers of scientific mistakes and frauds. He called them "The Nine Circles of Scientific Hell."

Limbo. When you are just overlooking errors, superficiality, and sloppiness.
Overselling. Appears when you exaggerate the relevance of your results.
Post hoc storytelling. Interpreting the results as if there were a hypothesis.
p value fishing. Slightly preferring $p < 0.05$ over 0.06.
Creative outliers. Excluding problematic cases, referring to technicalities.
Plagiarism. Taking texts or theories from others.
Non-publication. Not publicizing results against your expectations.
Partial publication. Publishing only what reinforces your theory and position.
Inventing data. This really happens. The most famous case being Diederik Stapel of Tilburg University, who fabricated the data for a few dozen papers and several frequently cited books (https://en.wikipedia.org/wiki/Diederik_Stapel).

There are many social and scientific reactions to all these tensions. On a descriptive level, sensitive behavioral research has called for greater responsibility with data. This does not imply the end of science, or a radical constructionism, but a greater research rigor and a return to one classical value of science, namely, to public transparency in science. Recent discussions on statistical methods and on the difficulties of replicating experiments resulted in more rigorous research standards and an increase in the public aspects of science. The most interesting suggestions derived from these debates are not hopeless reactions but the advice of the scientific community. A more open science is needed, and a system of recognition and publication practice that makes the null effect research visible and fosters the replication studies as well. The very context-sensitive behavioral research taught all of us to be more careful with our data. It does not bring an end to science or to total relativism but brings more rigor and a re-establishment of one classical value of science, its public nature.

Multiplicity of psychological explanations: a comprehensive look at the three aspects

From the last third of the 19th century on, following the hermeneutic debates around Windelband and Dilthey (see Chapter 10 in Volume 1), a leading vision of doing research on the mind was to follow the example of natural science methodically and, regarding content or substance, to interpret the mind as a natural phenomenon. In one of these natural science approaches, the mind was interpreted as "natural" due to an assumed continuity between bodily, neural, and mental processes, which sometimes even claimed that mental processes would be identical to some neural excitation, or at least reducible to it. This was certainly a program of physiological materialism. There was another naturalistic perspective, however. As a continuation of the Darwinian heritage, several generations of psychologists would claim that mental processes are similar to bodily processes in the sense that they are the results of an evolutionary selection of the past several million years, and they were stabilized because they had an adaptive function. For a century, philosophers – starting with Husserl (1910/2002) – as well as psychologists with a softer engagement concentrating on culture, from Spranger (1926) on, debated that both of these kinds of reductionism were false. The novelty of the latest generation of naturalists is not the mere fact that the idea of a neurobiological and evolutionary reduction or anchorage comes up again but the fact that now these reductions are clustered together. Psychologists started to think in a quadrangle of evolution-experience-culture-nervous system. It is an attempt to overcome the naivety and one-sidedness of the 150-year-old reductionist attempts. This combination is illustrated in Figure 10.3.

During the work of the last generation, many of the traditional vicissitudes and traps of these approaches seem to have been resolved or at least softened. There are several basic reasons for this change, which all have to do with a more complex image, replacing traditional dualities with at least triangles, and models of multiple causation. As Andler (1992) pointed out in his recent summary of the cognitive trends, naturalization has become a new brand for the scientific interpretation of the mind, working from the direction of neuroscience and evolutionary biology in parallel and from cooperation.

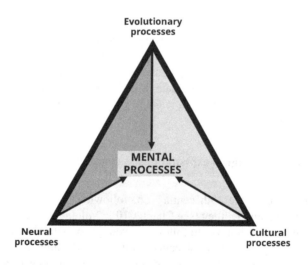

Figure 10.3 The multiple determination in present-day psychology.

Evolutionary psychology: a new paradigm, indeed?

The triple Darwinian message – animal/human continuity, selection, and individual differences – was treated in a compartmentalized manner by traditional Darwinists of psychology. Each Darwinist sub-camp emphasized only one of the issues (see Chapter 7 in Volume 1). Either they dealt with comparative psychology with some outlook on child development or, as in the tradition of instrumental conditioning (and behaviorism), with the mechanisms of adaptive selection in learning, or the genetic determination of individual differences.

For a redefinition of psychological issues within an evolutionary framework, a great step was taken when a new generation of researchers in experimental cognitive psychology realized that, for a better understanding of the human mind, one must find a biological interpretation, along the lines of interpreted cognition outlined at the end of Chapter 9. We know better today what it is exactly that we have to explain due to experimental cognitive psychology. But for a serious explanation, a distant time frame and a functionalist attitude should be used. This realization was met with the emancipation of human ethology as a subfield along with the discussions concerning sociobiology. The differences and continuities between sociobiology and later evolutionary psychology are not particularly trivial. While sociobiologists were reductionist naturalists, ignoring the mind (Wilson, 1975), evolutionary psychology realized a need for a new biological vision that deals with the inner world. Evolutionary psychology does not ignore the mind, as behaviorism and radical sociobiology did, and does not treat it as a mere shadow, as some models in neuroscience tend to do. Evolutionary psychology takes the psychological side to belong to the proximal stage of explanation in the sense of the evolutionary system theorist Ernst Mayr (1982), and it takes up the relations between mind and evolution as it was dropped a century earlier. This return to the classic attitude was a drastic change compared to the attitude of sociobiology, which tended to treat the mental realm as an epiphenomenon.

The "evolutionary psychology" brand was started by the programmatic book of the Santa Barbara group (Barkow et al., 1992). It launched the entire brand name as a self-identifying movement in the 1990s, which was strengthened in the next decade, as shown in Figure 10.4.

There are two important underlying aspects shown on Figure 10.4. First, while "evolutionary psychology" certainly has a shining career in the last two decades, the broader biological discipline, ethology, remains a more stable reference point, even within psychology. Second, though "evolutionary psychology" suddenly became important, "cultural psychology" was not forgotten. It is another, gradually increasing, new synthetic discipline (see the international survey in the volume edited by Jovanovic et al., 2019). Similarly, the rise of evolutionary psychology did not outgrow cognitive psychology, which still remains a stronger self-identifying logo.

Contemporary evolutionary psychology, as outlined in a programmatic way by the books edited by Barkow, Cosmides, and Tooby (1992) and by Buss (1994,

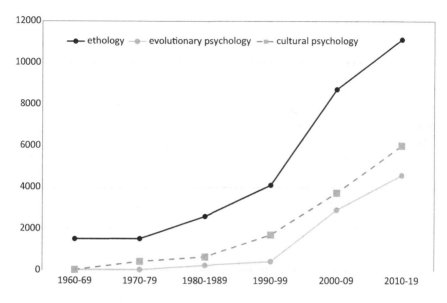

Figure 10.4 The fate of the terms *ethology, cultural psychology*, and *evolutionary psychology* in the psychological literature.

Source: Based on the PsycINFO database.

1999, 2009), considers humans and the experience-laden phenomena of the human mind to be central in understanding evolution compared to earlier comparative psychology and to ethology, which did not. The refreshing, new features of evolutionary psychology in applying the Darwinian heritage are:

- Studying modern humans with an evolutionary commitment (in contrast to studying only animals).
- Interpreting the architecture of the human mind and our preferences as the results of a long history of adaptation.
- The capacity to develop culture is also interpreted as a result of adaptive processes through hundreds of thousands of years.

While many critics interpreted evolutionary psychology's focus on humans to be a limitation, it is not a defect of the endeavor. Evolutionary psychology deals with humans not because of narrow-mindedness but rather because it seeks answers to questions that are inherently connected to the human condition: How do we see colors? Why are there so many languages? What is the origin, function, and role of personality differences? Why are we jealous? So on and so forth.

For the birth of an integrated evolutionary psychology, the analysis of social processes was also a missing point. A new social mentality appeared with individualized and biologically anchored social mind (Humphrey, 1976). Many evolutionary psychologists see continuity between biological evolution relying on selective advantages and the unfolding of the basic parameters of culture. This attitude entails a commitment to postulating a social mind with culture-building capabilities as a biological heritage. In this regard, contemporary evolutionary psychology returns to the original Darwinian message and sharply criticizes the separation of evolution and culture/society by most of 20th-century social science. At the same time, unlike sociobiology, it does not consider mental experiences and social organizations as mere epiphenomena. Providing an evolutionary explanation for our partner preferences, for example, does not eliminate the very feeling of attraction. Attraction and love are mediating factors providing for the success of evolutionary determinants of partner choice and maintenance in everyday life. Contemporary evolutionary psychology treats the internal world as itself an agent of evolution. Finally, evolutionary psychology is not exclusive. It tries to connect the three crucial issues of psychology: organization and change of knowledge, including intentionality; the factors of feelings and moving behavior; and the issue of individual differences. Thus, it promises to deliver a unified vision of humans. In this effort toward unification, it treats evolution as a general integrative principle for all of psychology.

As Barker and Buss (2006, p. 69) put it in a didactic interview, in the vision of evolutionary psychology, all psychological mechanisms originate from and owe their existence to evolutionary processes at some basic level. Darwin's theories of natural and sexual selection are the most important evolutionary processes responsible for creating evolved psychological mechanisms. It is a real novelty in psychology that they combine both kinds of selections into a single model. At the same time, alongside the inspiration of modern cognitive psychology, they use an information processing metaphor as well. Evolved psychological mechanisms can be described as algorithmic devices. They are designed to take inputs, transform them through a series of procedures, and produce outputs at various points throughout an organism's life span. The output of evolved psychological mechanisms can be physiological activity, like heightened sexual arousal, information that serves as input to other psychological mechanisms (writing a poem for your beloved one), or manifest behavior (kissing an attractive partner). Evolved psychological mechanisms are instantiated in the brain in the wiring and activation patterns of neural structures. These mechanisms are formed in an epigenetic process during the individual lifetime. They serve to solve statistically recurrent adaptive problems that our ancestors confronted; thus, they are tied to a stone age mind.

Evolutionary psychology treats itself as a general metatheory of psychology. The "central promise of evolutionary psychology starts from the idea that the main non arbitrary way to identify, describe and understand psychological mechanisms is to articulate their functions – the specific adaptive problems they were designed by selection to solve" (Buss, 1995, p. 6). Table 10.1 shows some examples from Buss how this way of thought operates with adaptations.

The achievements of evolutionary psychology have transformed many chapters of modern psychology. They have provided a new adaptationist frame to interpret the architecture of the human mind (how memory systems or human communicative systems developed), offered a Darwinian frame to interpret specific

Table 10.1 Some examples from the list of Buss (1995) for psychological mechanisms with an evolutionary base

Psychological mechanism	Function
Fear of snakes	Avoid poison
Better female location memory	Fruit collecting
Male sex jealousy	Paternity certainty
Female preference for mates with resources	Child-rearing
Male preference for young mates	Fertility
Savanna-like landscape preference	Provision for resources

achievements (face recognition, spatial memory), and interpreted our motivational preferences and avoidances (mate selection, food aversions, etc.). Evolutionary psychology has offered a new inspiration for developmental psychology as well, with its interest in universal patterns of infancy, and has given a novel approach for social psychology (pointing at the genesis of the primary social mind) and personality psychology (the adaptive role of individual differences). At the same time, this new trend, with its new journals (*Evolution, Mind and Behaviour* from 2000, *Evolutionary Psychology* from 2003), textbooks, like Barrett et al. (2001), and conference series, has created a lot of discussion and motivated a series of criticisms as well, as shown under CONTROVERSIES.

Controversies

Questioning evolutionary psychology

Besides all the success of evolutionary psychology, ironical and conceptual doubts have also appeared. One line of the criticism treats the issue of ultra-adaptationism, and another the super-modularity issue. Jerry Fodor, as a representative of the traditionalist cognitive camp, was on the forefront of both of these challenges. Fodor (1998, 2000) raised concerns in two books about the claims of radical evolutionary psychology, radical computational psychology, as well as their alliance. Fodor realized that the architecture of the human mind proposed by evolutionary psychology challenges the traditional Cartesian unified Ego when it dissolves the Ego in the world of modules. Fodor (1983) upheld his original claims in *Modularity of mind*, where he proposed modules to be domain-specific computational systems, but at the same time kept some sort of central processor. When these proposals showed up, Fodor (2000) emphasized that we have to keep the duality of specialized and general problem-solving modules in order to have a rational animal. Fodor also challenged the adaptationist program, the other central aspect of the new evolutionary psychology. According to the views of evolutionary psychology, all architectural, conceptual, and preferential aspects of the human mind must have a specific adaptationist story – and they are there because they have a biological function. In modern evolutionary talks, the God-like planner is replaced by the planner of Mother Nature. However, Mother Nature should also be eliminated from a consistent Darwinism. "Psychological Darwinism is a kind of conspiracy theory. . . . [W]hat seemed to be your, after all, unsurprising interest in your child's well-being turns out to be your genes' conspiracy to propagate themselves. Not your conspiracy, notice, but theirs" (Fodor, 1998, p. 211.)

Fodor (2000) basically claimed that the mind is neither entirely modular nor strictly based on adaptive usage. Contrary to Pinker (1997) and his British pair, Plotkin (1997), Fodor claimed that a computational theory of mind is not easy to reconcile with evolutionary ideas. Remain innatist without accepting the adaptationist tales! Fodor tried to show that innate structures are Platonic universals that have no clear evolutionary or ontogenetic explanation. He treated the issue of the coherence of thoughts more importantly than simple explanatory tales. He realized that many of the evolutionary cognitive proposals like those of Dennett (1997a) are basically metaphoric. Later, Fodor even challenged the Darwinian program of biology (Fodor, 2008; Fodor and Piattelli-Palmarini, 2010), claiming that "selection" and "selection for" were not equivalent and there is a certain circularity in Darwinian explanations. Fodor's fights against evolutionary psychology could, in fact, be argued to have had an anti-Darwinism almost of religious fervor. As the Hungarian cognitive scientist Gábor Bródy (2010) mentioned, on the basis of Fodor, the logical trouble with Darwinian selectionist explanations is certainly the difficulty to differentiate adaptations from mere by-products. There always remains a feeling of "just-so stories" in the adaptationist explanations. However, in the traditionally minded cognitive challenges toward evolutionary explanations, there seems to be an issue of perfect design as well. Some cognitivists would like to see a motivated "perfect design," which is certainly not true of real existing biological systems, that were developed under local constraints, using "cludges" and tinkering (Marcus, 2008).

The challenging neo-Darwinian program met criticisms of a more methodical kind as well. Buller (2005) claimed to have identified four fallacies of the aforementioned program of evolutionary psychology, especially in the use of arguments derived from studies on present-day university students toward the old adaptive environment. I list his critiques with some soft interpretive commentary.

Fallacy 1: Analysis of Pleistocene Adaptive Problems Yields Clues to the Mind's Design. This critique is a commitment toward total social constructionism: we are the way we are because our society is as it is.

Fallacy 2: We know, or we can discover, what distinctively human traits are. This critique is a statement about the futility of looking toward human universals, as done, for example, in the descriptive work of Brown (1999).

Fallacy 3: "Our Modern Skulls House a Stone Age Mind." This critique is rather strong. It questions the presupposed mental continuity over 50,000 years.

Fallacy 4: The psychological data provide clear evidence for pop EP. This is a methodical criticism. It is hard to believe, for example, that an analysis of the sexual behavioral patterns of contemporary college students really tells something about the way humans universally are.

Buller argued that a basic fallacy of evolutionary psychology is its inability to find strong supports because it postulates universals of human nature that were never really proven. Methodically, its main fallacy is a reverse engineering attitude: it stars off from a Pleistocene mind and tries to find with soft questionnaire methods their supports in present-day life. This is true, however, of most modern psychology. We study WEIRD people (White, educated, industrialized, rich, and Democratic) to arrive to universals. This can be remedied by combining cultural and evolutionary approaches.

Ketellar and Ellis (2000) raised some more methical philosophical issues. They claimed that EP should develop testable predictions in the technical sense or realize that it is more a fruitful compass for a research program rather than a hypothesis-testing enterprise. At the same time, it should also allow for co-development and environmental optimization. Evolutionary psychology should postulate rigid and flexible, early and late closing processes.

We could add to this list that we should not necessarily postulate an adaptation story for everything, we should not entertain total modularity, and we should not expect engineering perfection. As emphasized half a century ago by Lévi-Strauss (1958, 1966), later by Jacob (1977, 1982), and today by Marcus (2008), both somatic evolution and mental evolution have to work with what is available; it is characterized by **tinkering** and therefore with less than engineering optimization. We use whatever is available.

Contemporary evolutionary psychologists certainly have to face the challenge raised by Gould and Lewontin (1979). We all should certainly be suspicious of "just-so stories." This is a reference to the famous book of Kipling for children, published in 1902, where the British colonial author explains the origin of animal-specific features with *ad hoc* stories. For example, one just so story is that the *camel got his hump* because he was punished after some wrongdoing, and this beating resulted in a hump. The avoidance of stories such as these should not mean, however, that the reverse engineering and adaptationist approach should be dropped altogether. It merely has to be more systematic and rely on different types of evidences, such as how we see today in the combination of evolutionary ideas with neuroscience.

Alternative versions of evolutionary psychology

Especially regarding the modularity issue promoted by evolutionary psychology, which is criticized sharply by Buller and Fodor, an alternative was taking shape in another group of psychologists committed to the evolutionary case. Many critics of evolutionary psychology pointed out that a more flexible vision is necessary. First, one should consider the unfolding of niches and, in this way, gene–environment co-evolutions. One should also look for broader adaptations, not merely explanations of single behavioral traits, and in this process, the understanding of ontogenetic development should be central, as well as a consideration of the proximal mechanisms of functions, that is, the underlying neural structures and processes. Thus, evolutionary explanations should not be dropped but should be done with a broader attitude.

At the end, two contemporary interpretations of evolutionary psychology emerged. One is the view of the path-breaking Santa Barbara school that is headed by Cosmides and Tooby and taken up by Buss (1995, 1999, 2009) and Pinker (2002). In this group, a connection is proposed between modular brain organization and mosaic-like selective adaptations for different cognitive domains and functions, in the form of the so-called Swiss army knife model of evolution and cognitive organization. There is a specialized adaptation for all problems in all species (Tooby & Cosmides, 1990, 1992; Cosmides & Tooby, 1994; Pinker, 2002). This is the **standard-view evolutionary psychology**, or EP for short. This approach ties a peculiar interpretation of Darwin to computational or algorithmic concepts of cognitive psychology and a conservative social vision since it assumes rather fixed adaptations.

The other approach is softer and, at the same time, broader. We can call this more comprehensive approach **evolutionary attitude**, EA. This approach tries to be a proponent of Darwinian thinking in any field of psychology, as represented, for example, by an early textbook of Gaulin and McBurney (2001), who described "general psychology" from the perspective of evolution. It does not entail an ultra-adaptationist attitude, and regarding the architecture of the mind, it combines modular organization with general cognition. This view is more generous from a historical point of view as well. It establishes a continuity between the earlier Darwinian ideas that arose in psychology: the biological, down-to-earth functionalism of late-19th-century comparative psychology with a tradition spanning over a hundred years; the evolutionary epistemology proposed by the followers of Karl Popper (Campbell, 1974); and contemporary evolutionary concepts. The novelty of the present situation is not our questions (curiosity about whether animals can think or what is the role of social contacts in the human mind existed 150 years ago as well as today) but, in the greater data sets, more sophisticated methods on animals, children, and humans of diverse cultures.

Many central questions of the leading psychological theories are shown in two distinctively different but in an equally evolutionary light in the framework of the two varieties of new evolutionary psychologies. Table 10.2 shows some features of the two frameworks. The evolutionary attitude is most clearly represented today

Table 10.2 Two approaches on the application of evolutionary ideas to psychology

Issues	Evolutionary psychology (EP)	Evolutionary attitude (EA)
Adaptationism	Every mental feature is an adaptation	Adaptations and exaptations
Architecture of the mind	Entirely modular	Modules and general cognition
Determinant features	Early environment, Pleistocene mind	Epigenetic programs, interactions
Focus	Sexual attraction, motivation	All of human psychology
Computation	Adaptations as programs	Neuro-developmental

by Tomasello (1999, 2009, 2014) and Csibra and Gergely (2009). It is very telling that in the critical frame of Buller, neither Tomasello nor Dennett (1994) appeared at all.

The relationship between evolutionary prehistory, advocated by EP, and "real human history" also become a respected and interesting question again. There are some avant-garde efforts to create this connection. One of them is the conception of Merlin Donald (1991, 2001, 2018), a Toronto-based cultural evolutionist. For him, the key to continuity between prehistory and history is the fact that the crucial moments both in hominid evolution and in cultural change are always parallel and corollary changes in mental representation and communicational tools in the construction of the human mind.

As for the future of Darwinian psychology, there are a few challenges to meet.

- Clarifying multiple mappings between evolutionary tools and social roles. We would also hope to find new explanatory mechanisms of the relationships between models of biological change and the spread of cultural knowledge.
- Offering an accurate interpretation of the EvoDevo-brain-genes interface. One of the interesting central topics today is to see how patterns of gene activation and individual life events "correlate" in the unfolding of the brain and behavioral individuality.
- Creating possibilities to combine theoretical functionalism with individual variation research; discovering how genetics and "'embriology' contribute to the unfolding of psychological individuality" (Pléh & Boross, 2015, pp. 12–13).

Social life as a biological adaptation

During the past three decades, with the advent of evolutionary psychology and its gradually developing contacts with developmental issues, a new and serious challenge has emerged regarding **the biological routing of some of the most cherished cultural achievements and features of humans**. This challenge involves the idea that some of our cultural habits and propensities are the results of interactions between biological constraints and cultural shaping, rather than being constructed by culture alone.

Psychologists as well as naturalistically minded social scientists entertain a double-faced biology today, treating proximal and distal factors as proposed by Mayr (1982) together. They tend to combine the neuro and the evolutionary attitude. Genes and plasticity are treated together in certain research programs, not as exclusive factors. This happens both in biology and in developmental studies in psychology (Ellis & Bjorklund, 2005; Marcus, 2001, 2004, 2005).

Elementary sociality is treated in the last generation as a basic starting point rather than as a result of external constraints (Tomasello, 1999, 2009; Gergely & Csibra, 2006; Csibra & Gergely, 2009, 2011). We do not have to believe in "supraindividual minds" or the like to deal with the social aspects of human life. Even the social aspects of the human mind should be found in the mind itself.

The optimistic naturalists of today emphasize three new issues. Primary sociality, the emergence of a ToM, and the ability to create cultures based on a social mind.

Sociality is a primitive, initial biological fact. It is not a secondary result of socialization, but a result of evolutionary adaptations, or exaptations. The traditional divisions in this regard were rather straightforward (Chapter 5). According to one of the possible interpretations, the human mind, as an individual biological organization, is controlled by a social-cultural environment and develops a secondary social attribute (see SSSM as mocked by Pinker, 1997). This approach saw no continuity between evolution and history and treated our social nature as entirely constructed. The other interpretation, which is becoming more visible today, presents a similarity or continuity between biological evolution and social history and would differentiate between elementary biological sociality and the societal mind as a secondary product. Nicolas Humphrey (1976) initiated the renewal of this biological theory more than a generation ago – this is true even in anthropogenesis. According to this vision, during anthropogenesis, the original function of hominid intellect was to give orientation in social life, either in a positive way, via imitation, empathy, role modeling, and similar functions, or in a "negative way," by means of manipulation, by development of what is called today a Machiavellian intelligence. In the vision of Humphrey, social intelligence became the leading form of intelligence in social primates:

> [T]hey must be able to calculate the consequences of their own behavior, to calculate the likely behavior of others, to calculate the balance of advantage and loss.... "[S]ocial skill" goes hand in hand with intellect, and here at last the intellectual faculties required are of the highest order. The game of social plot and counter-plot cannot be played merely on the basis of accumulated knowledge, any more than can a game of chess.
> (Humphrey, 1976, p. 312)

The social intellect in this vision has contributed to the development of subsistence intelligence in leading toward better technologies, and also social and societal organizations, especially organizations intended to teach the young for the subsistence technologies in social settings.

The anthropologist Dan Sperber (1996), *horribile dictu*, even talked about a double materialistic stance of the social and human sciences. They deal with representations that are functional states of the brain, and these representations are shared. Sperber has also spelled out that this attitude makes the cognitive sciences and psychology central players in the foundations of social sciences. "Mental phenomena are present everywhere in social processes, and in an essential manner.... The materialistic program for the social sciences needs a materialistic vision of mental phenomena. This conception is developed by the cognitive sciences" (Sperber, 1996, p. 12).

Recruiting the existing brain to do new tasks is an interesting example of the interactions involved here. A cortical area is dedicated to a cognitive task but not strictly prewired for it. This logic shown, for example, in bilingual brains might be valid in cultural systems and brain relations as well. Stanislaw Dehaene, the French cognitive neuroscientist, demonstrated the process with regards to reading. A common neural network at the intersection of parieto-occipito-temporal areas is activated when reading words in different writing systems. This sensitive area could not have naturally formed by evolution to make a sight for reading. It was most likely formed to all sharp vision of textures under small angles, like in working with instruments and face recognition. Reading as a cultural system recruited this system that was there for wider purposes.

According to Dehaene and Cohen:

The neuronal recycling hypothesis consists of the following postulates:

1. Human brain organization is subject to strong anatomical and connectional constraints inherited from evolution. Organized neural maps are present early on in infancy and bias subsequent learning.
2. Cultural acquisitions (e.g., reading) must find their 'neuronal niche,' a set of circuits that are sufficiently close to the required function and sufficiently plastic as to reorient a significant fraction of their neural resources to this novel use.
3. As cortical territories dedicated to evolutionarily older functions are invaded by novel cultural objects, their prior organization is never entirely erased.

(Dehaene & Cohen, 2007, pp. 384–385)

One might speculate that similar processes may have been present regarding the genesis of language as well. The Broca's area might have been selected for producing quickly changing movements, and the Wernicke area for the analysis of quickly changing acoustic patterns. Language might have been recycling these existing neural modules, and the combinations would be recruited in a stabilized manner that had the best, that is, fastest, and most reliable results.

Cultural learning as a species-specific adaptation

The entire issue of culture has become central both for the naturalistic and for the more humanistic trends. The very notion of **cultural psychology** as a self-identity has become popular around the turn of the century. The term appears sporadically in the 1960s, is gradually reinforced over a generation, shows up over 1,000 times in the 1990s, and has 2,300 references in the first decade of the new millennium, as shown on Figure 10.3. James Mark Baldwin (1909, 1911) already proposed a century ago that one peculiar feature of humans is **cultural learning**. We spend quite a few years in all sorts of cultural contexts, even in preliterate societies, as Humphrey (1976) also highlighted it, with acquiring arbitrary cultural systems. As young children, we struggle with language and with our family relationships, while as adolescents, we struggle with social order, moral regulations, friendships, and gender contacts. Cultural learning and brain development go hand in hand.

The assumption as a biologically based primary sociality is central to these triple connections. Our culture-forming ability is a key biological adaptation. Some cultural theorists talk about the specificity of this ability (Boyd & Richerson, 1985) and even claim that there is a biological adaptation for building cultures (Tooby & Cosmides, 1992). Still others believe that there is no special cultural "preadaptation." Rather, the extreme cultural richness of humans is not a biological heritage but a by-product. "Humans are not particularly cultural animals; it is human populations that have become extremely cultural" (Morin, 2016, p. 245). In this vision, social learning as a basic mechanism incidentally leads to culture in dense populations. "We do not need any particular talent for cultural transmission. Culture is not of the human essence. It is, in the context of human sociability, an accident that was quite likely to occur" (Morin, 2016, p. 252).

Cultural learning is intimately tied to the interpretation of intentional action of others in the human species. Thus, in this regard, there is no difference between biology and culture. According to arguments like that of Baldwin's, learning agents can influence the evolution of the genes or their culture. Barrett et al. (2002) show in their textbook that even the comparison of nearly exact (genes) versus the much less exact (culture) reproduction is rather questionable. They mockingly compare the "heritabilities" in biological and cultural traits. Interestingly enough, some of the cultural traits show as much correlation within human populations as biological traits do. The heritability of height is 0.86, and that of religion is 0.71. "Cultural transmission, it seems, is both reliable and surprisingly robust by comparison with genetically transmitted traits" (Barrett et al., 2002, p. 356). The same is true for the comparison of the speed of cultural and evolutionary change.

Selectionist models of cultural learning showed up as well. One can postulate four cycles about the determination of human life. The first Darwinian phase is responsible for creating new reactions to environmental challenges, while the second phase, individual learning, is responsible for adequacy, for the accommodation to the environment. In humans, this is supplemented by internal manipulation and selection, by thought selection, and by culture. Culture can be interpreted as a subsystem that combines learned habits with rational insight and representation, that is, thinking. This combination is based either on imitation or on rational argument and on specific mechanisms, like constrained imitation emphasized by Richerson and Boyd. One can take a reversed vision of the cycles as well. Starting from the cycle of culture, some subsystems, such as science, create socialization patterns which direct the learning systems through the world of thinking. We teach the new generation to read, write, and count in order to provide them with representational systems that allow for faster mental selection and more efficient planning.

Several new proposals of the last generation, the most notable among them being that of Tomasello (1999) and Gergely and Csibra (2006), pointed out that a striking feature of humans, even in contrast with other primates, is the presence of a **teaching attitude that supplements cultural learning**. We are a teaching and learning species, prepared to learn from our seniors and to teach the juniors: we apply a **pedagogical stance** from early on, as Gergely and Csibra (2006) phrase it. Our infants have expectations that older teachers will direct the learning systems according to comprehensive systems of expectations. The world of thinking will come through such a teaching–culture interaction.

Human infants are prewired with a natural pedagogy stance. They form a peculiar learning niche together with the environment, causing species-specific, peculiar ways of learning. The natural pedagogy approach of Gergely and Csibra (2006) and Csibra and Gergely (2009) presupposes that, using the evolutionarily given constraints of mutuality and learning from adult cues, cultures are built up and maintained by an evolutionary learning process.

> Human infants are prepared to be at the receptive side of natural pedagogy by being sensitive to ostensive signals that indicate that they are being addressed by communication,
>
> (i) by developing referential expectations in ostensive contexts and
> (ii) by being biased to interpret ostensive-referential communication as conveying information that is kind-relevant and generalizable.
>
> (Csibra & Gergely, 2009, p. 158)

Theory of mind as the central aspect of social cognition

The central point of the new theory of biologically based sociality is the assumption of a naive theory of mind, or ToM. The **theory of mind attribution** is a feature where sociality and the intentional aspects of the mind do become attached to each other: when paying attention to others, humans try to discover their intentions, and that would be the royal way of social integration as well. As a continuation of the Humphrey program, new approaches assign sociality to the individual mind and try to elaborate a theory of primary sociality on a biological basis. These attempts usually rely on the analysis of primary attachment processes, the formation of the theory of mind, and the unfolding of intention attribution for and by conspecifics.

The assumed theory of mind is a commitment not merely to adapt to others but to treat others as beings who also entertain beliefs and desires and who are feeling and thinking beings. From a historical point of view, this is a social learning theory that moves folk psychology into the focus of thinking about the human mind. Psychology finally openly admits its attachment to folk psychology.

In the 1960s and 1970s, it rarely showed up in the psychological literature, and if it did, it usually did so with meanings different from the present-day usage. It started to gain ground in the 1980s (100 appearances), got boosted in the 1990s (800 references), and has become a star in the first decade of our century, with over 2,700 appearances in the psychological literature, and over 4,000 times between 2010 and 2015.

This research initiated by Leslie (1987) and Perner (1991), in fact, followed the steps of the comparative issues raised by Premack and Woodruff (1978) and the philosophical issues raised by Dennett (1978b, 1987). Premack showed videotapes of disrupted actions (e.g., to open a cage) of human agents for a human-raised chimpanzee. The chimpanzee was able, for example, to realize what was necessary to escape from a cage. Thus, the human-raised animal understood the "epistemic situation" of the social agent seen on the video. The interpretation had interesting consequences for human psychology and for knowledge attribution in general.

> In assuming that other individuals *want, think, believe*, and the like, one infers states that are not directly observable, and one uses these states anticipatorily, to predict the behavior of others as well as one's own. These inferences, which amount to a theory of mind, are, to our knowledge, universal in human adults.
> (Premack & Woodruff, 1978, p. 525)

The study of the **mentalizing ability of different animals** resulted in a large experimental literature. As two participant researchers summarized a generation of studies, the picture emerging is rather complex.

> On the 30th anniversary of Premack and Woodruff's seminal paper asking whether chimpanzees have a theory of mind . . ., there is solid evidence from several different experimental paradigms that chimpanzees understand the goals and intentions of others, . . . but there is currently no evidence that chimpanzees understand false beliefs. Our conclusion for the moment is, thus, that chimpanzees understand others in terms of a perception–goal psychology, as opposed to a full-fledged, human-like belief–desire psychology.
> (Call & Tomasello, 2008, p. 187)

The entire issue of human mentalization initiated by the works of Leslie (1987) and Perner (1991) is based on the fact that we are especially good at attributing knowledge and desires to our partners, which goes under the names of folk psychology, mentalizing ability, or commonsense psychology. Our ability to attribute mental states to various agents, in order to interpret, explain, and predict their actions, plays a central role in complex human social life and intentional communication. There were many classic proposals showing that children achieved this complex ability between 3 and 4 years of age (Perner, 1991). At the same time, autism started to be interpreted as a missing theory of mind module-based disorder, even as a "mind blinded" state (Baron-Cohen, 1995). Most of these studies used a false belief task: the human observer, usually a child, sees that an actor changed an object, or its place. When another actor, who went out, comes back, the child has to guess what the misguided actor would think. Children up to 3–4 years of age are unable to entertain two perspectives, and they respond as if they assumed that the other also knows the truth. The role of ToM is certainly central; it should be clear at the same time that "human social cognition" cannot be identical with "theory of mind ability" as shown in false belief tasks. ToM research led to a more structured conception of this ability, its development, the underlying cognitive/neural machinery, and consequentially, of social cognition. In several studies, a much earlier gradual emergence of this ability was revealed, involving qualitatively different and much earlier stages. Ágnes Kovács et al. (2010) showed that infants, already at 7 months old, are sensitive to the mental states of others, as evidenced by their looking patterns. This capacity may be a crucial factor of the unfolding of a social sense in humans. A rather structured image of social cognition and ToM ability, as a part of it, is suggested by empirical findings. Bartsch and Wellman (1995) showed, analyzing the spontaneous talk of children, that after the early spontaneous attention to the mental state of others, in the later, more "conscious" consideration, children first concentrate on the desires of people, which is supplemented around 4 years with a consideration of beliefs as well in their speech.

The idea of a ToM and the accompanying belief–desire psychology moves toward a more abstract, and therefore more general, conception of human sociality than the one treated by classic social psychology. For classic social psychology, the differential attribution of intentions to others was the issue, the attribution of personality-based intentions to others, and bad luck to ourselves (Kelley, 1967, 1992). Lee Ross (1977), in a very influential paper, cited over 3000 times, even talked about "intuitive psychologists" but was still mainly interested in the varieties and modulations of attribution. In the new cognitive theories, the general theory of mind and the folk psychology image of a belief–desire, naive psychology appearing in all human interpretations are at the center (Dennett, 1987) and not the situational modulations of attributing goodwill or good luck. While in classical psychology the genesis of desires was the key issue from the libido theory of Freud to neobehaviorist theories of extrinsic and intrinsic motivation, the new cognitive theories showcase the general assumption that under every behavioral act there is a desire, and the central idea is not the analysis of the genesis of these desires.

New aspects of brain/mind relations

Classical approaches re-emerging

To understand the new situation of brain/mind relation interpretations in the last three decades' half century, it is worth remembering that the recent proposals all started off from traditional attitudes, not to be forgotten.

Dualism classically talks about two irreducible substances. That seemed to belong to the Cartesian past. The dualistic attitude, however, reappeared in secular scientific discourse in the second half of the 20th century and provided a background to newer "spiritualistic" approaches. It was present, for example, in the attitude of the Nobel Prize–winning researcher of synapses Sir John Eccles in the Popper and Eccles (1977) dialogue book, and in the contributions of the French phenomenological philosopher Paul Ricoeur (1913–2005) in the Changeux and Ricoeur (2000) debate book. Ricoeur analyzed the difference between a physicalist and a mentalist way of talk as a semantic irreducibility. Ricoeur's position is all the more interesting since this modern French hermeneutician expressed his worries about experimental psychology itself, not merely about neural reductionism. "For me, the real differentiation is not between psychology and neuroscience. The real cliff might be between psychology and the phenomenal experience" (Ricoeur, in Changeux & Ricoeur, 2000, p. 142).

Functionalisms provided the central ideas of brain–mind relations from the 1960s on in cognitive psychology as well. In the broad functionalist view taken over from Aristotle, the mind is interpreted as the organization, the "form" of matter (see Chapters 2 and 8 in Volume 1). The traditional cognitive interpretation of this notion proposed that mental processes are always realized by a material system, yet they are not identical with it. There are different varieties of these ideas today, such as **psychological functionalism**, **machine functionalism**, and **language-embedded functionalism**. Cognitive functionalism took shape in the 1960s, combining the aforementioned inspirations, and was at the peak of its success at the end of the 1970s. (See the reader edited by Ned Block, 1980, 1996.) It revived the Aristotelian philosophical heritage, and it also gave credibility to the autonomous investigation of the inner world. In their computer-inspired versions, modern functionalists interpreted the mind on the analogy of a software. In their linguistic philosophy-inspired versions, they were talking about **token identity** (there is always a physical event behind a mental event) rather than **type identity** (the same mental event would always correspond to the same physical event). In the mainstream vision, the same mental function is not always based or performed by the same physical process. Think of the difference of imagining writing a word on the blackboard in left- and right-handed people. In left-handed people, the right hemisphere is activated; in right-handed people, the left hemisphere. Their brains are still doing the same thing.

This kind of physical neutralization was important because cognition for this school was – in contrast to the early 21st-century embodied slogans – deliberately disembodied. By the end of the 20th century, this kind of functionalism became outdated. Radical identity theories emerged, and most importantly, a cross-talk between ideas about the neural systems and the mind showed up in psychological research as well.

Eliminative materialism is a new type of identity theory practiced by the Churchland couple at UC–San Diego (Churchland, 1986, 1995). This kind of eliminativism tends to treat psychological concepts as concepts like the ones cultivated in astrology. Paul Churchland (1995) even stated that all aspects and issues of human inner mental life would, in the long run, be simply identified with neural models. Every subjective or cultural thing, from "red," through "noun," to "love," would disappear. They usually show this for simple issues, like isomorphies between color names and the cortical representation of colors (Paul Churchland, 1981). As a research strategy, eliminativism as a radical neuroscience doctrine appeals to many people in the interpreted cognition moves. They are, however, rarely as open as the Churchland couple.

More complex brain/mind relations

For all naturalistic visions of the mind and behavior, starting from classic materialism, there are two key issues. The basic one is always the postulated relationship between neuronal and psychological levels, and the supplementary one is the issue of determinism. The novelty is related to the changing methods, the cross-disciplinary cooperation, and the challenges posed by the development of neuroimaging.

Today, there are new aspects of the relations between neuroscience and psychology, all of which relate to an increased methodical sophistication.

Contemporary human neuroscience research starts off from complicated behavioral and mental concepts. Compared to earlier decades, it is trying to find answers or suggestions for much more complex issues when, for example, looking for the brain foundations of mental images (Kosslyn, 1994), of linguistic rules (Pinker, 1991), or for the neurobiological regulation of moral behavior (Damasio, 1994), researchers start off from really detailed psychological, linguistic, and even ethical theories. At the same time, they consider systemic properties of the neural tissue.

> To understand the neural organization of such complex behaviors as perception or speech requires an understanding not only of the properties of individual cells and pathways but also of the network properties of functional circuits in the brain. Such network properties, although obviously dependent on the properties of individual neurons in the network, go well beyond these properties and provide for the emergent properties that are commonly referred to as higher brain functions.
>
> (Cowan et al., 2000, p. 353)

Psychophysiology is directly tied to complex task settings. Complex psychological experiments are combined with time-sensitive physiological indicators. Some of them are combined bodily markers of emotional activation, like skin conductance changes accompanying the emotional aspects of decision-making in the studies of Damasio (1994), but most of them are directly related to the brain. The event-related potential method has become central within cognitive psychology due to its high temporal resolution, which is connected to assumed processing steps. The great event of the last 30 years has become the use of high-spatial-resolution neuroimaging in psychological e research (Posner & Raichle, 1994).

Brain imaging: a new phrenology?

The traditional approach to study relations between higher brain functions and complex psychological processes from the time of Broca on had been a detailed neuropsychological description of the consequences of brain damage. Classical textbooks followed this damage-based interpretation well into the 1980s (Luria, 1966). This approach had two limitations. The brain traumas, strokes, and tumors do not follow the biological articulation of the brain, and many studies did use a very limited number of patients. Due to brain imaging, brain functioning related to mental performance was studied with stimulus conditions manipulated by the experimenter in intact brains in order to look for natural neural units underlying the performance. The issue of small n-s, however, remained, due to the cost of the new methods.

In the beginning, in the 1990s, the great discovery was that, using positron-emission tomography, one could identify the activation of areas known from classical neuropsychology to be involved in word processing, for example, the Wernicke area of the left temporal lobe in acoustic word recognition (Posner & Raichle, 1994). Over the span of 25 years, brain imaging has become a must and a dominant technology even within psychology. There are two constant debates in the field. One concerns the **complexity of the data**, which implies many statistical traps. The other issue is a peculiar self-deception in localization. The danger of localization is the neglect of individual differences and the belief in a unique universal configuration of higher cognitive processes (Uttal, 2001). A more substantial issue is that complex cognitive functions usually involve many subprocesses, even dealing with seemingly simple issues like word recognition. Neuroimaging in itself does not provide a model for the neurobiological organization of mental processes. For approaching the answers, you have to have complex psychological experiments with complex questions. The new technologies, in fact, force the psychologists to raise the entire issue of neural reduction and interpretation into a more sophisticated frame.

By knowing where something happens, we do not necessarily know what happens there. As Kéri and Gulyás (2003), two Hungarian neuroscientists and psychiatrists, summarized the issues two decades ago, brain activity is not merely metabolic activity that is measured by the imaging technologies. It has a behavioral aspect, an electrical aspect, and a neurotransmitter aspect as well.

> Neuroimaging studies are devoted to find correlation between behavior and neuronal activity. However, the fundamental terms of such neuronal correlation approaches, . . . are poorly defined. First, what kind of neuronal activity are we looking for? We must take into consideration the complex dynamics of neurotransmitter functions (synthesis, transport, release, receptor actions, and reuptake), electric activity, underlying metabolic processes, and blood flow changes. . . . [T]he relationship among them is not sufficiently understood, although many studies are built on the assumptions that they are even interchangeable.
> (Kéri & Gulyás, 2003, p. 1,103)

To avoid a new phrenology, one has to combine neuroimaging, especially functional neuroimaging, with clear ideas about the functional organization of a given cognitive domain. Cartography is merely the first step that has to be followed by a consideration and precise modeling of the procedures involved, keeping in mind that usually there are many-to-many relations between mental processes and the brain rather than simple phrenological maps. Imaging must be used as a tool to develop theories of cognition and never to substitute interpreting the visualization for a real understanding of what is happening (Dehaene, 2007).

Theoretical brain models and the human mind

Alongside the new technologies, an important novelty of the last 30 years comes from a combination of comprehensive models of brain function and human mental architectures. Without always realizing the similarity, the Hebb-style (1949) conceptual nervous system models are once again in vogue. There is more at stake here than psychologists using concrete brain indices. The modularist, the Chomsky–Marr-type computational, and the connectionist visions all have their equivalents in overall brain models.

An interesting theoretical brain model is **neural Darwinism**. These models entail a strong developmental component and are open toward interpreting cultural learning as well. They propose that one basic feature of higher neural development is that an initial **abundance** is followed by a **pruning** and **selection** in the neural systems. In competition between different network connections, the winner is based on repeated uses. The connections that are strengthened are the ones that have a real-world equivalent, that are activated through perception (Edelman, 1987). Repeated patterns are selectively stabilized. The selection is Darwinian, but there is no Darwinian reproduction, merely a strengthening within an organism. The selected neural templates do not self-reproduce. Thus, the analogy with Darwinian selection is only partial. At the same time, these models are analog to the multiple-selection-level models promoted by Bühler, Popper, and Dennett. Neural Darwinism corresponds to their habit and idea selection (see Chapter 5).

The neural Darwinist models are promoted by the 1972 Nobel Prize–winning immunologist Edelman (1929–2014) and by the French neuroscientist Changeux (1985), winner of the 2018 Albert Einstein World Award for Science. Edelman (1987) extended his selectionist immunological work to the domain of neuronal systems. In this vision, experience, at least on the level of basic networks, selects between existing connections. Development can be seen as "degeneration," the shrinking of the abundant possibilities, as already introduced by another Nobel Prize winner (1984), the Danish immunologist Niels Jerne (1911–1994), who even talked about the generative grammar of the immune system in his selectionist theories (Jerne, 1985). David Hull et al. (2001) show a modern biological variety of the multiple selection model, combining genetics, immunology, and behavior. Jablonka (2006) provides an even broader image of multiple selection, similar to the evolutionary epistemology promoted by Campbell (1974) a generation earlier.

These theories postulate several cycles in the nervous system over the course of individual development. The first cycles are responsible for the setup of the neural net itself, and the second and later cycles for synaptic tuning would correspond to certain concepts or ideas. In these new models, the selective agent is a perceptual learning cycle based on repetition. Figure 10.5 illustrates this model.

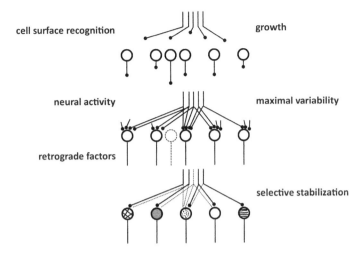

Figure 10.5 The abundance-selection model of neural development proposed by Changeux in 1985. Redrawn.

Neural selectionist models assume an active organism that creates internal models, and the environment selects the relevant models from the pool of these proposals. In relating biological, neural, and psychological theories, discussions regarding the ultimate driving forces of development have also re-emerged in a selectionist interpretation. These were already hinted at by Roman Jakobson (1899–1982), the Russian, Czech, and American formal linguist who claimed that, in the babbling of children, all possible speech sounds are produced first, and later, when children really start to acquire language, they follow a universal sequence. They begin with large contrasts, such as between *m* and *a*. The first sound is nasal, labial, and a consonant, the second a back oral vowel. In the gradual unfolding of finer contrasts, they show a pattern of unlearning. Children start to limit their productions and contrasts to the features that are relevant in the environmental language (Jakobson, 1941).

Thus, the idea that children start with universal assumptions and limit their scope later on was present in early child language research. The novelty after three generations was twofold. From the 1980s on, many researchers postulated these preparations to be there in an evolutionary manner to start with, and they proposed that selective adaptations are present much earlier than previously thought, namely, during the first year of life. Jakobson, on the other hand, put this selective adaptation only to the second and third years of life. Speech development has become one of the areas to illustrate the general idea of development as a gradual selection. Development does not create structures *ex nihilo*. It consolidates the parameters of the system that are activated as options available within the system; they are evolutionarily given organism-based hypotheses (Gervain & Mehler, 2010).

Dual cognitive systems and dual brain systems

A non-trivial affinity has been developing since the 1980s between some assumed qualitative dualities in cognitive processing and dualities in the underlying brain structures. They proposed a duality between action-based and implicit systems on the one hand and category-based explicit systems on the other hand. The first and most influential proposal has come around as a division of labor in the higher levels of visual processing. A difference was found in mammals in two projections coming from the occipital lobes. The **dorsal stream**, the visual role of the parietal lobes, and a **ventral stream**, the visual role of the temporal lobes, were differentiated both anatomically and functionally. The dorsal stream is responsible for location (WHERE system). The temporal lobes, on the other hand, are responsible for representing objects (WHAT system). Monkeys with lesions on the ventral stream do not recognize objects, but they remember their locations, while animals with a dorsal stream lesion recognize the objects but do not remember their location (Ungerleider & Mishkin, 1982). Goodale and Milner (1995) studied human neuropsychology patients with dorsal stream and ventral stream lesions. The ventral stream–damaged patients could not recognize different objects, but they did accommodate their hand movements to them. Dorsal stream–damaged patients could not organize their hand movements according to object shapes, while they did correctly recognize the objects. Therefore, Goodale and Millner proposed a distinction between action and perception, as functions of the dorsal and ventral stream, respectively.

The French neuroscientist Marc Jeannerod (1935–2011) went further. He claimed that these distinctions, in fact, correspond to a differentiation between **semantic (recognition)** and **pragmatic (action) systems**. "The former is at the service of the identification and recognition of visually presented objects. The latter is at the service of actions directed upon visually presented objects" (Jeannerod, 1994, p. 188). This visual and brain duality corresponds to a basic duality in human cognition. The ventral system and semantic processing correspond to a world-to-mind fit, while the dorsal system and pragmatic processing correspond to a mind-to-world fit. In higher cognition, action and perception are no more separated. "[Tool using] schemas are in turn formed on the basis of the observation of the actions of others . . . involving the use of tools by other agents" (Jeannerod & Jacob, 2005, p. 311).

This duality of WHAT and WHERE had been extended to the study of language as well. Landau and Jackendoff (1993) proposed that the ventral–dorsal asymmetry of visual processing corresponds to a distinction between a shape-sensitive and abundant system of nouns, with tens of thousands of nouns, and a relatively shaped insensitive spatial language system (suffixes, adverbials, postpositions, and prepositions) with 100 elements. This proposal has created a large number of empirical studies on the spatial linguistic marking system in many languages.

Ullman (2001) combined the action–perception distinctions with the issue of rule-based and item-based language representations central in interpreting language since the works of Pinker (1991). In Ullman's interpretation, the qualitative differences in linguistic representations relate to two memory systems. An action- and skill-related procedural system in the basal ganglia and motor cortex, responsible for actions and rules, contrasted to temporal lobe and hippocampus, which are related to episodic memory, to objects and specific events, and item storing vocabulary.

The majority of psychologists and neuroscientists acknowledge the coexistence of a dual system in human cognition: an action-based one and a knowledge-based one. Some of these solutions are **emergentists**. In this view, rules emerge from a large number of items (Smolensky, 1988). According to **competitive versions**, the dual systems compete with one another, giving alternative solutions to cognitive demands with different temporal delays. The item-based system is faster, but limited in scope (Pinker, 1991). **Cooperative** proposals assume the coexistence of the dual systems for solving cognitive and environmental tasks, and they are correction systems for each other. Episodic recall would correct the overgeneralizing tendencies of semantic memory, providing a correction over our own stereotypes, similar to the stored item *went* correcting the overuse of the rule system in forms like *goed*.

There are many fine grading issues involved here, questioning absolute dualities and the like. Table 10.3 shows a summary of the proposed dual systems. The sometimes radically divisive initial models provided important sources of heuristic ideas for our search of brain–mind relations during the last few decades. These often resulted in more flexible models as a second step. Several of the new neuroscience proposals are returning to an interpretation of the philosophical "KNOWING WHAT, KNOWING HOW" distinction of Ryle (1949).

Table 10.3 Some proposed mental dual systems and their prosed brain equivalents

Theory	System I	System II	Reference
Functionalism	TO KNOW WHAT	TO KNOW HOW	Ryle, 1949
Episodic–semantic	Episodic events, hippocampus	Semantic knowledge, cortex	Tulving, 1972
Rules–items	Items, temporal lobe	Rules, Broca's area	Pinker, 1991
Explicit–implicit	Conscious, hippocampus	Priming subcortex, cortex	Schacter, 1987
Action–perception	WHAT temporal	WHERE parietal	Goodale & Milner, 1995
Knowledge–skills	Declarative hippocampus	Procedural fontal, basal	Ullman, 2001
Types of consciousness	Phenomenal posterior cortex	Access frontal cortex	Block, 2007
Fast–slow	Intuitive	Reasoning	Kahneman, 2011

Note: Read it by columns arranged in a temporal order.

Neuroscience and elementary sociality

Neuroscience has become connected with the study of elementary sociality as well. These efforts had a long tradition and past, from the end of the 19th century on. The novelty has become the use of more sophisticated theories of the social mind and better neuroscience methodologies a hundred years later. Neurolinguistic research, as one example, obtained evidence for a differentiation between strictly linguistic coherence and coherence based on social cognition and social knowledge base. There are classically observed communication problems following traumatic brain injuries. Prefrontal damages cause a tendency in the affected patients to stick to the literal meanings of expressions, and an inability to entertain multiple readings. This suggested a social interpretation function to be connected to the prefrontal lobes. A French group at Salpetrière in Paris has shown that **managerial knowledge**, as they call it, has a specific role in cognition and has a special brain localization. This managerial knowledge is used for representing goal hierarchies, temporal order of events, causal links between actions, etc. (Crozier et al., 1999). With card sorting and other sequence-related methods, they obtained a double dissociation. When required to make up sentences from cards (dog, bites, men), Broca patients (traditional agrammatic aphasics) made 64% sequencing errors and only 6% story sequencing errors. Prefrontal patients, on the other hand, made only 4% sentence sequencing errors, with 62% story sequencing errors. A specific goal hierarchy function can be connected to the anterior cortical areas. The prefrontal areas deal with a wider time window, with natural causality, and social reasons that are different from the sequencing issues involved in syntax and grammar in general, related to classical Broca's area. "[C]omplex goal-directed actions may require specific mechanisms to cope with the long-range temporal frame within which they typically unfold, while assembling words to form a sentence takes place in a comparatively much smaller time frame" (Sirigu et al., 1998, pp. 771–772).

A generation earlier, the Russian neuropsychologist Luria (1966, 1973) also elaborated a theory for the role of the prefrontal areas in social cognition. His prefrontal-damaged patients were unable to treat texts as holistic units, messing up the order of elements and being uncertain about the importance of different parts. This deficit was accompanied by similar disorders in interpreting complex pictorial information depicting several protagonists and complicated human actions (Luria, 1973).

Damasio (1994) studied relations between emotional coding, social responsibility, and some prefrontal areas. He showed that prefrontal damage leads to a loss of responsibility and a lack of processing "somatic markers," emotionally regulated coding of risky situations. After the pioneering work of Damasio on social consequences of frontal lobe injuries, studies on both impaired and non-impaired human and non-human subjects, using various methodologies (traditional neuropsychological methods, neuroimaging, etc.), have made significant steps toward identifying brain structures playing a central role in various aspects of social cognition. The most important of such structures in the case of a theory of mind functioning are the medial prefrontal cortex, the temporal pole, the amygdala, and the supra-temporal sulcus, though the entire "social brain" involves other structures and other sociocognitive functions too.

The identification of **mirror neurons** in the brains of monkeys and their assumed relations to social learning created much echo. Neurobiological studies during the last 20 years have shown a possible anchorage for the postulated mechanisms of motor empathy. Rizzolatti et al. (1996) showed that in the monkey premotor cortex, there were neurons which reacted basically the same way when the monkey started a voluntary goal-directed intentional movement (grasping food) and when the monkey saw another monkey making the intentional movement. Thus, the so-called mirror neurons were active for intentional self-movement and seen movement in social mates.

Many speculations started that raised the possibility that this mapping between intention-movement-sight might be crucial in the development of language, self-consciousness, and empathy, both in evolution and in ontogenetic development. Arbib (2005) tried to show that from the face-controlling mirror neuron system, human language evolved in a stepwise manner. First, a hand-controlling system developed, and later an acoustic protolanguage. There are critical voices regarding the issue of understanding the goals of others implied in the mirror neuron ideas. Csibra (2007) proposed that mirror neurons might be important in coordinating movements rather than in attributing goals to actions. Goal interpretations should not be based on this postulated automatic system. The details are still debated. For a historical perspective, it is remarkable that in the mirror neuron proposal, we have a factual integration of the social learning, neuroscience, and evolutionary as well as cultural research traditions (Andler, 1992).

EvoDevo: a combination of evolution and development

One novelty of the last quarter of century is the combination of the ideas on child development with considerations of our evolutionary heritage. This is not a peculiar idea in psychology. Relying on traditional recapitulation theories and their critical evaluation, recent biological thought also considers how mechanisms of embryological development themselves evolved, and how, considering embryology, one might reconstruct evolution itself (see the reader edited by Laubichler & Maienschein, 2007). Robert (2008) proposed that, in fact, the adequate way to introduce evolution into psychology would not be through the now "traditional" evolutionary psychology but through a serious consideration of the lessons of developmental biology.

Two types of genetic reasoning in modern psychology

In order to interpret the present fate of genetic ideas within psychology, we have to go back to the 1960s. The popularity of notions related to genetics changed drastically during the last half century. Figure 10.6 shows the changes of the key concepts over half a century.

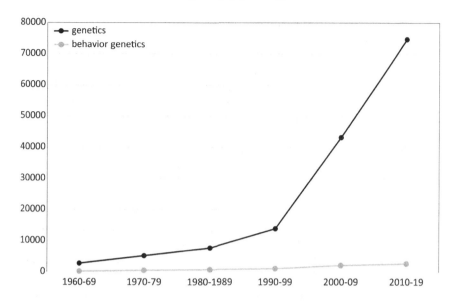

Figure 10.6 Changes in the popularity of **genetics** and **behavior genetics** in the psychological literature.

Source: PsycINFO database.

Genetic determination that became a specific issue of the psychometric tradition, with the debates on intelligence in the 1920s–1930s, was lost to theoretical psychology in the 1950s. It reappeared in American psychology in the 1960s, but in two rival and different forms, as summarized in Table 10.4 as two theories of development. One was the innatism proposed by Chomsky (1959, 1965, 1968), mainly an analogy with ethology and other European inspirations, suggesting that complex human behaviors may be under genetic control. The other trend was the re-emergence of genetic interpretation of individual differences that was mainly interested in the unfolding of differences.

The psychological interests were continuously divided from the 1930s on. Some people were and are mainly interested in the genetic components of individual differences, while others in the generic, species-specific, supposedly innate determination of certain functions. In a comprehensive biological theory, these two issues are certainly not separated. In the Darwinian mode, variations are all over the place, and the extended Darwinian model, the "modern synthesis" of Sir Ronald Fisher (1890–1962), responsible for a combination of Darwinism with population genetics from the 1930s on, connected the idea of variation to genetics in a clear population statistical manner (Fisher, 1930/1999).

Innatism and the factors of development

The work of the **"generic innatist" group** followed the liberal argumentation initiated by Chomsky and applied it to psychology in a universalistic manner. Most of

Table 10.4 New biological ideas about the determination of development in the 1960s

Type of innovation	Key novelty	Opponents	Leading representatives
Universal nativism	Cognitive structures are *a priori*	Learning theories	Chomsky, Fodor
Inheritance of differences	Individual differences are heritable	Differences based on nurture	Hans Eysenck, Arthur Jensen
Critical periods	Experience is efficient only at certain times	Cumulative experience	Konrad Lorenz, Eric Lenneberg

the research was interested in the early development of some particular abilities, or **domains**, as they preferred to call it later on, like language, numbers, face recognition, and the like. The main arguments for a generic genetic determination were based on early developmental manifestations, cross-species comparisons, content-specific developmental disorders, and less frequently, real cross-cultural comparisons. Innatism was one way to overcome the "empty organism" and "black box" metaphor of the behaviorists. Innate organizing principles of language and other complex human achievements belong to "species-specific behaviors." For Chomsky and his followers, this kind of genetic determination is not a mechanical determinism in the traditional sense. Language, while it is genetically determined, is by far not a constraint on thought. Rather, by its very structure and due to its openness, language, both as a system and in its actual use, is unbound and unlimited, thereby ensuring the unlimited free development of humanity (Chomsky, 1972b, 1978, 1988). In the hand of his followers, this general innatism claim was usually transformed into the specific innatism claims of the modularists, as we have witnessed in Chapter 9. The critical period theories were an accommodation of the innatist theories. Before the formation of recent epigenetic theories of development, they allowed for the influence of individual experience factors supplementing the innate mechanism, usually talking about species-specific stable environmental factors in the sense of Donald Hebb (1949, 1958).

Psychology, similarly to biology, recognizing the importance of the embryological notion of critical periods, soon realized the options in the new EvoDevo biology for psychological development. During the last generation, modern developmental psychology tried to relate its evolutionary commitments to the issues of developmental mechanisms. There were earlier attempts toward this program. Challenges to the simple "prewired ideas of modularity" were already proposed in the 1990s. The efforts of Annette Karmiloff-Smith (1938–2016), a British developmental psychologist at Birkbeck College and University College, London, were central to these efforts. Karmiloff-Smith (1992, 1998) tried to interpret modularity as a developmental achievement based on innate preferences rather than ready-made innate modular solutions. In her view, human development was not the unfolding of prewired modules but rather modularization itself. Certain preparations that are based on evolution help develop content-specific modules during development.

Elman et al. (1996) compiled an entire list of possible neural and evolutionary mechanisms of innateness with a strong learning flavor.

The newer approaches started off with a theoretical critique of a simple blueprint image of genetic determination. In a way, as presented among the first ones by Gary Marcus (2001, 2004, 2005) of New York University and by the edited volume of Ellis and Bjorklund (2005), the new aim was, and is, to relate proximal mechanism of development with distal mechanisms of evolution. This has been the eternal dream since the time of Haeckel (1866) and J. M. Baldwin (1894), through the evolutionary epistemology of Karl Popper (1963, 1972) and Donald Campbell (1974).

The new approaches have two basic novelties. They do not merely look for analogies but for causal relations connecting the two changes, and they rely on clear notions of modern genetics. There are interesting analogies between developmental processes of psychology and biological processes regarding the "preparedness" of organisms for change.

> Evolutionary biology possessed not only an analogue to trial and error learning, but also an analogue to cognitive psychology in the theory of developmental constraints! Cognitivists insisted that trial and error was mediated by complex internal states that could speed up, slow down, or channel the effects of environmentally mediated learning. Advocates of developmental constraints said the same thing about the operation of natural selection. Embryological development biased the set of 'options' that were available to selection.
>
> (Amundson, 2006, p. 10)

As Gary Marcus (2001, 2005) emphasized, nativism can be reconciled with the effect of experience. The brain can be assumed to have an initial structure, at the same time emphasizing that during development, there are factors such as gene expression, interaction between cellular structure, chemoaffinity, and gradual differentiation that all play a role in the unfolding of the genetic make-up. In the last 25 years, we have witnessed the appearance of a new synthesis, whereby innate mechanisms, learning and experience, perception, as well as social factors have all been acknowledged to play important roles in the development of higher-order cognition and language. In this new perspective, the question is shifted from a simple **nature-versus-nurture** dichotomy to exploring the mechanisms that are responsible for aspects of cognitive development and their interaction with one another.

Heredity of intelligence: Galton reloaded

For the attitude emphasizing individual differences, I present two lines of research and argumentation. The inheritance of intelligence issue is the most telling and most visible one. This is the issue where the social embedding continues to be seen most clearly, and that is where the entire issue was discussed for most of modern psychology, for over 100 years. For the more specific inheritance claims, I show the difficulties with the logic of neurodevelopmental dissociation pathology-based researches.

With the birth of modern genetics, psychologists were looking toward explanation of individual differences in genetics. Watson and Crick seemed to be great promises even before the Human Genome Project. The new psychogeneticians denied that the behaviorists' simple life history empiricism could be a possible way to explain individual differences. To explain individual differences, they referred to the Galtonian paradigm that proposed heredity to be crucial in determining individual differences in behavior and basically presupposed an additive role of nature (genetic) and nurture (environment). The followers of Galton considered even interaction as a mere statistical term and did not consider the possibilities of substantial proactive visions of interaction, where human agents as environmental factors factually enter the causal chain, in changing schooling patterns, for example.

There is a further important aspect of the revival of Galton's theory, namely, that it assumes **one single feature of excellence**, which is in clear contrast to the modular ideas. A hot new debate regarding the validity of the Galtonian paradigm started half a century ago when Arthur Jensen (1923–2012), a Berkeley-based educational psychologist, published a paper claiming the genetic intellectual inferiority of African Americans (Jensen, 1969). Jensen claimed that intellectual differences are inherited, and it is hardly possible to raise intelligence by interventions. Table 10.5 shows the basic arguments promoted by this much-discussed review and program paper and the opponent opinions.

Jensen's paper started intensive debates that lasted for two generations. The paper, by 2023, has over 6,500 references. The leading evolutionist, paleontologist, and science popularizer of the egalitarian group at Harvard University, Stephen Jay Gould, was a key player in the field with an emotionally committed antiracist environmentalist attitude who openly claimed that scientific objectivity should not mean a lack of preferences. In his frequently cited (over 15,000 references) and republished book *Mismeasure of man*, where he surveyed all the allegedly distorted use of intelligence testing for social discrimination and related racist psychology, he expressed his opinion in emotional terms, which he kept later on as well, even in his criticism of evolutionary psychology.

> We pass through this world but once. Few tragedies can be more extensive than the stunting of life, few injustices deeper than the denial of an opportunity to strive or even to hope, by a limit imposed from without, but falsely identified as lying within.
> (Gould, 1981, pp. 61–62)

The **intervention issue** was historically crucial. All of this debate about interpreting individual differences was raised in the middle of the New Society campaigns of compensatory education in America, under Presidents John F. Kennedy and Lyndon B. Johnson, where many programs were created in the frames of the Head Start movement, partly based on theories about the effect of early experience

Table 10.5 Some value choices of the claims about the genetic determination of intelligence promoted by Arthur Jensen

Jensen's thesis	Consequences	Opponents
IQ is a key for social differences	Cognitive structures are unified	Multiplicity of cognitive differences
IQ differences inherited	Key to schooling; IQ cannot be raised	IQ differences result of early experience
Social differences inherited	No social injustice in schooling	The school and social cult of IQ is unjust

Source: Arthur Jensen (1969).

to compensate for the lack of parental education and poverty. Jensen (1969), already with his title – *How Much Can We Boost IQ and Scholastic Achievement?* – was challenging the idea of these compensatory interventions. The interventions relied on the notion of "impoverished environment" taken over from animal studies and proposed by J. M. Hunt (1906–1991). The book of Hunt (1961) on the importance of early experience was central in several regards. Hunt was, by training and experience, a Freudian developmental psychologist and was originally interested in early childhood to explain pathology. He gradually became interested in the impact of early experience on cognitive development. Hunt did not rely on the 60-year-old psychometric tradition of intelligence. In the new cognitive atmosphere, he tried to interpret intelligence as an information processing ability. As part of this effort, Hunt also postulated that this information processing ability was profoundly influenced by early experience, in line with the idea of critical periods.

Hunt's book was significantly influential in setting the stage for the social intervention programs in the United States initiated in the mid-1960s. He served in presidential committees under Lyndon B. Johnson, was one of the authors of a policy document, *The Children's Bill of Rights*, and even acted as a promoter of educational television programs, such as *Sesame Street*. The interventions, at the same time, were not sophisticated enough in an educational sense and treated some social groups in a rather condescending manner, such as lacking culture or even lacking a proper language, like the ideas regarding Black English in the United States. As many social critics saw it, the entire idea that a program was successful only if it raised the IQ of the participants was socially questionable. There might be other gains, like in learning motivation, strategic life planning, and so on. Hunt (1969) himself argued that the failure of educational intervention was due to a lack of serious educational strategy and the ignorance of the effects of early experience (Hunt, 1979). Around the same time, when Jensen published his provocative paper, Richard Herrnstein (1930–1994), a Harvard psychologist, who was an old-time pigeon psychophysicist and historian of psychology, published a paper in the *Atlantic* magazine spelling out the social aspects of the genetic argumentation (Herrnstein, 1971). He claimed that (inherited) IQ was a determinant of social success in America. Therefore, social distribution of wealth, power, and so on was becoming more and more based on IQ. And these social differences would increase further. The logic of this paper was straightforward and later resulted in a book on meritocracy (Herrnstein, 1973).

The controversies between the two camps had an assumed opposite causal chain in their social argumentation, but the macro sociological-level relations between social status and intelligence were accepted by both camps. The politically left-wing "environmentalists" claimed that these differences are caused by cumulative effects of the environment, from childhood undernutrition to intellectually unchallenging environments. For the researchers claiming inheritance, the social differences in intelligence would be a result of a long history in liberal societies of social class position becoming tied to inherited intellectual differences, including selective mating strategies. Due to an assumed equal-opportunity schooling in liberal societies, social stratification would be more and more stabilized and would historically mirror inherited individual differences in general intellectual ability.

Sir Cyrill Burt (1961) was the British proponent of these "inherited class differences." Burt (1883–1971) was a star of British statistical psychology, professor of University College London, and the first psychologist to be knighted in 1946, in fact, for his research on intelligence testing in children. Burt, as a school psychologist and as an academic psychologist, started from the early 1900s with a conception of general intelligence taken over from Spearman. Burt interpreted the social correlations of measured intelligence as showing that social mobility corresponds to the amount of variance in intelligence not explained by inheritance. According to Burt, social stratification in a liberal society mirrors the inheritance of intelligence.

The interpretation Burt gave for the social distribution created a lot of tension, both within British psychology and in the United States as well. Burt (1958, 1966, 1972) supported his general claims about inheritance of intellectual differences on the basis of his own studies on twins. Comparing monozygotic twins and siblings in the correlation of their IQ levels and the contributions of shared and different environments, Burt claimed that the variance due to heredity in a very much genetically determined feature like height was 89 versus 11%, while in IQ, it was 82 vs. 18% (Burt, 1972). This was the major support for the idea that the recent social mobility of 15 to 20% in industrial societies mirrors genetic determination. Those working-class children move upward who had a higher IQ. Otherwise, over a few hundred years of social freedom in democratic societies, the social class distribution, and therefore wealth distribution, basically would mirror the distribution of innate abilities.

There were several issues involved here. One was specifically related to generalizing from within-group differences to the between-group differences of subgroups or races. In the immediate discussion of the Jensen paper, also relying on the twin data, the Harvard developmental psychologist Jerome Kagan (1969) suggested that twin research does not allow us to make intergroup comparisons. These arguments raised the possibility that inheritance does not determine more than a mere response range and argued for taking environmental interventions, such as the Head Start program, and other early education programs seriously. Way before genomics, the issues that were raised were similar to those regarding the relationships between epigenesis and heritability in our post-genomics era (Grigorenko, 2018).

A further issue was raised after Burt died, and it questioned the reliability of his basic twin data. Detailed research by Burt's biographer, Hearnshaw (1979), showed that the twin correlations reported by Burt were numerically identical over publications during 20 years, while he claimed to have included new data. The outstanding British researcher on animal learning and intelligence Nicholas MacKintosh (1935–2015) took up the challenge and edited an entire book on the several aspects of the Burt scandal (MacKintosh, 1995). The conclusion was that it is hard to determine if Burt was deliberately falsifying or merely being careless. In any case, the Burt affair did not serve the genetic arguments well. MacKintosh (1998) also produced a comprehensive survey of a 100 years of research on human intelligence, similar to the edited book of Sternberg (2018) from a later perspective. In the middle of the debates on nature versus nurture in intelligence, and bias in testing a task force lead by Neisser et al. (1996) and by Sternberg and Grigorenko (1997), provided a balanced scientific view both on the concept of intelligence and its measurement issues.

In an interesting way, as the analysis of Weidman (1996, 1997) clearly showed it, the new debate fired up the cultural war between progressives and conservatives in psychology and in social science again. The first group stood for nurture, the second for nature. One aspect of the hereditary determination group's claims was almost forgotten. They did claim that with economic growth, there was a standardization of the environment, including cultural environment, with things like universal education, reading, and numeracy – which actually raises heritability. This last point is especially important in modern societies, with their intense efforts to **equalize opportunity**. As a general rule, as environments become more uniform, heritabilities rise.

> It is the central irony of egalitarianism: uniformity in society makes the members of families more similar to each other and members of different families more different. . . . The flaw in its logic is obvious: it is impossible for Herrnstein and Murray to prove that our society presents a "uniform" environment to all people.
>
> (Weidman, 1997, pp. 142–143)

As Dickens and Flynn (2001) showed in a formal model, high heritability and environmental influences are not contradictory. People select environments that correspond to their IQ the same way as they selectively chose partners, fitting to their own intelligence (assortative mating). These influences increase the effect of heredity in a peculiar way.

> Most environmental effects are relatively short-lived. . . . Enrichment programs may nonetheless be worthwhile because at least some seem to have long-term effects on achievement and life outcomes, and the temporary IQ boosts they provide may mediate those effects. . . . [S]uch programs would be most likely to produce long-term IQ gains if they taught children how to replicate outside the program the kinds of cognitively demanding experiences that produce IQ gains while they are in the program and motivate them to persist in that replication long after they have left the program.
>
> (Dickens & Flynn, 2001, p. 366)

Thus, the success of interventions depends on the success of motivational changes.

Bronfenbrenner and Ceci (1994) proposed a framework along these lines, by distinguishing systematically between proximal and distal influences. This was one of the last papers of the famous cultural developmental psychologist Uriel Bronfenbrenner (1917–2005). He was one of the intellectual moving forces of the Head Start movement in the 1960s. A generation later, they concluded that the better environmental conditions, in fact, provide for a fuller development of genetic potential; thus, in a paradoxical manner, there is more observed heredity effects under good developmental conditions. That is an argument for social improvement and intervention in their view.

> When proximal processes are weak [i.e., in poverty, CsP], genetically based potentials for effective psychological functioning remain relatively unrealized but that they become actualized to a progressively greater extent as proximal processes increase in magnitude.... [U]nrealized capacities might be actualized through social policies and programs that enhance exposure to proximal processes in environmental settings.
> (Bronfenbrenner & Ceci, 1994, pp. 569, 583)

Thus, the debate that continued for two generations has two interesting messages. First, to interpret the effects of genetic and environmental differences, a sophisticated developmental theory is necessary. Second, both progressive and conservative theorists agree that **the impact of the genetic potential increases in better and/or homogenous environments** (Kccs-Jan et al., 2013). The social policy implications are differentially interpreted. The conservatives think that these better environments are already attained, while the liberals and progressives argue for interventions to achieve these favoring environments.

The messages of these debates have the concept of general intelligence underlying these ideas from the time of Galton. Recently, the challenge is how to relate modularity of function to the psychometric claims regarding general intelligence. Gary Marcus and his colleagues made an interesting secondary reanalysis of the many – over 200 – available brain imaging studies of general cognitive functions. They proposed that basically there is always an overlap between the different brain areas which are supposed to be responsible for a given task. This is due to the fact that even simple-looking cognitive tasks would involve different modules.

> We suggest a potential way of reconciling a central finding in human individual differences, both with modern conceptions of neural function and with some forms of modularity and functional specialization in cognitive science.... [A]ny given task will most likely necessarily call upon the operation of hypothesized modules.
> (Rabaglia et al., 2011, p. 301)

Thus, they basically propose something like what was proposed by the neuropsychology of Luria in the 1960s: complex human function involves an entire array of brain regions. Kovács and Conway (2016) made an even more detailed region overlap analysis, showing that g might be related to prefrontal functions.

Innatism and the smart babies

During the last generation, a new **developmental science** has been taking shape. It is reminiscent of pedology a good hundred years earlier. The similarity is due mainly to methodology. Developmental science is an interdisciplinary enterprise that tries to understand child development with a combination of the methodical and conceptual tools of the genetics, biology, and psychology of development. One implication of innatism was that innate components of mental life should be present very early on. These efforts resulted in conceptions of the **competent infant**. The usual starting point is the mocking of an idea of William James (1890, p. 487) about the disordered sensory confusion of objects in the sensations of babies. "The baby, assailed by eyes, ears, nose, skin, and entrails at once, feels it all as one great blooming, buzzing confusion," and the babies would take a long time to learn to differentiate these sensory impressions to be parts of objects. This image was prevalent in all empiricist theories of child development, including behaviorism and Piaget. The earliest efforts to question this entirely constructed image were proposed by psychoanalytic theories of Ego development in the 1930s, such as Mélanie Klein or Michael Balint. These psychoanalysts, discussed in Chapter 1, were not taken seriously by mainstream developmentalists. The real innovation and the discovery of smart babies have come with the literal psychological interpretation of theoretical innatist claims. The new proposals emphasize what complex achievements regarding the world of objects and the world of communication are available even for neonates and how domain-specific these hidden competencies are. How early, for example, infants acquire complex skills, such as getting tuned to the phonological system of the mother tongue, after starting with a broader innate sensibility (Mehler & Dupoux, 1994).

There were two crucial inroads for this new vision: research technology developments and the claims of innatism.

Development of infancy research technologies. It is impossible to give verbal instructions to babies and to ask them about their experiences. Infancy research has taken indirect routes, from the time of John B. Watson, with his controversial study of fear conditioning in little Albert, an infant (Watson & Rayner, 1920). Conditioning techniques and learning were central for infancy research for half a century. From the 1970s on, new, refined technologies for the indirect study of baby preferences, like habituation and selective looking and the like, played a crucial role in developing the conception of "smart babies." One central technique has been the use of **habituation**. Habituation has been a central tool in studying animal learning, perception, and attention. You can study discrimination with repeated stimulation until boredom (habituation), and changing one aspect of the stimulus afterward to see if it still evokes the habituated response (Sokolov, 1960, 1963). This research tool was extended to babies from animals. The first method still in use was introduced by the team of Peter Eimas (1934–2005) at Brown University.

He made babies listen to repetitive syllables, like *da, da, da*, while their sucking frequency was measured by a pacifier provided with a sensor. In general, babies react with increased sucking frequency to new stimuli. After a while, as a result of habituation, the reaction to the repeated [da] syllable decreased. When the stimulus was changed to [ta], the sucking frequency increased again. Thus, babies could differentiate between voiced [d] and voiceless [t] (Eimas et al., 1971).

Another frequently used technology is the measurement of **looking times** with a peculiar double presupposition. With very elaborate stimulus procedures, the researchers suppose that children look more either at familiar stimuli or in other arrangements, that they look more at the unexpected, surprising stimuli. For example, children look at targets speaking their environmental language, showing a familiarity effect (Gervain & Mehler, 2010). At the same time, children look more at unfamiliarly arranged face targets because they have an expectation for the face arrangement. With much setting elaboration, the two interpretations can be differentiated. Looking times and selective turning toward one source are useful measures for discrimination. With looking time technologies, one can study, for example, understanding words in preverbal children. The baby listens to the word *apple* and is shown an apple on the left and a banana on the right. If the baby looks more frequently to the left, this implies the baby "understands" the word *apple*.

Another class of technologies uses **brain-evoked potentials and imaging**. Csibra et al. (2000), for example, showed that a change in object perception might be detectable between 6 and 8 months old by a more regularized gamma band activity around 40 Hz in the infant brain. Or to take another example, research using the so-called **near-infrared spectroscopy** of infant brain imaging compared different reactions in newborns to

> repetition-based AAB (e.g., *babamu, nanape*) and ABB (e.g., *mubaba, penana*) patterns as compared to random ABC controls (e.g., *mubage, penaku*) in the bilateral temporal areas, with a somewhat stronger response in the left hemisphere, as well as in the left frontal regions. The processing of structural regularities thus appears to be clearly left-lateralized at birth.
> (Gervain, 2014, p. 212)

A literal interpretation of innatism. Psychologists interpreted innatism not as a mere general philosophical self-explaining doctrine but as something that has to be checked empirically, possibly on very young children. Very young children, following the way Chomsky introduced grammatical knowledge into the mind of every speaker, were presented not merely as knowers but also as theory builders, little scientists, and philosophers. The original linguistic innatism proposed by Chomsky in the 1960s was generalized from the 1980s on into a general "cognitive innatism."

A special version of these "babies as theoreticians" idea is the **core knowledge** vision promoted by Sue Spelke at Harvard University (2000). According to this innatist model, the innate ideas do not relate to specific concepts as Fodor (1983) proposed but only to some basic systems of knowledge. The theory proposed by

Susanne Spelke assumes some content-specific modular systems, but they are presented as a compromise between the general cognition and the overmodular conceptions.

> The human mind is not a single, general-purpose device that adapts itself to whatever structures and challenges the environment affords. Humans learn some things readily, and others with greater difficulty, by exercising more specific cognitive systems with signature properties and limits. The human mind also does not appear to be a "massively modular" collection of hundreds or thousands of special-purpose cognitive devices . . . [but it is] built on a small number of core systems.
> (Spelke & Kinzler, 2007, pp. 91–92)

The first core system is **object representation**. It centers on the spatio-temporal principles of cohesion, continuity, and contact. The second one is **agency**. The intentional actions of agents are directed to goals, and agents achieve their goals through means that are efficient. **Numerosity** and **geometry**, and maybe **social representation** of others, make the list full.

At the same time, the new developmental studies have also shown that several procedures in many areas, which seemed to develop very early, do take much more time. Visual integration, for example, develops until rather late, into early puberty (Kovács, 2004). Related to these timing issues, several practical questions are also integrated into contemporary developmental science, like the reopening of the issue of sensitive periods. Some practically interesting issues are what remain relatively open throughout our entire life, such as learning new words or recognizing and storing new faces. The crucial age in the consolidation of value systems and self-regulation, the specific importance of a "second critical period," is adolescence.

Determining factors of development

The traditional nature/nurture issue had become complex due to the self-conscious development of the modern natural sciences of development. William Stern, in his book on language acquisition (Stern & Stern, 1907), already proposed a convergence theory of development. According to the convergence theory, nature and nurture not merely interact in determining development but determine development in a convergent manner, somehow relying on common proximal causal mechanisms. For Stern, this joint integrating field was the concept of personality, where environmental and genetic factors do relate to each other (Stern, 1914, 1938).

The novelties due to the Human Genome Project do entail real empirical consequences as well, not merely a renewal of theoretical speculations about the factors that determine development. Modern genetics promoted both in theory and in practice a complex image of organic individual development, including mental development. Some of these non-trivial consequences are due to the structure of genetic determination. They did overwrite former simplistic systems of psychogenetics relying on a direct, blueprint-readout metaphor.

Limitations of the genome. Psychologists themselves have been challenged in their psychogenetic models by the fact born out of the Human Genome Project, where the basic issue is how so few genes (numbers were moving from 32,000 down to 23,000 over the decade) can be responsible for so many cognitive adaptations (Marcus, 2005, 2006). Both in behavior genetics and in the genetic interpretation of psychological processes, we have to forget the idea of a biunique correspondence between genes and preferences or species-specific behaviors. Most behavioral and cognitive features must have a polygenic determination, supplemented by epigenetic mechanisms (Grigorenko, 2018).

Fostering regulatory genes. These do play trivial roles in organic development, like in the development of body symmetries, but they may as well be crucial in neural development and therefore in determining sensitive developmental periods (Charney, 2012).

Genetics in an open system. Philosophers have emphasized for centuries that man is an open project. Nowadays, research on mental development also realized the centrality of this issue. The most characteristic human processes, such as language or culture, though they do follow interesting universals, do assume an adjustment during individual lifetime. Thus, when looking for genetic determinants of behavior and cognition, we must look for genetic models that entail the existence of environmental interactions as a sort of species-wide expectation, which have a stabilizing role, for example, for the sound system of the mother tongue, kinship relations, and so on. Evolution paves the way for individual development, where genetics and ecology, such as the cultural environment of primary and secondary socialization, determine the way of "choosing individual" routes made possible by the evolutionary landscape. The intense study of epigenetic unfolding, as shown by Charney (2012), indicates the implications of the still-relevant landscape metaphor proposed by Waddington (1942, 1957) to illustrate the concept of epigenesis. Evolution, development, genetics, and ecology together allow for multiple developmental pathways.

> Epigenetics [is] associated with the interaction of genes, their products, and the internal and external environment. . . . [It focuses] on alternate developmental pathways, on the developmental pathways underlying stability and flexibility, and on the influence of environmental conditions on what happens in cells and organism.
> (Jablonka & Lamb, 2002, pp. 88–89)

Epigenesis as a term has several meanings. In some of its loose psychological usage, it merely means the idea that environment-driven development is important. It is also used to refer in an evolutionary sense to gene–culture co-evolutions, such as lactose tolerance in human adults and cattle breeding. It is often used in the interpretation of genetic vulnerability and environmental interactions in the genesis of different psychopathologies (Jablonka & Lamb, 1995, 2002). In the modern genetic interpretation, however, the very term *epigenesis* also implies a definite genetic notion, namely, that the activation of the genome, or more precisely, parts of the genome, is experience-dependent as well (Charney, 2012).

Epigenesis has several meanings regarding behavioral development as well. It does imply some kind of intricate sensitivity to environmental effects, in the form of sensitive periods or the like. Grigorenko (2018) summarized how this concept might be useful in understanding some puzzles of the assumed inheritance of intelligence.

Critical periods of development

The new developmental studies re-raise the issue that was already asked by Eric Lenneberg (1967): Are there life periods that are characterized by easier or faster acquisition of certain skills and types of information? Are there **critical periods of human development**? The original notion of embryological and ethological critical periods manifested certain built-in tensions and certain empirical concerns when applied to psychological development. Behavioral critical periods in ethology have to have a rather clear developmental window assigned to them, like 12 to 36 hours after hatching in chickens, and they have to have a clear biological reason for their closure. Some of the proposed human critical periods, however, have rather unclear temporal boundaries, and their closure mechanisms are rather unspecified. Let us stay with the example of language development: the native sound system typically develops during the first two years of life, yet the acquisition of native-like sound systems is not closed by that time boundary. Some studies claim that this window closes around five years of age, while others that it lasts until puberty. These large differences show up even in clinical brain damage data. There certainly is a relearning of the native language until about 12 years. However, until 5, this relearning is faster and goes on with less efforts. Thus, the very early acquisition does not close the window. That is one of the reasons that people prefer to talk about sensitive rather than critical periods. The closing factors are also frequently debated. From the time of Lenneberg (1967) on, relying on clinical developmental aphasia data, the basic idea was that the critical period for language acquisition was somehow related to the development of brain asymmetries, the specialization of the left hemisphere for language. Left hemisphere preference for language, however, is already present at birth. Thus, the sensitive period might rather be related to the stabilization of the *use* of the left hemisphere for language processing.

> Over the first few years of life, the initial language network, already in place at birth, extends and becomes more lateralized, developing the adult pattern. This corresponds to an attunement to the native language, with certain perceptual distinctions turning from merely acoustic into linguistic features. As a result of this neural commitment to the native language, the initial plasticity is gradually reduced, with a critical or sensitive period for native-like speech perception and production closing during childhood or early puberty. . . . Whether all aspects of language have a sensitive period, when this period ends and under what circumstances (amount and type of input, etc.) are still heatedly debated.
> (Gervain, 2014, p. 216)

Disordered populations and the logic of modular dissociation

At the turn of the millennium, the successes of the Human Genome Project and the technical development of non-invasive genetic screening have led to leaps in psychogenetic research as well. During the last decades, psychologists started to look for associations between unique variations in the genome (so-called SNPs, single-nucleotide polymorphisms) and formulated specific hypotheses regarding systemic variations, for example, in the genetic alleles regulating the production and reception of certain key neurotransmitters, and related them to behavioral and personality variations.

The "psychogenetic mode" basically was and still is practiced in three ways.

1. **Twin studies.** One can find genetic similarities and differences of a very broad nature without explaining the exact causal mechanisms that are responsible for the similarities found.
2. **Combining molecular genetics and the study of individual differences.** In this regard, the first enthusiastic research applied two attitudes. Either a candidate gene design, supposing, for example, that an allelic variation in the coding for dopamine, an energizing neurotransmitter, and coding for its receptors would be correlated with an outgoing personality type. As a large genetics consortium – where the psychological part is represented by Steven Pinker – highlighted in a critical self-review, these studies usually predicted sensational but largely non-reproducible results (Rietveld et al., 2014). For the future, the group proposed a design that makes strong hypotheses on the basis of a random search in large samples and then tests these hypotheses on other samples.
3. **Using disordered populations that have a typically gene-related neurodevelopmental disorder.** In this research type, genomic variations are sought for in a pathological population, which is then related to brain or neurotransmitter variations.

The genetic universalist research logic has become attached to the issue of individual differences from the 1980s on, through the dissociative logic of the modularist claims. Several extreme individual variations were studied in the "generic inheritance" group of researchers that has led, if not to a synthesis, then to some rapprochement between the two traditions.

Let us take the example of language again. The original Chomskyan philosophical claims about innatism were turned into empirical claims by ambitious psychologists. Chomsky himself has become ambivalent regarding the interpretation of these scientific developments initiated by him. Under the influence of the basic modularity ideas being anchored in an innatist philosophy, a deduction was drawn that there should be specific non-acquired, genetic disorders in each broad area covered by the modularity claims. That was the time of ideas on **dissociative developmental disorders**. Interpretations of Fodor in the 1990s looked for specific dissociative disorders. This domain-specific approach of the mind has its own peculiar interpretations for psychopathology as well. Since major behavioral and cognitive adaptations would mainly be innately organized, one can look for specific developmental disorders that would support the specificity of the cognitive and behavioral organization of an innate modular system. Notice that all these arguments reintroduce the study of cognition into the domain of biological sciences.

The most traditional and most widely used method for decomposing mind/brain into component systems builds on interpreting these populations as cases of **double dissociation**. *Double dissociation*, as a term, was originally introduced by Teuber (1955) in analyzing animal lesion studies and in arguing alongside Karl Lashley (1929) that sometimes it is hard to differentiate whether an effect of a lesion is a general decrease of function or something more specific. "What is needed for conclusive proof is "double dissociation," i.e., evidence that tactile discrimination can be disturbed by some other lesion without loss on visual tasks and to a degree comparable in severity to the supposedly visual deficit after temporal lesions" (Teuber, 1955, p. 283).

Following this logic, the entire human neuropsychology tradition, going back to Broca and Wernicke, was reinterpreted as an issue of double dissociation, specific patterns of disorders being tied to specific brain parts. The important ideas were modularity and a subtractive idea: if a module is damaged, the rest remains intact. This idea has enough problems in adult neuropsychology, mainly related to the issue of executive control-based compensations. Think of prospective memory disturbances compensated for by relying on blackboards, magnetic tables, and other external metacognitive aids. Other issues showed up, however, when the qualitative attitude of double dissociation in brain damage–based human neuropsychology was transferred to the developmental logic, supposing that there are developmental modules that can be damaged in a similar "subtractive" manner.

One clear-cut example is the interpretation of **social cognition**. Studying neurodevelopmental disorders with genetic background, and with specifically impaired or specifically preserved social cognition, has gained particular importance in understanding the origins of human social cognition. Finding groups that are developmentally challenged in social cognition is crucial for several reasons. They are relevant in an evolutionary context due to their genetic background. Because there are some neurodevelopmental changes in these people, they are relevant in understanding the neural basis of social cognition. By showing selective impairments/preservation of various aspects of social cognition, they offer insights about how these functions are organized and embedded within the overall architecture of the mind/brain. Moreover, they offer a window into the developmental unfolding of social cognition.

Autism promises to be a primary case, where impaired social cognition is combined with relatively intact other cognitive domains. The study of **autism spectrum disorders** combined with preserved other aspects of cognition has become essential in our knowledge of the structural, developmental, and neural aspects of human social capacities (Baron-Cohen, 1989, 1995; Győri, 2006). Some researchers were even taking about **mind blindness** in their case (Frith, 2001). To take another favored example, dyslexia could be a disorder specific to word form consciousness, with other aspects of cognition unimpaired, Williams syndrome would be an inherited disorder specific to spatial cognition (Bellugi et al., 2000). The general interpretation for all these disorders has been in line with the modularist claims:

- They leave all other cognitive functions intact.
- They are all or none, since they are caused by a missing presumed gene.
- They can only be compensated for, but never cured.

As a consequence of the innatist argumentation of Chomsky, the idea of a **genetic organization of language disorders** was strengthened in the 1990s. The proposal goes back to Eric Lenneberg (1967). The nativist vision of language as a system by him gave a direct genetic interpretation: the innate system should somehow be coded in the genome. Lenneberg argued mainly for the fact that over a certain brain size threshold, all children seem to acquire language. Later, a direct exploration was initiated to search for children with specific language impairment (SLI). The famous papers of Mira Gopnik and Crago (1991) did find such a familial aggregation, where the basic phenomenological issue were difficulties with grammatical morphology that seemed to show a general familial inheritance. The affected family members, even as adults, made mistakes in English regarding agreement, saying things like "He go," "They goes."

SLI, as proposed by Gopnik, has become popular in the developmental dissociation literature. In the 1980s, specific language impairment figures merely 27 times in the psychological literature, in the next decade 347 times, and in the first decade of our century, 933 times.

Along the double-dissociation logic applied to language disorders, there was an interest toward a theoretical interpretation of SLI as well. One of the sharpest dissociations was originally proposed by Pinker (1991, 1999), and later supported by Clahsen (1999). One can decompose the underlying modularity of language claims into two sub-claims, big and little modularity. There is an issue of "big modularity." Specific language impairment with troubles of language would leave the rest of cognition intact. The "little modularity" would suggest a specific impairment of grammar, with a relatively intact vocabulary. In a famous double-dissociation comparison, SLI children have a very specific issue with grammar, while within the relatively good language skills, Williams syndrome subjects show a better grammar–weaker lexicon pattern (Bellugi et al., 2000). This would show up within the Williams syndrome group, especially when one contrasts Williams syndrome subjects with the SLI condition. English Williams syndrome subjects have a stronger tendency for morphological overgeneralization, replacing *went* with the overgeneralized *goed*, and show an overuse of rules of grammar. SLI subjects would acquire rule-based, regular items such as *learned* only as items, just as irregulars (*went*). These data are usually explained with reference to an anterior cortical, rule system (later supplemented by a basal ganglia–related subcortical skill system by Ullman, 2001), as opposed to a posterior cortical, item-based memory system. In the case of Williams syndrome, the posterior system was challenged, while in SLI, the anterior system was supposed to be challenged. This interpretation has been criticized on the basis of detailed developmental data by Karmiloff-Smith and her coworker Thomas. Instead of the **rules-versus-items** model, they offered a rivaling theoretical explanation. Instead of a contrast between items and rules, there would be a universal learning mechanism with different "tuning curves," that is, slowdowns in the impaired population (Thomas and Karmiloff-Smith, 2003). Cognitively impaired children would be seemingly unable for some kinds of learning due to the time constraints of learning.

The logic of modular dissociations, which also showed up in connection with SLI, was severely questioned.

1. The double dissociation in the sense that SLI children would have all other cognition intact is questionable. They do show peculiar **other cognitive impairments, which questions the specificity of the impairment**. As Bishop (2001) showed, they do have limited acoustic working memory, and as Tallal and Piercy (1973) demonstrated, they also have specific problems with processing quickly changing acoustic input. Thus, their language problems might be related to general fine memory learning pattern and acoustic issues. Ullman (2001, 2006) claimed that in line with this general model of procedural learning being responsible for grammar, SLI children had a problem with their procedural learning, related to anterior cortical parts and some basal ganglia.
2. Bishop (2001) also showed by family genetic association studies that while there was strong evidence for a genetic component, it was mainly related to a subtype of SLI that was connected to reduced working memory; thus, the acoustic issues might have a more developmental origin.
3. **Microgenetics of SLI.** SLI, for a decade, was mainly interpreted as a genetic disorder on the basis of classical behavioral genetic data. Eventually, in the family Gopnik identified, Lai et al. (2001) found a genetic deviation in all affected family members: the lack of the FOXP2 gene, which created a huge sensation. Subsequent animal studies and gene transplantations showed, however, that this gene was not responsible simply for some aspect of grammar but for organized complex movements in general. It has a version in more ancient mammals, and it had a mutation certainly a few hundred thousand years ago that allowed for the fine motor control necessary for speech articulation. Thus, it does not seem to be built specifically for grammar.

The presence of FOXP2 in other animals does not diminish its relevance for speech and language, but rather represents another example of recruitment and modification of existing pathways in evolution. Although the genetic pathways implicated in language may have in part been recruited from genetic cascades involved in other brain systems, this does not mean that they necessarily draw on the same neural substrates as these other systems. It is quite possible, for example, that the development of an ability to represent hierarchical grammar might be influenced by some of the same genes as those influencing representation of hierarchical plans in other domains.

(Marcus & Fisher, 2003, p. 261)

Thus, the hopes for SLI, which were so high, to support both innatism and modularity were spoiled. Today, SLI seems to be much less specific on the behavioral level, but also much less specific on the genetic level. This observation supports theories that call for a gradual epigenetic development instead of a blueprint reading determination of phenotype, as conceived originally. A developmental mechanism is replacing strict innatism that relies on interactions rather than on a simple one-way determination. By now, even the name was replaced by **specific developmental language disorder** (Bishop et al., 2017).

This turn has broader implications as well. It is hard to imagine a simple Mendelian genetics for (supposed) modular cognitive organizations. In addition, we must recognize that there are not only opponent systems in cognition but supplementary systems as well, such as nighttime and daytime vision, or grammar and the lexicon. Finally, specific cultural learning mechanisms show up in humans as a procedure that is prepared to acquire relatively unmotivated, arbitrary systems in a flexible manner (Csibra & Gergely, 2009).

This all relates back to the history of modularity.

Descent-with-modification suggests that there should be shared properties between modules, but if there are no modules at all, there would still be shared properties between underlying neural substrates; at best the current arguments put descent-with-modification modularity on a par with a domain-general view; they don't independently affirm it. Affirming modularity (of any sort) in any domain remains an empirical challenge.

(Marcus, 2006, p. 462).

Tasks

CA

Find new behavioral data gathering methods.
Uncertainties in psychological data and the post-truth mentality.
Data reliability and the gender and culture issues.
EvoDevo, Baldwin, Stern, and Piaget.
Selectionist psychological and neuroscience models.
IQ heredity and the theory of multiple intelligences.
The essence of the nature/nurture debate today.
Innatism and genetics.
The concept of social mind.

DSA

"Heredity," "learning," and "development" in common discourse (Google Ngram).

Jensen, Gould, and Burt and Herrnstein from the 1970s in public discourse (Google Ngram).

Pinker, Ullman, and Marcus from 1990 to 2020 in psychology (PsycINFO).

Co-occurrences of "genetics" and "innatism" in psychological texts (PsycINFO).

"IQ" over 120 years in psychology (PsycINFO).

"Modularity" and "development," 1985 to 2020, in the psychological literature (PsycINFO).

"Social mind" and "empathy" in public discourse, 1970–2020 (Google Ngram).

11 The future of psychology

> Science . . . is the source of a deep tension in the modern world. On the one hand, we have been formed by the traditions of our culture. . . . On the other hand, modern empirical sciences have reshaped our world and the way this whole world is interpreted.
>
> (Gadamer, 1983, p. 209)

Changes in psychology as a profession

Applied psychology, both regarding its impact on society and its mere size, has become an important profession in the Western world in the decades following the Second World War. Today, it seems to be a trivial fact of life that research and teaching are merely a small subdomain that is built upon the much larger base that is the profession of psychology as we know it. This process had already started at the end of the 19th century. It involved schoolteachers in the child study movements, with early sporadic clinical interventions, and with the beginnings of business psychology. School counseling, and later school psychology, became widespread in the 1920s, not only in the United States, and in the UK with Cyril Burt as a leading school psychologist, but, with the involvement of Piéron and Wallon, two leading academic psychologists, in the French setting as well. William Stern in Germany, Carlotte and Karl Bühler in Austria, László Nagy and Ferenc Mérei in Hungary, and Basov, Blonskij, and others in Soviet Russia promoted a child-centered educational applied psychology under the logo of pedology (see Chapter 4 for more) well. Together with psychotherapies, school psychology as a continuation of these efforts has gradually become a leading accredited program type in the 1960s.

There was an overall **general shift of the importance of professional compared to academic jobs and activities within psychology**. One of these social aspects was the **impact of wars and big-scale politics on applications of psychology**. The First World War, as we will see, resulted in the massive use of intelligence testing, and led to its spread in civilian life, as well as the treatment of "shell shock," post-traumatic disorders. The Second World War resulted in the formation of new group dynamic methods and theories, the consolidation of modern

DOI: 10.4324/9781032625805-13

neuropsychology, and on the end of the scale, the information processing vision of man.

There was an increasing professional orientation and commitment due to wartime cooperation from the part of academic psychology as well. Capshew (1999) reviewed the direct involvement of psychologists in the war efforts. A constant hope was that psychology can become an aid toward social and international peace. Gordon Allport and many other social psychologists had already expressed their hopes that social engineering worked toward social peace during the war (Allport et al., 1943).

The wars also changed everyday life. As the French psychologist and sociologist Pierre Naville recounted in the book edited about him by Blum (2007), modern wars radically changed life with the upheaval they caused. They directly impacted families, changed working habits by causing women to work, changed dressing habits and hairstyles, among a number of other ramifications. This had many consequences for psychologists.

Another important aspect is the **relations of psychology to important social and political movements**. That is most trivial in the Soviet Russian model with the constant optimistic image of man infiltrating psychology in the form of different culturalisms. At the same time, this optimistic psychology was later questioned by the same political authorities, in the name of even more dramatic educational indoctrination (Chapter 7). Optimism was also present in the American New Deal politics, where psychology tried to live up to the dream of democratizations and increasing opportunities for all. The emerging Fascism had direct and indirect influences on psychology. Jewish psychologists, an entire generation of Gestalt and psychoanalytic colleagues, had to leave Germany and many countries under its influence, bringing over their ideas and approaches to Western Europe and especially the United States. At the same time, in Germany, new racist psychologies were promoted. As these changes were occurring, left-wing psychologies elaborated theories about the psychological aspects and even addressed the causes of the rise of fascism in personality dynamics and the role of prejudice in social life (Chapter 6). The war years created a crucial alliance in two regards. The moral engagement for social service and helping the government was high in the United States, as well as the belief in a behavioral social science that could possibly be used for social engineering. This easy alliance lasted until the 1970s. By the 1970s, the governmental alliance of psychologists in the United States was shaken by the Vietnam War, the divisive interpretations of the success of minority equality efforts, and by the feminist movement. The disengagements between government and psychologists in the United States and several European countries did not question the very social success of psychology as a profession; they merely changed its direct alliances within society.

Technology itself with **mass production, automatization, and computerization has drastically changed applied psychology**. Handcrafted, tailored psychological instruments were gradually replaced, first, by electric tools, then by special electronic circuits, and finally by multipurpose computer programs. Methodological moves of sophistication led to the appearance of statistics, then, with the developments of Sir Raymund Fisher's methods, ANOVA appeared, and the 1950s–1960s showed the spread of significance testing for all effects and differences, partly under the impact of marketing research. This also implied a reconsideration of the "variables" in psychological research into independent, organismic, and dependent variables, as done by Woodworth in his textbooks, the latest version being Woodworth and Schlossberg (1954). This was followed by the spread of multivariate statistics due to the software packages. It resulted in reporting differences as well. In touchy issues, such as gender or national differences, size effects in meta-analytic reviews have become an expectation by now. This was followed by critiques of significance testing (Chapter 10).

On the basis of the data of Tryon (1963), membership in the APA professional divisions rose much faster compared to other academic fields. While in 1940, 75% of the American psychologists were occupied in an academic position, by 1959, the two employment types were equalized roughly (52 vs. 48%), and later on, the applied fields became dominant in employment as well. Today, these ratios appear in huge absolute numbers. Practicing psychologists in the United States numbered well over 50,000 in the 1970s, compared to a minority of academic people which numbered 20,000. Figure 11.1 shows the changes of the *American Psychological Association* membership over half a century.

Similar processes went on in Europe as well, but a decade or two later. According to data of the EFPA, the Organization of European Associations of Psychology, academic work is about 20% and clinical work is almost 80% around the beginning

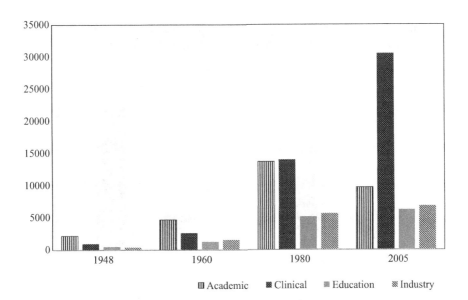

Figure 11.1 Membership in the APA sections in the second half of the 20th century.
Source: http://www.apa.org/about/division/numbers.pdf with simplifications.

450 *On the road toward contemporary psychology*

of the 21st century. Organizational psychology numbers about 23%, with multiple assignments allowed.

The gradual professionalization of psychology was true for a small community, within Hungarian psychology as well, as shown in Figure 11.2. The clinical profession has increased the fastest, and its percentage is around 53%, while the academic profession is a silent minority, around 17%.

One key aspect of the rise of applied psychology as a mundane profession were the changes in the **collective representations of psychology**. This has been most clearly spelled out and analyzed in the case of the French public representation of psychoanalysis. It is an important detail of French psychology that psychoanalysis has been slow to gain impact there (see Chapter 1), and it mainly spread after the Second World War. This spread was perceived by many as a consequence of American influence, labeled by the French Communists as American colonialization, and later by historians of social movements as self-colonialization as well. The French social psychologist Serge Moscovici (1961) elaborated his concept of **social representation** (Chapter 6) with the example of the impact of Freud and psychoanalysis on French public image. The theory showed that the spread of psychology was not merely a question of its spread in actual meeting of clients and psychologists but a question of its spread and role in changing the self-representation of people. Moscovici tried to reveal this image through an analysis of the French press and by using interviews with people of different social status. He showed a rather structured image of psychoanalysis. In this public representation, a structure of consciousness-unconscious-repression complex emerged. The general message was an image of the determining force of early childhood, the importance of desires, and the inaccessibility of our unconscious life to ourselves as defining features of psychoanalysis. There was a social repression in this image of the disappearance of the sexual nature of the libido itself from the public image.

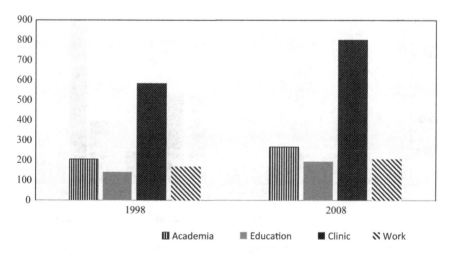

Figure 11.2 Psychology profession in Hungary around the millennium.

The crucial importance of the role of psychology in changing the image of humans was also emphasized by one of the founders of American cognitive psychology, by George Armitage Miller (1969, p. 1065). As president of APA, Miller emphasized: "I believe that any broad and successful application of psychological knowledge to human problems will necessarily entail a change in our conception of ourselves and of how we live and love and work together." The new applied paradigm envisioned by Miller would not be behavioral technology. It would leave options for choice, competencies, and the like, intending mainly to change our image of ourselves. It would see humans as motivated to work, to practice competencies as active agents and masters of their own lives.

A generation later, the Stanford-based social psychologist Philip Zimbardo summarized why this optimistic vision of George Miller has never come true.

> I think for four reasons: Excessive modesty about *what* psychology really had of value to offer the public, ignorance about *who* was "the public," cluelessness about *how* to go about the mission of giving psychology away, and lack of sufficient concern about *why* psychology needed to be accountable to the public.
>
> (Zimbardo, 2004, p. 340)

An important divisive issue in the march of applied psychology would be the realization that applied psychology **concentrated too much on the individual**. Most applied psychologists – clinicians, guidance centers, etc. – with a humanistic engagement concentrate on the individuals turning to them for help. This attitude has its own logic, ethical standards, and *raison d'être*. At the same time, many interventions targeting the individual would use social relations and social networks to deal with the client. The group therapies, psychodrama, and other interventions, while they aim to change the individual, use the image of a self being mainly manageable from a centripetal perspective, from the social roles constituting the outer layer of the self. Psychology, at the service of personal guidance in this regard, has become socially a rival of religious practices. Yet even if the original unit and target was the individual, psychologists oftentimes realized that the problems of their clients were related to several people: systemic methods to deal with couples or families, with schools and other systems, also emerged. In non-clinical domains, like in the military, in industry, in education, the need to propose **system-related interventions** has risen. Make communication more efficient in our company, make the organization interested in innovations, and change the school system rather than children. The tension between individuum-centered and institution-centered applied psychology continues to be with us.

Tensions between academic and professional fields

With the numerical and, in many countries, financial victory of applied psychology, the issue of the relationship between research and practice emerged again. There are disgruntled labels that are trivially related to the competition for financial and public attention resources. "Academic psychology is not worth of anything" *versus* "applied psychologists are disoriented gurus." The recent rise of the psychological society, combined with the promises of behavioral technologies, also led to public skepsis toward applied psychology from the public. Lilienfeld (2011) identified a series of basic criticisms. Some of them are semantic excursions, such as "Psychology is merely commonsense." Psychology sometimes expresses semantic truisms, like, "Opposites attract each other." Sometimes, psychology claims that it cannot generalize because individuals differ; at other times, it promises easy reductionist solutions. The way to improve the image of psychology is to involve more teaching for non-psychologists and to engage leading academic researchers to address their public. Stars of contemporary American psychology, like Csíkszentmihályi, Gardner, Sternberg, or Pinker, already initiated this commitment.

In American psychology, these tensions even led to institutional separations. A hundred years ago, Titchener had already tried to establish a rather modest society of experimentalists (see Chapter 9 in Volume 1). Then in 1959, the *Psychonomic Society* was established to cultivate research, mainly research in experimental psychology. This society became stabilized with a journal, society, and conferences (now more than 60). In the 1970s, the American practitioners moved. They created so-called professional schools, first in clinical psychology, and later, more broadly, with a new degree of Doctor of Psychology (Psy.D) that has about the same number of students as programs offering a more traditional PhD, indicating an end to the combined research and practitioner training in clinical psychology. As a follow-up to this, several committees were formed within the *American Psychological Association* to resolve the tension between professional practitioners and experimentalists. This did not work. Finally, in 1988, a separate new society, *Association for Psychological Science* (APS), was formed, first under the name of *American Psychological Society* that changed its name in 2005.

The separation should not come as a surprise. As Simonton (2000) analyzed excellence in psychology, there always were and continue to be two basic trends. He differentiated qualitative people (like Freud, Jung, Adler, James, G. Allport, and Rogers) and experimentalists and mathematizers (like Skinner, Estes, Harlow, and Thurstone). These two trends both have independent success within psychology. Both soft and hard people may be very successful in psychology according to the number of citations. Only the middle-of-the-road ones do not have a substantial impact. Thus, in psychology, both the holistic, interpretive trends and the experimentalists have a great impact. Nevertheless, as the separations showed, they do not coexist in a state of complete symbiosis, cooperation, and overlap.

In clinical practice, traditional theoretical divisions showed up within the applied field itself. They basically touch upon the issue of causality and understanding. One aspect of this division is **intervention as opposed to understanding**. While behaviorism as a theory of the human condition and as a leading experimental school was losing its impact from the 1970s on, the ethics of behavior-based interventions and its technologies continued flourishing (Spear, 2007). The different protocols of behavior therapy represent a need for direct intervention, though mainly by softening the passive image of man. Instead of conditioning, the cognitive aspect of behavior modification started to mean a life project requiring the cooperation on the part of the client most of the time as well. Figure 11.3 shows the popularity of **behavior therapy** and **cognitive behavior therapy** over two generations of psychology. What one can see is that in the 1970s, when behaviorism as a theoretical approach had its fall, the popularity of behavior therapy, in fact, increased for a time and cognitive behavior therapy caught up in the last decade.

At the same time, in the public mind, psychotherapy came up in the 1960s as the sign of the psychological society. Within the public domain, psychoanalysis is still the dominant vision.

On the institutional level, psychology in its professional practice is involved both in understanding and helping the individuals and helping institutions.

> The prototypical healers that the twentieth century has bequeathed us are the psychotherapist and the management expert. The former heals persons, but has the larger ambition of remodeling the society after the psychotherapist's clinic. The other heals groups, but in practice has the narrower ambition of healing corporate structure.
>
> (Ashis, 2001, p. 28)

It is a general characteristic of that time from the 1970s in affluent Western societies that besides these models of professional psychology, with the advent of self-help and pop psychology literature, a mundane "psychological culture" developed. Psychology has become part of a "leisure time culture," with its popular magazines

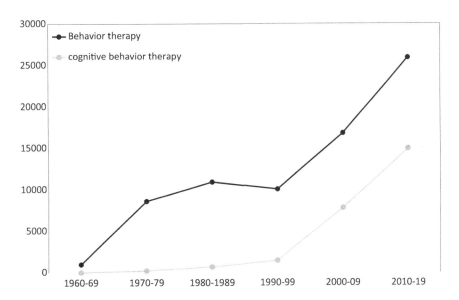

Figure 11.3 The fate of the notions "behavior therapy" and "cognitive behavior therapy" in the PsycINFO database.

and later websites, going on the track of the *Homo Psychologicus* (Cohen, 1970). We cannot deal with this merely from the higher stance of academic psychology, since even academic psychology admits that the main route for the social impact of psychology is its influence on our self-image. Essentially, the helping attitude extended its reaches toward everyday life, beyond the clinic, and this kind of secularization put psychology on the menu of everyday life problems and their solutions. Table 11.1 summarizes the typical divisions in the helping aspects of applied psychology of the last half century. In contemporary society, the two images coexist. A certain market of ideas and practices has been formed, no matter how bad the very idea of a "market" in mental health may sound for many who believe in single principles.

This situation is enriched by the strong and noisy alternative social movements from the 1980s on. From the critique of a one-dimensional man in the student movement in the 1960s, through feminism and multiculturalism, all had a not-too-tolerant inspiration toward psychology demanding what used to be called in the 1960s and 1970s by the neo-Marxist approaches a critical theory of society through a **critical psychology** (see the edited volume by Fox & Prilleltensky, 1997).

Determinism and the "third force" movements

A central issue that is often discussed for the position of psychology in modern society has become the amount of determinism in human life and the role of biological and social moments clinical and guidance work. On the one hand, **biological theories of personality disorders and mental troubles have become more articulated**, mainly in line with the development of our understanding of the biochemistry of the brain, the Human Genome Project, and pharmacological developments with the introduction of major tranquilizers that go along with this. This is most clearly expressed in the mental disorder classification systems DSM since 1952.

The **discovery of neuroleptics** was a crucial moment in the development of modern biological psychiatry. Jean Delay (1907–1987), the French psychiatrist, and his coworkers tried the drug chlorpromazine in 1952 originally designed for anesthesiology on agitated psychotic patients. This event, which Delay originally labeled the discovery of neuroleptics, initiated the pharmacological revolution in psychiatry, the birth of an alliance between pharmaceutical industry, and the

Table 11.1 Some alternative visions of applied psychology during the last decades

Classical image	Alternative
Individuum-centered	Organization-centered
Selection	Support
Professionals-based	Self-help
Determined humans	Self-managing humans
Explanation	Understanding
Adaptation	Self-actualization

psychiatric profession (Delay & Deniker, 1955). Delay was already a very influential biological psychiatrist and biologist of memory at that time; in the footsteps of Janet (Delay, 1942), he was an expert on alleged amnesia of some of the accused Germans during the Nuremberg trials. At the same time, he was a successful writer, a member of the French Academy, and a personal mentor of Michel Foucault. Delay even gave a place for Jacques Lacan at the Sainte Anne hospital in Paris, while he was the director of the hospital. Through the success of chlorpromazine, he has become responsible for the first international classification of psychiatric drugs.

For the biological psychiatrists, the use of major tranquilizers became a symbol of a more human biological treatment, but for the revolting youth, a symbol of the further biologization of mental disorders. In the late 1960s, many manifestations accompanied these tensions that were anti-pharmaceutical as well, while they were fighting for a more psychological treatment of patients. Several artistic representations of the inhumanity of mental treatments also appeared, like the novel *One Flew Over the Cuckoo's Nest* of Ken Kesey and the movie based on it by Milos Forman. The more human treatment – compared to psychosurgery and shock therapy – did not stop left-wing criticism. The hospital of Delay was attacked in May of 1968 in Paris, and within two years, Delay retired. He continued to follow his literary work. Driss Moussaoui (2002), a leading psychiatrist in Marocco, and a student of Delay, gives a detailed and passionate account both of the discovery of major tranquilizers, and the entire complex life course of Jean Delay, including his shock and alienation after his humanistic psychiatry ward was occupied by the revolting students as a symbol of social power.

Antipsychiatry emerged in a context in America where rather than biological psychiatry, it was in fact psychoanalytic "soft" interpretation that was dominant in the 1960s. Psychoanalytic treatment, which mainly ignored psychotic patients, dominated American clinical life in the 1960s. It is also interesting that the major movement leaders, Szasz in the United States and Laing in Britain, were themselves psychoanalytically trained. In their approach to mental disorder, they offered an even more radical psychodynamic view of mental illness than Freudians ever dreamed of. One leading opponent both of psychoanalysis and biological psychiatry was the **antipsychiatry movement** initiated by Thomas Szasz (1920–2012), who, in a famous book, claimed that mental illness was merely a fabrication about misunderstandings of human behavior and communication. There is no biological basis for mental disorders (Szász, 1961). There were other "soft interpretations" of the psychotic experience in the 1950s–1970s. One was proposed by the British anthropologist and communication researcher Gregory Bateson (1904–1980). Bateson was an innovative social researcher, always wishing to look at social behavior from unusual angles. Among his many topics of research, many of them anthropological, one was the study of relationships between social disease and communication, with the use of communication theory and the theory of logical types taken from Bertrand Russell. In Palo Alto, California, Bateson became associated with issues of psychiatry. On the basis of his hospital fieldwork, he proposed a **double-bind** theory of the genesis of schizophrenia. The family pattern underlying schizophrenia would be a contradiction between direct communication and metacommunication, as between literal and ironical meanings, when, for example, a mother tells a child appearing in torn jeans something like, "How well are you dressed."

> When the individual is involved in an intense relationship, and is caught in a situation in which the other person in the relationship is expressing two orders of message and one of these denies the other. . . . [H]e may defend himself in ways which have been described as paranoid, hebephrenic, or catatonic.
>
> (Bateson et al., 1956, pp. 5, 7)

The theory has remained more an interpretive theory than a real causal one that is supported by empirical studies. This approach fits those theories at large – some of them within psychoanalysis – that were making mothers responsible for schizophrenia and in general blamed working women for the many troubles of modern American social adaptation.

Szasz and Bateson were more theoreticians and intellectual debaters. Robert Laing (1927–1989), the British psychiatrist, poet, and social critic, on the other hand, became a symbol figure for combining a radical critique of psychiatry with radical social movements. Laing claimed that the essence of mental disorders was to be searched for in family socialization practices and family oppression, which led to alienation and an alternative interpretation of reality. This family explanation may sound rather Freudian. However, according to Laing, the family structure leads not to neurosis but to alternative realities. These alternative realities correspond to what traditional psychiatry called psychosis and delusions. In the interpretation of Laing (1960, 1961), psychosis is not a mental illness but a real different vision of reality that should be respected and even accepted as a possible vision of the world. Originally, Laing wanted to prove empirically this etiology, but after a while, he took up an entirely "understanding" attitude. There has to be no controlled studies of the families, merely an interpretation of the message of the clients. Mental illness would be a provocative alternative interpretation of the world and of communication itself, based on family experience.

In the 1970s, the views of Laing, and partly also those of Bateson, were combined with the civil rights and civil disobedience movements. These efforts contributed to many tensions over the mental health and clinical professions, especially in the United States and Britain, but also in France. In its practice, the antipsychiatry movement combined social psychiatry with the antiauthoritarian message of actual cultural critiques, critical social science like Foucault (1978, 1988) and Goffman, and the use of mind-altering substances. Some of these alternatives did promote drugs, but not with an intention to cure, but with an intention to open the mind to new experiences. Out of this came a new psychiatric practice in London in the Kingsley Hall ward, which was soon closed because of the disruptive behavior of the patients (about 100 were there during a five-year period), and the theoretical disorganization of the boss, Laing himself, preaching for an acceptance of a new disintegrated self.

There was a clinical attitude toward social issues as well in the 1950s under the influence of psychoanalytic ideas. In the 1950s, both American applied psychology and psychiatry were dominated by psychoanalytic ideas and practices. On the initiative by psychologists, the public even started to talk about nations as being "insane," and the need to change their "character" to improve the chances for peace. The longtime Freudian influence, and the spread of clinical practices, underwent a gradual value reorientation in the 1960s. The psychotherapy notion was extended in the "third force" trends, with the advent of humanistic psychology that was extending psychotherapy toward the healthy person, using psychology as a tool toward self-development. On the other hand, "critical psychology" movements appeared that combined some of the earlier neo-Freudian moves with Bateson and Laing and started to question the social adaptation programs implied in the idea of a "therapeutic society." Parallel to this, they again questioned all sorts of reductionisms and claimed for a joint recognition of the internal world of the mind and its objective social embedding.

From a historical perspective, antipsychiatry was born at the same time as modern biological psychiatry. Both offered challenges toward the dominant socialization visions of mental disorders promoted by psychoanalysis. The biological approach claimed to treat unbalanced biological conditions of brain neurotransmitters. Antipsychiatry, on the other hand, challenged the entire idea of "balance" and "adaptation" and claimed that mental patients were crazy but not ill. In essence, patients were reacting to a defective world, and their message has to be listened to.

The cultural criticism of the adaptation message of clinical work and its suppression of the supposed challenge to the social order is constantly re-emerging. There is also an emergent critique of pharmaceuticals, its lack of success, and the unfounded nature of psychiatric classification. There are also New Age movements, like the anti-psychiatric campaigns of scientology.

New flexible theories of personality and psychotherapy

While these rather intense intellectual debates went on, there was another differentiation within groups that claimed a softer determination of life paths and possible pathologies as well. One was the **identity theory proposed by Erik Erikson** (1902–1994). Erikson was a German-born psychoanalyst trained by Anna Freud. In the United States, he was affiliated with Yale, Berkeley, and Harvard Universities. His influence, however, has mainly come not from his teaching but from his writings on identity and the stages of personality development. He was a well-read and widely cited author, with over 200,000 references to his work. His *Childhood and Society* (Erikson, 1950, 60,000 references) won the Pulitzer Prize and the National Book Award in the United States. His main theory was extending the psychoanalytic stages of individual development into a fuller stage theory of human development that includes adult development as well. He proposed a developmental theory where each stage has its own "main tasks" and positive or negative outcomes. Erikson's vision had two crucial features that made him attractive for many practical directions. The **formation and crisis of identity** outlined by him in studies of famous people like Luther has made the concept of identity central to many future psychologies (Erikson, 1958). With the advent of feminist movement and the issues surrounding gender and national identity a generation later, this became a central topic for broader social movements as well. By treating adulthood also as having its own stages, Erikson became a pillar of lifelong developmental theories in humanistic directions of psychology. The development goes over an open system (Erikson, 1968). It has its own challenges and risks and involves personal decisions, as shown in Table 11.2. Psychotherapy is also centered on issues of identity and developmental stages.

Since the 1960s, the social roles so central to social psychology also showed up as bases of personality theory and psychotherapy. Eric Berne (1910–1970) developed a transactional theory of layers of personality, classifying social interactions from mere pastimes, through personally not committing "games," to a deeper layer, committing the full personality (Berne, 1964). In a way, Berne replaced the tripartite layers postulated by Freudian theory by interpersonal layers. His **transactional analysis** is a further communicative approach to psychotherapy that intends to analyze and suppress life-threatening games and dangerous life scripts. Berne was a popular writer in the 1970s, and his transactional analysis was still popular in the early 1980s. In an intellectual sense, his therapeutical approach promised to combine a loose topological model taken over from psychoanalysis with the American social interactionist tradition.

Schools of depth psychology and the behavioral and cognitive therapy practices developed in detail the ideas about the experience or habit-based determination of personality, while always taking personality to be determined by life history. The so-called **third force options** were articulated as an opposition to this determination. Besides the antipsychiatry movement seen earlier, there were softer, third force varieties that emphasized instead of criticism new experiences and personal enrichment. **Humanistic psychology** was to become the cover name for several efforts. The leading figure of the movement was Carl Rogers (1902–1987). Rogers, himself a practicing psychoanalyst, advocated an approach that concentrated on human options and self-initiative compared to traditional deterministic Freudian approaches. Robert Kramer (1995) showed that some ideas of Rogers were routed

Table 11.2 The main stages of development according to Erikson

Stage	Age	Feature	+ Outcome	– Outcome
Hope	1.5 years	Predictability	Trust	Mistrust
Will	1–3 years	Efficiency	Autonomy	Shame
Purpose	3–6 years	Planning	Initiative	Guilt
Competence	6–11 years	Social comparison	Industry	Inferiority
Adolescence	12–18 years	Fidelity	Identity	Role confusion
Adulthood	18–35 years	Love	Intimacy	Isolation
Late adult	35–64 years	Care	Generativity	Stagnation
Old age	65– years	Wisdom	Integrity	Despair

Source: Erikson (1950, 1968).

by the innovative attitude of the dissident psychoanalyst Otto Rank (1884–1939), who came to the United States and developed a more person-centered approach. Psychotherapy in the vision promoted by Rogers became more client-centered and did not follow a prescribed script. It was a practice based on the full acceptance of the client as a person and on creating an open, accepting atmosphere on fostering learning and new developments of the self rather than reducing its antiquated tensions. The basic features of his approach to psychotherapy were intended to create acceptance and warmth: congruence, unconditional positive acceptance, and empathetic understanding characterized his open attitude.

Besides his influential books (Rogers, 1953, 1972), Rogers spelled out his views in several public discussions, with theologians and religious leaders and also with psychologists, among them B. F. Skinner (see Chapter 8). Rogers clearly saw that issues of social value orientation are also involved here. Significant problems of social philosophy underlie the diverging attitudes regarding therapy. If objective study supports the conclusion that dependence, guidance, and expert direction of the client's therapy and life are necessary, then a social philosophy of expert control – like the social philosophy of Skinner – is clearly implied. If research indicates that the client has at least the latent ability to understand and guide himself, then a psychological basis for democracy is demonstrated.

In the debate between Skinner and Rogers, after summarizing their agreements (the goal of behavioral science is to control behavior), Rogers listed his issues of disagreements: "Who will be controlled? Who will exercise control? What type of control will be exercised? Most important of all, toward what end or what purpose, or in the pursuit of what value, will control be exercised?" (Rogers in Rogers & Skinner, 1962, p. 20).

Rogers proposed to have other goals than mere behavioral technology. He preferred

> man as a process of becoming, as a process of achieving worth and dignity through the development of his potentialities, the individual human being as a self-actualizing process, moving on to more challenging and enriching experiences the process by which the individual creatively adapts to an ever-new and changing world.
> (Rogers in Rogers & Skinner, 1962, p. 25)

The therapeutic or intervention goal is self-reliance of the client and a move toward internal control. Skinner wanted to start from strong control and claimed in the debate that he had proposed gradual reduction of control already in his *Walden Two* (Skinner, 1948).

The humanistic movements also encompassed the works of Charlotte Bühler (1893–1974), a Viennese émigré working in California (Bühler & Melanie, 1972), who extended her original ideas about lifelong development and the centrality of value formation on the human life course (Bühler, 1933).

Some of these elevated humanistic goals, when they became a movement, concluded regarding psychotherapy and the formation of personality in the **encounter**

group movement that acceptance and laissez-faire attitude should prevail. This moved the emphasis away from painful self-knowledge and the fight against negative forces, such as anxiety. Eastern practices, yoga, and meditation also reached the palette of mental health services offered (Rogers, 1970).

The way the psychological society developed in the last three decades was threefold.

1. Psychoanalysis and behavior therapy developed on their own, and they were the most frequently offered help in institutional and private settings for clients and patients.
2. The softer therapies gradually developed into helping practices not for disordered people but became constituents of leisure time activities, helping the mood regulation of modern society and shaping for specific situations by coaches.
3. Many self-help movements developed form Alcoholics Anonymous through different parents and victim associations to support people in need.

New applied psychologies: technological changes of the profession

The social embedding of contemporary psychology gives new directions to applied psychologies as well. The traditional disciplinary boundaries become loosened not only on a theoretical level but in practice as well. One trend is the widening of classical domains. Besides changes in traditional individuum-centered clinical psychology, **health psychology** also appeared partly under the influence of behavioral medicine as well. Figure 11.4 shows that the whole notion of health psychology is born in the 1980s and soon becomes a strong partner or rival of clinical psychology.

Besides the changes of classical domains, entirely new applied fields also appeared. Modern **economic psychology** had its early initiative by George Katona (1951), started massively in the late 1970s, and has appeared as a term 1,300 times in the PsycINFO database for over four decades. Its twin term, **behavioral economics**, is almost as popular. It covers in a parallel manner the social psychology of local economic market interactions and the representation and internal mediators of macro-processes, including the determinants of consumer and investor decisions.

Architectural changes and contemporary information society

During the last generation, the advent of new information technologies was supplemented by the overall presence of new networks and social media. On the first hand, this meant an **architectural change**. Gestures, spoken language, and writing-based information architectures characterized the last centuries, and this was suddenly supplemented by the accessible distant knowledge and distant contacts. This has brought along many new theoretical issues and issues for applied psychology. The modern network-based knowledge carriers propose that network-based knowledge provides for real constant accessibility. Donald (2014) raised three basic changes due to the new information society: personal autonomy under the shadow of external knowledge systems, the recreation of trust in a networked

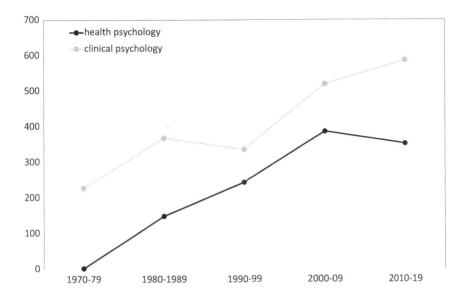

Figure 11.4 **Health psychology** and **clinical psychology** as titles of papers in the PsycINFO database during the last decades.

society, and the tensions between machine-centered and human-centered governance. "The future development of memory technology cannot be predicted with any certainty. A consequence of this is that the future forms of cultural memory are also uncertain" (Donald, 2017, 37).

The psychological issue that touches architectures and mentalities seems too simple: in order to regain our personality, we may again regulate our communicative patterns ourselves and reconsider what time we spend with what. A simple aspect of this is how much time we spend on **finding and obtaining** the constantly refreshing pieces of knowledge (search and paste) and how much time is spent on **using this valuable information**. There is no easy solution, but there certainly is an intellectual task and a social problem that touches on the ecology of mental resources.

There is an ongoing debate between pessimists, like the Oxford pharmacologist Susan Greenfield (2015), who claims that the easily accessible information leads to shallow processing and that constant clicking leads to search for dopamine-based brain happiness, and the optimists, who claim that the new data management leads to new memory economy and faster learning. There are many tasks here for future applied psychology. Besides the entirely internalist and entirely externalist views of the mind, there are some trends that emphasize that even the most modern technologies, in a way, become accepted and widespread because they somehow become harmonized with the **ethological constraints of the mind**. Theoreticians in this group believe in the stability of biological systems that can only be slightly modified by new technologies. Evolution built in some fairly stable needs and possibilities into human beings that cannot be changed by cultural influence. The nightmare of Orwell cannot be realized because human beings are unable to suffer loneliness or restriction of information spread for longer periods of time. Dunbar (2003, 2021), along these lines, described several examples of chat rooms that fit into long-established motivational and cognitive systems.

Theories of secondary orality and the re-personalization of technological communication imply that the new media uses the old, available tools of network formation, which are then used to build an inner world that becomes very much new due to **cognitive ecology**. The task of the scientist here is to analyze the universal aspects of this process. In order to do this, there is a need for more cross-talk between disciplines and communicative tolerance, exactly what these new tools were meant for. There is still a long way to go, of course, until we become as flexible and versatile in our science dealing with communicative media as we are in our subjective judgment and in our mental architectures.

Tensions between the scientific and interpretive attitudes

The issue of psychology as a natural science re-emerging

Is psychology a natural science? This is a traditional issue of the 19th century from at least Comte on that can be raised both regarding substance and regarding method. It has become increasingly relevant today again (Hatfield, 2002). The Vienna school of neopositivistic philosophy was the first to claim systematically that there is unity of science based both on method and on substance, and psychology had to be reoriented along these lines. This attitude has customarily been referred to as **physicalism** (Carnap, 1932). This physicalist comprehensive attitude has been much criticized already in its own time. Interestingly, after two generations, the naturalistic unification re-emerged in a finer variety. Quine (1951, 1953, 1969), the Harvard analytic philosopher, in a way brought the Vienna school spirit to our times, without its physicalism. Even the philosophical discipline of **epistemology will, at some point, be naturalized**. The argumentation is reversed in relation to Carnap. Rather than psychology looking for a philosophical foundation, psychology is, by its nature, interpreted as a natural science and is going to be the foundation of the study of knowledge, that is, epistemology.

This is still contrasted with another view. According to this view, natural science is radically different from human or social sciences. This was the claim of the 19th-century German school of historiography, where authors claimed that history was idiographic while science was nomothetic, as we saw in Chapters 8 and 10, in Volume 1. This opposition is more or less accepted by contemporary hermenuticians. This is expressed in the logo of this chapter by the famous German hermeneutic philosopher Hans George Gadamer (1900–2002) as an essential tension of the human condition, where humans are citizens of two worlds: the world of meaningful experience and of causal laws (Gadamer, 1983, 1984).

Hermeneutics, phenomenology, and contemporary psychology

The most clear-cut critics of naturalistic psychology today bring back the understanding tradition of the late 19th century. One trend is basically an unhappy meditation based on ontological or metaphysical realization that nature has no meaning. In some efforts, like the one proposed by the French hermeneutical philosopher Paul Ricoeur (in Changeux & Ricoeur, 2000) and by the philosopher and cognitive scientist Rom Harré, there is a general criticism that treats natural science as meaningless and that interprets both nature and human affairs as lacking intrinsic meaning (Harré, 1988). According to these phenomenologists, humans and their affairs should be treated as meaning carriers.

Intentionality

Both for the naturalists and for the social and spiritual constructionists, the place of intention is a crucial issue in the interpretation of life and mind. Concentrating on intentionality may lead us to three types of psychologies: folk psychology, intentional system theory, and sub-personal cognitive psychology, the latter being a neuronal theory of cognition (Dennett, 1987). The greatest problem with classical hermeneutics was to present intentionality as a royal way to replace explanation with interpretation. The issue of intentions has become central in several branches of natural science–minded psychology and their philosophical interpretations as well. One is the trend initiated by Jerry Fodor (1968) that treats intentions as really existing causal agents. The other is the intentional stance introduced by Dennett (1987), where intentions are postulated as soft attitudes in the mind of the interpreter. However, Dennett does not treat intentions as ghosts or other imagined phenomena. They are abstract relations, but at the same time, they are objective, like gravitational forces, or the equator of the earth.

Phenomenological social science and psychology

The "understanding attitude" tries to reconstruct the internal relations of mundane, everyday thought in seemingly difficult cases. An interesting trend is represented by the interpretations of social constructivism that start off form an interpretation of the heritage of Wittgenstein (1958) and the role of rules in mental life by the New Zealand British American philosophical psychologist Rom Harré (1927–2019). He is a characteristic representative of a constructionist trend in the intersection of philosophy, theoretical psychology, and cognitive science. His overall anthropological conception started off as a critique of cognitive revolution (Harré, 1988, 1990). He compared Vygotsky and Wittgenstein to the then-dominant machine image of human thinking. Harré claimed the following deviations on the paths of Wittgenstein and Vygotsky from a machine-based image of cognition.

1. **Mind is historical**(ly changing). This is the message of Kenneth Gergen as well. Regarding the structure of social psychology in a volume edited together with his wife, they campaigned for more historical sensitivity in social psychology (Gergen & Gergen, 1984).
2. **"Mind" is a collective production,** mainly mediated by language. The same is insisted by Kennett Gergen (1985) in his call for constructionism in psychology.

3. Linguistic meaning is not fixed. **Linguistic productions are more or less indeterminate.**
4. Mentality is formed discursively. Due to this conversational origin, **contradiction is sometimes to be tolerated.**
5. Mind and Self belong to **skill-type organizations** and to a holistically skill-based person.

Harré represents a language-centered social constructionism. This vision has some inherent problems. First of all, the aforementioned are upheld by many new naturalist psychologists. One can also question the entire constructionist attitude by emphasizing how loosely the entire movement is organized. Harré proposed a theory where the mind should be studied in a discursive manner, making mind entirely flexible, not necessarily postulating a constant internal theater. There is a further issue regarding the very meaning of "social" used in these exercises. One interpretation of "social" is the immediate social relations that shape the mental world, where these immediate social networks mediate the normative moments coming from the wider context of society. The other interpretation is more directly societal; it interprets "social" as the direct determining impact of society on the mental realm and in the mind. Harré concentrates on normativity many times, like in 1 and 2 earlier.

Regarding the substantial message of this social constructivism, the social interpretation of **rule application** plays a central role. Societal rules would determine the meanings of interactive events. These trends moved nearer to everyday life, not merely in its technical sense, but also in the strategies and ideologies of research. The Wittgenstein-based (1958) ideology of a rule-based social life, the regularities of ordinary life, besides ordinary language, shows up in theoretical proposals.

They follow a new phenomenology of social life, partly relying on the works of the Austrian German phenomenological sociologist **Alfred Schütz** (1899–1950), whose work was discovered in the 1960s–1970s in the English-speaking world (Schütz, 1967). His attitude of pursuing a naive phenomenological attitude appeared as a task of reconstructing the world of the layman from ethnogeny to ethnomethodology. In an interesting manner, the issue of rule-based organization is as crucial for them as for the cognitivists. The cognitive research looks for rules in very transparent issues, like "They goes home," and starts from the analysis of ungrammaticality (Chapter 9). The phenomenologists look for more hidden social rule, in behaviors that seemed to be not under social control. But they reveal the existence of rules also by breaking the rules. They study or create deviant cases where rule following is somehow broken.

Traditionally anomic events have become their center of attention. New terminologies appeared to deal with these efforts. Harré and Secord (1972) called their new approach **ethnogeny**, namely, the analysis of social interaction episodes combined with their verbal accounts on the part of the participants. Their examples to study rule-like regularities were found in mundane behaviors, like soccer hooliganism. At the other end of the world, in California, a new method or school of sociology, **ethnomethodology**, developed at about the same time. This trend intended to reconstruct a naive sociology, that is, the study of the way people, participants in interaction, interpreted their own behavior in terms of rules. In a method initiated by Harold Garfinkel (1917–2011) at UCLA, the ethnomethodologists studied rules by disobeying assumed regularities. Garfinkel (1967) outlined an entire program of what could be considered "happening sociology." The behavior of people is always rule-regulated, and one way to recognize the rules is to see what happens if you break them. Their most interesting results came from studying conversations in telephone calls, emergency situations, and the like (Sacks et al., 1974). As the innovative social theorist Ervin Goffman (1922–1982) spelled out, even in language, one has to look for the interpersonal regulation rather than merely for representation or expression of thought (Goffman, 1974).

The two visions, the objective and the phenomenological and understanding visions, of human life remain to be complementary approaches rather than being exclusive of each other. The same duality was accepted by the cognitive psychologist George Mandler (1996) when he pointed out that it might be true that following the dual approach of Wundt, not all psychology should try to be experimental; some should remain interpretive, like archeology or history. One interesting aspect of this duality is that the academic attitude, especially from the works on language in the cognitive frame, also relied on the notion of rules, but stripping it from its phenomenological flavor. If one studies the understanding of indirect requests in the laboratory (*Why don't you close the door?*) or the interpretive schemata used in story understanding (Clark, 1979; Noveck & Sperber, 2004; Noveck, 2018), the researchers may process their data as if they were pedal pressings or recall patterns of nonsense syllables. Brought to the laboratory, the most elusive phenomenological data also lose their mysterious nature. The interpretative attitude should keep in mind the need to explain the individual, in its everyday world. As George Mandler (1996, p. 27) mentioned it:

[T]he question about doing psychology without experiments is about psychology and the everyday world. . . . A search for the mechanisms and processes that eventuate in everyday human thought and action must, I believe, involve the rejection of facile explanations of complex human behavior, frequently couched in appeals to innateness, and to apparently inevitable evolutionary adaptations. Complex human actions and thoughts are unlikely candidates for unique, singular evolutionary events.

We have to keep in mind that contemporary research regarding its methods is moved by both forces with relatively little connections between the two. This duality also implies that the unity of psychology seems to be more and more an illusion (Sternberg, 2004). We may have to realize that the irreducibility of the causal and the interpretive frameworks will have to stay. What changed compared to a hundred years ago is what domains are touched by this duality (e.g., relationships of clinical work and research) and what domains can be studied by both attitudes in parallel (e.g., language and social life). Regarding the repeated claims of this book, we claim that folk psychology exists as a "naive theory" used by human agents. It is not self-explanatory, however, as the contemporary hermeneuticians would like to believe, but has to be explained by naturalistic explanations.

Does psychology have a unified future?

Psychology certainly was a victorious science and profession of the 20th century, with booming programs, societies, and professional practices over five continents. Still, in turning to the new millennium, several of its troubles a hundred years ago seem to re-emerge. Questions of unity, assumed intellectual dryness, practical sterility, or, the other way around, issues of unclear boundaries and practical looseness, do re-emerge. The novelty in our century is not self-inquiry but rather the situations of abundance that are prevalent nowadays. Thus, we are entitled to relate to them in an ironical manner.

Classical proposals and questioning of unity

Classical psychology, already at its birth, was questioned from many sides, as we saw in Chapters 9 and 10, in Volume 1. The most consequential skepticism was the attitude of Auguste Comte (1830), who, besides questioning the reliability of introspection and any inner observation, also claimed that in a hierarchy of knowledge types and sciences, all positive knowledge about the human mind should be distributed between physiology and sociology. There was no place left for psychology. Interestingly, the early independent psychologists and even the sociologists responded with a pattern-based vision to that two generations later, though they themselves did not call their attitude pattern-based. In this vision, there are different levels of organization in nature. One can talk in a positivistic manner about these levels without making the levels independent realities. In chemistry, compounds show new features, but the fact that water, H_2O, is chemically different from hydrogen (H) and oxygen (O_2) does not question the unity of the universe and does not lead to a postulation of compounds as being an independent realm from elements. One also talks about phenomena of life and living beings without postulating something like a *vis vitalis*, an essence of life. In a similar manner, we can talk about mental phenomena without talking about the soul or the mind as a reified entity responsible for these phenomena. The "pattern principle" of psychology is that certain bodily processes – we would call them today certain "neuronal processes" – are organized in a certain pattern that corresponds to the mental level. Regarding the higher level, partially on inspirations from Wundt, Durkheim proposed a pattern-based vision of what is a social fact. In the conception of Durkheim (1894), there is an analogy between experimental psychology and sociology. Psychology treats patterns of physiological phenomena as being psychological. Sociology treats social phenomena as patterns of individual mental events. We have three levels or representations in a hierarchy – the physiological, the mental, and the social – and the "lower" levels produce patterns that lead to new levels, where new causalities emerge. The pattern vision was responsible for the unity of psychology in this vision.

Thus, psychology started off 150 years ago with a distantiation from brain reductionism, and with an assertion of inner life, by claiming that **psychology has a place on the palette of sciences, without being committed to a "soul" as an explanatory principle**. The unity was partly questioned by the methodical triality we saw throughout the book. The laboratory, the market, and the couch represented different domains for gaining psychological knowledge (Danziger, 1990). The serious doubts regarding the independence/autonomy and/or unity of psychology were openly raised in the late 19th-century German "mental science debates." The new issues during the last half century in these debates are related to the constantly re-emerging issue of the unity of psychology, in the midst of its diversification and multiplicity. Can one keep together the personal of such a vessel with so many diverging navigators?

During the last generation, these concerns were supplemented with questioning the independence, or at least the leading role, of psychology on the part of neuroscience. To deal with possible futures of psychology is a serious contemporary issue. In the PsycINFO database, there are 300 items dealing with these issues, 70 with these words in the title, and about 30 in our last decade.

Two versions of modern questioning of psychology

The one and a half century of psychology's "independent life" has shown that psychology both as a science and as a profession has two recurring problems. The first is that **psychology is theoretically too multiple**. There are basically two versions of treating this tension and march toward unification. The first one is a unifying, or a merely theory-oriented, use of the paradigm notion within psychology. Theoretical psychology in the midst of the multiplicity has looked for authority many times, for basic principles to reduce everything in the hope of creating a theoretical unity, sometimes postulating paradigm shifts (Palermo, 1971; Weimer & Palermo, 1973). The other option is to recognize and accept the inherent multiplicity. Many people, including myself, are more careful in overextending the use of the scientific paradigm notion and believe in the coexistence of various research and applied practices.

The other recurring topic, also since the late 19th century, is the challenge mainly coming from applied psychology claiming that **academic psychology is too united, too scientific**, as practiced in universities and research institutes, compared to the varied nature of applied psychology. Mainstream academic psychology tends to forget the multiple embedding of humans, the varying central points of applications of psychology, and the pragmatic embedding of the profession itself. Thus, the other challenge is that due to its practice, psychology is a divided profession, and this should be accepted.

There are two pairs of metaphors used to describe these uncertainties. The first metaphor popular in the 1930s goes back to the Bible, specifically to *Matthew 25:31–46*, where the sheep are presented as the believers and the goats are the symbols of the non-believers. This was taken up by William James as a difference between the tender-minded philosophical experience–based approaches and the obstinate scientific approaches to the mind. Stevens (1939) rejuvenated the metaphor for psychology, claiming that the quietly grazing empiricists are the down-to-earth goats, and the speculative theoreticians are the high-nosed sheep. The novelty of his time was that the two would be united in a neopositivistic theory of science.

> The rational and the empirical elements in science are disentangled and then reassembled. . . . The formal, rational, *a priori*, deductive side of creative thinking, which has always been so dear in the hearts of James's "tender-minded" neither rules nor is ruled by the empirical, synthetic, *a posteriori*, inductive wing.
>
> (Stevens, 1939, p. 250)

We remain goats with our experimentation and constrain the speculation of the sheep into a strict mathematical frame of deduction.

Isaiah Berlin (1953) rejuvenated another metaphor that goes back to the ancient Greek poet Archilochus: "A *fox* knows many things, but a *hedgehog* one important thing." Berlin used this metaphor for all human culture and philosophy. Some cultural actors do see everything under a single light, under the torch of a defining idea, like the hedgehog. Examples include Plato, Hegel, Marx, Dostoevsky, Nietzsche, Freud, and Skinner. The other pole is formed by cultural actors who see the world as being varied. They are the foxes. These include people like Aristotle, Shakespeare, Balzac, W. James, or Jerome Bruner. Using these metaphors, one can argue that psychology, taken in its entire complexity, belongs more to the fox types than to the hedgehog types, while the great schools, from Freud and Watson on, always tried to propose that they were hedgehogs who found THE unifying principle of the mental world.

The issue of unification and multiplicity

As we have seen in Chapter 10 of Volume 1, since the late 19th century and the crisis of positivism, the tension between natural science and mental science, the duality of explanatory and understanding attitudes, continues to be a tension within psychology as well. This tension might also be characterized as a tension between scientific and philosophical psychology in the sense promoted by the historically minded French experimentalist Paul Fraisse (1988). This tension has touched upon many existential and intellectual aspects as well and went on through 20th-century psychology, usually implying not only methodical differences but also differences related to the goals of research as well. The aim of the scientific attitude was, and continues to be, to put behavior and experience into the frames of a natural science canon. Its practical aims are changed, shaped, and directed through behavioral interventions. The other pole, emphasizing either the spiritual aspects of humans (like Dilthey and Spranger) or the social nature of humans (like the social frames discussed in Chapter 5 and in this chapter earlier), emphasized that the world of meanings cannot be deduced from nature; it is constructed (Harré, 1986) or exists in a separate spiritual mental domain (Spranger, 1926). The practical aim of psychology, according to this vision, is not instrumental intervention but interpretation of experience.

These two conceptions in their different versions have had institutional consequences that can still be observed today. For over a century, psychology is institutionally classified or moved alternatively near or into faculties of humanities, social sciences, education, or to natural science and medical faculties. The dichotomy is made more complex by what Cronbach (1957) referred to as the **two disciplines of scientific psychology**. There is an experimental tradition and a tradition starting from Galton and Spearman that uses statistical machinery to study individual differences. Today, this century-old bifurcation is made even more complex by the extension of sophisticated statistical machineries in the domain of social and personality psychology. "Number crunching" can be seen as an extension of the second discipline of scientific psychology to originally "meaning-based" mental science issues, forming there a natural science methodology that relies on soft data. A further complication comes from different versions of "critical psychology." They are also anti-science but, at the same time, do not aim toward "understanding" human mentality. Rather, they would like to change human mentality, alongside changing society (Teo, 2005).

The psychology of the 21st century starts to overcome its positivistic and technological shyness and courageously admits again that it has an **image of humans.** Expressions like "worldview" and "human nature" become eligible again in the psychological literature as well. Many psychologists start to believe that underlying the huge number of specific research and transcending their peculiarities, they have an emerging image of the human mind and the human being. Contemporary experimental psychologists also see these dilemmas. George Mandler (1996), the cognitive memory psychologist who turned toward the history of psychology at the end of his career, clearly showed that there is a clear underlying dual picture of human nature involved in the debates about the causal and the humanistic approaches to human phenomena.

> Our psychology reflects abiding traditions of Western society. . . . The deterministic and scientistic view sees humans as flawed, often close to the Augustinian sense, whereas the free, and humanist view requires a more optimistic and ameliorative view of human society. . . . An understanding by social scientists of these problems, of the consequences of constraint and of freedom, should help us to resolve some of these problems, without in the process coming under the control of those who would wish to determine the outcome of that resolution.
>
> (Mandler, 1996, pp. 27–28)

This is, in one regard, a rather classic statement of the opposition. It assumes that according to the deterministic image, humans only have bad, negative biological features. The hope of the 1960s, "Make love, not war," and the message of the cooperative nature of humans of modern evolutionary psychology (Tomasello, 2009) seem to be left out from this duality. Many naturalists today see humans as cooperative and competitive, rational and irrational at the same time.

As one of the key modern historians of psychology, David Leary (1980, p. 186) mentioned there were many attempts over a century and half for unification, but there were many worries as well.

Psychologists and scholars made a series of reflections which highlighted a number of points:

1. The discipline has not made linear progress toward a systematic, unified psychology. . . .
2. The epistemological assumptions and methodological strictures which have provided the foundation of modern psychology during much of the past century deserve a critical review and reformulation.
3. There have been shifting emphases as regards the subject matter psychology over the past century. . . .
4. Having achieved the status of an independent science, psychology is now moving towards the utilization of more complex, interdisciplinary approaches to the study of its phenomena and,
5. There is a growing recognition that, throughout its history, psychology as a discipline has existed within, been shaped by, and contributed to the maintenance or change of particular socio-cultural concepts.

Is there a crisis today? Two types of psychology or two types of psychologists?

From the 1920s on, there has been a repeatedly returning crisis literature in psychology, though it has become really self-conscious in our century. There is a new crisis literature starting from the 1980s. Interestingly, this self-reflection does not use the label of *crisis* to describe its own efforts (for a review, see the thematic issue edited by Mülberger & Sturm, 2012). It tries to interpret the situation of the science and disciplines of psychology in a sociological and philosophical manner, as an issue of **unity of science**.

As a consequence of the classic crisis years initiated by Driesch (1925) and Bühler (1927), several attempts were proposed to overcome it. Bühler (1927) claimed that the crisis feeling was the result of diversification; it was an *embarras de richesses*, an embarrassment of riches, a multiplicity challenge. Thus, he proposed a unifying principle based on holism and sign-based regulations. Vygotsky (1926), with his cultural psychology, and Piaget (1972), with his genetic epistemology, tried to overcome the natural-versus-human-science duality by moving ahead, by making psychology a central switch point of all disciplines, a so-called hub discipline, as recently was claimed. If we attempt to combine them, their foundations can be minced into a slightly eclectic synthesis of communication, development, and operations-based functionalism.

Piaget (1979), in a talk held in 1966 at an international conference in Moscow, tried to show that psychology has a central position in the system of sciences. It is epistemologically in between the subject and the object, and methodically between the formal and the strictly empirical sciences. Regarding the content of the relations, a combination of external (accommodation) and internally initiated (assimilation) biological processes in the model of Piaget (1950, 1972) resulted in a mental adaptation that continues biological adaptation. There was a crucial "progress image" promoted by Piaget both for individual development and for cultural processes in moving toward decentration and comparison of points of views.

In the mid-20th century, the neobehaviorists tried to find the desired unity in an extended notion of learning, including symbolic processes (Mowrer, 1960). The neobehaviorist hope for a synthesis was best presented by the ambitious six-volume overall handbook edited by Sigmund Koch (1959–1963). The approach was a result of many years of discussions, panel works, and committees toward a cross-talk across fields and domains and an emergence of theoretical conceptions and actual summaries of research field. The behavioral metatheory is best seen in the proposals for discussion. They mainly cover issues of what are the independent, intervening, and dependent variables in a system, what is the formal structure of the behavioral system, all in accord with a Hull-style science theory attitude. Neobehaviorists already believed that they were able to integrate *Gestalt* psychology and psychoanalysis, which they showcased as a special chapter of equilibration among emotional and behavioral/adaptive aspects.

These behavioral unificationist tendencies continued from the mid-1960s, namely, from the assumed cognitive revolution (Kimble, 2005a, 2005b). The cognitive trend entertained an idea of unity with its image of humans as modeling their environment. Its basic unifying idea was to interpret all mental life as a model of reality, and behavior as being driven by these internal models. The human nature corresponding to this conception was a belief–desire folk psychology that tried to integrate in a subtractive manner the emotional and driving force issues into this new image of man (Stich et al., 1994). From the 1950s to the 1970s, mainstream psychology lived under the impression that there was a unity either under the umbrella of learning or, later, under the banner of cognition.

Is there **a crisis in present-day psychology**? asked the renown cognitive psychologist George Mandler (1924–2016).

> Current experimental psychology cannot be characterized as typical of normal science activity in general. In contrast to the situation that concerned Bühler [in 1927], today there are not three but no general theory that commands wide attention. Normal science is concerned with the testing (confirming and falsifying) general theories about a particular field. Today there are few general propositions that are applicable across the related fields of psychology. . . . Much of experimental psychology is characterized as "cognitive" but apart from stressing the importance of knowledge and information in the structure of human minds, the appellation does not provide any theoretical propositions. . . . [O]ur journals and organizations spend too much time on applauding our field, and too little on examining its shortcomings. Examinations like Bühler's are needed in order to encourage further progress.
>
> (Mandler, 2011, p. 246)

The last quarter of century is certainly full of worries and discussions about unity. The monograph of the leading behaviorist theoretician of the University of Hawaii, Arthur Staats (1924–2021), who became famous for proposing "time-out" as punishment for children (Staats, 1968), campaigned for unity on two levels. There is a need for a unified organizational form, institutional frames where theories can be discussed, and there is a need for a unified ontology (what the proper subject of psychology is), and methodology (Staats, 1983, 1999). Staats (1999) campaigned for a positive unifying program trying to combine different organizational levels and domains (personality, psychophysics, clinical psychology, and so on), in a way trying to repeat the dream of Sigmund Koch a good generation earlier.

In the French context, there was the traditional dream of unity promoted by Daniel Lagache (1903–1972), founder of the Sorbonne degree program and, at the same time, a leading classical psychoanalyst before the Lacanian times. He believed in unity of psychology combining neobehaviorism with psychoanalysis, learning theory, and clinical psychology (Lagache, 1949, 1993), not unlike the spirit of the Koch unifying program. Ohayon (2006, as well as Carroy & Ohayon, 1999), in their detailed, partly interview-based book about the articulation of French clinical psychology, and the specific role of Lagache and psychoanalysis, showed that the clinical profession as a specialty did take form in France after the Second World War. There was an intricate dual campaign of psychologists and psychoanalysts for the creation of clinical psychology against the medical profession. Lagache, in fact, was trying to unify psychology under the banner of clinical practice. This was to be a unification of the first-person psychologies of traditional psychology and the third-person psychologies of behaviorism, in the name of a psychology of the second person, that is, an interactionist psychology.

> For the psychology of the "second person" the concept of behavior is preserved but for this psychology behavior is not reduced to material data; it has an intrinsic meaning and on the other hand, it "expresses" the psychological reality of the subject; the psychologist can understand it through his psychological knowledge via mental representations; the psychological interview thus moves in the frames of a personal relationship between the psychologist and the subject whom the psychologist assumes to be existing and having a value as a person. Clinical psychology is thus basically a psychology of the second person, and for this psychology psychological facts are behaviors that have their own meaning and express the person.
> (Lagache, 1949, pp. 435–436)

Lagache tried to establish the identity of the clinical psychologist both as a diagnostician and as a psychoanalytical therapist (Lagache, 1949). This resulted in tensions over the strictly medical establishment of the French psychoanalytic association, from which Lagache separated originally together with Lacan. Their later practical tensions were related to Lagache being too attached to the cause of clinical psychology over psychoanalysis. The separation of experimentalists and clinicians was also related to internal tensions within the newly establishing French psychologist identity.

The new generation of experimentalists were no longer medical doctors, even if Lagache still was. Thus, the issue articulated was how much experimental and how much clinical preparation was needed for would-be practitioners. Clinicians went for a while toward a clinical humanities specialty, under the leadership of Anne-Marie Rocheblave-Spenlé (1923–2000), an early feminist and adolescent clinical psychologist. Paul Fraisse (1911–1996) remained the experimentalist at the Sorbonne, becoming more and more influential in the 1960s in curricular development, requesting academic preparation for all to obtain a license.

Questioning unity: from Koch to Kendler

During the last quarter-century, several criticisms reached the entire unifying tradition and the specific efforts. The critics of unification do not question the underlying idea that psychological theories have an open or hidden conception of human nature. They merely question if that is or should be really a single one. A first strong voice in questioning unity was Sigmund Koch (1917–1996). The ironical aspect is that Koch started off in the 1950s with a great hope of unifying everything in the great handbook of a mostly Hull-inspired neobehaviorism (Koch, 1959–1963). On the basis of his experience as editor, Koch started already in the 1960s, and then very harshly in the 1980s, to claim that there are several psychologies rather than a single one (Koch, 1961, 1964, 1969, 1985, 1999). His change of mind was already expressed in his chapter in a volume comparing behavioristic and phenomenological visions of the human condition (Koch, 1964).

All the issues raised by the sometimes-pessimistic evaluations promoted by Koch are related to **what psychology is as a science**. Koch (1961) put this into the frames of the then-new challenges raised by the talks and book of C. P. Snow (1959) proposing two cultures, a (natural) science-based and a humanistic culture rephrasing the Windelband–Dilthey style dualities. According to Koch, the real trouble of psychology was that, while during the 20th century it tried to be **scientific** in its methods, it tended to forget that in its content it should belong to the **humanities**. Psychology may form that third force that may mediate between the drastically separated two cultures outlined by Snow (1959/1964). The real debt of psychology in taking this mediating role would be toward the humanities.

> In its search for scientific respectability, psychology has erected a widely shared epistemology, and a conceptual language which render virtually impossible the exploration of the content of man in a differentiated way. . . . [P]sychology *must* be that science whose problems lie closest to those of the humanities. . . . Relative to the present divisive situation in the world of knowledge, psychology, then, might be seen as a third force.
>
> (Koch, 1961, pp. 629, 630)

The conception of Koch was trying to set new goals, and as he himself noticed it, he was rather normative. Psychology should be more open, he claimed, at the imagined *zenith* and actual downfall of behaviorism. Koch, in a lamenting paper, *Reflections on the State of Psychology*, started to claim that we have to realize that part of it, or most of it, can never become part of science. It has to be a domain of the humanities. In his later papers, he even called for **psychological studies** rather than **psychological science**.

Gregory Kimble (1917–2006) rephrased the vision of Koch, and the issue of the place of psychology in the culture wars, as an internal division within the discipline. It might be that we, psychologists, are sometimes hard-headed, sometimes soft-headed, not constantly hard-headed, as Koch proposed. As a next step, in line with an empiricist behaviorist credo, Kimble operationalized the distinction and made it a subject of empirical research. He studied undergraduates and members as well as officers of the APA (more than 300 subjects) regarding humanistic and scientific values, on scales similar to the ones shown on Table 11.3 (Kimble, 1984). Notice that these opponent pairs are, in many regards, similar to the ones used by Robert Watson (1967) to compare psychological theories.

The subjects were presented with a ten-point semantic differential-like scales along these dimensions. Kimble (1984) found that with increasing experience and sophistication, his subjects tended to move toward the scientific pole. Undergraduates slightly preferred the humanistic pole, professionals slightly the scientific. The real sharp divisions were observed among professionals: 95% of experimental psychologists veered toward the scientific, and 75% of clinicians toward the humanistic pole. Experimentalists were deterministic and objectivistic, but they were divided between the analytic and holistic poles.

John Conway (1992), as president of the *Canadian Psychological Association*, went even further and related these differences to differences in personality. He essayistically surveyed proposed personality styles from the early 20th century on and life stories of famous psychologists like William James, Carl Rogers, Donald Hebb, Burrhus Skinner, Gordon Allport, and Herbert Simon to arrive to a suggestion that the hard and soft scientific and humanist styles imply different personalities. Analytic people are scanners, using narrow categories, and they are field-independent. They are more paradigmatic-descriptive in the sense of Bruner (1990), and they are more convergent. Holists, on the other hand, are more field-dependent, use broad categories with little scanning, are more intuitive in the Jungian sense, and are more narrative in the sense of Bruner (1990). In the interpretation of Conway, the hard and soft styles of thought proposed by William James correspond to an analytic and a holistic personality. There are "considerable conceptual similarities between scientific values and an analytic style, and between humanistic values and a holistic style of information processing. Measures of metatheoretical values and measures of cognitive style appear to be in search of related constructs" (Conway, 1992, p. 6).

Dean Simonton (2004), a longtime creativity researcher, in his detailed analysis of hundreds of life paths, proposed two characteristic creative life paths for all sciences. One he refers to as the **more constrained route**. In their lifestyle, these

Table 11.3 The scales used by Kimble to differentiate scientific and softer psychological attitudes

Scale	Opposed ideas
Values: scientific vs. human	Increasing knowledge vs. improving life
	Methodological strength vs. relevance
	Obligation to apply vs. no such obligation
Lawfulness of behavior	Lawful vs. not lawful
Determinism vs. indeterminism	Understandable vs. incomprehensible
	Predictable vs. unpredictable
	Controllable vs. incontrollable
Source of knowledge	Sense data vs. empathy
Objectivism vs. intuitionism	Observation vs. self-report
	Operational definition vs. linguistic analysis
	Investigation vs. common sense
Methodological strategy	Investigation vs. interpretation
Data vs. theory	Induction vs. deduction
	Evidence vs. argument
Setting for discovery	Experimentation vs. survey
Laboratory vs. field	Manipulation vs. naturalistic observation
	Hypothesis testing vs. correlation
	Control vs. realism
	Precision vs. ecological validity
Temporal aspects	Developmental vs. descriptive approach
Historical vs. ahistorical	Longitudinal vs. cross-sectional
Heredity – environment	Physiology vs. situation
	Biological vs. social
Generality of laws	Species-general vs. species-specific
Nomothetic vs. idiographic	"Standard man" vs. individual uniqueness
	Universalism vs. contextualize
Concreteness of concepts	Biological reality vs. abstract conception
Elementary – holism	Molecular–molar
	Part–whole
Action regulation	Reason vs. emotion thinking
Cognition vs. affect	Intellect vs. impulse
	Rational vs. irrational
Creativity of organisms	Automaticity vs. voluntary control
Reactivity vs. creativity	Associations vs. constructivism

Source: Kimble (1984).

people are characterized by looking for conventional solutions, are usually eminent in school, rarely have dyslexia or attention disorders, and tend to be firstborn. They usually only have one mentor during their career. Their political visions are stable, be it conservative or left-wing, and they do not change camps. In their dispositions, they are more logical and narrower, and there is less problem in their life histories. As scientists, they tend to follow one paradigm. They rarely become revolutionary scientists. The other route is more **accidental**. Their life paths tend to be much more varied and dramatic. These people tend to be second-born or later-born. They do experience many failures in schooling. Within their own creative domain, they frequently do have several sequential mentors. Their political visions are unstable, and they may frequently change their allegiance. In their personality dispositions, they seem to be more intuitive, more varied, and changing. The revolutionary scientist and the abstract artist are somewhere at the edges of these prototypes, on the boundaries.

This more empirical analysis of dualities in sciences and in psychology reminds one of the debates regarding idiographic and nomothetic trends and the discussion between Dilthey (1894) and Ebbinghaus (1896) regarding natural science and human science–based psychology. The first one would look for individuals and meanings, while the second one for context-free laws. In a way, as mentioned by Bálint Forgács, the disciplines seem to attract certain personality types, except psychology, which attracts both types of people, as shown by Simonton (2002). That might be the reason of the bridging role of psychology in the "war of the faculties."

During the half century since the issue was raised again by Koch (1961), there were many changes. Koch, for example, complained that experimental hard-nosed psychologists were not interested in the arts. Since then, there has been an entire school of creativity research interested in the arts. It attempts to study art with a rather natural science attitude, combining it with an interest toward meaning in art. Colin Martindale (1943–2008) at the University of Maine, for example, worked on explaining changes of artistic style in painting, poetry, novels. He identified Darwinian shifts of primary and secondary process dominance and changes between Romantic and classical art by analyzing the content of painting, sculpture, poetry, prose with sophisticated methods of content analysis (Martindale, 1990). He summarized his views by predicting the end of classical art because of a tension between communicative message and the constant need for change in the community.

Art in these visions would be a constant effort to grasp constancies of visual experience amid a constantly changing visual world. The French neuroscientist Jean-Pierre Changeux (2009) is more sensitive to art history. He supplemented the idea of decomposition with the idea of a tinkering (*bricolage*) coming from Lévi-Strauss (1958) and taken over to biology by Francois Jacob (1977). Artists, according to Changeux, would also tinker, that is, decompose and reassemble. The success of new tinkering depends both on cognitive attractors and on the involvement of emotional systems in the brain. The third addition of Changeux concerns historical changes in art. In his view, what is studied by traditional art history are spatial and temporal selections regarding certain visual elements and memes. Cultural selection and individual selection are connected in his proposal. Cultural-perceptual cultivation within one brain would result into cultural innovation.

Another example of the interest of hard-nosed scientists toward art is the new work of the Nobel Prize–winning neuroscientist Eric Kandel (2006, 2012; Kandel & Mack, 2003). Kandel even tried to combine neurobiology and psychoanalysis in interpreting the paintings of Klimt, Schiele, and Kokoschka and their relation to the turn-of-the-century Vienna and their personal lives. He presented his interpretation as based on the dual routes of perceptual integration, one being conscious, the other unconscious.

One aspect of these changes is the postulation of a meaning-creating and meaning-interpretive human nature. Thus, what used to be the privilege of the hermeneutic trend is now taken as a characteristic of humans at large. The new idea is that the humanistic pole imagined by Koch is a feature not merely of a peculiar disciplinary attitude but of humans at large, living in culture and creating culture.

Innovative unifying efforts: Campbell and Sternberg

The fragmentation of psychology is not unlike a marriage crisis, that is, it is related to a lack of communication and mutual misunderstandings. This interpretation has been in the air already since the 1960s. Donald Campbell (1916–1996), a social psychologist, published somewhat-ironical papers on the fate of social sciences among many of his contributions. Campbell was a member of the American National Academy of Sciences, and he was a key player in the methodologies of social psychology by developing the multi-trait/multimethod approach to personality assessment, and at the same time, he was a promoter of the evolutionary epistemology approach to a Darwinian philosophy (Campbell, 1959, 1974, 1977). He described the rivalry of the disciplines as a tribal rivalization, with the scientist as the myth of omniscience (Campbell, 1969). The patchwork of disciplines and departmental boundaries should be replaced by an overlapping structural arrangement. There should be less constraints among departments and disciplines and more flexible interdepartmental communications. We should not be misled and imagine a world with omniscient individual knowers. All disciplines in themselves are patchworks of knowledge compared to the comprehensive social life. "Thus, psychology is a hodgepodge of sensitive subjective biography, of brain operations, of school achievement testing, of factor analysis, of Markov process mathematics, of schizophrenic families, of laboratory experiments on group structure in which persons are anonymous, and so forth" (Campbell, 1969, p. 337).

Campbell did not expect to find a common underlying principle like a hedgehog would act. The rivaling topics are indeed different aspects of human behavior. Thus, new ideals should be followed, he claimed. Students should be socialized with **an open eye for easy interdisciplinary reading**, and scientists should remain eternal students while also being teachers. Institutions, he claimed half a century ago, should support *ad hoc* interdisciplinary programs and trainings going back to the multiplicity and fragmentation issues.

The optimism over the multiplicity that characterized Bühler a century ago is also coming back. There are several phrasings of this optimistic multiplicity. A most characteristic example is Robert Sternberg (2005, Sternberg & Grigorenko, 2001, 2002; Sternberg et al., 2001). Sternberg is an established researcher on intelligence, creativity, and emotions, as well as cognitive psychology of thinking styles and social governance. His constant emphasis is questioning unification efforts in the history of our discipline. According to Sternberg, fragmentation is a result of devaluing, ignorance, and competition. This should be replaced with living together in a tolerant optimism stance (Sternberg, 2005).

In his view, the divisive tension can only be resolved if our presumptions are related in an eclectic manner. This tolerant optimism has as its starting point that psychology is a complex, interdisciplinary field of science that studies the multiple embedding of humans. It looks at humans as behaving, motivated, and knowing beings. All these aspects do belong to human nature; thus, the same way as the subdisciplines (school psychology, industrial psychology, clinical psychology, etc.) make many types of psychologies due to the multiplicity of determining factors, theoretical psychology also has to presuppose different visions of human nature. Psychology unavoidably has a multiplicity of models, not only due to domains, but also due to the highlighted causal relations and determinations as well. Sternberg and his group basically campaign for an eclectic combination of approaches that he calls a **phenomenon-based proposal**. Both in teaching and in research, one should not start off from chapters (fields) but rather from phenomena. If one realizes, for example, that emotional development plays a central role in adult coping strategies, it does not follow that we have to decide if we are dealing with developmental, personality, clinical, or general psychology, or even psychophysiology. The phenomenon and the problems coexist for all these, and we should concentrate on problems and phenomena. This would lead to an eclectic **theory knitting**. The theory-knitting approach has advantages over the segregated approach. It aims toward cognitive integration, it realizes the importance of theory, and it is more explicit in what it aims to explain, and how. Theory knitting is not afraid of combining a criticist attitude with the motto of *Vive la différence!*

Disunity and the funeral mood

There are attempts to provide a logical analysis for the real or assumed disunity. Zittoun, Gillespie, and Cornish (2009) suggested two coordinated reasons for a feeling of fragmentation. The first is the lack of communication and collaboration; the other is the challenge of (not) meeting real social issues, such as the impact of an aging population on the psychological agenda. A new type of social organization could lead out of the impasse, with **teamwork**. Teamwork should be real and not merely the following of mentors by a large group of students. The other crucial issue would be concentrating on *key concepts*. This is, in fact, smuggling back the hedgehog into the world of the foxes.

Many self-critical suggestions also realized that the disunity and disintegration issue also has a **rhetorical aspect**. Different disciplines make "different cuts of the same domain," as Koch (1985) observed in one of his last papers. The different universes of discourse sometimes even use diverging lexicons for the same issues. A new, more elaborate analysis of the rhetoric of psychological language even claimed that schools of psychology create language communities. In the dominant experimental approach, all is presented as an issue of dependent and independent variables. Life is presented as merely a function of the few variables that are considered. However, in real life, there are many factors. It is an error to think that the fragmentation is merely a rhetorical issue. It is an issue of mistreating variability as being bad. Danziger (1997) has shown the importance of the language community aspect under another light. He showed that in the establishment of professional psychology, the very effort to stabilize the talk about emotion, motives, behavior, and the likes was the result of longtime developments, even independently of schools. In the sense of Michel Foucault (1970), the establishment of an order between the words, the lexical categories, and the categories of things (in this case mental objects) has certainly taken a long time.

A **mood of funerals** also showed up in the middle of the debates around unity or disunity due to its external relations, due to the highly praised interdisciplinary relations. Howard Gardner (1992), the well-known essayistic researcher of multiple intelligences and disciplinary historian, expressed in a rather cynical manner the possible strategies in the midst of diversification and disunity.

1. Maintain the status quo, since no one will announce that we are dead.
2. Declare victory.
3. Let us hope that there will be integration; the savior theory shall arrive.
4. We were too romantic. Other disciplines are also divided. Economy, for example, also has its schools, and geneticists and taxonomists also do different things (ironically, the latter claim is no longer true).

At the same time, while Gardner showed that many chapters of psychology are taken away by cognitive science and neuroscience, the core center, which was already the core for William James (1890), that of personality and the self, remains the possession of psychology. Interestingly, however, this domain belongs to psychology, to philosophy, and to literature at the same time. This would entail an interesting combination of the interest of psychologists and that of the writers in understanding the human condition, as emphasized by Bruner (2006). The positions of the novelist and that of the psychologist may come closer, approaching the humanistic and the scientific vision of humans. Along the same lines, as a reaction to Gardner, Woodward (1992, p. 193) claimed that "for the scientific study of personality the study of persons would do well to include the context, including the author *and* the reader *and* the cultural setting."

Janet Spence (1987, p. 1053), the former behaviorist anxiety researcher, presented her worst nightmares:

> I foresee a decimation of institutional psychology as we know it. Human experimental psychologists desert to the emerging discipline of cognitive science; physiological psychologists go happily to departments of biology and neuroscience; industrial/organizational psychologists are snapped up by business schools; and psychopathologists find their home in medical schools. Clinicians, school psychologists, and other health care practitioners have long since gone, training their own in freestanding professional schools or schools of education. Only personality-social psychologists and certain developmental psychologists would have no place else to go. In universities with doctoral programs, departments of psychology would be pale shadows of their former selves, their members outnumbered and outclassed by the natural sciences on the one hand and the humanities on the other hand.

She goes on to protect an action-based behavioral approach to psychology:

> What of value would be lost if this nightmare were to become reality? In my view, it would be the glue that holds us together, however tenuously, the common ground that justifies carving out psychology as a separate scientific discipline. The heart, the centerpiece, of the science of psychology, as I see it, is or should be a theory of *action,* what people actually do. . . . If the implications for behavior of the insights of the cognitive and neurosciences fail to be exploited, both science and society would be the losers.
>
> (Ibid)

The issue of **relations between psychology and morality** is raised again. Kendler (1999), starting from the example of relations between holism and *Gestalt* psychology on the one hand, and holism and fascism on the other hand, claimed that, in fact, one has to keep in mind the separation of value from fact. That does not imply that as psychologists we should not realize that our morality also has empirical consequences. We also have to keep in mind that when we speak up for moral principles, we are doing it as citizens, not always or not necessarily on the basis of science.

> The place of value in the science of psychology has been analyzed from the combined perspective of the fact/value dichotomy and the inevitable ascendancy of moral pluralism. . . . Four constants in particular should be recognized. First, one should realize that in a moral pluralistic society, monistic convictions need not be abandoned or attenuated; a monistic theology or secular philosophy can be practiced without necessarily being compromised by its minority status. . . . Second, the conclusion that psychology cannot validate moral principles does not force psychologists to avoid investigating morality. The whole gamut of moral behaviors, from developmental changes to religious beliefs, is fair game for scientific investigations. Third, the inability of the science of psychology to discover the right values for humankind does not require psychotherapists to avoid treating the moral conflicts of their patients. . . . [F]inally, the failure of natural-science methodology to validate moral principles that should guide human conduct does not free scientists in a democracy from moral obligations.
>
> (Kendler, 1999, pp. 834–835)

In the debate, many claimed against Kendler that science should be influenced by value. In his reply, he protected the separation of values and facts while simultaneously committing psychology to progressive social issues.

The state of the art of neuroreduction

In the mid-20th century, there were French proposals of either neuroreductionism or neuropuzzles. Georges Canguilhem (1958/2016), the French science historian, claimed that psychology was, in a way, trapped by being a shallow philosophy and an unfounded natural science. His opponent, Daniel Lagache (1949, 1993), proposed a unity of psychology based on its methods at that time.

> The unity of psychology is here sought in its possible definition as general theory of behavior: a synthesis of experimental psychology, clinical psychology, psychoanalysis, social psychology, and ethnology. On a closer look, however, we notice that perhaps this unity looks like a pact of peaceful coexistence signed by professionals more than a logical essence obtained by the revelation of constancy across a variety of cases. Of the two tendencies between which Professor Lagache want to find a solid accord i.e. the naturalist one (experimental psychology) and the humanist (clinical psychology); one gets the impression that the second carries, for him, more weight. . . . [I]t is inevitable that in presenting itself as the general theory of behavior, psychology will incorporate some idea of Man. Hence, it is necessary that we allow philosophy to question psychology about where this idea comes from, and whether it may not be, ultimately, from some philosophy.
> (Canguilhem, 2016, pp. 201–202)

> A philosopher can also address himself to the psychologist in the form of offering orientation advice . . . and say to him: when one leaves the Sorbonne by the street Saint-Jacques, one can ascend or descend; if one ascends, one approaches the Panthéon, the conservatory of great men [and takes the spiritualist stance regarding psychology, CsP]; but if one descends, one heads directly to the Police Department [taking the naturalistic stance regarding psychology, CsP].
> (Canguilhem, 2016, p. 213)

That modern psychology has to choose between the two attitudes seemed to be the conclusion half a century ago. We can nevertheless say that the prophecy of Canguilhem was challenged by new developments. What happened since then was that the panthéon attitude was articulated as a modern, non-spiritualistic philosophy of mind and cognitive science, while the prefecture attitude articulated itself as modern neuroscience.

The dualistic attitude expressed by Canguilhem caused a neglect of psychology for half a century in French philosophy as Canguilhem's words were taken as an indication that psychology should not be taken seriously, as Braunstein (1999) analyzed this history in detail. On the other hand, among psychologists in the same journal issue, the French social psychologist, and originally a student of Canguilhem, Robert Pagés (1958) had a radical critique of Canguilhem by claiming that experimentation was not only an issue of the prefecture but also an issue of social studies. It is a pseudo-controversy to believe that one can only experiment with lower phenomena.

Roudinesco (1993), the French philosopher and historian of psychology, analyzed the impact of this paper in this regard. She claimed that there was, in fact, an irony in the negative attitude of Canguilhem against psychology. That was a reaction against the dream of Lagache to entertain a unified psychology that would combine psychoanalysis, learning theory, and psychology as a helping profession. In a later paper, Canguilhem (1980) was specifically against psychoanalysis and its introduction as a new psychology of selfhood.

> Whenever Canguilhem speaks of psychology, he has something else in his mind than what we call psychology today. His criticism of psychology is an ethical critic, almost political, based on a theory of the subjecthood that corresponds, though with another terminology, to that of Foucault. For him, psychology corresponds to a submissive spirit that justifies everything in the name of a serious science. The psychologist and the philosopher represent for Canguilhem two possible relations to the world: one accepts the world in the name of the serious, the other resist it in the name of a revolting spirit.
>
> (Braunstein, 1999, p. 189)

The crucial issue in contemporary theoretical psychology, as it was a hundred years ago as well, is **the issue of neuroreductionism** (see Chapter 10 for more technical details). The issue of neuroreductionism today also relates to the **independence of psychology**. Some new intellectual developments and changes in the financial situation poise the psychology of the new millennium to become a branch of cognitive neuroscience. A lot of challenges do appear here. There is the danger of reductionism but also the danger of having all psychology just being absorbed by biology. This is a real danger. As the French historians of psychology Ohayon and Plas (2016) mentioned in an interview, psychology is in a danger of becoming just a chapter of biology. There is plenty of re-emerging discussion about the "final nature" of the relationships between biological and psychological approaches due to the new brain research methods, and great branding phrases, such as the "decade of the brain" between 1991 and 1999 in the United States, and the Human Brain project, started in Europe in 2013. Gregory Miller (2010), a clinical research psychologist, has shown in a critical survey paper ten years after the decade of the brain that, in the talk about the causation of mental disorders, the errors of deducing identity from correlations, or using loose predicates for brain and mind relations in interpreting hallucinations, delusions, and the like with concepts such as "underlies," "interacts," and so on. Miller (2010, pp. 735, 736) highlighted that:

> [W]e should not frame biology and psychology in a way that forces a choice between those kinds of explanations or attempts to juxtapose or blur them without spelling out a coherent relationship between them. . . . [W]e must be vigilant against indefensible but popular and pervasive claims that mental illness is simply a brain disorder, a chemical imbalance, or a genetic problem. . . . [A] mental disorder need not be triggered by, due to, or explained by brain

pathology any more than a software bug must be a consequence of hardware failure. Even if the specific etiology of a psychological disorder were to include brain mechanisms (or gene expression affecting brain mechanisms) in the causal chain, it is possible that the brain mechanism (or gene expression) is itself driven by psychological events.

This same attitude is expressed by the French neuroscientist Changeux (2017) when he shows on the basis of 40 years of studies that, in the organization of the brain, the genome is responsible merely for the formation of large neuronal nets. These nets themselves become organized in an epigenetic manner, by cycles of proliferation and tuning, leading to networks that last over the entire life of the person, even if they are based on cultural input, like the reading network.

Interestingly, amidst the many debates, some leading neuro researchers, like Gazzaniga (2013) and Ramachandran (2011), also warned us against such reductionism. V. Ramachandran is a brilliant neuropsychologist and neuroscientist of the Salk Institute who contributed to the neuronal interpretation of complex visual phenomena, synesthesia, and even art (Ramachandran & Hirstein, 1999). At the same time, he claims that the neuroscientist has to live with a dual attitude. He should not be afraid of reduction, but at the same time, he should start out of considerations of function.

> Psychologists often promote black-box functionalism and attack reductionist neuroscience – a syndrome I have dubbed neuron envy. The syndrome is partly a legitimate reaction to the fact that most funding from grant-giving agencies tends to be siphoned off, unfairly, by neuroreductionists. . . . [T]he problem with the pure black-box approach (psychology) is that sooner or later you get multiple competing models to explain a small set of phenomena, and the only way to find out which is right is through reductionism – opening the box(es). Unfortunately, for many physiologists reductionism becomes an end in itself, a fetish almost.
> (Ramachandran, 2011, pp. 323–325)

The historian of science and philosopher Gary Hatfield, in his millennial survey, mockingly emphasized that psychology is here to stay, even if it is disguised as neuro talk.

> The study of those brain functions of interest for cognitive science *is* the study of the psychological processes of organisms. The structure of those processes is not read off single cell recordings or images of brain activity. Rather, those recordings and images gain meaning by being related to a theory of what's being done functionally. Psychology is here to stay even if disguised to fool the money lenders.
> (Hatfield, 2002, p. 229)

Everything experimental, and where are we?

After a hundred years, psychology, with its pioneering experimental spirit among the social sciences, has become an attractive means by which many fields can employ an experimental rhetoric. While some trends in contemporary social and human sciences are characterized during the last generation by a re-emergence of the hermeneutic spirit and a renewed attitude of case-based interpretation, a parallel balancing process is the wide spread of the experimental spirit. People talk of experimental linguistics (the Linguistic Society of America even has a journal devoted to this), experimental pragmatics, experimental economics, experimental epistemology, and even experimental philosophy. A general characteristic of this broad move is the **search for certainties**. As Noveck (2018, p. 224) tells regarding experimental pragmatics, "[e]xperimentation provides the forum in which the exchange of ideas can be rigorously tested. Once engaged in the same forum, researchers can agree on the contours and contrasts that they see in the phenomena."

Psychology, in a way, has to redefine its own place in the middle of all these efforts. How does it begin to place itself among the rival integrators, like cognitive science, and between downward integrators, like the neurosciences, and upward integrators as network studies? The new experimental studies of feeling, cognition, and behavior should be reintegrated by psychology. Linda Smith (2011) from Indiana University has surveyed the varieties of psychology, the publication, the hiring, and the naming practice changes. Her positive program is that psychology **has to own the integration efforts**. Rather than wandering between the different points of views such as cognitive neuroscience, networks theories, psychogenetics, and so on, it has to acquire or subsume all this and should accommodate them. In her presentation, there are "two futures: bring it under one roof, behavior does the integration therefore, 'psychology' owns the integrative question." She prefers this solution. The other is to "break it up" into the component disciplines.

To put it succinctly, the **future of psychology is embedded into the coexistence of the profession and of the science underlying the profession**. Applied psychology today lives in the middle of new tensions. The traditional theoretical issues of where to position psychology also entail characteristic associate/rival relations regarding the professions as well. The psychology-psychiatry-pedagogy-sociology quartet has to be committed toward cooperation rather than competition in solving issues of developmental pathways and developmental problems or disorders. The role of psychology in this domain should be fearless initiative, forgetting some of its traditional feelings of inferiority. Models of behavior, knowledge, and feeling, that is, the central issues of psychology, provide the things to be explained for the reductionist models. For example, regarding the organization of the mental lexicon, the psychologist provides "working models" inserted between the neurologist and the linguist. For people studying higher-order social organizations, the psychological models of agents, of actors moving the economy, and of law will be sort of "lower order constraints." In the middle of interdisciplinarity, the issue of levels of organization is recognized again, and psychology is represented as an in-between discipline not with shame and with survival anxieties but with due pride.

Three aspects should be remembered from the 150 years of professionalized psychology as the message of applied psychology in all this turmoil.

1. **Strict following and dissemination of ethical principles.** Many times, this involves limitations for social roles. Psychologists follow much more individualistic ethics than many institutions would expect them to do, for example, regarding sharing data about their clients and the like. Or think of the famous Goldwater rule of the mental health professions. Avoid comment on the mental health of anyone you did not investigate yourself (American Psychiatric Association, 2013).
2. **Educational expectations.** Science and profession should go hand in hand, even if the majority of graduate training is applied by necessity.
3. **Strict competence ordering**. It is important to care for skills and practical competencies.

Tasks

CA

Compare antipsychiatry and scientology.
Humanistic psychology and the meaning of life.
The debate on "shallow processing" in contemporary WEB culture.
Rogers and classical psychoanalysis.
Role theory and transactional psychology.
Compare Bateson, Laing, and Berne.
Nature/nurture and biological psychiatry today.
Rules in psycholinguistics and in ethnomethodology.

DSA

Bateson, Berne, and Laing in psychological discourse: 1960–2020.
Canguilhem, Lagache, and Lacan in French public discourse, 1960–2020 (Google Ngram).
"Crisis of psychology" in psychology from 1980 (PsycINFO).
Co-occurrences of "antipsychiatry" and "humanistic psychology" in psychological texts (PsycINFO).
"Games" over a hundred years in psychology (PsycINFO).
"Ergonomy" and "information technology," 1990 to 2020, in the psychological literature (PsycINFO).
Harré and Wittgenstein in psychology (PsycINFO).

General references

Some contemporary resources for the history of psychology

Handbooks

Baker, D. B. (Ed.). (2012). *The Oxford handbook of the history of psychology: Global perspectives*. Oxford Academic. https://doi.org/10.1093/oxfordhb/9780195366556.001.0001. Twenty-nine chapters mainly on the international perspectives, organized by countries.

Freedheim, D. K., & Weiner, I. B. (Eds.). (2012). *Handbook of psychology: Vol. 1. History of psychology* (2nd ed.). Wiley.

Rieber, R. W. (Ed.). (2012). *Encyclopedia of the history of psychological theories*. Springer. Reference book of 46 chapters. It covers many theories of general psychology, but also a dozen individuals. https://link.springer.com/referencework/10.1007/978-1-4419-0463-8

Sternberg, R. J., & Pickren, W. E. (Ed.). (2019). *The Cambridge handbook of the intellectual history of psychology*. Cambridge University Press. The 19 chapters go by topics from sensation and attention to health psychology.

Watson, R. I. (1978). *The history of psychology and the behavioral sciences: A bibliographic guide*. Springer. It is a rich source to start reading the classics.

Readers

Gentile, B. F., & Miller, B. O. (2009). *Foundations of psychological thought. A history of psychology*. Sage. 37 well commented readings, arranged into topics like *Nativism and empiricism*, from Descartes to Chomsky, or *Perceiving* from Berkeley to David Marr.

Herrnstein, R. J., & Boring, E. G. (Eds.). (1965). *A source book in the history of psychology*. Harvard University Press. Still a rather useful reader with over 100 short excerpts translated from many sources arranged into content chapters (perception, memory etc.) with informative introductions to each chapter.

Portraits of important figures

Kimble, G. A., Boneau, C. A., & Wertheimer, M. (Eds.). (1991–2006). *Portraits of pioneers in psychology* (Vols. 1–6). Lawrence Erlbaum and Routledge. Analytic life histories, that go into the details of the professional activity as well.

Watson, R. I. (1976). *Eminent contributors to psychology* (Vols. 1–2). Springer.

Standard textbooks

Most of them have a rather specific vision. I try to point out these in the short remarks.

Boring, E. (1942). *Sensation and perception in the history of experimental psychology.* Appleton Century Crofts. https://archive.org/details/in.ernet.dli.2015.52372/page/n3/mode/2up

Boring, E. (1950). *A history of experimental psychology* (2nd Rev. ed.). Appleton Century Crofts. https://ia801605.us.archive.org/26/items/in.ernet.dli.2015.87639/2015.87639.A-History-Of-Experimental-Psychology.pdf

The two classics that are criticized as being one sided with their concentration on experimental psychology, and within that on the tradition initiated by Wundt. Still a rich source especially about early German laboratory psychology.

Greenwood, J. D. (2009). *A conceptual history of psychology.* McGraw Hill. Its strength is the overview of theories. One third analyzes classical psychology and the scientific revolution in early modernity.

Hearnshow, L. S. (1987). *The shaping of modern psychology.* Routledge. A slightly revisionist book. It takes into account the new challenges regarding unity and uniformity of science, but still preserves a rationalist attitude. In most questions presents a rather fresh, longitudinal image tracing the attitudes over centuries. philosophical but still science centered.

Leahey, T. H. (1987). *A history of psychology* (2nd ed.). Prentice Hall. Still the best modern text showing the advent of the cognitive revolution and the impact of the paradigm notion in doing history of psychology.

Richards, G. (2010). *Putting psychology in its place: Critical historical perspectives* (3rd ed.). Routledge. The clearest exposition of the new history approach. Goes more into earlier history, and in 20th Century concentrates on social and insitituional aspects rather than merely theories.

Some life histories in autobiographies

Murchison, C. (Ed.). (1936). *A history of psychology in autobiography* (Vols. 1–3). Clark University Press. (Original work published 1930) Vols. 4–7: edited by Boring and Lindzey and others, Prentice Hall and Stanford University Presses. Vols. 8–9 published by APA and edited by Gardner Lindzey and William M. Runyan. Personal life histories, several times of foreign authors as well, besides the Americans.

Parot, F., & Richelle, M. (Eds.). (1992). *Psychologues de Langue Française* [Psychologists of French language]. Presses Universitaires de France. 17 French autobiographies, from Piéron to Paul Fraisse. Mainly academic psychologists, but also some clinical psychologists as well who had academic functions.

Journals

There are several journals devoted to the history of psychology. I only list the most important English language modern journals.

Journal of the History of the Behavioral Sciences, from 1965, in four issues a year it covers the history of psychology and related fields, such as anthropology, sociology, psychiatry and psychoanalysis, economics, linguistics, communications, political science, and the neurosciences. http://onlinelibrary.wiley.com/journal/10.1002/-28ISSN-291520-6696

History of Psychology, since 1998, four times a year. Mainly covers psychology, but extends to non-English speaking countries. http://psycnet.apa.org/index.cfm?fa=browsePA. volumes&jcode=hop

History of the Human Sciences, since 1988, an alternative voice that emphasizes the interrelationships between the different human sciences, "sociology, psychology, anthropology and politics, and link their interests with those of philosophy, literary criticism, art history, linguistics, psychoanalysis, aesthetics and law." http://hhs.sagepub.com/ European Yearbook of the History of Psychology. Published since 215, publishes sources, analysis. Edited by Mauro Antonelli. https://www.brepolsonline.net/loi/eyhp

Electronic resources

Classics in the History of Psychology. A collection of classic readings searchable by title and author, developed by C. D. Green: http://psychclassics.yorku.ca/.

History and Theory of Psychology e print archive. Also edited by C. D. Green: http://htpprints.yorku.ca/. It is surprisingly rich in philosophical discussions.

George Boeree, C. *The History of Psychology* – e-text about the historical and philosophical background of psychology: http://webspace.ship.edu/cgboer/historyofpsych.html

References

Years of newer versions or translations are listed in the references, with the original publication year indicated at the end of the item. Translations are given in squared brackets. In the main texts, the usual reference is for the original year of publication.

Ádám, G. (1967). *Interoception and behaviour*. Akadémiai.
Ádám, G. (1998). *Visceral perception, understanding internal cognition*. Plenum Press.
Adler, A. (1928). *Understanding human nature*. G. Allen and Unwin.
Adorno, T. W., Frenkel-Brunswik, E., Levinson, D. J., & Sanford, R. N. (1950). *The authoritarian personality*. Norton.
Agnew, S. T. (1971, November 27). The assault on individuality. *Human Events, 31*, 48.
Alexander, F. (1950). *Psychosomatic medicine*. Norton.
Alexander, F. (1960). *The Western mind in transition: An eyewitness story*. Random House.
Alexandre, J. (1948). Maurice Halbwachs. *L'Année sociologique, 1*, 3–10.
Allport, F. (1920). The influence of the group upon association and thought. *Journal of Experimental Psychology, 3*, 159–182.
Allport, F. (1924a). *Social psychology*. Houghton Mifflin.
Allport, F. (1924b). The group fallacy in relation to social science. *American Journal of Sociology, 29*, 688–706.
Allport, F. (1937). Toward a science of public opinion. *Public Opinion Quarterly, 1*, 7–23.
Allport, F. H., & Allport, G. W. (1921). Personality traits: Their classification and measurement. *The Journal of Abnormal Psychology and Social Psychology, 16*(1), 6–40.
Allport, G. W. (1937). The functional autonomy of motives. *American Journal of Psychology, 50*, 141–156.
Allport, G. W. (1953). The trend in motivational theory. *American Journal of Ortho-Psyhiatry, 25*, 107–119.
Allport, G. W. (1954). *The nature of prejudice*. Addison-Wesley.

Allport, G. W. (1985). The historical background of modern social psychology. In G. Lindzey & E. Aronson (Eds.), *A handbook of social psychology* (Vol. I, 3rd ed., pp. 1–46). Addison-Wesley. (Original work published 1954)

Allport, G. W. (1961). *Pattern and growth in personality*. Harcourt.

Allport, G. W. (1968). *The person in psychology*. Beacon Press.

Allport, G. W., & Odbert, H. S. (1936). Trait names. A psycholexical study. *Psychological Monographs, 47*(Whole No. 211).

Allport, G. W. et al. (1943). Psychological considerations in making the peace. *Journal of Abnormal and Social Psychology, 38*(2), 131.

American Psychiatric Association. (2013). *The principles of medical ethics with annotations especially applicable to psychiatry*. American Psychiatric Association.

Amundson, R. (2006). EvoDevo as cognitive psychology. *Biological Theory, 1*, 10–11.

Ananiev, B. (1931). On nekotorih voprosah marxistko-leninskoj rekonstrukcii psichologii. [On some questions of the Marxist-Leninist reconstruction of psychology]. *Psihologia, 4*(3–4), 325–44.

Ananiev, B. (1948). Achievements of Soviet psychologists. *The Journal of General Psychology, 38*, 257–62.

Anderson, J. R. (1983). *The architecture of cognition*. Cambridge University Press.

Anderson, J. R., & Bower, G. H. (1973). *Human associative memory*. Winston and Sons.

Andler, D. (1992). *Introduction aux sciences cognitives* [Introduction to cognitive sciences]. Gallimard.

Angell, J. R. (1929). Yale's institute of human relations. *Yale Alumni Weekly, 24*, 583–588.

Anokhin, P. K. (1974). *Biology and neurophysiology of the conditioned reflex and its role in adaptive behavior*. Pergamon Press.

Anonymous. (1953). *Documents of psychology meeting* (Vol. 45). Izvestija Pedag Nauk.

Appleton, P. (2016). Jerome Bruner (1915 2016). *BPS Homepage*. https://thcpsychologist.bps.org.uk/jerome-bruner-1915-2016

Arbib, M. (2005). From monkey-like action recognition to human language: An evolutionary framework for neurolinguistics. *Behavioral and Brain Sciences, 28*, 105–167.

Arendt, H. (1951). *The origins of totalitarianism*. Harcourt.

Asch, S. E. (1952). *Social psychology*. Prentice Hall.

Ash, M. (1980). Academic politics in the history of a science: Experimental psychology in Germany 1879–1941. *Central European History, 13*(3), 255–286.

Ash, M. (1988). Die Entwicklung des Wiener Psychologischen Instituts 1922–1938 [The development of the department of psychology in Vienna 1922–1938]. In A. Eschbach (Ed.), *Karl Bühler's theory of language* (pp. 303–325). Benjamins.

Ashby, R. (1956). *An introduction to cybernetics*. Chapman and Hall.

Ashis, N. (2001). The twentieth century: The ambivalent homecoming of homo psychologicus. *Hitotsubashi Journal of Social Studies, 33*, 21–33.

Asmolov, A. G. (1997). The social biography of cultural-historical psychology. *Journal of Russian & East European Psychology, 35*(2), 48–65.

Asmolov, A. G. (2016). From LS Vygotsky's "mind in society" to A. A. Leontiev's "active mind": An essay on the cultural hero. *Voprosy Psikhologii*, (6), 95–104.

Asratian, E. A. (1953). *I. P. Pavlov. His life and work*. Foreign Languages Publishing House.

Assmann, J. (1992). *Das kulturelle Gedächtniss* [Cultural memory]. Beck.

Assmann, J. (2008). Communicative and cultural memory. In A. Erll & A. Nünning (Eds.), *Cultural memory studies: An international and interdisciplinary handbook* (pp. 109–118). Springer.

Assmann, J. (2012). *Cultural memory and early civilization: Writing, remembrance, and political imagination.* Cambridge University Press.
Atkinson, R., & Shiffrin, R. M. (1968). Human memory: A proposed system and its control processes. *Psychology of Learning and Motivation, 2,* 89–195.
Attneave, F. (1959). *Applications of information theory to psychology.* Holt.
Austin, J. L. (1962). *How to do things with words.* Oxford University Press.
Baars, B. J. (1986). *The cognitive revolution in psychology.* Guilford Press.
Bäckman, L., & Holsten, von, C. (Eds.). (2002). *Psychology at the turn of the millennium* (Vols. 1 and 2). Taylor and Francis.
Baddeley, A. (1976). *The psychology of memory.* Basic Books.
Baddeley, A. D., & Hitch, G. J. (1974). Working memory. In G. A. Bower (Ed.), *Recent advances in learning and motivation* (Vol. 8, pp. 47–90). Academic Press.
Bakhtin, M. (1986). *Speech genres and other essays* (V. W. McGee, Trans.). University of Texas Press.
Baldwin, J. (1909). *Darwin and the humanities.* Review publications. http://archive.org/stream/darwinandthehuma00balduoft#page/n5/mode/2up
Baldwin, J. M. (1894). *Mental development in the child and the race: Methods and processes.* Macmillan Publishing.
Baldwin, J. M. (1911). *Individual and society or psychology and sociology.* Badger.
Balint, A. (1954). *The early years of life* (1st ed.). Basic Books.
Balint, M. (1965). *Primary love and psycho-analytic technique.* Tavistock.
Balint, M. (1968). *The basic fault.* Tavistock.
Bandura, A. (1962). Social learning through imitation. In M. R. Jones (Ed.), *Nebraska symposium on motivation* (pp. 212–269). University of Nebraska Press.
Bandura, A. (1963). *Social learning and personality development.* Holt, Rinehart, and Winston.
Bandura, A. (1973). *Aggression: A social learning analysis.* Prentice-Hall,
Bandura, A. (1977). Self-efficacy: Toward a unifying theory of behavioral change. *Psychological Review, 84,* 191–215.
Barker, L., & Buss, D. (2006). Teaching evolutionary psychology: An interview with David M. Buss. *Teaching of Psychology, 33,* 69–76.
Barkóczi, I., & Putnoky, J. (1968). *Tanulás és motiváció* [Learning and motivation]. Tankönyvkiadó.
Barkow, J. H., Cosmides, L., & Tooby, J. (Eds.). (1992). *The adapted mind.* Oxford University Press.
Baron-Cohen, S. (1989). The autistic child's theory of mind: A case of specific developmental delay. *Journal of child Psychology and Psychiatry, 30*(2), 285–297.
Baron-Cohen, S. (1995). *Mindblindness: An essay on autism and theory of mind.* MIT Press.
Barrett, L., Dunbar, R., & Lycett, J. (2001). *Human evolutionary psychology.* Palgrave.
Bartlett, F. C. (1916). An experimental study of some problems of perceiving and imaging. *British Journal of Psychology, 8,* 222–226.
Bartlett, F. C. (1920). Psychology in relation to the popular story. *Folklore, 31,* 264–293.
Bartlett, F. C. (1923). *Psychology and primitive culture.* Cambridge University Press.
Bartlett, F. C. (1932). *Remembering.* Cambridge University Press.
Bartlett, F. C. (1936). Frederic Charles Bartlett [autobiography]. In C. Murchison (Ed.), *A history of psychology in autobiography* (Vol. III, pp. 39–52). Clark University Press.
Bartlett, F. C. (1940). *Political propaganda.* Cambridge University Press.
Bartlett, F. C. (1951). The bearing of experimental psychology upon human skilled performance. *British Journal of Industrial Medicine, 8,* 209–217.

Bartlett, F. C. (1958). *Thinking: An experimental and social study*. Allen Unwin.
Bartsch, K., & Wellman, H. M. (1995). *Children talk about the mind*. Oxford University Press.
Basov, M. J. (1932). *Obshije osnovi pedologii* [General principles of pedology]. Gosudarstvennoje isdatel'stvo.
Bastide, R. (1970). Mémoire collective et sociologie du bricolage [Collective memory and tinkering]. *Année Sociologique, 21,* 65–108.
Bates, E., & MacWhinney, B. (1989). Functionalism and the competition model. In B. MacWhinney & E. Bates (Eds.), *The crosslinguistic study of sentence processing* (pp. 3–76). Cambridge University Press.
Bateson, G., Jackson, D. D., Haley, J., & Weakland, J. (1956). Towards a theory of schizophrenia. *Behavioral Science, 1,* 251–264.
Bauer, R. A. (1952). *The new man in Soviet psychology*. Harvard University Press.
Bechterew, W. (1957). *La Réflexologie collective*. Delachaux et Niestle. (Original work published 1921)
Beckermann, A., McLaughlin, B. P., & Walter, S. (Eds.). (2009). *The Oxford handbook of philosophy of mind*. Oxford University Press.
Bekhterev, V. (1909). La méthode de la psychologie objective [The method of objective psychology]. *J de Psycho Normale et Pathol, 6,* 481–505.
Bekhterev, V. (2007). *La psychologie objective*. Alcan, New edition L'Harmattan. (Original work published 1913)
Bekhterev, V. (1923). *Obschiee osnovi refleksologii cheloveka* [General foundation of human reflexology]. Gosizdat.
Bekhterev, V. (Ed.). (1925a). *Novoe v refleksologii i fiziologii nervnoj sistemi* [New results in reflexology and physiology of neural systems]. Gosizd.
Bekhterev, V. (1925b). *Psihologia, reflexologia, i Marxism* [Psychology, reflexology and Marxism]. Nauka.
Bekhterev, W. (1973). *General principles of human reflexology*. Jarrolds. (Original work published 1932)
Bekhterev, W. (2001). *Collective reflexology*. Routledge. (Original work published 1921)
Bellugi, U., Lichtenberger, L., Jones, W., & Lai, Z. (2000). The neurocognitive profile of Williams syndrome: A complex pattern of strengths and weaknesses. *Journal of Cognitive Neuroscience, 12,* 17–29.
Bergman, E. T., & Roediger, H. L., III. (1999). Can Bartlett's repeated reproduction experiments be replicated? *Memory & Cognition, 27,* 937–947.
Berko, J. (1958). The child's learning of English morphology. *Word, 14,* 150–177.
Berko-Gleason, J., & Ratner, N. B. (2024). *The development of language* (10th ed.). Pearson.
Berkowitz, L. (1969). Frustration-aggression hypothesis: Examination and reformulation. *Psychological Bulletin, 106,* 59–73.
Berlin, I. (1953). *The hedgehog and the fox: An essay on Tolstoy's view of history*. Weidenfeld & Nicolson.
Berlyne, D. E. (1954). A theory of human curiosity. *British Journal of Psychology, 45,* 180–191.
Berlyne, D. E. (1960). *Conflict, arousal, and curiosity*. McGraw-Hill.
Berne, E. (1964). *Games people play*. Grove Press.
Bever, T. G. (1970). The cognitive basis for linguistic structures. In: Richard Hayes. (ed.) *Cognition and language development*. Wiley, 279–362.
Bickerton, D., & Szathmáry, E. (Eds.). (2009). *Biological foundations and origin of syntax*. MIT Press.

Biederman, I. (1987). Recognition-by-components: A theory of human image understanding. *Psychological Review, 94*, 115–147.
Billig, M. (2015). Kurt Lewin's leadership studies and his legacy to social psychology: Is there nothing as practical as a good theory. *Journal for the Theory of Social Behaviour, 45*, 440–460.
Binet, A. (1888). *The psychic life of micro-organisms.* Longmans.
Binet, A. (1890). *On double consciousness: Experimental psychological studies.* Open Court Publishing Co.
Binet, A. (1891). *Animal magnetism* (3rd ed.). Kegan Paul.
Binet, A. (1896). *Alterations of personality.* D. Appleton.
Binet, A. (2010). *La psychologie individuelle* [Individual psychology]. L'Harmattan. Reedition of his papers on individual differences with a preface by S. Nicolas.
Binet, A., & Féré, C. (1888). *Animal magnetism.* Appleton.
Binet, A., & Henry, V. (1894). La mémoire des phrases. Mémoire des idées [Memory of sentences. Memory of ideas]. *Année Psychologique, 1*, 24–59.
Binet, A., & Henry, V. (1896). La psychologie individuelle [Individual psychology]. *L'Année Psychologique, 1*, 411–465.
Binet, A., & Simon, T. (1916). *The development of intelligence in children (The Binet-Simon scale).* Williams & Wilkins Co.
Bishop, D. V. M. (2001). Genetic influences on language impairment and literacy problems in children: Same or different? *Journal of Child Psychology and Psychiatry, 42*, 189–198.
Bishop, D. V. M., Snowling, M. J., Thompson, P. A., Greenhalgh, T., & CATALISE Consortium. (2017). Phase 2 of CATALISE: A multinational and multidisciplinary Delphi consensus study of problems with language development: Terminology. *The Journal of Child Psychology and Psychiatry, 58*, 1068–1080.
Bleuler, E. (1950). *Dementia Praecox or the group of schizophrenias.* International Universities Press. (Original work published 1911)
Block, N. (Ed.). (1980). *Readings in the philosophy of psychology.* Harvard University Press.
Block, N. (1996). What is functionalism? In Donald M. Borchert (ed.) *Encyclopedia of Philosophy Supplement.* Macmillan.
Block, N. (2007). Consciousness, accessibility, and the mesh between psychology and neuroscience. *Behavior and Brain Sciences, 30,* 481–548.
Blodgett, H. C. (1929). The effect of the introduction of reward upon the maze performance of rats. *University of California Publications in Psychology, 4*, 113–134.
Blondel, C. (1914). *La conscience morbide* [The morbid consciousness]. Alcan Digitized. https://ia600204.us.archive.org/28/items/laconsciencemorb00blon/laconsciencemorb-00blon.pdf
Blondel, C. (1924). *La psychanalyse* [The psychoanalysis] Alcan.
Blondel, C. (1928). *Introduction a la psychologie collective* [Introduction to collective psychology]. Colin.
Blondel, C. (1933). *Le suicide* [The suicide]. Librairie Universitaire d'Alsace.
Blonski, P. P. (1920). *Reforma nauki* [Science reform]. Gosizd.
Blonski, P. P. (1921). *Ocherk nauchnoj psihologii* [An outline of scientific psychology]. Ogiz.
Blonski, P. P. (1925). *Pedologia* [Pedology]. Ogiz.
Blonski, P. P. (1934). The subject of psychology and psychopathology from a genetic standpoint. *Pedagogical Seminary and Journal of Genetic Psychology, 35*, 356–373. (Original work published 1928)
Blonski, P. P. (1935). *Pamjat'i mislenie* [Memory and thinking]. Ogiz.

Blonski, P. P. (1930). Zur Psychologie der monoandrischen und der polyandrischen Frau in der modernen Kultur [The psychology of the monandrous and the polyandrous woman in modern civilization]. *Zeitschrift für Sexualwissenschaft und Sexualpolitik, 17,* 1–13.

Blonski, P. P. (1977). The problem of recall. *Journal of Russian & East European Psychology, 15,* 3–14.

Bloomfield, L. (1926). A set of postulates for the science of language. *Language, 2,* 153–164.

Blum, F. (Ed.). (2007). *Les vies de Pierre Naville* [The lifes of Pierre Naville]. Presses Universitaires de Septentrion.

Blumenthal, A. (Ed.). (1970). *Psychology and language: A historical introduction to psycholinguistics.* Wiley.

Blumenthal, A. (1987). The emergence of psycholinguistics. *Synthese, 72,* 313–323.

Boas, F. (1911). *The mind of primitive man.* Macmillan. Revised edition 1938. https://archive.org/details/mindofprimitivem031738mbp/page/n5/mode/2up

Bobrow, D. G., & Collins, A. (Eds.). (1975). *Representation and understanding. Studies in cognitive science.* Academic Press.

Boden, M. A. (Ed.). (2006). *Mind as machine: A history of cognitive science* (Vols. I–II). Oxford University Press.

Boole, G. (1958). *An investigation into the laws of thought.* Cambridge University Press. (Original work published 1854)

Borgatta, E. F. (2007). Jacob L. Moreno and sociometry: A mid-century reminiscence. *Social Psychology Quarterly, 70,* 330–332.

Boring, E. G. (1923). Intelligence as the tests test it. *New Republic, 36,* 35–37.

Boring, E. G. (1940). Was this analysis a success? *Journal of Abnormal and Social Psychology, 35,* 4–10.

Boring, E. G. (1945). The use of operational definitions in science. *Psychological Review, 52,* 243 245.

Bosc, O. (2010). Gustave Le Bon, un mythe du xxe siècle? [Gustave Le Bon, a myth of 20th century?] *Mil neuf cent. Revue d'histoire intellectuelle, 28*(1), 101–120.

Bourdieu, P. (1977). *Outline of a theory of practice.* Cambridge University Press.

Bousfield, W. A. (1953). The occurrence of clustering in the recall of randomly arranged associates. *Journal of General Psychology, 49,* 229–240.

Bower, G. H. (1994). A turning point in mathematical learning theory. *Psychological Review, 101,* 290–300.

Bowlby, J. (1969). *Attachment and loss* (Vol. 1.). Hogarth Press.

Boyd, R., & Richerson, P. J. (1985). *Culture and the evolutionary.* University of Chicago Press.

Brady, W. J., Julian A. W., John T. J., & Van Bavel, J. J. (2017). Emotion shapes the diffusion of moralized content in social networks. *Proceedings of the National Academy of Sciences, 114,* 7313–7318.

Braunstein, J. F. (1999). La Critique Canguilhemienne de la Psychologie [The critic of psychology by Canguilhem]. *Bulletin de Psychologie, 52*(2), 181–190.

Brewer, W. F. (1974). There is no convincing evidence for operant or classical conditioning in normal, adult human beings. In W. Weimer & D. Palermo (Eds.), *Cognition and the symbolic processes.* Erlbaum.

Bridgman, P. W. (1927). *The logic of modern physics,* Macmillan.

Broadbent, D. E. (1958). *Perception and communication.* Pergamon.

Broca, P. (1861). Sur le volume et la forme du cerveau suivant les individus et suivant les races [The volume and form of the brain accordingg to individuals and races]. *Bulletin de la Société d'Antropologie, 4,* 200–204.

Broca, P. (1865). Sur le siége de la faculté du language articulé [On the site of the abilty of articulated language]. *Bulletin de la Société d'Antropologie, 6,* 337–393.

Bródy, G. (2010). Darwin és Napóleon [Review of Jerry Fodor – Massimo Piattelli-Palmarini: What Darwin got wrong]. *Századvég, 56,* 121–130.

Bronfenbrenner, U., & Ceci, S. J. (1994). Nature-nurture reconceptualized in developmental perspective: A bioecological model. *Psychological Review, 101,* 568–586.

Brown, D. E. (1999). *Human universals.* McGraw–Hill.

Brown, R. (1958). *Words and things.* Free Press.

Brown, R. (1970). *Psycholinguistics: Selected papers.* Free Press.

Brown, R. (1973). *A first language: The early stages.* Harvard University Press.

Brown, R. (1986). *Social psychology* (2nd ed.). Free Press.

Brown, R., & Bellugi, U. (1964). Three processes in the child's acquisition of syntax. *Harvard Educational Review, 34,* 133–151.

Brown, R., & Berko, J. (1960). Word association and the acquisition of grammar. *Child Development, 31,* 1–14.

Brown, R., & Gilman, A. (1960). The pronouns of power and solidarity. In T. Sebeok (Ed.), *Aspects of style in language.* The MIT Press. Reprinted in Brown, 1970.

Brown, R., & Kulik, J. (1977). Flashbulb memories. *Cognition, 5,* 73–99.

Brown, R., & Lenneberg, E. H. (1954). A study in language and cognition. *Journal of Abnormal and Social Psychology, 49,* 454–462.

Brown, R., & McNeill, D. (1966). The "tip of the tongue" phenomenon. *Journal of Verbal Learning and Verbal Behavior, 5,* 325–337.

Brown, R. E., & Milner, P. M. (2003). The legacy of Donald O. Hebb: More than the Hebb synapse. *Nature Reviews Neuroscience, 4,* 10–13.

Bruner, J. (1957). On perceptual readiness. *Psychological Review, 64,* 123–152.

Bruner, J. (1960). *The process of education.* Harvard University Press.

Bruner, J. (1974). *Beyond the information given.* George Allen & Unwin Ltd.

Bruner, J. (1975). The ontogenesis of speech acts. *Journal of Child Language, 2,* 1–19.

Bruner, J. (1983). *In search of mind: Essays in autobiography.* Harper and Row. http://pubman.mpdl.mpg.de/pubman/faces/viewItemOverviewPage.jsp?itemId=escidoc:2301309

Bruner, J. (1984). Notes on the cognitive revolution. *Interchange, 15,* 1–8.

Bruner, J. (1990). *Acts of meaning.* Harvard University Press.

Bruner, J. (1991). The narrative construction of Reality. *Critical Inquiry, 18,* 1–21.

Bruner, J. (1997). Celebrating the divergence: Piaget and Vygotsky. *Human Development, 40,* 63–73.

Bruner, J. (2004). Ignace Meyerson and cultural psychology. In C. E. Erneling & D. M. Johnson (Eds.), *The mind as a scientific object: Between brain and culture* (pp. 402–412). Oxford University Press.

Bruner, J. (2006). La culture, l'esprit, les récits [Culture, mind, narratives]. *Enfance, 58,* 118–125.

Bruner, J. S. (1997). Will cognitive revolutions ever stop? In D. M. Johnson & C. E. Erneling (Ed.), *The future of the cognitive revolution* (pp. 279–292). Oxford University Press.

Bruner, J. S., Goodnow, J. J., & Austin, G. A. (1956). *A study of thinking.* Wiley.

Bruner, J. S., Olver, R. R., & Greenfield, P. M. (1966). *Studies in cognitive growth.* Wiley.

Brunswik, E. (1934). *Wahrnehmung und Gegenstandswelt: Grundlegung einer Psychologie vom Gegenstand her* [Perception and the world of objects: Foundations of a psychology of objects]. Deuticke.

Brunswik, E. (1943). Organismic achievement and environmental probability. *Psychological Review, 50,* 255–272.

Brunswik, E. (1952). *The conceptual framework of psychology: International encyclopedia of unified science.* University of Chicago Press.
Brunswik, E. (1955). Representative design and probabilistic theory in a functional psychology. *Psychological Review, 62,* 193–217.
Bugental, J. F., Wegrocki, H. J., Murphy, G., Thomae, H., Allport, G. W., Ekstein, R., & Garvin, P. L. (1966). Symposium on Karl Bühler's contributions to psychology. *Journal of General Psychology, 75,* 181–219.
Bühler, C. (1933). *Der menschliche Lebenslauf als psychologisches Problem* [The human life course as a psychological problem]. Hirzel.
Bühler, C., & Hetzer, H. (1932). *Kleinkindertests. Entwicklungstests für das erste bis sechste Lebensjahr* [Tests on small children. Developmental tests fron the first to the 6th year]. Hirzel.
Bühler, C., & Melanie, E. (1972). *Introduction to humanistic psychology.* Brooks, Cole Publication Company.
Bühler, K. (1908) Tatsachen und Probleme zu einer Psychologie der Denkvorgänge. II. Über Gedankenzusammenhänge. II. Über Gedankeneinnerungen. *Archiv für die gesammte Psychologie, 12,* 1–23, 24–92. Part of it translated as on thought connections, in Rapaport, 1951, pp. 39–57.
Bühler, K. (1913). *Die Gestaltwahrnehmungen* [Gestalt perceptions]. W. Spemann.
Bühler, K. (1918) Kritischer Musterung zu einer neuer Theorie der Satzen [Critical anaysis of a new theory of sentences]. *Indogermanische Jahrbücher, 6,* 1–20.
Bühler, K. (1930). *The mental development of the child: A summary of modern psychological theory.* Routledge. (Original work published 1922)
Bühler, K. (1927). *Die Krise der Psychologie* [The crisis of psychology]. Fischer.
Bühler, K. (1990). *Theory of language: The representational function of language* (D. F. Goodwin, Trans.). Benjamins. (Original work published 1934)
Bühler, K. (1936). *Die Zukunft der Psychologie und die Schule* [The future of psychology and the school]. Deutscher Verlag für Jugend und Volk.
Bühler, K. (1960). *Das Gestaltprinzip im Leben des Menschen und der Tiere* [The Gestalt principle in the life of humans and animals]. Huber.
Bühler, K. (2009). *Théorie du langage.* Agone.
Buller, D. J. (2005). Evolutionary psychology: The emperor's new paradigm. *Trends in Cognitive Sciences, 9,* 277–283.
Burt, C. (1958). The inheritance of mental ability. *American Psychologist, 13,* 1–15.
Burt, C. (1961). Intelligence and social mobility. *British Journal of Statistical Psychology, 14,* 3–24.
Burt, C. (1966). The genetic determination of differences in intelligence. *British Journal of Psychology, 57,* 137–153.
Burt, C. (1972). The *inheritance of general intelligence. American Psychologist, 27,* 175–190.
Buss, D. M. (1984). Evolutionary biology and personality psychology toward a conception of human nature and individual differences. *American Psychologist, 39,* 1135–1147.
Buss, D. M. (1994). *The evolution of desire: Strategies of human mating.* Basic Books.
Buss, D. M. (1995). Evolutionary psychology: A new paradigm for psychological science. *Psychological Inquiry, 6,* 1–30.
Buss, D. M. (1999). *Evolutionary psychology. The new science of the mind.* Alyn Bacon.
Buss, D. M. (2009) The great struggles of life: Darwin and the emergence of evolutionary psychology. *American Psychologist, 64,* 140–148.
Buzsáki, G. (2006). *Rhythms of the brain.* Oxford University Press.

Bykov, K. M. (1959). *The cerebral cortex and the internal organs* (W. H. Gantt, Trans.). Chemical Publishing.

Calkins, M. W. (1915). The self in scientific psychology. *American Journal of Psychology, 26*, 495–524. Electronic version in *Classics* . . .

Call, J., & Tomasello, M. (2008). Does the chimpanzee have a theory of mind? 30 years later. *Trends in Cognitive Sciences, 12*, 187–192.

Campbell, D. T. (1959). Methodological suggestions from a comparative psychology of knowledge processes. *Inquiry, 2*, 154–182.

Campbell, D. T. (1969). Etnocentrism of disciplines and the fish-scale model of omniscience. In M. Sherif & W. Sherif (Eds.), *Interdisciplinary relations in the social sciences* (pp. 328–348). Alidine. Reprinted in Campbell, 1988.

Campbell, D. T. (1974). Evolutionary epistemology. In P. A. Schlipp (Ed.), *The philosophy of Karl Popper* (pp. 413–463). Open Court.

Campbell, D. T. (1977). *Descriptive epistemology: Psychological, sociological, and evolutionary*. William James lectures. Harvard University.

Campbell, D. T. (1988). *Methodology and epistemology for social science: Selected papers Donald T. Campbell*. University of Chicago Press.

Canetti, E. (1962). *Crowds and power* (C. Stewart, Trans.). Viking Press.

Canguilhem, G. (2016). Qu'est-ce que la psychologie? *Revue de Métaphysique et de Morale, 63*, 12–23. (Original work published 1958)

Canguilhem, G. (1980). Le cerveau et la pensee [The brain and thinking]. *Prospectives de Santé, 14*, 81–98.

Canguilhem, G. (2016). What is psychology? *Foucault Studies, 21*, 200–213.

Capshew, J. H. (1999). *Psychologists on the march: Science, practice, and professional identity in America, 1929–1969*. Cambridge University Press.

Carnap, R. (1959). Psychology in physical language. In A. J. Ayer (Ed.), *Logical positivism* (pp. 102–142). Glencoe. (Original work published 1932)

Carnap, R. (1937). *The logical syntax of language*. Harcourt. (Original work published 1934)

Carroll, J. B. (1993). *Human cognitive abilities: A survey of factor-analytic studies*. Cambridge University Press.

Carroll, J. B., & Casagrande, J. B. (1958). The function of language classification in behavior. In E. Maccoby, F. Newcomb, & E. Hartley (Eds.), *Readings in social psychology* (pp. 18–31). Holt.

Carroy, J. (1991). *Hypnose, suggestion, et psychologie* [Hypnosiis, suggestion and psychology]. Presses Universitaires de France.

Carroy, J. (1993). Foules expérimentales, psychologie des foules et psychologie sociale expérimentale de Bernheim à Milgram [Experimental crowds. Crowd psychology and experimental social psychology from Bernheim to Milgram]. *Sociétés contemporaines, La psychologie sociale et ses histoires, 13*, 167–172.

Carroy, J., & Ohayon, A. (1999). L'unité de la psychologie dans l'œuvre de Daniel Lagache. L'idéal scientifique et compromis politique [The unity of psychology in the work of Daniel Lagache. Scientific ideals and political compromise]. *Bulletin de Psychologie, 52*(440), 191–202.

Carroy, J., Ohayon, A., & Plas, R. (2006). *Histoire de la psychologie en France* [History of psychology in France]. La Découverte.

Carroy, J., & Plas, R. (2000). How Pierre Janet used pathological psychology to save the philosophical self. *Journal of the History Behavioral Science, 36*, 231–240.

Cattell, R. B. (1965). *The scientific analysis of personality*. Penguin.

Cattell, R. B. (1967). *Intelligence: Its structure, growth and action: Its structure, growth and action*. North Holland.
Changeux, J.-P. (1985). *The neuronal man*. Princeton University Press.
Changeux, J. P. (2009). *The good, the true, and the beautiful: A neuronal approach*. Yale University Press.
Changeux, J. P. (2017). Climbing brain levels of organisation from genes to consciousness. *Trends in Cognitive Sciences, 21*, 168–181.
Changeux, J. P., & Danchin, A. (1976). Selective stabilisation of developing synapses as a mechanism for the specification of neuronal networks. *Nature, 264*, 707–712.
Changeux, J. P., & Dehaene, S. (1989). Neuronal models of cognitive functions. *Cognition, 33*, 63–109.
Changeux, J. P., & Ricoeur, P. (2000). *What makes us think?: A Neuroscientist and a philosopher argue about ethics, human nature, and the brain*. Princeton University Press.
Charney, E. (2012). Behavior genetics and postgenomics. *Behavioral and Brain Sciences, 35*, 331–410.
Chelpanov, G. I. (1924). *Psihologia i Marxism* [Psychology and Marxism]. Russkij Kniznik.
Cherry, C. (1966). *Human communication: A review, a survey, and a criticism*. MIT Press.
Chomsky, N. (1957). *Syntactic structures*. Mouton.
Chomsky, N. (1959) Review of B. F. Skinner's verbal behavior. *Language, 35*, 26–58.
Chomsky, N. (1965). *Aspects of a theory of syntax*. The MIT Press.
Chomsky, N. (1967). Recent contributions to the theory of innate ideas. *Synthese, 17*, 2–11.
Chomsky, N. (2006). *Language and mind* (3rd ed.). Harcourt, Cambridge University Press. (Original work published 1968)
Chomsky, N. (1972a). Psychology and ideology. *Cognition, 1*, 11–46.
Chomsky, N. (1972b). *Problems of knowledge and freedom: The Russell lectures*. Vintage Books.
Chomsky, N. (1978). Language development, human intelligence, and social organization. In W. Feinberg (Ed.), *Equality and social policy* (pp. 120–143). University of Illinois Press.
Chomsky, N. (1980). *Rules and representations*. Columbia University Press.
Chomsky, N. (1986). *Knowledge of language*. Praeger.
Chomsky, N. (1988). *Language and problems of knowledge*. The MIT Press.
Chomsky, N. (2005). Three factors in language design. *Linguistic Inquiry, 36*, 1–22.
Chomsky, N. (2016). *What kind of creatures are we?* Columbia University Press.
Chomsky, N., & Miller, G. A. (1963). Introduction to the formal analysis of natural languages. In R. D. Luce, R. R. Bush, & E. Galanter (Eds.), *Handbook of mathematical psychology* (Vol. II, pp. 269–322). Wiley.
Churchland, P. (1986). *Neurophilosophy*. MIT Press.
Churchland, P. M. (1981). E liminative materialism and the propositional attitudes. *The Journal of Philosophy, 78*(2), 67–90.
Churchland, P. M. (1995). *The engine of reason, the seat of the soul. A philosophical journey into the brain*. MIT Press.
Clahsen, H. (1999). Lexical entries and rules of language: A multidisciplinary study of German inflection. *Behavior and Brain Sciences, 22*, 991–1060.
Clark, A. (1989). *Microcognition*. The MIT Press.
Clark, A. (1994). *Associative engines*. The MIT Press.
Clark, C. J., & Winegard, B. M. (2020). Tribalism in war and peace: The nature and evolution of ideological epistemology and its significance for modern social science. *Psychological Inquiry, 31*, 1–22.

Clark, H. H. (1979). Responding to indirect speech acts. *Cognitive Psychology, 11*, 430–477.
Clark, K. B. (1988). The Brown decision: Racism, education, and human values. *The Journal of Negro Education, 57*, 125–132.
Clark, K. B., & Clark, M. P. (1947). Racial identification and preference in Negro children. In T. Newcomb & E. Hartley (Eds.), *Readings in social psychology* (pp. 169–178). Holt.
Cofer, C. N. (1978). Origins of the Journal of Verbal Learning and Verbal Behavior. *Journal of Verbal Learning and Verbal Behavior, 17*, 113–126.
Cofer, C. N., & Appley, M. H. (1964). *Motivation: Theory and research*. Wiley.
Cofer, C. N., & Musgrave, B. S. (1961). *Verbal learning and verbal behavior*. McGraw Hill.
Cohen, J. (1970). *Homo psychologicus*. George Allen and Unwin.
Cohen, J. (1994). The earth is round (p < 0.05). *American Psychologist, 49*, 997–1003.
Cohen-Cole, J. (2005). The reflexivity of cognitive science: The scientist as model of human nature. *History of the Human Sciences, 18*(4), 107–139.
Cohen-Cole, J. (2007). Instituting the science of mind: Intellectual economies and disciplinary exchange at Harvard's center for cognitive studies. *British Journal for the History of Science, 40*, 567–597.
Cole, M. (1996). *Cultural psychology: The once and future discipline*. Harvard University Press.
Cole, M., & Maltzmann, I. (Eds.). (1969). *A handbook of contemporary Soviet psychology*. Basic Books.
Cole, M., & Scribner, S. (1974). *Culture and thought*. Wiley.
Collins, A. M., & Quillian, M. R. (1969). Retrieval time from semantic memory. *Journal of Verbal Learning and Verbal Behavior, 8*, 240–247.
Coltheart, M. (1999). Modularity and cognition. *Trends in Cognitive Sciences, 3*, 115–120.
Comte, A. (1975). *Auguste Comte and positivism: The essential writings* (G. Lenzer, Ed.). Harper and Row. (Original work published 1830)
Confino, A. (1997). Collective memory and cultural history: Problems of method. *The American Historical Review, 102*, 1386–1403.
Conway, J. B. (1992). A world of differences among psychologists. *Canadian Psychology, 33*, 1–24.
Cosmides, L., & Tooby, J. (1994). Beyond intuition and instinct blindness: Toward an evolutionarily rigorous cognitive science. *Cognition, 50*, 41–77.
Cowan, W. M., Harter, D. H., & Kandel, E. R. (2000). The emergence of modern neuroscience: Some implications for neurology and psychiatry. *Annual Review of Neuroscience, 23*, 343–391.
Craig, W. (1918). Appetites and aversions as constituents of instincts. *Biological Bulletin, 34*, 91–107.
Craik, K. J. W. (1943). *The nature of explanation*. Cambridge University Press.
Cronbach, L. J. (1957). The two disciplines of scientific psychology. *American Psychologist, 12*, 671–684.
Crozier, S., Sirigu, A., Lehéricy, S., van de Moortele, P.-F., Pillon, B., Grafman, J., Agid, Y., Dubois, B., & LeBihan, D. (1999). Distinct prefrontal activations in processing sequence at the sentence and script level: An fMRI study. *Neuropsychologia, 37*(13), 1469–1476.
Csibra, G. (2007). Action mirroring and action understanding: An alternative account. In P. T. Harrad, Y. Rossetti, & M. Kawato (Eds.), *Sensorimotor foundations of higher cognition. Attention and performance XXII* (pp. 435–479). Oxford University Press.
Csibra, G., Davis, G., Spratling, M. W., & Johnson, M. H. (2000). Gamma oscillations and object processing in the infant brain. *Science, 290*, 1582–1585.

Csibra, G., & Gergely, G. (2009). Natural pedagogy. *Trends in Cognitive Sciences, 13,* 148–153.
Csibra, G., & Gergely G. (2011). Natural pedagogy as evolutionary adaptation. *Philosophical Transactions of the Royal Society of London. Series B, Biological Sciences, 366*(1567), 1149–1157.
Cutler, A. (Ed.). (2005). *Twenty-first century psycholinguistics: Four cornerstones.* Erlbaum.
Dahrendorf, R. (1967). *Society and democracy in Germany.* Doubleday.
Damasio, A. (1994). *Descartes's error.* Basic Books.
Danziger, K. (1983). Origins and basic principles of Wundt's Völkerpsychologie. *British Journal of Social Psychology, 22,* 303–313.
Danziger, K. (1990). *Constructing the subject.* Cambridge University Press. https://www.researchgate.net/publication/312940536_Constructing_the_Subject_Historical_Origins_of_Psychological_Research
Danziger, K. (1997). *Naming the mind: How psychology found its language.* Sage.
Danziger, K. (2000). Making social psychology experimental: A conceptual history, 1920–1970. *Journal of the History of the Behavioral Sciences, 36,* 329–347.
Danziger, K. (2008). *Marking the mind: A history of memory.* Cambridge University Press.
Danziger, K. (2010). *Problematic encounter: Talks on psychology and history.* http://www.kurtdanziger.com/Problematic%20Encounter.pdf
Deese, J. (1965). *The structure of associations in language and thought.* Johns Hopkins University Press.
Dehaene, S., & Cohen, L. (2007). Cultural recycling of cortical maps. *Neuron, 56,* 384–398.
DeLamater, J. (2013). Preface. In J. DeLamater & A. Ward (Eds.), *Handbook of social psychology* (2nd ed., pp. i–viii). Springer.
DeLamater, J., & Ward, A. (Eds.). (2013). *Handbook of social psychology* (2nd ed.). Springer.
Delay, J. (1942). *Les dissolutions de la mémoire* [Dissolutions of memory]. Presses Universitaires de France.
Delay, J., & Deniker, P. (1955). Neuroleptic effects of chlorpromazine in therapeutics of neuropsychiatry. *Journal of Clinical and Experimental Psychopathology, 16*(2), 104–112.
Dennett, D. (1978a). Skinner skinned. In *Brainstorms: Philosophical essays on mind and psychology* (pp. 53–70). The MIT Press.
Dennett, D. (1978b). Beliefs about beliefs. *Behavioral and Brain Sciences, 1,* 568–570.
Dennett, D. (1987). *The intentional stance.* The MIT Press.
Dennett, D. (1994). *Darwin's dangerous idea.* Simon and Schuster.
Dennett, D. (1997a). *Kinds of minds: Towards an understanding of consciousness.* Basic Books.
Dennett, D. (1997b). Darwinian fundamentalism: An exchange. *The New York Review of Books, 44*(13).
Dennett, D., & Kinsbourne, M. (1992). Time and the observer: The where and when of consciousness in the brain. *Behavioral and Brain Sciences, 15,* 183–247.
Der Große Brockhaus. (1931). 15. Edition. Brockhaus.
Dewey, J. (1910). *The influence of Darwin on philosophy.* Holt.
Dewsbury, D. A. (1994). The comparative psychology of Paul Schiller. *Psychological Record, 44,* 307–350.
Dewsbury, D. A., & Bolles, R. C. (1995). The founding of the Psychonomic Society. *Psychonomic Bulletin & Review, 2,* 216–233.
Dickens, W. T., & Flynn, J. R. (2001). Heritability estimates versus large environmental effects: The IQ paradox resolved. *Psychological Review, 108,* 346–369.

Dilthey, W. (1894). Ideen über eine beschreibende und zerglierdendre Psychologie [Ideas about a descriptive and segmenting psychology]. *Sitzungberichte der Akademie der Wissenschaften zu Berlin, 2*, 1309–1407.

Dilthey, W. (1977). *Descriptive psychology and historical understanding*. Nijhoff. Translation of Dilthey, 1894 and another paper on understanding others.

Dixon, N. F. (1971) *Subliminal perception: The nature of a controversy*. McGraw-Hill.

Dollard, J., Doob, L. W., Miller, N. E., Mowrer, O. H., & Sears, R. R. (1939). *Frustration and aggression*. Yale University Press.

Dollard, J., & Miller, N. E. (1950). *Personality and psychotherapy: An analysis in terms of learning, thinking and culture*. McGraw-Hill.

Donald, M. (1991). *Origins of the modern mind: Three stages in the evolution of culture and cognition*. Harvard University Press.

Donald, M. (2001). *A mind so rare: The evolution of human consciousness*. W. W. Norton & Company.

Donald, M. (2014). The digital era: Challenges for the modern mind. *Cadmus, 2*(2), 68–79.

Donald, M. (2017). Key cognitive preconditions for the evolution of language. *Psychonomic Bulletin & Review, 24*, 204–208.

Donald, M. (2018). The evolutionary origins of human cultural memory. In B. Wagoner (Ed.), *Handbook of culture and memory* (pp. 19–40). Oxford University Press.

Donders, F. C. (1969). On the speed of mental processes. *Acta Psychologica, 30*, 412–431. (Original work published 1868)

Draaisma, D. (2000). *Metaphors of memory. A history of memory research*. Cambridge University Press.

Dreyfus, H. (1972). *What computers can't do*. MIT Press.

Driesch, H. A. E. (1925). *The crisis in psychology*. Princeton University Press.

Ducret, J. J. (1990). *Jean Piaget: Biographie et parcours intellectuel* [Jean Piaget: Biography and intellectual road]. Delachaux et Niestlé.

Dunbar, R. (1998). The social brain hypothesis. *Evolutionary Anthropology, 6*, 178–190.

Dunbar, R. (2003). The social brain: Mind, language, and society in evolutionary perspective. *Annual Review of Anthropology, 32*, 163–181.

Dunbar, R. (2021). *Friends*. Little Brown.

Dupuy, J. P. (2009) *On the origins of cognitive science: The mechanization of the mind*. The MIT Press.

Durkheim, E. (1886). La philosophie dans les universite's allemandes [Philosophy in German universities]. *Revue Internationale de l'Enseignement, 11*, 313–338, 423–440.

Durkheim, E. (1982). *The rules of sociological method* (1st American ed.). Free Press. https://monoskop.org/images/1/1e/Durkheim_Emile_The_Rules_of_Sociological_Method_1982.pdf (Original work published 1894)

Durkheim, E. (1951). *Suicide: A study in sociology* (J. A. Spaulding & G. Simpson, Trans.). The Free Press. (Original work published 1897)

Durkheim, E. (1965). Individual and collective representations (D. F. Pocock, Trans.). In *Sociology and philosophy* (pp. 1–34). Cohen & West. (Original work published 1898)

Durkheim, É., & Mauss, M. (2009). *Primitive classification*. Taylor and Francis. (Original work published 1903)

Durkheim, É., & Tarde, G. (1904). La sociologie et les sciences sociales [Sociology and the social sciences]. *Revue internationale de sociologie, 12*, 83–84. http://www.uqac.uquebec.ca/zone30/Classiques_des_sciences_sociales/index.html

Ebbinghaus, H. (1896). Über erklärande und beschreibende Psychologie [On explanatory and descriptive psychology]. *Zeitschrift für Psychologie und Physiologie der Sinnesorganne, 9*, 162–205.

Edwards, D., & Middleton, D. (1987). Conversation and remembering: Bartlett revisited. *Applied Cognitive Psychology*, *1*, 77–92.

Eimas, P. D., Siqueland, E. R., Jusczyk, P. W., & Vigorito, J. (1971). Speech perception in infants. *Science*, *171*, 303–306.

Elkonin, D. (1972). Toward the problem of stages in the mental development of the child. *Soviet Psychology*, *10*, 225–251.

Elkonin, D. (2016). Intermediary action and development. *Cultural-Historical Psychology*, *12*(3), 93–112.

Ellenberger, H. F. (1970). *The discovery of the unconscious*. Basic Books.

Ellis, B. J., & Bjorklund, D. F. (2005). *Origins of the social mind: Evolutionary psychology and child development*. Guilford Press.

Elman, J. L., Bates, E. A., Johnson, M. H., Karmiloff-Smith, A., Parisi, D., & Plunkett, K. (1996). *Rethinking innateness: A connectionist perspective on development*. MIT Press.

Engel, P. (1998). The psychologists return. *Synthese*, *115*, 375–393.

Erdélyi, M. H. (1985). *Psychoanalysis: Freud's cognitive psychology*. W. H. Freeman.

Erdélyi, M. H. (2006). The unified theory of repression. *Behavioral and Brain Sciences*, *29*, 499–511.

Ericsson, K. A., & Kintsch, W. (1995). Long-term working memory. *Psychological Review*, *102*, 211–245.

Erikson, E. (1950). *Childhood and society*. Norton.

Erikson, E. (1958) *Young man Luther: A study in psychoanalysis and history*. Norton.

Erikson, E. (1968) *Identity: Youth and crisis*. Norton.

Erős, F. (1983). Freudo-Marxism in Hungary: Some parallels between Wilhelm Reich and Attila József. In S. Bem, H. Rappard, & W. van Horn (Eds.), *Studies in the history of psychology and the social sciences* (pp. 223–234). Psychologisch Instituut van de Rijksuniversiteit.

Erős, F. (1991). Fromm's theory and the problems of "real existing" socialism. In *Erich Fromm und die Kritische Theorie. Wissenschaft vom Menschen – Science of Man. Jahrbuch der Internationalen Erich Fromm Gesellschaft* (pp. 315–323). Lit Verlag.

Erős, F. (1992). Wilhelm Reich, Erich Fromm and the analytic social psychology of the Frankfurt school. In M. Kessler & R. Funk (Hrsg.). *Erich Fromm und die Frankfurter Schule* (pp. 69–73). Francke Verlag.

Erős, F. (2010). Review of Moscovici and Markova, 2006. *Journal of Community and Applied Social Psychology*, *20*, 532–533.

Erős, F. (2017). Social psychology in formation in Hungary: 1960–1990s. *European Yearbook of the History of Psychology*, *3*, 201–218.

Ervin, S. (1961). Changes with age in the verbal determinants of word association. *Amer J of Psychol*, *74*, 361–372.

Ervin, S. (1964). Imitation and structural change in children's language. In E. Lenneberg (Ed.), *New directions in the study of language* (pp. 163–189), MIT Press.

Eschbach, A. (Ed.). (1984). *Bühler Studien* [Bühler studies] (Vol. 2). Suhrkampf.

Espagne, M. (2009). Le cercle positiviste de Leipzig: une anthropologie en germe? [The positivist circle of Lepizig: An anthropology being born?]. *Revue Germanique Internationale*, *10*, 81–95.

Estes, W. K. (1950). Toward a statistical theory of learning. *Psychological Review*, *57*, 94–107.

Estes, W. K. (1959). The statistical approach to learning theory. In S. Koch (Ed.), *Psychology: A study of a science* (Vol. II, pp. 380–491). McGraw-Hill.

Etkind, A. (1994). How psychoanalysis was received in Russia, 1906–1936. *Journal of Analytical Psychology*, *39*, 191–202.

Etkind, A. (2020). *Eros of the impossible: The history of psychoanalysis in Russia* (N. Rubins & M. Rubins, Trans.). Routledge. (Original work published 1997)
Eysenck, H. (1973) *The biological basis of personality*. Transaction Publishers.
Farr, R. (1990). Waxing and waning of interest in societal psychology: A historical perspective. In H. T. Himmelweit & G. Gaskell (Eds.), *Societal psychology* (pp. 46–64). Sage.
Farr, R. (1991). The long past and the short history of social psychology. *European Journal of Social Psychology, 21,* 371–380.
Farr, R. (1996). *The roots of modern social psychology, 1872–1954*. Blackwell.
Feest, U. (2005). Operationism in psychology: What the debate is about, what the debate should be about. *Journal of the History of the Behavioral Sciences, 41,* 131–149.
Feldman, J. A., & Ballard, D. H. (1982). Connectionist models and their properties. *Cognitive Science, 6,* 205–254.
Ferenczi, S. (1989). *Thalassa: A theory of genitality*. Karnac Books. (Original work published 1924)
Ferenczi, S. (1995). *The clinical diary of Sándor Ferenczi*. (J. Dupont, Ed.). Harvard University Press. (Original work published 1932)
Ferenczi, S. (1949). The confusion of tongues between adults and children: The language of tenderness and of passion. *International Journal of Psycho-Analysis, 30,* 225–230. (Original work published 1933)
Festinger, L. (1957). *A theory of cognitive dissonance*. Stanford University Press.
Festinger, L., Riecken, H. W., & Schachter, S. (1964). *When prophecy fails: A social and psychological study of a modern group that predicted the destruction of the world*. Harper Collins.
Fisher, R. A. (1930/1999) *The genetical theory of natural selection*. Edited by Henry Bennett. Oxford University Press.
Fisher, R. A. (1935). *The design of experiments*. Oliver.
Flavell, J. (1963). *The developmental psychology of Jean Piaget*. Van Nostrand.
Fleck, L. (1979). *Genesis and development of a scientific fact* (T. J. Trenn & R. K. Merton, Trans.). University of Chicago Press. (Original work published 1935)
Fodor, J. (1968). *Psychological explanation*. Random House.
Fodor, J. (1975). *The language of thought*. Random House.
Fodor, J. (1983). *The modularity of mind*. The MIT Press.
Fodor, J. (1985). Fodor's guide to mental representation: The intelligent auntie's vademecum. *Mind, 94,* 76–100.
Fodor, J. (1998). *In critical condition: Polemical essays on cognitive science and the philosophy of mind*. The MIT Press.
Fodor, J. (2000). *The mind doesn't work that way*. The MIT Press.
Fodor, J. (2008). Against Darwinism. *Mind and Language, 23,* 1–24.
Fodor, J., & Piattelli-Palmarini, M. (2010). *What Darwin got wrong*. Profile Books.
Fodor, J. A., & Pylyshyn, Z. W. (1988). Connectionism and cognitive architecture. *Cognition, 28,* 3–71.
Forster, K. I. (1999). The microgenesis of priming effects in lexical access. *Brain and Language, 68,* 5–15.
Foucault, M. (1970). *The order of things: An archeology of the human sciences*. Pantheon.
Foucault, M. (1978). *The history of sexuality: Vol. 1. An introduction* (R. Hurley, Trans.). Pantheon, Allen Lane. https://suplaney.files.wordpress.com/2010/09/foucault-the-history-of-sexuality-volume-1.pdf (Original work published 1976)
Foucault, M. (1988). *Technologies of the self*. University of Massachusetts Press.
Fox, D. R., & Prilleltensky, I. (Eds.). (1997). *Critical psychology: An introduction*. Sage.

Fraisse, P. (1988). *Pour la psychologie scientifique: histoire, théorie et pratique* [For a scientific psychology: History, theory, and practice]. Margada.
Fraser, C., Bellugi, U., & Brown, R. (1963). Control of grammar in imitation, comprehension, and production. *Journal of Verbal Learning and Verbal Behavior, 2,* 121–135.
Fraser, J., & Yasnitsky, A. (2015). Deconstructing Vygotsky's victimization narrative: A reexamination of the "Stalinist suppression" of Vygotskian theory. *History of the Human Sciences, 28,* 128–153.
Frege, G. (1892). Über Sinn und Bedeutung [On meaning and reference]. *Zeitschrift fuir Philosophie und philosophische Kritik, 100,* 25–50.
Freud, A. (1928). *Introduction to the technique of child analysis.* Nervous and Mental Diseases Publishing Co.
Freud, S. (1916). *Leonardo da Vinci* (A. A. Brill, Trans.). Moffat, Yard & Co. (Original work published 1910)
Freud, S. (1921). Group psychology and the analysis of the ego. In *The standard edition of the complete psychological works of Sigmund Freud, Volume XVIII (1920–1922)* (pp. 65–144). Hogarth Press.
Friederici, A. D. T. (2002). Towards a neural basis of auditory sentence processing. *Trends in Cognitive Sciences, 6,* 78–84.
Frisch, J. von. (1950). *Bees, their vision, chemical senses, and language.* Cornell University Press.
Frith, U. (2001) Mind blindness and the brain in autism. *Neuron, 32,* 969–979.
Frobenius, L. (1968). *The voice of Africa.* B. Blom. (Original work published 1933)
Fromm, E. (1941). *Escape from freedom.* Farrar & Rinehart.
Fromm, E. (1947). *Man for himself: An inquiry into the psychology of ethics.* Holt.
Fromm, E. (1956). *The art of loving.* Harper & Row.
Gadamer, H. G. (1983). Citizens of two worlds. In H. G. Gadamer (Ed.), *On education, poetry, and history: Applied hermeneutics.* State University of New York Press.
Gadamer, H. G. (1984). *Truth and method.* Crossroad.
Galperin, P. Y. (1969). Stages in the development of mental acts. A handbook of contemporary soviet psychology. In M. Cole & I. Maltzman (Eds.), *A handbook of contemporary soviet psychology* (pp. 249–273). Basic Books.
Galperin, P. Y. (1976). *Vvedenie v psihologiu* [Introduction to psychology]. Moscow State University.
Galperin, P. Y. (2009). Uchenie o pamjati [The study of memory]. *Kulturno-istoricheskaja Psichologia, 2,* 109–113. (Original work published 1938)
Gardner, H. (1983). *Frames of mind: The theory of multiple intelligences.* Basic Books.
Gardner, H. (1985). *The mind's new science: A history of the cognitive revolution.* Basic Books. The paperback edition of 1987 has a new epilogue: *Cognitive science after,* 1984.
Gardner, H. (1992). Scientific psychology: Should we bury it or praise it? *New Ideas in Psychology, 10,* 179–190.
Gardner, H. (2000). *Intelligence reframed: Multiple intelligences for the 21st century.* Basic Books.
Garfinkel, H. (1967). *Studies in ethnomethodology.* Prentice-Hall.
Gauld, A., & Stephenson, G. M. (1967). Some experiments related to Bartlett's theory of remembering. *British Journal of Psychology, 58,* 39–49.
Gaulin, J., & McBurney, F. (2001). *Psychology. An evolutionary approach.* Prentice-Hall.
Gazzaniga, M. S. (2013). Understanding layers: From neuroscience to human responsibility. Neurosciences and the human person: New perspectives on human activities. *Pontifical Academy of Sciences: Scripta Varia, 121,* 1–14.

Geldern, J. von. (1993). *Bolshevik festivals, 1917–1920*. University of California Press.

Gentner, D. (2010) Psychology in cognitive science: 1978–2038. *Topics in Cognitive Science 2*, 328–344.

Gergely, G., Bekkering, H., & Király, I. (2002). Rational imitation in preverbal infants. *Nature, 415*, 755.

Gergely, G., & Csibra, G. (2006). Sylvia's recipe: The role of imitation and pedagogy in the transmission of cultural knowledge. In S. Levenson & N. Enfield (Eds.), *Roots of human sociality: Culture, cognition, and human interaction* (pp. 229–255). Berg Publishers.

Gergely, G., Nádasdy, Z., Csibra, G., & Bíró S. (1995). Taking the intentional stance at 12 months of age. *Cognition, 56*, 165–193.

Gergen, K. (1973). Social psychology as history. *Journal of Personality and Social Psychology, 26*, 309–320.

Gergen, K. (1978). Experimentation in social psychology: A reappraisal. *European Journal of Social Psychology, 8*, 507–527.

Gergen, K. (1985). The social constructionist movement in modern psychology. *American Psychologist, 40*, 266–275.

Gergen, K. J., & Gergen, M. M. (Eds.). (1984). *Historical social psychology*. Erlbaum.

Gervain, J. (2014). Developmental science and the nature–nurture issue: The case of language. In C. Pléh, G. Csibra, G., & P. Richerdson (Eds.), *Naturalistic approaches to culture* (pp. 209–221), Akadémiai.

Gervain, J., & Mehler, J. (2010). Speech perception and language acquisition in the first year of life. *Annual Review of Psychology, 61*, 191–218.

Gesell, A. (1926). *Mental growth of the pre-school child*. MacMillan.

Geuter, U. (1992). *The professionalization of psychology in Nazi Germany*. Cambridge University Press.

Gibson, J. J. (1950). *The perception of the visual world*. Houghton Mifflin.

Gibson, J. J. (1960). The concept of stimulus in psychology. *American Psychologist, 15*, 694–703.

Gibson, J. J. (1966). *The senses considered as perceptual systems*. Houghton Mifflin.

Gibson, J. J. (1979). *The ecological approach to visual perception*. Houghton Mifflin.

Gigerenzer, G. (2000). *Adaptive thinking: Rationality in the real world*. Oxford University Press.

Gigerenzer, G. (2004). Mindless statistics. *The Journal of Socio-Economics, 33*, 587–606.

Ginneken, J. van. (1992). *Crowds, psychology, and politics. 1871–1899*. Cambridge University Press.

Goffman, E. (1959). *The presentation of self in everyday life*. Doubleday.

Goffman, E. (1974). *Frame analysis: An essay on the organization of experience*. Harper and Row.

Golden, C. J. (2004). The adult Luria-Nebraska neuropsychological battery. In G. Goldstein, S. R. Beers, & M. Hersen (Eds.), *Comprehensive handbook of psychological assessment, Vol. 1: Intellectual and neuropsychological assessment* (pp. 133–146). John Wiley & Sons Inc.

Goldstein, J. (1987). *Console and classify: The French psychiatric profession in the nineteenth century*. Cambridge University Press.

Goldstein, K. (1940). *Human nature in the light of psychopathology*. Harvard University Press.

Gombocz, Z. (1903). *Nyelvtörténet és lélektan. Wundt néplélektanának ismertetése* [Language history and psychology. A review of the Völkerpsychology of Wundt]. Athenaeum.

Goodale, M. A., & Milner, B. (1995). *The visual brain in action*. Oxford University Press.

Gopnik, A., Meltzoff, A. N., & Kuhl, P. K. (1999). *The scientist in the crib: What early learning tells us about the mind*. Morris.

Gopnik, M., & Crago, M. B. (1991). Familial aggregation of a developmental language disorder. *Cognition, 39*, 1–50.

Gould, S. J. (1981). *The mismeasure of man*. Norton.

Gould, S. J., & Lewontin, R. C. (1979). The sprandels of San Marco and the Panglossian paradigm: A critique of the adaptationist program. *Proceedings of the Royal Society, B205*, 581–598.

Grastyán, E. (1961). The significance of the earliest manifestations of conditioning in the mechanism of learning. In *Brain mechanisms and learning*. Blackwells.

Grastyán, E. (1967). A tanulás alapvető paradoxonai és idegélettani feloldásuk [Basic paradoxes of learning and their resolution by neurophysiology]. *Pedagógiai Szemle, 8*, 893–914.

Grastyán, E., & Buzsáky, G. (1979). The orienting-exploratory response hypothesis of discriminative conditioning. *Acta Neurobiologiae Experimentalis, 39*, 491–501.

Grastyán, E., Karmos, G., Vereczkey, L., & Kellényi, L. (1967) The hippocampal electrical correlates of the homeostatic regulation of motivation. *Electroencephalography and Clinical Neurophysiology, 21*, 34–53.

Greco, A. (2012). Cognitive science and cognitive sciences. *Journal of Cognitive Science, 13*, 471–485.

Green, C. D. (1992). Of immortal mythological beasts: Operationism in psychology. *Theory & Psychology, 2*(3), 291–320.

Green, C. D. (1996). Where did the word "cognitive" come from anyway? *Canadian Psychology, 37*, 31–39.

Greenfield, S. (2015). *Mind change: How digital technologies are leaving their mark on our brains*. Random House.

Greenspoon, J. (1955). The reinforcing effect of two spoken sounds on the frequency of two of responses. *The American Journal of Psychology, 68*, 409–441.

Greenwood, J. D. (1999). Understanding the "cognitive revolution" in psychology. *Journal of the History of the Behavioral Sciences, 35*, 1–22.

Greenwood, J. D. (2003). Wundt, *Völkerpsychologie*, and experimental social psychology. *History of Psychology, 6*, 70–88.

Greenwood, J. D. (2004). *The disappearance of the social in American social psychology*. Cambridge University Press.

Gregory, R. (1966). *Eye and brain: The psychology of seeing*. Weidenfeld and Nicolson.

Gregory, R., & Gombrich, E. (1973). *Illusion in nature and art*. Duckworth.

Grigorenko, E. L. (2018). Puzzled intelligence: Looking for missing pieces. In R. J. Sternberg (Ed.), *The nature of human intelligence* (pp. 152–166). Cambridge University Press.

Guilford, J. P. (1950). Creativity. *American Psychologist, 5*, 444–454.

Guilford, J. P. (1967). *The nature of human intelligence*. McGraw Hill.

Gurvitch, G. (1966). *Les Cadres sociaux de la connaissance* [The social frames of knowledge]. Presses Universitaires de la France.

Guthrie, E. R. (1935). *The psychology of learning*. Harper & Row. Revised edition 1960.

Guthrie, E. R. (1959). Association by contiguity. In S. Koch (Ed.), *Psychology: A study of a science* (Vol. 1, pp. 158–95). McGraw-Hill.

Gyáni, G. (2012). Changing relationship between collective memory and history writing. *Colloquia: Journal for Central European History, 19*, 128–44.

Győri, M. (2006). *Autism and cognitive architecture. Domain specificity and cognitive theorizing on autism*. Akadémiai.

Habermas, J. (1990). *Moral consciousness and communicative action*. The MIT Press. (Original work published 1983)
Haeckel, E. (1866). *Generelle Morphologie der Organismen* [General morphology of organisms]. Georg Reimer.
Haeckel, E. H. P. A. (2020). *The history of creation*. Routledge. (Original work published 1892)
Haggbloom, S. J., Warnick, R., Warnick, J. E., Jones, V. K., Yarbrough, G. L., Russell, T. M., Borecky, C. M., McGahhey, R., Powell, J. L., III, Beavers, J., & Monte, E. (2002). The 100 most eminent psychologists of the 20th century. *Review of General Psychology, 6,* 139–152.
Haidt, J. (2013). *The righteous mind: Why good people are divided by politics and religion*. Vintage Books.
Halbwachs, M. (1912). *La classe ouvrière et les niveaux de vie* [The working class and life standards]. Felix Alcan.
Halbwachs, M. (1918). La doctrine d'Émile Durkheim [The doctrine of d'Émile Durkheim]. *Revue Philosophique de la France et del'Étranger, 85,* 353–411.
Halbwachs, M. (1925). *Les cadres sociaux de la mémoire* [Social frames of memory]. Alcan.
Halbwachs, M. (1978). *The causes of suicide*. Free Press. (Original work published 1930)
Halbwachs, M. (1938). Individual psychology and collective psychology. *American Sociological Review, 3,* 615–623.
Halbwachs, M. (1939). Individual consciousness and collective mind. *American Journal of Sociology, 44,* 812–822.
Halbwachs, M. (1941). *La topographie légendaire des Évangiles en Terre Sainte: étude de mémoire collective* [The legendary topography of the Evangils on the Saint Land: A study of collective memory]. Presses Universitaires de France.
Halbwachs, M. (1950). *La mémoire collective* [Collective memory]. Presses Universitaires de France.
Halbwachs, M. (1968). *La mémoire collective* [Collective memory] (2nd ed.). Presses Universitaires de France.
Halbwachs, M. (1992). *On collective memory* (L. Coser, Trans.). University of Chicago Press. Translation of Halbwachs, 1925, and also includes some chapters of Halbwachs, 1941.
Hall, G. S. (1911). *Adolescence* (Vols. I–II). Appleton. http://psychclassics.asu.edu/Hall/Adolescence/chap17.htm
Hammond, K. R. (1966). *The psychology of Egon Brunswik*. Holt.
Harkai Schiller, P. (1940). *A lélektan feladata* [The task of psychology]. MTA.
Harkai Schiller, P. (1944). *Bevezetés a lélektanba. A cselekvés elemzése* [Introduction to psychology. The analysis of action]. MTA. Digital version: http://mtdaportal.extra.hu/books/schiller_pal_bevezetes_a_lelektanbaL.pdf.
Harlow, H., Harlow, M., & Meyer, D. (1950). Learning motivated by a manipulation drive. *Journal of Experimental Psychology, 40,* 228–234.
Harmat, P. (1987). Psychoanalysis in Hungary since 1933. *International Review of Psycho-Analysis, 14,* 503–508.
Harré, R. (1986). Social sources of mental content and order. In J. Margolis, P. T. Manicas, R. Harré, & P. F. Secord (Eds.), *Psychology: Designing the discipline* (pp. 91–127). Blackwell.
Harré, R. (1988). Wittgenstein and artificial intelligence. *Philosophical Psychology, 1,* 105–115.
Harré, R. (1990). Vygotsky and artificial intelligence: What could cognitive psychology possibly be about? *Midwest Studies in Philosophy, 15,* 389–399.

Harré, R., & Secord, P. F. (1972). *The explanation of social behaviour*. Blackwell.
Harrington, A. (1996). *Reenchanted science: Holism in German culture from Wilhelm II to Hitler*. Princeton University Press.
Harris, Z. (1951). *Methods in structural linguistics*. University of Chicago Press.
Hartmann, H. (1939). *Ego psychology and the problem of adaptation*. International Universities Press.
Harzing, A. W. (2011). *The publish or Perish book*. https://harzing.com/publications/publish-or-perish-book
Hatfield, G. (1995). Remaking the science of the mind. Psychology as natural science. In C. Fox, R. Porter, & R. Wokler (Eds.), *Inventing human science: Eighteenth-century domains* (pp. 184–270). University of Calfornia Press.
Hatfield, G. (2002). Psychology, philosophy and cognitive science: Reflections about the history and philosophy of experimental psychology. *Mind & Language, 17*, 207–232.
Hathaway, S. R., & McKinley, J. C. (1940). A multiphasic personality schedule (Minnesota). I. Construction of the schedule. *Journal of Psychology, 10*, 249–254.
Hauser, A. (1959). *The philosophy of art history*. Knopf.
Hauser, M. D., Chomsky, N., & Finch, W. D. (2002). The faculty of language: What is it, who has it, and how did it evolve? *Science, 298*, 1569–1579.
Head, H. (1920). *Studies in neurology, in two volumes*. Oxford University Press.
Hearnshaw, L. S. (1979). *Cyril Burt, psychologist*. Cornell University Press.
Hebb, D. O. (1949). *The organization of behavior*. Wiley.
Hebb, D. O. (1955) Drives and the C. N. S. (conceptual nervous system). *Psychological Review, 62*, 243–254.
Hebb, D. O. (1958). *A textbook of psychology*. Saunders.
Hebb, D. O. (1960). The American revolution. *American Psychologist, 15*, 735–745.
Heider, F. (1944). Social perception and phenomenal causality. *Psychological Review, 51*, 358–374.
Heider, F. (1958). *The psychology of interpersonal relations*. John Wiley & Sons.
Heider, F. (1983) *The life of a psychologist: An autobiography*. University of Kansas Press.
Heider, F., & Simmel, M. (1944). An experimental study of apparent behavior. *American Journal of Psychology, 57*, 243–259.
Heinroth, O., & Heinroth, M. (1958). *On birds*. Ann Arbor. (Original work published 1924–1934)
Held, R., & Hein, A. (1958). Adaptation of disarranged hand-eye coordination contingent upon re-afferent stimulation. *Perception & Motor Skills, 8*, 87–90.
Held, R., & Hein, A. (1963). Movement-produced stimulation in the development of visually guided behavior. *Journal of Comparative and Physiological Psychology, 56*, 872–876.
Hellpach, W. (1938). *Einführung in die Völkerpsychologie* [Introduction to folk psychology]. Enke.
Hempel, C. G. (1997). The logical analysis of psychology. In P. Morton (Ed.), *A historical introduction to the philosophy of mind*. Readings with commentary (pp. 164–173). Broadview Press. (Original work published 1935)
Hempel, C. G. (1954). A logical appraisal of operationism. *The Scientific Monthly, 79*, 215–220.
Hempel, C. G. (1965). *Aspects of scientific explanation*. Free Press.
Hermann, I. (1963). *Die Psychoanalyse als Methode* [Psychoanalysis as a method] (2nd ed.). Westdeutscher Verlag. (Original work published 1929)
Hermann, I. (1943). *Az ember ősi ösztönei* [The ancient insticts of man]. Pantheon.
Heron, W. (1957). The pathology of boredom. *Scientific American, 196*(1), 52–56.

Herrnstein, R. J. (1971). I.Q. *Atlantic Monthly, 228*(3), 43–64.
Herrnstein, R. J. (1973). *I.Q. in the meritocracy*. Little Brown.
Hick, W. E. (1952). On the rate of gain of information. *Quarterly Journal of Experimental Psychology, 4*, 11–26.
Hilgard, E. (1948). *Theories of learning*. Appleton.
Hilgard, E. (1962). The scientific status of psychoanalysis. In E. Nagel, P. Suppes, & A. Tarski (Eds.), *Logic, methodology and philosophy of science* (pp. 375–390). Stanford University Press.
Hilgard, E. R., & Marquis, D. M. (1940). *Conditioning and learning*. Appleton-Century-Crofts.
Himmelweit, H. T. (1980). Societal psychology: Implications and scope. In H. T. Himmelweit & G. Gaskell (Eds.), *Societal psychology* (pp. 17–45). Sage.
Hochberg, J. E. (1962). Nativism and empiricism in perception. In L. Postman (Ed.), *Psychology in the making* (pp. 255–330). Knopf.
Hofstadter, D. (1979). *Gödel, Escher, Bach: An eternal golden braid*. Basic Books.
Holst, E. von. (1937/1973). On the nature and order of central nervous system. In E. Holst, *Collected papers* (pp. 120–145). University of Miami Press.
Holt, J. (1915). *The Freudian wish and its place in ethics*. Holt. Electronic version http://ia700305.us.archive.org/24/items/freudianwishitsp007914mbp/freudianwishitsp007914mbp.pdf
Holt, J. (1931). *Animal drive and the learning process*. Holt.
Holt, R. R. (1964). Imagery: The return of the ostracized. *American Psychologist, 19*, 254–266.
Horney, K. (1937). *The neurotic personality of our time*. Norton.
Houdé, O., & Meljac, C. (Eds.). (2000). *L'esprit piagétien. Hommage international à Jean Piaget* [The Piagetian spirit. International respect of Jean Piaget]. Presses Universitaires de France.
House, J. S. (1977). The three faces of social psychology. *Sociometry, 40*, 161–177.
Hubel, D. H. & Wiesel, T. N. (1959). Receptive fields of single neurones in the cat's striate cortex. *The Journal of Physiology, 148*, 574–591. https://www.ncbi.nlm.nih.gov/pmc/articles/PMC1363130
Hull, C. L. (1920). Quantitative aspects of evolution of concepts: An experimental study. *Psychological Monographs, 28*(1), i-86.
Hull, C. L. (1935). The conflicting psychologies of learning. A way out. *Psychological Review, 42*, 491–516.
Hull, C. L. (1937). Mind, mechanism, and adaptive behavior. *Psychological Review, 44*, 1–32.
Hull, C. L. (1943). *Principles of behavior*. Appleton.
Hull, C. L. (1945). The place of innate individual and species differences in a natural-science theory of behavior. *Psychological Review, 52*(2), 55–60.
Hull, C. L. (1952). *A behavior system*. Yale University Press.
Hull, D. L., Langman, R. E., & Glenn, S. S. (2001). A general account of selection: Biology, immunology and behavior. *Behavioral and Brain Sciences, 24*, 511–573.
Humboldt, W. von. (1999). *On language. On the diversity of human language construction & its influence on the mental development of the human species* (M. Losonsky, Ed., P. Heath, Trans.) Cambridge University Press. (Original work published 1836)
Humphrey, N. K. (1976). The social function of intellect. In P. P. G. Bateson & R. A. Hinde (Eds.), *Growing points in ethology* (pp. 303–317). Cambridge University Press.
Hunt, E., & Agnoti, F. (1991). The Whorfian hypothesis: A cognitive psychology perspective. *Psychological Review, 98*, 377–389.
Hunt, J. M. (1961). *Intelligence and experience*. Ronald Press.

Hunt, J. M. (1969). Has compensatory education failed? Has it been attempted? *Harvard Educational Review*, *39*, 278–300.
Hunt, J. M. (1979). Psychological development: Early experience. *Annual Review of Psychology*, *30*, 103–143.
Hunyady, G. (2001). A nemzeti karakter talányos pszichológiája [The puzzling psychology of national character]. In G. Hunyady (Ed.), *Nemzetkarakterológiák: Rónay Jácint, Hugo Münsterberg és Kurt Lewin írásai* (pp. 7–50). Osiris Kiadó.
Hunyady, G. (2006). *A szociálpszichológia történeti olvasatai* [Historical readings of social psychology]. ELTE Eötvös Kiadó.
Husserl, E. (2010). *Logical investigations* (J. N. Findlay, Trans.). Routledge. (Original work published 1900–1901)
Husserl, E. (2002). Philosophy as a rigorous science. In Burt C. Hopkins, Steven Crowell (eds.). Routledge. *The new yearbook for phenomenology and phenomenological philosophy II* (pp. 249–295). (Original work published 1910)
Husserl, E. (1965). *Phenomenology and the crisis of philosophy* (Q. Lauer, Trans.). Harper and Row. (Original work published 1911)
Ivanov-Smolensky, A. G. (1933). *Metodika issledovania uslovnih refleksov u cheloveka* [Methods of studying conditioned reflexes in man]. Medgiz.
Ivanov-Smolensky, A. G. (1954). *Essays on the patho-physiology of the higher nervous activity*. Foreign Languages Publishing House.
Jablonka, E. (2006). *Evolution in four dimensions: Genetic, epigenetic, behavioral, and symbolic variation in the history of life*. The MIT Press.
Jablonka, E., & Lamb, M. J. (1995). *Epigenetic inheritance and evolution: The Lamarckian dimension*. Oxford University Press.
Jablonka, E., & Lamb, M. J. (2002). The changing concept of epigenetics. *Annals of the New York Academy of Sciences*, *981*, 82–96.
Jackson, H. J. (1884, March). Evolution and dissolution of the nervous system. Croonian lectures delivered at the Royal College of Physicians. *Lancet*, 555–558, 649–652, 739–744.
Jacob, F. (1977). Evolution and tinkering. *Science*, *196*, 1161–1166.
Jacob, F. (1982). *The possible and the actual*. University of Washington Press.
Jaensch, E. R. (1930). *Eidetic imagery and typological methods of investigation*. Harcourt Brace.
Jaensch, E. R. (1933). Die Lage und die Aufgaben der Psychologie, ihre Sendung in der deutschen Bewegung und an der Kulturwende [The position and problems of psychology; its mission in the German movement and at the new cultural turning-point]. In *Zeitschrift für Psychologie und Physiologie der Sinnesorgane* (Abt. 1). Supplement. Also as a separate book.
Jaensch, E. R. (1934). Der Gegentypus der deutschen völkischen Bewegung [The countertype against the German national movement]. *Bericht über den Kongress der Deutschen Gesellschaft für Psychologie*, *13*, 56–58.
Jaensch, E. R. (1937). Wege und Ziele der Psychologie in Deutschland [Ways and goals of psychology in Germany]. *The American Journal of Psychology*, *50*, 1–22.
Jaensch, E. R. (1939). Der Hühnerhof als Forschungs- und Aufklärungsmittel in menschlichen Rassenfragen [The chicken yard as a research and explanation tool of the human race question]. *Zeitschrift für Tierpsychologie*, *2*, 223–258.
Jahoda, G. (1993). *Crossroads between culture and mind: Continuities and change in theories of human nature*. Harvard University Press.
Jahoda, G. (2000). Piaget and Lévy-Bruhl. *History of Psychology*, *3*, 218–238.

Jahoda, G. (2007). *A history of social psychology: From the eighteenth-century enlightenment to the Second World War*. Cambridge University Press.
Jaisson, M., Marcel, J-C., Martzion, O., Muchielli, L., Steinmer, P., & Topalov, C. (Eds.). (1999). *Maurice Halbwachs et les sciences humaines de son temps* [M. Halbwachs and the human sciences of his time]. Presses Universitaires de Septentrion.
Jakobson, R. (1968). *Child language: Aphasia and phonological universals*. Mouton. (Original work published 1941)
Jakobson, R. (1960). Closing statement: Linguistics and poetics. In T. Sebeok (Ed.), *Style in language* (pp. 350–377). The MIT Press.
James, W. (1890). *Principles of psychology*. Holt. http://www.bahaistudies.net/asma/principlesofpsychology.pdf or https://archive.org/details/theprinciplesofp01jameuoft/page/n6/mode/2up
Janet, P. (1920). *The major symptoms of hysteria* (2nd ed., with New Matter). Macmillan.
Janet, P. (1923). *De l'angoisse a l'extase* [From anxiety to extasis]. Alcan.
Janet, P. (1928). *L'évolution de la mémoire* [The evolution of memory]. Flammarion.
Janet, P. (1930). The autobiography of Pierre Janet. In C. Murchison (Ed.), *A history of psychology in autobiography* (Vol. I, pp. 123–133). Clark University Press. Electronic version in Greeen *Classics* . . .
Janet, P. (1936). *L'intelligence avant le langage* [Intelligence before language]. Flammarion.
Janet, P. (1994). Les troubles de la personnalité sociale [Troubles of social personality]. *Bulletin de Psychologie, 414,* 156–183. (Original work published 1937)
Janis, I. L. (1972). *Victims of groupthink: A psychological study of foreign-policy decisions and fiascoes*. Houghton Mifflin.
Jeannerod, M. (1994). The representing brain neural correlates of motor intention and imagery. *Behavioral and Brain Sciences, 17,* 187–246.
Jeannerod, M. (2004). La création de l'Institut des sciences cognitives du CNRS (1992–1998) [The creation of the institute of cognitive science at CNRS]. *La Revue pour l'histoire du CNRS, 10,* 16–22.
Jeannerod, M., & Jacob, P. (2005). Visual cognition: A new look at the two-visual systems model. *Neuropsychologia, 43,* 301–312.
Jennings, H. S. (1906). *Behavior of the lower organisms*. Columbia University Press.
Jensen, A. R. (1969). How much can we boost IQ and scholastic achievement? *Harvard Educational Review, 39,* 1–123.
Jensen, A. R. (1998). *The g factor: The science of mental ability*. Greenwood.
Jensen, A. R., & Rohwer, W. D. (1963). Verbal mediation in paired-associate and serial learning. *Journal of Verbal Learning and Verbal Behavior, 1,* 346–352.
Jerne, N. K. (1985). The generative grammar of the immune system. *Science, 229,* 1957–1959.
John-Steiner, V. (1997). *Notebooks of the mind: Explorations of thinking* (Rev. ed.). Oxford University Press.
Johnson, D., & Erneling, C. E. (Eds.). (1997). *The future of the cognitive revolution*. Oxford University Press.
Johnston, E. (2001). The repeated reproduction of Bartlett's *Remembering*. *History of Psychology, 4,* 341–366.
Jones, E. (1910). The Œdipus-complex as an explanation of Hamlet's mystery: A study in motive. *The American Journal of Psychology, 21,* 72–113.
Joravsky, D. (1977). The mechanical spirit: The Stalinist marriage of Pavlov to Marx. *Theory and Society, 4,* 457–477.
Joravsky, D. (1987). L. S. Vygotskii: The muffled deity of Soviet psychology. In M. G. Ash & W. R. Woodward (Eds.), *Psychology in twentieth-century thought and society* (pp. 189–211). Cambridge University Press.

Joravsky, D. (1989). *Russian psychology: A critical history*. Blackwell.
Joravsky, D. (1992). Comparative psychology in Russia. *International Journal of Comparative Psychology, 6*, 56–62.
Jost, T., & Kruglanski, A. W. (2002). The estrangement of social constructionism and experimental social psychology: History of the rift and prospects for reconciliation. *Personality and Social Psychology Review, 6*, 168–187.
Jovanovic, G., Allolio-Näcke, L., & Ratner, C. (Eds.). (2019). *The challenges of cultural psychology: Historical legacies and future responsibilities*. Routledge.
Jovchelovitch, S. (1996). In defence of representations. *Journal for the Theory of Social Behaviour, 26*, 121–135.
Jung, C. G. (1917). *Psychology of the unconscious*. Moffat. https://ia700402.us.archive.org/23/items/psychologyuncon00junggoog/psychologyuncon00junggoog.pdf
Jung, C. G. (1923). *Psychological types*. Pantheon.
Jung, C. G., & Kerényi, C. (1969). *Essays on a science of mythology: The myth of the divine child and the mysteries of Eleusis*. Princeton University Press. (Original work published 1941)
Jung, K. (1910). The association method. *American Journal of Psychology, 21*, 219–269.
Kagan, J. S. (1969). Inadequate evidence and illogical conclusions. *Harvard Educational Review, 39*, 274–277.
Kagan, J. S. (1994). *Galen's prophecy: Temperament in human nature*. Basic Books.
Kahneman, D. (1973). *Attention and effort*. Academic Press.
Kahneman, D. (2003). Maps of bounded rationality: Psychology for behavioral economics. *The American Economic Review, 93*, 1449–1475.
Kahneman, D. (2011). *Thinking fast and slow*. Farrar, Strauss and Girow.
Kahneman, D., & Tversky, A. (1973). On the psychology of prediction, *Psychological Review, 80*, 237 251.
Kail, M., & Vermè, G. (Eds.). (1999). *La psychologie des peuples et ses dérives* [Folk psychology and its derivatives]. Centre National de Documentation Pedagogique.
Kandel, E. R. (2001). The molecular biology of memory storage: A dialogue between genes and synapses. *Science, 294*, 1030–1038.
Kandel, E. R. (2006). *In search of memory: The emergence of a new science of mind*. Norton.
Kandel, E. R. (2009). The biology of memory: A forty-year perspective. *Journal of Neurosciences, 29*(41), 12748–12756.
Kandel, E. R. (2012). *The age of insight: The quest to uderstand the unconsious in art, mind, and brain, from Vienna 1900 to the present*. Random House.
Kandel, E. R., & Mack, S. (2003). A parallel between radical reductionism in science and art. *Annals of the New York Academy of Sciences, 1001*, 272–294.
Kandel, E. R., & Squire, L. R. (2009). *Memory: From mind to molecules* (2nd ed.). Scientific American.
Kapás, I. (2020). *Pszichoanalízis, ideológia, társadalom* [Psychoanalysis, ideology, society]. Oriold.
Karady, V. (1976). Durkheim, les sciences sociales et l'Université: bilan d'un semi-échec [Durkheim, social sciences and the university: Survey of half a century]. *Revue française de sociologie, 17*(2), 267–311.
Kardos, L. (1960). *Die Grudfragen der Psychologie und die Forshungem Pawlow's*. Akadémiai.
Kardos, L. (1988). *Az állati emlékezet* [Animal memory]. Akadémiai.
Kardos, L., Da Pos, O., Dellantonio, A., & Saviolo, N. (1978). Discrimination learning and visual memory. *Italian Journal of Psychology, 5*, 101–133.

Karmiloff-Smith, A. (1981). *A functional approach to child language: A study of determiners and reference*. Cambridge University Press.
Karmiloff-Smith, A. (1992). *Beyond modularity*. The MIT Press.
Karmiloff-Smith, A. (1998). Development itself is a key to understanding developmental disorders. *Trends in Cognitive Sciences, 2*, 389–398.
Kashima, Y. (2000). Recovering Bartlett's social psychology of cultural dynamics. *European Journal of Social Psychology, 30*, 383–403.
Katona, G. (1951). *Psychological analysis of economic behavior*. McGraw-Hill.
Katz, J. J., & Fodor, J. A. (1963). The structure of a semantic theory. *Language, 39*, 170–210.
Kees-Jan, K., Wicherts, J. M., Dolan, C. V., & van der Maas, H. L. J. (2013). On the nature and nurture of intelligence and specific cognitive abilities: The more heritable, the more culture dependent. *Psychological Science, 24*, 2420–2428.
Kelley, H. H. (1967). Attribution theory in social psychology. In D. Levine (Ed.), *Nebraska symposium on motivation* (Vol. 15, pp. 192–238). University of Nebraska Press.
Kelley, H. H. (1992). Common-sense psychology and scientific psychology. *Annual Review of Psychology, 43*, 1–23.
Kendler, H. (1999). The role of value in the world of psychology. *American Psychologist, 54*, 828–835.
Kendler, H. H., & Kendler, T. S. (1962). Vertical and horizontal processes in problem solving. *Psychological Review, 69*, 1–16.
Kéri, S., & Gulyás, B. (2003). Four facets of a single brain: Behaviour, cerebral blood flow/metabolism, neuronal activity and neurotransmitter dynamics. *Neuroreport, 14*, 1097–1106.
Kesserling, T. (1994). A comparison between evolutionary and genetic epistemologies or: Jean Piaget's contribution to post-Darwinian epistemology. *Journal for General Philosophy of Science, 25*, 293–325.
Ketellar, D., & Ellis, W. (2000). Are evolutionary explanations unfalsifiable? *Psychological Inquiry, 11*, 1–6.
Key, E. (1900). *The century of the child*. Putnam's Sons.
Kimble, G. A. (1984). Psychology's two cultures. *American Psychologist, 39*, 833–839.
Kimble, G. A. (2005a). Functional behaviorism: A plan for unity in psychology. *American Psychologist, 54*, 981–988.
Kimble, G. A. (2005b). Paradigm lost, paradigm regained: Toward unity in psychology. In R. Sternberg (Ed.), *Annual convention of the American Psychological Association* (pp. 91–106). American Psychological Association.
Kinsey, A., Pomeroy, W., & Martin, C. (1948). *Sexual behavior in the human male*. Saunders.
Kinsey, A., Pomeroy, W., Martin, C., & Gebhard, P. (1953). *Sexual behavior in the human female*. Saunders.
Kintsch, N. (1974). *The representation of meaning in memory*. Erlbaum.
Kintsch, W. (1978). Comprehension and memory of text. In W. K. Estes (Ed.), *Handbook of learning and cognitive processes* (Vol. 6, pp. 57–58). Erlbaum.
Kintsch, W. (1998). *Comprehension: A paradigm for cognition*. Cambridge University Press.
Kintsch, W., & Mangalath, P. (2011). The construction of meaning. *Topics in Cognitive Science, 3*, 346–370.
Kitchener, R. F. (1986). *Piaget's theory of knowledge: Genetic epistemology and scientific reason*. Yale University Press.
Kitchener, R. F. (1991). Jean Piaget: The unknown sociologist? *The British Journal of Sociology, 42*, 421–442.

Kitchin, R. (2014). *The data revolution: Big data, open data, data infrastructures and their consequences*. Sage.

Klages, L. (1929). *The science of character*. Allen and Unwin.

Klautke, E. (2013). *The mind of the nation: Völkerpsychologie in Germany, 1851–1955*. Berghahn.

Klein, M. (1921/1975). *Love, guilt and reparation and other works 1921–1945: The writings of Melanie Klein* (Vol. 1). Hogarth Press.

Klix, F. (1971). *Information und Verhalten. Kybernetische Aspekte der organismischen Informationsverarbeitung* [Information and behavior. Cybernetic aspects of organismic information processing]. Huber.

Klix, F., & Hagendorf, H. (Eds.). (1985). *Human memory and cognitive capabilities: Mechanisms and performances: Symposium in Memoriam Hermann Ebbinghaus 1885*. North-Holland.

Klix, F., & Hoffmann, J. (1980). *Cognition and memory*. North Holland.

Koch, S. (Ed.). (1959–1963). *Psychology: A study of a science* (Vols. 1–6). McGraw-Hill.

Koch, S. (1961). Psychological science versus the science-humanism antinomy: Intimations of a significant science of man. *American Psychologist, 16*, 629–639.

Koch, S. (1964). Psychology and emerging conceptions of knowledge as unitary. In T. W. Wann (Ed.), *Behaviorism and phenomenology: Contrasting bases for modern psychology* (pp. 1–41). University of Chicago Press.

Koch, S. (1969). Psychology cannot be a coherent science. *Psychology Today, 14*(3), 64–68.

Koch, S. (1985). The nature and limits of psychological knowledge: Lessons of a century qua 'science'. In S. Koch & D. Leary (Eds.), *A century of psychology as science* (pp. 75–99). McGraw-Hill.

Koch, S. (1999). *Psychology in human context: Essays in dissidence and reconstruction*. University of Chicago Press.

Koffka, K. (1935). *Principles of Gestalt psychology*. Harcourt.

Kohlberg, L. (1971). *From is to ought: How to commit the naturalistic fallacy and get away with it in the study of moral development*. Academic Press.

Kohlberg, L. (1981–1984). *Essays on moral development (Vols. 1–2)*. Harper & Row.

Kohlberg, L., Yaeger, J., & Hjerthholm, E. (1968). Private speech: Four studies and a review of theories. *Child Development, 39*, 691–736.

Köhler, W. (1925). *The mentality of apes*. Penguin. (Original work published 1921)

Konorski, J. (1948). *Conditioned reflexes and neuron organization*. Cambridge University Press.

Konorski, J., & Miller, S. (1937). On two types of conditioned reflex. *Journal of General Psychology, 16*, 264–272.

Kornilov, K. N. (1921). *Uchenie of reakcijah cheloveka s psichologicheskoj tochki zrenia* ("reaktologia") [A theory of human reactions from a psychological point of view]. Ogiz.

Kornilov, K. N. (1923). Psihologia is Marxism [Psychology and Marxism]. *Pod Znamenem Marxizma, 1*.

Kornilov, K. N. (1930). Psychology in the light of dialectic materialism. In *Psychologies of 1930* (pp. 243–278). Clark University Press.

Kornilov, K. N. (1955). O zadachakh sovetskoĭ psikhologii [On the tasks of Soviet psychology]. *Voprosy Psychologii, 1*(4), 16–28.

Kornilov, K. N. (1957). Printsipy izucheniia psikhologii lichnosti sovetskogo cheloveka [Principles of studying the personality of Soviet people]. *Voprosy Psychologii, 3*, 131–141.

Kosslyn, S. M. (1980). *Image and mind*. Harvard University Press.

Kosslyn, S. M. (1994). *Image and brain: The resolution of the imagery debate*. The MIT Press.
Kosslyn, S. M., & Pomerantz, J. R. (1977). Imagery, propositions and the form of internal representations. *Cognitive Psychology, 9*, 52–76.
Kostyleff, N. (1911). *La crise de la psychologie expérimentale: le présent et l'avenir* [The crisis of experimental psychology: The present and the future]. Alcan.
Kovács, Á. M., Téglás, E., & Endress, A. D. (2010). The social sense: Susceptibility to others' beliefs in human infants and adults. *Science, 330*, 1830–1834.
Kovács, I. (2004). *Visual integration: Development and impairments*. Akadémiai
Kovács, K., & Conway, A. R. A. (2016). Process overlap theory: A unified account of the general factor of intelligence. *Psychological Inquiry*, (3), 151–177.
Kovács, K., & Pléh, C. (2023). William Stern: The relevance of his program of 'Differential Psychology' for contemporary intelligence measurement and research. *Journal of Intelligence, 11*, 41. https://doi.org/10.3390/jintelligence11030041
Kozulin, A. (1982). Peter Blonsky and Russian progressivism: The early years. *Studies in Soviet Thought, 24*, 11–21.
Kozulin, A. (1984). *Psychology in Utopia: Toward a social history of Soviet psychology*. The MIT Press
Kozulin, A. (1985). Georgy Chelpanov and the establishment of the Moscow institute of psychology. *Journal of the History of the Behavioral Sciences, 21*, 23–32.
Kramer, R. (1995). The birth of client-centered therapy: Carl Rogers, Otto Rank, and "the beyond". *Journal of Humanistic Psychology, 35*, 54–110.
Krasner, L. (1958). Studies of the conditioning of verbal behavior. *Psychological Bulletin, 55*, 148–170.
Krech, D., Crutchfield, R., & Ballachey, E. S. (1962). *The individual in society: A textbook of social psychology*. McGraw-Hill.
Krech, D., Rosenzweig, M. R., Bennett, E. L. (1960). Effects of environmental complexity and training on brain chemistry. *Journal of Comparative and Physiological Psychology, 53*, 509–519.
Krechevsky, I. (1932). 'Hypotheses' in rats. *Psychological Review, 39*, 516–532.
Kretschmer, E. (1925). *Physique and character*. Kegan Paul.
Kruglanski, A. W., & Stroebe, W. (Eds.). (2012). *Handbook of the history of social psychology*. Psychology Press.
Kuhn, T. (1962). *The structure of scientific revolutions*. University of Chicago Press.
Kuhn, T. (1970). *The structure of scientific revolutions* (2nd English ed.). University of Chicago Press.
Külpe, O. (1912). Über die moderne Psychologie des Denkens [On the modern psychology of thinking]. *Internationale Monatsschrift für Wissenschaft, Kunst und Technik, 6*, 1069–1110.
Kundera, M. (1986). *The art of the novel*. Grove Press.
Kuo, Z. Y. (1921). Giving up instincts in psychology. *The Journal of Philosophy, 24*, 645–664.
Kuo, Z. Y. (1924). A psychology without heredity. *Psychological Review, 31*, 427–448.
Kutas, M. (1993). In the company of other words: Electrophysiological evidence for single-word and sentence context effects. *Language and Cognitive Processes, 8*, 533–557.
Lacan, J. (1977). *The four fundamental concepts of psycho-analysis*. Norton. https://archive.org/details/EbooksclubEbooksclub.orgTheFourFundamentalConceptsOfPsychoanalysisTheSeminarOfJacquesLacanBook11
Lachman, R., Lachman, J. L., & Butterfield, E. R. C. (1979). *Cognitive psychology and information processing: An introduction*. Erlbaum.

Laffal, J. (1955). Response faults in word association as a function of response entropy. *Journal of Abnormal and Social Psychology, 50,* 265–270.
Lagache, D. (1949). *L'unité de la psychologie* [The unity of psychology]. PUF.
Lagache, D. (1993). *The work of Daniel Lagache.* Karnac Books.
Lai, C. S. L., Fisher, S. E., Hurst, J. A., Vargha-Khadem, F., & Monaco, A. P. (2001). A forkhead-domain gene is mutated in a severe speech and language disorder. *Nature, 413,* 519–523.
Laing, R. D. (1960). *The divided self: An existential study in sanity and madness.* Penguin.
Laing, R. D. (1961). *The self and others.* Tavistock Publications.
Lamiell, J. T. (2003). *Beyond individual and group differences: Human individuality, scientific psychology, and William Stern's critical personalism.* Sage.
Lamiell, J. T. (2012) Introducing William Stern (1871–1938). *History of Psychology, 15,* 379–384.
Lamiell, J. T. (2020). William Stern (1871–1938), eclipsed star of early 20th century psychology. In *Oxford research encyclopedia of psychology.* Oxford University Press. http://dx.doi.org/10.1093/acrefore/9780190236557.013.523
Landau, B., & Jackendoff, R. (1993). 'What' and 'Where' in spatial language and spatial cognition. *Behavioral and Brain Sciences, 16,* 217–265.
LaPiere, R. T. (1934). Attitudes vs. actions. *Social Forces, 13,* 230–237.
Lashley, K. S. (1923). The behavioristic interpretation of consciousness. *Psychological Review, 30,* 237–272, 329–353.
Lashley, K. S. (1929). *Brain mechanisms and intelligence.* University of Chicago Press.
Lashley, K. S. (1938). Experimental analysis of instinctive behavior. *Psychological Review, 45,* 445–471.
Lashley, K. S. (1950). In search of the engram. In J. F. Danielli & R. Brown (Eds.), *Society of experimental biology symposium, no. 4: Psychological mechanisms in animal behavior* (pp. 454–482). Academic Press.
Lashley, K. S. (1951). The problem of serial order in behavior. In L. A. Jeffres (Ed.), *Cerebral mechanisms in behavior* (pp. 112–136). Wiley.
László, J. (2004). Narrative psychology's contribution to the second cognitive revolution. *Journal of Cultural and Evolutionary Psychology, 2,* 337–354.
László, J. (2008). *The science of stories.* Routledge.
László, J., & Wagner, W. (Eds.). (2003). *Theories and controversies in societal psychology.* New Mandate.
Latour, B. (1987). *Science in the making.* Harvard University Press.
Latour, B. (1993). *We have never been modern.* Harvester.
Latour, B. (2005). *Reassembling the social: An introduction to actor-network-theory.* Oxford University Press.
Laubichler, M. D., & Maienschein, J. (Eds.). (2007). *From embryology to Evo-Devo: A history of developmental evolution.* The MIT Press.
Lavabre, M-C. (2000). Usages et mésusages de la notion de mémoire [Uses and misuses of the concept of memory]. *Critique Internationale, 7,* 48–57.
Lazarsfeld, P. F. (1959). Amerikanische Beobachtungen eines Bühler-Schülers [American observations of a Bühler student]. *Zeitschrift für Experimentelle und Angewandte Psychologie, 6,* 69–76.
Lazarus, M., & Steinthal, H. (1860). Einleitende Gedanken über Völkerpsychologie [Introductory thoughts on Völkerpsychologie]. *Zeitschrift für Völkerpsychologieu und Sprachwissenschaft, 1,* 1–73.
Leary, D. E. (1980). One hundred years of experimental psychology: An American perspective. *Psychological Research, 42*(Wundt Centennial Issue), 175–189.

Le Bon, G. (1894). *Les Lois psychologiques de l'evolution des peuples* [Psychological laws on the evolution of people]. Alcan.
Le Bon, G. (1903). *The crowd* (4th Impression). Unwin.
Lenin, V. I. (1972). *Materialism and empirio-criticism*. Progress Publishing House. *Lenin collected works* (Vol. 14, pp. 17–362). https://www.marxists.org/archive/lenin/works/1908/mec/index.htm (Original work published 1909)
Lenin, V. I. (1976). *Philosophical notebooks*. In *Collected works* (Vol. 38). Progress Publishing House. (Original work published 1929)
Lenneberg, E. H. (1967). *Biological foundations of language*. Wiley.
Le Ny, J-F. (1961). *Le conditionnement* [Conditioning]. Presses Universitaires de France.
Le Ny, J.-F. (1975). *Le conditionnement et l'apprentissage* [Conditioning and learning]. Presses Universitaires de France.
Le Ny, J-F. (1979). *La sémantique psychologique* [Psychological semantics]. Presses Universitaires de France.
Le Ny, J.-F., & Kintsch, W. (Eds.). (1982). *Language and comprehension*. North Holland.
Leontiev, A. N. (1932). Studies in the cultural development of the child: III. The development of voluntary attention in the child. *Journal of Genetic Psychology, 40*, 52–81.
Leontiev, A. N. (1981). *Problems of the development of the mind*. Progress Publishing House. https://www.marxists.org/admin/books/activity-theory/leontyev/development-mind.pdf (Original work published 1959)
Leontiev, A. N. (1978). *Activity, consciousness, and personality*. Prentice-Hall. https://www.marxists.org/archive/leontev/works/activity-consciousness.pdf
Leontiev, A. N. (2005). Oral autobiographic note. In A. A. Leontiev, D. A. Leontiev, & E. E. Sokolova (Eds.), *Aleksej Nikolajevich Leontiev. Dejatelnost, soznanie, lichnost* [A.N. Leontiev. Activity, consciousness, personality] (pp. 367–385). Smysl.
Le Rider, J. (1992). Viennese modernity and crises of identity. *Psychohistory Review, 21*, 73–106.
Leslie, A. (1987). Pretense and representation: The origins of the "theory of mind". *Psychological Review, 94*, 412–426.
Lessing, H-U. (2004). Le rapport critique der Dilthey a la *Völkerpsychologie* de Lazarus et Steinthal [Dilthey's critical relation to the *Völkerpsychologie* of Lazarus and t Steinthal]. In C. Trautmann-Waller (Ed.), *Quand Berlin pensait les peuples: anthropologie, ethnologie et psychologie 1850–1890* [When Berlin thought of people: Anthropology, ethnology and psychology 1850–1890] (pp. 149–164). CNRS.
Levelt, W. J. M. (1989). *Speaking: From intention to articulation*. The MIT Press.
Levelt, W. J. M. (2013). *A history of psycholinguistics: The pre-Chomskyan area*. Oxford University Press.
Levinson, S. C. (1996). Language and space. *Annual Review of Anthropology, 25*, 353–382.
Lévi-Strauss, C. (1949). *Les structures élémentaires de la parenté* [Elementary structures of family]. Presses Universitaires de France.
Lévi-Strauss, C. (1958). *Anthropologie structurale* [Structural anthropology]. Plon.
Lévi-Strauss, C. (1966). *The savage mind*. University of Chicago Press.
Lévy-Bruhl, L. (1922). *The mentality of primitive people*. Allen and Unwin. (Original work blished 1910)
Lévy-Bruhl, L. (1949). *Les Carnets de Lucien Lévy-Bruhl* [Notebooks of Lévy-Bruhl] (M. Leenhardt, Ed.). Presses Universitaires de France.
Lewin, K. (1926). *Vorsatz, Wille und Bedurfnis (mit Vorbemerkungen uber die psychische Krafte und Energien und die Struktur der Seele)* [Intention, volition, and need. With preliminary remarks about mental strength and anargy and the struxture of the mind] Springer.

Lewin, K. (1931). The conflict between Aristotelian and Galileian modes of thought in contemporary psychology. *Journal of General Psychology, 5,* 141–177.
Lewin, K. (1935). *A dynamic theory of personalty.* McGraw Hill.
Lewin, K. (1951). *Field theory in social science.* Harper.
Lewin, K., Lippitt, R., & White, R. K. (1939). Patterns of aggressive behavior in experimentally created social climates. *Journal of Social Psychology, 10,* 271–299.
Likert, R. (1932). A technique for the measurement of attitudes. *Archives of Psychology, 140,* 1–55.
Lilienfeld, S. O. (2011). Public skepticism of psychology: Why many people perceive the study of human behavior as unscientific. *American Psychologist, 66,* 1–19.
Lindholm, G. (1992). Charisma, crowd psychology and altered states of consciousness. *Culture, Medicine and Psychiatry, 16,* 287–310.
Lindner, G. (1871). *Ideen zur Psychologie der Gesellschaft als Grundlage der Sozialwissenschaft* [Ideas about the psychology of society as the foundation of social science]. Herold.
Lindsay, P. H., & Norman, D. (1977). *Human information processing: An introduction to psychology* (2nd ed.). Academic Press.
Lindzey, G. (Ed.). (1954). *Handbook of social psychology.* Addison-Wesley.
Lindzey, G., & Aaronson, E. (Eds.). (1968). *Handbook of social psychology* (3rd ed.). Addison-Wesley.
Lippman, W. (1922). "The mental age of Americans," "The mystery of the 'a' men," "The reliability of intelligence tests," "The abuse of the tests," "Tests of hereditary intelligence," "A future for the tests". *New Republic, 32,* 213–215, 246–248, 275–277, 297–298, 328–330, and *33,* 9–11.
Lodge, D. (2002). *Consciousness and the novel.* Penguin Books.
Loeb, J. (1993). *Comparative physiology of the brain and comparative psychology.* Routledge. http://ia600304.us.archive.org/22/items/comparativephysi00loeb/comparativephysi00loeb.pdf (Original work published 1900)
Loeb, J. (1912). *The mechanistic conception of life.* University of Chicago Press. New edition Harvard University Press, 1964.
Loftus, E. (1975). Leading questions and the eyewitness report. *Cognitive Psychology, 7,* 560–572.
Lombroso, C. (1891). *The man of genius.* Walter Scott.
Lombroso, C. (1911). *Crime: Its causes and remedies.* Little, Brown, and Company.
Lo Monaco, G., Delouvée, S., & Rateau, P. (Eds.). (2016). *Les représentations sociales. Théories, méthodes et applications* [Social representations. Theory, methods, and applications]. DeBoeck.
Lorenz, K. (1962). Kant's doctrine of the a priori in the light of contemporary biology. In L. von Bertalanffy & A. Rapoport (Eds.), *General systems: Yearbook of the society for general systems research* (Vol. VII, pp. 23–35). Society for General Systems Research. (Original work published 1941)
Lorenz, K. (1942). Induktive und teleologische Psychologie. *Die Naturwissenschaften, 30*(9–10), 133–143.
Lorenz, K. (1965). *Evolution and modification of behavior.* University of Chicago Press.
Lorenz, K. (1966). *On aggression.* Methuen.
Lorenz, K. (1970). *Studies in animal and human behaviour.* Harvard University Press,
Lorenz, K. (1996). *The natural science of the human species: An introduction to comparative research: The "Russian manuscript" (1944–1948).* The MIT Press.
Lubek, I. (1993). Some reflections on various social psychologies, their histories and historiographies. *Sociétés contemporaines, La psychologie sociale et ses histoires, 13,* 33–56.

Luce, R. D., Bush, R. R., & Galanter, E. (Eds.). (1963). *Handbook of mathematical psychology* (Vols. I–III). Wiley.
Luria, A. R. (1977). Psychoanalysis as a system of monistic psychology. *Soviet Psychology, 16*(2), 7–45. (Original work published 1925)
Luria, A. R. (1928). Psychology in Russia. *The Pedagogical Seminary and Journal of Genetic Psychology, 35*, 347–355.
Luria, A. R. (1932). *The nature of human conflicts* (2nd ed.). Liveright, Grove Press.
Luria, A. R. (1933). The second psychological expedition to Central Asia. *Science, 78*, 191–192.
Luria, A. R. (1961). *The role of speech in the regulation of normal and abnormal behavior*. Pergamon Press.
Luria, A. R. (1965). L.S. Vygotsky and the problem of localization of functions. *Neuropsychologia, 3*, 387–392.
Luria, A. R. (1966a). *Higher cortical function in man*. Basic Books.
Luria, A. R. (1966b). XVIII international congress of psychology. *American Psychologist, 21*, 747–753.
Luria, A. R. (1968). *The mind of a mnemonist*. Basic Books.
Luria, A. R. (1970). *Traumatic aphasia*. Mouton.
Luria, A. R. (1973). *The working brain: An introduction to neuropsychology*. Basic Books.
Luria, A. R. (1974). Scientific perspectives and philosophical dead ends in modern linguistics. *Cognition, 4*, 374–385.
Luria, A. R. (1987). *The man with a shattered world: The history of a brain wound*. Harvard University Press.
Luria, A. R. (2003). *Psihologicheskoe nasledie. Izbrannie trudi po obschej psichologii* [Psychological heritage. Selected works in general psychology]. Smysl.
Luria, A. R. (2010). *The making of mind*. Harvard University Press. A new politically corrected edition in 2010 *The autobiography of Alexander Luria*. Psychology Press. (Original work published 1979)
Luria, A. R., & Vinogradova, O. S. (1959). An objective investigation of the dynamics of semantic systems. *British Journal of Psychology, 50*(2), 89–105.
Luria, A. R., & Vygotsky, L. S. (1992). *Ape, primitive man, and the child: Essays in the history of behavior*. Harvester. (Original work published 1930)
Luria, A. R., & Yudovich, F. (1959). *Speech and the development of mental processes in the child*. Staples.
Maccoby, E. E., & Jacklin, C. N. (1974). *The psychology of sex differences*. Stanford University Press.
Maccoby, E. E., Newcomb, T., & Hartley, E. (Eds.). (1958). *Readings in social psychology*. Holt.
MacCorquodale, K. (1970). On Chomsky's review of Skinner's *verbal behavior*. *Journal of the Experimental Analysis of Behavior, 13*, 83–99.
MacCorquodale, K., & Meehl, P. E. (1948). On a distinction between hypothetical constructs and Intervening variables. *Psychological Review, 55*, 95–105.
Mach, E. (1976). *Knowledge and error: Sketches on the psychology of enquiry*. D. Reidel. (Original work published 1905)
MacKay, D. (2003). *Information theory, inference, and learning algorithms*. Cambridge University Press.
MacKintosh, N. J. (Ed.). (1995). *Cyril Burt: Fraud or framed?* Oxford University Press.
MacKintosh, N. J. (1998). *IQ and human intelligence*. Oxford University Press.

MacWhinney, B., & Bates, E. (Eds.). (1989). *The crosslinguistic study of sentence processing*. Cambridge University Press.
MacWhinney, B., & Snow, C. (1985). The child language data exchange system. *Journal of Child Language, 12,* 271–296.
MacWhinney, B., & Snow, C. (1990). The child language data exchange system: An update. *Journal of Child Language, 17,* 457–472.
Maiorov, F. P. (1948). *The history of the theory of conditioned reflexes*. Medical Academy.
Maiorov, F. P. (1951). The problem of the interrelation of the subjective and the objective in research on the higher nervous activity of man. *Fiziologicheskii Zhurnal SSSR, 37,* 133–139.
Malinowski, B. (1927). *Sex and repression in savage society*. Kegan Paul.
Mandler, G. (1967). Organization and memory. *Psychology of Learning and Motivation, 1,* 327–372.
Mandler, G. (1996). The situation of psychology: Landmarks and choicepoints. *American Journal of Psychology, 109,* 1–35.
Mandler, G. (2002a). *Interesting times: An encounter with the 20th century*. Erlbaum.
Mandler, G. (2002b). Origins of the cognitive (r)evolution. *Journal of the History of the Behavioral Sciences, 38,* 339–353.
Mandler, G. (2007). *A history of modern experimental psychology: From James and Wundt to cognitive science*. The MIT Press.
Mandler, G. (2011). Crises and problems seen from experimental psychology. *Journal of Theoretical and Philosophical Psychology, 31,* 240–246.
Mandler, J. M., & Mandler, G. (1964). *Thinking: From association to Gestalt*. John Wiley & Sons.
Mandler, J. M., & Mandler, G. (1968). The diaspora of experimental psychology: The Gestaltists and others. In D. Fleming & B. Bailyn (Eds.), *The migration-Europe and America, 1930–1960: Vol. 2. Perspectives American history*. Harvard University, Charles Warren Center.
Mannheim, K. (1936). *Ideology and Utopia*. Harcourt.
Mannheim, K. (1952). *Essays on the sociology of knowledge*. Oxford University Press.
Marcus, G. (2004). *The birth of the mind*. The MIT Press.
Marcus, G. F. (2001). Plasticity and nativism: Towards a resolution of an apparent paradox. In S. Wermter, J. Austin, & D. Willshaw (Eds.), *Emergent neural computational architectures based on neuroscience* (pp. 368–382). Springer.
Marcus, G. F. (2005). What developmental biology can tell us about innateness. In P. Carruthers, S. Laurence, & S. Stich (Eds.), *The innate mind: Structure and content* (pp. 22–33). Oxford University Presss.
Marcus, G. F. (2006). Cognitive architecture and descent with modification. *Cognition, 101,* 443–465.
Marcus, G. F. (2008). *Cludges. The haphasard construction of the human mind*. Houghton Mifflin.
Marcus, G. F., & Fisher, S. E. (2003). FOXP2 in focus: What can genes tell us about speech and language? *Trends in Cognitive Sciences, 7,* 257–262.
Marcus, G. F., Pinker, S., Ullman, M., Hollander, M., Rosen, T. J., Xu, F., & Clahsen, H. (1992). Overregularization in language acquisition. *Monographs of the Society for Research in Child Development, 57*.
Marcus, G. F., Vijayan, S., Bandi Rao, S., & Vishton, P. M. (1999). Rule-learning in seven month-old infants. *Science, 283,* 77–80.
Marcuse, H. (1955). *Eros and civilization*. Beacon Press.
Marcuse, H. (1964). *One dimensional man*. Routledge.

Marr, D. (1982). *Vision*. Freeman.
Marslen-Wilson, W. D., & Tyler, L. K. (1980). The temporal structure of spoken language understanding. *Cognition, 8,* 1–71.
Martindale, C. (1990). *The clockwork muse*. Basic Books.
Marton, L. M. (1972). Theory of individual differences in neobehaviorism and in typology of higher nervous activity. In V. D. Nebylitsyn & J. A. Gray (Eds.), *Biological bases of individual behavior* (pp. 221–235). Academic Press.
Marton, L. M. (1996). Harkai Schiller tudományos szemlélete harminc év néhány tudományos felismerésének tükrében [The scientific vision of Harkai Schiller in the light of 30 years of scientific discoveries]. *Pszichológia, 16,* 115–131.
Marton, L. M., & Urbán, J. (1971). An electroencephalographic investigation of individual differences in the process of conditioning. In H. J. Eysenck (Ed.), *Readings in extraversion-introversion*. McGibbon and Kee.
Marx, K. (1932). *Economic & philosophic manuscripts of 1844*. https://www.marxists.org/archive/marx/works/1844/manuscripts/preface.htm (Original work published 1844)
Marx, M. H., & Hillix, W. A. (Eds.). (1963). *Systems and theories in psychology*. McGraw Hill.
Maslow, A. (1943). A theory of human motivation. *Psychological Review, 50,* 370–396.
Maslow, A. (1954). *Motivation and personality*. Harper.
Maslow, A. (1968). *Toward a psychology of being*. Wiley.
Masters, W. H., & Johnson, V. E. (1966). *Human sexual response*. Little and Brown.
Mauss, M. (1924). Rapports réels et pratiques de la psychologie et de la sociologie [Real and practical connections of psychology and sociology]. *Journal de Psychologie Normale et Pathologique*, 892–922. Electronic version in 2002 from the Classique des Sciences Sociales.
Mauss, M. (1966). *The gift*. Cohen. (Original work published 1925)
Mauss, M. (1985). A category of the human mind: The notion of person; the notion of self (W. D. Halls, Trans.). In M. Carrithers, S. Collins, & S. Lukes (Eds.), *The category of the person: Anthropology, philosophy, history* (pp. 1–25). Cambridge University Press. (Original work published 1938)
Mauss, M. (1979). *Psychology and sociology: Essays*. Routledge.
Mayo, E. (1933). *The human problems of an industrial civilization*. Macmillan.
Mayr, E. (1982). *The growth of biological thought*. Belknap Press.
McClelland, D. C. (1953). *The achievement motive*. Appleton.
McClelland, D. C. (1961). *The achieving society*. D van Nostrand.
McClelland, J. L., & Rumelhart, D. E. (1986). *Parallel distributed processing* (Vol. 2). The MIT Press.
McCulloch, W., & Pitts, W. (1943). A logical calculus of the ideas immanent in nervous activity. *Bulletin of Mathematical Biophysics, 5,* 115–133.
McDougall, W. (1908). *An introduction to social psychology*. Methuen.
McDougall, W. (1920a). *The group mind*. Holt.
McDougall, W. (1920b). *An introduction to social psychology* (15th ed.). Methuen.
McLeish, J. (1975). *Soviet psychology: History, theory, content*. Methuen.
Mead, G. H. (1934). *Mind, self and society*. University of Chicago Press. Digital version http://livros01.livrosgratis.com.br/bu000001.pdf
Mead, M. (1928). *Coming of age in Samoa*. Morrow. https://ia802701.us.archive.org/26/items/comingofageinsam00mead/comingofageinsam00mead.pdf
Mead, M. (1975). *Male and female*. W. Morrow.
Meehl, P. E. (1954). *Clinical versus statistical prediction: A theoretical analysis and a review of the evidence*. University of Minnesota Press.

Mehler, J. (1969). Psycholinguistique et grammaire générative [Psycholingustics and generative grammar]. *Langages, 4*(16), 1–13.
Mehler, J., & Dupoux, E. (1994). *What infants know: New cognitive science of early development.* Blackwell.
Melton, A. W., & Martin, E. (1972). *Coding processes in human memory.* Winston.
Mercier, D. (1925) *Les origines de la psychologie contemporaine* [The origins of contemporary psychology] (3rd ed.). Alcan. (Original work published 1897)
Mercier, H., & Sperber, D. (2017). *The enigma of reason.* Harvard University Press.
Mérei, F. (1948). *Gyermektanulmány* [Pedology]. Új Nevelés Könyvtára.
Mérei, F. (1949). Group leadership and institutionalization. *Human Relations, 2,* 23–29.
Mérei, F. (1971). *Közösségek rejtett hálozata* [The hidden network of communities]. Közgazdasági.
Mérei, F. (1994). Social relationships in manifest dream content. *Journal of Russian and East European Psychology, 32,* 46–68.
Mérei, F. (1997). Allusion as a semiotic surplus of joint experience. *Journal of Russian & East European Psychology, 35,* 6–48.
Merleau-Ponty, M. (1963). *The structure of behavior* (A. Fisher, Trans.). Beacon Press. (Original work published 1942)
Merton, R. K. (1957). *Social theory and social structure.* Free Press.
Meskil, D. (2004). Characterological psychology and the German political economy in the Weimar period (1919–1933). *History of Psychology, 7,* 3–19.
Mészáros, J. (2009). Sándor Ferenczi and the Budapest School of psychoanalysis. *Psychoanalytic Perspectives, 6*(2), 31–51.
Mészáros, J. (2010). Progress and persecution in the psychoanalytic heartland: Antisemitism, communism and the fate of Hungarian psychoanalysis. *Psychoanalytic Dialogues, 20,* 600–622.
Mészáros, J. (2012). Effect on dictatorial regimes on the psychoanalytic movement in Hungary before and after World War II. In J. Damousi & M. B. Plotkin (Eds.), *Psychoanalysis and politics. Histories of psychoanalysis under conditions of restricted political freedom* (pp. 79–108). Oxford University Press.
Mészáros, J. (2014). *Ferenczi and beyond. Exile of the Budapest school and solidarity in the psychoanalytic movement during the Nazi Years.* Karnac.
Mészáros, J. (2017, November). The saga of psychoanalysis in Eastern Europe: Repression and rebirth in Hungary, and in former Czechoslovakia and Yugoslavia. *Ciências, Saúde – Manguinhos,* 24(suppl.) 91–103.
Meumann, E. (1913). *The psychology of learning* (J. W. Baird, Trans.). D. Appleton.
Meyer, A. (1928). Thirty-five years of psychiatry in the United States and our present outlook. *American Journal of Psychiatry, 8,* 1–36.
Meyerson, I. (1948). *Les fonctions psychologiques et les oeuvres* [Psychological functions and the works]. Vrin.
Meyerson, I. (1952). L'entrée dans l'humain [Entering the human stage]. *Revue Philosophique de la France et de l'Étranger, 142,* 1–13.
Meyerson, I. (1954). *La psychologie du XX. Siecle* [Psychology of 20th Century]. Presses Universitaires de France.
Meyerson, I. (1987). *Ecrits. Pour une psychologie historiques* [Writings for a historical psychology]. Presses Universitaires de France.
Middleton, D., & Crook, C. (1996). Bartlett and socially ordered consciousness: A discursive perspective. Comments on Rosa. *Culture & Psychology, 2,* 379–396.
Middleton, D., & Edwards, D. (Eds.). (1990). *Collective Remembering.* Sage.

Milgram, S. (1963). Behavioral study of obedience. *Journal of Abnormal and Social Psychology, 67,* 371–337.
Milgram, S. (1974). *Obedience to authority: An experimental view.* Harper and Row.
Miller, G. A. (1951). *Language and communication.* McGraw Hill.
Miller, G. A. (1956). The magical number seven, plus or minus two. *Psychological Review, 63,* 81–97.
Miller, G. A. (1962). Some psychological studies of grammar. *American Psychologist, 17,* 748–762.
Miller, G. A. (1963). Thinking, cognition, and learning. In B. Berelson (Ed.), *The behavioral sciences today* (pp. 139–150). Basic Books.
Miller, G. A. (Ed.). (1964). *Mathematics and psychology.* Wiley. https://archive.org/details/MathematicsAndPsychology/page/n1/mode/2up
Miller, G. A. (1969). Psychology as a means of promoting human welfare. *American Psychologist, 24,* 1063–1075.
Miller, G. A. (1991). *The science of words.* Freeman.
Miller, G. A. (2003). The cognitive revolution: A historical perspective. *Trends in Cognitive Sciences, 7,* 141–144.
Miller, G. A. (2010). Mistreating psychology in the decades of the brain. *Perspectives on Psychological Science, 5,* 716–743.
Miller, G. A., & Chomsky, N. (1963). Finitary models of language users. In R. D. Luce, R. R. Bush, & E. Galanter (Eds.), *Handbook of mathematical psychology* (Vol. II, pp. 419–491). Wiley.
Miller, G. A., Galanter, E., & Pribram, K. A. (1960). *Plans and the structure of behavior.* Holt, Rinehart, & Winston.
Miller, J. G. (1965). Living systems: Basic concepts. *Behavioral Science, 10,* 193–237.
Miller, M. A. (1998). *Freud and the Bolsheviks: Psychoanalysis in imperial Russia and the Soviet Union.* Yale University Press.
Miller, N. E. (1941). The frustration-aggression hypothesis. *Psychological Review, 48,* 337–342.
Miller, N. E. (1944). Experimental studies of conflict behavior. In J. McV. Hunt (Ed.), *Personality and behavior disorders: A handbook based on experimental and clinical research* (pp. 431–465). The Ronald Press Company.
Miller, N. E. (1948). Theory and experiment relating psychoanalytic displacement to stimulus-response generalization. *Journal of Abnormal and Social Psychology, 43,* 155–178.
Miller, N. E. (1957). Experiments on motivation. Studies combining psychological, physiological and pharmacological techniques. *Science, 126,* 1271–1278.
Miller, N. E. (1959). Liberalization of basic S-R concepts. In S. Koch (Ed.), *Psychology: The study of a science* (Vol. 2, pp. 196–292). McGraw-Hill.
Miller, N. E. (1963). Some reflections on the law of effect produce a new alternative to drive reduction. In *Nebraska symposium on motivation* (pp. 65–112). University of Nebraska Press.
Miller, N. E. (1969). Learning of visceral and glandular responses. *Science, 163,* 434–445.
Miller, N. E., & Dollard, J. (1941). *Social learning and imitation.* Yale University Press.
Minkova, E. (2013). *The history of Russian pedology: Dreams and reality.* Lambert.
Mironenko, I. A. (2013a). Concerning interpretations of activity. *Integrative Psychological and Behavioral Science, 47,* 376–393.
Mironenko, I. A. (2013b). Contemporary Russian psychology in the context of international science. *Procedia – Social and Behavioral Sciences, 86,* 156–161.

Mironenko, I. A. (2014). Integrative and isolationist tendencies in contemporary Russian psychological science. *Psychology in Russia: State of the Art, 7*(2), 4–13.
Mischel, W. (1973) Toward a cognitive social learning reconceptualization of personality. *Psychological Review, 80,* 252–283.
Moede, W. (1920). *Experimentelle Massenpsychologie* [Experimental crowd psychology]. Hirzel.
Moessinger, P. (2000). Piaget: From biology to sociology. *New Ideas in Psychology, 18,* 171–176.
Montgomery, K. C. (1954). The role of the exploratory drive in learning. *Journal of Comparative and Physiological Psychology, 47,* 60–64.
Morawski, J. G. (2012). The importance of history to social psychology. In A. W. Kruglanski & W. Stroebe (Eds.), *Handbook of the history of social psychology* (pp. 19–41). Psychology Press.
Moreno, J. L. (1934). *Who shall survive? A new approach to the problem of human interrelations*. Beacon House.
Moreno, J. L. (1946). *Psychodrama* (Vol. 1). Beacon House.
Moreno, J. L. (1985). *The autobiography of J. L. Moreno, M. D. Abridged Moreno archives*. Harvard University.
Morgan, C. L. (1894). *An introduction to comparative psychology*. Walter Scott.
Morgulis, S. (1914). Pavlov's theory of the function of the central nervous system and a digest of some of the more recent contributions to this subject from Pavlov's laboratory. *Journal of Animal Behavior, 4,* 362–379.
Morin, O. (2016). *How traditions live and die*. Oxford University Press.
Morris, C. (1938). *Foundations of the theory of signs: International encyclopedia of unified science* (Vol. 1, No. 2). University of Chicago Press.
Morton, J. (1969). The interaction of information in word recognition. *Psychological Review, 76,* 165–178.
Moruzzi, G., & Magoun, H. W. (1949). Brain stem reticular formation and activation of the EEG. *Electroencephalography and Clinical Neurophysiology, 1,* 455–473.
Moscovici, S. (2008). *Psychoanalysis: Its image, its public*. Polity Press. (Original work published 1961)
Moscovici, S. (1984). *The phenomenon of social representations*. Cambridge University Press.
Moscovici, S. (1985). *The age of the crowd*. Cambridge University Press.
Moscovici, S. (1988). Notes towards a description of social representations. *European Journal of Social Psychology, 18,* 211–250.
Moscovici, S. (1993). Which histories to write? What stories to tell!/Quelles histoires? *Sociétés contemporaines, La psychologie sociale et ses histoires, 13,* 25–32.
Moscovici, S. (1998). Social consciousness and its history. *Culture & Psychology, 4,* 411–429.
Moscovici, S., & Marková, I. (2006). *The making of modern social psychology: The hidden story of how an international social science was created*. Polity Press.
Moussaoui, D. (2002). *A biography of Jean Delay*. Excerpta Medica.
Mowrer, O. H.(1936). Stimulus-response theory of anxiety and its role as a reinforcing agent. *Psychological Review, 46,* 553–565.
Mowrer, O. H. (1947). On the dual nature of learning: A re-interpretation of "conditioning" and "problem-solving." *Harvard Educational Review, 17,* 102–148.
Mowrer, O. H. (1950). *Learning theory and personality dynamics*. Ronald Press.
Mowrer, O. H. (1954). The psychologist looks at language. *American Psychologist, 9,* 660–694.
Mowrer, O. H. (1960). *Learning theory and the symbolic processes*. Wiley.

Mowrer, O. H. (1961). *The crisis in psychiatry and religion*. D. Van Nostrand.
Mowrer, O. H. (1972). Integrity groups: Basic principles and objectives. *The Counseling Psychologist, 3*, 7–32.
Mucchielli, L. (1998). *La Découverte du social. Naissance de la sociologie en France* [The discovery of the social. Birth of sociology in France]. La Découverte.
Muchielli, L. (1999). Pour une psychologie collective. La héritage durkhemien d'Halbwachs et sa rivalité avec Blondel l'entre-deux-guerres [Towards a collective psychology. The Durkheim heritage of Halbwachs and its rivalry with Blondel between the two wars]. *Revue d'Histoire des Sciences Humaines, 1*, 103–141.
Mülberger, A. (2012). Wundt contested: The first crisis declaration in psychology. *Studies in History and Philosophy of Science Part C: Studies in History and Philosophy of Biological and Biomedical Sciences, 43*, 433–444.
Mülberger, A., & Sturm, T. (Eds.). (2012). Psychology, a science in crisis? A century of reflections and debates. *Studies in History and Philosophy of Science Part C: Studies in History and Philosophy of Biological and Biomedical Sciences Special Section II, 43*, 425–521.
Müller, G. E., & Pilzecker, A. (1900). *Experimentelle Beitrage Zur Lehre Vom Gedachtniss* [Experimental contributions to the study of memory]. Barth.
Müller, U., Carpendale, J. I. M., & Smith, L. (Eds.). (2009). *The Cambridge companion to Piaget*. Cambridge University Press. https://www.cambridge.org/core/books/cambridge-companion-to-piaget
Murray, H. A. (1938). *Explorations in personality*. Oxford University Press.
Musil, R. (1995). *The man without qualities*. Knopf. (Original work published 1930)
Namer, G. (1987). *Mémoire et société* [Memory and society]. Klinkskieck.
Namer, G. (1994). Postface. In M. Halbwachs, *Les cadres sociaux de la mémoire* [Social frames of memory] (pp. 297–367). Reedition of Halbwachs, 1925, Albin Michel.
Namer, G. (1999). La Mémoire Culturelle chez Maurice Halbwachs [The cultural memory in Maurice Halbwachs]. *L'Année sociologique (1940/1948), 49*, 223–235.
Nánay, B. (2011). Popper's Darwinian analogy. *Perspectives on Science, 19*, 337–354.
Nebylitsyn, V. D., & Gray, J. A. (Eds.). (1972). *Biological bases of individual behavior* Academic Press.
Neisser, U. (1967). *Cognitive psychology*. Prentice-Hall.
Neisser, U. (1976). *Cognition and reality*. Freeman.
Neisser, U. (Ed.). (1982). *Memory observed: Remembering in natural contexts*. Freeman.
Neisser, U., Boodoo, G., Bouchard, T. J., Jr., Boykin, A. W., Brody, N., Ceci, S. J., Halpern, D. F., Loehlin, J. C., Perloff, R., Sternberg, R. J., & Urbina, S. (1996). Intelligence: Knowns and unknowns. *American Psychologist, 51*, 77–101.
Nelson, K. (1977). The syntagmatic-paradigmatic shift revisited: A review of research and theory. *Psychological Bulletin, 84*, 93–116.
Némedi, D. (1995). Collective consciousness, morphology, and collective representations: Durkheim's sociology of knowledge 1894–1900. *Sociological Perspectives, 38*, 41–56.
Neumann, J. von. (1951). The general and logical theory of automata. In L. A. Jeffries (Ed.), *Cerebral mechanisms in behavior*. Wiley.
Neumann, J. von. (1958). *The computer and the brain*. Yale University Press.
Neurath, O. (1987). Unified science and psychology. In B. McGuinness (Ed.), *Unified science* (pp. 1–23). Reidel. (Original work published 1933)
Neuroskeptic. (2012). The nine circles of scientific hell. *Perspectives on Psychological Science, 7*, 643–644.
Newell, A. (1980). Physical symbol systems. *Cognitive Science, 4*, 251–283.
Newell, A. (1989). *Unified theories of cognition*. Harvard University Press.

Newell, A., Simon, H. A., & Shaw, J. J. (1958). Elements of a theory of problem soving. *Psychological Review, 65,* 151–165.

Nicolas, S. (2002). *Histoire de la Psychologie Française* [History of French psychology]. In Press.

Nisbett, R. E. (2003) *The geography of thought: How Asians & Westerners think differently & why.* The Free Press.

Nisbett, R. E., Pang, K., Choi, I. & Norenzayan, A. (2001). Culture and systems of thought: Holistic versus analytic cognition. *Psychological Review, 108,* 291–310.

Nisbett, R. E., & Miyamoto, Y. (2005). The influence of culture: Holistic versus analytic perception. *Trends in Cognitive Sciences, 9,* 467–474.

Noble, C. E. (1952). An analysis of meaning. *Psychological Review, 59,* 421–430.

Noll, R. (1994). *The Jung cult: Origins of a charismatic movement.* Princeton University Press.

Nora, P. (1989). Between memory and history: Les Lieux de Mémoire. *Representations, 26,* 7–24.

Norman, D. A. (1980). Twelve issues for cognitive science. *Cognitive Science, 4,* 1–32.

Norman, D. A. (Ed.). (1981). *Perspectives on cognitive science.* Lawrence Erlbaum.

Norman, D. A. (1988). *The design of everyday things.* Basic Books.

Noveck, I. (2018). *Experimental pragmatics. The making of a cognitive science.* Cambridge University Press.

Noveck, I., & Sperber, D. (Eds.). (2004). *Experimental pragmatics.* Palgrave Macmillan.

Núñez, R., Allen, M., Gao, E., Miller Rigoli, C., Relaford-Doyle, J., & Semenuks, A. (2019). What happened to cognitive science? *Nature Human Behavior.* https://doi.org/10.1038/s41562-019-0626-2

Nye, R. (1975). *The origins of crowd psychology: Gustave LeBon and the crisis of mass democracy in the third republic.* Sage.

Nyíri, J. C. (1992). *Tradition and individuality.* Kluwer.

Ogden, R. M. (1911). The unconscious bias of laboratories. *Psychological Bulletin, 8,* 330–331.

Ohayon, A. (2006). *Psychologie et psychanalyse en France. L'impossible rencontre (1919–1969)* [Psychology and psychoanalysis in France. The impissible meeting. 1919–1969]. La Découverte.

Ohayon, A., & Plas, R. (2016). Questions contemporaines en psychologie [Contemporary questions in psychology]. *Le Journal des Psychologues, 7*(339), 51–58.

O'Keefe, J. (1976). Place units in the hippocampus of the freely moving rat. *Experimental Neurology, 51,* 78–109.

O'Keefe, J., & Nadel, L. (1978). *The hippocampus as a cognitive map.* Clarendon Press.

Oldfield, R. C. (1954). Memory mechanisms and the theory of schemata. *British Journal of Psychology, 45,* 14–23.

Olds, J., & Milner, P. (1954). Positive reinforcement produced by electrical stimulation of septal area and other regions of rat brain. *Journal of Comparative and Physiological Psychology, 47,* 419–427.

Ong, W. J. (1982). *Orality and literacy: The technologizing of the word.* Methuen.

Open Science Cooperation. (2015). Estimating the reproducibility of psychological science. *Science, 349,* 6251, aac4716. doi:10.1126/science.aac4716

Osgood, C. E. (1949). The similarity paradox in human learning: A resolution. *Psychological Review, 56,* 132–143.

Osgood, C. E. (1952). The nature and measurement of meaning. *Psychological Bulletin, 49,* 197–237.

Osgood, C. E. (1953). *Method and theory in experimental psychology*. Oxford University Press.

Osgood, C. E. (1957). A behavioristic analysis of perception and language as cognitive phenomena. In J. S. Bruner, E. Brunswik, L. Festinger, F. Heider, K. F. Muenzinger, C. E. Osgood, & D. Rapaport (Eds.), *Contemporary approach to cognition* (pp. 75–118). Harvard University Press.

Osgood, C. E. (1960). Cognitive dynamics in the conduct of human affairs. *The Public Opinion Quarterly, 24*, 341–365.

Osgood, C. E. (1962). *An alternative to war or surrender*. University of Illinois Press.

Osgood, C. E. (1963). On understanding and creating sentences. *American Psychologist, 18*, 735–751.

Osgood, C. E., May, W. H., & Miron, M. S. (1975). *Cross-cultural universals of affective meaning*. University of Illinois Press.

Osgood, C. E., & Sebeok, T. (Eds.). (1954). *Psycholinguistics: A survey of theory and research problems*. Indiana University Press.

Osgood, C. E., Suci, G., & Tannenbaum, P. (1957). *The measurement of meaning*. University of Illinois Press.

Ovcharenko, V. (1999). The history of Russian psychoanalysis and the problem of its periodisation. *Journal of Analytical Psychology, 44*(3), 341–353.

Pagés, R. (1958). Quelques remarques sur " Qu'est-ce que la *psychologie*? [Some remarks on What is psychology]. *Revue de Métaphysique et de Morale, 63*, 26–31.

Paivio, A. (1971). *Imagery and verbal processes*. Holt.

Paivio, A. (1986). *Mental representations: A dual coding approach*. Oxford University Press.

Paivio, A. (2007). *Mind and its evolution: A dual coding theoretical approach*. Lawrence Erlbaum.

Palermo, D. (1971). Is a scientific revolution taking place in psychology? *Science Studies, 1*, 135–155.

Palermo, D. S., & Jenkins, J. J. (1963). Frequency of superordinate responses to a word association test as a function of age. *Journal of Verbal Learning and Verbal Behavior, 1*, 378–383.

Palermo, D. S, & Jenkins, J. J. (1964). *Word association norms: Grade school through college*. University of Minnesota Press.

Parot, F. (2000). Psychology in the human sciences in France, 1920–1940: Ignace Meyerson's historical psychology. *History of Psychology, 3*, 104–121.

Pataki, F. (1998). *A tömegek évszázada* [The century of crowds]. Osiris.

Paul, H. (1888). *Prinzipien der Sprachgeschichte* [Principles of language history] (2nd ed.). Halle.

Pavlov, I. P. (1898). *Die Arbeit der Verdauungsdrüsen* [The work of the digestive glands]. J. F. Bergmann.

Pavlov, I. P. (1901). *Le travail des glandes digestives* [The work of the digestive glands]. Masson.

Pavlov, I. P. (1902). *The work of the digestive glands*. Griffin.

Pavlov, I. P. (1927). *Conditioned reflexes: An investigation of the physiological activity of the cerebral cortex* (G. V. Anrep, Trans.). Oxford University Press.

Pavlov, I. P. (1928). *Lectures on conditioned reflexes: Twenty-five years of objective study of the higher nervous activity (behaviour) of animals*. Liveright Publishing Corporation.

Pavlov, I. P. (1932). The reply of a physiologist to psychologists. *Psychological Review, 39*, 91–127.

Pavlov, I. P. (1955). *Selected works*. Foreign Language Publishing House.
Pavlov, I. P. (2014). *Ob ume voobsche, o russcom ume v chasnost'i. Zapiski fiziologa* [On the mind in general, on the Russian mind in particular. Notes of the physiologist]. AST Publishers.
Pavlov Session. (2001). *Scientific session on the physiological teachings of academician Ivan P. Pavlov: June 28–July 4, 1950*. Academy of Sciences of the USSR Academy, University Press of the Pacific. (Original work published 1950)
Pearson, K. (1892). *The grammar of science*. Dover Publications.
Pearson, K. (1895). Notes on regression and inheritance in the case of two parents. *Proceedings of the Royal Society of London, 58*, 240–242.
Pearson, K. (1900). On the criterion that a given system of deviations from the probable in the case of a correlated system of variables is such that it can be reasonably supposed to have arisen from random sampling. *Philosophical Magazine Series, 5, 50*, 157–175.
Pedological distortions in the commisariats of education. (1936, July 4). Resolution of the central commnittee of the communist party of the Soviet Union. Wortis, 1950, 242–245.
Peirce, C. S. (1883). *Studies in logic, by members of the Johns Hopkins University*. Little Brown.
Perner, J. 1991. *Understanding the representational mind*. The MIT Press.
Perreault, C. (2012). The pace of cultural evolution. *PLoS ONE, 7*(9), e45150. doi:10.1371/journal.pone.0045150
Philippe, J. (1897). Sur les Transformations de nos Images Mentales [On the transformation of our menatl images]. *Revue Philosophique de la France et de l'Étranger, 43*, 481–493.
Piaget, J. (1920). La psychanalyse dans ses rapports avec la psychologie de l'enfant. I-II [Psychoanalysis in its relations with child psychology. I-II]. *Bulletin mensuel de la Société Alfred Binet, année, 20*(1–3), 18–34, 41–58.
Piaget, J. (1959). *The language and thought of the child* (3rd Rev. and English ed.). Routledge. (Original work published 1923)
Piaget, J. (1951). *The child's conception of physical causality*. Humanities Press. (Original work published 1927)
Piaget, J. (1928). Logique génétique et sociologie [Genetic logic and sociology]. *Revue Philosophique de la France et de l'Étranger, 105*, 167–205.
Piaget, J. (1965). *The moral judgment of the child*. Free Press. (Original work published 1932)
Piaget, J. (1950). *The origins of intelligence in children*. Basic Books. (Original work published 1936)
Piaget, J. (1962). *Play, dreams and imitation in childhood*. Norton. The original French title was talking about symbol formation in children. (Original work published 1945)
Piaget, J. (1950). *The psychology of intelligence*. Harcourt Brace. (Original work published 1947)
Piaget, J. (1972). *Psychology and epistemology: Towards a theory of knowledge*. Penguin. (Original work published 1950)
Piaget, J. (1981). *Intelligence and affectivity*. Annual Reviews. (Original work published 1954)
Piaget, J. (1960). *Logic and psychology*. Basic Books.
Piaget, J. (1971). *Insights and illusions of philosophy*. World Publishing Company. (Original work published 1965)
Piaget, J. (1972). *The principles of genetic epistemology*. Basic Books.
Piaget, J. (1975). *Sociological studies*. Routledge.
Piaget, J. (1977). *Psychology and epistemology*. Penguin.
Piaget, J. (1978). *Behavior and evolution*. Random House.
Piaget, J. (1979). Relations between psychology and the other sciences. *Annual Review of Psychology, 30*, 1–8.

Piaget, J., Inhelder, B., & Szeminska. A. (1956). *The child's conception of space*. Routledge. (Original work published 1948)

Piaget Foundation (1976). *Mainly French texts of Piaget Foundation*. http://www.fondation-jeanpiaget.ch/fjp/site/crypt/verifier.php?DOCID=828

Piatelli-Palmarini, M. (1989). Evolution, selection and cognition: From "learning" to parameter setting in biology and in the study of language, *Cognition, 31*, 1–44.

Piattelli-Palmarini, M. (Ed.). (1980). *Language and learning: The debate between Jean Piaget and Noam Chomsky*. Harvard University Press.

Piattelli-Palmarini, M. (1994). Ever since language and learning: Afterthoughts on the Piaget-Chomsky debate. *Cognition, 50*, 315–346.

Pickering, M. J., & Garrod, S. (2004). Toward a mechanistic psychology of dialogue. *Behavioral and Brain Sciences, 27*, 169–226.

Pinker, S. (1989). *Learnibility and cognition: The acquisition of argument structure*. The MIT Press.

Pinker, S. (1991). Rules of language. *Science, 253*, 530–555.

Pinker, S. (1994). *The language instinct*. William Morrow.

Pinker, S. (1997). *How the mind works?* Norton.

Pinker, S. (1998). Obituary for Roger Brown. *Cognition, 66*, 199–213.

Pinker, S. (1999). *Words and rules: The ingredients of language*. Harper Collins.

Pinker, S. (2002). *The blank slate*. Penguin.

Pinker, S., & Mehler, J. (Eds.). (1988). *Connections and symbols*. The MIT Press.

Pinker, S., & Prince, A. (1988). On language and connectionism. *Cognition, 28*, 73–193.

Pinker, S., & Ullman, M. T. (2002). The past and future of the past tense. *Trends in Cognitive Sciences, 6*, 456–463.

Pizarroso, N. (2018). *Ignace Meyerson*. Les Belles Lettres.

Pizzarroso, N. (2013). Mind's historicity: Its hidden history. *History of Psychology, 16*, 72–90.

Pléh, C. (2003). Narrativity in text construction and self construction. *Neohelicon, 30*, 187–205.

Pléh, C. (2008). *History and theories of the mind*. Akadémiai.

Pléh, C. (2019). Narrative psychology as cultural psychology. In G. Jovanovic, L. Allolio-Näcke, & C. Ratner (Eds.), *The challenges of cultural psychology: Historical legacies and future responsibilities* (pp. 237–249). Routledge.

Pléh C., & Boross, O. (2015). Darwinism as a decryption key for the human mind. In R. Scott & S. Kosslyn (Eds.), *Emerging trends in the social and behavioral sciences: An interdisciplinary, searchable, and linkable resource*. Wiley Online Library.

Pléh, C., & Gurova, L. (2013). Existing and would-be accounts of the history of cognitive science: An introduction. In C. Pléh, L. Gurova, & L. Ropolyi (Eds.), *New perspectives on the history of cognitive science* (pp. 1–34). Akadémiai.

Plotkin, H. (1997). *Evolution in mind*. Allen Lane.

Polanyi, M. (1946/1964). *Science. Faith and society* (2nd ed.). University of Chicago Press.

Politzer, G. (1994). *Critique of the foundations of psychology: The psychology of psychoanalysis* (M. Apprey, Trans.). Duquesne University Press. https://www.marxists.org/archive/politzer/works/1928/intro.ht (Original work published 1928)

Politzer, G. (2000). *After the death of M. Bergson*. https://www.marxists.org/archive/politzer/works/1941/bergson.htm (Original work published 1941)

Politzer, G. (1947). La crise de la psychologie contemporaine [The crisis of contemporary psychology]. Edition Sociale.

Poole, R. (2008). Memory, history and the claims of the past. *Memory Studies, 1*, 149–166.

Popper, K. R. (1934). *Logik der Forschung* [The logic of research]. Julius Springer.

Popper, K. R. (1945). *The open society and its enemies*. Routledge.
Popper, K. R. (1959). *The logic of scientific discovery*. Basic Books.
Popper, K. R. (1963). *Conjectures and refutations*. Routledge.
Popper, K. R. (1972). *Objective knowledge: An evolutionary approach*. Clarendon Press.
Popper, K. R. (1976). *Unended quest: An intellectual autobiography*. Fontana.
Popper, K. R. (1994). *Knowledge and the body-mind problem: In defense of interaction*. Routledge.
Popper, K. R., & Eccles, J. C. (1977). *The self and its brain*. Springer.
Posner, M. I. (1976). *Chronometric explorations of mind*. Oxford University Press.
Posner, M. I., & Raichle, M. E. (1994). *Images of mind*. Scientific American Books.
Postman, L., Bruner, J. S., & McGinnies, E. (1948). Personal values as selective factors in perception. *J Abnormal Psychology, 43*, 142–154.
Premack, A., & Premack, D. (1972). Teaching language to an ape. *Scientifc American, 272*(4), 1–11.
Premack, D. (1959). Toward empirical behavior laws: I. Positive reinforcement. *Psychological Review, 66*, 219–233.
Premack, D., & Woodruff, G. (1978). Does the chimpanzee have a theory of mind? *Behavioral and Brain Sciences, 4*, 515–526.
Prinzhorn, H. (1928). Les courants principaux de la psychologie allemande contemporaine [Principal currents in contemporary German psychology]. *Journal de Psychologie, 25*, 828–848.
Prohászka, L. (1935). *A Vándor és a Bújdosó* [The wanderer and the fugitive]. Minerva.
Pulvermüller, F. (2002). A brain perspective on language mechanisms: From discrete engrams to serial order. *Progress in Neurobiology, 574*, 1–27.
Putnam, H. (1960). Minds and machines. In S. Hook (Ed.), *Dimensions of mind* (pp. 138–164) Collier Books.
Putnam, J. J. (1917). The theories of Freud, Jung and Adler. *Journal of Abnormal Psychology, 12*, 145–160.
Putnoky, J. (1979). "Motority" in three functional domains of word meaning. *Journal of Psycholinguistic Research, 8*, 543–558.
Pylyshyn, Z. W. (1973). What the mind's eye tells the mind's brain: A critique of mental imagery. *Psychological Bulletin, 80*, 1–25.
Pylyshyn, Z. W. (1981). The imagery debate: Analogue media versus tacit knowledge. *Psychological Review, 88*, 16–45.
Pylyshyn, Z. W. (1984). *Computation and cognition*. The MIT Press.
Pylyshyn, Z. W. (2003). Return of the mental image: Are there really pictures in the brain? *Trends in Cognitive Sciences, 7*, 111–118.
Quine, W. V. (1951). Two Dogmas of empiricism. *The Philosophical Review, 60*, 20–43. Reprinted in Quine, 1953.
Quine, W. V. (1953). *From a logical point of view*. Harvard University Press.
Quine, W. V. (1969). *Ontological relativity and other essays*. Columbia University Press.
Rabaglia, C. D., Marcus, G. F., & Lane, S. P. (2011). What can individual differences tell us about the specialization of function? *Cognitive Neuropsychology, 28*, 288–303.
Ramachandran, V. S. (2011). *The tell-tale brain: Unlocking the mistery of human nature*. Heinemann.
Ramachandran, V. S., & Hirstein, W. (1999). The science of art: A neurological theory of aesthetic experience. *Journal of Consciousness Studies, 6*(6–7).
Ramat, P. (2010). The (early) history of linguistic typology. In J. J. Song (Ed.), *The Oxford handbook of linguistic typology*. Oxford University Press, Oxford Handbooks Online.
Rapaport, D. (1942). *Emotions and memory*. Williams and Wilkins.

Rapaport, D. (Ed.). (1951). *Organization and pathology of thought.* Columbia University Press.

Rapaport, D. (1960). *The structure of psychoanalytic theory: A systematizing attempt.* International Universities Press.

Razran, G. H. S. (1939). A quantitative study of meaning by a conditioned salivary technique (semantic conditioning). *Science, 90,* 89–90.

Reich, W. (1973). *The function of the orgasm: Sex-economic problems of biological energy.* Farrar, Strauss and Giroux. http://www.wilhelmreichtrust.org/function_of_the_orgasm.pdf (Original work published 1927)

Reich, W. (1945). *Character analysis.* Farrar, Strauss and Giroux. http://www.wilhelmreichtrust.org/character_analysis.pdf (Original work published 1933)

Reich, W. (1970). *The mass psychology of fascism.* Farrar, Strauss and Giroux. http://www.wilhelmreichtrust.org/mass_psychology_of_fascism.pdf (Original work published 1933)

Remembering Bruner. (2017, February). Remembering Jerome Bruner. *APS Observer.*

Renan, E. (2018). *What is a nation? And other political writings.* Columbia University Press. (Original work published 1882)

Rescorla, R. A., & Wagner, A. R. (1972). A theory of Pavlovian conditioning: Variations in the effectiveness of reinforcement and non-reinforcement. In A. H. Black & W. F. Prokasy (Eds.), *Classical conditioning II* (pp. 64–99). Appleton-Century-Crofts.

Ribot, T. (1890). *The psychology of attention.* Open Court.

Ribot, T. (1899). *The evolution of general ideas.* Open Court.

Richard, N. (2013). *Hippolyte Taine: Histoire, psychologie, littérature* [Hippolyte Taine: History, psychology, literature]. Garnier.

Ricoeur, P. (1970). *Freud and philosophy, an essay on interpretation.* Yale University Press. (Original work published 1965)

Ricoeur, P. (2004). *Memory, history, forgetting.* University of Chicago Press.

Riesman, D. (1950). *The lonely crowd: A study of the changing American character.* Yale University Press.

Rietveld, C. A. et al. (2014). Common genetic variants associated with cognitive performance identified using the proxy-phenotype method. *Proceedings of the National Academy of Sciences USA, 111,* 13790–13794.

Rioux, J-P., & Sirinelli, J-F. (1998). *Le temps des masses. Le XXe siècle* [The time of the crowds. 20th century]. Seuil.

Rizzolatti, G., & Arbib, M. A. (1998). Language within our grasp. *Trends in Cognitive Sciences, 21,* 188–194.

Rizzolatti, G., Fadiga, L., Fogassi, L., & Gallese, V. (1996). Premotor cortex and the recognition of motor actions. *Cognitive Brain Research, 3,* 131–141.

Robert, J. S. (2008). Taking old ideas seriously: Evolution, development, and human behavior. *New Ideas in Psychology, 26,* 387–404.

Roediger, H. L., III. (2000). Sir Frederick Charles Bartlett: Experimental and applied psychology. In G. A. Kimble & M. Wertheimer (Eds.), *Portraits of Pioneers in Psychology.* American Psychological Association (Vol. IV, pp. 149–161).

Roediger, H. L., III. (2004). What happened to behaviorism. *APS Observer, 17,* 40–42.

Roediger, H. L., III. (2010). Reflections on intersections between cognitive and social psychology: A personal exploration. *European Journal of Social Psychology, 40,* 189–205.

Roediger, H. L., III, Meade, M. L. Galloc, D. A. S., & Olson, K. R. (2014). Bartlett revisited: Direct comparison of repeated reproduction and serial reproduction techniques. *Journal of Applied Research in Memory and Cognition, 3,* 266–271.

Rogers, C. R. (1953). *Client-centered therapy: Its current practice, implications and theory.* Constable.

Rogers, C. R. (1970). *Carl Rogers on encounter groups*. Harper & Row.
Rogers, C. R. (1972). *On becoming a person*. Houghton Mifflin.
Rogers, C. R., & Skinner, B. F. (1962). Some issues concerning the control of human behavior: A symposium. *Science, 124*, 1057–1066. Reprinted in *Pastoral Psychology*, 1962, *13*, 12–40. (Original work published 1956)
Róheim, G. (1930). *Animism, magic, and the divine king*. Kegan Paul.
Róheim, G. (1974). *Children of the desert*. Basic Books.
Róheim, G. (1992). *Fire in the dragon and other psychoanalytic essays on folklore*. Princeton University Press.
Rokeach, M. (1960). *The open and closed mind*. Basic Books.
Rokeach, M. (1973). *The nature of human values*. Free.
Rorschach, H. (1942). *Psychodiagnostics: A diagnostic test based on perception* (P. Lemkau & B. Kronenberg, Trans.). Hans Huber. (Original work published 1921)
Rosa, A. (1996). Bartlett's psycho-anthropological project. *Culture & Psychology, 2*, 355–378.
Rosch, E. (1978). Principles of categorization. In E. Rosch & B. B. Lloyd (Eds.), *Cognition and categorization* (pp. 27–48). Lawrence Erlbaum.
Rosch, E., & Mervis, C. B. (1975). Family resemblances: Studies in the internal structure of categories. *Cognitive Psychology, 7*, 573–605.
Rosenthal, R. (1966). *Experimenter effects in behavioral research*. Appleton-Century-Crofts.
Rosenthal, R., & Jacobson, L. (1968). *Pygmalion in the classroom: Teacher expectation and pupils' intellectual development*. Holt, Rinehart & Winston.
Rosenzweig, S. (1937). The experimental study of psychoanalytic concepts. *Journal of Personality, 6*, 61–71.
Rosenzweig, S. (1985). Freud and experimental psychology: The emergence of idiodynamics. In S. Koch & D. E. Leary (Eds.), *A century of psychology as science* (pp. 135–207). McGraw-Hill.
Rosenzweig, S. (1997). Letters by Freud on experimental psychodynamics. *American Psychologist, 52*(5), 571.
Ross, E. A. (1908). *Social psychology: An outline and source book*. Macmillan.
Ross, L. (1977). The intuitive psychologist and his shortcomings: Distortions in the attribution process. *Advances in Experimental Social Psychology, 10*, 173–220.
Roudinesco, É. (1993). Situation d'un texte: Qu'est-ce que la psychologie? [The situation of a text: What is psychology?] In *Georges Canguilhem* (pp. 135–144). Albin Michel.
Roudinesco, É. (1994). *Généalogies* [Geneealogies]. Fayard.
Roudinesco, É. (2016). *Freud, in his time and ours*. Harvard University Press.
Roudineso, É. (1990). *Jacques Lacan & Co: A history of psychoanalysis in France, 1925–1985*. University of Chicago Press.
Rubinstein, S. L. (1987). The problems of psychology in the works of Carl Marx, 1934. *Studies in Soviet Thought, 33*, 111–130. (Original work published 1934)
Rubinstein, S. L. (1940). *The principles of general psychology*. Uschpedgiz. Second, revised edition 1946.
Rubinstein, S. L. (1945). Consciousness in the light of dialectical materialism. *Science & Society, 10*(3), 252–261.
Rubinstein, S. L. (1965). *Sein und Bewusstsein* [On being and consciousness]. Deutscher Verlag Der Wissenschaften. (Original work published 1957)
Rubinstein, S. L. (1958). *O myshlenii i putyakh ego issledovaniya* [On thinking and the ways of its investigation]. Izd. AN SSSR Publisher.

Rumelhart, D. (1980). Schemata: The building blocks of cognition. In R. J. Spiro, B. C. Bruce, & W. F. Brewer (Eds.), *Theoretical issues in reading comprehension* (pp. 33–58). Erlbaum.

Rumelhart, D. E., McClelland, J. L., & Hinton, G. E. (1986). *Parallel distributed processing* (Vol. 1). Bradford Press.

Russell, B. (1921). *The analysis of mind*. Allan and Unwin. http://www.gutenberg.org/files/2529/2529-h/2529-h.htm

Ryle, G. (1949). *The concept of mind*. Hutchinson.

Sacks, H., Schegloff, E. A., & Jefferson, G. (1974). A simplest systematics for the organization of turn-taking for conversation. *Language, 50*, 696–735.

Sacks, O. (1995). *An anthropologist on Mars*. Knopf.

Saffran, J. R., Aslin, R. N., & Newport, E. L. (1996). Statistical learning by 8-month-old infants. *Science, 274*, 1926–1928.

Sapir, E. (1921). *Language*. Harcourt, Brace and Company.

Saussure, F. de. (1965). *Course in general linguistics*. McGraw Hill. (Original work published 1922)

Schacter, D. L. (1987). Implicit memory: History and current status. *Journal of Experimental Psychology: Learning, Memory, and Cognition, 13*, 501–518.

Schank, R., & Abelson, R. P. (1977). *Scripts, plans, goals, and understanding*. Erlbaum.

Schiller, P. von. (1948). *Die Aufgabe der psychologie*. Springer.

Schiller, P. H. (1950). Analysis of Detour behavior: IV. Congruent and incongruent detour behavior in cats. *Journal of Experimental Psychology, 40*, 217–227.

Schiller, P. H. (1951). Figural preferences in the drawings of a chimpanzee. *Journal of Comparative and Physiological Psychology, 44*, 101–111.

Schütz, A. (1967). *The phenomenology of the social world*. Northwestern University Press.

Scott, J. P. (1962). Critical periods in behavioral development. *Science, 138*, 949–957.

Scribner, S. (1997). *Mind and social practice: Selected writings of Sylvia Scribner*. Cambridge University Press.

Scribner, S., & Cole, M. (1981). *The psychology of literacy*. Harvard University Press.

Searle, J. R. (1980). Minds, brains, and programs. *Behavioral and Brain Sciences, 3*, 417–457.

Sears, R. R. (1943). *Survey of objective studies of psychoanalytic concepts*. Social Science Research Council.

Sears, R. R. (1959). Identification, sex-typing, and guilt. *Acta Psychologica, 15*, 462–468.

Sears, R. R., Maccoby, E. E., & Levin, H. (1957). *Patterns of child rearing*. Stanford University Press.

Sears, R. R., Rau, L., & Alpert, R. (1957). *Identification and child rearing*. Stanford University Press.

Sechenov, I. M. (1965). *Reflexes of the brain*. The MIT Press. (Original work published 1863)

Segal, E. M., & Lachman, R. (1972). Complex behavior or higher mental process: Is there a paradigm shift? *American Psychologist, 27*, 46–55.

Semprun, J. (1994). *L'Écriture ou la Vie* [Writing or life]. Gallimard.

Shannon, C. (1948). A mathematical theory of communication. *Bell System Technical Journal, 27*, 379–423. http://plan9.bell-labs.com/cm/ms/what/shannonday/shannon1948.pdf

Shannon, C. E., & Weaver, W. (1949). *A mathematical model of communication*. University of Illinois Press.

Shapin, S. (1996). *The scientific revolution*. University of Chicago Press.

Sheldon, W. H. (1940). *The varieties of human physique (an introduction to constitutional psychology)*. Harper & Brothers.

Shepard, R. N. (1978). The mental image. *American Psychologist, 33*, 125–137.
Shepard, R. N., & Chipman, S. (1970). Second-order isomorphism of internal representations. *Cognitive Psychology, 1*, 1–17.
Shepard, R. N., & Cooper, L. (1982). *Mental images and their transformations*. The MIT Press.
Shepard, R. N., & Metzler, J. (1971). Mental rotation of three dimensional objects. *Science, 171*, 701–703.
Sherif, M. (1936). *The psychology of social norms*. Harper.
Sherif, M., Harvey, O. J., White, B. J., Hood W., & Sherif, C. (1961). *Intergroup conflict and cooperation: The Robbers cave experiment*. University of Oklahoma Book Exchange. (Original work published 1954)
Sherrington, C. S. (1906). *The integrative action of the nervous system*. Yale University Press. Digitized version. https://liberationchiropractic.com/wp-content/uploads/research/1906Sherrington-IntegrativeAction.pdf
Sighele, S. (1891). *La Folla delinquente* [The criminal crowd]. Bocca. http://www.uqac.ca/Classiques_des_sciences_sociales/
Sighele, S. (1903). *L'intelligenza délia folla* [The intelligence of the crowd]. Bocca.
Simmel, G. (1982). On the relationship between the theory of selection and epistemology. In H. C. Plotkin (Ed.), *Learning, development and culture: Essays in evolutionary epistemology* (pp. 63–71). Wiley. (Original work published 1895)
Simmel, G. (1972). *On individuality and social forms*. University of Chicago Press. Edited by and with an introduction by D. Levine. (Original work published 1917)
Simon, H. A. (1977). *Models of discovery*. Reidel.
Simon, H. A. (1981). Otto Selz and information- processing psychology. In N. H. Frijda & A. de Groot (Eds.), *Otto Selz: His contribution to psychology*. Mouton.
Simon, H. A. (1982). *Models of bounded rationality* (Vols. 1–2). The MIT Press.
Simon, H. A., & Newell, A. (1972). *Human problem solving*. Prentice Hall.
Simonton, D. K. (2000). Methodological and theoretical orientation and the long-term disciplinary impact of 54 eminent psychologists. *Review of General Psychology, 4*, 13–24.
Simonton, D. K. (2002). *Great psychologists and their times: Scientific insights into psychology's history*. American Psychological Association.
Simonton, D. K. (2004). *Creativity in science: Chance, logic, genius, and Zeitgeist*. Cambridge University Press.
Sirigu, A., Cohen, T., Zalla, T., Pradat-Diehl, P., van Eeckhout, P., & Grafman, J. (1998). Distinct frontal regions for processing sentence syntax and story grammar. *Cortex, 34*, 771–778.
Sirotkina, I. (2006). When did "scientific psychology" begin in Russia? *Physis, 43*, 239–271.
Sirotkina, I. (2007). V. M. Bekhterev and the beginnings of experimental psychology in Russia. *Rivista di Historia di Psicologia, 28*, 315–320.
Sirotkina, I., & Smith, R. (2010). Psychological society and social change: Russia in transition. *Psychology in Russia: State of the Art, 3*, 626–645.
Sirotkina, I., & Smith, R. (2012). Russian federation. *The Oxford handbook of the history of psychology: Global perspectives*, 412–441.
Sirotkina, I., & Smith, R. (2016). Istoria psihologii v Rossii [History of psychology in Russia: Short outline with authors characterization]. *Humanities Studies*. Preprint WP6/2016/01.
Skinner, B. F. (1938). *The behavior of organisms*. Prentice Hall.
Skinner, B. F. (1945). The operational analysis of psychological terms. *Psychological Review, 52*, 270–277, 290–294.
Skinner, B. F. (1948). *Walden two*. Doubleday.

Skinner, B. F. (1950). Are theories of learning necessary? *Psychological Review*, *57*, 193–216.
Skinner, B. F. (1953). *Science and human behavior*. Macmillan.
Skinner, B. F. (1956). A case history in scientific method. *American Psychologist*, *11*, 221–233.
Skinner, B. F. (1957). *Verbal behavior*. Prentice Hall.
Skinner, B. F. (1963). Operant behavior. *American Psychologist*, *18*(8), 503–515.
Skinner, B. F. (1968). *The technology of teaching*. Appleton.
Skinner, B. F. (1971). *Beyond freedom and dignity*. Knopf.
Skinner, B. F. (1981). Selection by consequences. *Science*, *213*, 501–504.
Skinner, B. F. (1984). Methods and theories in the experimental analysis of behavior. *Behavioral and Brain Sciences*, *7*, 511–523. A condensation of two famous papers: Skinner, 1950, and flight from the laboratory which is in his cumulative record in its different versions, e.g. Skinner, 1972.
Skinner, B. F., & Ferster, C. B. (1969). *Contingencies of reinforcement: A theoretical analysis*. Meredith Corporation.
Slobin, D. I. (1985). Crosslinguistic evidence for the language-making capacity. In D. I. Slobin (Ed.), *The crosslinguistic study of language acquisition* (Vol. 2, pp. 1157–249). Erlbaum
Slobin, D. I. (2003). Language and thought online: Cognitive consequences of linguistic relativity. In D. Gentner & S. Goldin-Meadow (Eds.), *Language in mind: Advances in the study of language and thought* (pp. 157–192). The MIT Press.
Slobin, D. (2004). From ontogenesis to phylogenesis: What can child language tell us about language evolution? In J. Langer, S. T. Parker, & C. Milbrath (Eds.), *Biology and knowledge revisited: From neurogenesis to psychogenesis* (pp. 255–285). Lawrence Erlbaum Associates.
Slobin, D., & Bever, T. (1982). Children use canonical sentence schemes: A crosslinguistic study of word order and inflections, *Cognition*, *12*, 229–265.
Smith, L. (2011). *Challenges facing psychology departments*. http://www.apa.org/ed/governance/elc/2011/elc-lsmith2011.pdf
Smolensky, P. (1988). On the proper treatment of connectionism. *Behavioral and Brain Sciences*, *11*, 1–74.
Snow, C. P. (1964). *The two cultures: And a second look: An expanded version of the two cultures and the scientific revolution*. Cambridge University Press. (Original work published 1959)
Sokolov, E. N. (1960). Neuronal models in the orienting reflex. In M. A. Brazier (Ed.), *The central nervous system and behavior* (pp. 187–271). Macy Foundation.
Sokolov, E. N. (1963). *Perception and the conditioned reflex*. Pergamon Press.
Sokolov, E. N. (1975). *Neuronal mechanisms of the orienting reflex*. Erlbaum.
Sontag, S. (1975, February 6). Fascinating fascism. *The New York Review of Books*.
Spear, J. H. (2007). Prominent schools or other active specialties? A fresh look at some trends in psychology. *Review of General Psychology*, *11*, 363–380.
Spearman, C. E. (1904a). Proof and measurement of association between two things. *American Journal of Psychology*, *15*, 72–101.
Spearman, C. E. (1904b). 'General intelligence', objectively determined and measured. *American Journal of Psychology*, *15*, 201–293.
Spearman, C. E. (1907). Demonstration of Formulæ for true measurement of correlation. *The American Journal of Psychology*, *18*(2), 161–169.
Spearman, C. E. (1927). *The abilities of man: Their nature and measurement*. Macmillan.

Spelke, E. (2000). Core knowledge. *American Psychologist, 55*, 1233–1243.
Spelke, E., & Kinzler, K. D. (2007). Core knowledge. *Developmental Science, 10*, 89–96.
Spence, J. T. (1987). Centrifugal versus centripetal tendencies in psychology. Will the center hold? *American Psychologist, 42*, 1052–1054.
Spence, K. W. (1956). *Behavior theory and conditioning*. Yale University Press.
Sperber, D. (1985). Anthropology and psychology: Towards an epidemiology of representations. *Man* (London)*, 20*, 73–89.
Sperber, D. (1996). *Explaining culture: A naturalistic approach*. Blackwell.
Sperber, D., & Hirschfeld, L. A. (2004). The cognitive foundations of cultural stability and diversity. *Trends in Cognitive Sciences, 8*, 40–46.
Sperber, D., & Wilson, D. (1995). *Relevance: Communication and cognition* (2nd ed.). Blackwell.
Sperling, G. (1960). The information available in brief visual presentations. *Psychological Monographs: General and Applied, 74*(11, Whole No. 498), 1–29.
Sperry, R. W. (1963). Chemoaffinity in the orderly growth of nerve fiber patterns and connections. *Proceedings of the National Academy of Sciences of the United States of America, 50*(4), 703–710.
Sperry, R. W. (1995). The future of psychology. *American Psychologist, 50*, 505–506.
Spielrein, I. (1933). Zur Theorie der Psychotechnik [Towards the theory of psychotechnics]. Talk at the VIIth internatiaonal psychitecnic conference, Moscow, September 9th, 1931. *Zeitschrift für Angewandte Psychologie, 44*, 31–51.
Spielrein, S. (1994). Destruction as the cause of coming into being. *Journal of Analytical Psychology, 39*, 155–186. (Original work published 1912)
Spielrein, S. (1923). Quelques analogies entre la pensée de l'enfant celle de l'aphasique et la pensée subconsciente [Some analogies between the thought of the child, the aphatic patient and the subcoinscious thought]. *Archives de Psychologie, 18*, 305–322.
Spitz, R. A. (1945). Hospitalism. In R. S. Eissler (Ed.), *The psychoanalytic study of the child* (Vol. I). International Universities Press.
Spranger, E. (1926). Die Frage nach der Einheit der Psychologie [The issue of the unity of psychology]. *Sitzungsberichte der Preussischen Akademie der Wissenschaften. Philosophisch-Historische Klasse, 21–24*, 172–199.
Spranger, E. (1927). *Lebensformen: Geisteswissenschaftliche Psychologie und Ethik der Persönlichkeit* [Life forms. Mental science psychology and the ethics of personality] (6th ed.). Niemeyer.
Spranger, E. (1928). *Types of men*. Stechert.
Staats, A. W. (1968). *Learning, language and cognition*. Holt.
Staats, A. W. (1983). *Psychology's crisis of disunity: Philosophy and method for a unified science*. Praeger.
Staats, A. W. (1999). Unifying psychology requires new infrastructure, theory, method, and research agenda. *Review of General Psychology, 3*, 3–13.
Steinthal, H. (1881). *Einleitung in die Psychologie und Sprachwissenschaft* [Introduction to psychology and linguistics]. Dümmler. https://archive.org/details/einleitungindiep00steiuoft
Steinthal, H., & Lazarus, M. (Eds.). (1860). *Zeitschrift für Völkerpsychologie und Sprachwissenschaft*.
Stern, C., & Stern, W. (1907). *Die Kindersprache* [Child language]. Barth.
Stern, W. (1910). Abstracts of lectures on the psychology of testimony and on the study of individuality. *The American Journal of Psychology, 21*, 270–282.
Stern, W. (1911). *Die differentielle psychologie in ihren methodologischen Grundlagen* [Differential psychology in its methodological foundations]. Barth.

Stern, W. (1914). *The psychological methods of testing intelligence*. Warwick & York. Translation of Ster, 1912. https://openlibrary.org/books/OL7093967M/The_psychological_methods_of_testing_intelligence

Stern, W. (1938). *General psychology from the personalistic standpoint* (H. D. Spoerl, Trans.). Macmillan.

Sternberg, R. (2004). The role of biological and environmental contexts in the integration of psychology: A reply to Posner and Rothbart. *Canadian Psychology, 45*, 280–283.

Sternberg, R., & Grigorenko, E. L. (2001). Unified psychology. *American Psychologist, 56*, 1069–1079.

Sternberg, R., & Grigorenko, E. L. (2002). E pluribus unum. *American Psychologist, 57*, 1129–1130.

Sternberg, R., Grigorenko, E. L., & Kalmar, L. (2001). The role of theory in unified psychology. *Journal of Theoretical and Philosophical Psychology, 21*, 99–117.

Sternberg, R. J. (Ed.). (2005). *Unity in psychology: Possibility or pipedream?* American Psychological Association.

Sternberg, R. J. (Ed.). (2018). *The nature of human intelligence*. Cambridge University Press.

Sternberg, R. J., & Grigorenko, E. (Eds.). (1997). *Intelligence, heredity and environment*. Cambridge University Press.

Stevens, S. S. (1935). The operational basis of psychology. *American Journal of Psychology, 47*, 323–330.

Stevens, S. S. (1939). Psychology and the science of science. *Psychological Bulletin, 36*, 221–263.

Stevens, S. S. (1946). On the theory of scales of measurement. *Science, 103*, 677–680.

Stevens, S. S. (1951). *Handbook of experimental psychology*. Wiley.

Stevens, S. S. (1957). On the psychophysical law. *Psychological Review, 64*, 153–181.

Stevens, S. S. (1986). *Psychophysics: Introduction to its perceptual, neural and social prospects*. Routledge. (Original work published 1975)

Stich, S., & Ravenscroft, I. (1994). What is folk psychology? *Cognition, 50*, 447–468.

Student [William Sealy Gosset]. (1908). The probable error of a mean. *Biometrika, 6*, 1–25.

Sturm, T. (2012). Bühler and Popper: Kantian therapies for the crisis in psychology. *Studies in History and Philosophy of Biological and Biomedical Sciences, 43*, 462–472.

Sturm, T., & Mülberger, A. (2012). Crisis discussions in psychology – new historical and philosophical perspectives. *Studies in History and Philosophy of Science Part C: Studies in History and Philosophy of Biological and Biomedical Sciences, 43*, 425–433.

Sullivan, H. S. (1953). *The interpersonal theory of psychiatry*. Norton.

Sulloway, F. K. (1996). *Born to rebel: Birth order, family dynamics, and creative lives*. Pantheon.

Szász, T. (1961). *The myth of mental illness: Foundations of a theory of personal conduct*. Harper & Row.

Szentágothai, J. (1975). The 'module-concept' in cerebral cortex architecture. *Brain Research, 95*, 475–496.

Szondi, L. (1937). Contributions to "fate analysis": I. An attempt at a theory of choice in love. *Acta Psychologica, 3*, 1–80.

Szondi, L. (1952). *Experimental diagnostics of drives*. Grune & Stratton.

Taine, H. (1876a). Note sur l'acquisition du langage chez les enfants et dans l'espèce humaine [Remarks on the acquisition of language in children and in the human race]. *Revue Philosophique de la France et de l'Étranger, 1*, 5–23.

Taine, H. (1876b). *The origins of contemporary France*. Holt.

Talankin, A. (1932). Protiv menshevistycshchevo idealizma v psikhologii [Against menshevik idealism in psychology]. *Psikhologia, 1–2,* 38–62.
Talankin, A. A. (2000). On the Vygotsky and Luria group. *Journal of Russian and East European Psychology, 38*(6), 10–11. (Original work published 1931)
Tallal, P., & Piercy, M. (1973). Defects of non-verbal auditory perception in children with developmental dysphasia. *Nature, 241,* 468–469.
Tanner, W. P., Jr., & Swets, J. A. (1954). A decision-making theory of visual detection. *Psychological Review, 61,* 401–409.
Tarde, G. (1903). *The laws of imitation.* Holt. (Original work published 1890)
Tarde, G. (1901). *L'Opinion et la foule* [Opinions and the crowd]. Alcan. http://classiques.uqac.ca/classiques/tarde_gabriel/opinion_et_la_foule/tarde_opinion_et_la_foule.pdfb
Tarde, G. (1903). Inter-psychology: The interplay of human minds. *International Quarterly, 7,* 59–84.
Taylor, F. V. (1911). *The principles of scientific management.* Harper.
Taylor, J. A. (1956). Drive theory and manifest anxiety. *Psychological Bulletin, 53,* 303–320.
Teo, T. (2005). *The critique of psychology. From Kant to postcolonial theory.* Springer.
Teplov, B. (1985). Um polkovodtsa [The mind of the military leader]. In *Izbrannije trudi* (pp. 223–305). Pedagogika. (Original work published 1941)
Teplov, B. M. (1947). *Sovietskaja psihologicheskaja nauka za 30 let* [Soviet psychological science in 30 years]. Pravda.
Teplov, B. M. (1956–1967). *Tipologicheskie osob ennosti visshej nervnopj dejatelnosti cheloveka* [Typological features of human higher nervous activity] (Vols. 1–5). Nauka.
Ter Hark, M. (2007). *Popper, Otto Selz and the rise of evolutionary epistemology.* Cambridge University Press.
Terman, L. (1916). *The measurement of intelligence.* Riverdale Press; Gutenberg project. http://www.gutenberg.org/files/20662/20662-h/20662-h.htm
Teuber, H. L. (1955). Physiological psychology. *Annual Review of Psychology, 6,* 267–296.
Teuber, H. L. (1966). Kurt Goldstein's role in the development of neuropsychology. *Neuropsychologia, 4,* 299–310.
Thomas, M. C., & Karmiloff-Smith, A. (2003). Modeling language acquisition in atypical phenotypes. *Psychological Review, 110,* 647–682.
Thomas, W. I., & Znaniecki, F. (1927). *The Polish peasant in Europe and America* (Vol. 1, 4th ed.). Knopf
Thorndike, E. L. (1898). *Animal intelligence: An experimental study of the associative processes in animals.* Psychological Review, monograph supplements, no. 8. Macmillan. Electronic version in *Classics* . . .
Thorndike, E. L. (1911). *Individuality.* Houghton, Mifflin.
Thorndike, E. L. (1920). Intelligence and its uses. *Harper's Magazine, 140,* 227–235.
Thorndike, E. L. (1924). Measurement of intelligence. *Psychological Review, 31,* 219–252.
Thorndike, E. L. (1931). *Human learning.* Century.
Thorndike, E. L. (1932). *The fundamentals of learning.* Teachers College, Columbia University.
Thurstone, L. L. (1928). Attitudes can be measured, *American Journal of Sociology, 33,* 529–554.
Thurstone, L. L. (1952). L. L. Thurstone. In G. Lindzey (Ed.), *A history of psychology in autobiography* (Vol. VI, pp. 294–321). Prentice Hall.
Tinbergen, N. (1951). *The study of Intinct.* Clarendon Press.
Tinbergen, N. (1963). On aims and methods in ethology. *Zeitschrift für Tierpsychologie, 20,* 410–433.

Todes, D. P. (2012). *Pavlov's physiology factory. Experiment, interpretation, laboratory enterprise*. John Hopkins University Press.

Todes, D. P. (2014). *Ivan Pavlov: A Russian life in science*. Oxford University Press.

Tolman, E. C. (1932). *Purposive behavior in animals and men*. Century.

Tolman, E. C. (1935). Psychology versus immediate experience. *Philosophy of Science, 2*, 356–380.

Tolman, E. C. (1936). An operational analysis of "demands". *Erkenntnis, 6*, 383–391.

Tolman, E. C. (1948). Cognitive maps in rats and men. *Psychological Review, 55*, 189–208.

Tolman, E. C. (1951a). The intervening variable. In M. H. Marx (Ed.), *Psychological theory* (pp. 81–102). Macmillan.

Tolman, E. C. (1951b). *Behavior and psychological man*. University of California Press.

Tolman, E. C. (1959). Principles of purposive behaviorism. In S. Koch (Ed.), *Psychology: A study of a science* (Vol. 2, pp. 92–157). MacGraw Hill.

Tolman, E. C., & Brunswik, E. (1935). The organism and the causal texture of the environment. *Psychological Review, 42*, 43–77.

Tomasello, M. (1999). *The cultural origins of human cognition*. Harvard University Press.

Tomasello, M. (2000). The item based nature of children's early syntactic development. *Trends in Cognitive Sciences, 4*, 156–163.

Tomasello, M. (2003). *Constructing a language: A usage-based theory of language acquisition*. Harvard University Press.

Tomasello, M. (2009). *Why we cooperate*. The MIT Press.

Tomasello, M. (2014). *A natural history of human thinking*. Harvard University Press.

Tooby, J., & Cosmides, L. (1990). On the universality of human nature and the uniqueness of the individual: The role of genetics and adaptation. *Journal of Personality, 58*, 17–68.

Tooby, J., & Cosmides, L. (1992). Psychological foundations of culture. In J. H. Barkow, L. Cosmides, & J. Tooby (Eds.), *The adapted mind* (pp. 19–136). Oxford University Press.

Toulmin. S. (1978, September 28). The Mozart of psychology. *New York Review of Books, 25*, 51–57.

Towsey, P. M. (2009). More than a footnote to history in cultural-historical theory: The Zalkind summary, experimental study of higher behavioural processes, and "Vygotsky's blocks". *Mind, Culture, and Activity, 16*, 317–337.

Trautmann-Waller, C. (Ed.). (2004). *Quand Berlin pensait les peuples: anthropologie, ethnologie et psychologie 1850–1890* [When Berlin thought of people: Anthropology, ethnology and psychology 1850–1890]. CNRS.

Tryon, R. C. (1963). Psychology in flux: The academic-professional bipolarity. *American Psychologist, 18*, 134–143.

Tucker, R. C. (1955). *Stalin and the uses of psychology*. U.S. Air Force project rand research memorandum 1441. Rand Corporation.

Tucker, R. C. (1956). Stalin and the uses of psychology. *World Politics, 8*, 455–483.

Tulving, E. (1972). Episodic and semantic memory. In E. Tulving & W. Donaldson (Eds.), *Organization of memory* (pp. 381–402). Academic Press.

Turgenev, I. (1948). *Fathers and sons*. Hutchinson. http://intersci.ss.uci.edu/wiki/eBooks/Russia/BOOKS/Turgenev/FathersandSonsTurgenev.pdf (Original work published 1861)

Tversky, A., & Kahneman, D. (1974). Judgment under uncertainty: Heuristics and biases. *Science, 185*, 1124–1131.

Uexküll, J. von. (1926). *Theoretical biology*. Harcourt, Brace & Co.

Ullman, M. T. (2001). A neurocognitive perspective on language: The declarative/procedural model. *Nature Reviews Neuroscience, 2*, 717–726.

Ullman, M. T. (2004). Contributions of memory circuits to language: The declarative/procedural model. *Cognition, 92*, 231–270.

Umrihin, V. V. (1989). "Nachalo konca" povendencheskoj psihologii v SSSR [The "beginning of the end" of behavioral psychology in the USSR]. In M. G. Yarosevsky (Ed.), *Repressirovannaja nauka*. [Opressed Science]. Nauka (pp. 136–145).

Ungerleider, L. G., & Mishkin, M. (1982). Two cortical visual systems. In D. J. Ingle, M. A. Goodale, & R. J. W. Mansfield (Eds.), *Analysis of visual behavior* (pp. 549–586). The MIT Press.

Uttal, W. R. (2001). *The new phrenology: The limits of localizing cognitive processes in the brain*. The MIT Press.

Valsiner, J. (2005a). Towards a new science of the person: The potentials of the critical personology of William Stern. *Theory & Psychology, 15*, 401–406.

Valsiner, J. (Ed.). (2005b). *Heinz Werner and developmental science*. Kluwer.

Vargas, E. V., Latour, B., Karsenti, B., Aït-Touati, F., & Salmon, L. (2008). The debate between Tarde and Durkheim. *Environment and Planning D: Society and Space, 26*, 761–777.

Vargha, A. (1994). New data on the psychometry of the Szondi test. *Pszichológia, 14*, 199–268.

Vasilieva, J. (2010). Russian psychology at the turn of the 21st century and post-Soviet reforms in the humanities disciplines. *History of Psychology, 13*, 138–159.

Velichkovsky, B. M. (1982). *Contemporary cognitive psychology*. Moscow University Publishing House.

Velichkovsky, B. M. (1988). *Wissen und Handeln* [Knowledge and behavior]. Deutsche Verlag der Wissanschenften.

Veresov, N. (1999). *Undiscovered Vygotsky*. Lang.

Vernant, J. P. (1991). *Mortals and immortals*. Princeton University Press.

Vidal, F. (1994). *Piaget before Piaget*. Harvard University Press.

Vidal, F. (2000). Piaget avant Piaget. Pour une relécture de l'œuvre piagétiennne [Piaget before Piaget. Towards a new reading of the work of Piaget]. In O. Houdé & C. Meljac (Eds.), *Hommage international à Jean Piaget* [Internatiolan commemorizatioin of Piaget] (pp. 21–37). Presses Universitaires de France.

Vidal, F. (2001). Sabina Spielrein, Jean Piaget – going their own ways. *Journal of Analytical Psychology, 46*, 139–153.

Virués-Ortega, J., & Pear, J. J. (2015). A history of "Behavior" and "Mind": Use of behavioral and cognitive terms in the 20th century. *Psychological Record, 65*, 23–30.

Volosinov, V. N. (1976). *Freudianism: A Marxist critique* (I. R. Titunik, Trans.). Academic Press. (Original work published 1927)

Voyat, G. (1984a). The work of Henri Wallon. In G. Voyat (Ed.), *The world of Henri Wallon*. (pp. 33–58). Aronson.

Voyat, G. (Ed.). (1984b). *The world of Henri Wallon*. Aronson.

Vygodskaia, G. L., & Lifanova, T. M. (1996). *Lev Semenovich Vygotskii. Zhizn'. Deiatel'nost'. Shtrikhi k portretu* [Lev Semenovich Vygotsky. Life. Career. Brushstrokes of a Portrait]. Smysl.

Vygotsky, L. S. (1925). *Consciousness as a problem of the psychology of behavior*. Vygotsky, 1982, 78–98. https://www.marxists.org/archive/vygotsky/works/1925/consciousness.htm

Vygotsky, L. S. (1992). *Educational psychology*. St Lucie Press. (Original work published 1926)

Vygotsky, L. S. (1987). *The historical meaning of the crisis in psychology: A methodological investigation*. Plenum Press. Vygotsky, 1997, 233–343. (Original work published 1927)

Vygotsky, L. S. (1997). The instrumental method in psychology. In R. W. Rieber & J. Wollock (Eds.), *The collected works of L. S. Vygotsky* (Vol. 3, pp. 85–90). Plenum Press. https://www.marxists.org/archive/vygotsky/works/1930/instrumental.htm (Original work published 1930)

Vygotsky, L. S. (1986). *Thought and language*. The MIT Press. (Original work published 1934)

Vygotsky, L. S. (1962). *Thought and language*. The MIT Press.

Vygotsky, L. S. (1978). *Mind in society*. Harvard University Press.

Vygotsky, L. S. (1996–1999). *The collected works of Vygotsky* (Vols. 1–3). Plenum Press.

Vygotsky Archives. (1999). https://www.marxists.org/archive/vygotsky/

Waddington, C. H. (1942). The epigenotype. *Endeavour, 1*, 18–20.

Waddington, C. (1957). *The strategy of the genes*. George Allen & Unwin.

Wagoner, B. (2013). Bartlett's concept of schema in reconstruction. *Theory & Psychology, 23*(5), 553–575.

Wagoner, B. (2017a). *The constructive mind. Bartlett's psychology in reconstruction*. Cambridge University Press.

Wagoner, B. (Ed.). (2017b). *Handbook of culture and memory*. Oxford University Press.

Wagoner, B., & Gillespie, A. (2014). Sociocultural mediators of remembering: An extension of Bartlett's method of repeated reproduction. *British Journal of Social Psychology, 53*, 622–639.

Wallon, H. (1934). *Les Origines du Caractère chez l'Enfant* [The origins of character in children]. Boivin.

Wallon, H. (Ed.). (1938). *La Vie mentale. Encyclopédie Francaise: Vol. VIII* [The mental life: Vol. VIII of the French encyclopedia]. Larousse.

Wallon, H. (1942). *De l'acte à la pensée* [From action to thought]. Flammarion.

Wallon, H. (1947). *Projet de réforme Langevin-Wallon* [The Langevin-Wallon school reform project]. Institut Pédagogique Nationale.

Wallon, H. (1963). Pavlovisme et Psychologie [Pavlovism and psychology]. *Enfance, 16*, 79–85. (Original work published 1955)

Wallon, H. (1959). Le role de l'autre dans la construction du moi [The rôle of the other in the construction of the Me]. *Enfance, 12*, 277–286.

Wallon, H. (1968). Écrits et souvenirs. Including Entretien avec Henri Wallon [Writings and memoirs. Including an interview]. *Enfance, 21*, 1–154.

Wallon, H. (1990). *Psychologie et Dialectique. La Spirale et le Miroir* [Psychology and dialectics. The helix and the mirror]. Éditions Sociales.

Wason, P. C. (1968). Reasoning about a rule. *Quarterly Journal of Experimental Psychology, 20*, 273–281.

Watson, J. B., & McDougall, W. (1928). *The battle of behaviorism an exposition and an exposure*. Kegan Paul. Electronic version in *Classics*...

Watson, J. B., & Rayner, R. (1920). Conditioned emotional reactions. *Journal of Experimental Psychology, 3*, 1–14.

Watson, R. I. (1967). Psychology: A prescriptive science. *American Psychologist, 22*, 435–443.

Weber, M. (1958). *The protestant ethic and the spirit of capitalism*. Scribner. (Original work published 1905)

Weber, M. (1981). Some categories of interpretive sociology. *Sociological Quarterly, 22*, 151–180. (Original work published 1913)

Wechsler, D. (1939). *The measurement of adult intelligence*. Williams & Witkins.

Weidman, N. (1996). Psychobiology, progressivism, and the anti-progressive tradition. *Journal of the History of Biology, 29,* 267–308.
Weidman, N. (1997). Heredity, intelligence and neuropsychology; or, why The Bell Curve is good science. *Journal of the History of the Behavioral Sciences, 33,* 141–144.
Weidman, N. M. (1999). *Constructing scientific psychology. Karl Lashley's mind-brain debates.* Cambridge University Press.
Weimer, W. B., & Palermo, D. S. (1973). Paradigms and normal science in psychology. *Social Studies of Science, 3,* 211–244.
Werner, H. (1940). *Comparative psychology of mental development.* International Universities Press, Inc.
Werner, H., & Kaplan, B. (1963). *Symbol formation: An organismic developmental approach to language and the expression of thought.* John Wiley.
Werner, H., & Wapner, S. (1949). Sensory-tonic field theory of perception. *Journal of Personality, 18,* 88–107.
Wernicke, C. (1874). *Der aphasische Symptomenkomplex* [The aphasic symptom complex]. Cohn and Weigert.
Wertsch, J. V. (2008). The narrative organization of collective memory. *Ethos: Journal of the Society for Psychological Anthropology, 36,* 120–135.
Wertsch, J. V., & Roediger, H. L., III. (2008). Collective memory: Conceptual foundations and theoretical approaches. *Memory, 16,* 318–326.
White, R. W. (1959). Motivation reconsidered: The concept of competence. *Psychological Review, 66,* 297–333.
Whorf, B. L. (1956). *Language, thought, and reality.* MIT Press.
Wieczorek, O., Unger, S., &. Riebling, J. (2021). Mapping the field of psychology: Trends in research topics 1995–2015. *Scientometrics, 126,* 9699–9731.
Wiener, N. (1948). *Cybernetics or control and communication in the animal and the machine.* MIT Press.
Wiener, N. (1950). *The human use of human beings: Cybernetics and society.* Houghton Mifflin.
Wilson, E. O. (1975). *Sociobiology: The new synthesis.* Harvard University Press.
Winch, R. F. (1947). Heuristic and empirical typologies: A job for factor analysis. *American Sociological Review, 12,* 68–75.
Wirchow, R. (1872). Über die Methode der wissenschaftlichen Anthropologie [On the methods of scientific anthropology]. *Zeitschrift für Ethnologie, 4,* 300–320.
Wittgenstein, L. (1958). *Philosophical investigations* (2nd ed.). Macmillan, Blackwell. (Original work published 1953).
Wolf, P., & Holmes, K. J. (2002). Linguistic relativity. *Trends in Cognitive Sciences, 2,* 253–265.
Woodward, W. R. (1992). On opening the psychology of personality to philosophy and literature in our time. *New Ideas in Psychology, 10,* 191–194.
Woodworth, R. S. (1918). *Dynamic psychology.* Columbia University Press.
Woodworth, R. S. (1927). Dynamic psychology. In C. Murchison (Ed.), *Psychologies of 1925* (pp. 111–128). Clark University Press.
Woodworth, R. S. (1930). Dynamic psychology. In C. Murchison (Ed.), *Psychologies of 1930* (pp. 327–336). Clark University Press.
Woodworth, R. S. (1931). *Contemporary schools of psychology.* Appleton.
Woodworth, R. S. (1939). *Psychological issues: Selected papers of Robert S. Woodworth.* Columbia University Press.
Woodworth, R. S. (1948). *Contemporary schools of psychology.* Ronald Press.
Woodworth, R. S., & Schlossberg, H. (1954). *Experimental psychology* (2nd ed.). Holt.

Wundt, W. (1912). *Lectures on human and animal psychology*. Macmillan. https://archive.org/details/lecturesonhumana00wund/page/n4/mode/2up (Original work published 1863)

Wundt, W. (1888). Über Ziele und Wege der Völkerpsychologie [On the goals and roads of Völkerpsychologie]. *Philosophische Studien, 4*, 1–27.

Wundt, W. (1900). *Völkerpsychologie: Vol. I. Sprache* [Völkerpsychologie: Vol. 1. Language]. Engelmann. Other volumes and revisions until 1920.

Wundt, W. (1903). *Naturwissenchaft und Psychologie* [Natural science and psychology]. Engelmann.

Wundt, W. (1973). *An introduction to psychology*. Arno Press. https://ia700301.us.archive.org/7/items/introductiontops032004mbp/introductiontops032004mbp.pdf (Original work published 1912)

Wundt, W. (1916). *Elements of folk psychology* (E. L. Schaub, Trans.). Allen and Unwin and Macmillan.

Wundt, W. (1973). *The language of gestures*. Mouton. With additional chapters from G. H. Mead & K. Buhler.

Xypas, C. (2001). *L'autre Piaget. Cheminement intellectuel d'un éducateur d'humanité* [The other Piaget. The intellectual road of an educator of humanity]. L'Harmattan.

Yarbus, A. L. (1967). *Eye movements and vision*. Plenum Press.

Yarosevsky, M. G. (Ed.). (1989). *Repressirovannaja nauka* [Opressed science]. Nauka.

Yaroshevsky, M. G. (1968). I. M. Sechenov – the founder of objective psychology. In B. B. Wolman (Ed.), *Historical roots of contemporary psychology* (pp. 77–110). Harper and Row.

Yasnitsky, A. (2011). Vygotsky circle as a personal network of scholars: Restoring connections between people and ideas. *Integrative Psychological and Behavioral Science, 45*, 422–457.

Yasnitsky, A., & van der Veer, R. (Eds.). (2015). *Revisionist revolution in Vygotsky studies*. Routledge.

Yerkes, R. M., & Dodson, J. D. (1908). The relation of strength of stimulus to rapidity of habit-formation. *Journal of Comparative Neurology and Psychology, 18*, 459–482.

Yerkes, R. M., & Morgulis, S. (1909). The method of Pavlov in animal psychology. *Psychological Bulletin, 6*, 257–273.

Zawadzki, P. (2004). Halbwachs est-il notre contemporain? [Is Halbwachs our contemporary?] In Y. Deloye & C. Haroche (Eds.), *Maurice Halbwachs. Espaces, mémoires et psychologie collective* (pp. 181–203). Presses de la Sorbonne.

Zazzo, R. (1984). The two sources of intelligence for Henri Wallon. In G. Voyat (Ed.), *The world of Henri Wallon* (pp. 165–176). Aronson.

Zeigarnik, B. (1927). Das Behalten Erledigter Und Unerledigter Handlungen [Remembering finished and unfinished behaviors]. *Psychologische Forschung, 9*, 1–85.

Zeigarnik, B. V. (1972): *Experimental abnormal psychology*. Plenum Press.

Zimbardo, P. G. (1973). On the ethics of intervention in human psychological research: With special reference to the Stanford prison experiment. *Cognition, 2*, 243–256.

Zimbardo, P. G. (2004). Does psychology make a significant difference in our lives? *American Psychologist, 59*, 339–351.

Zinchenko, P. I. (1983). The problem of involuntary memory. *Soviet Psychology, 22*, 55–111. (Original work published 1939)

Zinchenko, V. P., & Vergiles, N. Y. (1972). *Formation of visual images*. Consultants Bureau.

Zittoun, T., Gillespie, A., & Cornish, F. (2009). Fragmentation or differentiation: Questioning the crisis in psychology. *Integrative Psychological and Behavioral Science, 43*, 104–115.

Author Index

Note: Page numbers in *italics* indicate pages in the references

Abelson, R.P. 209, *532*
Ádám, G. 238, *488*
Adler, A. 5, 9–11, 20, 28, 452, *488*
Agnoti, F. 137, *508*
Aït-Touati, F. *539*
Alexander, B. 14
Alexander, F. 12, 14, 245, *488*
Alexandre, J. 113, *488*
Allen, M. *525*
Allolio-Näcke, L. *510*
Allport, F. 64, 193–195, 198, *488*
Allport, G. W. 24, 30–32, 37, 51, 60, 71–72, 150, 166–167, 194, 205, 208, 314, 336, 448, 452, 574, *488–489*
Alpert, R. *532*
Ananiev, B. 230, 259, 262, 264, 268, *489*
Anderson, J. R. 146, 312, 365, *489*
Anokhin, P.K. 270, *489*
Appleton, P. 341, *489*
Arendt, H. 200, 207, *489*
Aronson, E. 167, *489*
Asch, S.E. 192, 200, 207, 402, *489*
Ash, M. 151, *489, 510*
Ashis, N. 453, *489*
Asmolov, A.G. 256, *489*
Asratian, E. A. 232, 238, *489*
Assmann, J. 122–123, *489, 490*
Austin, G.A. *494*
Austin, J. L. 341, *490*

Bailyn, B. *519*
Baker, D. B. *486*
Bakhtin, M. 4, 172, 243, *490*
Ballachey, E.S. *514*
Bandi Rao, S. *519*

Bandura, A. 189, 192, 304, 311, 316–317, *490*
Barkóczi, I. 275, *490*
Barkow, J.H. 362, 405, *490*
Baron-Cohen, S. 417, 442, *490*
Bartlett, F. C. xiii, 1, 102, 106, 117, 120, 137–150, 210, 224, 338, 352, *490*, 521, 530
Basov, N.J. 265, 447, *491*
Bastide, R. 117, *491*
Bates, E. 373–377, 382, 390, *491, 501, 518*
Bateson, G. 455–457, *491*
Bauer, R. A. 219–220, 237, 239, 246, 263, 267, *491*
Bekhterev, V. (Bechterew, W.) 185, 217–220, 226–231, 237, 264, *491*
Bekkering, H. *503*
Bellugi, U. 376–377, 443, *491*
Bennett, E.L. *514*
Berdyaev, N. 218
Berger, H. 329
Bergman, E. T. 146, *491*
Beritov-Beritasvili, I.S. 270, 278
Berko, J. 34, 321, 376–377, 390, *491*; see also Berko-Gleason, J
Berko-Gleason, J. 376, *491, 494*
Berlin, I. xii, 1, 468, *491*
Bever, Th. 337, 371, 377, 383, 390, *491, 534*
Billig, M. 200, *492*
Binet, A. 35, 54, 78, 80–82, 102, 145, 181, *492*
Bíró, S. *504*
Black, A. H. *530*
Bleuler, E. 6, 80, 83, 129, *492*
Blodgett, H. C. 296, *492*

Author Index

Blondel, C. i, xiii, 13, 96, 103, 106, 109–110, 112, 115, 161, 189, *492*, 523
Blonski, [Blonsky] P.P. 222–224, *492–493*
Blum, F. 448, *493*
Blumenthal, A. 177, 343, *493*
Boas, F. 102, 135, 172, *493*
Boden, M.A. 344, *493*
Boneau, C.A. *486*
Boole, G. 367, *493*
Borgatta, E.F. 203, *493*
Boring, E. G. 3, 283–284, 301, *487*, *493*
Boross, O. 412, *528*
Botkin, S. 235
Bourdieu, P. 102, 179, *493*
Bower, G.H. 146, 312, 351, *489*, *490*, *493*
Boyd, R. 419, *493*
Braunstein, J.F. 481–482, *493*
Breton, A. 4, 13
Brewer, W. F. 306, *493*
Bridgman, P.W. 15, 283–285, *493*
Broca, P. 169, 420, 426, 442, *493*
Brown, D. E. 409, *494*
Brown, R. 321, 351, 371, 375–378, *494*, 528
Bruner, J. 91, 115, 128, 132, 276, 334, 336–343, 345–346, 351, 364, 366, 378–379, 393, 468, 474, 479, 489, *494*, 530
Brunswik, E. 66, 151, 159, 288–290, 295–296, 327, *494*, 506, 525
Bugental, J. F. 150, 158, *495*
Bühler, C. 161, 459, *495*
Bühler, K. xiii, 1, 23, 62, 68, 76–77, 102, 150–162, 102, 178, 288, 295, 303, 422, 447, 460, 471, 477, *495*
Bukharin, N.I. 230, 239, 248
Bush, R.R. 312, *497*, *517*
Buss, D. M. 53, 405–407, *490*
Buzsáki, G. 392, *495*
Bykhovsky, B. 243–244
Bykov, K. M. 238, 270–271, *495*

Calkins, M. W. 35, 320, *495*
Campbell, D. T. 160, 297, 411, 422, 430, 477–480, *496*
Canetti, E 186, *496*
Canguilhem, G. 359, 480–482, 493, *496*, 531
Cantril, H. 186
Capshew, J.H. 446, *498*
Carnap, R. 298, 462, *496*
Carpendale, J.I.M. *524*
Carroll, J. B. 57, 136, *496*
Carroy, J. 12, 105, 180, 472, *496*

Casagrande, J. B. 136, *496*
Cattell, R.B. 53, 57, *496*
Changeux, J.P. 93, 352, 419, 422–423, 476, 483, *496–497*
Chelpanov, G.I. 218–224, 228–230, 232, *497*, 514
Cherry, C. 328, 359, *497*
Chipman, S. 348, *532*
Chomsky, N. 81, 91–94, 136, 177, 189, 275–276, 294, 304–310, 336–337, 341, 347, 351, 365, 369–372, 374–380, 390–392, 422, 428–429, 437, 441, 443, 486, *497*, *507*, *522*, 527–528
Clark, A. 358, 387, *497*
Clark, C. J. 200, *497*
Clark, H. H. 465, *497*
Clark, K.B. 340–341, *497*
Clark, M.P. 340–341, *497*
Cohen, J. 402, 454, *498*
Cohen, L. 257, 414, *499*
Cohen-Cole, J. 336, 354, 364, *498*
Cole, M. 134, 275, 277, *498*, *532*
Collins, A.M. 349, 368, 381, *493*, *498*
Comte, A. 102, 124, 164, 166, 462, *498*
Conway, A.R. 436, *514*
Conway, J.B. 474, *498*
Cooper, L. 348, *532*
Cornish, F. 478, *542*
Cosmides, L. 101, 394, 505, 411, 425, *490*, *498*, *538*
Crago, M. B. 443, *504*
Craig, W. 60–61, 369, *498*
Craik, K. W. 140, 352, *498*
Crook, C. 148, *521*
Crozier, W. 301
Crutchfield, R. *514*
Csibra, G. xvi, 189, 257, 374, 380, 412–413, 416, 427, 437, 445, *498*, *504*
Csíkszentmihályi, M. 452

Da Pos, O. 511
Dahrendorf, R. 179, *499*
Dali, S. 4
Damasio, A. 420, 426, *499*
Danchin, A. 93, *497*
Danziger, K. 141, 143, 175, 193–194, 196, 201, 467, 478, *499*
Deborin, A.M. 263
Dehaene, S. 93, 256, 257, 414, 421, 424, *497*, *499*
DeLamater, J. 190, 499
Delay, J. 105–106, 454–455, *499*, 523
Dellantonio, A. 511
Delouvée, S. 517

Author Index 545

Dennett, D. xvi, 59, 160, 255, 294, 303, 343, 379, 409, 412, 417–418, 422, 463, *499*
Dewsbury, D. A. 71, 349, *499*
Dilthey, W. 35–38, 44, 126–128, 153, 168, 172, 176, 252, 403, 468, 473, 476, *499*, 516
Dolan, C.V. 512
Dollard, J. 23, 189, 192, 200, 287, 293, 311, 315–318, *500*, *522*
Donald, M. 135, 412, 460–461, *500*
Donaldson, W. 538
Donders, F. C. 347, *500*
Doob, L. W. 200, *500*
Draaisma, D. 143, *500*
Driesch, H.A.E. 154, 158, 470, *500*
Ducret, J.J. 78, 80, *500*
Dunbar, R. 204, 462, *490*, *500*
Dupoux, E. 436, *520*
Dupuy, J. P. 344, *500*
Durkheim, E. i, 13, 38, 100, 102–103, 106–113, 125, 129–130, 168, 173, 179, 183, 187–189, 195, 211, 466, *500*, 511, 533, 539

Ebbinghaus, H. 32, 142–143, 145, 172, 212, 319, 476, *500*, 513
Eccles, J.C. 418, *529*
Edwards, D. 108, 147–148, *500*, *521*
Eichenbaum, B. 247
Eimas, P.D. 436–437, *500*
Ekstein, R. 495
Elkonin, D. 248, 253, 276, *501*
Ellenberger, H. F. 13, *501*
Ellis, B. J. 413, 430, *501*
Ellis, W. 410, *501*
Endress, A.D. *513*
Engels, F. 225, 229, 241, 259
Erdélyi, M. H. 19, 148, 393, *501*
Erikson, E. 313, 457–458, *501*
Ermakov, I. 242
Erős, F. 168, 206, 212, 245, *501*
Eschbach, A. 158, *501*
Espagne, M. 173, *501*
Etkind, A. 218, 240–243, *501*
Eysenck, H. 48–49, 53, 312–313, 429, *501*

Farr, R. 164, 167–168, 208–209, 212–213, *501–502*
Feest, U. 286, *502*
Féré, C. *492*
Ferenczi, S. 15–18, 26, 28, 245, *502*, 521
Ferster, C.B. 302, *534*
Festinger, L. 186, 191–192, 209, *502*, 525
Feuerbach, L. 229

Fisher, R., Sir 55, 428, 449, *502*
Fisher, S.E. 445, *514*
Fitch, T. 371, *507*
Flavell, J. 90, 344, *502*
Fleck, L. 162, *502*
Fleming, D.F. 519
Fodor, J. 81, 93–94, 326, 334, 356–358, 361, 368, 386, 388, 391–395, 408–409, 411, 429, 437, 441, 463, 493, *502*
Forgács, B. xvi–vii, 476
Forman, M. 455
Foucault, M. 272, 455–456, 479
Fox, D. R. *502*
Fraisse, P. 352, 468, 473, 487, *502*
Fraser, C. 377, *502*
Fraser, J. 250, *502*
Freedheim, D.K. *486*
Frege, G. 88, 385, *503*
Frenkel-Brunswik, E. 23, *488*
Freud, A. 18, 457, *503*
Freud, S. xii, 3–9, 109–114, 142, 150, 184–186, 201, 230–245, 302, 312, 315, 406, 408, 412, 432, 450, 452, 456–457, 468, 501, *503*, 522, 529, 539
Frisch, J. von 69, 503
Frobenius, L. 38–39, *503*

Gadamer, H. G. 447, 462, *503*
Galanter, E. 312, 497, *522*, *527*
Galperin, P. Y. 248, 253, 257–258, *503*
Gao, E. *525*
Gardner, H. 55, 334, 336, 452, 479, *503*
Garfinkel, H. 465, *503*
Gaskell, G. *501*, *508*
Gauld, A. 146, *503*
Gazzaniga, M. S. 483, *503*
Gebhard, P. *512*
Geldern, J. von 185, *503*
Gentile, B. F. *486*
Gergely, G. xvi, 82, 189, 257, 374, 380, 412–413, 416, 445, *498*, *503*, *504*
Gergen, K. 210, 402, 403, *504*
Gergen, M. M. 403, *504*
Gesell, A. 75, *504*
Geuter, U. 46, *504*
Gibson, J. J. 320, 338, 350, *504*
Gigerenzer, G. 55, 288, *504*
Gillespie, A. 478, *542*
Gilman, A. 375, *494*
Ginneken, J. van 165, *504*
Glenn, S. S. *508*
Goffman, E. 464–465, *504*
Goldstein, J. 30, 102, *504*

546 Author Index

Goldstein, K. 157, 344, *504*, 537
Gombocz, Z. 177–178, *504*
Gombrich, E. 338, *505*
Gonseth, W.S. (Student) 55
Goodale, M. A. 424, *504*, *538*
Goodnow, J.J. *494*
Gopnik, A. 335, 341, *504*
Gopnik, M. 443, *504*
Grastyán, E. 275, 330, *505*
Gray, J. A. 48, *519*, *524*
Green, C. D. 286, 354, *484*, *505*
Greenfield, P.M. *494*
Greenfield, S. 461, *505*
Greenspoon, J. 306, *505*
Greenwood, J. D. 176, 213, *505*
Gregory, R. 338, *505*
Grigorenko, E.L. 433–434, 439–440, 477, *505*, *535–536*
Guilford, J.P. 55, 57, *505*
Gulyás, B. 421, *512*
Gurova, L. 384, *528*
Guthrie, E. R. 300–301, 312, *505*
Gyáni, G. 121, *505*

Habermas, J. 89, 131, *505*
Haeckel, E. H.P.A. 124, 175, 385, 430, *505–506*
Haggbloom, S. J. 302, *506*
Halbwachs, M. i, xiii, 103, 106, 108–109, 110–124, 143, 146, 161–162, 214, 488, *506*, 509, 523, 524, 542
Haley, J. *491*
Hall, G. S. 75, *506*
Hammond, K. R. 66, *506*
Harkai Schiller, P. 20, 60, 64–65, 70–71, 159, 297, *506*, 519; *see also* Schiller, P.
Harré, R. 277, 463–464, 468, *506*
Harrington, A. 66, *506*
Hartley, E. *518*
Harzing, A.W. 192, 349, *507*
Hatfield, G. 398, *507*
Hathaway, S. R. 52, *507*
Hauser, A. 4, *507*
Hauser, M.D. 371, *507*
Head, H. Sir 139, 144, *507*
Hearnshow, L. S. *487*
Hebb, D. O. 67, 294, 326, 329–332, 345, 353, 364, 387, 422, 429, 474, *507*
Heider, F. 191–192, 209, *507*, 525
Heinroth, M. 64–65, *507*
Heinroth, O. 60, 62, 64–65, 6, 153, *507*
Hellpach, W. 179, *507*
Hempel, C. G. 40, 283, 355, *507*
Henry, V. 35, 145, *492*

Hermann, A. 17
Hermann, I. 15, 17, 285, *507*
Heron, W. 208, *507*
Herrnstein, R. J. 432–434, *486*, *507*
Hetzer, H. 151, *495*
Hilgard, E. 294, 366, *508*
Hillix, W. A. 282, *520*
Himmelweit, H. T. 212, *501*, *508*
Hirschfeld, L.A. 149, *535*
Hirstein, W. 483, *529*
Hjerthholm, E. *513*
Hochberg, J. E. 343, *508*
Holmes, K.J. 136–137, *541*
Houdé, O. 81, *508*, *529*
House, J. S. 190, *508*
Hull, C.L. 287–291, 297–300, 312–316, 322–323, 345, 403, *508*
Hull, D L. 422, *508*
Humboldt, W. von 34, 39, 44, 135, 171, 174, 352, 379, *508*
Humphrey, N. K. 117, 406, 413, 415, *508*
Hunt, E. 137, *508*
Hunt, J. M. 432, *508*
Hunyady, Gy. xvi, 182, *508–509*
Hurst, J. A. *514*
Husserl, E. 115, 155, 404, *509*

Ingle, D. J. *538*
Inhelder, B. 89–90, *523*, *527*
Ivanov, V. 218, 240
Ivanov-Smolensky, A. G. 237, 270–271, *509*

Jablonka, E. 422, 439, *509*
Jackendoff, R. 424, *515*
Jacklin, C. N. 318, *518*
Jackson, D. D. *491*
Jackson, H. J. 12, 105, 139
Jacob, F. 410, 476, *509*
Jacob, P. 424, *510*
Jacobson, L. 402, *531*
Jaensch, E.R. 45–49, *509*
Jaensch, W. 46
Jahoda, G. 131, 164, 169, 173, 192, *509*
Jaisson, M. 117, *509*
Jakobson, R. 154–155, 159, 329, 344, 370, 379, 423, *509*
James, W. 112, 301, 436, 452, 467–468, 474, 479, *509*
Janet, P. 13, 102, 103–106, 109, 146, 162, 224, 245, 252, 315, 455, 496, *510*
Janis, I. L. 198, *510*
Jeannerod, M. 352, 424, *510*
Jenkins, J. 320–321, *526*
Jennings, H.S. 68, 292, *510*

Jensen, A.R. 56, 30, 429, 431–433, *510*
Jerne, N.K. 422, *510*
John-Steiner, V. 251, *510*
Johnston, E. 137, *510*
Jones, E. 4, *510*
Joravsky, D. 217, 226, 249, 269, *510*
Jost, T. 210, *510*
Jovanovic, G. 405, *510*
Jovchelovitch, S. 213, *511*
József, A. 4, 501
Jung, C. G. 5–9, 20, 28, 44–45, 47–49, 501, 63, 71, 80, 124, 218, 241–242, 320, 452, 474, *511*, 525
Jusczyk, P.W. *500*

Kafka, F. 30
Kagan, J.S. 43, 433, *511*
Kahneman, D. 348–349, 362–363, 425, *511*, *538*
Kail, M. 169, 182, *511*
Kalinin, M. 267
Kalmar, L. *536*
Kandel, E.R. 236, 476, *498*, *511*
Kant, I. 44, 47, 92, 258–259, 286, *517*, *534*
Kapás, I. 245, *511*
Kaplan, B. 76, *541*
Karady, V. 108, *511*
Kardos, L. 22, 151, 159, 273, 297, *511*
Karmiloff-Smith, A. 85, 94, 379, 429, 444, *501*, *511*, *537*
Karmos, G. *505*
Karsenti, B. *539*
Kashima, J. 19, *511*
Katin, B. 226
Katona, G. 460, *511*
Kees-Jan, K. 435, *512*
Kellényi, L. *505*
Kelley, H. H. 192, 209, 418, *512*
Kendler, H. H. 344, 473, 480, *512*
Kendler, T.S. 344, *512*
Kerényi, C. 8, *511*
Kéri, S. 421, *512*
Kesey, K. 455
Kesserling, T. 91, 160, *512*
Ketellar, D. 410, *512*
Key, E. 75, *512*
Killborne, K. 376
Kimble, G. A. 471, 474–477, 486, *512*
Kinsbourne, M. 343, *499*
Kinsey, A. 165, *512*
Kintsch, W. 143, 349, 352, 360–361, *501*, *512*, *516*
Kinzler, K. D. 438, *534*
Király, I. xvi, *503*
Kiss, T. 89

Kitchener, R.F. 84, 91, 130, *512*
Kitchin, R. 401, *512*
Klages, L. 40–41, 48, *512*
Klautke, E. 170, 173, 179, *512*
Koch, S. 471–478, *513*
Kohlberg, L. 88, 13, *513*
Köhler, W. 60, 85, 157–158, 251, 350, *513*
Konorski, J. 270–271, 293, *513*
Kornilov, K. N. 220, 222–226, 228, 230–231, 241, 247–248, *513*
Kosslyn, S. M. 297, 327, 349, 361, 386, 420, *513*
Kostyleff, N. 154, *513*
Kotin, B. 226
Kovács, Á. M. 418, *513*
Kovács, I. xvi, 438, *514*
Kovács, K. xvi–vii, 35–36, 436, *514*
Kozulin, A. 218–219, 222, *514*
Kramer, R. 458, *514*
Krasner, L. 306, *514*
Krech, D. 307, 207, 296, *514*; see also Krechevsky, I.
Krechevsky, I. 296, *514*
Kretschmer, E. 43–45, 48, *514*
Kruglanski, A. W. 165, 191, 21, *510*, *514*
Krupskaja, N. 223, 247
Kubrick, S. 310
Kuhl, P.K. *504*
Kuhn, T. 346, *514*
Kulik, J. 375, 494
Külpe, O. 150, 155, *514*
Kundera, M. 342, *514*
Kuo, Z. Y. 66–67, *514*
Kutas, M. 382, *514*

Lacan, J. 12, 455, *514*, 531
Lachman, J. L. 335, 358, 367, *514*, *532*
Lachman, R. 358, *514*
Lagache, D. 20, 472–473, 481–482, 496, *514*
Lai, C. S. L. 446, *514*
Laing, R.D. 455–457, *514*
Lamb, M.J. 439, *509*
Lamiell, J. T. 34, 37, *515*
Landau, B. 424, *515*
Lange, N. 218, 258
Langman, R. E. *508*
LaPiere, R. T. 205, *515*
Lashley, K.S. 54, 67, 70, 314, 329, 331–332, 442, *515*
László, J. 147, 168, *515*
Latour, B. xv, 149, 366, *515*, *539*
Laubichler, M. D. 427, *515*
Lavabre, M-C. 119, 515
Lavater, J.K. 41

548 *Author Index*

Lazarsfeld, P. F. 23, 151, 160, *515*
Lazarus, M. 32, 170–177, *515*, *516*, *535*
Lazurskiy, A.F. 218
Leahey, T. H. *487*
Leary, D. E. 470, *515*
Le Bon, G. 64, 165, 167, 170, 180–187, 197, 493, *515*
Lenin, V. I. 11, 185, 221, 223, 231, 260, 263, *515*
Lenneberg, E. H. 344, 370, 375, 379, 429, 440, 443, *494*, *516*
Le Ny, J.-F. 236, 351–352, *516*
Leontiev, A. N. 220, 247–248, 250, 253–257, 259, 261–262, 268–269, 275, 353, *516*
Le Rider, J. 30, *516*
Lessing, H.U. 172, *516*
Levelt, W.J.M. 177, 323, 370, 374, *516*
Levin, A. *532*
Levinson, D. 23, *488*
Levinson, S. C. 136, *516*
Lévi-Strauss, C. 126, 410, 476, *516*
Lévy-Bruhl, L. i, xiii, 38, 83, 96, 103, 124–126, 135, 140, 161–162, 169, 211, 213, 252, 509, *516*
Lewin, K. 23, 53, 60, 65, 70, 191–193, 197–201, 206, 253, 295–296, 314, 317, *516*
Lifanova, T.M. 250, *539*
Likert, R. 205–206, *516*
Lilienfeld, S. O. 452, *517*
Lindenberg, S. xvi
Lindholm, G. 180, 185, *517*
Lindner, G. 172, *517*
Lindsay, P.H. 350, 366, *517*
Lindzey, G. xvi, 167, *487*, *517*
Li Ping, C. 376
Lippitt, R. 199, 200, *516*
Lippman, W. 33, 54, *517*
Lodge, D. 129, *517*
Loeb, J. 88, 292, 301, 303, *517*
Loftus, E. 402, *517*
Lo Monaco, G. 118, *517*
Lombroso, C. 41–42, 187, *517*
Lomov, B. 275
Lopatin, L. M. 222
Lorenz, K. 60–71, 153, 158–159, 331, 371, *517*
Lubek, I. 166, *517*
Luce, R.D. 312, *517*
Lunacharsky, A. 221
Luria, A.R. 37, 84, 132–135, 161–162, 223–229, 237, 241–244, 247–250, 253, 256–257, 353, 435, *518*

Maccoby, E. E. 167, 318, *518*
MacCorquodale, K. 287, 307, *518*
Mach, E. 30, 36, 157, 181, *518*
Mack, S. 476, *511*
MacKay, D. 327, *518*
MacWhinney, B. 373, 376–377, 382, *491*, *518*
Magoun, H. W. 329, *523*
Maienschein, J. 427, *515*
Maiorov, F. P. 237, *518*
Makareno, A.S. 267
Malenkov. G. 269
Malinowski, B. 4, *518*
Maltzmann, I. 275, *498*
Mandler, G. 320, 343–344, 349, 354–355, 382, 465, 469, 471, *519*
Mandler, J. M. 343–344, *519*
Mangalath, P. 361, *512*
Mannheim, K. 112, 162, *519*
Marcus, G. F. 390, 395, 409–410, 413, 430, 435, 439, 445, *519*
Marcuse, H. 26–28, *519*
Marková, I. 212, *523*
Marquis, D. M. 236, 294, *508*
Martin, C. *512*
Martin, E. 320, *520*
Martindale, C. 476, 519
Marton, L. M. 48, 71, 273, *519–520*
Martzion, O. *509*
Marx, K. 97, 164, 195, 201, 225, 229, 245, 258–260, 468, 510, *520*, 531
Marx, M.H. 282, *520*
Maslow, A. 9, 72–73, *520*
Mauss, M. 107–110, 197, *500*, *520*
Mauthner, F. 172
May, W. H. *526*
Mayo, E. 204, *520*
McClelland, D. C. 11, 72, 208, *520*
McClelland, J.L. 390, *520*
McCulloch, W. 332, 386, *520*
McDougall, W. 8, 60, 62–67, 73, 108, 124, 183, 194–195, *520*
McGinnies, E. *529*
McKinley, J. C. 52, *507*
McLeish, J. 216, 220, 267, *529*
McNeill, D. 375, *494*
Mead, G.H. 27, 84, 108, 116, 170, 172, 178, 192, 213, *520*
Mead, M. 4, *520*
Meade, M.L. *530*
Meehl, P. E. 287, 363, *518*, *520*
Mehler, J. 337, 369, 383, 388, 390, 423, 436, 437, *504*, *520*
Melanie, E. 459, *495*
Meljac, C. 81, *508*

Melton, A. W. 320, *520*
Meltzoff, A.N. 342, *504*
Mercier, D. 362, *521*
Mercier, H. 70, *521*
Mérei, F. 22, 78, 98, 203–204, 273, 447, *520–521*
Merezhkovsky, D. 218
Merleau-Ponty, M. 66, 80, *521*
Mervis. C.B. 349, *531*
Meskil, D. 41, *521*
Mészáros, J. xvi, 12, 14–17, *521*
Metzler, J. 349, *532*
Meumann, E. 33, 198, *521*
Meyerson, I. 123, 125–129, 161, 252, *521*, 560
Middleton, D. 108, 147–148, *500*, *521*
Milgram, S. 165, 192, 200, 207–208, 402, 496, *521*
Miller, B.O. *486*
Miller, George Armitage [G.A.] 4–5, 324, 328, 334–338, 340, 344–346, 349–351, 358–359, 370, 372, 381, 390, 451, *521–522*
Miller, Gregory, A. 482, 522
Miller, J.G. 311, *522*
Miller, M.A. 244
Miller, N. E. 23, 189, 192, 200, 287, 293, 311, 315–318, *500*, *522*
Miller, S. 270–271, 293, *513*
Milner, P.M. 331, 424, *504*
Miron, M. S. *526*
Mironenko, I.A. 262, 277, *522*
Mischel, W. 53, *522*
Mishkin, M. 424, *538*
Miyamoto, Y. 211, *525*
Moede, W. 198, *522*
Moessinger, P. 131, *522*
Monaco, A. P. *514*
Montgomery, K.C. 331, *522*
Morawski, J. G. 167, *523*
Moreno, J. L. 192, 201–204, 273, 493, *523*
Moreno, Z. 203
Morgan, C. L. 209, *523*
Morgulis, S. 292, *523*, *542*
Morin, O. xvi, 147, 415, *523*
Morris, C. 325, *523*
Morton, J. 387, *523*
Moruzzi, G. 329, *523*
Moscovici, S. 4, 112, 129, 166–168, 179–180, 186, 189, 209, 211–213, 450, 501, *523*
Mowrer, O. H. 60, 109, 200, 284, 304, 312–316, 318–322, 351, 374, 471, *500*, *523*
Mucchielli, L. 181, *523*

Mülberger, A. 154, 470, *524*, *536*
Müller, G. E. 145, 172, 320, *524*
Müller, U. 81, *524*
Murchison, C. *487*
Murphy, G. *495*
Murray, H. A. 52, 71–72, 314, 434, *524*
Musil, R. 30, 41, *524*
Myers, C. 124, 138–140

Nádasdy, Z. *504*
Nadel, L. 297, *525*
Nagy, L. 447
Namer, G. 116–118, *524*
Nánay, B. xvi, 160, *524*
Nebylitsyn, V. D. 48, *524*
Neisser, U. 147, 350–351, 360, 434, *524*
Nelson, K. 321, *524*
Némedi, D. 107, *524*
Neumann, J. von 322, 358, 365, 367–368, *524*
Neurath, O. *524*
Neuroskeptic 403, *524*
Newcomb, T. *518*
Newell, A. 336, 358, 361, 365, 386, 391, *524*, *533*
Nicolas, S. 12, *524*
Nietzsche, F. 40–41, 218, 240, 468
Nisbett, R.E. 211, *524–525*
Noll, R. 7, 9, *525*
Nora, P. 119–120, 397, *525*
Norman, D.A. 350, 366, *517*
Noveck, I. 465, 484, *525*
Núñez, R. *525*
Nye, R. 180, *525*
Nyíri, J. C. xvi, 114, 134, 135, *525*

Odbert, H.S. 51, *489*
Ohayon, A. 472, 482, *496*, *525*
O'Keefe, J. 297, *525*
Oldenburg, A. 233
Oldfield, R. C. 145, *525*
Olds, J. 331, *525*
Olson, K.R. 530
Olver, R.R. 494
Orbeli, L. 270
Ortega, Y. G. 186
Osgood, C.E. 205, 297–298, 300, 323–327, 344, 351, 374, *525–526*
Ovcharenko, V. 240, *526*

Pagés, R. 481, *526*
Paivio, A. 326–327, 386, 526
Palermo, D. 320–321, *526*
Parot, F. 128, *487*, *526*
Pataki, F. 186, *526*

550 Author Index

Paul, H. 172–175, 178, *526*
Pavlov (Pawlow), I. P. 48, 69, 217, 219, 222–226, 232–239, 244, 246, 253, 256–257, 269–276, 292–294, 301, 322, 330, 352, 489, 510, *526*
Pavlov session 269–272
Pear, J.J. 355, *539*
Pearson, K. 55, *526–527*
Peirce, C.S. 340, *527*
Perner, J. 417, *527*
Philippe, J. 144, *527*
Piaget, J. I, xiii, 1, 3, 70, 76, 78–94, 97–99, 103, 129–132, 160–162, 213, 242, 245, 251, 276, 382–384, 432, 470–471, 494, 500, 502, 508, 509, 524, *527*
Piaget Foundation 81, *527*
Piattelli-Palmarini, M. 93, 378, 409, 493, *527–528*
Pickren, W.E. *486*
Pilzecker, A. 145, 320, *524*
Pinker, S. 101, 343, 376, 378, 386, 388–391, 394, 409, 411, 413, 420, 425, 441, 443, 452, *519*, *528*
Pitts, W. 386, *520*
Pizarroso, N. 128, *528*
Plas, R. 105, 482, 496
Pléh, Cs. 35, 147, 275, 412, *514*, *528*
Plotkin, H. 409, *521*, *528*
Polanyi, M. 162, *528*
Politzer, G. 13–14, 95, *528*
Pomerantz, J. R. 327, *513*
Pomeroy, W. *512*
Poole, R. 120, *528*
Popper, K. R. 11, 157–160, 169, 189, 200, 207, 346–347, 362, 411, 418, 422, 430, *528–529*, 536–537
Posner, M.I. 347, 349, 360, 420–421, *529*
Postman, L. *529*
Potebnja, A. 172
Premack, A. *529*
Premack, D. 349, 351, 417, *529*
Pribram, K.A. *522*
Prilleltensky, I. 454, *502*
Prince, A. 388, 519
Prinzhorn, H. 40, *522*
Prinzhorn, M. xvi
Prohászka, L. 39, *529*
Prokasy, W. F. *530*
Pulvermüller, F. 326, *529*
Putnam, H. 93, 380, 392, *529*
Putnam, J.J. 5, *529*
Putnoky, J. 275, 326–327, *490*, *529*
Pylyshyn, Z. W. 327, 361, 365, 388, *502*, *529*

Quillian, M.R. 349, 368, *498*
Quine, W. V. 380, 462, *529*

Raichle, M. E 374, *529*
Ramachandran, V.S. 483, *529*
Ramat, P. 39, *529*
Rapaport, D. 19–20, *529*
Rateau, P. *517*
Ratner, C. *510*
Ratner, N. B. 376, *491*
Rau, L. *532*
Razran, G. 323, *529*
Reich, W. 23, 501, *530*
Relaford-Doyle, J. *525*
Renan, E. *530*
Renouvier, C. 35
Rescorla, R. A. 236, *530*
Ribot, Th. 104, 169, 181, 399, *530*
Richard, N. 102, *530*
Richards, G. 487
Richelle, M. *487*
Richerdson, P. 419, *493*
Ricoeur, P. 4, 120, 419, 463, *497*, *530*
Rieber, R. W. *486*
Riefenstahl, L. 186
Riesman, D. 206, *530*
Rioux, J-P. 180, *534*
Rivers, W. 124
Roediger, III. H.L. 120–122, 143, 145–146, 148, 355, 491, *530*
Rogers, C.R. 452, 458–460, 474, 514, *530*
Róheim, G. 3–4, 124, *530–531*
Rohwer, W.D. 320, *510*
Rokeach, M. 207, *512*
Rorschach, H. 48, 51–52, *531*
Rosa, A. 148–150, 521, *531*
Rosch, E. 38, 40, 136, 349, *531*
Rosenthal, R. 210, 402, *531*
Rosenzweig, M. R *514*
Rosenzweig, S. 19, *531*
Ross, E A. 167, *531*
Ross, L. 209, 218, *531*
Roudinesco, E. 6, 13–14, 481, *531*
Rubinstein, S. L. 221, 244–245, 262, 267–272
Rumelhart, D.E. 209, 300–301, 360, 368, 382, 387, 390, *520*
Russell, B. 139, 141, 282, 301, 455, *531*
Ryle, G. 71, 139, 281, 425, *531*

Sacks, H. 465, *532*
Sacks, O. 37, 257, *532*
Salmon, L. *539*
Sanford, N. 23

Sapir, E. 135–137, *532*
Saussure, F. de. 321, 347, *532*
Saviolo, N. *511*
Schank, R. 209, *532*
Schegloff, E. A. *532*
Schiller, F. 38
Schiller, P. von (Schiller, P.H.) *532*
Schlossberg, H. 62, 449, *542*
Schütz, A. 464, *532*
Scott, J.P. 68, 331, *532*
Scott, R. *528*
Scribner, S. 134, *498*, *532*
Sears, R. R. 3, 200, 318, *498*, *532*
Sebeok, T. 327, *509*, *526*
Sechenov, I. M. 217, 232, 271, 399, *532*, *542*
Secord, P.F. 464, *506*
Segal, E. M. 335, 367, *535*
Semenuks, A. *525*
Semprun, J. 13, *532*
Shannon, C. E. 150, 320, 327, *532*
Shaw, J.J. *524*
Shchukin, S. 218
Sheldon, W. H. 44–45, *532*
Shepard, R. N. 337, 348, 349, *532*
Sherif, M. 191, 192, 198, *533*
Shklovsky, V. 247
Shpet, G. (Spet) 249
Sighele, S. 180, 182, *533*
Simmel, G. *533*
Simmel, M. 209, *507*
Simon, H. A. 348, 363, 367, 386, 391, 474, *524*, *533*
Simon, T. 54, 80, *492*
Simonton, D. K. 452, 474, 476, *533*
Siqueland, E.R. 500
Sirinelli, J-F. 180, *534*
Sirotkina, I. 217–218, 222, 232, 264, 277, *533*
Skinner, B.F. xv, 274–275, 281, 285–294, 301–313, 319, 329, 337, 349, 371, 374, 452, 459, 468, 499, *530*, *533*
Slobin, D.I. 136, 376, 378, 390, *533*
Smith, L. 484, *534*
Smith, R. 217–218, 222, 232, 264, 277, *533*
Snow, C. 376, *518*
Snow, C.P. 376, 473, *534*
Sokolov, E. N. 253, 436, 454, *534*
Sontag, S. 186, *534*
Spear, J.H. 357, 452, *534*
Spearman, C.E. 56, 433, 469, *534*
Spelke, E. 94, 379, 437–438, *534*
Spence, J. T. 312, 479, *534*
Spence, K. W. 212, 312, 351, *534*

Sperber, D. xvi, 149, 162–163, 362, 374, 414, 465, *520*, *525*, *534*
Sperling, G. 349, 351, *534*
Sperry, R. W. 37, 348, 397, *535*
Spielrein, I. 225, 264, *535*
Spielrein, S. 80–83, 225, 242–243, *535*
Spinoza, B. 247
Spitz, E. xvi
Spitz, R. A. 17, *535*
Spranger, E. 36–40, 71, 153, 404, 468, *535*
Squire, L.R 236, *511*
Staats, A.W. 472, *535*
Stalin, J. V. 220–221, 230, 242, 244, 263–264, 269, 271, 273, 314, 538
Steiner, R. 218
Steinmer, P. *509*
Steinthal, H. 170–177, *515*, *516*, *535*
Stephenson, G. M. 146, *503*
Stern, C. 438, *535*
Stern, W. 32–37, 57, 77, 197, 438, 447, *535*
Sternberg, R.J. 434, 452, 465, 477–478, *486*, *535–536*
Stevens, S. S. 283–286, 337, 467–468, *536*
Stich, S. 471, *536*
Stroebe, W. 165, 191, *514*
Student [William Sealy Gosset] 55
Sturm, Th. 154, 470, *524*, 536
Suci, G. 325, *526*
Sulloway, F.K. 11, *536*
Swets, J.A. 339, *536*
Szász, T. 455–456, *536*
Székely, A. 376
Szeminska, A. 89, *527*

Taine, H. 102–103, 165, 530, *536*
Talankin, A. A. 263–264, *536*
Tannenbaum, P. 325, *526*
Tanner Jr., W.P. 339, *536*
Tarde, G. 42, 102, 167, 170, 180–182, 186, 187–190, 199, 316, *500*, *536–537*, 539
Taylor, F.V. 225, *537*
Téglás, E. *513*
Teo, T. 469, *537*
Teplov, B.M. 231, 259, 267, 269, 271, 273, *537*
Ter Hark, M. 159, *537*
Terman, L. 54, 318, 537
Teuber, H.L. 344, 382, 442, *537*
Thomae, H. *495*
Thorndike, E.L. 54, 157–158, 293, 301, 319, *537*
Thurstone, L.L. 57, 205, 452, *537*
Tinanov, B. 247
Tinbergen, N. 65–69, *537*

Todes, D. P. 226, 232–233, *537*
Tolman, E. C. 3, 20, 64, 152, 158, 285–289, 295–298, 300, 313, 327, *537–538*
Tomasello, M 277, 374, 378–379, 412–413, 416–417, 469, *496*, *538*
Tooby, J. 101, 394, 505, 411, 425, *490*, *498*, *538*
Topalov, C. *509*
Towsey, P.M. 264, *538*
Trautmann-Waller, C. 171, *516*, *538*
Trotsky, L. 230, 242, 244–245, 248
Tryon, R.C. 449, *538*
Tucker, R.C. 219–221, 239, 246, 263, 270–272, *538*
Tulving, E. 110, 425, *538*
Turgenev, I. 216, *538*
Tversky, A. 348–349, 362, *511*, *538*

Uexküll, J. von 60, 65–70, 153, *538*
Ullman, M.T. 326, 386, 389, 391, 424–425, 444, *519*, *528*, *538*
Umrihin, V.V. 222, *538*
Ungerleider, L. G. 424, *538*
Urbán, J. 273, *520*
Uttal, W. R. 421, *538*

Valsiner, J. 34, 76, *539*
van der Maas, H.L.J. *512*
van der Veer, R. 249, *542*
Vargas, V. *539*
Vargha, A. 21–22, *539*
Vargha-Khadem, F. *514*
Várkonyi, H.D. 89
Vasilieva, J. 242, 277, *539*
Velichkovsky, B.M. 276, *539*
Vereczkey, L. *505*
Veresov, N. 250, *539*
Vergiles, N. Yu. 255, *542*
Vermè, G. 169, 182, *511*
Vernant, J.P. 128, *539*
Vidal, F. 79–80, 130, *539*
Vigorito, J. *500*
Vijayan, S. *519*
Vinogradova, O. S. 237, 323, *518*
Virués-Ortega, J. 355, *539*
Vishton, P. M. *519*
Volosinov, V.N. 4, 243, *539*
Voyat, G. 98, *539*
Vygodskaia, G.L. 250, *539*
Vygotsky, L. S. 76–77, 84–85, 106–108, 116, 131–135, 161–162, 224–225, 245–258, 260, 264–268, 340, 344, 384, 389, 463, 470, 494, 506, 518, 538, *539–540*
Vygotsky Archives 540

Waddington, C. H. 439, *540*
Wagner, A. R. 236, *530*
Wagner, V. 226
Wagner, W. 226, *515*
Wagoner, B. 140, 144–147, *540*
Wallon, H. 77, 84, 89–90, 94–98, 108, 110, 129, 162, 272–273, 447, *539–540*
Wann, T.W. *513*
Wapner, S. 76, *541*
Ward, A. 190, *499*
Ward, J. 139
Wason, P. C. 349, 362, *540*
Watson, J. B. xii, 3, 66–67, 75, 224, 281–282, 285, 290–291, 302, 369, 436, 468, *540*
Watson, R. I. 474, *486*, *540*
Weakland, J. *491*
Weaver, W. 327, 532
Weber, M. 38–40, 112, 168, 186, 540
Wechsler, D. 56
Wegrocki, H. J. *495*
Weimer, W. B. 467, *541*
Weiner, I. B. *486*
Werner, H. 76–77, 539, *541*
Wernicke, C. 115, 414, 421, 442, *541*
Wertheimer, M. *486*
Wertsch, J. V. 118–122, *541*
White, R.K. 199, 200, *516*
Whorf, B.L. 135–137, 161–162, 541
Wicherts, J.M. *512*
Winch, R F. 40, *541*
Winegard, B. M. 201, *497*
Wirchow, R. 169, *541*
Wittgenstein, L. 139, 158, 176, 466–464, 506, *541*
Wolf, P. 136–137, *541*
Woodruff, G. 349, 351, 417, *529*
Woodward, W. R. xvi, 479, *541*
Woodworth, R. S. 60–62, 73, 81, 281, 449, *541*
Wundt, W. 56, 60, 70, 106, 141, 157, 164, 169–170, 171–180, 182–183, 218, 326, 354, 465–466, 499, 504, 505, 524, *541–542*

Xypas, C. 129, *542*

Yaeger, J. *513*
Yarbus, A. L. 255, 399, *542*
Yarosevsky, M.G. 276, *542*
Yasnitsky, A. 249, *542*
Yerkes, R. 70, 92, 314, 330, *542*
Yudovich, F. 256, *518*

Zalkind, A.B. 244–245, 264–265
Zawadzki, P. 119, *542*
Zazzo, R. 98, *542*
Zimbardo, P.G. 165, 208, 402, 451, *542*
Zinchenko, P. I. 220, *542*
Zinchenko, V.P. 255, *542*
Zittoun, T. 478, *542*

Subject Index

abilities 41, 54–57, 85, 97, 102, 376, 392, 429, 433, 496, 534
accommodation and assimilation (Piaget) 89–90, 471
achievement motivation 11, 72, 208, 398
achievements of humans (*oeuvres*, Meyerson) 126–127, 421
activation theories 53, 329–331, 523
activity theory 253–255, 518, 260–262; Leontiev 253–255; Rubinstein 246, 260–262
adaptation 28, 47, 50, 53, 61, 64, 78, 128, 234, 317, 406, 410–414, 423, 498, 538; evolutionary psychology 64, 217, 234, 317, 406, 410–414, 423, 457, 471; Piaget 78, 89
Aha experience (Bühler) 150
alienation 25, 456
alternative social movements 210–212; critical psychology 454–455; *see also* antipsychiatry
analytic (complex) psychology (Jung) 5–9
animism 83
animus/anima (Jung) 9
Annales school of history writing 112, 126, 179
anomia (Durkheim) 109
anthropology i, xii, 3, 27, 102, 124–126, 129, 148, 164, 168, 364, 380, 383, 487, 488, 501, 518; social 168–175; universals 126
anthropomorphism 235, 296
anticipated goal reactions 300
anxiety 24–25, 53, 287, 312–318, 479, 523, 534
appetitive and consummative stages (Craig) 61, 69
applied psychology 75, 95, 138, 225, 231, 265, 275, 279, 291, 337, 447–457; determinism 454–457; growth 457–460; individuum/system 447–451; tensions with academia 451–454; *see also* behavioral economics; 'third force' movements
archetypes (Jung) 7–8, 28
architecture (cognitive) 358–361, 363–369, 386–389, 395, 406–407, 408–411, 489, 502, 505; classical 358–361; connectionist 386–389
artificialism 83
associations 158, 174, 183, 226–227, 274, 319–322, 388–394; formation 319–320; mediation; paradigmatic-syntagmatic 321–322; semantics 321
associative memory 146, 389
athletic type 43
attachment theory 15, 68, 72, 493, 496
attitudes 165, 169, 191, 205–210, 325, 398, 515, 416, 537; dynamics 209–210; *see also* cognitive dissonance
attribution theories 12, 192, 208–210
authoritarianism 23–24, 49, 179, 199–200, 206–209; *see also* open-closed mind
authoritarian personality 24–25, 49–50, 488
autism 83, 93, 130, 417, 442, 490, 502, 505
automatic and controlled processes 368

Bakhtin-circle 4, 162, 243, 490
Bartlett-paradigm 145; memory construction and traces 146–150; story schematization 144–145, 147
basic fault (Bálint) 16, 560
Behavior and Brain Sciences (journal) 383
behavioral dispositions (Janet) 104–105
behavioral economics 460, 511

behavioral science 291, 298, 300, 311–314, 459, 486, 487
behavior therapy 310, 452–453; *see also* descriptive behaviorism
belief-desire psychology 59–60, 296, 417–418, 471
Big Five (personality) 53
biogenetic theory 15
birth order effects 11
bodily fluids and personality 43
bodily types and personality 43–45
brain imaging 326, 374, 420–422, 435, 437
brain-mind relations 418–427; eliminative materialism 419; emergence 419; functionalism 419; identity 419; *see also* dualism; functionalism; neural Darwinism
brain washing 208
Budapest school (psychoanalysis) 14–17, 20–21, 521

character 26, 30–31, 40–41, 43; national 169, 179–182, 208, 295, 508, 512, 514
child language 33, 922, 177, 341, 374–380, 534; errors in 389–390; experimental studies 376–377, grammar building 377–379; observational studies 372, 375; psycholinguistics 374–380; *see also* language acquisition
child psychology 75–76, 80–81, 96, 150, 223, 241, 344
CHILDES 376
choleric (personality) 48–49
Chomsky's critic of Skinner 306–307
Christiahonity 9, 169, 277; Jung 9; Meyerson 128
classification of human motives 71–73; *see also* deficiency and growth motives
clinging instinct (Herrmann) 15–17
clinical method (Piaget) 81–83
clinical psychology 12, 22, 311, 352, 452, 459–461, 472, 478, 481; dominant profession 449–450; *see also* health psychology
CNRS 352, 510
CNS (Conceptual Nervous System) 329
cocktail party situation 360
Cognition (journal) 383
cognitive dissonance 209, 354, 502; *see also* attitudes

Subject Index 555

cognitive maps (Tolman) 291, 295–298, 312, 333,; hippocampus 297; neural 414, 422
Cognitive Psychology (journal) 383
cognitive psychology 276, 279, 282, 290, 297, 311–312, 327–329, 333, 334–396; birth of 334–343; cognitive paradigm 346–353; journals 348–349; language acquisition 374–380; language processing 369–380; mental chronometry 347–348; parallels in other fields 335; societies 347–348; spread geographically 352–353; textbooks 349–350
cognitive revolution 334–336; questioning 353–359
Cognitive Science (journal) 383
cognitive science 380–395; abstract 383–384; institutions 382–383; interpreted 384–385; representational-non representational 385–386; *see also* connectionism; representations
cognitive social psychology 192, 204, 209; *see also* attitudes; attribution
CogSci *see* cognitive science
Cold War 24, 95, 192, 205, 311, 326, 327; cognitive research 345–346; social psychology 200, 206–208, 327; Sputnik shock 345–346
collative variables 330
collective memory 111, 113–116, 118–119, 505, 506, 541 (Halbwachs); history writing 119–122
collective psychology 109–110, 115, 117, 187 (Blondel) 103, 526, 523
collective representations 8, 107–108, 113, 125, 172, 179, 183, 188 (Durkheim, Halbwachs) 500, 524
collective representation of psychology 450
collective unconscious (Jung) 7–8
Collège de France 13, 94, 104, 108, 111–112, 126, 187, 352
compensation (Adler) 10, 28
competence-performance (Chomsky) 371, 377
competent infant *see* smart babies
computational theory 344, 346, 363, 369–372, 409
computer models: cognition 363–369; limitations 367–369; sequential processing 368

Conceptual Nervous System (CNS) 303, 329
concrete operations (Piaget) 86, 94
concrete psychology (Politzer) 13–14
conditioning 236–237, 270, 272–74, 292–294, 436, 452, 505, 514, 520; classical (S) and instrumental (R) 272–274, 292–294; human 310–312; language 319–323, 374; neo-behaviorism 292–293; Pavlov 237–238; Skinner 300–310; passive organism *vs.* activity in Eastern Europe 272–274
conduct (Janet) 103–106
conformism 198, 207–208, 210, 296
connectionism 301, 528, 534; Guthrie 301; PDP 386–389, 528, 534; Rumelhart 387
consciousness 172–178, 343, 425, 443, 492, 497, 500; Dennett 343, 499,; group 107–108, 113–114; historical 117, 121; Janet 104; Jung 28; Soviet theories 220–227, 231, 245–262, 275, 314; *Völkerpsychologie* 172–178, 193
consensual validation (Sullivan) 28
conservation (quantity & number, Piaget) 86–87
constructionism 108–109, 143–148, 340–343, 403, 409, 463–464, 510; Bartlett 143–148; Bruner 340–343; Piaget 94; social 108–109, 143, 214, 259, 409, 463–464; Vygotsky 108, 132–135, 246–253; Wallon 90–96; *see also* SSSM
context effects 53, 140–141, 191–193, 211, 338; memory 137, 140–141; perception 338, 393; social psychology 33, 53, 70, 191–193, 198–200, 211–212
contiguity (learning) 300–301, 505
convergence (Stern) 34, 77, 438
conversation 134, 147–148, 464–465; *see also* ethnomethodology
core knowledge 94, 437, 534
countertransference (psychoanalysis) 14
crisis of psychology 152–154, 156, 245–246, 470–473; Bühler 152–154; Vygotsky 245–246
critical periods of development 331, 429, 432, 440–442
critical psychology 167, 212–213, 454–457, 469; Frankfurt 212–213

cross cultural psychology 38, 102, 123–124, 124–137, 139–140, 211, 325–326, 398, 415; East-West (holistic – localistic) 211, 524–525; *see also* relativism; WEIRD
crowd psychology 164–165, 168, 170, 180–186, 496, 517, 522, 525; group mind 64, 141; irrationality 14, 182–184; political influence 185–186
cultural learning 414–418; teaching attitude 416; *see also* natural pedagogy
cultural memory 116, 122–123, 255, 461, 489–490, 500, 524; *see also* collective memory
cultural psychology 148, 153, 168, 179, 213, 277, 342, 398, 405, 470, 494, 498, 510, 528; *see also* cross cultural psychology; cultural learning; narrative psychology

data 281–282, 286, 320–321, 347–348, 363, 368, 374–377, 398–401; big data 499–401, 512; debates 401–403; statistical issues 402–403
decentration 83, 88–90, 131, 471 (Piaget)
decision theory 201, 349, 363; cognitive psychology 361–364; errors 362–364; fast and slow 363–364, 561; *see also* prisoners dilemma
deficiency and growth motives (Maslow) 72
depth psychology, schools 3–21
descriptive behaviorism (Skinner) 285–286, 300–303; critic of flights from laboratory 303; language 304–308; social utopia 303–311; *see also* Chomsky's critic of Skinner; programmed learning
determinism 15, 219–221, 320, 420, 429, 475; Skinner 294; Soviet psychology 219–221, 229, 336, 244, 252, 270, 272–274; 3rd force 454–460
developmental language disorders 441–445; FOXP2 444–445; SLI 442–444
developmental psychology xvi, 33, 75–78, 82, 91, 94, 152, 341, 353, 376, 408, 502
developmental science 384, 436–438

developmental theories 33–34, 75–98, 436–438, 504
development of thought (Piaget) 85–89
dialogical approach to literature (Bakhtin) 243
differential psychology (Stern) 34–37, 514–515, 535; trait analysis 35
discrimination (learning) 236, 238, 285, 292, 294, 312
discrimination (social) 12, 211, 341, 431, 436, 442
dissociations: developmental 431, 441–444; double dissociation 426, 442; pathology 13, 46, 109, 180, 426
dorsal and ventral stream (vision) 424
drive (Woodworth) 60–62
drive reduction 300, 318; brain (N. Miller) 331, 522; Grastyán 330, 505; Hull 300
dual coding (Paivio) 326–327, 526
dual cognitive systems 424–425; *see also* dorsal and ventral stream; procedural memory
dualism 70, 418
dual memory (Bergson) 111–113
dynamic psychologies 59–74

Ebbinghaus paradigm 142, 145
École Normale Supérieure 109
ecological psychology 147, 163, 255, 288–290, 350
ectomorph type 44
egocentric speech (Piaget)
egocentrism
Ego theory (psychoanalysis); A. Freud; Budapest school
eidetic imagery (Jaensch)
emotions; in development (Wallon)
encounter group
endomorf type
episodic memory
equilibration (Piaget)
equipotentiality (Lashley)
essentialistic thinking
ethnomethodology (Sacks) 464–465, 503
ethogeny (Harré) 464
ethology xiii, 15, 60, 64–71, 73, 158–159, 255, 303, 307, 330–335, 341, 344, 379, 405–406, 428, 440, 508, 537; biological functionalism 60, 159; psychoanalysis 15, 68, 70–71; *see also* instinct; imprinting;

sensitive periods of development; *Umwelt*
European Journal of Social Psychology 192, 211
evolution and progress 54, 169, 540
evolutionary attitude 411–412
evolutionary epistemology 159–160, 411, 422, 430, 477, 496, 533, 537
evolutionary psychology 64, 101, 384, 394, 412–418; adaptations 407–408, 411–412; levels of behavior selection (Bühler, Dennett, Popper) 157–160, 422–423, 294, 303; questioning 408–410; Schiller 159; *see also* EvoDevo; evolutionary attitude; evolutionary epistemology; genetics in psychology
excitation 227, 236–238, 388, 404
experimental spirit 383, 484; social psychology 194, 198
explanation (psychology) 100, 348, 395; evolutionary 348, 407, 409, 411, 512; external 28, 100, 383, 395; internal 73, 348; neural 222, 348, 419; social 100
extinction 236, 292
extraversion 47–51, 53, 520; Eysenck 49–51; Jung 47–49, *see also* Big Five

F (ascism) scale 24–25
factor analysis 53, 56–58, 325, 401, 477, 571
false belief tasks 136, 417–418
fate analysis (Szondi) 21–22, 536
flashbulb memories 375, 494
folk psychology (cognitive) 14, 28, 42, 59–60, 62, 82, 107, 127, 220, 227, 230, 235, 239, 240, 255, 282–286, 287, 291, 295–296, 303, 334, 345, 364, 367, 416–418, 463, 465, 471, 507, 536
formal operations (Piaget) 86–87
Frankfurt school 22–25, 207, 212, 245, 501
freedom 25, 186, 217, 233, 249, 275, 304–310, 370; Chomsky 370, 469; neo-freudianism 25–26, 560; Skinner 304–310, 534
French sociological school in psychology 95, 102–123, 146
freudomarxism 22–26, 239–245; Fromm 25; Marcuse 26; Soviet 239–245; *see also* neo-freudianism

frustration-aggression 313, 315, 491, 522
functional analysis in cognitive systems (Marr) 365, 369–371, 422, 519
functionalism (brain-cognition); language embedded; machine; psychological
functional organ (Luria) 257; *see also* neuronal recycling
function pleasure 71, 150

generalization 236, 271–272, 292, 313, 317, 319, 323, 362, 371, 379
generative grammar (Chomsky) 177, 389, 392, 422, 510, 520; *see also* Chomsky's critic of Skinner
genetic epistemology (Piaget) 91, 470, 527
genetics in psychology 48, 51, 236, 269–270, 412, 422, 427–440, 497, 538; epigenesis 407, 429, 439, 445, 483, 560; Human Genome Project 399, 431, 438–441, 454; individual differences 428–436; universality 436–440; *see also* EvoDevo; innatism
Gestalt theory and cognition 335, 343–344
Gift (Mauss) 108, 520
group dynamics (Lewin) 60, 191, 193, 199–201
group effects on behavior 198–199
group mind 8, 64, 107–108, 115, 117–118, 141, 146, 172, 174, 183, 190–191, 193, 195–196, 520
group structure 197–200, 477; leadership 191, 197–200; networks 204, 464, 483–484, 493; sociometry 201–204; *see also* leadership style; sociometry
groupthink 198–199, 510

habitus (Bourdieu) 102, 179
health psychology 459–460
hermeneutics in psychology 15, 463, 503; Harré 463–464, 468; Ricoeur 4, 120, 419, 463, 497, 530; understanding attitude 456, 463–466; *see also* ethogeny; ethnomethodology
higher mental activity (Luria, Vygotsky) 106, 132, 246, 256–257, 270, 334
higher nervous activity (Pavlov) 48, 231–232, 235–239, 269, 271, 509, 518–519, 526
hippocampus 227, 297, 330, 425, 525

historical psychology (Meyerson) 126–129; achievements (*oeuvres*) 126–127, 521; person 128
historical relativism xi–ii, 124, 126–129, 132–135, 252, 356; Dilthey 252–253; Lévy-Bruhl 121, 124–126; Meyerson 126–129; Vygotsky 132–135
hormic psychology (McDougall) 62–64
hospitalization 17
human factors (industry) 204
humanistic psychology xv, 9, 26, 37, 72–73, 152, 256, 346, 457, 495; *see also* encounter group
human nature 4, 25, 79, 127–128, 207–208, 267–268, 274, 356, 410, 469–471, 473, 477–478, 488, 495, 497, 498, 509, 511, 529, 560
hypotheses 88, 157–159, 362, 401–402, 423; cognition (Bruner, Wason) 340, 362; rat learning (Kreshevsky) 296; science (Popper) 160–161, 362; *see also* hypothetico-deductive method; statistics
hypothetico-deductive method (Hull) 298–299, 312

iconic memory 347–348
iconic representation (Bruner) 91, 340
ideal types (Weber) 38–40, 50
identification 311–317; learning theory 192, 311–314, 316–317, 490
identity 119–123, 128, 179; Erikson stages 457–458
idiographic attitude 36, 50, 71, 462, 475–476; Allport, G. 37, 50, 71; Luria 37, 257
imagery 326–327, 353, 513, 529; debate 327, 361, 529; *see also* dual coding
imitation 42, 90, 191–192, 311–313, 413–415, 490, 503; child language 374, 377, 502; development (Wallon) 98, 527; neobehaviorism 192, 308, 311–313, 316–317, 520; social cohesion (Tarde) 182, 187–190, 536, 539
imprinting 68
individual psychology (Adler) 10–11
individualism 102, 114, 174, 195, 308–309, 311; social psychology 194–197
infancy 408, 414, 436–438; attachment 15, 68, 72, 416; experimental studies 436–438; psychoanalysis 16–18;

research technology; sexuality;
see also smart babies
inferiority complex 10
information processing theory of cognition 360–361; coding 359; filters 360; representations 360–361, 365–366; limitations 366–367; stores 359–360; symbol processing 358, 367, 386–389, 390, 395
information theory 154, 157, 327–328, 335, 336–337, 344, 348, 358, 490; see also statistical behaviorism
inhibition 217, 236–238, 318
innatism 93–94, 372, 379–380, 392, 428–429, 436, 445; Chomsky 93–94, 309, 372, 379–380; factors of development 438–440; Fodor 392–393; see also child language; connectionism; core knowledge; developmental language disorders; EvoDevo; genetics in psychology; modularity; modularization; smart babies
inner speech 104, 251; Vygotsky 84–85, 251–252, 256, 389
instinct 15–17, 20–22, 61–68, 528; debates 64–66, 162, 157–158; ethology 64–68; McDougall 62–64; psychoanalysis 3, 15–17, 27; Szondi 20–22
Institute of Human Relations (Yale) 314–316
instrumental method (Vygotsky) 246–252, 539
integrative therapy (Mowrer) 318
intelligence 32–34, 53–57, 429–436; environmental effects 435; heredity debates 429–436; Piaget 82–88
intentionality 59, 70, 115, 155–156, 292, 407, 463
intentional stance (Dennett) 62, 227, 255, 335, 348, 463, 499, 504
interiorization 88, 252; Luria 256–257; Piaget 88; Vygotsky 84, 252
interpsychology (Tarde) 188; Durkheim debate 188–189
intervening variables 286–288, 290–291, 295–299; dispositional concepts 287; vs. hypothetical constructs 287, 518
introversion 47–51, 53, 520; Eysenck 49–51; Jung 47–49

irrationality 182–184; crowd psychology 14, 182–184, 141, 198; primitive mentality 124–126; 129–135, 137, 140; unconscious

Journal of Abnormal and Social Psychology 192, 194
Journal of Personality and Social Psychology 192
Journal of Verbal Learning and Verbal Behavior 321, 350

Kantianism 92, 258–259
KNOWING WHAT - KNOWING HOW 391, 425

language (system) 370–371, 424
language acquisition 374–379
language functions (Bühler) 154–156, 159
Language of Thought (LOT) 365; mentalese 365
language types 39, 136
latent learning 281, 296, 330
law of small numbers 363
laws of learning 236, 290, 294
leadership style 191, 197–201
learning theory 3, 20, 192, 281–333, 344, 355, 377, 390, 416, 472, 482, 493, 501
leptosome type 43–44
linguistic relativity 135–137, 534
linguistic turn (philosophy) 181, 298, 385
Lonely Crowd (Riesman) 206
long term memory (LTM) 110, 349, 501

Machiavellian intelligence 413
Marxism in psychology 23–27, 207, 222–225; Politzer 13–14; Soviet 222–225, 239–268; Wallon 94–98; see also Frankfurt school
materialism 217–222, 404, 419; in Soviet psychology 218–220, 230, 233, 239, 263, 513, 531; see also reductionism
mathematical theories of learning 312
mediation theories 298–300, 250; Hull 298–299; representative mediation (Osgood) 323–327; Vygotsky 250–253
melancholic (personality) 43
mentalism 93, 310, 345, 354, 369; language 93, 369

mentality (social) 83, 97, 102, 103, 112, 124–126; changes in history 126–129
mesomorph type 44–45
milieu theory 102–103
millennium, psychology 397–398
mirror neurons 384, 427
modularity 368, 429, 435, 441–445, 502–571; brain 392; Fodor 391–395; input systems 393; radical 408–409; *see also* connectionism; evolutionary psychology
modularization (Karmiloff-Smith) 94, 394, 429
motivation 59–73, 255, 272, 282, 293, 296, 300, 313, 331, 398, 418; *see also* classification of human motives drive; function pleasure; instinct
motor development (Wallon) 97
motor theories of cognition 104, 217, 291, 399; Osgood 324–325; Putnoky 326
mythology (Jung) 7

narrative psychology 105, 118–121, 147, 342–343; Bruner 132, 147, 342–343; László 147
narratives 103–105, 115, 122; Bartlett 143–146; Bruner 342–343, 494; social psychology of human action 147–148; social story telling (Janet) 103–106
naturalistic psychology 259, 462
natural pedagogy 416; *see also* cultural learning
neobehaviorism 281–332; conceptual, logical, ontological 281; descriptive 301–303; learning theories 282, 290–295; methodical behaviorism 281–282; molecular and molar 287; neurophysiology 329–333; progressivism; psychopathology 314–316; schools of 295–311; social learning 316–317; *see also* descriptive behaviorism; frustration-aggression; mathematical theories of learning; neopositivism and psychology; operationalism; purposive behaviorism; verbal learning
neo-freudism/neofreudianism 22–28, 346; *see also* authoritarian personality; alienation; freudomarxism

neopositivism and psychology 282/90
nervism (Botkin, Pavlov) 235
networks 484; associative 386; connectionist 390–392; neural 93, 387, 422, 497; semantic 118, 237, 323, 337, 349, 368, 375; socio-cultural 14–15, 22, 118, 201, 203–204, 401, 451, 460, 464, 483, 393
Neumann architecture 358, 365, 367–368, 524
neural Darwinism 422–423
neuroleptics 454
neuronal recycling (Dehaene) 257, 414, 499
neuropsychology 109–110, 256–257, 330, 420, 424, 435, 442, 448, 518; Damasio 420, 426, 499; Dehaene 256, 257, 414, 421, 424, 499; Luria 253, 256–257, 353, 435, 518
New Look (perceptual research) 19, 335, 338–339, 340, 343, 393
New Man (Soviet) 219–221, 244, 262, 267, 271; malleability of humans 267–269
nomothetic attitude 33–38, 40, 50, 71, 91, 289, 462, 476

obedience (authority) 24, 165, 184, 192, 200, 206–208, 402, 521
object permanence (Piaget) 86–87
object relations theory (psychoanalysis) 14, 16, 18
Oedipal conflict (psychoanalysis) 3–5, 17–18, 222
open-closed mind (Rokeach) 207, 512
operant learning 291, 293–294, 300–306, 312, 319, 351; *see also* conditioning
operationalism 281, 283–286; Boring 283–284; Bridgmann 283; Skinner 285–286; Stevens 280–285; *see also* intervening variables; scaling theory
opinion leaders 189, 212
oral history and memory 116
organon model (language) 154–155
orientation reaction (OR) 276, 330, 436; Hebb 330; Pavlov 330; Sokolov 276, 330, 436, 454
orienting activity (Galperin) 258
origin of language 177–178; Chomsky 429–430; G. H. Mead 178; Tomasello 374, 413, 538; Wundt 177–178

Pavlovism 95, 233, 237, 269–275, 540; *see* Pavlov school of reflexology
Pavlov school of reflexology 231–239; *see also* conditioning; reflexology debates; signalization systems; typology
Pavlov Session of the Soviet academies 269–272
pedology 33, 75, 89, 151, 273, 436, 447, 491; pedology-pedagogy-psychology relations 268–273; Soviet pedology 223–224, 225, 242, 247; Soviet antipedology decision 264–266, 532
perceptual learning 338–339, 352, 422
personalism (Stern) 32–33, 35–37, 41, 197, 515
personality 1, 3, 7, 8–12, 14, 20–28, 30–58, 60, 71–72, 75, 77, 96–97, 105, 128–129, 144, 180, 182, 190, 192–194, 199–203, 207, 221, 234, 237–238, 255–262, 272, 297, 311, 313–316, 318, 400–401, 406–408, 441, 448, 454, 457, 458–461, 469, 472, 474, 488, 489, 490, 492, 495, 496, 501, 507, 508, 510, 513, 520, 522, 523, 524, 535
personality dynamics (Lewin) 60
personality measurement 51–54
personality types 40–51
phenocopy (Piaget) 94
phenomenology in psychology 462–466, 513, 532
philosophy of mind 59, 71, 309, 380, 481, 491, 502
phlegmatic (personality) 43, 49
phrenology 392, 420–422
physiognomy 41
Piaget-Chomsky debate 93–94
picnique type 44
primitive mentality (Lévy-Bruhl) 83, 103, 124–126; coherence 129–131; universality (Lévi-Strauss) 126, 516
prisoners dilemma 208
procedural learning 326, 365, 390–391, 425, 444, 538
procedural memory 326
programmed learning 304
projective tests 48, 51–52, 71–73; thematic and structural 51
propositions 85–86, 92, 297, 306, 327, 358, 360–361, 365, 385–386; *see also* Language of Thought

psychiatry 3, 11–13, 27, 80, 82, 105, 180, 231–232, 456–457, 484; biological 455; antipsychiatry 456–457; *see also* clinical psychology; neuroleptics; psychoanalysis; psychotherapy
psychoanalysis 3–30; clinical psychology 472–473; culture 3–5; folklore and anthropology 3–5; France 13–14, 472–473; institutions 12; medical world 12; neobehaviorism 315, 317–318; *see also* Budapest school; Ego theory; object relations theory; psychosomatics; unconscious
psychodrama 203–204, 451
psychography 35
psycholinguistics 34, 92, 157, 177, 321, 326, 337, 369–380, 391, 493, 498, 516
psychological reality of grammar 307, 369–372; *see also* psycholinguistics
psychosomatics 13
psychotechnics (Soviet) 221, 225, 264
psychotherapy 8–9, 16–17, 25, 203, 275, 317–318, 457–460; behavioral/cognitive behavioral 311, 317–318; *see also* humanistic psychology; psychoanalysis; psychodrama; 'third force'
public opinion 189, 191; critic 196
purposive behaviorism (Tolman) 84, 295–298
Pygmalion effect 402, 531

questionnaires (personality) 24, 52–53, 400

racism 129, 182, 431; colonialism 122, 211; hierarchy 169–170, 182; Jaensch 45–46; monogetic and poligenetic theories 169; progress 169
reductionism biological 348, 407, 409, 411, 512; neural 222, 348, 419; social 100
reflexology (Bekhterev) 226–228; *see also* collective reflexology; reflexology debates
reflexology debates (Soviet) 228–230
relativity (thought) 124–126; Vygotsky and Luria 132–135; *see also* linguistic relativity
releasing stimuli 61, 66, 154

Subject Index

remembering 110–119, 137–150, 500, 503; group effects 122–123, 148–150; reconstructions 144–145
representations 360–366, 385–386; collective 107–108, 113, 125, 172, 179, 183, 188; imagery 326–327; propositional 85–86, 360–361
reversibility (Piaget) 85
Rorschach Test 48, 51–52, 531
rules 389–390; grammatical 389–390; moral 131; reality debates 389–391

sanguine (personality) 43, 49
Sapir-Whorf hypothesis 135–137
scaling theory (Stevens) 284–285
schema theory (Bartlett) 210, 137–150
schemata 81, 85, 89, 96, 141–143, 209–210, 352, 378; Bartlett 137–150; Rumelhart 209, 531; Schank and Abelson 209, 532
second system of signalization (Pavlov) 236–237, 271, 322–323; *see also* semantic conditioning
seduction theory (neurosis) 25, 27
Self 30, 36, 73, 90, 105, 170, 343, 464, 490; dissolution 30, 36, 105; historical psychology 128; literary theory 129, 517; preservation from mass 183
semantic conditioning 322–323
semantic differential 325–326
semantic memory 337, 350–351, 368, 425, 498, 538
semantics 155/6, 325, 374, 385, 391, 516
semiotic conception of the mind (Bühler) 150–161
sensitive periods of development (ethology) 68, 438–440; *see also* critical periods of development
sensory deprivation 208, 330
sensorymotor intelligence (Piaget) 86–87
sexual repressions 23
short term memory (STM) 336, 360
sibling rivalry 10
signal detection theory 339
signalization systems (Pavlov) 236–237
sign Gestalts (Tolman) 291
Skinner box 274, 292–293
smart babies 436–438
social behaviorism 27, 189–192, 200, 314–318; Bandura 304, 311, 490; Dollard-Miller 23, 189–192, 200, 311, 315, 316–318, 500, 522; G. H. Mead 27, 84, 108, 162, 168, 178, 213

social classification (Durkheim) 107–108, 172
social facts (Durkheim) 107, 172, 188–189
social frames of memory (Halbwachs) 110–119, 506; group mind 107–108, 117, 141; historical memory debates 199–123; spaces 114, 119–120
social memory 102, 105; Bartlett 143–148; Blonsky 224; Delay 106; Janet 105–106
social mind 341, 406–408, 413–418; biological adaptation 413–418; *see also* decentration; EvoDevo; Machivellian intelligence; societal psychology
social psychology 100–102, 164–213; ancestors and founders 164–168; European emancipation 192, 211–213; *see also* Frankfurt school
social representations (Durkheim, Moscovici) 106–111, 113–114, 179–180, 188, 191, 197, 204, 209, 213, 310, 523
societal psychology 100, 103, 168, 189, 190, 192, 194, 212–214, 464, 501, 515
sociobiology 64, 405–407
sociologism 96, 100, 102–103, 108–124
sociology i, xiii, 22, 25, 38, 102–129, 131, 139, 166–168, 172–173, 187, 190, 197, 204–205, 208, 213, 314, 361, 380, 401, 464–466
sociometry 201–204; Mérei 203; Moreno 201–202
Soviet/Russian psychology 215–275; activity theory (Leontiev) 253–255; beginnings of Russian psychology 218–219; behavioral schools 222–226; community principle 216, 220, 267; critical stance 263–265; instrumental school 246–252, 539; Marxism 222–225, 239–268; mysticism 217; New Man 219–221, 244, 262, 267, 271; pedology 223–224, 225, 242, 247; personality 253, 255–256, 261–262; psychoanalysts 239–245; radicalism 216–217; reactology 222–228; reflection theory (Lenin) 260, 263; reflexology schools 221–239; Stalinism 220, 225, 233, 236, 239, 244; typology 255, 261, 271; Vygotsky school

246–258; *see also* Pavlovization of psychology; reactology debates
stages in mental development (Piaget) 86–89
Stalinism in psychology 239, 262–264; Pavlov cult 269–272; transformism 262–264
stances (Dennett) 82, 371
Standard Social Science Model (SSSM) 101–102, 108, 118, 136
statistical behaviorism 327–329
statistics in psychology 55–57, 92, 98, 402–403; *see also* factor analysis
suicide 109, 111–112, 188, 492
surface and deep structure (Chomsky) 371–372
surrealists 13
symbol formation 76, 90–92; Piaget 527; Wallon 90, 97–99, 540; Werner 76
syncretism (Wallon) 97
Szondi test 21–22, 536, 539

TAT Test 52
tension regulation (Janet) 105
Theory of Mind (TOM) 42, 152, 155, 191, 282, 344, 351, 371, 416–418, 426, 519, 529; attribution 416–418; autism 417, 442, 490, 502, 505; children 351, 417–418; mentalizing in animals 417; *see also* false belief tasks
thinking 85–89, 90–93, 340–341, 494, 496, 510, 514, 531; computers 364–369; errors 362–363; development 85–89; 90–93, 340–341; strategies 340
'third force' movements 454–460; antipsychiatry 455–457; double bind 455–456; humanistic psychology 458–460; transactional analysis 458–459
tip-of-the-tongue 375, 560
Torres Straits cultural expedition 124, 139
tower of selection 294, 303
traditions and memory 116–118
traits (personality) 35
transactional analysis 458–459
transference (psychoanalysis) 240
Trends in Cognitive Sciences (*TICS* journal) 383
Trotskyism 242, 244–245; Soviet psychoanalysis 244–245; Vygotsky 230, 242, 248
typology(ies) 37–51; bodily 40–45; Pavlovian 48–49; personality 47–51; positivism debates 37–40; racist (Jaensch) 45–47; value issues 49–51; *see also* language types

Umwelt (Uexküll) 60, 65–68
Unconscious 5–8, 13–20, 21; collective 5–8; experimental studies 19–20
understanding sociology (Weber) 38
unity of psychology 465, 466–480; behavioral unification 472–473; eclectic unification 477–478; interdisiplinarity 478; multiplicity 474–477; questioning unity 478–480

vacuum behavior 63–65
verbal learning 319–323
Völkerpsychologie 172–179, 189; cultural evolutionism 175–176; group mind and individualism debate 171–173; language 177–179; Lazarus-Steinthal national mentality 171; *Volksgeist* 170–171; Wundt 173–179; *see also* origin of language; Wundt's theory of sentence
Voprosi Psihologii 267, 272
Vygotsky school 246–258; debates of its structure 253–255; *see also* instrumental method; Soviet psychology; zone of proximal development

WEIRD (Western, educated, industrialized, rich, democratic) 210–211, 410
WHAT and WHERE (vision) 424
worldview 82–84; preschool children (Piaget) 82–84; primitive mentality 124–126
WUG test (Berko) 377

zone of proximal development (Vygotsky) 252

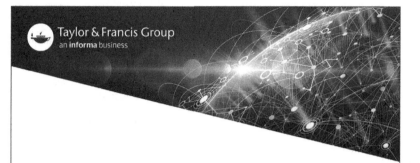